Public Sector Economics:
Theory, Policy and Practice

Public Sector Economics: Theory, Policy and Practice

Second Edition

Stephen J. Bailey

Professor, Division of Economics and Enterprise
Glasgow Caledonian University

palgrave
macmillan

First edition 1995
Second edition 2002

Published by
PALGRAVE
Houndmills, Basingstoke, Hampshire RG21 6XS and
175 Fifth Avenue, New York, N.Y. 10010
Companies and representatives throughout the world

PALGRAVE is the new global academic imprint of
St. Martin's Press LLC Scholarly and Reference Division and
Palgrave Publishers Ltd (formerly Macmillan Press Ltd).

ISBN 10: 0-333-92953-5
ISBN 13: 978 0-333-92953-7

This book is printed on paper suitable for recycling and made from
fully managed and sustained forest sources.
Logging, pulping and manufacturing processes are
expected to conform to the environmental regulations
of the country of origin.

A catalogue record for this book is available from the British Library.

Copy-edited and typeset by Povey–Edmondson
Tavistock and Rochdale, England

Printed and bound in Great Britain by
CPI Antony Rowe, Chippenham and Eastbourne

Contents

List of Figures and Tables   ix

Preface to the Second Edition   xi

PART I THEORY

1 The Role of Economic Theory   3

1.1   Introduction   3
1.2   The Nature of the Consumer   5
1.3   The Nature of the Market   6
1.4   The Nature of 'Public'   8
1.5   Governments and the Public Interest   13
1.6   Conclusions   14

2 The Economic Rationale for Government   17

2.1   Introduction   17
2.2   Economic Roles of Government   18
2.3   The Presumption in Favour of Market Provision   19
2.4   Market Failure: The Rationale for Government
      Intervention   26
2.5   Misuses of the Theory of Market Failure   42
2.6   Conclusions   44

3 Theories of Public Sector Growth   46

3.1   Introduction   46
3.2   Public Expenditure Categories   47
3.3   Explaining the Growth of Exhaustive Public
      Expenditures   48
3.4   Explaining the Growth of Transfer Expenditures   57
3.5   Conclusions   60

4 The Economic Effects of Taxation   62

4.1   Introduction   62
4.2   Classification of Taxation   62
4.3   Economically Optimal Taxes   63

4.4	Tax Incidence	66
4.5	The Welfare Effects of Taxation	69
4.6	Incentive and Disincentive Effects of Taxation	71
4.7	Empirical Evidence	77
4.8	Conclusions	82

5 The Economic Effects of Public Sector Borrowing   **84**

5.1	Introduction	84
5.2	The Crowding-out Hypothesis	85
5.3	Conclusions	93

6 Charging for Public Sector Outputs   **95**

6.1	Introduction	95
6.2	The Roles of Charges	95
6.3	Charging in Relation to Marginal Cost	97
6.4	Charges Adjusted for Externalities and Merit Goods	101
6.5	Charges Adjusted for Equity Criteria	102
6.6	Problems in the Payment of Subsidy	103
6.7	Charges Adjusted for their Institutional Context	105
6.8	Charging in Relation to Benefit	106
6.9	Charges Combining Cost, Benefit, Equity and Environmental Considerations	109
6.10	Conclusions	110

7 Public Choice Theory of Government Intervention   **112**

7.1	Introduction	112
7.2	Models of Government	113
7.3	Behavioural Problems of Leviathan Governments	115
7.4	Categorising Inefficiency	119
7.5	Conclusions	121

PART II POLICY AND PRACTICE

8 Rolling Back the Frontiers of the State   **127**

8.1	Introduction	127
8.2	Categorising the Major Reforms During the 1980s and 1990s	129
8.3	Demand-side Policy and Practice	131
8.4	Supply-side Policy and Practice	132
8.5	Supply-side Policies for Private Markets	136
8.6	Supply-side Policies for the Public Sector	147
8.7	The Purchaser–Provider Split	152
8.8	Private Financing of Public Sector Projects	154
8.9	Conclusions	160

9   Public Expenditure Policy and Practice   163

9.1   Introduction   163
9.2   The Public Expenditure/GDP Ratio   165
9.3   Cutting the Public Expenditure/GDP Ratio   168
9.4   Expenditure Components   172
9.5   Controlling Social Security Expenditures   180
9.6   Is Social Security Spending Out of Control?   198
9.7   The Changing Philosophy for the Welfare State   199
9.8   Conclusions   202

10   Tax Policy and Practice   206

10.1   Introduction   206
10.2   Principles of Taxation   208
10.3   The 'Burden of Taxation'   209
10.4   The Balance between Direct and Indirect Taxes   214
10.5   The Main Principles of UK Tax Policy During the 1980s
       and 1990s   215
10.6   Extending the VAT Base   225
10.7   Earmarked Taxes   231
10.8   Integration of Income Tax and National Insurance   242
10.9   Conclusions   247
Appendix 10.1   UK Taxes   248
Appendix 10.2   The Impact of Applying VAT to Newspapers   259
Appendix 10.3   Abolition of the Local Domestic Property Tax   260
Appendix 10.4   Tax Harmonisation   262

11   Public Sector Borrowing: Policy and Practice   267

11.1   Introduction   267
11.2   The Changing Economic Role of Budget Deficits   269
11.3   Defining and Measuring Public Sector Borrowing   271
11.4   A Structural or Cyclical Budget Deficit?   280
11.5   Forecasting the Budget Deficit/Surplus   283
11.6   Financing a Budget Deficit   284
11.7   Medium-term Debt Targets   286
11.8   Stocks and Flows of Debt   288
11.9   Conclusions   290

12   Income Inequalities and Economic Restructuring   293

12.1   Introduction   293
12.2   Definitions of Poverty   296
12.3   The Distribution of Income and Wealth   300
12.4   Limits of Principle and Practice   312
12.5   The Distributional Effects of Economic Policy   321
12.6   Dispelling Distributional Myths   325
12.7   Conclusions   326

PART III   CASE STUDIES OF THEORY, POLICY AND PRACTICE

13   Nationalisation, Privatisation and Regulation   333

13.1   Introduction   333
13.2   Privatisation Versus Nationalisation   334
13.3   The Efficiency Case for Nationalisation   341
13.4   The Efficiency Case for Privatisation   344
13.5   Comparing Efficiency under Nationalisation and Privatisation   345
13.6   Forms of Privatisation   350
13.7   Privatisation and Industry Structure   353
13.8   The Rationale for Regulation   357
13.9   Alternative Forms of Regulation   359
13.10   Regulatory Philosophy in the UK   361
13.11   The Form of Regulation in the UK: RPI minus X   362
13.12   Reconsideration of Rate of Return Versus Price Cap
        Regulation   367
13.13   Allocatively Inefficient Regulation   369
13.14   Conclusions   371

14   Water – A Case Study of Regulation and Charging   374

14.1   Introduction   374
14.2   General Characteristics   376
14.3   Economic Characteristics   377
14.4   Dealing with Market Failure   380
14.5   Regulation   383
14.6   Restructuring Water and Sewerage in Scotland   399
14.7   Charging for Water and Sewerage Services   401
14.8   Other Forms of Demand Management   417
14.9   Conclusions   420

15   Market Testing and Contracting Out   424

15.1   Introduction   425
15.2   Market Testing in Central Government   425
15.3   Market Testing in Local Government   427
15.4   Is Contracting Out Privatisation?   429
15.5   The Degree of Competition   432
15.6   The Extent and Nature of Cost Savings   432
15.7   Justifying the Choice of Services Subject to Market
        Testing   438
15.8   Interactions between Competition and Service Objectives   440
15.9   Conclusions   441

Index   445

List of Figures and Tables

List of figures

2.1	The Efficiency Case for Perfect Competition	20
2.2	The Production Possibility Frontier	22
2.3	Indifference Curves	23
2.4	Maximising Welfare	24
2.5	Negative Externalities	35
2.6	Positive Externalities	39
3.1	The Median Voter Demand Model	51
3.2	The Service Environment and Productivity Differential Models	54
4.1	Economically Optimal Taxes on Commodities	64
4.2	Taxation of Monopolisitic Rent	65
4.3	Tax Incidence	67
4.4	Price Elasticity of Demand and Tax Incidence	68
4.5	Welfare Effects of Taxation	69
4.6	Incentive and Disincentive Effects of Income Tax	72
4.7	Income and Substitution Effects	73
4.8	Comparing a Poll Tax and an Income Tax in Efficiency Terms	75
4.9	The Impact of Tax Changes on Tax Revenue	81
5.1	The Relationship between the PSBR and Interest Rates	87
5.2	The Relationship between Interest Rates and Investment	87
6.1	Marginal Cost Pricing	97
6.2	Subsidies for Allocative Efficiency and Equity	100
6.3	Welfare Comparison of In-kind and In-cash Subsidies	104
6.4	Two-market Price Discrimination	108
7.1	Bureaucratic Empire Building	118
8.1	The Purchaser–Provider Split	153
12.1	Redistribution of Original Income	303
12.2	Distribution of Income around the Mean	305
12.3	Integration of Income Tax and Social Security: Negative Income Tax	315
14.1	A Continuous Water Rate Schedule	408
14.2	A Stepped Water Rate Schedule	409

List of tables

2.1	A Taxonomy of Market Failure	30
7.1	Political Exploitation of Majority Voting Rules	117
9.1	The Growth of Public Expenditure 1963–4 to 2001–2	166
9.2	Public Expenditure 1997–8 to 2001–2: Summary	174
9.3	Total Managed Expenditure (TME) for Major Services 1984–5 to 1999–00	178–9
9.4	Major State Benefits by Category	181
9.5	Social Security Total Managed Expenditure 1994–5 to 1999–00	182
10.1	The Burden of Taxation in the UK 1996	213
10.2	The Main UK Taxes 2000/1	248
13.1	Nationalisation and Privatisation in the UK	337
13.2	Regulatory Bodies and Formulae	363
14.1	Average Unmeasured Household Water and Sewerage Bills 1994/5	389
14.2	Charge Limits for Water and Sewerage 1995–2000	391
14.3	Price Limits for 2000–1 to 2004–5	393
14.4	Average Expected Household Bills	395
14.5	Water and Sewerage Charges, West of Scotland Water, 2000/1	405
15.1	Cost Savings from Competitive Contracting: International Evidence	430

Preface to the Second Edition

The aim of this book is to produce a rather more comprehensive, wide-ranging treatment of public sector economics than is usual. It deals with theory, policy and practice within the broad context of political economy and attempts a more general integration of them than is found in most other economics texts. It recognises that students invariably study other subjects simultaneously with economics and so attempts to provide more of a multi-disciplinary approach than is usually the case.

The level of analysis is aimed at second and third year students taking degrees in public administration, public sector management, accountancy, social policy and social science. It provides only as much economic theory as is required in order for the student to gain a reasonable understanding of policy and practice in the UK during the 1980s and 1990s. All chapters in this second edition have been updated to take account of the election of the Labour government in 1997 and its implementation of policies up to the very end of the year 2000. The increasingly supply-side orientation of policy is emphasised throughout the book.

Most existing texts provide only very brief coverage of the practical aspects of policy. Where they do discuss policy implementation, they tend to retreat behind non-specific comments and points of principle. This book does neither. It provides a cogent appraisal of policy and practice in a readable and policy-relevant way. Hopefully, it will enable the reader to appreciate the arguments both supporting and questioning such developments as the reform of taxation and social security, of trade union and minimum wage legislation, of local government and the civil service and of former state industries through privatisation and regulation.

The very nature of 'public' is being so fundamentally changed that the conventional public sector economics textbook also has to be made less technical and mechanistic and more appreciative of political economy. An attempt is made to show how alternative economic theories become politicised and are used to provide intellectual justifications for ideological, moral and ethical beliefs. A serious effort is also made to make the practical detail relevant to the issues being discussed, in order that the student can appreciate the theoretical and conceptual underpinnings of policy and practice.

Chapter titles and subheadings avoid use of economists' jargon in an attempt to make the book more immediately comprehensible to the browser of contents pages and more suitable to students of multi-disciplinary undergraduate programmes. In-text references are generally avoided in order to expedite reading. Further reading is referenced at the end of each chapter.

Some of the traditional areas of public sector economics are excluded (for example, cost–benefit analysis) because they do not directly underpin an understanding of the development of policy and practice. In turn, this text includes general topics which are not treated extensively in other public sector economics texts (for example charges) and it also provides detailed case studies of nationalisation/privatisation, water and market testing and contracting out.

Part I deals almost exclusively with microeconomic theory. Chapter 1 provides a critical appraisal of the methodological approach adopted by economics in order that the student may appreciate the strengths and the limitations of economic theory relating to the public sector. Chapter 2 sets out the efficiency argument for allowing perfectly competitive markets to function and provides the broad efficiency rationale for government intervention based on 'market failure'. Whilst Chapter 2 provides the efficiency rationale for intervention, it does not specifically explain the growth of public expenditure. Hence, Chapter 3 examines the alternative economic theories of public expenditure growth.

Public expenditure has to be financed by taxation, by borrowing or by charges. Each of these sources of finance may lead to economic effects that counteract the economic efficiency benefits expected from government intervention. They are considered in the following three chapters. Chapter 4 examines the *prima facie* efficiency and welfare cases against taxation (unless used to correct market failure). Chapter 5 considers the possible adverse economic impacts of government borrowing to finance budget deficits. Chapter 6 reviews the economic case for charges and considers the subsidies often associated with them.

Part I is completed by Chapter 7, which reconsiders the validity of the assumption of benevolent government intervention in dealing with the problems of market failure. In particular, it reviews the economic arguments concerning excessive government and the need to restrain the growth of the public sector.

Part II provides a detailed analysis of the UK Conservative and Labour governments' economic policy and practice for the public sector during the 1980s and 1990s. It illustrates the relevance of the theory in Part I. Chapter 8 outlines the development of supply-side policies intended to increase the flexibility of aggregate supply. Chapter 9 considers the attempts to control the growth of public expenditure and the implications for individual expenditure programmes such as social security. Chapter 10 examines tax policy and practice and critically appraises possible reforms, for example the use of 'ear-marked' taxes for health.

Chapter 11 deals with public sector borrowing and public debt. Chapter 12 assesses the implications of economic restructuring and government policy for the distribution of income and wealth.

Part III contains case studies providing detailed practical illustrations of the integration of the theory of Part I with the policy and practice of Part II. The common theme of all three chapters is privatisation. Chapter 13 compares and contrasts the cases for nationalisation and privatisation of major industries. It also considers the rationale for regulation (subsequent to privatisation) and considers alternative regulatory arrangements. Chapter 14 illustrates the applicability to the water and sewerage industries of market failure concepts, the economic theory of pricing, and privatisation. Chapter 15 provides a case study of market testing and contracting out the provision of public sector services. It demonstrates how greater competition can be introduced for those services that remain within the public sector.

Having read this book, it is hoped that the student will have a much broader understanding of the nature of public sector economics, particularly in terms of its implications for supply-side policies. It is not merely a heavily theoretical and abstract area of intellectual enquiry. It is also an area of study that is directly relevant to our everyday lives. It affects the buses and trains on which we travel, the workers who empty our bins, the gas and electricity delivered to our homes, even the water coming out of our taps! It affects the taxes we pay to central and local government, the charges we pay at the local sports or leisure centre, the social security benefits we receive. It affects the agencies with which we register our cars or motorcycles or to which we apply for passports.

Whether we realise it or not, public sector economics is not confined within the covers of a textbook. It is out there, influencing the small and seemingly insignificant details of our everyday lives.

STEPHEN J. BAILEY

Part I

Theory

The Role of Economic Theory

1.1 Introduction
1.2 The Nature of the Consumer
1.3 The Nature of the Market
1.4 The Nature of 'Public'
1.5 Governments and the Public Interest
1.6 Conclusions

1.1 Introduction

The reader may be hoping to find answers to questions such as why does the public sector exist, is it too big or too small, are higher taxes bad, is more public spending good, is improved efficiency contrary to equity, can economic theory justify the substantial changes to the welfare state during the 1980s and 1990s? Whilst the book directly addresses these and other questions, it is not able to provide definitive answers. It can only show which theories support or refute economic and political arguments, which facts provide corroborative evidence in support of economic theories and how changes in policy and practice reflect belief in the validity of those theories rather than proven fact.

The distinction between **normative** and **positive** economics supposedly makes clear the scientific basis of economics. Normative statements incorporate value judgements, beliefs and moral stances, what **should** happen (e.g. to wage levels or benefits). Positive economics shows what **will** happen if certain specified conditions are met and if certain changes occur (e.g. if the price of labour rises in a perfectly competitive economy). Economic theories based on such deduction cannot be tested by means of experiments in laboratory situations. Instead they can be empirically tested through statistical analysis of large numbers of observations following changes in economic conditions. However a myriad of other factors simultaneously influence the economy and so results must be interpreted: data never 'speaks for itself', despite the colloquialism. Hence, it is rarely the case that definitive answers are provided to support or refute competing theories. Nonetheless it is usually implicitly assumed that positive economics can be presented in a value-free way, economists acting as independent, objective, scientific advisers on economic matters. Economic advisers can supposedly remain aloof from policy formulation and equity issues by simply showing the effects of policy and practice in a non-judgemental way.

The writings of early economists were suffused with a sense of ethics and morals. Modern economics, however, attempts to prove its claims to scientific objectivity and theoretical rigour. This can only be achieved by basing economic theory on a set of assumptions that simplify and abstract from reality. The fundamental underpinning of almost all economic theory is the assumption that individuals are calculatively rational, self-interested consumers whose every decision and action seeks to maximise their personal well-being based upon clear and consistent preferences. In the economics jargon, this is referred to as (economic) 'rent-seeking'. This is the adoption of behaviour patterns that achieve the maximisation of individual welfare or utility through calculation and equalisation of marginal rates of benefit and cost. Producers are assumed to act likewise, firms pursuing profit maximisation through the calculation and equalisation of marginal revenue and marginal cost. Those with other objectives are either bankrupted by the market system or subjected to takeover by other profit-maximising firms.

The 'rational economic man' model assumes consumer behaviour is selfish and single-minded. Whilst this may be thought an extreme view of behaviour, it is no more extreme than the 'selfish gene' model of evolutionary biology. Both models assume selfish behaviour in order to derive rich analytical insights and to advance those disciplines. Nevertheless, the 'rational economic man' model remains a highly partial explanation of the behaviour of consumers, producers and market economies even though this self-maximising behavioural pattern underpins the teaching of most economics at undergraduate level.

Whilst other branches of economic theory (e.g. institutional economics) can improve on these simplistic representations of human behaviour, a fuller explanation of human behaviour requires recourse to other academic disciplines, including philosophy, political science, psychology, social anthropology and sociology. The integration of economics with these other disciplines probably provides more potential than the further development of economic theory within its existing analytical straitjacket. Not surprisingly, other disciplines regard economic theory as esoteric if not arcane, an abstraction from reality based on a multitude of untenable assumptions within an incomplete analytical framework. Economics is not a pure, objective, clinical science (if, indeed, such an approach were appropriate to the policy-making arena) and the prescriptions of economists are no more valid than those of other interest groups schooled in other disciplines.

1.2   The nature of the consumer

Economic theory has a purely instrumental view of human action, behaviour being consistently rational and solely influenced by economic incentives. Maximisation of economic welfare requires incentives to be the same as those provided by economy-wide perfect competition. A polar opposite of this view is that human behaviour is influenced by moral principles, social norms, altruism and idealism. The results of multidisciplinary research funded during the later 1990s by the Economic and Social Research Council (ESRC) within its 'Economic Beliefs and Behaviour' programme challenge the two key assumptions of 'rational economic man' and set preference patterns. The research results suggest that human behaviour is influenced by both economic and non-economic factors and that preferences are not as clear and consistent as is assumed. In particular, altruism seems to coexist with self-interest in attitudes towards public expenditure and taxation. It may be the case that non-economic influences (such as group norms and culture) are decisive where economic incentives are weak, or even that they override strong economic incentives. The weaker the economic incentives (both absolutely and relative to non-economic factors) the less the predictive power of economic theory.

The economics of voter behaviour provides an illustrative example (see Chapter 7). A calculatively rational voter has little economic incentive to vote where there is little difference between political parties, where parties cannot be trusted to carry out the manifestos for which they were elected, where the probability that his or her vote will be pivotal in determining the outcome of the election is insignificant, and where the cost (in terms of effort and time forgone) of voting is high relative to the potential benefits. However the predictions of this economic theory of voter abstention are not substantiated by voter turnout. Clearly there are other non-economic influences on people's decision to vote. For example one may be disillusioned with politicians and policies but not with the democratic system itself.

Despite these caveats, purchasing and consumption are all-pervasive human actions. Economic models of consumer decision-making assume homogeneous products and *ceteris paribus* (all other factors remaining unchanged). The only relevant factors are the price of the commodity in question, the prices of other commodities and any changes in consumers' incomes or tastes. Consumption increases to the point where price paid equals marginal benefit. In practice, however, consumer decisions are not mono-attribute but rather multi-attribute. For example, whilst recurrent purchases of salt or carrots involve very few factors other than price, infrequent purchases of consumer durables such as houses and cars account for substantial proportions of disposable incomes and involve multiple attributes including risk taking. For example potential purchasers will be concerned about the reliability of a particular car and the investment value of a particular house. Such purchases involve complex cognitive processes which require resort to consumer psychology. Behavioural and institutional factors are also important for house purchase (e.g. the operating rules of mortgage grantors).

Even if all possible future outcomes were known, together with their associated probabilities, individuals may have limited abilities to process such information. In addition to the possibility of 'rational ignorance', psychological experiments suggest that people may use information incorrectly or fail to use all information relevant to decision-making. For example research evidence suggests that consumers do not simply equate marginal benefits with price but also consider what they have already spent (i.e. sunk costs). In other words, 'bygones are **not** bygones'. Consumers also appear to respond differently to prices according to whether they are described as discounts (positively valued) or surcharges (negatively valued), a form of 'money illusion'. Similar errors of judgement may be incurred by those in the public sector making decisions on behalf of individuals (e.g. doctors). Limited memory and inattentiveness may compound such errors. In practice most decision-making is characterised not by quantifiable risk but by uncertainty (i.e. all possible future outcomes and/or their associated probabilities are not known).

Hence consumer decisions may not obey the predictions of expected utility theory. Instead they may reflect 'bounded rationality' where individuals reduce decision-making problems to a modest number of variables, making 'reasonable' rather than 'optimal' decisions. Such 'satisficing' (rather than 'optimising') decisions then become the outcomes of 'rules of thumb' rather than of calculatively rational self-maximising rules. Whilst the choice between alternative rules of thumb would seem to depend on their relative costs (in terms of effort) and accuracy (relative to an optimising solution), once again the information required for such comparisons may also be subject to bounded rationality. These caveats should be borne in mind when reading Chapter 2.

1.3   The nature of the market

Capitalism is based on an accumulative dynamic constrained by scarcity. This leads to a bias in favour of economic growth that can best be delivered by the private competitive market. Neoclassical economic theory demonstrates that prices in unconstrained private markets are clearly superior to non-market planning systems in achieving an efficient allocation of resources (i.e. one that maximises economic welfare). In general, allocative efficiency requires the greatest possible output and the greatest aggregate benefit to be derived from the finite level of resources available to an economy. This will only be the case if a set of highly abstract marginal conditions are satisfied (see Chapter 2). It must not be possible to reallocate either productive resources (such as capital and labour), or the output that is gained from their employment, so as to increase the level of economic well-being. Any reallocation that is necessary to satisfy this condition can almost always be achieved within the market system simply by using taxes and subsidies to adjust demand and supply. Such allocative efficiency is predicated on the resulting income distribution being acceptable.

Allocative efficiency is technical, mechanistic, free of cultural and institutional context and therefore claims to be the universal positive science of economic behaviour. In fact orthodox economics has to progress from a highly sophisticated technical intellectual construct towards a more comprehensive and relevant model that combines the socio/politico and cultural contexts with economic constructs. The acclaimed market model operates within an institutional vacuum. However it is not markets *per se* that distribute resources but rather institutions such as modern corporations acting within the constraints imposed by the market system. Large corporations face many of the same organisational problems as governments (see Chapter 2), even if they are subject to a different set of constraints and incentives. The direct comparison of government with markets is therefore *methodologically invalid* and leads to a distorted set of conclusions that inevitably cast market systems in a favourable light.

The allocative efficiency case for the market allocation of scarce resources in almost all circumstances is mere economic dogma. Their inherent superiority arises, by definition, out of the assumptions upon which the economic model is based. Government intervention is only required where private markets fail to achieve such an efficient allocation and subsidy is only justifiable in **efficiency terms** in order to counteract market failure.

Most economists avoid equity issues, regarding them as judgemental (i.e. normative) and yet these are often a major influence on policy and practice (see Part II). Some attempt has been made to integrate equity and efficiency issues through the assumption of 'inequality aversion' and its resulting negative utility. In other words, increased inequality may reduce the welfares of those who are made better off in terms of income distribution. However this line of analysis is still set within the conventional approach of economic theory.

Conventional economic analysis usually concludes that there is a trade-off between equity and efficiency, for example because highly redistributive income taxes may reduce the incentive to work (see Chapter 4). Nevertheless, society may regard the market allocation of resources as unacceptable in **equity terms** and hence payment of subsidy may also be determined by political considerations. The distribution of income is significantly affected by the provision of free or heavily subsidised public sector services as much as by the levying of taxes on earnings and expenditures or the payment of state benefits in cash (see Chapter 12). However equity is not solely concerned with the distribution of income; nor is it the only aspect of the nature of 'public'.

1.4   The nature of 'public'

In the literature of subjects other than economics there is a pragmatic or common-sense view of the public sector. It is regarded as the outcome of historical processes and political compromise, an evolving organic institution that has changed in response to the imperatives of national security and changing social expectations regarding the welfare state.

Such a pre-theoretical interpretation of the nature of 'public' is not shared by neoclassical economic theory. Instead the nature of 'public' is determined purely on theoretical grounds and becomes an accidental residual of the failings of private markets to achieve an economically efficient allocation of resources (see Chapter 2). The need for public and collective action arises out of the limitations of private allocative processes and so economics has an essentially negative rationale for government intervention that is quite distinct from the more positive approaches of other academic disciplines such as political science. The efficiency justification for government intervention is based on two interdependent parts, first that markets fail to achieve an efficient allocation of resources, and second that government intervention corrects rather than exacerbates the degree of allocative distortion. Both these conditions must be fulfilled for intervention to be justified; failure in just one rules it out.

In principle, the theoretical rationale for government intervention provided by economics, and the nature and scope of that intervention, can be determined by technical criteria. In this analytical framework, the essence of 'public' is that it is merely the sum of actions necessary to correct private distortions. Such a rationale for government intervention clearly does not explain much of what governments and the public sector do. Neoclassical economic theory provides at best only a partial explanation of the need for a public sector. Similarly any economic rationale for the increased use of service charges by central and local government set in allocative efficiency terms is also partial (see Chapter 6).

Economic theory also requires public sector decision rules to yield the same choices that would result from the aggregation of individual preferences. In other words public sector decisions should mimic those of private markets after allowing for any of the technical measures (i.e. taxes and subsidies) required to cope with market failure. If voting systems fail adequately to reflect the aggregate of private wants, or if politicians and public sector bureaucrats ignore those wants, then government failure becomes quite profound. It is no longer simply a question of which institutional framework (private market or public sector) can deliver a particular output at lowest social cost. Now it is a question about the legitimacy of providing particular (levels of) services.

Here the economics of both public choice and public provision suggests that collective action is something of a disaster area. Opportunism and the pursuit of self interest in a calculatively rational way means that the users and providers of public services will always seek to promote their individual interests at the expense of the collective interest. Such behaviour ultimately leads to the inefficient and excessive provision of public services that are of low value relative to their costs (see Chapter 7). This will be exacerbated by the largely random decisions resulting from imperfect voting systems. The analytical framework utilised by economic theory yields a dismal appreciation of public and an overriding preference in favour of private markets where competition and prices can be relied on to avoid or minimise such distortions.

However it could be argued that this perspective is the inevitable outcome of taking private maximising market activity as the natural order of things and then building the theoretical rationale for government activity on that foundation. In other words, it is assumed that markets are natural, provide the most efficient framework for the growth/welfare-maximising allocation of resources, and everything else is a problem. But this makes two questionable assumptions: that the driving force pervading all human activity is the maximisation of economic materialism and that scarcity is a pervasive constraint on the availability of resources required to facilitate that maximisation. However it is arguable that welfare is not directly related to one's ownership of resources (or property rights) and that psychological, spiritual and relational (distributional) factors are of greater importance. Moreover the notion of scarcity is cultural rather than naturally given: it is the social, political and philosophical invention of classical liberal man.

It is instructive to invert the conventional approach of public sector economics textbooks, which almost invariably begin with a demonstration of the primacy of perfectly competitive private markets in allocative efficiency terms and then demonstrate the special and restrictive cases in which government intervention is required. An alternative approach would be to attempt to theorise adequately the nature of 'public', which would yield a clear and unambiguous definition of what activities should be undertaken by the public sector according to the set of criteria derived. All other activities could, in principle, be left for private markets to provide. The problem then becomes one of whether market systems are competitive enough to deliver such outputs in an allocatively efficient way. In this approach it is the private sector that becomes the residual. The fact that markets could provide the service by means of the price system does not necessarily mean that they should do so. In practice it is not possible to define the essential nature of public nor to draw such a clear dividing line between 'public' and 'private' (see Chapters 13 and 14). Nor is it possible adequately to theorise either one.

Government is not only a regulatory arrangement for the achievement of allocative efficiency. It promotes pluralism, participation and public choices as well as the provision of services, the so-called '4 Ps'. It has for centuries been argued (by J. S. Mill and others) that government is concerned with the discussion of public ideas whereby democratic deliberation (deliberative government) identifies and develops common interests in order to civilise the masses, constrain selfishness and promote the public interest. The emphasis on deliberation has been superseded within economic analysis by the idea that the pursuit of self-interest can be relied on to promote the public interest through the 'invisible hand' of market forces much more effectively than deliberative democracy. These ideas were developed during the Scottish Enlightenment by Adam Smith (1723–90) and others and imply a minimal **instrumental** (rather than **deliberative**) role for government, which is restricted to controlling the abuse of market power.

The prevailing view underpinning economic theory is that all individuals (in both the public and private sectors) pursue their own self-interest and that the collective interest is simply the aggregate of individual interests. The government simply has to find this out in order to maximise welfare. This is a very narrow, mechanistic view. Public choice theory identifies a democratic defect in that voting systems necessarily fail to represent accurately the aggregate of individual choices (see Chapter 7). However such problems arise from a misrepresentation of government that is not simply a vote-counting mechanism but is rather a dialectic forum in the Socratic tradition. Ideally governments comprise a set of individuals who can be trusted to take the right decisions and whose decisions may not in fact correspond to the aggregate or even to the majority of individual preferences at the time the decision is made. There is clearly a different meaning of the nature of 'public' here compared with the narrower economic meaning, which allows no deliberative role.

Time and place are important influences on the nature of public and private and they make it impossible to determine a clear, categorical definition of each sector that will stand the test of time. Instead the boundary between public and private is both fluid and hazy, not just in terms of interest but even in terms of ownership. Many services currently provided free by government have their origins in Victorian times and are still largely predicated by the sets of socioeconomic circumstances and morals of that period. Many of the changes to the scope and financing of the public sector during the 1980s and 1990s reflect a different moral view of the rights and responsibilities of the individual and an emphasis on equality of opportunity rather than of outcome (see Chapters 9, 10 and 12).

Although it may have arisen as a result of changes in the balance of political power, the privatisation debate (see Chapter 13) is essentially an empirical question regarding the efficiency of different institutional forms, not of market versus non-market allocative systems. It is argued that political interference distorted both decision-making and the policing mechanism within the public sector, with the result that both management incentives and the policing function provided by the threat of bankruptcy or takeover were severely distorted or nullified. There is a presumption that the transfer of property rights to the private sector reinstates such incentives and imperatives, even if this is not strictly true. For example it can be argued that where a former public monopoly becomes a private monopoly the latter is easier to control by means of regulation. Such a perceived need for continuing control through a regulatory framework effectively admits the continuing public nature of the privatised industry and the need to ensure minimum standards of safety, availability of service, quality of output, acceptability of tariff structure and so on. Even when services remain within the public sector publicness does not necessarily require direct provision by central or local government (see Chapter 15).

Hence the form of institution and the mode of intervention are crucial to the public–private debate. It is not just a question of which sets of abstract criteria give a particular service publicness or privateness, it is also an empirical question regarding the efficiency of the particular alternative organisational forms that could be used for service delivery. The major public utilities such as gas, electricity and water are no less public and no more private simply because ownership rights have been restructured by privatisation. All continue to have the essence of publicness in that they are crucial to the well-being of the nation's citizens. The same could be said for other services such as leisure and recreation, education and health, irrespective of how property rights are organised. Publicness is not the sole prerogative of a particular set of services; it is a concern for access and quality that goes beyond the purely selfish needs of the individual. It implies some form of deliberation about what is proper, rather than simply assessing what the populace of consumers or voters demand. Making up for past under-investment in sewerage treatment is a case in point (see Chapter 14).

The nature of public is therefore not defined in terms of a particular set of service characteristics. Nor is it defined on the basis of services being on the 'commanding heights' of the economy (a phrase used to justify nationalisation – see Chapter 13). The nature of public is not to be found in either technical or relative criteria. Rather the nature of public is the need for deliberation and reconsideration of both the appropriateness of uncontrolled outcomes and of the extent and nature of government intervention. Hence there is no static dividing line between public and private that is constant over time. Indeed there is such a large degree of overlap between the public and private sectors that it is invalid to consider them as mutually exclusive. Capitalism can only survive as long as the state enforces contracts and protects private property through legislation. Furthermore, many private companies could not exist without government contracts (e.g. for armaments or for domestic refuse disposal).

On the one hand the nature of public is conceptual and abstract and crucially dependent on the particular set of socioeconomic conditions and the moral values that exist at any one point in time. This theme is made evident in the discussion of the welfare state (Chapter 9). On the other hand the nature of public is also pragmatic and institutional and depends on technological and organisational imperatives. This theme is made evident in the discussion of the increasing scope for further liberalisation of regulated industries (see Chapter 13). Public is not simply that which cannot be private. Local government provides many services that could be (and indeed are) provided by the private sector, such as leisure and recreation services. Nor does public necessarily require a complete rejection of the market system for a particular set of services in whole or in part (see Chapter 15). Nor does public require public ownership as distinct from control. Regulation of privatised, formerly state-owned public utilities is increasingly common (see Chapter 13). Nor does it deny use of charges (see Chapters 6 and 14) or of other forms of private finance (see Chapter 8).

The belief that public services are in some sense distinctive and should therefore be free at the point of consumption has no objective analytical base. Continued payment of subsidy is often justified in terms of initial endowments, i.e. that those who have received free services in the past should continue to receive them in the future. Alternatively it is sometimes argued that services should continue to be provided free in the future simply because they have been provided free in the past, even when different groups of people use the service in different time periods. However the circumstances of future users may be radically different from those of previous users. It is also sometimes asserted that charging for services would in some way destroy their very publicness or collective nature, although this is not self-evident. Free services are sometimes claimed to promote democratic decision-making, for example in respect of local government functions, again of questionable validity.

None of these rationales has any clear intellectual or objective basis in terms of 'the nature of public'. The real objection to the increased use of charges for public sector services is based on custom and practice, the fact that they have almost exclusively depended on tax-financed support. There is a legitimate concern for the welfare of service users but this does not preclude consideration of charges where they promote rather than detract from the achievement of service objectives. It is those objectives that encapsulate the nature of public, not the form in which the service is organised nor the way in which it is financed. This is made evident in the case studies of Part III.

1.5 Governments and the public interest

Economics textbooks are replete with the assertion that democratically elected governments act in accordance with promoting the 'public interest'. The public interest is either defined vaguely as the well-being of its citizens or specifically in terms of a social welfare function (an aggregation of all individuals' welfare). However one of the lessons of history is that popular sovereignty cannot be trusted to guarantee human rights ('rights' being a value-laden concept). It is a liberal illusion to trust democratically elected governments with the protection of minorities. It is democratic institutions, together with their legal and constitutional safeguards, that enshrine human rights and protect the public interest rather than elected governments *per se*. A plurality of such institutions provides the 'division of powers' and 'checks and balances' against creeping totalitarianism. This is aided in many developed countries by traditional civil society, including religious, voluntary, charitable, labour and local community organisations, all of which enmesh individuals in the social and moral order of society.

The general public may assume that national governments are capable of managing their economic welfares. However there appears to be a decline in the capacity of nation states to act as political and economic powers within the economic and political unions of Western Europe and elsewhere. An idealised view of democracy along the lines of Rousseau, J. S. Mill and others is that of active and ongoing deliberative participation in political life. The reality, however, is limited to a democracy of infrequent passive participation, usually limited to casting one's vote (if at all) at election time. Active participation is confined to a small minority that is often unrepresentative of society in general. Power is 'brokered' in most modern democracies by a largely closed political class that tends to exclude or under-represent the working classes, poor, ethnic groups, women, and so on. The majority of members of parliament (Houses of Commons and Lords), of ministers and of senior public officials are men from the professional and propertied classes.

Whatever the reason for under-representation (discrimination or apathy), the fact is that politically marginalised groups on the socio-economic periphery cannot be sure that governments will protect their interests. Indeed if groups with political power have a different set of preferences then it is *methodologically contradictory* to assume that they will promote the interests of others whilst those others pursue calculatively rational, self-maximising decision rules. In terms of this analytical framework, the only check on the self-interested behaviour of those working within the institutions of government is provided by a number of political parties actively competing for office. Even here, collusion may arise to constrain political competition. Clearly it is naive to assume that governments necessarily act in the public interest, even if such a concept can be defined in practical terms.

The meaning of 'public interest' varies between academic disciplines. Within economics it relates to market failure. Within social policy it relates to the welfare state. Within political philosophy it relates to the constitutional relationship between the state and the individual, the liberal tradition of Aristotle, Saint Thomas Acquinas, John Locke and others emphasising the primacy of the individual (Aristotle's view of government being 'the art of governing free men'). In practice, the 'public interest' is a multidisciplinary, politicised concept.

The interpretation and emphasis placed on market failure concepts is derivative of the government's political perspective. Socialists may prefer Keynesian theory since it can be used to justify very detailed intervention in the economy and society, for example how much to spend, when, where and on whom. Non-socialists may prefer monetarist theory since it can be used to justify reduced government intervention (*laissez-faire*). They may also choose to believe theories that justify allowing people to keep what they earn (e.g. the theory that taxation causes disincentive-to-work effects; see Chapter 4). This is the political economy aspect of economic theory. Rather than politicians being the slaves of some defunct economist (as Keynes claimed), different economic theories may become the politicised intellectual rationales of different political parties.

1.6 Conclusions

Economic policies may be based on economic theories (even if those theories are open to question) but they are also influenced by morals, ethics and ideological beliefs. Hence, whilst the intention of this book is to enable the student to appreciate the theoretical framework within which economic policy and practice are set, it must always be borne in mind that their formulation and practical application are influenced by a myriad of factors.

Rather than being unnecessarily rejectionist of the analytical framework of much economic theory, this chapter has attempted to clarify the nature and extent of its contribution to the understanding of the public sector. Economic theory can claim no intellectual or practical superiority over other academic disciplines. It is simply another conceptual framework by which to understand economy and society. It provides no definitive answers to economic and social problems. Its explanatory power is necessarily limited by the simplifying assumptions and abstractions from reality that must be made in order to clarify key issues.

Alternative economic theories are also imbued with moral propositions regarding the roles and responsibilities of the state and of the individual. Those differing propositions yield differing definitions of the public and private sectors. Hence, whilst the foregoing discussion of the nature of public and private could be criticised for providing no clear alternative definitions, such an attempt would be unnecessary and probably futile, in that it would reflect the author's own normative views.

The next chapter sets out the conventional neoclassical rationale for government intervention in the economy, simply in order that the reader may appreciate the highly abstract model upon which many economic prescriptions are based. It attempts to simplify this intellectual construct without losing its coherence. The analysis assumes that consumer decision-making is optimal, not subject to bounded rationality or lack of computational ability. Assuming away all these decision-making constraints for market systems necessarily gives an overwhelming bias in favour of markets and consumer sovereignty. Similarly, applying the same self-serving behavioural assumptions to the actions of politicians and public sector bureaucrats and officials, necessarily yields a strong sense of mistrust of public sector intervention. The reader should bear in mind the caveats of this chapter and, in particular, remember that economic analysis is necessarily partial as an explanation of the behaviour of people, firms and governments.

These caveats are not new to the economics profession. They have been voiced over the years by the likes of Veblen, Galbraith, Leontief and, most recently, Ormerod. However they tend to be underplayed in undergraduate text books which, irrespective of such qualifications, still aspire to scientific positivism based on an overly elaborate set of theories based on mathematical models. This approach gives a grossly misleading impression of the lack of practicality of economics, not just for students but also for the non-economist layperson, public service professional and politician. In fact economics is not only useful, it is central to policy making as **both** Conservative and Labour governments increasingly work with (rather than against) markets to achieve their social and economic objectives. Examples range from differential licence fees for cars to reduce pollution (see Chapter 10) to work-based welfare for the unemployed and low-income groups (see Chapter 12).

The reader is encouraged to go back to the preface in order to appreciate the very wide area of policy and practice falling within the remit of public sector economics. Clearly, there is a high degree of overlap with other academic disciplines in terms of the topics analysed. Government intervention to deal with allocative inefficiency necessarily impinges upon, and is affected or constrained by, the pursuit of multiple objectives. Therefore, public sector economics cannot be studied in isolation from other academic disciplines.

Unless these methodological limitations are recognised there will be unrealistically high expectations of the contribution economic theory can make to the resolution of economic problems. Resulting disappointments will then lead many people to reject economics as irrelevant. Such an outright rejection would be as invalid as a belief that a study of economics provides the route to a panacea for economic ills. Economists specialising in such areas as housing, transport and local government have long recognised the limitations of the neoclassical model and have typically adopted a multidisciplinary approach to the study of these areas. With the exception of Chapter 2, subsequent chapters try to set the neoclassical approach within a multidisciplinary framework.

Further reading

Economic and Social Research Council (online). Available at <http://www.esrc.org.uk>.

Eichner, A. (1983) *Why Economics is Not Yet a Science* (London: Macmillan).

Gerrard, B. (1995) 'The Scientific Basis of Economics: A Review of the Methodological Debates in Economics and Econometrics', *Scottish Journal of Political Economy*, vol. 42, no. 2, pp. 221–35.

Ormerod, P. (1994) *The Death of Economics* (London: Faber & Faber).

2 The Economic Rationale for Government

2.1 Introduction
2.2 Economic Roles of Government
2.3 The Presumption in Favour of Market Provision
2.4 Market Failure: The Rationale for Government Intervention
2.5 Misuses of the Theory of Market Failure
2.6 Conclusions

2.1 Introduction

The public sector (i.e. the institutions and activities of government) is conventionally treated as an alternative to 'the market'. These are often regarded as mutually exclusive, the decision being which sector should undertake a particular productive activity. The market sector is stereotyped as **private**, unregulated, economic activity providing output in accordance with consumers' willingness to pay, allocation of goods and services ultimately depending on the existence or not of **profits**. The public sector is stereotyped as planned non-market services, provision of which is determined **collectively** through democratic decision-making processes, and whose allocation is according to the assessed **needs** of the final recipient. The crucial difference is that the user of market outputs pays a direct cost (market price) whereas the user of public sector outputs pays no direct cost, instead sharing the tax cost with all other taxpayers. This strict categorical distinction is extremely useful as a conceptual framework when analysing the relative roles of markets and governments. However it is fundamentally unsound in terms of the actual structure of the economy. Planning and markets are **not** mutually exclusive. If perfect competition could exist in practice there would be no need for firms to exist. The model of perfect competition is a theory of markets, **not** a theory of the firm. It is an abstraction devoid of institutional form, used to predict changes in price and output that result from changes in demand and supply conditions. If the assumptions of perfect competition existed (such as perfect information and freedom of entry to and exit from the market), then all economic transactions such as the assembly of inputs and production and sale of outputs could be handled instantaneously.

So why do firms (i.e. modern corporations) exist? The answer (in efficiency terms) is that imperfect information and the resulting uncertainty means that transactions involve costs. The costs of agreeing and enforcing transactions may be so high that it becomes cheaper and more efficient to organise internally within the firm – investment finance, the hiring of inputs, production processes and marketing – rather than depend on market provision. Put simply, the modern corporation is a planning mechanism for private production.

Hence the supposed clear, categorical divide between markets and planning is false. The discussion of the previous chapter suggested that the public–private divide is fluid, a matter of degree rather than a clear categorical difference. Free markets simply could not exist without government defining and regulating property rights and laws of contract. In policy terms, what is important is not the existence of planning but rather its scale and its sector.

2.2   Economic roles of government

The four main economic roles of government are:

1. **The allocative role:** the government pursues that allocation of resources which maximises economic welfare. This is generally referred to as allocative efficiency or the 'first best' allocation of resources. The government has to deal with the market distortions caused by monopoly power and other forms of 'market failure' (see below).
2. **The distributive role:** the government balances allocative efficiency with equity in the allocation of resources by using taxation, social security and the distribution of public sector services to influence the distribution of income.
3. **The regulatory role:** the government legislates and enforces laws of contract, consumer protection, justice and so on, in order that the market economy may function.
4. **The stabilisation role:** whereas the allocative, distributive and regulatory roles are microeconomic in nature, the stabilisation role is macroeconomic in using fiscal, monetary and other economic policies to pursue objectives for the control of inflation, unemployment, and so on.

These four roles interact with each other. For example fiscal policy intervention under the stabilisation role involves changes to taxation and public expenditure that affect the distribution of income in cash and in kind (i.e. the monetary value of health, education and other public sector services received).

2.3   The presumption in favour of market provision

For economic welfare to be maximised, it must not be possible to increase output by reorganising the factors of production (including the removal of monopoly power) or to increase welfare by redistributing commodities used for consumption. It is generally accepted that more competition is better than more monopoly because the former is an effective means of maximising both economic growth and the welfare that can ultimately be derived from it. However this does not give the 'efficiency advocate' automatic priority over other forms of advocacy (e.g. democracy). The free market is only optimal in terms of efficiency rules. Society is concerned with many other issues against which allocative efficiency may have to be traded off (e.g. equity).

Perfect competition maximises economic welfare by definition, because of the assumptions and objectives upon which the market model is based. The intuitive explanation is that, in perfectly competitive market conditions, firms have to be as competitive as possible, buying all their inputs at the lowest possible cost (economy), using them to maximise output (productive efficiency), and selling them for a price that only just allows the firm to remain in business (i.e. earning 'normal profits'). Moreover, since all consumers purchase those outputs in accordance with their personal preferences and finances, then output is automatically allocated so as to maximise utility. No rearrangement of production or consumption is possible that will increase economic welfare **for given sets** of production conditions and personal preferences. This is because all producers and all consumers face the same sets of prices. Hence any reallocation of inputs or outputs will reduce allocative efficiency. This intuitive explanation can now be shown diagrammatically.

Figure 2.1(a) shows the standard diagram for a perfectly competitive *firm* producing an homogeneous product in pursuing maximum profits. Price (p) is shown on the vertical axis and quantity (q) on the horizontal axis, with zero at the origin. The usual U-shaped cost curve shows average cost (AC), which is total cost divided by output. If c denotes unit cost and q denotes output then AC equals cq/q. AC initially falls (e.g. because indivisible capital costs are spread over a larger rate of output) but ultimately rises as the rate of output increases (due to the law of diminishing marginal returns). The marginal cost schedule ($MC = \Delta cq/\Delta q$, where Δ denotes 'marginal change in') cuts the lowest point of the AC schedule since when MC is below AC the latter falls, and when MC is greater than AC the latter rises.

Being insignificant in relation to market size, the firm is a price taker, unable to exert any market power on price levels. The firm can sell all its output at $p1$, hence the horizontal price line. Price $p1$ therefore equals

Figure 2.1 The efficiency case for perfect competition: (a) the perfectly competitive firm; (b) the individual consumer's demand; (c) market equilibrium

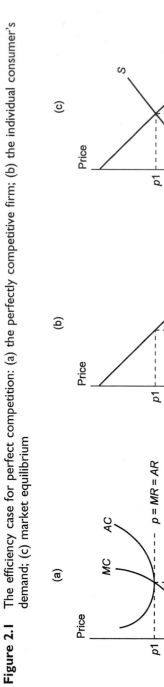
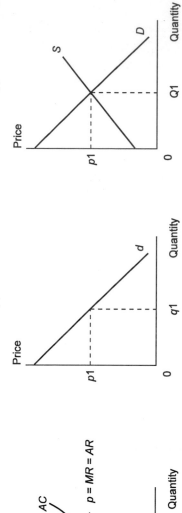

both average revenue (pq/q) and marginal revenue ($\Delta pq/\Delta q$). For levels of production less than $q1$, MR exceeds MC, so that the firm is not maximising profits. MC is greater than MR for levels of production higher than $q1$, so reducing profits. Hence $q1$ maximises profits because $MR = MC$.

Figure 2.1(b) shows that the **consumer** demands more output as the price of the commodity falls. The consumer equates marginal valuation of the commodity, shown by the slope of the demand curve (d), with price. Marginal valuation is greater than price ($p1$) for levels of consumption below $q1$ and less than price for levels of consumption above $q1$. The horizontal aggregation of all quantities demanded at given prices for all consumers yields the market demand schedule D in **Figure 2.1(c)**. The market supply curve S shows that supply rises in response to higher prices (because of the profit maximisation assumption). Equilibrium quantity is at $Q1$ where aggregate demand from all consumers equals aggregate supply from all firms at $p1$. Hence the market clears, there being no excess demand to force price up, nor excess supply to force it down.

Competition minimises costs, equal to $p1$ in **Figure 2.1(a)**. In addition, there is no possibility of monopoly power being used to raise price by reducing output (in order to earn excess profits). Hence output is maximised. In facing the lowest possible price, the consumer can maximise consumption from a fixed income, therefore maximising economic welfare. Hence both production and consumption are maximised within the constraints imposed by finite resources.

This is a **partial** equilibrium situation for a single industry. If perfect competition exists everywhere then economy-wide production and consumption will both be maximised and it will not be possible to increase either by reallocating resources. This **general** equilibrium situation is derived using **Figures 2.2 to 2.4**.

In maximising output from given resources, perfect competition results in the economy being located on its production possibility frontier (PPF). This is shown in Figure 2.2 which assumes that the economy only produces two commodities, X and Y, shown on the vertical and horizontal axes respectively. Zero is at the origin. If all factors of production were devoted to the production of X, the maximum amount that could be produced would be X_{max} with zero Y. Similarly, the maximum amount of Y is Y_{max}, with zero X. The PPF shows all maximum possible combinations of X and Y that the economy can produce from its finite resources (e.g. combination S with Xs and Ys).

The PPF is concave to the origin, showing that the rate at which X can be transformed into Y (a measure of 'opportunity cost') changes as production switches between the two commodities. For example, starting

Figure 2.2   The production possibility frontier

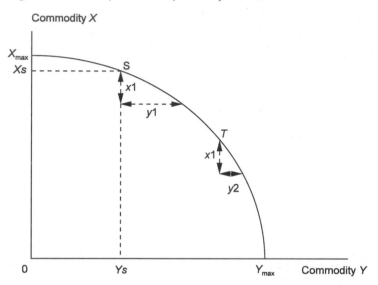

at point S, if the economy reduces production of X by $x1$ the resources so released can be used to produce more of Y, an extra amount of $y1$. If, however, the switch from X to Y had started at point T, then giving up the same amount of X as before ($x1$) yields only $y2$ more of Y ($y2$ is less than $y1$). The production ratios $y1/x1$ and $y2/x1$ measure the **marginal rate of transformation** (MRT) of X into Y. The MRT of X into Y falls as successive equal amounts of X are given up. This occurs because increasing use is made of some factors of production that are more suited for production of X than of Y (i.e. not all factors are homogeneous).

The PPF only shows the distribution of **production** between X and Y. The preferred pattern of **consumption** is shown by the indifference curves in **Figure 2.3** (which uses the same axes as **Figure 2.2**). The indifference curves are convex to the origin showing that, in order to keep an individual consumer at a constant level of welfare (utility or satisfaction), an increasing amount of Y must compensate for equal successive reductions in consumption of X. For example, starting at point U, if the individual gives up amount $x1$ of commodity X an extra amount $y1$ of commodity Y is required in order that the individual has the same level of satisfaction. However, if the switch had begun at point V a larger amount of Y ($y2$) would be required to compensate for the same loss of $x1$. This assumes that the more of a particular commodity a person consumes, the less additional utility is gained from successive equal increments in its consumption (the law of diminishing marginal utility).

Figure 2.3   Indifference curves

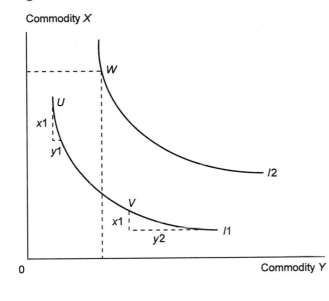

The consumption ratios $x1/y1$ and $x1/y2$ measure the **marginal rate of substitution** (MRS) between the two commodities.

Figure 2.3 also shows that indifference curves further from the origin represent higher levels of welfare. For example the individual prefers combination W (on $I2$) to combination U (on $I1$) because W has more of both X and Y (compare the dashed lines from W with a similar set, not shown, from U). Similarly, combination W is preferred to V (which has more Y but less X than combination W) because the individual is indifferent between U and V (both being on the same indifference curve) and so must prefer W to V, since W is preferred to U. (This logical result means that any one *individual's* indifference curves never cross.)

Figure 2.4 combines the PPF with two sets of indifference curves, $Ia1$ to $Ia4$ for individual A and $Ib1$ to $Ib4$ for individual B. The origin for A's set of indifference curves is at the junction of the X and Y axes (i.e. at 0) but the origin for B's is at point N. In both cases the indifference curves are convex to their respective origins. Starting at point 5, where $Ia1$ cuts $Ib3$, the welfare of individual B can be increased whilst holding that for individual A constant by moving to point 1 (A is on the same indifference curve but B has moved from $Ib3$ to $Ib4$). Hence, the points of tangency between the indifference curves (i.e. at 1, 2, 3 and 4) trace out all the combinations of X and Y at which it is not possible to make B better off without making A worse off. At these points of tangency, the rate at which X is substituted for Y is the same for both individuals A and B. In

Figure 2.4   Maximising welfare

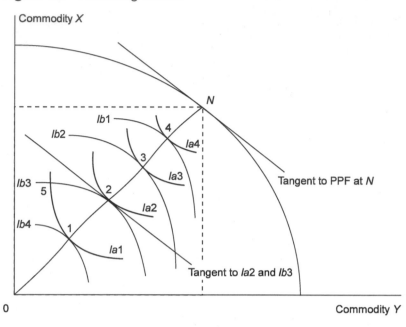

other words the MRS between the two commodities is the same for both individuals at any point lying on the 'contract curve' 0N.

Total efficiency for the economy requires maximisation of both output and the welfare derived from its consumption. This occurs when MRS in consumption equals MRT in production. For example, assume MRS is 1.5X for 1Y but MRT is 3X for 1Y. Consumers are therefore willing to give up 1Y as long as they receive an extra 1.5X in compensation. However if production of Y were to be reduced by one unit they could receive an extra 3X. Hence welfare can be increased by reducing the output of Y to allow that of X to be increased. This shift in production (i.e. movement along the PPF from right to left) should continue until MRS = MRT. At this point any change in production will reduce total welfare since the opportunity cost is too high. **Figure 2.4** shows that MRS = MRT when the slopes of the tangents to the indifference curves and PPF are the same, i.e. at points 2 and N. Point 2 achieves total efficiency as follows:

1.   **Efficiency in production** because the economy is on its PPF. For a fixed supply of inputs it is not possible to produce more of one commodity without producing less of another, nor is it possible to reduce the use of one input without increasing the use of another to

produce a given output. The economy is on its PPF because the MRT of any two factors of production is equal for all products.

2. **Efficiency in consumption** because it is not possible to increase welfare by altering the distribution of commodities between consumers. All consumers have the same MRS and so cannot increase their welfare by trading X and Y with each other.

3. **Total efficiency** because MRS = MRT. There is efficiency in both production and consumption *and* all consumers and producers face the same set of (perfectly competitive) prices (so MRS = MRT). Hence no person can be made better off without at least one other person being made worse off.

Total (or allocative) efficiency describes an optimal welfare situation known as a 'Pareto optimum' (after the Italian economist who defined it). For the optimum to exist **all** of the above three marginal conditions must be satisfied **simultaneously**. This is demonstrated by **Figure 2.4**. Starting at point 2, individual A can only be made better off (e.g. moving from $Ia2$ to $Ia3$) by making B worse off (moving from $Ib3$ to $Ib2$). Hence no person can be made better off without someone else being made worse off. Perfect competition therefore delivers a Pareto optimum automatically without any need for planning, the so-called 'invisible hand' of market forces. There is no need for government intervention as long as:

• the assumptions underpinning the model of perfect competition are valid; and
• the distribution of income is acceptable.

The Pareto optimum and the diagrams used to illustrate it make a number of philosophical and behavioural assumptions. **First**, the welfare of society is the sum of the welfares of all individuals in it. **Second**, welfare is idiosyncratic (i.e. a private phenomenon), each individual being the best judge of his or her own welfare and of the choices of activities that promote it. **Third**, individuals pursue the maximisation of personal welfare in a calculatively rational way (see Chapter 1). In combination, these assumptions imply a moral presumption in favour of the allocation of resources by voluntary exchange. In turn, this requires a purely capitalistic economy, rather than a centrally planned or a mixed economy. However the criterion for a welfare improvement (i.e. that at least one person be made better off without someone else being made worse off) is too strict. It requires unanimity in agreeing any socio-economic change and so confers a universal right of veto to those who do not benefit from any policy initiative but are still required to contribute towards its cost. This welfare rule effectively entrenches the status quo and so has little practical relevance for policy making.

One modification of the unanimity rule would be to allow change where the gainers could compensate the losers and still be better off than before the policy initiative was introduced. This 'compensation test' does not necessarily require the gainers to actually compensate the losers. Such a requirement would be based on a normative statement (i.e. *should* compensate). Maximisation of efficiency only requires the possibility of compensation.

The Pareto optimum effectively accepts whatever distribution of income arises out of the free market system and then constructs the 'first best' situation from it. It is clear from **Figure 2.4** that the distribution of welfare between individuals *A* and *B* varies between points 1, 2, 3 and 4. Which particular point is chosen depends on the distribution of income since this affects the relative purchasing power of individuals. The more a person earns (or inherits) the higher the indifference curve that can be attained (see Chapter 4 for a formal treatment). Hence if *A* is rich and *B* is poor then the point of tangency between their respective indifference curves will move away from 0 towards *N*, representing a higher level of welfare for *A* and a lower level for *B*. Total efficiency then requires a movement along the PPF in order to make MRS = MRT.

The Pareto optimum is developed in isolation from the social, moral and political conceptions of justice relating to resource endowments (i.e. income and wealth). These value-laden, normative, **equity** issues are disregarded by the **efficiency** prescriptions of the Pareto optimum, making it only a partial measure of welfare and therefore not the only influence on practical policy issues. Governments also intervene for **social** purposes in order to achieve a more equal distribution of income. Nevertheless it provides a very forceful intellectual efficiency rationale for a preference in favour of *laissez-faire*, i.e. **competitive markets** rather than government planning and control. It also implies that any redistribution of income and wealth should not be made by attempting to control prices or outputs, explaining economists' oft-stated preference for redistribution by means of cash transfers.

2.4   Market failure: the rationale for government intervention

The economic rationale for the existence of the public sector can only be understood in terms of the degree to which government intervention improves allocative efficiency. Such improvement is only possible if markets fail to achieve a Pareto optimum (a situation of allocative inefficiency). However, this is a necessary but not sufficient condition for government intervention. Intervention is only worthwhile in efficiency terms if government planning reduces rather than increases the degree of market failure. **Figure 2.4** demonstrates the enormous amount of information that would be needed for a **centrally-planned** economy to achieve a Pareto optimum. Information would be required relating to the preferences for different commodities (and the rates of trade-off between them) for every individual (i.e. each person's indifference curves) and the productivity of every factor input (and the rates of trade-off between them) for every commodity (i.e. the PPF). All the perfectly competitive market requires is that all product prices equal their respective marginal costs and the rest follows automatically through the 'invisible hand'. However, there are two possible causes of market failure.

First, when price does not equal marginal cost in all sectors of the economy. Price equals marginal cost under perfect competition. However, perfect competition may fail to exist because producers have monopoly power and can therefore control prices ('price makers' rather than 'price takers'). This may be because economies of scale (where average cost falls as the rate of output increases) are so substantial in relation to market size that one producer can supply the whole market. In this case a 'natural monopoly' exists. Alternatively it may be because of restrictive trade practices amongst a few large suppliers (i.e. oligopoly). Competition may also be constrained because markets are not contestable (e.g. where freedom of exit is constrained due to high fixed costs, in turn limiting freedom of entry) or because information is imperfect.

Selective government intervention in particular sectors of the economy (e.g. in a 'mixed economy') is problematic. The government cannot be confident that, in choosing to intervene in only a few sectors, it will improve allocative efficiency. The 'theory of second best' shows that once price departs from marginal cost in any sector, the best approach may be to cause all prices to diverge from their respective marginal costs. In other words, once any one of the three conditions for the Pareto optimum fails to be satisfied, the best strategy may be to abandon one or both of the other two.

The intuitive explanation is that as many prices should be adjusted as necessary in order to mimic the 'first best' allocation of resources attained by a Pareto optimum. Account has to be taken of the relationships between commodities and of the impact of changes in their price on real incomes. For example, if the price of commodity X is greater than its marginal cost, because it is produced by a monopolist, then demand will be less than that under perfect competition (where $p = MC$). In addition, demand for its complements will be suboptimally low and demand for its substitutes suboptimally high. The appropriate response would be to reduce the prices of its complements (by payment of a subsidy) and/or increase the price of its substitutes (by imposition of a commodity tax). The degree of price adjustment required depends on the sensitivity of demand to price change. For example the greater the price elasticity of demand the smaller the price adjustment required to bring demand back to its 'first best' level. Besides price elasticities of demand for the relevant commodities, account must also be taken of cross and income elasticities of demand. For example energy prices can take a substantial proportion of household income so that any change in (say) the price of electricity can have a significant impact on real income and therefore on demand.

The information requirements for such an approach are enormous. Not only would it be necessary to have all the information depicted in **Figure 2.4** for all individuals and commodities; it would also be necessary to have information on price, cross and income elasticities of demand for all commodities. At best, only piecemeal adjustments could be made in practice. Partial responses based on insufficient or inaccurate information may lead to intervention being counterproductive in efficiency terms. However intervention may pursue social aims as well, so that the policy relevance of the second-best theorem is limited in practice. Government decision-making is incremental in approach, rather than an all-embracing single step to attain general equilibrium optimisation.

Second, when prices fail to incorporate all costs and benefits. Besides equating prices and marginal costs, perfect competition also assumes perfect knowledge. However market equilibrium will be distorted if individual consumers are poor judges of their own welfare with the result that they are unwilling to pay for economically optimal levels of consumption of particular commodities (the merit goods case). Alternatively markets may simply not exist at all for commodities because producers are unable to enforce payment to recover costs and because consumption does not deplete supply (the public goods case). Even if costs are recoverable and the full personal benefit of consumption is recognised, market price may fail to incorporate the wider costs and benefits to society accruing from the production and consumption of a particular commodity (the externalities case).

Merit goods

The Pareto optimum assumes that individuals are the best judges of their own welfare. However, allocative inefficiency will occur if individuals undervalue the **personal** benefits derived from consumption of a commodity. In other words, the individual attributes insufficient merit to the good or service, the **merit goods** case. For example people may make insufficient provision of personal insurance against ill-health and injury, a result of the 'it will never happen to me' syndrome. However, actuarial statistics show that people underestimate their susceptibility to certain incapacitating illnesses and accidents. People may also make inadequate provision for their old age (for example fail to take out a private pension) because it is so far into the future that it seems unimportant. In other words people may discount too heavily both personal risk and the future. There are three ways of removing such allocative inefficiency:

1. **Compulsion:** use the force of law to require people to take out adequate insurance against illness, accident and old age.
2. **Improve information:** make clear to individuals the personal risks they face.
3. **Subsidy:** encourage optimal personal levels of consumption by using subsidy to reduce the price paid by consumers.

These options are not necessarily mutually exclusive. For example, insurance is obligatory for vehicle drivers and for health care in some European countries. However **compulsion** may be contrary to civil liberties, a normative concept that underpins the voluntary exchange ethos of the Pareto optimum. **Improved information** may also be appropriate in certain cases, for example the UK's Health Education Council provides information on the health risks associated with unprotected sex with many partners (which increases the risk of incurring a sexually transmitted disease) and smoking (which increases the risk of lung cancer and respiratory illnesses). However this is more to encourage people to engage in low-risk activities rather than to increase their health insurance cover. Subsidy can be used to equate perceived benefits and market prices in order to achieve allocative efficiency. For example it is provided in some countries through tax relief on the purchase of private health insurance and private pensions. **Table 2.1** provides a summary of the main characteristics.

Public goods

In order to avoid confusion and misconception, it should immediately be noted that it is a common mistake on the part of students to categorise all public sector outputs as public goods. Nor is a service a public good simply because it is provided out of the public purse (i.e. free at the point of consumption). The term 'public goods' is also potentially misleading in that it relates primarily to services rather than to physical commodities *per se*. Moreover the term is free of normative statements, in that it says nothing about the desirability or otherwise of provision of the activity. For example, it will be shown below that nuclear defence has the economic characteristics of a public good and yet there is considerable disagreement about the effectiveness, morality and desirability of nuclear weapons.

Public goods are defined in terms of their **economic** rather than their administrative, physical, normative or financing characteristics.

Table 2.1 A taxonomy of market failure

Type of commodity	Pure public good	Mixed goods[1] with externalities	Merit goods	Pure private goods
Who benefits?	All in society	Consumers and society	Individual consumers	Individual consumers
Exclusion of non-payers	Technically impossible	Difficult or impossible	Feasible	Feasible
Feasibility of pricing	Not feasible	Feasible	Feasible	Feasible
Consumer choice	None	Some	Full	Full
Impact of use on supply	None	Depletes supply	Depletes supply	Depletes supply
Who pays on allocative efficiency grounds?	The taxpayer only	Consumers pay prices adjusted by taxes or subsidies[2]	Consumers pay prices subsidised by taxpayers	Consumers pay full costs
Relationship between payment and use	None	Close	Close	Full
Who decides whether to produce?	Government only	Modified market	Modified market	Market only

Notes:
1. Having elements of both public and private goods.
2. Taxes in the case of negative externalities; subsidies in the case of positive externalities.

Samuelson argued that markets will fail to exist for public goods because they are **both**:

- **non-excludable** – it is not possible to prevent use of (or benefit from) the service by those who do not pay for it (producers therefore being unable to recover costs); and
- **non-rival in consumption** in that one person's consumption of the commodity does not affect any other person's consumption of it.

These characteristics are not applicable to 'private goods' that are **both** excludable and rival in consumption; for example commodities that are physically consumed or where property rights confer exclusive use.

Examples of public goods include lighthouses, street lighting, information, national defence and the public health benefits of safe disposal of industrial, domestic and commercial wastes. In all these examples a potentially infinite number of users can benefit simultaneously and it is not possible to prevent people benefiting from the service. It is sometimes said that public goods are characterised by a third feature, namely that they are non-rejectable. For example, nuclear deterrence is non-rejectable by campaigners for nuclear disarmament. However information can be rejected as unacceptable or invalid.

Consumers' willingness to pay for marketable commodities is shown by demand curves. In **Figure 2.1** demand curves for individuals were added together to obtain the aggregate market demand curve for the commodity. Such aggregation has no meaning for a public good since consumption is non-rival. A given level of output can satisfy any number of consumers. Hence output of the public good has to be decided first and then the willingness to pay for all individuals can be added together. However, once consumers realise that they cannot be excluded from use of the public good there is no incentive for them to pay for it: they can take a 'free ride'. This means that the demand curve, or any point on it, is unknown. There is no incentive for consumers to reveal their willingness to pay to a potential supplier attempting to relate payment to benefit received from consumption of the public good.

Since Pareto's analysis of allocative efficiency does not confer moral principles or social constraints upon consumers, they will have no sense of guilt when 'free riding'. Indeed it would be inconsistent for them to pay for a public good since they are assumed to maximise their welfare. Avoiding payment allows them to increase consumption of other goods and so increase their welfare. Hence potential suppliers of the public good would not be able to cover the costs of production. The costs of protecting property rights through legally binding contracts for market transactions are so prohibitive that a market fails to exist. If the public good is to be produced, payment must be made compulsory via taxation.

Market failure is profound and absolute in the **pure** public goods example (i.e. where both non-excludability and non-rivalness exist simultaneously). However few examples of pure public goods exist. For example, hospital and education services are both excludable (e.g. to foreigners) and rival (there being a limited number of available places). Therefore the concept cannot be used to justify the free provision of all public sector services simply because very few are public goods. In practice, charges may recover all or part of the cost of a public good if it is provided in joint supply with a private good (which is both excludable and rival). For example ships passing lighthouses have to use ports and docks, both of which are rival and excludable. Hence harbour fees could (and usually do) contain an additional element to recover the cost of lighthouses, a crude approximation of charge and benefit. Similarly street lighting costs could be recovered by a combined toll imposed on road users. The costs of providing information could be recovered by a premium added to charges for computer printouts from bibliographic databases or from charges for photocopies from public library 'in-print' information sources.

It is clear that many services have some of the characteristics of public goods but do not wholly satisfy the definition. Therefore they are not **pure** public goods. This suggests the concept of **impure** public goods having either non-rivalness or non-excludability but not both or, alternatively, substantial (but not complete) elements of both. For example a public park may be non-excludable for practical purposes but if congestion is created by too many users then consumption of the services provided by the park becomes rival. For that reason, the public park could also be regarded as an impure private good, rather than an impure public good. Use of either term may reflect one's ideological preference, respectively, for justifying private provision and/or no subsidy or public provision and/or subsidy. Table 2.1 used the term 'mixed goods' in order to avoid any ideological predisposition and because non-excludability and non-rivalness are more a matter of degree than an absolute categorical difference. In practice, most outputs are mixed goods and they, rather than the polar cases of pure private and pure public goods, are the subject of major public policy debates regarding the payment of allocative efficiency subsidies. In order to address this issue it is simpler to make use of the concept of 'externalities'.

Externalities

The private sector sells many commodities that affect people other than the purchaser. **Social** costs and benefits extend beyond the purchaser's **private** costs and benefits and so are external to market prices. These 'externalities' lead to allocatively inefficient decisions **even if** individuals are the best judges of their own welfare (i.e. there are no merit good characteristics) and even if perfect competition exists (see **Table 2.1**). There are two cases.

Negative externalities

Production or consumption of a commodity may impose costs on non-users, for example through environmental pollution (see Chapter 14 in respect of pollution of water supplies). The costs of cleaning up the pollution, treating the illnesses that result from it and the working days and output lost due to illness are all examples of social costs. These costs are not reflected in firms' cost schedules; they are external to private costs, explaining use of the terms 'external costs' or 'negative externalities'.

Atmospheric pollution is mainly caused by smoke and sulphur dioxide arising from the burning of fossil fuels such as coal (largely burnt in power stations) and petrol and diesel (burnt by vehicles). Petrol and diesel engines emit carbon monoxide, nitrogen oxides, volatile organic compounds, particulates and other pollutants, road transport producing around half of total emissions in the UK. These 'chemical cocktails' cause summertime smogs (ground level ozone) which UK government experts estimate are responsible for up to 12500 premature deaths and up to 9900 extra hospital admissions in the UK every year. These estimates are subject to much uncertainty because of the complexity of chemical cocktails and the lack of knowledge of critical pollution/illness thresholds. None the less, they are thought to under-state the overall effects of air pollution because they relate to only a few pollutants at present. Local government monitoring of air quality (a statutory duty under the 1995 Environment Act) shows quality standards are frequently breached in cities throughout the UK.

Some pollutants are carcinogenic, whilst others are thought to account for the sharp increase in asthma and other bronchial complaints and diseases. Those most at risk include children, people with respiratory and coronary disease, pregnant women, older adults, and people allergic to pollution. Research for the British Lung Foundation calculated that the health costs arising from road transport air pollution alone total more than £11 billion per annum. This figure is based on what people are willing to pay to avoid risks of ill health. Whilst the 'willingness to pay' technique can be criticised on methodological grounds, the resulting figure takes no account of the separate NHS costs of treating pollution-related illness, nor of the health costs of road traffic accidents. Again, therefore, the figure is likely to understate the external costs of transport.

It is often argued that car drivers effectively pay for their use of public roads because the taxes they pay on cars and fuel more than cover the costs of providing the road network (see Chapter 10). However the private use of roads by vehicles creates negative externalities arising from pollution (e.g. exhaust emissions), accidents (e.g. medical costs and lost earnings), congestion (the extra costs of slower transport of people and goods) and from vehicle noise (nuisance costs).

Noise pollution (i.e. environmental, as distinct from workplace, noise) concerns excessive and unwanted sound that inflicts physiological and/or psychological harm on individuals. The former relates to damage to the ear and loss of hearing. The latter relates to interference with sleep, interruption of conversation and so on. These external costs imposed on others are difficult to measure in financial terms. However, noise pollution in areas surrounding major international airports can, in principle, be measured by the diminution of property values in the affected areas. As regards congestion costs, the Confederation of British Industry estimates that road congestion increases industrial costs by £19 billion per year.

Environmental groups' calculations suggest that the social costs of car use are more than three times greater than the direct costs of the construction, maintenance, administration and policing of roads. Hence the official figure for the cost of the road system is more than quadrupled. On the basis of these and other estimates, it appears that road users pay only about one third of the external costs they impose on others.

Since social costs are external to private costs they are not passed on in higher product prices. Prices are therefore too low (in relation to marginal cost) and so consumption and demand are too high. This results in allocative inefficiency. This case is shown in **Figure 2.5**, which includes both private and social marginal costs (*MC* and *SMC* respectively). The demand schedule is horizontal because perfect competition is still assumed to exist. For ease of exposition, the average cost curve is not shown. *SMC* lies above *MC*, showing that a given level of output $q1$ has a social cost $c2$ greater than private cost $c1$. The value of the negative externality is $c2 - c1$. The market equilibrium is $q2$ (where $MR = MC$) but the social optimum output is only $q1$. Hence there is excess production of $q2 - q1$, so that allocative inefficiency exists. Government intervention can therefore be justified. There are five options:

1. **Internalise the negative externality.** For example, assume that a private sewage company dumps untreated sewage in rivers used for water abstraction by a private water company. The latter would incur substantial costs in purifying the water for drinking and so on. Merger of the two companies into a combined water and sewerage operation would internalise the negative externality, this being the norm (see Chapter 14).
2. **Prohibit the negative externality.** Pass legislation to make illegal either the economic activity causing the pollution or the pollution itself, for example excessive noise. Noise pollution in the UK (levels in excess of 91 decibels of a given duration) is controlled, *inter alia*, by local government byelaws, by the Noise Abatement Act 1960, by the Control of Pollution Act 1974 (Part III), by the Environment Act 1995 and by various EU Directives. These limit (as distinct from completely prohibit) noise emissions from motorcycles, subsonic aircraft, lawnmowers, construction plant and so on.
3. **Regulate the negative externality.** For example, limit output of the polluting commodity to $q1$ in Figure 2.5.

Figure 2.5   Negative externalities

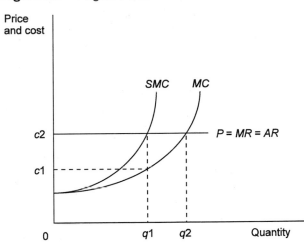

4. **Tax the negative externality.** For example, a tax equal to $c2 - c1$ would achieve the optimal level of output $q1$ in Figure 2.5 by equalising private and social costs. The optimal amount of tax therefore equals the vertical distance between SMC and MC (so that SMC equals MC plus the tax).

5. **Introduce a trading scheme in negative externality licences.** This combines the last two options, being based on both regulatory and market-based regimes. Licences are used to limit the maximum amount of pollution each company could emit. Companies investing in pollution-reducing technology can sell the consequently unused part of their licences to other companies in order to recover the costs of their investments. The reduction in the total of pollution is achieved by allowing companies to sell only part (e.g. half) of their unused pollution quota. The greater the proportion of the unused licence that can be sold, the greater the incentive for firms to invest in pollution reduction and the quicker that reduction. Companies slower to invest become relatively high cost (having to continue buying unused licences) and ultimately lose trade. Pollution is reduced, more quickly if the aggregate total of licences is progressively reduced over a period of years. This reduction also increases financial incentives to reduce emissions because the price of unused licences will rise as they become more scarce.

In general, **internalisation** of negative externalities is not feasible. For example it is difficult to internalise the health costs associated with the atmospheric pollution caused by car exhaust fumes. Furthermore, in practice, joint water and sewerage companies often continue to pollute the environment by dumping untreated (or only partially treated) sewage into rivers, lakes and the sea (see Chapter 14). **Prohibition** of car use in order completely to remove the polluting activity would be too draconian, in breach of civil liberties and economically inefficient (disrupting transport of people and goods and car manufacturing). Partial (rather than outright) prohibition may be feasible, particularly in the most affected areas. For example, the UK's 1995 Environment Act places a duty on local governments to monitor air quality in their area and they have powers to close roads or whole districts to traffic or particular types of vehicles if necessary (subject to central government approval). Such measures may merely displace traffic and related pollution to other areas. Despite the plethora of legislative acts to deal with noise pollution (noted above), traffic noise continues to rise inexorably.

Regulation is costly to monitor and enforce and, like prohibition, can lead to high legal costs being incurred in prosecuting offenders. Partial regulatory solutions may be possible, for example including an exhaust emission test in the UK's Ministry of Transport annual vehicle inspections and making the fitting of catalytic converters compulsory on all new cars. **Taxation** of the negative externality is the most appropriate economic solution since it makes use of market forces and minimises the need for government intervention (and its associated costs). It also makes the polluter pay for the social costs imposed on others (**the polluter pays principle**). For example, in the 1990s the tax on leaded petrol was much greater than that on unleaded petrol, the differential being introduced specifically to encourage the subsequent shift towards the latter and so reduce lead pollution (see Chapter 10). However, the above analysis of the social costs of road transport suggests higher petrol and diesel taxes are required (see Chapter 10).

A trading scheme in negative externality licences is feasible but there is a limit to the number of firms or plant for which governments can assess, set caps or targets, monitor and enforce. This restricts the extent to which trading schemes and other regulatory approaches can be applied to small and medium-sized enterprises. Examples exist at both national and international levels. In 1985 the USA introduced lead quotas for its oil refineries as part of a two-year plan to phase out lead in petrol. Refineries phasing out the metal before the end of the two-year period were allowed to sell their unused licences to other refineries taking longer. This trading scheme raised the money needed to finance the new investment to reduce lead in petrol and allowed refineries some flexibility in the timing of their investment programmes within the overall timetable. The USA's licence-trading initiative concentrated on the supply side of the market whereas the UK tax-differential initiative (referred to above) concentrated on the demand side. The USA later introduced a similar scheme to reduce pollution emissions from its power stations (particularly sulphur dioxide, which causes 'acid rain' that causes deforestation and destroys ecosystems). Power stations investing in new technology (e.g. flue gas desulphurisation equipment) or buying more expensive low-sulphur coal gained credits based on how many tonnes of sulphur dioxide were no longer released into the atmosphere. These credits could then be sold to other (still polluting) power stations in order to finance those higher costs. The environmental gain was achieved by allowing only part of each saved tonne of sulphur to be sold as a credit.

An international example is the **Kyoto Protocol**. The 1997 United Nations conference in Kyoto (Japan) agreed a scheme to introduce a trade in 'greenhouse-gas' (carbon dioxide) emissions. This is referred to as 'carbon trading' or 'emissions trading'. This international scheme allows each country a maximum amount of carbon pollution that it can discharge into the atmosphere each year. If a country emits less than its target it can sell the 'unused' emission amount to another country that wishes to exceed its target. For example, Japan could buy part of an Eastern European country's carbon quota, the latter using the money to modernise its old highly polluting power stations. This would reduce pollution more than if Japan spent the same amount of money trying to reduce the same amount pollution from its more modern (less polluting) power stations. Japan and other affluent countries can effectively buy the right to pollute the planet. However the Kyoto Agreement at least partly addressed this criticism. First, it limited the amount of trading to a maximum of 50 per cent of a country's target. Second, it requires industrialised countries to reduce their carbon dioxide emissions over time.

The UK's target reduction is 12.5 per cent below its 1990 level by 2010. In fact, the UK had already exceeded this target by 2000 mainly because of the rapid replacement of coal-fired by gas-fired power stations (see Chapter 13). In the longer term, further reductions are expected to result from energy efficiency programmes in homes, further tax differentials in favour of 'cleaner' car fuels (e.g. those with a low sulphur content – see Chapter 10), road pricing and other measures to restrict car use. The UK government expects to achieve a 20 per cent reduction by 2010 and so will have a 7.5 per cent excess – equivalent to 15 million tonnes of carbon credits for sale to other countries. Estimates vary about how much a tonne of carbon will be worth in international trade. Assuming the lowest estimate of £60 a tonne, this would raise almost £1 billion, all or part of which could be reinvested in other pollution control programmes.

To sum up, all measures other than outright prohibition can be criticised for allowing pollution to continue – even if at a reduced level. There is, however, an optimal level of pollution in efficiency terms.

Figure 2.5 demonstrates that, in principle, firms' cost functions can be modified so as to include the social costs of pollution. Environmentalists may object to this on the grounds that small but persistent levels of pollution can accumulate over the long term and, once past a threshold, lead to catastrophic ecological effects. They often argue that it is not possible to assess the long-term impacts before they occur so that there must to be a presumption in favour of environmental protection. Whilst this 'no risk' strategy may prove to be too restrictive of economic activity, it raises profound moral and philosophical issues regarding potentially harmful effects upon communities – especially those in the immediate vicinity of the polluting activity. These issues can only be addressed by public discussion (see Chapter 1). Profit-seeking market activities (even if modified) may not be the most appropriate instrument of control, especially if they are the *only* means of control. Nevertheless, the USA's scheme of tradeable sulphur dioxide emission credits was generally seen as a demonstration of the success of emissions trading. In its first two years, this scheme reduced sulphur dioxide emissions by more than a third and scheme costs were much less than expected. Whilst the bulk of trade was between power stations, there were instances of environmental groups buying the credits and cancelling them. The USA's experience was thought to demonstrate that emissions trading is much cheaper and more effective than 'command and control' regulation.

Positive externalities (also known as external benefits)

Market provision of a commodity will be too low where it has beneficial consequences for other people not involved in the transaction. For example a person paying for inoculation against a contagious disease also benefits others who are not party to the market transaction because their risk of contracting the disease is reduced as well. Similarly, if education makes individuals more economically productive, it benefits society (through faster economic growth) as well as the individual (through a better-paid job). Social benefits are external to the market and therefore are not incorporated in demand schedules. Individual consumers will ignore such positive externalities in making provision for themselves since they are assumed to maximise their own personal welfares. It would be illogical for consumers to take account of the social benefits of their activities since they would have to pay for more output than they require for themselves. Output will therefore be too low.

The demand schedule in **Figure 2.6** measures willingness to pay, that is, the marginal private valuation (MPV) for the commodity. The marginal social valuation (MSV) exceeds the MPV and so the private optimal output $q1$ is less than the social optimal output $q2$. Hence allocative inefficiency exists. There are two options:

1. **Compulsion:** the government could make consumption of the service compulsory. For example, parents of children of school age are compelled by force of law to send them to school. However compulsory inoculation would be both contrary to civil liberty and medically unnecessary since prevention of epidemics does not require **all** people to receive preventative treatment. It would also be economically inefficient (i.e. treating people unnecessarily).
2. **Subsidy:** willingness to pay is inversely related to price. Use of a subsidy to reduce the price paid by consumers could therefore be used to increase demand up to the optimal level. The optimal amount of subsidy equals the vertical distance between *MSV* and *MPV* (so that *MSV* equals *MPV* plus the subsidy) in **Figure 2.6**. This is the economic rationale for subsidising vocational education for 16 and 17 year olds in work or on an employer-based training scheme (see Chapter 9). The subsidy solution can work within the market system and is consistent with individual responsibility. For example people intending to travel to countries where diseases such as polio and yellow fever are rife are encouraged to be immunised, the cost of most immunisations being wholly subsidised by the state.

This efficiency logic does not necessarily provide the justification of all subsidies. Positive externalities may be so limited that the cost of government intervention would be greater than the resulting benefit in terms of improved allocative efficiency. For example, if local government leisure centres or libraries are mainly used by groups who are already healthy and productive members of society then the resulting positive

Figure 2.6   Positive externalities

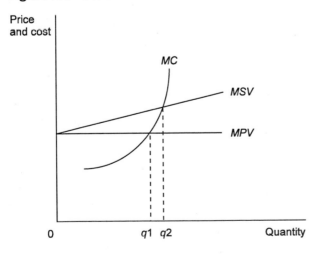

externalities would be so small that they could not be used to justify substantial subsidy. If clients are also relatively affluent then subsidy could not be justified on equity grounds either.

In addition to taxing activities that cause pollution (discussed above), those that reduce pollution could also be subsidised on efficiency grounds because of the environmental and health benefits they create. For example, the UK government seeks to meet a target of generating 10 per cent of electricity from renewable resources. So-called 'industrial crops' such as willow, straw and elephant grass can be used as fuel for power stations. Farmers could be encouraged to grow these crops (as well as others used for motor fuels, solvents, dyes, paints, cosmetics and so on.) by subsidising their production. Not only would this engender a switch to environmentally-friendly ('green') power generation, but it would also deal with many of the perverse subsidies created by the European Union's Common Agricultural Policy (CAP).

Many EU farmers receive livestock and crop subsidies, either paid directly by their governments or by consumers through the minimum price (price support) arrangements of the CAP. This is an income maintenance scheme for farmers, **not** a positive externality subsidy. However, since subsidy is paid per head of livestock or per ton of crop, the incentive is to increase farm output in order to maximise receipt of this production subsidy. This has led to over-production and consequent destruction of natural habitats through over-grazing and removal of hedgerows and woodland areas. In turn, this led to the development of 'set-aside' and other non-production subsidies, whereby subsidy is paid if farmers do not plant fields or over-graze moorland (e.g. with sheep).

Set-aside subsidies therefore have allocative efficiency benefits in terms of reducing surplus agricultural production (e.g. grain and beef 'mountains' and wine 'lakes') and so reducing environmental degradation, whilst simultaneously maintaining farmers' incomes. Nevertheless, it would probably be more effective to pay subsidies specifically to safeguard wild birds and flowers, rather than simply to stop producing surplus crops. Moreover, it is clear that the need for such an efficiency subsidy has been caused by the prior payment of an income-maintenance subsidy. Once paid, it may be politically difficult to abolish a subsidy scheme. In this example, the efficiency subsidy would probably not have been required had not the income-maintenance subsidy been paid in the first place. The justification for the subsidy and the subsidy scheme have changed but the payment of subsidy continues. That one subsidy should, in effect, be used to justify another subsidy may be considered bizarre. This example demonstrates how efficiency subsidies can become politicised in that the farming and environmental lobbies have considerable political power. This is an aspect of public choice theory (see Chapter 7). The same criticism applies to the positive externality subsidies to farmers for production of industrial crops to reduce an untaxed negative externality caused by burning fossil fuels.

It has to be realised that the need for subsidies encouraging environmentally friendly activities often arises because environmentally unfriendly activities do not pay their full social marginal costs. Whilst payment of subsidies for the former may be more politically expedient than taxes on the latter, political expediency does not negate the allocative efficiency case for taxing negative externalities. The resulting revenues could be used to finance allocative efficiency subsidies.

At the moment, most such subsidies are financed by general taxes which may themselves create allocative inefficiency (see Chapter 4). That a subsidy for an activity (e.g. use of cars) should justify another subsidy (e.g. use of public transport) to offset the undesirable effect of the first subsidy is perverse. If car drivers had to pay for the full social and private costs of motoring, the relative price of car use would rise and the relative price of use of public transport would fall. If use of private and public transport were highly price elastic and income elastic, there would be a large shift from use of cars to use of buses and trains, reducing the need for further road building. Higher revenues from fares would reduce the need for subsidies for rail and bus services paid in respect of the positive externalities they generate in reducing congestion and pollution.

Transaction costs

The public goods, merit goods and externalities cases are special cases of the more general problem of transaction costs. Transaction costs are incurred in attempting to establish and enforce property rights and the financial liability for use of a service. Property rights allow the owner exclusive rights to decide how to use an asset, to obtain the income from it and to transfer those rights to others. The costs of fully defining and enforcing property rights may be excessive such that contracts will be incomplete. Hence market failure is relative rather than absolute and depends on the costs of agreeing, monitoring and enforcing contracts relative to the value of the transaction. Transaction costs approach infinity for pure public goods (because of the 'free rider' problem) and approach zero for pure private goods.

Transaction costs occur where **bounded rationality** (i.e. imperfect information and decision-making) and difficulties of contract enforcement facilitate **opportunism**, where one party to the transaction exploits these contractual ambiguities and difficulties of enforcement to their own advantage. 'Free riders' are an extreme case. Opportunism may be further facilitated by **asset specificity**, where the resources used by a supplier in the provision of an output are so highly specific that they are not easily redeployable. This causes the seller to become heavily dependent on continuing purchases by the buyer in order to recover the costs of the original investment. It may also cause the buyer to become highly dependent on a single supplier. Hence the two contracting parties become locked into a bilateral exchange. However, contractual mis-specifications and ambiguities will encourage opportunistic behaviour on both sides, leading to joint losses.

This encourages internalisation of market functions within the modern private corporation in order to ensure property rights and avoid opportunism, and helps to explain why firms exist (see Chapter 1). Modern corporations are therefore efficient **governance structures** for highly idiosyncratic and recurrent exchanges where the human and physical assets used in production of the service are very specialised and transaction-specific. Markets are best suited to non-specific, standar-dised, one-off or short-term transactions involving little uncertainty and where property rights can be clearly established by the legal system. Hence transaction costs economics shows the limitations of the 'invisible hand' in promoting pursuit of self-interest through an unplanned market system. The modern private corporation is a planning mechanism, and where transaction costs are high, private interest is best served by the collective interest within the modern corporation. Of course some private corporations may be formed primarily for uncompetitive reasons. The extent of transaction costs is an empirical question. Nonetheless, high transaction costs lead to market failure even if the output is a private good and so explain why both governments and corporations are necessary governance structures.

To sum up, where used to correct market failure, taxes and subsidies can be justified on efficiency grounds. The economically optimal rate of subsidy is dependent on the degree of market failure, and so in most cases the subsidy would only cover a part of production costs. Charges or prices would continue to cover the bulk of costs in most cases. Hence, in the case of chargeable services provided by the public sector (e.g. local government leisure and recreation services), it is misguided to claim that people are being asked to 'pay twice', i.e. both a charge and a local tax contribution. In such cases, taxes and charges are complementary rather than mutually exclusive.

2.5   Misuses of the theory of market failure

1. **Using the concept of public goods to justify provision of the current set of services provided by the public sector.** Most public sector outputs are not pure public goods but rather private goods capable of being provided by private companies. For example there are both public and private sector libraries, information brokers,

leisure centres, residential care establishments for elderly people and rental housing. The private provision of such services may be supported by subsidies in respect of positive externalities. In the case of pure public goods, the government could agree supply contracts with private companies, their costs being fully financed by subsidy. A private national defence contractor may be problematic (commercial imperatives possibly overriding loyalty to the client country), but of course private companies are used to manufacture armaments and military vehicles.

2. **Using public goods, merit good and positive externality concepts to justify free services.** Only pure public goods require production costs to be **fully** subsidised, on the assumption they would otherwise not be provided because of private producers' inability to recover costs through charges. However, as already noted, subsidy may not be necessary where a public good is in joint supply with a private good. Merit good and external benefit characteristics only justify the partial subsidy of costs, the degree of subsidy depending on the magnitude of those characteristics. However the payment of subsidies in respect of the positive externalities derived from use of public transport are larger simply because the negative externalities relating to use of cars are not covered by charges or taxes, as demonstrated in the example above

3. **Using transaction costs as a blanket justification for the current set of public sector outputs on the grounds that private suppliers would exploit the public sector and/or the service user.** There are certainly many examples of bounded rationality, asset specificity, difficulties in defining property rights and scope for opportunism in many of the services currently provided by the public sector. Bounded rationality occurs where the individual and societal benefits of, say, education are unquantifiable. Asset specificity occurs in the form of highly trained labour (e.g. police officers or teachers) and highly specific assets (e.g. land-fill sites for refuse). However, the transaction costs rationale also suggests that some services should not be provided in-house at all because the market is a more efficient governance structure. Competitive tendering and the contracting out of cleaning, catering, refuse collection, grounds maintenance and other similar services can be justified in transaction costs terms because these services display little in terms of asset specificity, bounded rationality, indefinable property rights or bilateral exchange (see Chapter 15). Indeed, where services are not categorically different in the public and private sectors, whole services may be more efficiently provided by the private market, e.g. some sports, leisure and recreation facilities. Technical arguments are, of course, an insufficient explanation of the services currently provided by

government in that the actual framework of provision is more the outcome of political, historical and institutional factors, underpinned by equity (rather than by technical) issues (see Chapter 1).

4. **Government use of market failure concepts as scientific pretence to impose its own preferences on individuals and communities.** The difficulties of quantifying and valuing merit good and positive externality characteristics may facilitate political manipulation of the electorate. For example the government could exaggerate the personal and social benefits derived from the arts or from public libraries (i.e. their contribution to the development of education, literacy and culture) in order to justify levels of service greater than would be provided by private markets without financial assistance from the government. In financing the subsidies required to achieve such higher levels of service, taxpayers are forced to pay for services they may not wish to use. Higher taxes and lower (subsidised) charges effectively redistribute income from the generality of tax-payers to the specific groups who use such services. If low-income groups are paying taxes in support of services used by higher-income groups, then the outcome may be deemed to be inequitable. Inequity may be compounded if those higher-income groups possess more political power than do low-income groups. Such self-serving beha-viour is an aspect of public choice theory that suggests governments grow to serve their own interests and those of their supporters, rather than those of the wider community (see Chapter 7).

2.6 Conclusions

This chapter has shown that, under certain highly restrictive assump-tions, the efficient allocation of resources can best be achieved through competitive markets rather than by means of government planning. This is because the market system economises on information requirements and maximises both the economy's productive capacity and the welfare associated with it. However, markets fail to achieve allocative efficiency where monopoly power replaces perfect competition and/or where markets fail to include all social costs and benefits in the private cost functions of producers and consumers. Government intervention may be justifiable in such circumstances, but only if it results in a net improvement in allocative efficiency.

Forms of intervention include the taxation or subsidisation of private production and consumption, direct provision by the public sector, compulsion or prohibition. Whilst Pareto optimality implies a presump-tion in favour of the use of tax and subsidy solutions to modify the outcomes of market systems, a series of measures are used in practice. It is often not possible clearly to demonstrate which particular form of intervention is the best. Nor is it even possible to say, from these principles alone, whether the public sector is too big or too small. Chapter 7 demonstrates that the usefulness of market failure for policy making is limited by the possibility of self-serving behaviour by bureaucrats, local politicians and distributional coalitions.

In concentrating on allocative efficiency as the rationale for government intervention in the market economy, the neoclassical theory of the role of the state is incomplete. Chapter 1 noted the necessity of a multidisciplinary approach to assessing the need for government intervention. However, even within a purely economics perspective, the neoclassical theory is also incomplete because it is largely static and does not consider the potential for government intervention to improve the dynamic efficiency and technological capability of the economy. Such dynamic interactions are a major aspect of policy and practice and are the basis of the supply-side measures discussed in Parts II and III.

Further reading

British Lung Foundation (1998) *Transport and Pollution – The Health Costs* (London: British Lung Foundation).

Connolly, S. and Munroe, A. (1999) *Economics of the Public Sector* (Harlow: Prentice Hall).

Cullis, J. and Jones, P. (1998) *Public Finance and Public Choice: Analytical Perspectives*, 2nd edn (Maidenhead: McGraw-Hill).

Department of Health (1998) *Quantification of the Effects of Air Pollution on Health in the United Kingdom*, Committee on the Medical Effects of Air Pollutants (London: The Stationery Office).

Douma, S. and Schreuder, H. (1992) *Economic Approaches to Organisations* (Hertfordshire: Prentice Hall).

HM Government (1997) *The United Kingdom National Air Quality Strategy*, Cm 3587 (London: HMSO).

OECD (1999) *National Climate Change Policies and the Kyoto Protocol* (Paris: Organisation for Economic Co-operation and Development).

OECD (1999) *Action Against Climate Change – the Kyoto Protocol and Beyond* (Paris: Organisation for Economic Co-operation and Development).

Potter, S. (1997) *The National Air Quality Strategy*. Research Paper 96/33 (London: House of Commons Library).

The London Air Quality Network (1996) *Air Quality in London*. The Third Report of the London Air Quality Network (London).

3 Theories of Public Sector Growth

3.1 Introduction
3.2 Public Expenditure Categories
3.3 Explaining the Growth of Exhaustive Public Expenditures
3.4 Explaining the Growth of Transfer Expenditures
3.5 Conclusions

3.1 Introduction

Wagner's Law (named after a nineteenth century German economist) states that the public sector inevitably grows faster than the economy as a whole. Interpreted in its narrowest form, the Law requires the income elasticity of demand for public sector services to be greater than one so that demand grows faster than income. In fact, virtually all studies have found the income elasticity to be less than one, demand growing more slowly than income. This may be because the wrong measure of income was used in those studies (i.e. current income instead of 'permanent income') and/or because of methodological difficulties in measuring national income. Alternatively, income elasticity of demand may not be the only factor influencing the growth of the public sector.

Chapter 2 outlined the 'market failure' rationale for government intervention. The optimal degree of intervention is clear in principle: only that which is required to offset allocative inefficiency. In principle the economically optimal levels of subsidy and taxation can be calculated in respect of positive and negative externalities, and so on. However, these economic prescriptions are essentially static and so are insufficient as an explanation of the growth of the public sector. Dynamic explanations are required. For example, there may be supply-side as well as demand-side influences on public expenditure and income may not be the only demand-side factor.

Irrespective of whether government spending grows more quickly or more slowly than national income, the fact is it does grow virtually without exception in all economies over time. This chapter therefore examines the various economic theories of public sector growth to provide the context for later consideration (in Chapter 9) of attempts to control rising public expenditure.

3.2 Public expenditure categories

General government expenditure (GGE) includes the spending of all levels of government (national and local). GGE in the UK was only 9 per cent of gross domestic product towards the end of the nineteenth century. By the end of the twentieth century it was just over 40 per cent. This is remarkable growth, both in terms of the share of national output produced by the public sector and of the growth in real expenditures. **Cash expenditures** for different years have to be made directly comparable by taking account of inflation over the period. The resulting standardised figures are **real expenditures**. There are two main categories:

1. **Exhaustive expenditures.** These refer to government purchases that consume or exhaust the purchasing power of the money it spends, hence 'exhaustive expenditures'. They include purchases of inputs (e.g. labour) used in its own production of goods and services and purchases of outputs from the private sector (e.g. cleaning services). They also include investment in fixed assets such as machinery, land and buildings. Put simply, exhaustive expenditures use productive resources.

2. **Transfer payments/expenditures.** These refer to expenditures where the government does not purchase factors of production or use resources. Instead the money is transferred from taxpayers to recipients. They include subsidies to private sector firms (e.g. those receiving grants supporting investment in economically depressed regions or inner cities), payments of interest (to those from whom the government has borrowed), loans granted by the government (e.g. to tenants buying their council houses) and overseas aid (e.g. in support of economic development programmes). The largest component of transfer payments is welfare benefits such as income support, unemployment benefit and state pensions, growth of which has been substantial since about 1960.

Spending on goods and services accounted for about four-fifths of GGE in the UK at the end of the nineteenth century. A century later it accounted for only three-fifths: the share of spending on transfer payments had risen from one to two-fifths. Social security payments accounted for a third of GGE by 1991. Growth in the size of the public sector relative to GDP and a proportionate shift towards transfer payments are characteristic features of developed countries. Any comprehensive economic theory of public expenditure growth has to explain the long-term proportionate growth of public spending within the economy and the relative shift from exhaustive to transfer payments. No single economic theory is able to do this, nor even explain changes in exhaustive expenditures alone. Instead there are two broad groups of models:

- **Macro models** of public expenditure growth attempt to account for the long-term growth of GGE.
- **Micro models** of public expenditure growth attempt to explain changes in particular components of GGE, whether caused by increasing demand for individual services or by changes in their cost structures.

These models incorporate demand-side and/or supply-side factors. On the demand-side, public expenditure increases because citizens want more public spending as their incomes rise; if not all citizens then at least those with political power and influence. On the supply-side, it is those who work within the public sector (rather than the general public) who want more public spending, including government bureaucrats. The models discussed below are somewhat simplified, being based on a myriad of models developed in the nineteenth and twentieth centuries – many of which can only explain part of the growth of the public sector. They are particularly difficult to test because of the methodological problems discussed in Chapter 1.

3.3 Explaining the growth of exhaustive public expenditures

Macro models of public expenditure growth

Development model: public expenditure is a prerequisite of economic development, its level being directly related to the stage of development which a country has reached, transforming from a traditional to an industrial and then to a post-industrial (i.e. service) economy. The public sector initially provides physical capital (i.e. infrastructure) such as roads, railways, water supply and sanitation. As economic growth proceeds, the balance of public sector investment shifts towards **human capital** (i.e. a productive labour supply), providing educational, health and welfare services. This is because the increasing division of labour within an increasingly urbanised settlement pattern requires greater state intervention to deal with the administrative and protective functions of society (i.e. the regulatory role of government – see Chapter 2). Structural factors (industrial, demographic and social) therefore determine the growth of public expenditures, the rapidity of growth being determined by the pace of economic development. Such growth occurs independently of the wishes of citizens or governments.

Organic state model: the state is assumed to grow like an organism, reflecting changes in society and economy and making decisions on behalf (and to the benefit) of its citizens. Society's demands for services such as education and health grow as per capita incomes grow (i.e. they have high income elasticity of demand). Such services can be provided by the private sector. However, the manifestations of market failure noted in Chapter 2 (notably externality and merit good concepts) require government intervention (subsidy and/or direct provision) in order to make these services available to individuals in economically optimal amounts (i.e. the allocative role of government). The degree of market failure may increase as economy and society become more complex. The state may also have increasingly to manage the economy to provide a stable price system for the market system to function smoothly (i.e. the stabilisation role of government). Hence, there is a fairly steady long-term rise in public expenditure reflecting decisions by the state.

Political constraints model: it is assumed that taxpayers indicate through the democratic system of electoral representation what levels of taxation they are willing to pay to finance public sector services. A given tolerable tax rate yields increasing tax revenues when applied to growing personal and corporate income and expenditure. Public expenditure may increase further during war, famine or other national crises (the displacement effect), perhaps only slowly returning to its former level because of the time taken to repay borrowing to part-finance the crisis. However the crisis may also increase the tolerable level of taxation because of enhanced public expectations about what the state can do to improve people's living standards (the inspection effect). The net result is occasional short-term jumps in public expenditure within a rising long-term trend. Ultimately, however, citizens' willingness to pay taxes determines the relative size of the public sector. That willingness is not solely dependent upon income.

Fiscal illusion models: assumes citizens' preferences for tax-expenditure packages determine public expenditure but that they increasingly underestimate the amounts they pay in taxes due to 'fiscal illusion'. This can be caused by a number of factors. First, a progressive shift towards less 'visible' taxes, such as those levied on cigarettes and petrol – few people realising exactly how large a proportion of the price is made up of tax. Second, an increasingly complex tax system, few people realising how much total tax they pay on their incomes, expenditures, savings and investments and so on. Third, 'fiscal drag' which occurs when the levels at which incomes become (more highly) taxable are not increased in line with inflation, so resulting in increasingly elastic tax revenues. Fourth, increasing use of deficit finance, meaning current taxpayers either will not have to pay higher future taxes to repay public sector borrowing or, if they do have to repay debt, they discount future tax liabilities because they are 'myopic'. Examples for the first three factors are discussed further in Chapter 10 whilst Chapter 11 discusses those for the fourth factor.

Leviathan model: assumes that political constraints on public expenditure growth are limited and that the state seeks growth as much or more to benefit those who work in the public sector as to promote the public interest. Government departments and agencies have an in-built tendency to grow bigger because **bureaucrats and professional technocrats are predisposed to more spending,** improving service provision and professional standards for their own sake. Those working in the public sector **also tend to have more political influence** than the general public because they are 'closer to government' and know how to pressurise political decision-makers. That influence increases as public sector employment rises **and state workers account for more votes** and generally voting for more public spending than the general public. Hence the public sector becomes self-serving and grows like a leviathan (i.e. a monster). This *macro* model is comprised of a number of separate *micro* models relating to the behaviour of bureaucrats, politicians, pressure groups and individual voters (see below).

At best, whether jointly or singly, macro models can only explain the long-term rising trend of public expenditure. They are essentially aggregative (macro) in approach, providing insufficient explanation of the changing composition of public expenditure.

Micro models of public expenditure growth

Micro models attempt to identify the variables that directly influence the demand for and supply of specific public sector outputs and therefore they explain changes in public spending. There is at least one micro model for each group of main actors that influences the demand for and supply of public sector outputs. There are micro models of the behaviour of (a) voters, (b) politicians, (c) bureaucrats and (d) pressure groups. The last three are considered in Chapter 7 because of their relevance to the leviathan model of government. See also Chapter 1 on governments and the public interest. Hence the following section is restricted to exposition of a micro model of voters' preferences.

A voters' preferences micro model: the median voter model

This model assumes that voters have preferences for particular mixes and levels of public sector services. They can be expected to express those preferences through democratic processes. This assumption contrasts sharply with those of the macro models. In particular, the organic state macro model assumes that the state makes decisions independently of its citizens, whilst the leviathan macro model assumes that governments grow exogenously of their citizens. The political constraints macro model assumes that taxpayers are primarily concerned with tolerable levels of taxation, rather than with the services that taxes finance.

The voters' preferences micro model makes the simplifying assumption that voters are the primary determinants of both *total* public expenditure and its *distribution* between services. The model assumes that the voting system accurately reflects voters' demands for public sector services and it models the behaviour of the middle (i.e. median) voter. Hence the alternative name for this micro model is the **median voter model**.

Figure 3.1 adopts the usual analysis of demand and supply conditions. It shows typical demand schedules (*D*1 and *D*2) and a rising average cost schedule (*AC*). In the long run, *AC* could rise, fall or remain constant as the rate of output increases, depending (respectively) on the existence of diseconomies, economies or constant returns to scale. A rising *AC* schedule is assumed for purposes of exposition. It is assumed that the state provides public sector output as long as the median voter is willing to pay tax (the 'tax price') sufficient to cover average costs. These are represented by the horizontal and vertical axes respectively.

The measurement of quantity is problematic in that many public sector outputs are intangible (e.g. better health, protection against crime and against foreign enemies) and production and consumption are

Figure 3.1   The median voter demand model

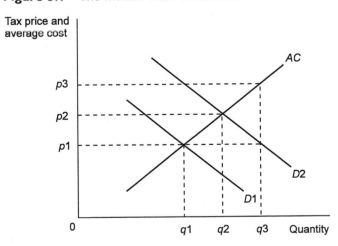

simultaneous (e.g. doctors' consulting services to patients). However this is also true of many private sector services (e.g. financial advice or hairdressing). Some public sector services have intermediate consumption goods that can be used as proxy outputs. For example, intermediate consumption goods for transport services are provision of roads (public sector) and cars (private sector). With the possible exception of status-symbol cars, neither are desired for their own sake but as facilitators of mobility. Hence problems of output measurement do not invalidate the following analysis.

In order to explain the growth of public expenditure, this micro model has to demonstrate which factors or variables influence demand for the output and which factors influence its supply.

Demand-side factors

The variables influencing demand are the preferences of the median voter, the total population and its demographic structure.

1. **The median voter.** For the median voter, public expenditure is initially $p1q1$, derived from the intersection of $D1$ and AC where demand equals supply. If the median voter's post-tax income rises the demand curve shifts to the right to $D2$, showing that at price $p1$ demand increases to $q3$. The greater the income elasticity of demand for that particular public sector service the greater the shift to the right. However the state will not provide $q3$ since willingness to pay ($p1$) is less than the tax price, $p3$. The new equilibrium is therefore $p2q2$, where tax price equals average cost. Public expenditure has therefore increased from $p1q1$ to $p2q2$.

   Causes of the shift from $D1$ to $D2$ include:

   (a) **An increase in the median voter's post tax income** through:
   - an increase in gross income, or
   - a reduction in liability to pay tax (which increases net income).
   Reduced tax liability is caused by:
   - an increase in tax free allowances, or
   - an increase in the economy's total tax base (which therefore reduces average tax payments, *ceteris paribus*);

   (b) **A rise in the relative price of substitutes** (e.g. private health care); and

   (c) **A fall in the relative price of complements** (e.g. cars, for roads).

2. **Total population.** The impact of a change in total population depends on the economic characteristics of the public sector commodity:
   - **Pure private goods:** output would normally *increase in proportion* to population because of their exclusive property rights.

- **Pure public goods:** output *will not need to be increased* at all because of their non-rivalness characteristic. However, whilst supply does not need to increase there may nevertheless be an increase in demand for a pure public good if it has a high income elasticity of demand and if rising population reduces the tax cost faced by the median voter (e.g. caused by an influx of working immigrants paying taxes). This result is represented in Figure 3.1 and may explain the association between increasing defence spending and increasing affluence quite independently of the need for additional military deterrence.

- **Impure public (mixed) goods:** *a less than proportional increase* in output would normally be required where there is a mix of non-exclusive but rival-use characteristics. However rivalness in use may require the outputs of pure private or mixed goods to increase *proportionately more* than population when there are indivisibilities in service supply.

3. **Demographic structure.** *Rising numbers of elderly people* increase demands on health care and personal social services whilst *more children* increase demands on health and educational provision. For example, in the UK health and personal social services costs per head in the 0–4 age group are twice those of working age. They are four times greater for those aged 65–75 and nine times greater for those over 75 years of age. Dramatic increases are forecast for the over 85s (rising by 78 per cent from 1987 to 2027) with moderate increases for the under-16 group (10 per cent over the same period). Even a fall in numbers may be more than offset by rising participation rates. For example, for higher education the 25 per cent fall in school leavers between 1989 and 1994 was more than offset by rising university entrance rates amongst women, ethnic groups, mature students and low-income groups.

Supply-side factors

These variables relate to the environment in which services are produced, the quality of goods provided and the productivity of the inputs used to provide them.

1. **Service environment.** A deteriorating service environment requires more inputs for a given standard of output whether the commodity in question is a pure private good, mixed good or pure public good. Examples (respectively) include increased pollution (e.g. of water supplies), increased congestion (e.g. of roads or swimming pools) and increased international military tension (which requires increased defence spending). Deterioration of the service environment requires more spending in order to maintain service quality,

Figure 3.2   The service environment and productivity differential models

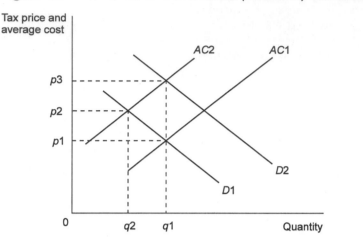

represented in Figure 3.2 by the shift from *AC*1 to *AC*2. Ignore *D*2 for the time being since demand conditions are assumed to remain constant. The tax costs of providing the same output (*q*1) rise from *p*1*q*1 to *p*3*q*1. Normally, however, the increase in tax cost would reduce median voter demand to *q*2 (i.e. staying on *D*1) so public expenditure falls from *p*1*q*1 to *p*2*q*2.

2. **Quality of service.** A higher quality generally requires a higher level of expenditure for a given volume of service. Analysis is similar to the service environment model and is represented by an upward shift in the average cost curve in Figure 3.2, leading to increased public spending. If there are expectations of continually improving the quality of public sector outputs such as health care and education, then expenditure will rise over time.

3. **Productivity of inputs.** In general, the lower the productivity of public sector inputs the greater the expenditure necessary to provide a given level or quality of service. It has often been claimed that factors of production are employed at lower levels of efficiency in the public sector than in the private sector because of management inefficiencies in the former. This criticism of public sector management provides the rationale for privatisation (see Chapter 13) and for contracting out (see Chapter 15). However there is also a more general hypothesis that technological differences in the production functions of the public and private sectors create a differential in the productivity of the inputs used by each sector. This is derived from Baumol's productivity differential model and is generally referred to as the relative price effect.

The relative price effect

Assume that the output of the public sector mainly comprises services with little or no scope for productivity improvements, whereas private sector outputs have considerable scope for productivity improvements. Under these conditions it can be shown that public spending will account for a rising share of gross domestic product.

Public service pay and pensions accounts for over half of UK exhaustive expenditures. If private sector pay increases are financed by productivity improvements then the unit cost of output remains constant, even though pay levels increase. Whilst the public sector has to match such pay increases (in order to prevent loss of workers to the private sector) it cannot finance them through improved productivity. Hence the price of public sector outputs rises relative to those of the private sector. This relative price effect is due to different technological conditions, namely the (assumed) greater scope for economies of scale and technological change in the private sector.

The increase in public expenditure will be greater the more price inelastic the demand for public sector services. Normally, however, the increase in relative prices would reduce demand (i.e. a movement along the demand curve). This will be partially or fully offset if rising real incomes lead to an increase in demand (i.e. a shift of the demand curve to the right). If the effect of income elasticity of demand is greater than price elasticity of demand then demand increases and, combined with the higher unit costs, public expenditure increases. This is represented in **Figure 3.2**. In this case, the shift in the average cost schedule from $AC1$ to $AC2$ is caused by the productivity differential and the shift from $D1$ to $D2$ is caused by the increase in personal incomes arising from pay settlements. Public expenditure is initially $p1q1$. The rise in average cost would reduce demand from $q1$ to $q2$ (moving along $D1$ represents price elasticity) but this is exactly offset in the diagram by the shift from $D1$ to $D2$ (representing income elasticity). Output therefore remains constant at $q1$ but total public expenditure rises from $p1q1$ to $p3q1$.

This model has a number of questionable assumptions. **First**, it is an empirical question whether the scope for productivity improvements is necessarily more limited in the public sector. There is no technical reason why production functions and/or technological possibilities should be static for public sector services but dynamic for similar private sector services. **Second**, the public and private sectors may not be in competition for a fixed supply of labour, especially if there is large-scale and long-term unemployment. **Third**, it may not necessarily be the case that pay rates are equalised in both sectors even if competition for labour occurs. For example, whilst it is methodologically difficult to compare pay and conditions, anecdotal evidence suggests that in the UK blue collar (manual) workers have received better pay and conditions in the public than in the private sector, the opposite having been the case for white collar (professional and administrative) workers (see Chapter 15). **Fourth**, there is no longer automatic inflation-indexing of input costs. The planning of UK public expenditure in real (or volume) terms was associated with a rise in public sector costs of about 0.5 per cent per annum more than private sector costs in the two decades up to the mid 1970s. Thereafter the introduction of 'cash limits' on about 60 per cent of public expenditure, followed by the shift to cash planning in 1982, meant that index-linking ceased to be automatic (see Chapter 9).

In effect the UK government refused to accommodate the relative price effect and no longer allowed for it in its allocations to government departments. It was argued that inflation-indexing provided managers with poor incentives to reduce costs. Many government departments have monopsonistic (sole buyer) powers that can be used to exert downward pressure on input prices (or constrain their increases). They are price makers rather than price takers. Changes in the mix of inputs in response to changing relative prices are also possible in many cases. To the extent that the model is valid, however, it suggests that public sector growth will restrain economic growth and that this will inevitably occur even if the public sector is as efficient as possible. Economic growth will be further constrained if the public sector is inefficient (see Chapter 7).

Interactions: multiple deprivation and fiscal stress

Interactions between variables may lead to much greater increases in public spending, the whole effect being greater than the sum of the individual parts. Local government provision of services (i.e. exhaustive expenditures) provides an illustrative example. The decline in manufacturing employment in major British cities has been associated with the emigration of economically viable socioeconomic groups (skilled and educated younger workers). This **selective out-migration** leaves behind a residual of unemployed, unskilled, relatively uneducated socioeconomic groups and of old (retired) and single parent households. Hence, in order to maintain a given quantity and quality of service per head of population, city local governments may need to spend more per capita because of **multiple deprivation** (i.e. the *simultaneous* occurrence of many aspects of social and economic disadvantage).

For example, as elderly groups account for an increasing proportion of the total population of cities, local government personal social services expenditures per head of *total* population will rise even if local government expenditure *per elderly person* is held constant. However, if the supportive sons and daughters of those elderly people have left the city in search of jobs, then city municipalities will have to *increase* their provision of services to the elderly. Similar processes may lead to increases in municipal per capita spending on subsidised council housing (e.g. for single parent families). Urban decay may lead city governments to incur increased spending to deal with industrial dereliction and local economic regeneration policies. Urban socio-economic decay may also be associated with increased crime rates and so increased need to spend on policing functions.

These interacting forces increase the *need* to spend per capita (and possibly in aggregate) in order to maintain constant quantity and quality of service. At the same time local voters may expect and demand continual improvements in service quality, so increasing city govern-ments' costs. However the out-migration of industry and affluent socioeconomic groups leads to constrained local tax revenues. Hence fiscal stress ensues as the costs of public service provision rise faster than the revenues needed to finance them. Such unbalanced growth of revenues and expenditures may be exacerbated by limited scope for improvements in the productivity of (labour-intensive) local government services whilst real labour costs rise (but see Chapter 15). This local government example can be seen to combine all of the preceding supply-side and demand-side factors, which in combination exert considerable upward pressure on *exhaustive* public expenditures.

3.4 Explaining the growth of transfer expenditures

The explanation of increasing transfer expenditures relates to changing demographic and economic structures interacting with notions of social and economic justice. Transfer payments are affected by a number of factors:

Demographic structure. This influences transfer payments through state old-age pensions and child benefit in particular (see Chapter 9). These transfer expenditures are in addition to the exhaustive expenditures on health and on personal social services such as residential care and day centres for elderly people.

Household structure. The increasing numbers and proportions of marriages ending in divorce have led to an increasing number of single parent families. Such families tend to be more heavily dependent on state benefits such as income support and housing benefit (see Chapter 9). Once again, these transfer expenditures are additional to their increased use of health and personal social services such as child care and social work services.

Economic recession. Increasing unemployment leads to increased public spending on transfer payments such as the 'jobseeker's allowance', income support and housing benefit. However, whilst recession can last up to a decade it does not explain the secular trend of rising public expenditure. Its influence is short to medium term.

Equity considerations. In general, the greater the desired degree of equality of living standards the greater the redistribution of income and wealth through transfer payments and taxation. The absolute level of transfer payments and taxes, their share of gross domestic product and their distribution between different socioeconomic groups will therefore depend on notions of social equity interacting with changing demographic and household structures and changing economic prosperity. However equity is a multifaceted concept and is not simply concerned with the achievement of increased equality of incomes and living standards. Equity also incorporates notions of justice and reward for merit. For example, if it is accepted that self-improvement and work effort should be rewarded, then equity will not lead to complete equality in living standards (see Chapter 12).

Moreover, if complete equality could be achieved, it may create such enormous disincentives to personal achievement that society, and everyone within it, would be substantially the poorer. Examples are the supposed disincentive-to-work effects of taxation and of high benefit payments (see Chapters 4 and 12). High transfer payments increase public expenditure whilst significant disincentive-to-work effects reduce gross domestic product. The combined result is that public expenditure rises sharply as a proportion of national income. This illustrates how efficiency and equity can interact in the form of a trade-off. The conventional neoclassical view is that the trade-off is negative, i.e. increased equity leads to decreased efficiency because it creates disincentives to productive effort. Nevertheless, a trend towards greater equality can be explained in terms of neoclassical economic theory using the median voter model.

Equity and the median voter model

If the median voter also has the median income then he or she will favour redistributing income from the mean to the median. This is because the mean is greater than the median when the distribution of income is skewed to the right by a relatively small number of people earning exceptionally high incomes (see Chapter 12). Thus the median voter will favour progressive taxes which tax more highly those with incomes greater than middle incomes; but will not favour taxes which also tax those on middle incomes more than those on lower incomes (see Chapter 10). Likewise, the median voter will also favour increased public spending on transfer payments. This is because, over time, extension of the voting franchise to lower income groups (non-propertied classes, women, younger people) has the effect of lowering the income of the median voter and so, *ceteris paribus*, increasing the gap between median income and mean income. Hence, the new median voter will demand even greater redistribution of incomes. This self-serving interest in a more equal distribution of income is quite distinct from **inequality aversion** (see Chapter 1).

The median voter model therefore provides at least a partial explanation of the growth of **both** exhaustive expenditures and transfer payments and predicts a growing preoccupation with redistribution. It yields essentially the same result as a political science model (based on Tocqueville and others) which states that, once granted, full political suffrage unleashes democratic pressures for the government to deal with the worst social and economic inequalities. However, some degree of inequality may be regarded as socially desirable because of the signals it sends to citizens about the benefits and costs of particular patterns of behaviour (i.e. the costs of not conforming with social and economic conventions).

Inequalities in the distribution of income were conceptualised in terms of the Paretian approach of **Figure 2.4**. In this neoclassical model, the point on the contract curve is effectively chosen by the median voter. However society may be more concerned with equality of *opportunity* than equality of *outcome*, with equality of *access* to public services rather than equality of *use* of those services, with *individual responsibility* rather than *central control* and direction. Such inequalities are not simply restricted to income. They also manifest themselves in quite profound differences in living conditions and life chances. Segregation of income groups occurs in terms of occupation, area of residence, schools attended by their children, entry to higher education, prevalence of particular illnesses, mortality statistics, consumption patterns, race and ethnicity and so on. So-called 'inner city' areas contain concentrations of socioeconomic and racial disadvantage (multiple deprivation) requiring government intervention which simply cannot be explained by the median voter model. As already noted, multiple deprivation provides a cost-based explanation of increasing public expenditure that interacts with notions of equity. In practice it is not possible to distinguish which part of intervention is required on equity grounds and which is required on efficiency grounds.

Whilst the distinction between transfer payments and exhaustive public expenditures appears to be clearly distinguishable in conceptual terms, many exhaustive expenditures have redistributive consequences because of their differential impacts on particular areas or socio-economic groups. Equity and cost-based factors become combined in their real impacts. For example, increases in exhaustive public expenditures by inner city local governments reflect both the rising costs of urban public services (an objective factor) and the implementation of social policies designed to improve equity (a normative factor). In allocating intergovernmental grants to local governments, central government inevitably finds it difficult to distinguish between the part of rising urban public expenditure that is due to local governments' own social policies and that which is due to the changing service environment. This is a particularly contentious issue when central and urban local governments are of different political persuasions and so have different views on social equity.

3.5 Conclusions

Economic models can be used to explain increased public expenditure independently of notions of equity. Macro and micro models of public expenditure growth can be used to explain both the increasing real level of exhaustive public expenditures and the rising share of gross domestic product for which they account. They do not attempt to explain increased public spending by reference to inefficiency in the production of public sector outputs (see Chapter 7). The median voter model suggests that the public spending on exhaustive expenditures will be too low (because market failure is ignored) and that public spending will become increasingly focused on redistribution of income. However, the median voter model does not provide the basis of a general model of public expenditure because it is only a model of demand for public sector outputs. A general model requires both a demand side and a supply side. Moreover, even as a demand-side model, the median voter model faces many theoretical criticisms. These criticisms are discussed in detail in the author's 1999 text *Local Government Economics*, which also discusses the division of responsibilities between central and local government.

Both macro and micro models of public expenditure growth are too mechanistic in that they ignore changes in culture and perceptions of government, for example the recent shift away from 'bigger is better' to 'small is beautiful'. Changes in the meaning and nature of 'public' (see Chapter 1) and in conceptions of social justice (see Chapter 12) can have profound influences on the relative size of the state. Whilst economic theory therefore only provides a **partial** explanation of the growth of the state and its expenditure much the same can be said of the theories of other disciplines. It is probably not possible to develop a totally comprehensive model of the growth of government and the public sector. Nor is it possible to say whether public expenditure is too large or too small, or growing too fast or too slow. Nonetheless the economic models do illustrate the wide range of value-free influences on public spending.

Further reading

Bailey S. J. (1999) *Local Government Economics: Principles and Practice* (Basingstoke: Macmillan).

Connolly, S. and Munroe, A. (1999) *Economics of the Public Sector* (Harlow: Prentice Hall).

Cullis, J. and Jones, P. (1998) *Public Finance and Public Choice: Analytical Perspectives*, 2nd edn (Maidenhead: McGraw-Hill).

Gemmell, N. (ed.) (1993) *The Growth of the Public Sector: Theories and International Evidence* (Aldershot: Edward Elgar).

Lybeck, J. A. and Henrekson, M. (eds) (1988) *Explaining the Growth of Government* (Amsterdam: North-Holland).

4 The Economic Effects of Taxation

4.1 Introduction
4.2 Classification of Taxation
4.3 Economically Optimal Taxes
4.4 Tax Incidence
4.5 The Welfare Effects of Taxation
4.6 Incentive and Disincentive Effects of Taxation
4.7 Empirical Evidence
4.8 Conclusions

4.1 Introduction

Taxation can be used for both efficiency and equity purposes as well as to finance the system of democracy. Besides simply raising money, taxation can be used to discourage consumption of commodities yielding negative externalities (see Chapter 2), to stabilise national income as part of discretionary or automatic fiscal policy (see Chapter 8) and to redistribute income and wealth (see Chapter 12).

However taxation is not the only means of financing government intervention. Finance is also derived from borrowing, charges for service use, the sale of capital assets and miscellaneous sources (e.g. charitable donations to hospitals and public–private partnerships for industrial and commercial development projects). The first two of these income sources are analysed in Chapters 5 and 6 respectively. Part II will deal with policy and practice and provides a detailed description of sources of finance and their recent reform. This chapter restricts itself to an examination of the economic theory of taxation.

4.2 Classification of taxation

Taxes fall into two main categories:

1. **Direct taxes**, levied *directly* on incomes, profits and wealth, including income tax, national insurance contributions, corporation tax, petroleum revenue tax and inheritance tax.
2. **Indirect taxes** on expenditures (therefore levied *indirectly* on incomes and so on), including value added tax, customs and excise duties on tobacco and alcohol, and local property taxes.

The distinction between direct and indirect taxes is not always obvious. For example, national insurance contributions (NICs) are paid by both employers and employees. Employees' NICs are a direct tax on earnings. Employers' NICs are a direct tax if they lead to workers accepting lower wages but an indirect tax if wages are unaffected, employers increasing product prices instead. Whilst such a distinction may seem artificial, in that ultimately a given total national tax bill will have the same average effect on individuals, households and firms, the structure of taxation can have considerable potential effects on efficiency and equity. For example, whilst direct taxes are capable of appropriating predetermined proportions of differing income levels, the impact of indirect taxes depends on the proportion of income spent on taxable commodities and the degree to which indirect taxes raise product prices rather than reduce wages or profits. Taxes of whatever form may also affect people's incentive to work and firms' incentive to invest.

4.3 Economically optimal taxes

An allocatively efficient (optimal) tax will have no impact on the allocation of resources other than those impacts specifically intended to overcome market failure (see Chapter 2). Hence, with this exception, optimal taxation does not alter the relative prices of outputs and inputs. It is useful to distinguish two cases.

Economically optimal taxes on commodities

Such taxes will only appropriate the **economic rent** earned by a factor. Economic rent has been defined as the excess earned by a factor of production over the sum necessary to induce it to do its work (the **Ricardian** definition), or as the excess earnings over the amount necessary to keep a factor in its present occupation (the **Paretian** definition). The **Ricardian** definition applies to natural resources such as coal, oil and gas, which have no alternative use if left in the ground. Compare two separate oil deposits whose product is sold under perfectly competitive conditions and whose factor supply is perfectly elastic, but whose costs differ as depicted in **Figure 4.1**. Deposit 1 is represented by $MC1$ and $AC1$, deposit 2 by $MC2$ and $AC2$. The least-cost rate of output is the same for both deposits at $q1$, but costs are assumed to be higher for deposit 2 because of geological or locational factors. Only deposit 1 will be exploited if price is $p1$, its rate of output being $q1$. If price rises to $p2$ then deposit 2 will produce $q1$. However, deposit 1 will now produce $q2$ (where its $MC = MR$) and so total supply will now be $q1 + q2$. Deposit 1 now earns an economic rent equal to the area $p2UVc1$ because it is now intramarginal.

Figure 4.1 Economically optimal taxes on commodities

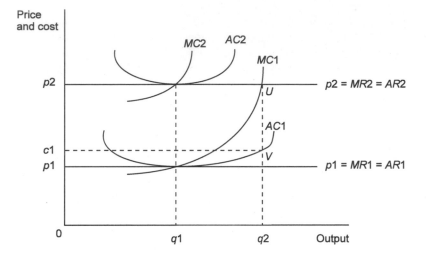

This economic rent is due to the unique nature of the deposit and is distinct from monopoly profits since it is consistent with perfect competition in the market for the product. In theory it may be taxed without affecting price or output as long as MR and MC are unchanged. Hence, taxation of economic rent has no allocative effects. An ideal tax would therefore only appropriate $p2UVc1$. The marginal deposit (i.e. deposit 2, when price is $p2$) would be free of taxation since it earns no economic rent. This is the theoretical basis of petroleum revenue tax (see Chapter 10, Appendix 10.1).

In practice oil resources can only be exploited using other factors of production (labour, capital and entrepreneurship). These other resources have alternative employments and so the **Paretian** definition of economic rent becomes relevant. The government must determine the minimum rate of return required to attract factors into oil production. This minimum rate is referred to as **transfer earnings** because it determines whether factors transfer from one use to another. **Economic rent is all earnings above transfer earnings**, and again it may be taxed without affecting allocative efficiency. Economic rents will be higher in the short run than in the long run because capital is fixed in the former. Taxation of short-run '*quasi-rents*' would deter further exploration for (and development of) further oil deposits. Hence an allocatively efficient tax only appropriates long-run (or true) economic rents, not short-run quasi-rents.

If producers have some control over oil prices then marginal fields will earn monopolistic rent (i.e. monopoly profits). In principle, taxation of monopolistic rent will also leave output unchanged. In **Figure 4.2**,

Figure 4.2 Taxation of monopolistic rent

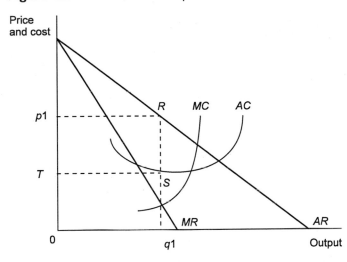

monopolistic rent is equal to the area $p1RST$ and its removal by an optimal tax would leave output unchanged at $q1$.

In practice, calculation of the optimal tax requires accurate knowledge of all the information depicted by **Figures 4.1** and **4.2**. This includes present and future values for the price per unit of output, the cost functions (for exploration, development and production), the rate of production and the rate of 'normal profits' (i.e. those consistent with transfer earnings). The government's lack of detailed knowledge of costs and normal profits, its wish to maintain the UK's self-sufficiency in oil whilst encouraging environmentally sustainable production, and the power of the multinational oil companies inevitably leads to ongoing negotiation between government and companies about the appropriate level of taxation. Hence, determination of the optimal level of taxation is rather more complicated in practical than in conceptual terms.

If oil production were to yield negative externalities (e.g. pollution) then taxation could also be used to reduce the rate of output by appropriating more than economic rent (e.g. by taxing quasi-rents). This would reduce oil production in the long run and can be compared with the direct regulation solution to pollution outlined in Chapter 2. Direct government control of production below $q1 + q2$ in **Figure 4.1** would dissipate the economic rent, so reducing the value of the resource available for taxation. Both the revenue loss and the administrative costs of regulation would reduce welfare. Hence, economists advocate market-based solutions using an indirect tax which raises revenue whilst restraining production.

Economically optimal taxes on people

A poll tax (a fixed lump-sum per head) is allocatively efficient because it does not change the relative prices of goods or services, including labour. An income tax may cause allocative inefficiency because it changes the relative prices of work and leisure. This will be formally demonstrated below. If it causes a net reduction in work effort then the economy moves within its production possibility frontier and welfare is correspondingly reduced (see Chapter 2). However, since it is related to income, an income tax is more acceptable on equity grounds than a poll tax.

A poll tax is severely **regressive**: the lower the income, the higher the proportion of income for which it accounts. Equity rules normally favour **progressive** taxation (i.e. where the proportion taken by tax rises with income), or at least **proportional** taxation (i.e. where the proportion of income taken by taxation stays the same at all income levels but where the rich still pay more tax than the poor in absolute terms). Hence, whilst allocatively efficient, a poll tax is usually deemed so inequitable that it is not politically acceptable as the sole or dominant form of taxation (see Chapter 10, Appendix 10.1). It may, however, be acceptable as a small part of a larger tax system.

4.4 Tax incidence

Whilst a firm may be legally liable to pay customs and excise duties on its products it may attempt to recover tax increases by raising product prices (**forward shifting**), reducing the prices paid for its inputs of land, labour and capital (**backward shifting**), reducing dividends paid to its shareholders (**lateral shifting**) or some combination of all three responses. Whilst it is very difficult to assess the total extent to which tax is actually shifted, it is possible to examine forward shifting onto consumers on an *a priori* basis.

Figure 4.3 shows the case for a commodity tax fixed in cash terms and applied to each unit produced for the good in question. The effect of imposition of the unit tax is represented by shifting the supply curve from $S1$ (pre-tax) to $S2$ (post-tax). This demonstrates that the price received by the producer must rise by the full amount of the tax for supply to remain unchanged. For example, the pre-tax equilibrium is $p1q1$ (where demand equals supply). The unit tax is $p3 - p1$ and the supplier would have to receive $p3$ in order to maintain supply at $q1$. However a rise in price to $p3$ reduces demand to $q3$, creating excess supply of $q1 - q3$. Price falls until the excess supply is removed at the post-tax equilibrium $p2q2$. It is clear that, whilst the supplier is legally liable to pay the tax, the economic incidence of the tax is shared between

Figure 4.3   Tax incidence

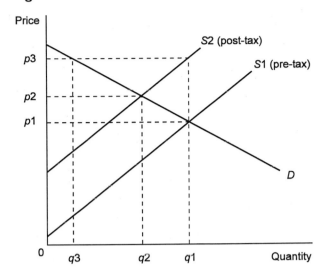

the supplier (who receives a lower 'net of tax' price) and the consumer (who pays a higher retail price). The incidence is as follows:

$$\frac{p3 - p2}{p3 - p1} \text{ on the producer} \qquad \frac{p2 - p1}{p3 - p1} \text{ on the consumer}$$

This particular pattern of incidence reflects the price elasticities of demand and supply. This is demonstrated by **Figure 4.4**. The two demand schedules $D1$ and $D2$ combine with the same pre- and post-tax supply schedules of **Figure 4.3**. The pre-tax equilibrium is shown by the intersection of $D1$ and $D2$ with $S1$. In both cases the pre-tax equilibrium is $p1q1$. The post-tax equilibrium is shown by the intersections of $D1$ and $D2$ with $S2$. Price rises more for $D2$ (to $p6$, with quantity traded falling to $q6$) than for $D1$, where the outcome is $p5q5$. This is because $D2$ is more price inelastic than $D1$.

If demand is **perfectly price inelastic** (i.e. a vertical demand schedule) price rises by the full amount of the tax because a change in price has no effect on quantity demanded. The consumer bears 100 per cent of the tax incidence. If demand is **perfectly price elastic** (i.e. horizontal demand schedule), an increase in price would cause demand to fall to zero so that the supplier has to bear 100 per cent of the tax. In this case supply traded falls. Similarly if supply is perfectly price inelastic the producer bears 100 per cent of the tax and if supply is perfectly price elastic the consumer bears 100 per cent of the tax. The final incidence clearly depends on the relative price elasticities of demand and supply.

Figure 4.4   Price elasticity of demand and tax incidence

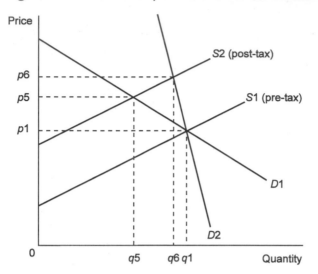

Besides determining the distribution of tax incidence between supplier and consumer, the price elasticities of demand and supply will also affect the amount of tax revenue raised. Tax revenues are clearly greater for D2 than for D1 in **Figure 4.4**, since quantity traded is greater, but unit tax (shown by the vertical distance between S1 and S2) is the same. In general, the greater the price elasticities the lower the tax revenue because of the greater reduction in quantity traded. Hence, only where demand or supply are perfectly price inelastic will total tax revenue equal the product of the unit tax multiplied by the level of sales before the introduction of (or an increase in) the tax.

Figures 4.3 and **4.4** refer to application of a unit tax in a situation of perfect competition. The analysis of incidence is essentially the same for a percentage (*ad valorem*) tax and for a monopoly situation. A tax that reduces monopoly profits (because the supplier bears some of the incidence) may be more politically acceptable than one that forces firms in competitive markets out of business. However perfect competition and monopoly are rare. Oligopoly is the most common form of market structure but also the one for which economic theory has least predictive power. Oligopolistic firms may recover more than 100 per cent of the tax if they treat it as a variable cost to which they apply their percentage mark-up to recover overheads and profits. This pricing behaviour magnifies the allocative distortion caused by taxation.

Whilst heavily simplified, the analysis of **Figures 4.3** and **4.4** demonstrates the factors that influence who really pays the tax and how much tax is received (Appendix 10.2 provides a more realistic example). Except in the extreme (and unlikely) cases of perfectly elastic demand and perfectly inelastic supply, indirect taxes increase commodity prices and so create inflationary pressures. Except for petroleum revenue tax and perhaps taxes on heavily polluting fuels (see Chapter 2), they are usually non-optimal taxes in that their impact on relative prices is not designed to correct market failures or to tax no more than economic rent (see Chapter 10).

4.5 The welfare effects of taxation

Indirect taxes can also be expected to reduce consumers' welfare since the quantity consumed is likely to fall (except in the extreme and unlikely cases of perfectly inelastic demand or perfectly inelastic supply). This is shown in **Figure 4.5**, which reproduces the demand and supply schedules of **Figure 4.3**. The demand schedule shows consumers' willingness to pay and its slope is a measure of their marginal valuation of the commodity. In the pre-tax equilibrium $p1q1$, marginal valuation (or benefit) equals price $p1$. This is the case for the last unit consumed, that is $q1 - (q1 - 1)$. For all other units (zero to $q1 - 1$), marginal valuation exceeds marginal price ($p1$). For example, for the pre-tax equilibrium, the excess is $A - p1$ starting from zero and $B - p1$ at $q2$. Consumers therefore retain a surplus of marginal valuation over price, measured by the vertical distance between the price line and the demand schedule. The **consumers' surplus** pre-tax is therefore measured by the area $ACp1$, bounded by the price line, the demand curve and the vertical axis. After tax it is reduced to $ABp2$ because the equilibrium price has risen.

Figure 4.5 Welfare effects of taxation

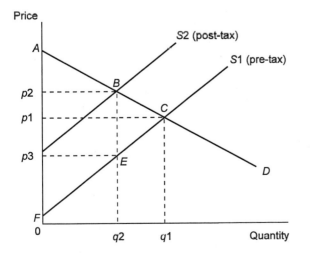

There is a similar loss of welfare on the part of the producers. The supply schedule shows the minimum prices that must be paid in order to call forth supply, but equilibrium price is greater than those minima for all but the marginal unit. For example, for the pre-tax equilibrium, the excess is $p1 - F$ starting at zero and $p1 - E$ at $q2$. The producers' surplus pre-tax is therefore measured by the vertical distance between the supply schedule and the **net of tax** price line. The **producers' surplus** pre-tax is therefore $p1CF$, measured by the area bounded by the price line, the supply curve and the vertical axis. After tax it is reduced to $p3EF$, $p3$ being the price received by the producer net of tax. Market price is $p2$ but not all of the tax $(p2 - p3)$ is borne by the consumer. This is because price has risen from $p1$ to only $p2$ with the result that the consumer only pays tax of $p2 - p1$. The remainder $(p1 - p3)$ is paid by the supplier so that the net price is $p3$. Hence producers' surplus is $p3EF$ post-tax, demonstrating a loss of producers' surplus.

Assume that total welfare is the sum of consumers' and producers' surpluses, together with the welfare gained from public sector outputs financed by the tax. Total welfare before tax is measured by ACF, tax revenue being zero. Assume that the value of public sector outputs is equal to their tax cost. On this assumption, post-tax welfare is measured by $ABEF$. This is made up of consumers' surplus ($ABp2$), plus producers' surplus ($p3EF$) plus tax revenue ($p2BEp3$) which equals the tax $(p2 - p3)$ multiplied by post-tax output ($q2$). Therefore welfare is reduced by BCE as a result of the tax, assuming that the *value of public sector outputs equals their tax cost*. BCE is known as the **excess burden** of taxation or the **deadweight loss** of welfare. It provides an *a priori* assumption against taxation. The results for *ad valorem* taxes and for monopoly are essentially the same.

In practice the deadweight loss of welfare will be reduced if the tax is used to finance services that yield substantial positive externalities (see Chapter 2). Similarly, public services that are complementary to private sector outputs may be valued more than their tax costs. In these cases the area BCE would be reduced, and possibly eliminated so that an excess benefit or gain of welfare results. If, however, tax revenues were to be used to finance public services yielding little or no positive externalities, and the production of which was at excessively high cost (inefficiency in production) or in quantities greater than citizens wish to consume (inefficiency in consumption), then the area BCE would underestimate the excess burden or deadweight loss. In other words $p2BEp3$ would be an overestimate of the value of public services. This is more likely when the provision of public services is characterised by bureaucratic empire building (see Chapter 7).

The practical application of the deadweight loss concept associated with taxation is to minimise tax levels whilst maximising the benefits of public sector outputs. This explains the current preoccupation with assessing the economy, efficiency and effectiveness of the provision of public sector services (see Chapters 8 and 9). It is possible to assess the technical aspects of economy and efficiency, for example through efficiency audits and competitive contracting (see Chapter 15). However assessment of externalities and of the complementary nature of public sector outputs is extremely difficult in practice and assessments of these characteristics tend to be highly judgemental and value-laden. Supporters of collective action through the public sector would naturally emphasise the wider benefits of public services whilst supporters of free markets would naturally emphasise inefficiencies, both in deciding which outputs to produce and in their production.

4.6 Incentive and disincentive effects of taxation

In deriving an *a priori* case against taxation, the foregoing analysis assumed that gross domestic product is independent of taxation. In other words, it assumed that the only effect is a **redistribution** of the pattern of production and consumption between market and tax-financed outputs. This is represented by a move along both the production possibility frontier and its associated contract curve (see **Figure 2.4**). However, if high levels of taxation create disincentive-to-work effects then gross domestic product will be lower as a result of taxation. In such a case the deadweight loss of welfare identified in **Figure 4.5** would severely understate the total welfare loss because the economy moves **inside** its production possibility frontier as factors of production are dissuaded from work. The same outcome would result if taxation of companies created a disincentive-to-invest effect (see Chapter 10, Appendix 10.1).

Figure 4.6 shows a **backward-bending supply curve of labour**, the derivation of which will be explained shortly. Income tax obviously affects take-home pay (i.e. post-tax wages). If an increase in income tax reduced wages from $w2$ to $w3$, then hours worked would fall from $h3$ to $h2$ (a disincentive-to-work effect). However, if the supply curve is backward bending and increased income tax reduced wages from $w1$ to $w2$, hours worked would increase from $h1$ to $h3$ (an incentive-to-work effect). Clearly income tax will affect the decision to work, which in turn affects output, but it is not self-evident whether those effects will be positive or negative. If work effort is reduced the economy moves within its production possibility frontier. Hence any such disincentive-to-work effect is important in that it reduces economic growth and therefore the capacity of the economy to improve living standards generally and to provide benefits for low-income and economically disadvantaged

Figure 4.6   Incentive and disincentive effects of income tax

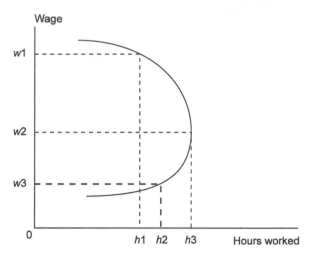

groups. It is important, therefore, to fully appreciate the incentive or disincentive effect of taxation. It is the net outcome of two effects:

1. **The substitution effect.** This refers to the substitution of leisure for work or vice versa. The opportunity cost of leisure is the income forgone by not working. This is the 'price' of leisure. Hence an increase in income tax (i.e. a fall in the post-tax wage rate) reduces the cost of leisure and increases demand for it (i.e. hours worked fall). The reverse occurs when post-tax wages rise. The substitution effect therefore depends on the price of leisure measured by changes in the marginal post-tax wage rate, i.e. the extra take-home pay arising from an extra hour's work (e.g. overtime). In turn, the marginal wage rate depends on the marginal rate of income tax, i.e. the extra tax paid divided by the extra income earned.
2. **The income effect.** Leisure is assumed to be a commodity with a high income elasticity of demand. Hence the income effect increases the demand for leisure as incomes rise, and increases work effort as income falls. The income effect depends on the average rate of income tax (i.e. total income tax paid divided by total earned income).

Hence the net impact of a change in income tax on hours worked depends on the relative size of the income and substitution effects. If the income effect is greater than the substitution effect, an increase in income tax will increase hours worked and reduce leisure time (i.e. $h1$ to $h3$ in **Figure 4.6**). If the income effect is less than the substitution effect then an increase in income tax will reduce hours worked and increase leisure time (i.e. $h3$ to $h2$). If the income and substitution effects are of exactly the same size then hours worked will remain constant.

Separation and measurement of income and substitution effects is provided in **Figure 4.7**. $I1$ and $I2$ are the usual indifference curves, explained in Chapter 2. However the trade-off is now between income earned by working (on the vertical axis) and leisure (on the horizontal axis). As before, the price of leisure is the income forgone by not working. Lines BA, CA and MN are budget lines showing the maximum combinations of income and leisure that can be achieved within a given budget. For example, beginning with budget line BA, maximum income is $0B$ if no leisure is taken, whilst maximum leisure is $0A$ if hours employed are zero. The line BA shows all maximum possible combinations of income and leisure, given their prices.

Assuming the objective is to maximise welfare, individuals try to locate on the highest possible indifference curve, $I1$ being preferred to $I2$. The particular combination of work and leisure chosen on $I1$ is determined by the point of tangency with the budget line, where the marginal rate of substitution (MRS) of work for leisure required to maintain a constant level of welfare equals the marginal rate of transformation (MRT) of work into leisure. MRS is measured by the slope of the indifference curve. MRT is measured by the slope of the budget line, which itself measures the ratio of the prices of work and leisure. As explained in Chapter 2, equilibrium exists when MRS equals MRT.

The original equilibrium point is $e1$. An increase in income tax reduces maximum post-tax income but has no effect on maximum leisure. Hence

Figure 4.7   Income and substitution effects

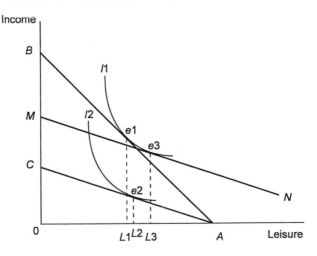

the line BA pivots on point A to CA. The rate of income tax is BC divided by 0B. The highest attainable indifference curve is now I2 and the equilibrium shifts from e1 to e2. Leisure increases from L1 to L2 meaning that hours worked fall. In this case the substitution effect is greater than the income effect. This is equivalent to the shift from h3 to h2 in **Figure 4.6**, both cases demonstrating the **net** outcome.

Figure 4.7 allows separation and estimation of the income and substitution effects by restoring the income to what it was before imposition of the income tax. This is achieved by giving the individual a lump-sum payment that shifts CA to MN (parallel to CA), which is tangential to the original indifference curve I1. This restores welfare back to its pre-tax position. However the slope of MN is now less than that of BA because the relative prices of work and leisure have been changed as a result of the tax. Hence a new point of tangency occurs at e3. The shift from e1 to e2 is the net effect of the income tax and depends on the relative sizes of the income and substitution effects. The movement from e1 to e3 is the substitution effect and is due to the change in the relative prices of work and leisure. The shift from e3 to e2 is the income effect.

The **income effect** of a lower post-tax wage reduces leisure and increases work effort, the movement from e3 to e2 reducing leisure from L3 to L2. The **substitution effect** of a lower post-tax wage decreases work and increases leisure, the movement from e1 to e3 increasing leisure from L1 to L3. In the diagram, the *net* effect of the increased income tax is the shift from e1 to e2 because the substitution effect is greater than the income effect. However, if the income effect is greater than the substitution effect then e2 will lie the left of e1, showing that the extra tax reduces leisure and increases work effort.

Note that this theory does **not** prove that income tax (or increases in it) creates disincentives to work. Whilst e2 must be to the left of e3, the position of e2 relative to e1 is indeterminate since it depends on which is bigger, the income or substitution effect. What the theory **does** demonstrate is that a poll tax is to be preferred to an income tax on efficiency grounds because it does not change the relative prices of goods or services (including labour). In other words a poll tax does not destroy the pre-tax marginal equality of $MRS = MRT$. An income tax does destroy that marginal equality because it is a selective tax on income.

This is shown in **Figure 4.8**, which compares an income tax with a poll tax **raising the same tax revenue**. The pre-tax budget line is BA. Imposition of a poll tax of BZ (equal to AY) creates budget line ZY, maximum post-tax income being 0Z and the maximum leisure being 0Y (YA amount of time having to be spent earning sufficient income to pay the poll tax). The budget line shifts parallel to BA to its new position at ZY because the poll tax does not affect the relative prices of work and leisure. It passes through e3 because it raises the same amount as the

Figure 4.8   Comparing a poll tax and an income tax in efficiency terms

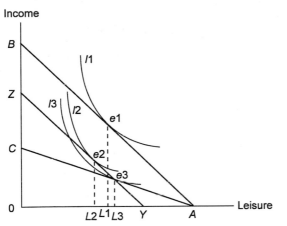

income tax. The poll tax reduces income by less than the income tax (which creates *CA* as before) because it has a wider tax base, being payable by those who were previously not working but who now have to work in order to pay it.

The poll tax equilibrium is *e2*, resulting in less leisure (i.e. more work) at *L2* than the income tax equilibrium *e3* and *L3*. This is because the marginal rate of tax for a poll tax is zero (i.e. payment is not related to income). Hence the poll tax has no substitution effect, only an income effect (measured by the shift from *e1* to *e2*) that increases work effort. The income tax creates a substitution effect precisely because payment of it is related to income (i.e. the marginal tax rate is positive). The substitution effect partially offsets the income effect. Therefore the net result is that the poll tax will increase work effort by more than the income tax.

In fact in **Figure 4.8** the substitution effect of the income tax more than offsets the income effect so that *L3* lies to the right of *L1*. There is a net disincentive-to-work effect created by the income tax compared with the incentive to work created by the poll tax. This assumes that people fulfill their legal obligations to pay both taxes and that there is work available for them as they seek to regain their original level of welfare. **Figure 4.8** also makes it clear that, relative to a poll tax, an income tax creates an excess burden because it results in the individual being on a lower indifference curve (*I3* rather than *I2*). This is effectively the same result as that obtained in **Figure 4.5**. It is the outcome of the substitution effect caused by the income tax.

It is clear that if the government wished to increase the level of income tax without creating or exacerbating disincentive-to-work effects, it should reduce the value of personal allowances (which exempt the first part of earnings from income tax). It could achieve this by not increasing allowances in line with inflation. There would be no substitution effect since the marginal rate of income tax would remain unchanged. There would be an income effect since the average tax rate increases, so increasing the incentive to work. Similarly, if the government wished to reduce income tax it would be more efficient to reduce the rates of income tax rather than increase personal allowances. Reducing rates would reduce the substitution of leisure for work and so reduce any disincentive-to-work effects. Whilst this substitution effect would be partly offset by an income effect (created by the increased post-tax income resulting from the cut in tax rates), increasing allowances would only create an income effect that would increase the amount of leisure (i.e. reduce work effort) relative to a reduction in tax rates.

The more progressive the income tax structure, the higher the marginal tax rates for successive bands of income. Hence progressive taxes have greater substitution effects than proportional taxes and are therefore more likely to create net disincentive-to-work effects with a greater excess burden. If this is the case then efficiency rules require cuts in top tax rates, contrary to equity rules which require increases in those rates. A proportional income tax therefore has many advantages. It avoids a proliferation of successive increases in marginal tax rates as income rises and so minimises allocative distortions. At the same time it ensures that more affluent income groups still pay more in pound terms than lower income groups since both pay the same percentage. Equity is further improved if personal tax allowances are introduced since they constitute a greater proportion of low incomes than of high incomes. However, increasing income tax by reducing the real value of personal allowances (as suggested above) would cause a greater proportionate reduction of low incomes than of high incomes.

So far the discussion has been in terms of formal income tax. However, if means-tested social security benefits are also withdrawn as incomes increase from very low levels, then the **effective marginal tax rates** could be much higher. For example, assume that total benefits are withdrawn at the combined rate of £0.70 for every increase in gross earnings of £1.00 (a not unreasonable assumption based on past experience) and that the rate of income tax above personal allowances is £0.20. The effective marginal tax rate is therefore 90 per cent. Hence no matter how hard an individual in receipt of such benefits tries to increase earnings from work he or she is trapped in poverty. The **poverty trap** occurs most frequently for unskilled, low-paid workers who are heads of household with four or more dependent children and are in receipt of means-tested benefits (see Chapter 9). The **unemployment trap** occurs for similar families but whose head of household is unemployed. The withdrawal of income tax and benefits, together with work-related costs (e.g. of travel to work) may result in the extra income gained from working being so small that it is simply not worth working 40 hours or so for a few extra pounds per week. In both cases an increase in gross wages is almost completely offset by withdrawal of tax and benefits.

The severity of the unemployment and poverty traps varies according to household type. Calculations of benefit entitlement in relation to changing earnings levels can be extremely complex. In general, however, these traps are most severe for tenants paying high rents, home owners with mortgages, lone parents and others having to pay for child care in order to accept a job, and those with partners and/or children to support.

This *a priori* analysis of the most appropriate tax reforms when there are disincentive-to-work effects provides an explanation of the various tax reforms in the UK during the 1980s and 1990s (see Chapter 10).

4.7 Empirical evidence

Whilst the theory does provide a guide to the most efficient tax changes, it is inconclusive about the existence or not of disincentive-to-work effects caused by high tax rates. Empirical evidence is required in order to determine which is larger: the income effect or the substitution effect. Incentive or disincentive effects of taxation can be assessed by the following.

Measuring the impact of tax changes on people's working patterns

Interviews. People could be asked how income tax affects their work effort. The problem here is that, unless questions are very carefully worded, respondents may simply repeat popular prejudices (e.g. the 'of course I pay too much tax' syndrome). They may also have little or no awareness of the value of their personal allowances, their marginal and average tax rates or their formal or effective tax rates. Hence, respondents may be more influenced by their perceptions of their tax rates than by the tax rates they actually pay. The tax rates published in the Inland Revenue's income tax schedule are typically greater than the rates actually paid because of the effect of tax allowances (see Chapter 10).

Econometric surveys. These surveys compare changing work effort subsequent to changes in income tax. Such studies have suggested that the effect of income tax on work incentives is small or non-existent and that cuts in higher rates of tax do not increase work incentives. This may be because income and substitution effects are largely offsetting, because some groups of workers receive no extra payment for extra hours of work (e.g. some salaried workers), because other factors besides wages influence work effort (e.g. family circumstances), or because working hours are fixed. In respect of the last point, in 1997 the *Economic Journal* published evidence that more than a third of male manual workers would prefer to work an average of 4.3 fewer hours per week. Of course, a distinction has to be made between the formal hours requirement and those actually worked, the difference being absenteeism. Absenteeism may be influenced by tax rates as well as by work culture and other factors.

Such studies necessarily exclude those who do not work and those who may not work precisely because of disincentive-to-work effects. For example spouses of working partners may not take up paid employment because of income taxation; workers taking early retirement may do so because they will not be made much worse off, through avoiding high levels of income tax; people may leave the country precisely because of high income taxes. If such cases are widespread then econometric studies severely underestimate the disincentive effects (and deadweight loss) of income taxation. A 1993 UK survey by Income Data Services found that more than 80 per cent of workers retire before reaching the retirement age of their occupational scheme, two-thirds retiring before the age of 60. However, this may also reflect organisations' strategic restructuring of human resources or other cultural factors, rather than simply disincentive effects.

In fact, other empirical evidence suggests that the greatest disincentive effects may be caused not by the tax system alone, but by its interaction with state benefits in creating the poverty and unemployment traps. Research results published by the Joseph Rowntree Foundation (JRF) in 1995 and by the National Housing Federation in 1997 identified state benefits supporting rent and mortgage payments as a major factor in widening and deepening both the unemployment trap and the poverty trap. This reflected government policy in raising rents for public sector housing and in deregulating the private sector (see Chapter 8). As rents increased so did the number of people eligible for housing benefit – and that eligibility extended further up the income scale (from lower to higher incomes). The same outcome followed sharp increases in monthly mortgage costs, state benefits paying mortgage interest repayments for unemployed mortgage holders. Hence, increasing numbers of people experienced loss of state benefits as their earned income rose, the result being little or no increase in net income.

Any resulting disincentive to work depends upon a number of conditions. **First**, those in receipt of means-tested benefits undertake detailed financial calculations. **Second,** those calculations are rational and based upon perfect information. **Third,** the product of those calculations is crucial regarding the decision to work. The JRF research was qualitative (based upon interviews), not large enough to be statistically representative, and hence its results should be treated only as indicative. Nevertheless, its results are broadly consistent with other such indicative, non-quantitative studies.

It found that of those receiving state benefits in respect of public and private sector rents and mortgage costs, a 'would the family be better off?' calculation was made by half of claimants and was decisive. Another quarter made such calculations but they were prepared to be worse off in work than as unemployed claimants. In the remaining quarter of cases the decision to work was not based upon financial calculations. In both the last two categories, the decision to work was based on household work strategies rather than on individualised financial calculations. These strategies include an unwillingness to live off state benefits in the long term, the fact that better jobs are easier to come by if one already has a job, and the domestic division of labour. Male partners typically prefer paid full-time employment to looking after the children – the latter usually being left to the female partner who therefore may prefer not to work or to work only part-time. Alternatively, lack (and cost) of child-care facilities may limit mothers' ability to work. This would explain why women with children below school age are less likely to be in paid employment, typically taking part-time work when their children begin attending school.

Hence, tax/benefit disincentives to work may be overstated and do not necessarily require changes in benefit levels – because other factors are known to cause a disincentive to work. **First,** the known loss of out-of-work benefits compared with the uncertain level of in-work benefits topping up low wages. **Second,** delays between stopping payment of out-of-work benefits and beginning payment of in-work benefits. Delayed benefit payments can result in extreme hardship and debt for the lowest income households. **Third,** the temporary (or otherwise insecure) nature of many low paid jobs, causing frequent switching between in-work and out-of-work benefits with associated bureaucratic hassle and disruption in benefit payments. **Fourth,** extra work-related costs (e.g. travel and meals costs, tools and so on). Only the last factor would require changes in levels of benefit payments.

Ultimately, therefore, the decision whether or not to work and whether to work full-time or part-time may reflect family, social and attitudinal factors as much as or more than any financial disincentives caused by the interaction of the tax and benefit systems. The econometric and other evidence is that taxation **on its own** has little impact on people's decisions to take paid employment and on the hours actually worked. The impact is greater in respect of 'secondary' income earners than for 'primary' earners within households (usually wives and husbands respectively). For primary income earners, the income tax system seems to influence decisions when to retire. These impacts are greater when income tax payments combine with loss of income-related benefits.

From a sociological perspective, work provides non-pecuniary (as well as pecuniary) benefits, including personal identity, status, social contacts, structured activity and variety. Moreover, for given tax and benefit structures, work incentives and disincentives vary between different household types (lone parent households, single person households, couples without children, and couples with children), between the old and young, between primary and secondary earners and between full-time and part-time workers. This suggests that it would be mistaken to place too much emphasis on marginal and average tax rates when deciding policy measures to encourage greater work effort. Attention has also to be paid to social, domestic and institutional factors concerning the decision to work.

Institutional factors limit the ability of individuals to adjust their work patterns in response to average and marginal tax rates, but these are ignored by the economic model of labour supply. An individual's decisions to start or continue in a job, to change between full time and part time, and to work overtime are affected by a number of institutional factors. **First**, collective bargaining between trade unions and employers to determine working hours, scope for paid overtime and so on. **Second**, 'career ladders', whereby one's decision to work today may be influenced by potentially higher after-tax pay in the future. **Third**, occupational pensions, entitlements to which may effectively be lost when quitting a job. **Fourth**, employers seem to prefer to recruit from those already in work, fearing that unemployed people are poorly motivated and lacking skills. **Fifth**, the 'labour market' is not a unitary market: it is heavily segmented (e.g. by the need for professional qualifications and by geography) such that one's choice of jobs is heavily constrained.

Consideration of the above social, domestic and institutional factors, in addition to the economic influences on labour supply, demonstrates the benefits of a multidisciplinary approach analysing incentives to work. People do not only work for money and their work (or non-work) patterns reflect many factors, not just the tax regime. The myriad of economic and non-economic constraints on people's work patterns has increasingly been reflected in the government's labour market policies (see Chapter 8) and its work-based welfare strategy (see Chapters 9 and 12).

Figure 4.9   The impact of tax changes on tax revenue

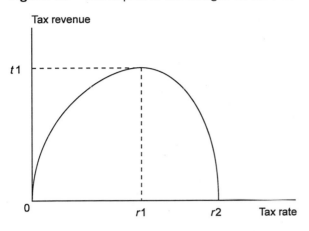

Measuring the impact of tax changes on tax revenues received

If higher income taxes cause disincentive-to-work effects then the amount of tax revenues received will fall when taxes are raised and rise when taxes are lowered. This relationship is shown in **Figure 4.9** and is usually referred to as the Laffer curve. At the origin, both the tax rate and tax revenues are zero. Thereafter both rise together up to a maximum tax revenue $t1$ for tax rate $r1$. Above $r1$, higher rates lead to lower revenues, ultimately falling to zero at $r2$. Hence the substitution effect is greater than the income effect between $r1$ and $r2$. The greater the elasticity of supply of labour (or of other factors of production), the lower the percentage rate of $r2$, possibly well below 100 per cent.

Tax revenues can increase as a result of tax cuts because existing labour works more hours (limited by the number of hours in the week), because other people are encouraged to become economically active (e.g. economically inactive spouses) or because lower tax rates lead to reductions in tax avoidance and tax evasion. High tax rates encourage **tax avoidance**, where wages and salaries are transformed into fringe benefits or perks (ranging from luncheon vouchers to company cars and to capital gains on share option schemes) which are either not taxed at all or are taxed at lower rates than incomes. High tax rates also encourage **tax evasion**, i.e. the illegal non-declaration of taxable income. The lower the rate of tax, the more the incentive for both tax evasion and tax avoidance is reduced.

Hence, if there were disincentive-to-work effects, then the income tax cuts of the 1980s should have been associated with a large increase in tax revenue. Once again, however, the evidence is ambiguous since the increases in tax revenues following the cuts in top income tax rates during the 1980s can be explained by other factors, including **fiscal drag** (where inflation increases earnings relative to fixed tax thresholds, so dragging earnings into higher tax brackets – see Chapter 10) and changes in economic activity unrelated to the tax change (e.g. rising exports and reduced imports induced by a depreciating currency).

4.8 Conclusions

This **partial** equilibrium analysis of direct and indirect taxation yields an *a priori* presumption against taxation. The efficiency rule therefore requires a comparison of the *a priori* allocative distortions of taxation (outlined in this chapter) with the *a priori* allocative benefits of government intervention to deal with externalities and so on (outlined in Chapter 2). Intervention is only justified in efficiency terms where intervention reduces market failure's allocative distortions by more than any allocative distortions caused by such intervention. Lack of empirical evidence on both counts results in the following 'rule of thumb' economic policy prescriptions. **First**, governments should only intervene in cases of gross market failure which seem relatively easy to remedy. **Second**, where possible, use lump-sum taxes and transfer payments. **Third**, otherwise minimise tax levels. **Fourth**, seek economy, efficiency and effectiveness in the provision of public services in order to minimise the tax revenues necessary for their financing.

However, allocative distortions may also be caused by other means of financing government intervention (namely borrowing and charges) and by leviathan governments. These issues are considered in the following chapters. In combination with the *a priori* deadweight loss of taxation, they provide an even more powerful theoretical case against government intervention except in the most severe cases of market failure.

Further reading

Atkinson, A. B. and Mogensen, G. V. (1993) *Welfare and Work Incentives: A North European Perspective* (Oxford: Clarendon Press).

Blundell, R. (1992) 'Labour Supply and Taxation: A Survey', *Fiscal Studies*, vol. 13, no. 3, pp. 15–40.

Bryson, A. and Mckay, S. (1994) *Is it Worth Working? Factors Affecting Labour Supply* (London: Policy Studies Institute).

Connolly, S. and Munroe, A. (1999) *Economics of the Public Sector* (Harlow: Prentice Hall).

Cullis, J. and Jones, P. (1998) *Public Finance and Public Choice: Analytical Perspectives*, 2nd edn (Maidenhead: McGraw-Hill).

Dilnott, A. and Wall, S. (1988) 'Top Rate Tax Cuts and Incentives: Some Empirical Evidence Survey', *Fiscal Studies*, vol. 9, no. 4, pp. 70–92.

Ford, J., Kempson, E. and England, J. (1995) *Into Work? The Impact of Housing Costs and Benefits on People's Decisions to Work* (York: Joseph Rowntree Foundation).

James, S. and Nobes, C. (2000) *The Economics of Taxation: Principles, Policy and Practice* 7th edn (Harlow: Pearson).

Kay, J. A. and King, M. A. (1996) *The British Tax System*, 6th edn (Oxford: Oxford University Press).

Stewart, M. B. and Swaffield, J. K. (1997) 'Constraints on the Desired Hours of Work of British Men', *The Economic Journal*, vol. 107, no. 441, pp. 520–35.

Wilcox, S. and Sutherland, H. (1997) *Housing Benefit, Affordability and Work Incentives: Options for Reform* (London: National Housing Federation).

5 The Economic Effects of Public Sector Borrowing

5.1 Introduction
5.2 The Crowding-out Hypothesis
5.3 Conclusions

5.1 Introduction

If tax revenues are less than net public expenditure (i.e. gross expenditure minus income from sales, fees and charges) a budget deficit will occur. This deficit has to be financed by public sector borrowing. Short-term borrowing will always be necessary in order to smooth out differences in the timing of expenditures and tax receipts during the course of the financial year. It is usually financed by the sale of 90-day treasury bills. The concern with public sector borrowing relates to long-term borrowing of several years or more, usually financed by the sale of gilt-edged securities ('gilts'). Gilts are fixed-interest British government securities traded on the stock exchange. They are a very secure financial asset since it is certain that interest will be paid, and that they will be redeemed (bought back) by the government on the due date. Hence they are almost as good as holding gold, almost 'gilt-edged'. However they are not totally risk-free since their market value can fall during the issue period. Sale prior to the redemption date could therefore lead to a capital loss (or gain) being incurred. Inflation also reduces their real interest rate and their real redemption value.

Government borrowing is likely to have economic effects even if it is used to finance socially progressive initiatives in pursuit of increased equity. The same caveat applies even if borrowing is used to finance infrastructural investments that increase the productive capacity of the economy or yield an excess of benefits over costs. These economic effects may even reduce productive capacity, such that the net impact is to create inefficiency. This chapter concentrates on the possible adverse consequences of public sector borrowing, ignoring the use to which revenues are put. It is therefore only a partial analysis and is based on the classical school.

5.2   The crowding-out hypothesis

This hypothesis states that government intervention leads to private activity being reduced, i.e. 'crowded out'. There are two forms of crowding out.

Real resource (direct) crowding out

Growth of public sector employment occurred simultaneously with the decline of manufacturing employment from the late 1960s and 'cause and effect' was claimed. In other words, it is argued that public sector production uses resources that could otherwise be used by the private sector. There are similarities with the 'productivity differential' micro model of public expenditure growth (see Chapter 3), which assumes that the private sector experiences productivity improvements whilst the public sector does not. If, therefore, the public sector replaces the private sector it can be expected to constrain economic growth. This displacement effect occurs directly as the public sector uses tax revenues to buy or hire resources that would otherwise be used by the private sector.

This has been challenged both as a matter of fact and as a matter of theory. **First**, government statistics (unintentionally) exaggerated the growth of public sector employment by counting part time jobs as full-time. Most of those part-time jobs were taken by females whereas the manufacturing sector mainly shed full-time male workers, only a quarter of whom took jobs in the public sector. Moreover lack of labour was hardly a problem during the recessions of the early 1980s and early 1990s. **Second**, the assumption is that public and private sector outputs are mutually exclusive substitutes, whereas many would appear to be complementary with private production. For example the public sector's provision of education and health care may sustain the capitalist system by making labour more productive. Its provision of roads eases the transport of both the inputs and outputs of economic activity. Its provision of law and order secures property rights to productive resources and the profits derived from their employment, both of which are essential for markets to work. More radically, the state may legitimise the capitalist system by bearing the costs it imposes on society whilst allowing the profits to accrue to individuals (the *O'Connor legitimation thesis*). **Third**, privatisation and contracting out transferred to the private sector former public sector employees and otherwise reduced public sector employment during the 1980s and 1990s (see Chapters 13 and 15). Hence direct crowding out would appear to be questionable in theory and of very limited impact in practice.

Financial (indirect) crowding out

Whereas direct crowding out occurs when the state uses tax revenues to appropriate productive resources, indirect crowding out occurs if public expenditure, taxation and borrowing cause disincentives to productive effort, namely to work or to invest. **Disincentive-to-work** effects created by the interaction of the tax and benefit systems were discussed in Chapter 4 and will be discussed further in Chapters 10 and 12. **Disincentives to invest** in other productive resources may occur if borrowing leads to higher interest rates or inflation. (Note that investment refers to the purchase of plant and machinery to produce output, **not** to putting one's money into an account at a bank, building society or other financial institution: that is saving.)

Higher interest rates

The sale of government debt in order to finance public sector borrowing may lead to a rise in interest rates, which indirectly crowds out private investment. Two conditions must hold for this to happen. **First**, increased public sector borrowing must lead to higher interest rates. **Second**, private sector investment must be highly interest-elastic, with the result that investment falls. This is demonstrated in **Figures 5.1** and **5.2**.

The demand and supply of investment funds depends on their price (i.e. the interest rate). **Figure 5.1** depicts supply and demand conditions for investment funds. The interest rate is shown on the vertical axis and quantity on the horizontal axis. Using $D1$, the initial equilibrium is $r1q1$ where demand equals supply. Assume the government finances increased expenditure by borrowing. The demand schedule therefore shifts from $D1$ to $D2$. There is now an excess demand for investment funds at $r1$ (of $q3 - q1$) and this drives up their 'price' to $r2$, at which point supply and demand are equal at $q2$. An alternative explanation is that the government floods the market with gilts, driving their prices down and their interest rates up. To illustrate this, assume for simplicity that gilts have been selling for £100, being redeemed 12 months later for £110. The interest rate is therefore 10 per cent per annum. Now the increased public sector borrowing increases the supply of gilts and drives down their selling price to £90. However the redemption value is fixed at £110 so the interest rate rises to 22 per cent. Interest rates on other financial assets are assumed to rise accordingly.

The impact on investment is shown in **Figure 5.2**. As the interest rate rises from $r1$ to $r2$ the amount of investment in real resources falls from $q1$ to $q2$. There are two possible explanations of this. **First**, higher interest rates increase the cost of borrowing used to finance investment, therefore reducing it. However most investment is financed by 'ploughed back' profits. **Second**, higher interest rates discount more heavily the future

Figure 5.1   The relationship between the PSBR and interest rates

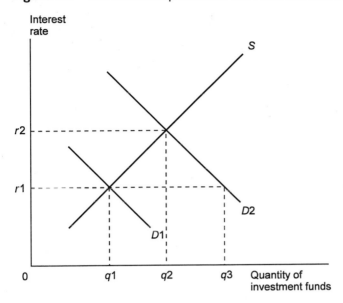

Figure 5.2   The relationship between interest rates and investment

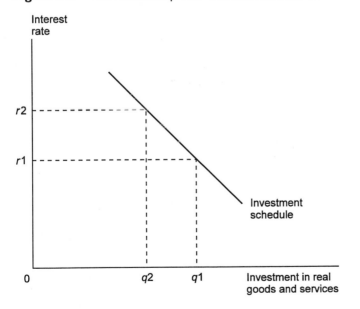

revenue streams arising from investment projects, so reducing their net present value and therefore their profitability.

For example, £100 received today will, if loaned at an interest rate of 10 per cent, be worth £110 in one year's time, £121 in two years' time and so on. This is compound interest. Discounting future sums is the opposite of compound interest. So, £121 receivable in two years' time has a present value of £100 when discounted at 10 per cent. The formula is $121/(1 + 0.10)^2$ where the numerator is the cash sum, the denominator is one plus the interest rate (in brackets) and 2 is the number of years into the future when the sum is received. Similarly, £121 receivable in two years' time has a present value of £109.75 when discounted at 5 per cent, that is $121/(1 + 0.05)^2$. Therefore the higher the interest (i.e. discount) rate the less profitable the investments because their future profits are discounted more heavily into smaller present values. Higher interest rates may therefore crowd out investment, depending on its sensitivity to them (i.e. its interest elasticity).

The total impact of an increase in public sector borrowing depends on:

1. the slope of the supply of investment funds function (**Figure 5.1**), and
2. the slope of the real investment schedule (**Figure 5.2**).

The greater the elasticity of supply of investment funds (i.e. the less the slope of S in **Figure 5.1**) the smaller the rise in interest rates caused by an increase in the government's borrowing requirement. The greater the interest inelasticity of the investment schedule (i.e. the steeper its slope in **Figure 5.2**) the smaller the impact of a rise in interest rates on the quantity of real investment. Hence, in the extreme case, indirect crowding out through interest rates will be zero if the supply of investment funds is perfectly elastic or if the investment function is perfectly inelastic.

Both could be the case in a severe and prolonged recession. In such a case firms are usually very reluctant to invest in plant and machinery and so the government can increase its own borrowing with little impact on interest rates. Very pessimistic expectations about the profits to be derived from investment in a recession may make the investment function totally unresponsive to changes in the interest rate. Alternatively, in a boom, expectations of future profits may be so optimistic that higher interest rates have little or no effect on firms' investment plans. This is most likely if they do not use the **discounted cash flow method** of investment appraisal described above. The evidence is that most firms assess projects in terms of the speed with which they are expected to earn sufficient profits to pay back the original investment. The faster the **payback period**, the more attractive the investment for many firms. The interest rate is irrelevant to decision making using this technique and so any influence of government borrowing on interest rates is not reflected in the level of investment.

Statistical evidence suggests that the link between public sector borrowing and interest rates and the link between interest rates and investment are both poor. The apparent insensitivity of fixed investment to interest rate changes by British manufacturing companies is contrary to evidence from North America. It may be due to a mis-specification of research (for example a lack of disaggregation between types of investment), the use of nominal rather than real interest rates, or the insensitivity of multinational and public corporations to domestic interest rates. Major UK firms can borrow from abroad if UK interest rates are relatively high, thereby reducing the impact of high UK interest rates on domestic investment. Nonetheless, there will be a transfer of resources abroad once debts are repaid – effectively crowding out. Private house construction and purchase is certainly sensitive to interest rates because of the impact on mortgage repayments. Hence the extent of indirect crowding out through interest rates remains unclear. In addition, it is arguable that the direction of causation is the reverse of that outlined above. In other words, a high deficit is the result (not the cause) of higher interest rates because of the resulting higher debt repayments.

Inflation

Despite the lack of irrefutable evidence, assume that the government believes that indirect crowding out through interest rates is potentially substantial or that it is afraid of political unpopularity arising from increasing interest rates (because of the effect on mortgage interest payments). It can avoid both outcomes whilst still increasing its borrowing. Government borrowing operates through the Bank of England. Assume that the government tells the Bank to sell only as much government stock as the market will bear at the present interest rate. This strategy avoids an excess supply of government stock and so prevents a fall in their prices and a subsequent rise in interest rates. Sale of gilts therefore takes time but the government needs money to spend immediately. Hence the Bank credits the government's account with the value of the unsold stock, effectively an overdraft facility. The government makes cheques payable to individuals and firms for transfer payments and for exhaustive expenditures.

The recipients of those government cheques pay them into their accounts at commercial banks, which in turn present them to the Bank for payment. The Bank then credits the commercial banks' accounts (held at the Bank) with the value of those cheques. The commercial banks' cash reserves therefore rise. For a given ratio of cash to financial liabilities (i.e. deposits) set by the Bank, these increased reserves allow a **multiple expansion of deposits**, the commercial banks granting loans and overdrafts to their customers. This is often referred to as '*the government is printing money to finance its expenditures*'. In fact the government is not printing money. Nevertheless the effect is the same since the value of bank deposits is part of most conventional definitions of the money supply.

The **quantity theory** of money contends that a rise in the money supply leads to inflation. The relationship $MV = PT$ states that total spending (i.e. MV) equals total purchases (i.e. PT). M is the money supply, V is its velocity of circulation (i.e. the speed at which it changes hands), P is the average price level and T is the volume of transactions (effectively output). Monetarists assume that V and T are fixed so that a change in M leads directly to a change in P. An increase in the money supply therefore leads to inflation. The theoretical basis of this link lies in the **real balance effect**, which assumes that people, firms and financial institutions hold portfolios of assets ranging from real goods, through financial assets (such as government stock and shareholdings in private companies) to building society and bank deposits and cash. Therefore the increased money supply not only leads to an increase in cash and deposits, it also increases demand for consumer goods and so on. Given that output (T) is assumed to be fixed, the increase in M therefore leads to an increase in P, i.e. inflation. Inflation reduces the real purchasing power of money and so crowds out private expenditure. In effect the government can always outbid the private sector for use of productive resources by 'printing money'. However this analysis can be challenged both in theory and in fact.

Theory

The theoretical basis of the quantity theory can be challenged. Keynesian economists argue that the $MV = PT$ identity is deficient because the pattern of demand is determined by **relative** prices, not the **average** price measured by P. The equation also has no interest rate component, which Keynesians argue may be crucial in determining the demand for money. For example, if interest rates are expected to rise then the price of government stocks and bonds must be expected to fall (see the gilts example above). In such a case people and firms will be unwilling to buy government stock because they would expect to incur a capital loss. Hence any increase in the money supply finds its way into **idle balances** (i.e. is not spent) and so inflation does not occur. In such an event the rise in M is directly offset by a fall in V, the famous Keynesian **liquidity trap**. Whilst this is an extreme case it shows why increases in the money supply may not be directly converted into inflation, because M, V, P and T are not independent of each other, as assumed by the quantity theory.

Keynesians also argue that T is only fixed during periods of full employment. UK unemployment was around the three million mark for most of the 1980s and early 1990s and still above one million by the end of the 1990s. Hence, increases in T would appear to have been available.

The counter-argument is that constraints on supply prevented increases in output even though surplus factors of production were available. For example it was argued that trade unions exploited their monopoly powers over the supply of labour, preventing surplus workers leading to downward pressure on wages and salaries and so blocking their re-employment. If supply-side constraints are binding then, whilst the control of government borrowing is necessary in the short term, the removal of those constraints is a necessary long-term measure. This explains much of both the Conservative and Labour governments' microeconomic and macroeconomic policies during the 1980s and 1990s (see Chapters 8 and 11).

Evidence

If increases in public sector borrowing do lead to increases in the money supply these two events should be highly correlated. A similar correlation would also have to be found between increases in M and increases in P. Note, however, that a statistical association between two variables does not necessarily prove causation from one event to another, nor indicate the direction of causation.

Borrowing and M. In Britain, use of multiple regression analysis suggested that a £1 change in the public sector borrowing requirement was only statistically associated with a £0.4033 change in the money supply (defined as £M3, i.e. sterling M3) during the 1980s. This statistical technique also found that only 35 per cent of changes in £M3 were 'explained' by changes in public sector borrowing. These results may be due to offsetting changes in other parts of £M3, for example non-bank purchases of government debt (e.g. by people), which transfer money from the commercial banks to the Bank of England so reducing deposit creation (i.e. the reverse of the 'multiple expansion of deposits' mechanism described above). These results may also come about because there are other influences on the money supply besides public sector borrowing (e.g. net external monetary flows arising from foreign trade). However monetarists argue that failure to find a strong relationship between changes in public sector borrowing and the money supply reflects failure to define money correctly. For example, should it include commercial bills of credit traded between companies, often outside the controlled banking system?

M and P. Empirical evidence from North America suggests that the relationship between M and P may not hold in practice. A clear link between changes in M and changes in P should be evident from time-series analysis. Monetarists take a 'base year' in which prices were stable but the money supply increased and find that this is subsequently followed by inflation. They therefore claim causality between M and P. However Keynesians say causation is reversed (i.e. from P to M rather than from M to P). They demonstrate this by taking a base year in which there is inflation but no increase in the money supply and find that this is subsequently followed by a rise in the money supply. They explain this result by arguing that inflation causes firms to experience rising input costs in advance of sales and so they ask commercial banks for loans during the interim period, the money supply rising as a consequence.

Overview

Neither the theory nor the empirical evidence is sufficiently robust to give unconditional support to either the monetarists or the Keynesians. There is no economic law which sets down a direct relationship between public sector borrowing and interest rates or inflation. Nonetheless, given its monetarist beliefs during the 1980s and 1990s, the then Conservative government clearly faced a dilemma. It believed that excessive borrowing pushes up interest rates and deters investment and consumption financed by borrowing. If the government attempts to avoid this expected outcome it loses control of the money supply and creates inflation (as explained above). It therefore cannot control both interest rates and inflation by these means, so indirect crowding out appears to be inevitable.

Of course there are other influences on interest rates, investment, growth of the money supply and inflation. For example a depreciating exchange rate makes pounds worth fewer francs, dollars, and so on. This has the effect of increasing the cost of imports in terms of domestic currency, leading to cost-push inflation. Similarly, given globalisation of capital markets, UK interest rates are influenced by those in other countries. For example high interest rates may be used to attract foreign funds to UK banks in order to increase the demand for pounds and so support the exchange rate in order to avoid inflation caused by the rising cost of imports as sterling depreciates. However, this makes UK manufactures relatively uncompetitive on home and foreign markets. In that case, government exchange rate policy crowds out manufacturing investment, possibly more so than the impact of borrowing. Such international pressures may explain the limited relationships between public sector borrowing and inflation or interest rates. Nevertheless, if the government wishes to control inflation and interest rates it will naturally concentrate on controlling those domestic influences over which it has some degree of control.

The 1997 Labour government continued the former Conservative government's policy of controlling inflation (*not* the money supply *per se*). It established the Monetary Policy Committee of the Bank of England, the MPC's remit being to control inflation by varying the interest rate (see Chapter 8). Meanwhile, the Labour government sought to control public sector borrowing as part of its 'prudent' fiscal policy (see Chapter 11).

It is therefore behavioural factors that explain the emphasis on controlling public sector borrowing, rather than the strength or weakness of any relationship between the borrowing and inflation or investment. Governments tend to try to control what they think they can, even though other factors outside their control may be much more influential, possibly frustrating that attempted control. Furthermore, governments generally find it easier to cut capital expenditure than current expenditure, on the grounds that voters do not miss expenditure that has not yet taken place. Cutting current expenditure would require service reductions and possibly redundancies of public sector employees – politically highly controversial. Nonetheless, cutting capital expenditure can have adverse consequences for economic growth because it leads to the private sector losing building contracts and because public sector capital expenditure often complements private sector expenditures. The 1997 Labour government recognised the force of these arguments and sought to make up for past cuts in capital spending (see Chapter 11).

5.3 Conclusions

Exhaustive public expenditures can cause crowding out both directly and indirectly whereas transfer expenditures can only cause indirect crowding out because the government merely redistributes (rather than exhausts) their purchasing power. Direct crowding out assumes that public and private expenditures are mutually exclusive substitutes and that public expenditure is (relatively) unproductive. However, many exhaustive public expenditures could be argued to be complementary to private expenditures and may even yield a greater return than private expenditures (e.g. because of positive externalities). Nevertheless, indirect crowding out may occur even where complementarity exists by reducing incentives to work or by creating other distortions in capital and labour markets. Although the costs of this distortion are not necessarily greater than the benefits (if any) of intervention, it is not possible to measure such distortionary costs nor the benefits of intervention with any accuracy, or even at all.

Higher interest rates disadvantage borrowers but benefit savers. Whilst these negative and positive income effects should cancel out, there will still be a substitution effect away from investment and towards saving. It may be thought that governments will be more amenable to higher inflation than to higher interest rates since the latter increases real public debt whereas the former reduces it. However, getting the rate of inflation back down again can impose substantial costs on the economy.

Whilst neither theory nor fact is conclusive, British governments during the 1980s and 1990s laid great emphasis on controlling the public sector borrowing. The classical school requires governments to do less borrowing in the belief that market forces will generate economic growth. This is in direct contrast to the Keynesian view that budget deficits are a strategic macroeconomic instrument used by interventionist governments in times of recession. The classical school views government deficits as a major cause of instability, Keynesians holding the reverse view as long as public sector borrowing is used wisely and so does not result in 'boom and bust'. If crowding out is close to 100 per cent, then running a budget deficit as a means of financing an expansionary Keynesian fiscal policy will be counter-productive in the longer term. In that case, immediate financial crowding out due to public sector borrowing will be exacerbated in the future by the disincentive-to-work effects of the higher taxes required to repay borrowing. These are the reasons for the monetarist claim that fiscal policy is impotent. Whilst 100 per cent crowding out appears to be an extreme case, so does 100 per cent crowding in (i.e. through multiplier effects).

Whilst the theoretical debate continues, even Keynesians agree that borrowing to finance consumption (rather than investments in the economic infrastructure) is inadvisable over the longer term and can only be justified in the short term (if at all) as a way of 'spending one's way out of a recession'. Hence there must be close scrutiny of borrowing and the uses to which it is put.

This intellectual justification is in addition to any moral or normative stance that borrowing is bad and that governments, like people, should 'live within their means'. Whilst it could be claimed that many infrastructural investments are self-financing in terms of their positive contributions to economic growth, such assertions are not provable and cannot simply be taken on trust. Borrowing may become a political tool manipulated by governments for political ends, leading to excessive expenditure (see Chapter 7). If so, then any allocative inefficiencies could be greatly exacerbated. Hence, the 1997 Labour government adopted the **sustainable investment rule**, only borrowing to finance investment in physical infrastructure (see Chapter 11).

Further reading

Cavanna, H. (ed.) (1988) *Public Sector Deficits in OECD Countries: Causes, Consequences and Remedies* (London: Macmillan).

Sturm, R. and Muller, M. M. (1999) *Public Deficits: A Comparative Study* (London: Longman).

6 Charging for Public Sector Outputs

6.1   Introduction
6.2   The Roles of Charges
6.3   Charging in Relation to Marginal Cost
6.4   Charges Adjusted for Externalities and Merit Goods
6.5   Charges Adjusted for Equity Criteria
6.6   Problems in the Payment of Subsidy
6.7   Charges Adjusted for their Institutional Context
6.8   Charging in Relation to Benefit
6.9   Charges Combining Cost, Benefit, Equity and Environmental Considerations
6.10 Conclusions

6.1 Introduction

Chapter 5 began by noting that the public sector deficit is the difference between net public expenditure and taxation. Gross spending is greater than net spending by the amount of income from sales, fees and charges. The term 'charge' refers to all of these payments.

Use of the term 'charge' rather than 'price' implies politico-administrative (rather than market) control in such a way that charges (and related subsidies) secure the publicness of the service (as discussed in Chapter 1). Whilst price and charge are used interchangeably in this book, they both refer to payments levied on the consumers of public sector outputs where there is a direct link between payment and consumption. Hence they refer to **requited** payments. However the link between payment and service provided may vary considerably in terms of the degree of cost recovery.

6.2 The roles of charges

Charges have to serve many different functions. These include raising revenue, covering costs, the need to meet financial targets or required rates of return on assets, checking abuse of service, the need to target subsidy and the pursuit of equity.

Advocates of the increased use of service charges (such as the Institute of Economic Affairs) see them as both efficiency instruments and an alternative to collective action. They argue that charges should replicate free market forces and 'roll back the frontiers of the state' (see Chapter 8). They argue that allocative inefficiency results from the use of taxes to finance public services. Tax payments are largely fixed in that common rules apply regarding liability to pay and payment does not vary directly or immediately with the individual's consumption of services. Hence demand rises until the marginal private benefit of increased consumption equals zero (since price is zero). This results in marginal social cost being greater than marginal social benefit, and so excessive public expenditures result. Put simply, free commodities are subject to excess demand (e.g. congested roads and motorways).

This argument assumes that taxpayers see no substantive connection between their consumption of free (i.e. tax-financed) public sector outputs and their tax liabilities. This assumption is more questionable the smaller the scale of government (e.g. local versus national) and the more evenly spread the liability for tax (e.g. a poll tax versus income tax). Furthermore the argument only applies to exhaustive public expenditures, not transfer payments (distinguished in Chapter 3). It assumes that the charge is the only influence on user demand and is qualified to the extent that service users incur other costs in using the service or in having to satisfy eligibility criteria. For example, service users incur travel and time costs when visiting a national museum and incur other costs in buying or renting sports equipment for use at local authority sports facilities. Moreover, access to health and personal social services is restricted to those judged by practitioners to be in need of service. Even otherwise free and unrestricted public services may have low take-up rates. For example by no means all of local authorities' citizens use their local public library, museum or art gallery.

Service providers may determine demand even when a user charge is levied. For example demand for secondary (i.e. hospital) health care may be price inelastic since admission to hospital is primarily determined by doctors. Moreover medical practitioners may have their own incentives to see health services expanded beyond economically optimal levels (the leviathan model of government, see Chapter 7). Such charges may also contradict both equity and the principle of access to health services on the basis of need, irrespective of ability to pay. Demand for primary (i.e. general practitioner) health care may be highly price elastic. In that case charges for medical consultations with general practitioners would discourage people from seeking early treatment for medical conditions. This may cause medical problems to get worse, so increasing the costs of remedial treatment. The net result would be increased inefficiency. Moreover inefficiency will result if charges are not based on costs. For example, monopoly providers of public health services could levy charges in excess of marginal costs, so destroying the conditions necessary for the attainment of a Pareto optimum.

6.3 Charging in relation to marginal cost

Chapter 2 demonstrated that marginal cost pricing maximises welfare. This is also shown in **Figure 6.1** (a partial, as distinct from general, equilibrium analysis) using the consumer and producer surplus concepts developed in Chapter 4. The average cost curve has been omitted for simplicity (i.e. it is assumed that the monopolist is making a profit). The profit-maximising price is $p1$ (where $MR = MC$). Consumers' surplus is $ABp1$ and producer's surplus is $FEBp1$, giving a total welfare of $ABEF$. Price $p2$ equals marginal cost at point C, the intersection of MC and D. Marginal cost pricing would therefore create a consumers' surplus of $ACp2$ and a producer's surplus of $FCp2$, giving a total welfare of ACF. Hence marginal cost pricing increases welfare since ACF is greater than $ABEF$ by the area BCE. The intuitive explanation is that output is greater for MC pricing (at $q2$) than for the profit-maximising price (at $q1$). Consumption is higher since price is lower but marginal cost is still covered by price, and so welfare is greater.

In theory, setting the charge equal to MC achieves allocative efficiency because it both maximises the output derived from finite productive resources and matches the distribution of that output with willingness to pay the full incremental costs of its production (see Chapter 2). This was the theoretical rationale for the suggested adoption of marginal cost pricing by the former UK nationalised industries during the late 1960s and 1970s. **Figure 6.1** also shows that output should be increased if price

Figure 6.1 Marginal cost pricing

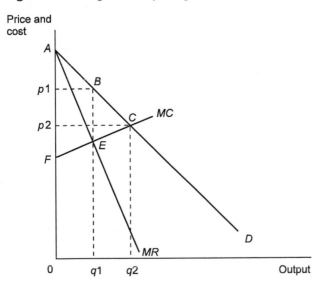

is greater than *MC* because willingness to pay exceeds incremental cost for all levels of output up to *q*2. *MC* exceeds willingness to pay for levels of output above *q*2 and so output should be contracted. Hence marginal valuation equals marginal cost at *q*2.

The theory underpinning **Figure 6.1** assumes that:

1. **The individual is the best judge of personal welfare and that individual welfares can be added together.** The first is consistent with the Paretian criterion for welfare but the second is not. Cardinal welfare analysis assumes that welfares can be both quantified and added together. This is not possible in practice. However the Paretian welfare criterion requires no absolute measurement (i.e. it is ordinal). A Paretian welfare improvement only requires at least one person to be made better off without anyone else being made worse off.
2. **Competitive forces operate throughout the economy.** In fact they do not and second best theory suggests that once any one price departs from its respective marginal cost then all prices have to do so (see Chapter 2, Section 2.4).
3. **There are no external effects in consumption or production** (i.e. market failure).
4. **The distribution of income and welfare resulting from marginal cost pricing is acceptable.**
5. **There are no indirect taxes** causing the prices faced by consumers and producers to diverge.

Chapters 2, 3 and 4 have shown that these assumptions are almost invariably invalid so the practical application of the theoretical rationale for marginal cost pricing is open to question. Besides these **theoretical** problems, there are also a number of **practical** problems in the application of *MC* pricing.

First, it can result in complex tariff structures. There are in fact two measures of marginal cost: (a) **long-run marginal cost** (LRMC), includes incremental capital and running costs; (b) **short-run marginal cost** (SRMC), excludes capital costs since, by definition, they are fixed in the short run. It only includes incremental running costs.

If the objective is to maximise profits, variation from the *LRMC* rule is only sanctioned during periods of excess capacity (i.e. where output demanded is less than available supply). Price should at least equal *SRMC* in such cases. *LRMC* and *SRMC* will only be equal if the productive facility is producing its output at its planned (optimal) capacity. If over-capacity is permanent, the productive facility should not be replaced upon its economic exhaustion since price is less than *LRMC*. The facility should be closed down immediately if price is insufficient to cover *SRMC*.

LRMC (e.g. for electricity generation) varies by time of day, week and year. It is greatest during periods of early morning peak demand and lower in the afternoons. LRMC pricing would require higher tariffs in the morning than in the afternoons since it is the morning peak that requires additional capacity. Such a tariff structure would be complicated. However, since electricity meters do not monitor household consumption by time of day, LRMC pricing is a concept not a practical retail pricing policy. Partial implementation of LRMC pricing is achieved through 'white meter' and 'Economy 7' retail tariffs, which charge discounted prices for electricity consumed during the night. Likewise, telecommunications charges also vary by time of day, generally being cheapest during evenings, night-time and weekends when spare capacity exists. They also differentiate between local, regional, national, international and other calls in reflecting costs.

More generally, the economic solution for public utilities such as energy and water is a **two-part tariff**, which has both a fixed component (a standing charge) recovering system capital costs and a variable component (a metered running rate) to recover variable costs (see Chapter 14). For other (non-utility) services, these economic concepts have been operationalised as: 'variable cost charging', 'full cost charging' and 'partial overhead charging'.

Variable cost charging (price = SRMC) covers all or part of running costs. It is justifiable in off-peak periods since capacity is fixed and surplus capacity is available. SRMC is the economic justification for cheaper telephone calls during the evenings and weekends and for cheaper fares for buses and trains outside the rush hour.

Full cost charging ($p = LRMC$) covers all fixed and variable costs. It is required in peak periods (e.g. the rush hour for commuting by bus or train) since peak-period users determine the capacity of the system.

Partial overhead charging covers all variable costs and a proportion of fixed costs. This is appropriate where some (but not full) contribution is required towards fixed costs, for example use of local government library fax services (where charges could cover the variable and overhead costs of the fax service but exclude physical accommodation costs).

Second, losses occur if the industry experiences economies of scale. LRMC is less than LRAC where average cost falls as the rate of output increases. Hence, setting $p = LRMC$ results in a loss being incurred because price (i.e. average revenue) is less than LRAC. This is demonstrated in **Figure 6.2** using demand curve $D1$ (ignore $D2$ for now). Price $p2 = LRMC$ is less than $p3 = LRAC$, resulting in a loss of $(p3 - p2)q1$. Output $q1$ is therefore financed both by consumers (paying $0p2Bq1$) and by a $p = LRMC$ **subsidy** (of $p3ABp2$). This subsidy is paid by taxpayers and so income effects occur, negative for taxpayers and

Figure 6.2 Subsidies for allocative efficiency and equity

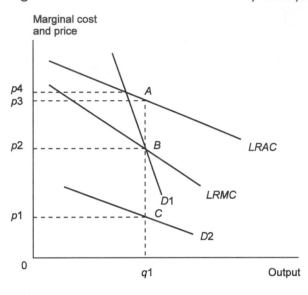

positive for subsidised consumers. Hence, assumption 3 above becomes invalid.

In practice, the need to avoid losses led many public utilities to adopt *LRAC* pricing and to maintain it even after the government expressed a policy preference for *LRMC* pricing in 1967. The intersection of *D*1 and the *LRAC* schedule in **Figure 6.2** yields *p*4, equal to *LRAC*. Note that output is less than *q*1 since *p*4 is greater than *p*3.

Third, profits accrue if there are diseconomies of scale. Where *LRMC* and *LRAC* are rising, *the p = LRMC* rule results in profits because *LRMC* is greater than *LRAC*. Profit maximisation may not be the relevant objective for public sector outputs, especially those with a social dimension (e.g. public transport in rural areas). In such cases profits may be regarded as politically unacceptable and lead to claims of 'monopoly exploitation' of consumers. This provides another practical rationale for *p = LRAC*.

Fourth, it is extremely difficult to measure marginal cost in practice. Accounting practices are not based on economic cost concepts. Hence it has long been recognised that marginal cost pricing is only one of a number of imperfect possibilities where the relevant information is simply not available.

Fifth, it is difficult to implement such a policy if firms are price takers. Firms are price takers, rather than price makers, where there is competition between, say, rail, bus and air travel.

Like other abstract economic constructs (such as the perfectly competitive market model) marginal cost pricing is an ideal, non-implementable in practice but, nonetheless, a valuable benchmark against which all feasible charging arrangements can be judged.

6.4 Charges adjusted for externalities and merit goods

Profit-maximising rules may be qualified by any subsidies paid in respect of market failure. For allocative efficiency to be achieved, pure public goods have to be fully financed by subsidy whilst pure private goods are fully funded by user charges. In other cases, charges should be adjusted in accordance with the size of positive externality or merit good characteristics (subsidy) or of negative externalities (tax). For example public transport fares may be subsidised on the grounds that increased use of buses and trains reduces the number of vehicles on roads, therefore reducing congestion and so providing a positive externality. Note, however, that the need for this subsidy could be substantially reduced if use of cars was taxed by an amount equal to the value of the negative externalities (congestion, pollution and accidents) it creates (see Chapter 2).

The price adjustments for merit good and positive externalities are demonstrated in **Figure 6.2**. $D2$ now represents the market demand curve, indicating the aggregation of willingness to pay for all individuals in the market economy. $D1$ now represents the social valuation of consumption of the commodity that coincides with $LRMC$ at point B. The slopes of $D1$ and $D2$ indicate that marginal social valuation is falling faster than marginal private valuation as the rate of output (and consumption) increases. Social valuation is greater than private valuation by (a) the amount of positive externalities not reflected in $D2$ and/or (b) the amount of undervaluation of the personal benefits of consumption of the good or service (merit good).

The size of these undervaluations is measured by the vertical distance between $D1$ and $D2$. Hence, for level of output $q1$, marginal private valuation is $q1C(=p1)$, positive externalities are CB, and so marginal social value is $q1B(=p2)$. Note that, compared with the discussion of $LRMC$ pricing above, the level of subsidy has been increased for output $q1$. The $p = LRMC$ **subsidy** remains the same as before at $p3ABp2$. However the **positive externalities/merit goods subsidies** total $p1p2BC$ so that consumers now only pay $0p1Cq1$. The combination of these subsidies gives the total **allocative efficiency subsidy** of $p1p3AC$.

Whilst clearly definable in abstract terms, externalities and merit good characteristics may be extremely difficult to quantify. In such cases, politicians and public sector bureaucrats may prefer to use a crude 'rule of thumb'. For example services that are judged to benefit the community more than users may receive 75 per cent subsidy, services benefiting users more than the community may receive 25 per cent subsidy and those where the benefits are judged to be equal may receive 50 per cent subsidy. However this approach is over-simplistic as well as essentially arbitrary and subjective in that it is based on bureaucrats' and politicians' impressions of the nature of benefits derived from individual services. This is a rather paternalistic approach and one that might be exploited by those wishing to see the public sector expand for reasons other than efficiency or even equity (see Chapter 7).

6.5 Charges adjusted for equity criteria

Charges may also be adjusted in order to take account of equity and access considerations. Assume that the demand curve $D2$ in **Figure 6.2** shows willingness, rather than ability, to pay. If the government thinks it desirable for low-income groups to have access to public services it could pay an **income maintenance subsidy** to low-income consumers equal to all or part of the area $0p1Cq1$. This subsidy requires assessment of individual consumers' incomes or financial means (called 'means testing'). Withdrawal of subsidy as gross income rises would exacerbate the poverty and unemployment traps discussed in Chapter 4.

The alternative is to give exemptions and discounts unrelated to income. They could be given to certain categories of people such as children, the elderly, the unemployed, students, etc. These **categoric concessions** are either a crude form of means testing or reflect a belief that some groups 'deserve' special status. For example the elderly may be exempted from charges either because they are assumed to have relatively low incomes, or because it is believed that they deserve exemption (even if affluent) simply because of their age. In practice such concessions may be amalgamated with the 'rule of thumb' subsidies for positive externalities described above.

A blanket opposition to charges on equity grounds assumes:

1. that only the poor consume public sector outputs (almost invariably untrue), or
2. that the administrative costs of means-testing are greater than any subsidy that is misdirected to affluent consumers (an empirical question), or
3. that means-testing itself deters claims for subsidy because of a negative association with 'charity', objection to invasions of privacy and so on (there is some evidence of this), and
4. that the government departments, tiers or agencies providing those outputs have responsibilities for income maintenance (in fact many do not).

6.6   Problems in the payment of subsidy

The analysis of **Figure 6.2** has to recognise that payment of subsidy is problematic. There are two approaches.

Direct in-cash income transfers

These payments would increase the real incomes of recipients, leading to increased demands for normal goods and services (i.e. those with positive income elasticities of demand), shifting $D2$ upwards towards $D1$ in **Figure 6.2**. However it is most unlikely that all of the subsidy would be spent on increased consumption of public services with positive externality and merit good characteristics such as that represented in **Figure 6.2**. This is because the in-cash transfer creates an income effect but no substitution effect (see Chapter 4). Moreover, by definition, individual consumers undervalue the personal benefits of consumption of services with merit-good characteristics. Hence a proportion of direct in-cash benefits will be spent on other goods and services. This means that the cash subsidy would have to be greater in order to achieve an allocatively efficient level of spending on the merit good. Those benefits may be offset by any negative externalities associated with the increased consumption of other goods or by any allocative inefficiency caused by the higher taxes necessary to fund those subsidies (see Chapter 4).

In general, in-cash subsidies are least effective in increasing the consumption of commodities with low income elasticities of demand and most effective where the objective is simply to increase poorer groups' total consumption of **all** goods and services, provided by both the public and private sector. Such a payment is perhaps best regarded as a redistributive rather than an allocative efficiency subsidy because it pays no attention to the existence or otherwise of externalities and so on. This is the case for social security benefits such as income support, which are not tied to consumption of particular services (see Chapter 9).

Indirect in-kind income transfers through subsidised service charges

Receipt of such price subsidies is conditional upon consumption of the service. Such 'tied' subsidies are more cost effective in that they are better targeted on the relevant service and its users. However they have two disadvantages.

First, the value of the subsidy is directly proportional to consumption. If public services are predominantly used by affluent groups then those groups receive disproportionate amounts of subsidy. For example there is some evidence that such 'middle-class capture' of subsidy occurs in subsidised local government leisure services such as museums and art galleries where middle-class groups are over-represented relative to their share of the population. In such cases, whilst well targeted on particular services or facilities, such subsidies are not well targeted on particular target groups of user (i.e. low-income or otherwise 'needy' groups). Hence charges may have much greater potential in promoting equity than is acknowledged by conventional wisdom, especially if they are given discounts or exemptions.

Second, price subsidies result in a lower level of welfare than in-cash subsidies of the same monetary value. **Figure 6.3** makes use of the analysis in Chapter 4. The pre-subsidy budget line is *BA*. Subsidising consumption of good X shifts the budget line to *CA*, the equilibrium moving from *e1* to *e2*. Note that consumption of **both** X and Y (representing all other goods) has increased. This is because the price subsidy has both an income and a substitution effect. It is more effective than an in-cash (income transfer) subsidy in shifting the balance of consumption towards good X because the latter only has an income effect. This is demonstrated in **Figure 6.3** by giving an in-cash subsidy of the same monetary value as the price subsidy, resulting in *DF* (cutting through *e2*). This results in a new equilibrium at *e3* which, being on a higher indifference curve (*I3* instead of *I2*), yields a higher level of welfare. Note that *e3* lies to the left of *e2*, indicating a lower level of consumption of good X compared with *e2*. This is because *DF* only

Figure 6.3 Welfare comparison of in-kind and in-cash subsidies

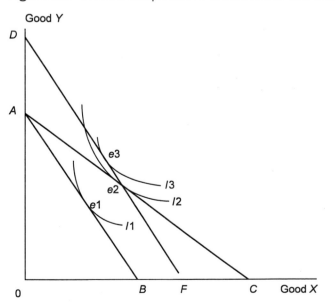

incorporates an income effect (relative prices remaining constant) whereas CA incorporates both an income and a substitution effect (the relative price of X being reduced).

The lower level of welfare associated with price (in-kind) subsidies compared with in-cash subsidies gives a presumption in favour of the latter, but only in terms of the welfare of the recipients. By definition, however, the government, and voter-taxpayers who both finance the subsidy and are assumed to choose the policy, experience greater increases in welfare as a result of price subsidies than of in-cash subsidies. This is precisely because all of the subsidy is used to increase consumption of good X, total consumption of which is greater than is the case for cash subsidies. Hence, taking account of these other welfares, the price subsidy is likely to increase social welfare by more than the in-cash subsidy. This assumes that only those eligible for subsidy actually receive it and that the costs of determining eligibility for subsidy are the same for both types of subsidy. It also assumes that those providing the subsidised service do not gain utility in its provision. If they do, then they can be expected to agitate for price (in-kind) subsidies rather than in-cash subsidies since the former lead to higher outputs of good X, so leading to increased budgets and greater employment in the service (see Chapter 7).

6.7 Charges adjusted for their institutional context

Charging rules have to be compatible with the objectives of the services to which they are applied. Hence a service-by-service approach is necessary if charges are to be introduced or increased in order to see who actually uses services. Account also has to be taken of service objectives and these are not solely to redistribute consumption in favour of low-income groups. The introduction of charges requires a more accurate identification of both service costs and service users. Hence, in tandem with means-tested and categoric subsidies, they could facilitate a more accurate targeting of service benefits on prioritised groups and secure a more equitable financing arrangement.

Charges must also be situationally relevant. They must be capable of being determined within the interactive, sequential and incremental environment of policy making. In practice, decisions about service characteristics are taken in a dynamic context. Decisions relate to what services to provide, to whom, and how they should be financed. Ideally at least, these decisions are taken simultaneously and are not bound by a particular set of rules regarding allocatively efficient pricing, whether on the basis of 'first best' or 'second best' criteria (see Chapter 2).

Charging rules cannot simply be transferred unamended from market to non-market systems of provision since their objectives differ radically (e.g. profit maximisation and securing equality of access respectively). The major problem with the efficiency rationale for charges is not the apparent conflict between equity and efficiency but rather its failure adequately to theorise the nature of 'public' (see Chapter 1). The efficiency rationale for charges and subsidies is based on market failure terms and so implicitly assumes that the public sector is simply an abstract efficiency instrument devoid of morals, ethics, behavioural characteristics and institutional form.

The pursuit of increased economic efficiency requires a much more sophisticated approach than simply the introduction of user charges based on incremental service costs, adjusted to take account of any wider social and economic benefits they confer. Charges have the potential to reduce allocative inefficiency. However they do little to reduce **X-inefficiency**, which is possibly of much greater magnitude than **allocative inefficiency** (see Chapter 7). Contracting out the supply of services within a competitive bidding system has more potential to improve efficiency through cost reduction (see Chapter 15). User charges will have little impact on allocative efficiency where service users have little real discretion over payment of charges, for example where a standing charge for connection to electricity, gas or water supplies is the major part of the total charge levied on low-volume users (see Chapter 14). The standing charge has many of the characteristics of a tax because its payment is largely unrelated to consumption.

In terms of the leviathan model of government (see Chapters 3 and 7), a public sector bureau's ideal charge would not affect its ability to produce an excessive output at excessive cost, would not reduce demand and would guarantee additional income for further service expansion. Charges would become coercive levies in much the same way as taxes. Hence the conventional argument for user charges (set out at the beginning of this chapter), that there will be excess demand for services provided free at the point of use, is too simplistic because it ignores the decision-making mechanism that determines supply. Charges intended to maximise efficiency may be manipulated by those who administer them, both to maximise bureaucratic utility and to secure gains for distributional coalitions (see Chapter 7).

6.8 Charging in relation to benefit

This charging rule avoids the conceptual and practical problems relating to costs discussed above. It can be used to maximise revenue. Unless the output is a merit good, benefit is measured by the demand schedule which shows willingness to pay. **Figure 6.1** was used to demonstrate profit maximisation and marginal cost pricing. Note that some consumers would have been willing to pay $p1$ under profit maximisation pricing rules but are now only required to pay $p2$ under marginal cost pricing rules. Indeed some consumers would be willing to pay a maximum price of $0A$. This is the same analysis as that used to derive consumers' surplus in Chapter 4. Charging in relation to benefit received would, in its extreme form, charge the maximum price that each and every consumer was willing to pay. The MR schedule in **Figure 6.1** would therefore pivot on point A and become coincident with the demand curve D. This results in $p = AR = MR$, an equality usually associated with perfect competition. Here it is achieved by a monopoly practising **perfect price discrimination**. In effect the producer appropriates the consumers' surplus.

It can be seen that revenue is greater under perfect price discrimination ($0ACq2$) than under both profit maximisation pricing ($0p1Bq1$) and marginal cost pricing ($0p2Cq2$). This pricing strategy may be favoured by bureaucrats who wish to see the service expanded as part of 'empire building' (the leviathan thesis again). In practice it is extremely difficult to identify each and every consumer's willingness to pay. However a similar result can be achieved by splitting the total market into two or more submarkets, each with different price elasticities of demand.

This is demonstrated in **Figure 6.4**. The combined market is represented in **Figure 6.4(c)**, the profit-maximising equilibrium being $p(c)q(c)$. Assume that output $q(c)$ is now split between two submarkets. The submarket with high price inelasticity of demand would be used to generate revenue by raising price. This is demonstrated in **Figure 6.4(a)**, $p(a)$ being substantially greater than $p(c)$. The submarket with high price elasticity of demand would face a lower price and be used to meet sales or use targets. This is demonstrated in **Figure 6.4(b)**, $p(b)$ being slightly less than $p(c)$. Total revenue $[p(a)q(a) + p(b)q(b)]$ is greater than $p(c)q(c)$. Hence profits have been increased since costs are assumed to be unaffected by splitting the market, $c1$ being kept constant in **Figures 6.4(a)** and **6.4(b)**.

Price discrimination is only possible where a single producer controls supply and where resale can be prevented between submarkets facing different prices. Hence it can only be practised by monopolists supplying services. It was used extensively by the former nationalised industry (British Rail) in terms of different fares for different types of passenger making the same journey at a particular point in time. For example passengers on a particular train travelling between the same two points have paid different fares according to whether they booked the ticket in advance or at the time of travel, whether they held a discount card as a student, senior citizen (i.e. over 65 years of age) or family group or

Figure 6.4 Two-market price discrimination: (a) price inelastic submarket; (b) price elastic submarket; (c) combined market

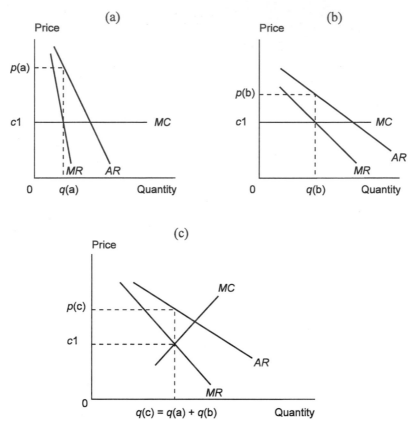

whether they did not qualify for such discounts. This allowed British Rail to compete with the long-distance coach service (e.g. for price-sensitive students) and with air-flights (e.g. for business travellers).

Price discrimination was further developed subsequent to privatisation of British Rail (see Chapter 13), franchises allowing the 25 private sector train operating companies monopoly control of their own services. The cost of return fares between any two major cities for a given rail company typically varied by a factor of between four and five. In 1999, 'Apex', 'Super Advance' and other such tickets booked (say, three days) in advance were typically between a quarter and a fifth of 'turn up and go' fares. The cheapest tickets are generally regarded as excellent value for money. Nonetheless, the Central Rail Users Consultative Committee (CRUCC) and others frequently criticise these cheap seats. They are limited, are often fully booked weeks in advance, are inflexible once booked, lead to an impenetrable jungle of complex fare pricing, have created huge differences between operators in the cost per mile travelled, and have allowed the companies disingenuously to claim they have cut fares. Most companies' 'turn up and go' fares increased faster than the retail price index in the five years following privatisation and, in some cases, they exceed the cost of flying between major British cities. The CRUCC found that there were 90 different ticket types by the year 2000. Even for a single operator, finding the cheapest ticketing option can be very difficult.

These price differences reflect, in part, the extra costs faced by the train operating companies in having to provide extra carriages for non-booked travel. However, they also enable companies to maximise revenue by taking advantage of the price inelastic demand of business people and others who are unable to plan their journeys in advance and so have to travel at short notice. Whilst such a pricing strategy is consistent with profit maximisation it has led to criticism of unfair fares (i.e. monopoly exploitation) and demands for greater regulatory control (see Chapter 13).

Price discrimination is generally not suitable for other public sector services where there is more than one producer (e.g. of sports facilities) or where willingness to pay cannot be identified (e.g. the 'free-rider' problem for public goods, see Chapter 2). This demand-based marketing strategy is clearly distinct from the cost-based $p = LRMC$ pricing rule.

6.9 Charges combining cost, benefit, equity and environmental considerations

Besides incorporating a standing charge and a running rate, the **two-part tariff** charging structure often has a **volume discount** where, above a threshold level of consumption, the cost per unit consumed falls. This can be justified in company cost terms because high volume consumption reduces average costs by spreading fixed costs over a larger output. It also benefits the public utility by increasing its revenues and, thereby, its profits. However, this form of tariff is regressive and environmentally unfriendly. It is regressive because poor households, in typically consuming less than affluent households, spread the standing charge over fewer units. They therefore pay more per unit consumed than richer households and the bill typically accounts for a higher proportion of their household incomes. It is environmentally unfriendly because it encourages consumption, energy and water use typically causing pollution. Volumetric discounts therefore abrogate the 'polluter pays' principle of Chapter 2, especially if there is a critical threshold level above which pollution causes increasingly severe ecological damage.

Whilst the social security system already helps benefit recipients pay their energy and water bills, a more equitable tariff structure would abolish the standing charge. This is something that some privatised energy companies are already doing in order to attract new customers. They could also charge a relatively low price for low levels of energy use, thereafter raising the unit price sharply. This could be justified in terms of allowing households enough cheap energy and water sufficient for basic health and comfort but thereafter encouraging households to be more discriminating in their use of these services. Rising unit prices would provide a financial incentive for consumers to adopt measures to save energy (e.g. loft insulation) and water (see Chapter 14).

To a greater or lesser extent, such a pricing structure would therefore reflect company costs, benefits of use, equity and environmental considerations. It could be criticised for partially abrogating the 'polluter pays' principle in that even low volume use is polluting and so should not be subsidised via cross-subsidy from high volume users to low volume users. It could also be criticised for not relating charges directly to long-run marginal costs, particularly ignoring the fixed infrastructure costs of connecting even low volume users to the system. Nor does it relate bills directly to ability to pay. The water regulator favours a multi-part tariff that responds to many of these concerns (see Chapter 14). Ultimately, however, any practical tariff structure is necessarily a trade-off between conflicting objectives.

6.10 Conclusions

The strong efficiency arguments supporting charging in accordance with marginal costs have been demonstrated in this chapter and in Chapter 2. However the efficiency ideal of marginal cost pricing can only work in mechanistic mathematical models where agents are programmed automatons operating within clearly defined utility and cost functions within competitive markets. This is obviously not the case for most public sector outputs, where charges are determined by the politico/bureaucratic process. In such cases the introduction of increased or new charges is not necessarily an effective way of achieving efficiency savings. If demand is perfectly price inelastic, or if individuals are compelled to consume a service (e.g. school education), their more immediate effect will be a redistribution of income in cash terms because demand is unaffected. If demand is highly price elastic and service take-up is voluntary, their more immediate effect will be a redistribution of income in-kind because demand collapses. Efficiency cannot be improved at a stroke.

Whilst there is a general conflict between efficiency and equity caused by charging, this does not necessarily hold in all cases. If free or subsidised public services are inequitably distributed at present because of 'middle-class capture' of their benefits, the incremental use of charges can be used to target more successfully subsidy on prioritised groups. Charges can therefore promote both equity and efficiency in such cases. However new or increased charges may be exploited by bureaucrats as a means of raising additional finance for service expansion beyond the point at which marginal social benefit equals marginal social cost. This is most likely to be the case where there is a large element of compulsion in payment of the charge, in effect a pseudo tax. This point is addressed in detail in Chapter 7.

Further reading

Bailey, S. J. (1999) *Local Government Economics: Principles and Practice* (Basingstoke: Macmillan). (Chapter 7 covers local authority charges.)

Bailey, S. J. and Falconer, P. (1999) 'A Councillor's Guide to Local Government Charges', *CIPFA Financial Information Service 18: Revenues* (London: Chartered Institute of Public Finance and Accountancy).

Bailey, S. J., Falconer, P. and McChlery, S. (1993) *Local Government Charges: Policy and Practice* (Harlow: Longman).

7 Public Choice Theory of Government Intervention

7.1 Introduction
7.2 Models of Government
7.3 Behavioural Problems of Leviathan Governments
7.4 Categorising Inefficiency
7.5 Conclusions

7.1 Introduction

Previous chapters have examined the efficiency rationale for government intervention, namely where markets fail to achieve allocative efficiency, and the means by which such intervention is financed. The basic Keynesian model of the management of aggregate demand is an example of how, in theory, intervention can be used during times of mass unemployment in order to maximise the output of the economy, so moving the economy back onto its production possibility frontier. Crowding out reduces the efficacy of intervention but, if less than 100 per cent, increased output may lead to a welfare improvement (see Chapter 5). However the analysis of Pareto optimality demonstrated that detailed knowledge of both production conditions and consumption preferences is required if allocative efficiency is to be attained through non-market systems (see Chapter 2). Moreover 'second best' theory suggests that piecemeal intervention may be counterproductive, increasing rather than reducing allocative inefficiency.

Critics argue that these technical and information problems are easily exaggerated in the practical policy context within which government intervention operates. However, besides these **technical** problems constraining the attainment of the 'first best' allocation of resources, there are also **behavioural** problems that may serve to deny both first best or second best solutions. Behavioural distortions of allocative efficiency arise from two areas. **First**, both taxation and government expenditure may change the behaviour of consumers and producers in ways that were neither intended nor foreseen by the government and its economic advisers when decisions to intervene were taken. **Second**, governments may themselves abuse their position of trust, no longer seeking to pursue allocative efficiency (or even equity) in promoting the public interest.

This chapter summarises the technical problems already addressed in previous chapters and goes on to analyse potential behavioural problems on the part of government and citizens. In so doing, it develops a theory of **government failure** (public choice theory) which parallels that of **market failure**.

7.2 Models of government

The allocative, distributive, regulatory and stabilisation roles of government (see Chapter 2) are set within a particular model of government: the despotic benevolent government model. However there are other economic models of government, not all of which assume benevolence.

1. **The despotic benevolent government model.** The government acts in the public interest, seeking the 'first best' allocation of resources so as to maximise welfare by offsetting specific instances of market failure. This model is consistent with both the development and organic state macromodels of public expenditure growth (see Chapter 3). It assumes (perhaps naively) that the government is both omniscient and benevolent. The government makes decisions on behalf of its citizens to promote their interests, hence 'despotic benevolent government'. The government may even know better than individual consumers what is best for them, for example where they undervalue the benefits of provision for health care (the merit goods concept of Chapter 2). This is clearly contrary to the Pareto optimum assumption that the individual knows best.
2. **The fiscal exchange model.** The government acts in the private interest, providing specific services for specific tax payments voluntarily agreed by citizens, hence 'fiscal exchange'. In this model the government is simply a service-delivery instrument responding to citizens' demands for collectively provided goods and services. This is the model implicit in the median voter demand micromodel of public expenditure growth (see Chapter 3). It assumes that demands can be expressed by individuals for discreet public sector outputs with attached tax payments. Equilibrium is obtained where the marginal tax price equals marginal benefit.
3. **The fiscal transfer model.** Whereas the fiscal exchange model was based on unanimity (citizens agreeing to service provision and the associated tax prices), the fiscal transfer model is based on compulsion. Here the majority-voting rule allows the majority to over-tax the minority and direct services to themselves, hence 'fiscal transfer'. Both the fiscal exchange model and the fiscal transfer model drop the assumption of benevolent government. Indeed government has no

existence of its own: it is non-organic, passively responding to the
wishes of voters.

4. **The leviathan model.** Here the government grows like a monster (i.e.
    a leviathan) because it is assumed to be made up of utility-maximis-
    ing, self-serving politicians, bureaucrats, professional groups and
    other pressure groups. It serves its own (rather than the public)
    interest and there are no effective constitutional constraints on its
    growth.

The political constraints macromodel of public expenditure (see
Chapter 3) assumes that governments like to spend money but are
constrained by citizens' dislike of paying taxes. The leviathan model of
government assumes that such a constraint on the size of the public
sector is weak and ineffectual because of the limited relationship
between those who vote for, those who pay for and those who use
public sector services, there being a general belief that someone else will
pay. Public sector outputs are generally free at the point of consumption,
being financed largely by taxation. The benefits of public expenditure
tend to be concentrated on particular socioeconomic or demographic
groups or on people living in particular geographic areas. Therefore
voting for increased expenditure for one's own group or area does not
incur a commensurate increase in liability to pay. Information tends to be
asymmetrical (i.e. heavily biased in favour of one's own interests) and
politicians compete for the votes of special interest groups rather than
serve the wider public interest. Bureaucrats may themselves determine
or influence supply independently of political decision-making. All these
factors combine to create a monstrous public sector, a leviathan.

The despotic benevolent government model dominated economic
analysis up to the 1960s and is still a common implicit assumption of
first-year economic text books (e.g. in analysing Keynesian macroeconomic management of aggregate demand). However, by the 1980s the
leviathan model had come into vogue. Whilst the monetarist school of
macroeconomics is distrustful of governments on the ground that they
lack the 'political will' to follow politically unpopular economic
prescriptions (i.e. are too prone to U-turns), the leviathan model assumes
government is made up of self-serving individuals who manipulate and
distort public choices to further their own ends (hence 'public choice
theory').

The despotic benevolent government model achieves allocative
efficiency because all its actions are, by definition, in pursuit of it. The
fiscal exchange model of government only achieves allocative efficiency
as long as there is no market failure arising from merit-good or
externality characteristics etc. The fiscal transfer model achieves neither
allocative efficiency nor equity since no account is taken of either market

failure or equity. The leviathan model is the worst-case scenario on both allocative and equity grounds, the government actively seeking to distort both equity and efficiency in its own interests.

Whilst apparently mutually exclusive, there may be elements of all four models in practice, none being a perfectly satisfactory explanation of public sector outcomes. Each model has aspects that do not accord with the way in which decisions are made. For example, in the UK the government is not the sole source of ideas for legislation (model 1), agreement of specific taxes for specific services is limited (model 2), those in the majority are not necessarily the same from one issue to the next (model 3) and there may be (written or unwritten) constitutional constraints on the growth of government (model 4).

In practice, the programmes that must be implemented in order to achieve those outcomes require prior enabling legislation, for example a finance act to raise revenue to finance an expenditure programme. Proposals for a new piece of legislation come from the political parties' manifestos, interest groups, professional bodies and government departments. Those proposals must be published in the form of a government bill, a private member's bill (from a member of parliament) or a private bill (dealing with issues that affect a particular group or a specific individual). These parliamentary bills are considered by relevant government departments and a cabinet committee and are subjected to parliamentary scrutiny by both Houses (readings, vote, committee and report stages). Governments are of course subject to periodic re-election.

Hence all four of the above models of government are gross simplifications or abstractions from reality. None is clearly superior to the other three, either in terms of its accordance with reality or in being able to be empirically tested. Empirical testing of public choice insights is especially difficult, particularly in terms of establishing their generality.

7.3 Behavioural problems of leviathan governments

Chapter 1 has already noted that those in positions of political power within government are unrepresentative of society in general. Bearing this caveat in mind, representative democracy is made necessary because voting systems are mechanically incapable of consistently aggregating a multitude of individual wishes into a single set of collective wants. Voting systems do not gauge the intensity of preferences, voters are known to be poorly informed about alternative policies on offer, it is quite rational for the voter not to bother to be well informed when voting or, given the insignificant impact of his or her vote on personal well-being, even not to vote at all. Furthermore the voter's knowledge may be heavily biased in favour of his or her special interests, reinforced by the political party system that is the cornerstone of representative democracy.

The imbalance between benefits and costs may lead to excessive public spending. It has been argued that public expenditure may be suboptimally low because tangible tax costs are more apparent (and more concentrated) than the intangible benefits of public services. However, as already noted, the alternative argument is that benefits are concentrated on particular groups of voters whilst tax costs are more widely dispersed. Hence, more people may vote for increased spending on particular programmes than against it.

For example, the supposed asymmetry in voter behaviour was said to be compounded in British **local** government by the lack of a direct relationship between those who vote for, those who pay for and those who use local government services. During the 1980s Conservative governments argued that there was a general belief that someone else would pay. The 'someone else' were national taxpayers financing intergovernmental grants, local businesses paying local non-domestic property taxes whilst having no vote, and the minority of local voters who paid full local domestic property taxes as heads of household. Hence the Conservative governments believed that there was an in-built tendency for voters to vote for excessive local government spending.

The significance of the voting problem is that it is not possible to construct a social welfare function that could be used to guide government intervention so as to achieve allocative efficiency. In reality, however, government actions are not rigidly determined by voting outcomes. Voters are themselves uncertain about the benefits of particular government actions and perhaps even uncertain about their own preferences. Indeed governments (and opposition parties) fulfil a deliberative role by debating social equity, moral, ethical and other issues. They are not just concerned with economic efficiency (see Chapter 1).

The voting problem is supposedly overcome by electing **politicians** who can be trusted to make the right decisions on behalf of citizens. However the idea of one ('honest broker') politician representing all individual citizens in his or her constituency irrespective of political persuasion is questionable. Moreover public choice theory suggests that the various parties to the public expenditure process pursue their own self-interest at the expense of the public interest. Politicians may seek to increase their chances of political survival rather than promote the public interest. For example they could exploit the majority voting rule in order to maximise their chances of re-election.

Table 7.1 shows the distribution of ranked preferences for three alternative policies. That particular distribution of preferences results in none of the alternatives having majority support. There is a clear lack of

Table 7.1 Political exploitation of majority voting rules

Preferences	Voter A	Voter B	Voter C
First choice	X	Y	Z
Second choice	Y	Z	X
Third choice	Z	X	Y

consensus amongst voters. Assume that the government adopts policy X. That policy is preferred by voter A but is the third choice for voter B and second choice for voter C. Both B and C prefer Z to X. Hence the opposition can defeat the government by proposing Z. Similarly, if the government chooses Y, the opposition can offer X to attract support from A and C (since both prefer X). If the government chooses Z it can again be defeated by the opposition offering Y (preferred by both A and B). Such a preference pattern may be infrequent and its importance reduced by uncertainty and political compromise. However it does demonstrate how majority voting may make reaching consistent collective decisions impossible. This indeterminacy may be exploited by politicians seeking to promote their own self-interest rather than the public interest. This is usually referred to as 'the Arrow problem' (after its originator).

Bureaucrats may also be self-serving, rather than the 'passionless grey figures' serving the public interest assumed in the early literature on bureaucracy. **Figure 7.1** displays the usual marginal cost and demand schedules (*MC* and *D* respectively). These schedules relate to the **users** of public sector outputs, **not** the bureaucrat. As already demonstrated for Figure 6.1, optimum output is where **marginal** benefit (i.e. willingness to pay shown by the demand curve) equals **marginal** cost. This is $q1$ in **Figure 7.1**. However bureaucrats' utilities are assumed to be positively and directly related to the size of their budgets, larger budgets enabling more staff to be hired, thereby extending career structures, improving prospects for promotion and enhancement of salaries and conferring status and prestige. Hence bureaucrats have incentives to increase output beyond $q1$.

For example, bureaucrats could advocate service expansion up to the point where **total** benefit equals **total** cost rather than where **marginal** benefit equals **marginal** cost. This may be an acceptable decision-making technique for the general public and specialists who are not economists, both groups being unfamiliar with the equilibrium and optimisation rules of marginal analysis. Indeed, the median voter demand model in **Figure 3.1** makes supply of public sector outputs available as long as *average* costs are covered by willingness to pay a tax price. It does not consider *marginal* equalities of costs and benefits. Alternatively, bureau-

Figure 7.1 Bureaucratic empire building

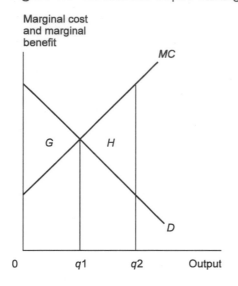

crats may deliberately understate the true marginal cost in order to persuade policymakers to expand output. This can be visualised in **Figure 7.1** by moving the marginal cost schedule down along the demand curve.

Total benefit equals total cost at $q2$ because area G (the excess of marginal valuation over marginal cost) equals area H (the excess of marginal cost over marginal valuation). In effect the bureaucrats have captured the consumers' surplus for themselves (see Chapter 4). In the extreme case output doubles from $q1$ to $q2$. Hence, inefficiency arises **even if cost per unit of output is minimised** because overproduction occurs. This outcome may result from use of either taxes or charges, payment of which is compulsory, as long as revenues from the latter are reinvested into the service as net additional funds (see Chapter 6).

This model of bureaucratic empire building can be criticised for giving too much power to bureaucrats. Bureaucrats' utility may not simply be dependent on maximising programme budgets, and in practice those budgets are constrained by the institutional framework (and its power structures) within which they operate. For example taxpayers may seek reductions in service output because marginal cost exceeds marginal benefit for output between $q1$ and $q2$ in **Figure 7.1**. Since politicians seek re-election they will be sensitive to the demands of voters. However bureaucrats themselves have votes and are perhaps more likely to use them than other groups. Hence they may acquire sufficient political power to guarantee self-preservation and self-interest. This is especially the case at local government level where local bureaucrats may account for a large proportion of the local electorate (especially in sparsely populated authorities) and they may themselves be local politicians.

7.4 Categorising inefficiency

Rather than doubling output (allocative inefficiency), bureaux may produce at excessively high cost (X-inefficiency). The distinction between these two concepts of efficiency was implicit in the analysis of Chapters 2, 3 and 6.

X-efficiency. This is an organisation-specific concept denoting general managerial and technological efficiency at the level of the firm, bureau or organisation. It is a corollary of the profit maximisation assumption that requires firms to use inputs, solve their organisational problems and produce output at least cost. However, X-inefficiency may occur if organisations are insulated from competition by natural or statutory monopolies (see Chapter 13). Being shielded from competition, bureaucrats may take 'on the job' leisure, for example attending highly prestigious international conferences in attractive foreign cities and using unnecessarily generous expense allowances. In such cases they express preferences for cost items besides output, causing X-inefficiency (also known as **'organisational slack'**).

Allocative efficiency. This is an aggregative, economy-wide concept that requires inputs and outputs to be priced at their respective marginal costs and allocated in accordance with the preferences and income constraints of consumers. It is a question about what point on the production possibility frontier is optimal. Chapter 2 (**Figure 2.4**) showed that consumers' preferences (shown by their indifference curves) determine the economy's location on its production possibility frontier. Allocative inefficiency occurs if the distribution of particular public sector outputs is not in accordance with those personal preferences, for example where a planner or monopolist distorts that allocation. In such a case it may be possible to redistribute resources making someone better off without making someone else worse off (i.e. a Pareto improvement is possible because a Pareto optimum does not exist).

Scope for discretionary behaviour by bureaucrats may be facilitated by a number of factors.

Asymmetric information. Voters and politicians may be heavily dependent on information provided by bureaucrats who face incentives to overstate benefits and understate the costs. External benefits (see

Chapter 2) may be exaggerated and/or accounting practices may understate costs (e.g. use of historic rather than current costs, see Chapter 13). Asymmetric information may therefore lead to excessive output.

Asymmetric tax liability. Formal liability for both national and local taxation varies, as does its economic incidence (see Chapter 4). Those who bear the least tax cost may be more amenable to increased public sector outputs.

Asymmetric consumption benefits. Public sector outputs tend to be concentrated on particular geographic areas or on particular socio-economic and demographic groups. Those who receive disproportionate benefits may be more amenable to increased public sector outputs.

Asymmetric voting patterns. Those most likely to benefit from additional services may be more likely to vote for them than those who benefit least yet also bear additional tax costs (e.g. middle and working classes respectively). This is more likely to be the case given that the composition of tax revenues is being shifted from direct to indirect taxes (see Chapter 10).

The combination of heterogeneous preferences, the asymmetry of effective political power, the inflexibility of tax payments for financing services and the largely discretionary nature of service take-up may facilitate excessive output. For example local government service 'prices' in the form of tax payments are largely fixed, in that common rules apply regarding liability to pay national and local taxes, and payment does not vary directly or immediately with the individual's consumption of services. Hence the major part of redistribution at the local government level is through service usage (i.e. exhaustive expenditures) and there is an incentive to seek to vary the level of output and/or to change its distribution within a given tax cost. Assuming an objective of utility maximisation, **'distributional coalitions'** of people, bureaucrats, politi-cians and firms may seek to increase the welfares of their members at the expense of the rest of society. For example, there is evidence of middle-class capture of subsidy through service usage and these 'upper' socio-economic groups (owner-occupiers, better qualified or educated) are more likely to both vote and participate in local political groups and meetings.

Distributional coalitions may constrain the ability of local government to adapt to changing socio-economic conditions. Services tend to be targeted (intentionally or otherwise) at particular groups or localities and any reduction of services would see a reduction in the benefits accruing to them but little or no change in tax liability. Hence local government services are difficult to cut back, half-empty schools in areas of falling pupil numbers for example. The result is over-capacity (for example in school accommodation) and, hence, allocative inefficiency. This is reinforced if employees are difficult to dismiss (e.g. because of strong trade union power) and where promotion prospects are not adversely affected by poor performance, especially when performance is difficult to measure and objectives are not clearly specified. The result is X-inefficiency caused by over-manning of public sector services, this being illustrated by the dramatic reductions in staffing levels when public services became subject to competitive contracting in the 1980s and 1990s (see Chapter 15).

Hence, public choice theory encompasses **demand-side** factors relating to voters' incentives, and **supply-side** factors relating to politicians' and bureaucrats' incentives. In combination, these factors may lead to both allocative inefficiency and X-inefficiency. In such cases, efficiency policy will be based on returning as many activities as possible to private competitive markets (i.e. privatisation, see Chapter 13). Those activities remaining within the public sector can be made more X-efficient by increasing internal competition through the creation of internal markets between competing bureaux, competitive contracting etc. However internal competition will not necessarily eliminate any allocative inefficiency since the decision to produce the output is not determined by consumer sovereignty. In general, therefore, there will be a preference for progressive privatisation and liberalisation of government departments and agencies so as to promote consumer sovereignty (see Chapter 8).

7.5 Conclusions

Public choice theory is based on an **inhospitality thesis** of government intervention. It suggests that intervention necessarily distorts economic activity to a greater extent than unregulated private markets, even if they are less than perfectly competitive. Not only is crowding out a possibility through disincentive-to-work effects, there is also the possibility of leviathan government. In other words, changing the distribution of income is not simply a case of redividing a given set of consumption possibilities between consumers and so redetermining the position of the Pareto optimum on the production possibility frontier. The very process of redistribution may cause the production possibility frontier to shrink (i.e. move closer to the origin) because of both disincentive-to-work effects and the inefficiencies caused by leviathan governments.

Whilst the crowding-out hypothesis received considerable attention during the late 1970s and early 1980s, by the 1990s increasing attention was being paid to the leviathan thesis based on the analytical framework of public choice. Public choice theory simply applies the assumptions and methodology of neoclassical analysis of the private sector to analysis of the operations of the public sector. The power of that framework lies in the clarity and simplicity of its logic. Ultimately, however, it is based upon the assumption of a single-minded pursuit of power, security and income by the bureaucrat, politician or pressure group. Whilst it is difficult to argue that individuals do not attempt to increase their own welfare, it may be equally difficult to accept that they will do so systematically and irrespective of the costs imposed on other groups. This may appear to be too cynical a view of public servants, many of whom do have a conception of the public interest and not all of whom are (economic) **rent seekers**.

Public choice theory is **positive** economics in that it adopts the leviathan model of government to predict the behaviour of public organisations. However, it has also been used for **normative** purposes by right-wing political groups as an intellectual justification for reducing government intervention, much in the same way that the despotic benevolent model of government has been used by left-wing ideologists to justify government intervention. In its positive economics context, public choice theory questions the transaction costs justification of internalisation of market transactions within public sector organisations (see Chapter 2). Instead, such internalisation may result from bureau-cratic empire building.

During the 1990s there seems to have been a sharp fall in the general public's trust in political institutions. There was increasing public concern about the need to promote and protect ethical standards in public life; to prevent political 'sleaze', misuse of public powers or misdemeanours by those in public office. Moreover the potential for conflicts of interest increased as large parts of the public sector were sold, became subject to contracting out or were reconstituted as self-regulating bodies such as quangos and Civil Service executive agencies (see Chapters 8, 13, 14 and 15).

Central and local government politics and the Civil Service are increasingly a complex world of professional–political connections, including company positions for friends and relatives, personal links with consultancy companies (e.g. finance or public relations), with political pressure groups etc. In the late 1980s and early 1990s there was increasing evidence of members of parliament (MPs) accepting cash from pressure groups as payment for parliamentary questions, ministers indulging in political nepotism when making public appointments to quangos or being influenced by conflicts of interest, and ex-cabinet members becoming directors of companies whose privatisation they oversaw. Such concerns were put on record in a 1994 report by the Public Accounts Committee which found evidence of mismanagement, nepotism and corruption in some self-regulating quangos. The Nolan Committee on Standards in Public Life reported opinion polls that found that politicians and government ministers vie with journalists for being the least trusted occupational groups in the UK, civil servants also being seen as generally untrustworthy. Nolan advocated seven principles of public life for the holders of public office to observe: selflessness, integrity, objectivity, accountability, openness, honesty and leadership. These principles are the foundations of the despotic benevolent model of government.

Trusting politicians always to promote the public interest (rather than their self-interest) and the concept of apolitical bureaucrats as passionless grey figures seems to be a peculiarly British trait. In many other democracies it is taken for granted that civil servants have political affiliations. In some other countries bribery and corruption are acknowledged to be widespread in public and political life. Subsequent to the Nolan committee report, legislation was passed requiring MPs to disclose earnings from consultancies derived from parliament and banning paid advocacy by MPs, including tabling questions, motions and amendments to legislation.

Public sector reform in the UK during the 1980s and 1990s included reform of the tax and benefit systems and, more generally, 'rolling back the frontiers of the state' through privatisation and other means. Whilst there are undoubtedly other explanations of such events (e.g. from a neo-Marxist political perspective), the economic models discussed in the preceding chapters can be used to explain (or at least provide intellectual justifications for) these reforms. The state and the economy go hand in hand.

Socialism requires political and economic institutions and processes that foster collective action. Conservatism requires the break-up of economic planning processes and political power. Rather than politicians being the slaves of some defunct economist (as Keynes once claimed), economists and their competing theories may be exploited by national and local politicians to provide intellectual (if not scientific) justifications of their policies. This *instrumental* view of economic theory is in sharp contrast with that of explanation and prediction (see Chapter 1). Economists may themselves develop economic theories which suit their own political preferences (e.g. for increased marketplace liberalism and reduced state intervention). Such policies are the subject of Parts II and III.

Further reading

McNutt, P. (1996) *The Economics of Public Choice: Contemporary Issues in the Political Economy of Governing* (Cheltenham: Edward Elgar).

Niskanen, W. A. (1996) *Bureaucracy and Public Economics* (Cheltenham: Edward Elgar).

Nolan, (1995) *Standards in Public Life. First Report of the Committee on Standards in Public Life*, Cm 2850-1 (London: HMSO).

Olson, M. (1965) *The Logic of Collective Action: Public Goods and the Theory of Groups* (Cambridge Mass: Harvard University Press).

Olson, M. (1982) *The Rise and Decline of Nations: Economic Growth, Stagflation and Social Rigidities* (New Haven: Yale University Press).

Pardo, C. J. and Schneider, F. (1996) *Current Issues in Public Choice* (Cheltenham: Edward Elgar).

Self, P. (1993) *Government by the Market? The Politics of Public Choice* (Basingstoke: Macmillan).

Part II

Policy and Practice

8 Rolling Back the Frontiers of the State

8.1 Introduction
8.2 Categorising the Major Reforms During the 1980s and 1990s
8.3 Demand-side Policy and Practice
8.4 Supply-side Policy and Practice
8.5 Supply-side Policies for Private Markets
8.6 Supply-side Policies for the Public Sector
8.7 The Purchaser–Provider Split
8.8 Private Financing of Public Sector Projects
8.9 Conclusions

The Government's economic objective is to promote sustained (economic) growth and higher living standards. In delivering this objective, fiscal and monetary policies are complemented by the Government's continuing programme of **microeconomic** reform. This reform is designed to improve the efficiency of markets and strengthen the long-term supply performance of the economy. . . The Government's strategy for strengthening the **supply side** aims to make the economy more responsive to market disciplines by enlarging the market sector, increasing competition, deregulating, and improving the climate for enterprise, particularly small businesses (*Financial Statement and Budget Report 1994–95*, London: HMSO, 1993, pp. 1–2, emphasis added).

The present Government will not resort to the interventionist policies of the past. In the industrial policy-making of the 1960s and 1970s, to be modern meant believing in planning. Now, meeting the requirements of the knowledge driven economy means **helping markets work better**. The Government believes strongly that open, transparent and effective markets are vital to encourage efficiency and innovation. (*Our Competitive Future: Building the Knowledge Driven Economy*, Cm 4176, London: Stationery Office, 1998, pp. 11 and 51, emphasis added).

8.1 Introduction

The public sector is a pervasive part of everyday life, providing people with services such as health care, education, law and order and redistributing income through taxation and payment of social security.

The economic rationale for government intervention in the market economy is based on allocative efficiency criteria, whatever actions are necessary to compensate for market failure (see Chapter 2). Hence some macromodels of public expenditure growth suggest that growth of the public and private sectors is complementary, the state providing the wherewithal for the market to function (see Chapter 3). However, crowding-out theory and the apparent trade-off between efficiency and equity suggests that growth of the public sector may be at the expense of economic growth (see Chapters 4 and 5). If so, growth of the public sector ultimately leads to living standards being less than they would otherwise have been if the public sector had not grown as fast or at all. Moreover, to the extent that a leviathan state exists and acts in its own (rather than the public) interest, then loss of economic potential may be exacerbated (see Chapter 7). This inhospitality thesis of government provides the basic rationale for the policy of 'rolling back the frontiers of the state', a phrase coined during the 1980s.

The loss of economic potential may occur even if standards of living have improved over time. It is undisputedly true that the average family or person is materially much better off now than in the 1980s or 1990s. Over the 26 years up to 1997, 'Social Trends' data show that, after taking account of inflation, household disposable income per head nearly doubled in real terms. Over the same period there were sharp increases in the proportions of households owning a telephone, television, washing machine, central heating system and so on. Ownership of new consumer durables such as videos, microwave cookers, compact disc players and home computers is increasing steadily.

Whilst there are continuing ideologically based arguments about deteriorating standards of service, the standards of most public services appear to have improved, sometimes dramatically. For example there have been considerable increases in the proportions of relevant age groups entering higher education. Improved medical practices have generally been regarded as having led to higher quality health care – although it is extremely difficult to measure quality. Poverty remains a controversial issue, but the poor of today are almost invariably better off in absolute terms than their counterparts of 20 or more years ago – although there is some more recent evidence of an absolute deterioration for the very poorest groups (see Chapter 12).

'Rolling back the frontiers of the state' is not simply a case of reducing the provision of services. There may be some aspects of service reduction where demands or perceived needs have changed, but generally the emphasis is on transferring (not reducing) service provision to the private sector. Indeed, the output of many of the transferred services has actually increased (see Chapter 13).

Improved access to services does not necessarily require direct provision by the state. Instead the state could enable provision to be made through market or pseudo-market systems (see Chapter 15). It is believed greater efficiency can be achieved by market systems and so existing resources can be made to go further. To that extent 'rolling back the frontiers of the state' is about improving access to service provision. However it is also a more fundamental moral issue regarding the rights and responsibilities of the individual and the legitimate role of the government in everyday life.

8.2 Categorising the major reforms during the 1980s and 1990s

Whatever their political persuasion, successive governments have acknowledged the need to control the growth of the public sector. However the solutions adopted during the 1980s and 1990s marked a distinct shift in approach. Whilst continuing to use the traditional **macroeconomic** instruments of the 1960s and 1970s, increasing emphasis was put on radical **microeconomic** reforms, and also on **supply-side** (as distinct from **demand-side**) measures to help markets work better, as made clear in the above quotations. The first is from the then Conservative government (in power 1979–1997) and the second from the Labour government (which came to power in 1997). Both governments share the same supply-side approach to economic policy, as will be made clear below.

The increasing emphasis on microeconomic measures does **not** mean that macroeconomic measures have been abandoned. It is simply that it has become clear that the competing macroeconomic views of monetarists and Keynesians are based on differing views of microeconomics, in particular the efficiency of markets in promoting market clearing (i.e. the equation of supply and demand). For example, despite massively increasing unemployment during the early 1980s, employment earnings continued to rise in real terms, wages rising faster than inflation. In other words, an excess supply of labour did **not** drive down the real price of labour. This outcome was contrary to the expectations of neoclassical economics, which assumes the instantaneous adjustment of markets to disequilibrium conditions through changes in factor and product prices. Hence macroeconomic events are effectively derived from the aggregation of micoeconomic relationships. Since supply creates its own demand (**Say's Law**) through price changes, then unemployment should be nothing more than a transient phenomenon. In direct contradiction of this microeconomic-based model of the economy, extreme Keynesians argue that markets may fail to clear in both the short and the long run.

Recession and unemployment can persist indefinitely because real wages do not fall, they are 'sticky', as are a number of other 'prices' in the economy.

Whilst this is a highly simplified account of the microeconomic differences between the two broad schools, it does illustrate the rationale underpinning the subsequent search for microeconomic solutions to the economic problems of the 1980s and 1990s. Unlike Keynesians, the neoclassical school believes that markets can work efficiently and that free unregulated markets do necessarily promote the social and economic interest. Hence macroeconomic policy cannot ignore micro-economics, and the major public sector reforms of the 1980s and 1990s have contained a mixture of macroeconomic and microeconomic elements. It is the increasing emphasis on supply-side and microeconomic reforms that clearly separates the reforms of the 1980s and 1990s from those of earlier decades and provides the key to understanding the strong links between economic theory, policy and practice in the reform of the public sector.

Microeconomic issues were the predominant focus of Part I, which considered the efficiency of markets, the efficiency rationale for government intervention, the microeconomic influences on public expenditures, the welfare and efficiency effects of taxation, the economic effects of public sector borrowing, charging for public sector outputs and models of government behaviour. The conclusions of Part I were that governments may intervene in pursuit of their own (rather than the public) interest, that public expenditure, taxation and borrowing may cause inefficiencies through crowding-out effects and that, whilst the efficiency rationale for charges may be subverted in practice, there is a general presumption against the payment of subsidies except for allocative efficiency purposes.

In effect Part I emphasised the possibility that government intervention may obstruct market clearing and so cause microeconomic inefficiencies. For example, if high marginal rates of income tax cause disincentive-to-work effects then labour markets will fail to clear. This disequilibrium situation will be exacerbated to the extent that means-tested social security benefits combine with income tax to cause severe **unemployment traps**. In other words, generous income maintenance schemes may raise the **reserve price of labour** (i.e. increase the wage that must be paid in order to make employment more financially worthwhile than unemployment). If so, the unemployed simply stop actively seeking work and therefore there is no downward pressure on wages and high levels of unemployment can persist. The neoclassical solution is to remove disincentive-to-work effects by reducing marginal tax rates, and also to reduce the reserve price of labour by restricting the eligibility for benefit of those who are capable of working (see Chapter 9). This approach denies the Keynesian explanation of unemployment (i.e. a deficiency of aggregate demand). Instead it continues to have faith in Say's Law (that supply creates its own demand) and attempts to make prices flexible enough to ensure market clearing. This is a **supply-side** policy and is in sharp contrast with the **demand-side** emphasis of Keynesians' management of aggregate demand to reduce unemployment.

8.3 Demand-side policy and practice

The macroeconomic sections of first-year economics textbooks typically develop a model of national income determination based on the circular flow of income between firms and households. Additions to the circular flow include government expenditures, investment by companies and export earnings. Withdrawals from the circular flow include taxation, savings by firms and households and expenditures on imports. If additions to the circular flow are greater than withdrawals from it the national output expands to meet the increased spending, leading to the recruitment of more workers. Hence, by varying the levels of government spending and taxation (discretionary fiscal policy) the government can control the level of aggregate demand and so control the levels of employment and unemployment. In this Keynesian analysis, demand calls forth supply (a reversal of Say's Law).

The use of fiscal policy supposedly gives the government more direct control over aggregate demand than any measures it can use to influence domestic and corporate savings, investment by companies and spending on imports and exports. Hence fiscal policy and its associated multiplier effects can be used to 'crowd in' private spending. However Part I demonstrated that government intervention may lead to crowding out because of the potential impact of high marginal rates of taxation on the incentive to work and because of the potential implications of public sector borrowing for interest rates (and therefore interest-sensitive expenditures) and the money supply (and therefore inflation). Hence, fiscal policy must be consistent with the needs of monetary policy (i.e. the control of interest rates, money supply and inflation), operating within a monetarist perspective.

Bearing this counter-argument in mind, demand-side policies would include increased government expenditures on welfare (low income groups having a high marginal propensity to consume) and other transfer payments (e.g. regional policy), and on exhaustive expenditures such as infrastructural investments in road building. Tax cuts could also be used to boost private consumption expenditures but are generally regarded by Keynesians as less effective than increases in public expenditure because some of the tax cut is saved whereas all of the public expenditure is spent. Hence, for the same monetary value, public expenditure generates larger multipliers than tax cuts. Both taxes and public expenditures could simultaneously be used to promote equity by altering the distribution of income (in cash and in kind).

However the crowding-out argument states that tax cuts and increased government spending do not constitute a net addition to aggregate demand because they simply lead to public expenditure replacing private expenditure. For example, higher public expenditure financed by borrowing may lead to expectations of higher future tax rates, which in turn may lead to increased savings rates (by consumers and producers) in order to meet those higher future tax liabilities. Hence rational private sector expectations of government policy may cause private spending to fall. In other words, the private sector's actions may compensate for public sector actions, with the effect that the public sector grows at the expense of the private sector.

Moreover, since it is asserted that the productivity of the private sector is greater than that of the public sector, the economy's productive potential is reduced, leading to lower economic growth (see Chapter 3). This is exacerbated to the extent that increased social security payments create a dependency culture, stifling individual enterprise on the part of those who are capable of supporting themselves. In summary therefore, demand-side policies are regarded as at best short-term measures and at worst counterproductive of long-term growth. The long-term strategy then becomes one of removing constraints on supply.

8.4   Supply-side policy and practice

Supply-side policies seek to remove constraints or impediments on output. In Keynesian analysis the greatest impediment on supply is lack of aggregate demand. Hence the most effective supply-side measure is the demand-side measure of expansionary fiscal policy to boost aggregate demand. This is a macroeconomic solution to supply-side constraints. However in the mid 1970s the then Labour prime minister conceded that the government could no longer spend its way out of a recession. In part, this reflected the increasing dominance of monetarism over Keynesian economics. However it also reflected the beginning of a shift from major reliance on macroeconomic solutions towards micro-economic measures. Hence the increasing disillusionment with fiscal policy was not restricted to the Conservative Party.

For four decades after 1945 macroeconomic policy was directed at the control of output and employment and microeconomic policy at the control of inflation (e.g. the control of credit creation by commercial banks). This was reversed during the 1980s and 1990s, when macroeconomic policy was used to control inflation and microeconomic policy was used to remove supply constraints. Control of inflation and improvements on the supply side of the economy became the two main objectives of the economic strategy of both Conservative and Labour governments. Control of inflation was not so much a faithful application of monetarist rules to control the money supply as a refusal to adopt Keynesian reflationary policies in response to unemployment (see Chapter 11). Supply-side measures involved the removal of impediments preventing people and firms responding quickly to changing market conditions.

The economic strategy reflected the dispute over the relative significance of demand and supply factors in determining output and employment. The dispute concerned whether stagnant or falling output and rising unemployment was due to restrictive fiscal and monetary policies or due to supply constraints (especially labour market rigidities). Frequent references were made during the early 1980s to the large amounts of spare capacity that existed in British industry and hence the potential for expansionary fiscal policy to boost output and employment. However, just as economics distinguishes between nominal and effective demand (the latter being backed by purchasing power), so must it distinguish between nominal and effective supply.

Effective supply is not the same as physical capacity. The former will be less than the latter if real labour costs are too high, if the requisite skills are in short supply or if the technology forming that capacity is obsolete. Hence it is **economic** capacity that is relevant and this will be dependent upon supply constraints in other factor markets. In other words, aggregate supply may be so inelastic that expansionary fiscal policy would have little impact on the level of unemployment. In this analysis, unemployment is the result of deficiencies in aggregate supply rather than a deficiency of aggregate demand. It can be argued that the policy makers of the 1950s, 1960s and 1970s tended to overestimate the elasticity of aggregate supply and that this explains the apparently increasing impotence of Keynesian demand management. In fact it never was potent in this analysis. It only worked if aggregate supply was highly elastic. Increasing government intervention in the economy and an increasing degree of monopoly power led to the accumulation over time of supply constraints. This hypothesis of an **increasing inelasticity of aggregate supply** could be used as an alternative to that of a **deficiency of aggregate demand** to explain the recurrent economic crises of the 1950s, 1960s and 1970s. Neither hypothesis is readily refuted.

In terms of the 'inelastic aggregate supply' hypothesis, Say's Law was increasingly being pre-empted by supply constraints. Here the solution is not to expand demand but rather to reduce the constraints on supply in each and every market in which they are binding. This explains the shift in the focus of economic policy from macroeconomic to micro-economic solutions to what had previously been seen as macroeconomic problems. The microeconomic sections of first-year economics textbooks begin by developing the model of perfect competition, whose basic assumptions are that there are many buyers and sellers, freedom of entry and exit and perfect knowledge. Hence supply adjusts immediately to changes in demand conditions (and vice versa). In other words there are no constraints on supply. Textbooks then go on to develop models of monopoly, monopolistic competition and oligopoly, all of which contain supply constraints.

The monopolist reduces output below the perfectly competitive level so as to raise prices and make monopoly profits. Monopolistic firms practising product differentiation also have a lower output because marginal revenue is less than price, as is the case for monopoly. Similarly, the output of oligopolistic firms tends to be constrained because the interdependence of a few large suppliers means that they are unwilling to engage in price competition (i.e. the demand curve is kinked). The achievement of long-run economic growth therefore depends on the removal of supply constraints caused by the various manifestations of monopoly power. Hence, in this context, economic policy must be concerned with supply-side rather than demand-side measures, with boosting of supply rather than demand. If fiscal policy is used to boost aggregate demand but supply constraints remain totally binding then the only result is inflation, not increased employment. Supply-side constraints therefore have the potential to explain the failure of expansionary fiscal policy for reasons beyond the theoretical disagreements between Monetarists and Keynesians regarding monetary and fiscal policy.

Rather than making a choice between monetarists and Keynesians, both the Conservative and Labour government in effect opted for a return to the pre-Keynesian neoclassical *laissez-faire* by leaving markets to allocate resources but improving their operations wherever possible. This explains why both Conservative and Labour governments of the 1980s and 1990s eschewed **both** extreme monetarism and extreme Keynesian economic policies in response to inflation and unemployment. They neither followed a strict monetary rule nor adopted fiscal reflation. The perceived problem and its supposed solution were much more pragmatic than choosing between the stereotyped 'mad monetarists' and 'wet liberal Keynesians'. Government policy became increasingly focused on maintaining macroeconomic stability whilst identifying and removing long-embedded impediments to supply.

Conservative governments' 'rolling back the frontiers of the state' and supply-side policies were maintained by the subsequent Labour government but the latter paid increasing attention to macroeconomic stability. Macroeconomic stability related to avoiding the 'booms and busts' of earlier decades, which were thought to reduce economic growth. This is because uncertainty is thought to discourage private sector investment, not just in machines and buildings but also in people and ideas. Monetary policy focused on securing low and stable levels of inflation through interest rate adjustments. The failure of earlier attempts to control the money supply and its uncertain influence on inflation led to the conclusion that control of the interest rate was the more pragmatic policy instrument. However, it was thought that the interest rate needed to be set free from political manipulation. Hence, control of the interest rate was handed over to the Bank of England's newly constituted Monetary Policy Committee (MPC), the MPC being given the task of using it to achieve a target rate of inflation of 2.5 per cent (measured by the retail price index minus mortgage interest payments). Fiscal policy became focused on the long term, way beyond the short time horizons of the trade cycle. Central governments eschewed use of taxation and public spending to control aggregate demand. Instead, they became increasingly focused on improving the nation's stock of human capital and enabling people to free themselves from welfare dependency by finding paid work. Rather than using fiscal policy to fine-tune the economy in the short term, the post 1997 Labour government used fiscal policy to promote economic growth in the long term by increasing both the supply of labour and its productivity. The traditional Labour government objective of full-employment was replaced by a broader socio-economic objective of reducing social exclusion by achieving employment opportunity for all whilst recognising the changing nature of work in the 'knowledge-driven economy'.

By such means, it was thought that the level of unemployment could be reduced much further than in the past before inflation began to occur. This would result in sustained periods of non-inflationary growth. In effect, the interest rate is a short-term monetary instrument for the control of inflation whilst public expenditure and taxation become long-term fiscal instruments by which to control inflation through their impact upon the supply and productivity of the factors of production. In terms of the macroeconomic jargon, supply-side policies reduce the **natural rate of unemployment** (a monetarist concept) or reduce the **non-accelerating inflation rate unemployment** (a Keynesian concept). Despite their theoretical differences, both monetarists and Keynesians accept that the equilibrium rate of unemployment can be reduced in the long term by supply-side policies.

The route to employment opportunity for all, and so to social inclusion, now goes through the supply-side of the economy, the demand-side route having failed to reach the desired destination. Fiscal policy under the Conservative and Labour governments of the 1980s and

1990s became increasingly concerned with making structural changes to the supply side of the economy – crucially and strategically different from its conventional demand-side orientation during the 1950s, 1960s and 1970s. For example, from a conventional demand-side perspective, investment is simply an injection into the circular flow of income to boost aggregate demand. The new supply-side perspective adopts a more strategic definition of investment to include education and training, because no amount of investment in physical capital can compensate for a poorly trained and educated workforce.

Removing impediments to supply required a plethora of both momentous and seemingly trivial reforms during the 1980s and 1990s, which in combination could liberate aggregate supply from its pervasive constraints. Those reforms will now be analysed for both public and private sectors. Note, however, that such a classification of supply-side policies is rather artificial since many reforms affect both sides of the economy.

8.5   Supply-side policies for private markets

Supply-side policies concentrated on 'helping markets work better'. This was the headline used for a succession of HM Treasury 'Economic Progress Reports' in the mid to late 1980s, the phrase subsequently reappearing from time to time in government documents (e.g. see the 1998 quotation at the beginning of this chapter). Better functioning markets keep prices and costs down, thus facilitating achievement of the government's inflation target in the long term (the MPC's use of interest rates being a short-term measure). Those focusing on private markets can be categorised as follows.

Labour markets

In its 1985 White Paper *Employment: The Challenge for the Nation*, the then Conservative government stated that 'the biggest single cause of the UK's higher unemployment is the failure of our jobs market, the weak link in the economy'. It argued that the cause of unemployment at the time was not lack of demand, nor lack of public investment nor technological change. Instead labour needed to be improved in terms of quality, cost and incentives, flexibility and freedom (including less regulation by government and unions). The subsequent Labour government likewise took the view that unemployment is caused by the 'unemployability' of the unemployed, rather than a lack of demand for their labour. Unemployability is apparently demonstrated by the coincidence of high levels of vacancies and high unemployment in particular geographic areas. Increasing emphasis was placed on creating a labour market flexible and adaptable enough to respond effectively to structural change. Measures during the 1980s and 1990s included the following.

First, making work pay and so increasing the incentives to work. This involves cuts in the rates of income tax, cuts in low-paid employees' national insurance contributions, introduction of a national minimum wage (in 1999), introduction of a tax credit for low-paid workers with families to support (the 1999 Working Families Tax Credit – see Chapters 10 and 12), reducing the rates at which in-work benefits are withdrawn as income increases and so on. The intention is to reward skills and responsibilities and to make more people better off in work than out of it by reducing the unemployment trap (see Chapters 4 and 9). Prior to the national minimum wage, the then Conservative government abolished 'wages councils' in 1993. These had previously set minimum legal wage rates for more than 2.5 million workers in a range of jobs in shops, hotels, catering and hairdressing establishments and so on. That Conservative government argued that wages were too high and employment too low as a result. Hence abolition of *sector-specific* minimum wages would allow workers to price themselves back into work. However, the subsequent Labour government took the view that very low wages didn't make work worthwhile and so introduced the *national minimum wage* in 1999. The Conservative Party subsequently dropped its opposition to the national minimum wage once it became apparent that it had not cost jobs.

Second, helping people move from welfare to work. Both Conservative and Labour governments believed that a strong welfare state should avoid creating a dependency culture. It should underpin, not undermine, a competitive economy. They therefore sought to remove barriers to work using a combination of 'carrots and sticks'. For example, in 1998 the Labour government introduced a New Deal initiative as part of its Welfare to Work programme. It consists predominantly of employment and training schemes. The New Deal (in its various forms) applies automatically to young people aged 18–24 who have been claiming Jobseeker's Allowance (see Chapter 9) for six months. Financed by a windfall tax on the privatised utilities, it provides a period of intensive counselling, after which participants either get a job (unsubsidised) or, alternatively, choose one of four options (the 'carrots'). These are a subsidised job with an employer (taken by 25 per cent), work on an environmental project (taken by 12 per cent), voluntary work (13 per cent), or full-time education or training (50 per cent). Individuals refusing to participate in the scheme have their benefits cut (the 'stick'). In other words, there was no fifth option of staying at home on full benefit. The New Deal was later applied (with varying 'carrots and sticks') to the long-term unemployed aged 25 and over, to lone parents, disabled people, and non-working partners aged under 25 of unemployed social security claimants without children.

Third, encouraging self-employment through provision of financial assistance, awareness seminars, business start-up courses and so on. Initiatives included the Enterprise Allowance Scheme, paying formerly unemployed people £40 a week for a year to help start up their own businesses.

Fourth, encouraging greater occupational mobility through reforms to occupational pensions. *Occupational pensions* are generally 'portable' within the public sector, meaning that public sector employees can take their pension entitlements with them if they change employer within the public sector (e.g. moving from one local government employer to another). In the private sector, however, *company pensions* are usually frozen when an employee changes jobs. The value of an employee's frozen pension is substantially reduced by even moderate levels of inflation if the ensuing period up to retirement is, say, ten or fifteen years. This has the effect of progressively reducing occupational mobility as an employee accumulates 'pensionable years' (and pension entitlement) with his or her current employer. This can act as a major supply-side constraint inhibiting the efficient operation of labour markets, especially for key white-collar and professional employees. Legislation passed in the mid 1980s required pension schemes to protect and increase early leavers' pension rights. Furthermore employees were given the right to join *personal pension* schemes, to which tax relief was applied and which, unlike company schemes, are portable between different employers and therefore do not deter movement. Employees were also enabled to make *additional voluntary contributions* (AVCs), with tax relief, to a scheme separate from their occupational schemes. Those remaining within their occupational scheme could purchase *additional years* of pensionable service, up to the prescribed maximum. '*Stakeholder*' *pensions* were introduced in the late 1990s to extend pension entitlements to those on low incomes and who do not benefit from occupational pension schemes. Besides removing a supply constraint, these pension reforms are also intended to help reduce the burden on the state retirement pension (see Chapter 9).

Fifth, encouraging greater geographical mobility through reform of the housing market. Minimum periods of residence in a local authority's area are usually required before a person qualifies to be put on waiting lists for council housing. This deters geographical mobility since the council tenant (head of household) moving to a job in another local authority would have additional accommodation expenses (e.g. of a private bed-sit or boarding house) until his or her family were allocated a council house in the new area. Hence the government encouraged the sale of council houses to sitting tenants in the belief that they would become more mobile as owner-occupiers, able to move from one area to another by selling and buying residential properties (see below). This was further encouraged by cuts in the stamp duty payable on house purchase and abolition of solicitors' monopoly on conveyancing. Increased mobility was also facilitated by measures such as assured and shorthold tenancies designed to increase the amount of privately rented accommodation by allowing landlords to receive a reasonable rate of return whilst safeguarding the interests of private tenants.

Sixth, abolition of the national insurance surcharge in 1984/5. This had been dubbed *'a tax on jobs'*, since it cost private sector employers several billion pounds a year in the early 1980s. Hence its abolition was expected to encourage employers to increase their recruitment of labour. Likewise, the 1997 Labour government reduced both employers' and employees' national insurance contributions for the lowest paid workers in order to encourage their employment (see Chapter 10).

Seventh, reducing the powers of trade unions. The early to mid 1980s was characterised by over three million unemployed, rising real wages and rising vacancy rates. Say's Law appeared to be contradicted by events, the excess supply of labour seeming to exert insufficient downward pressure on real wage levels for those job vacancies to be filled. Despite high job vacancy rates, the long-term unemployed were not pricing themselves back into work. One explanation could be that they were not being allowed so to do by trade unions. Hence the then Conservative government attempted to weaken the industrial power wielded by trades unions. Legislation was passed requiring *secret ballots* before taking industrial action (if unions are to retain immunity from legal action), for the election of union officials, and for the approval of 'closed shops' (which make union membership compulsory for all employees of a firm). These reforms could also be regarded as democratising trades unions. *Secondary picketing* was also made subject to civil litigation. These measures were expected to increase the flexibility of the price of labour. By the late 1990s, trade union membership was at its lowest level since 1945. The greatest fall in membership was amongst male, manual and industrial blue-collar workers, in part reflecting the decline of manufacturing employment. Decline in membership has been comparatively slow amongst women, part-time and white-collar workers, especially in the public sector. About a third of the workforce was still covered by union recognition agreements for collective bargaining on pay and conditions by the end of the 1990s.

Eighth, encouraging companies to develop profit-related pay and share option schemes by giving relief against income tax. This was intended to give employees a direct stake in their company's performance and hence improve labour flexibility over wages and other conditions of work (e.g. demarcation rules).

Ninth, filling the 'skills gap' by expanding further and higher education. Shortages of skilled labour can lead to inflationary pay increases even though unemployment is relatively high. This is because unemployment is disproportionately concentrated among unskilled workers. For example, in 1997 only 3.5 per cent of those with higher education qualifications were unemployed compared with 12.4 per cent of those with no qualifications. In between those extremes, the higher the qualification the lower the rate of unemployment. The free market tends to fail to provide training because the newly-skilled employees are easily 'poached' by rival employers. Hence, it is often argued that the UK's labour force is deficient in craft and technical skills. This leads to poorer quality manufactured goods and could explain the relatively poor performance of UK manufactured goods on home and world markets. Hence, there have been an almost bewildering number of training initiatives during the 1980s and 1990s. They have included increased and improved provision of vocational education and training in schools, colleges, the work place and so on, including adult training and retraining. Initiatives included the Technical and Vocational Education Initiative, city technology colleges, PICKUP (a programme to update work-force skills), the Youth Training Scheme (for school leavers), job clubs and the Job Training Scheme. All were expected to increase the availability of labour with skills appropriate to employers' needs.

Tenth, assistance searching for jobs. Long-term unemployment is not only positively correlated with lack of qualifications but also with lack of recent work experience. The long-term unemployed often lack motivation to find a job and employers are often reluctant to hire them because they fear they will not be productive workers. The long-term unemployed are therefore thought to need advice and guidance, the rationale for schemes such as Restart (counselling for the long-term unemployed), Jobclubs, Jobplan, Jobsearch and so on. Their titles being largely self-explanatory, they typically consist of workshops, seminars and interviews aimed at helping people identify and apply for suitable jobs, presenting themselves more effectively at interviews and in their curriculum vitae, giving and receiving support from others and so on.

Eleventh, employment subsidies. These are financial incentives to encourage employers to recruit workers from the ranks of the unemployed. They have included employers' national insurance contribution 'holidays' and Workstart (a pilot wage subsidy scheme for employers taking on people unemployed for two years or more).

Twelfth, encouraging employers to end ageism. Employers are more likely to shed ageing workers than younger employees and are less likely to recruit older workers. Combined with an increasing incidence of voluntary early retirement of older men, ageism was thought to be leading to an age imbalance in the work force with consequent loss of skills and experience. Hence, the New Deal programme (noted above) was also extended on a voluntary basis to the third of people aged 50 and over who were outside the labour market and in receipt of welfare payments for six months or more.

A brief evaluation. Although the details differed, the broad thrust of their various initiatives was common to the Conservative and Labour governments of the 1980s and 1990s. Typically, each new initiative responded to the criticisms regarding its predecessor(s). Whether those initiatives were successful is difficult to determine. There are severe methodological difficulties in separating out the effects of one initiative from another (there having been 42 welfare-to-work schemes in operation in the UK in 1997 alone) and from other exogenous influences on employment and so on. Even if that separation could be undertaken, counting people placed in jobs exaggerates a scheme's effectiveness if many of those people would have found work without the scheme, albeit not as quickly (referred to as *deadweight*). Exaggeration also occurs if the new recruit (bringing a wage subsidy for the employer) *substitutes* for an existing (but unsubsidised) employee or other person looking for work with the same firm, or if additional jobs in one firm *displace* jobs elsewhere. **Deadweight, substitution** and **displacement** reduce the **net additionality** of a scheme but their impact is hard to measure. Critics argue that whilst such schemes benefit particular individuals they do not create sustainable 'real' jobs and their net impact on overall unemployment is insignificant. The counter-response is that such schemes are not meant to be short-term fixes for unemployment but, instead, aim to improve the employment potential of their target groups in the long term, thus increasing the effective supply of labour. They have to be seen as only one part of a much more comprehensive and co-ordinated supply-side policy.

Studies by the National Institute for Economic and Social Research, the Institute for Employment Research, the Joseph Rowntree Foundation, the Institute of Fiscal Studies and the Industrial Society broadly judged the New Deal programmes to be a success. The NIESR concluded that the New Deal was effectively self-financing in terms of the unemployment and other benefits saved. The IER found participants to have very positive perceptions of the New Deal programmes (especially young people and single parents). The JRF also found that an 'encouraging proportion of the jobs were sustained and that the New Deal made a real difference to a range of different groups'. The IS and IFS found that the New Deal had a broader value in reconfiguring the employment service. The 1997 Labour government's own measure of the success of supply-side initiatives to help labour markets work better is *'employment opportunity for all'*. Not everyone will take advantage of the opportunities created by these various initiatives. The government regards employment opportunity for all as the modern definition of full employment. Supply-side measures are intended to help individuals compete effectively for jobs, create a secure transition from welfare to work and provide financially rewarding employment. These objectives underpin the policies analysed in Chapters 9, 10 and 12.

Capital markets

A series of measures were introduced during the 1980s and 1990s to remove central government controls (i.e. supply constraints) over financial markets. The objective was to allow financial capital to find its most efficient use. The main measures included the following.

First, abolition of foreign exchange controls in 1979, which was intended to allow finance to find the most profitable investments, even if overseas, rather than restrict investment opportunities to the domestic economy. Removal of those controls also allowed holiday-makers to take as much currency with them as they wished. Previously there were very strict limits on the amount of currency that could be taken abroad, requiring holiday-makers to pay for as much as possible before leaving the UK.

Second, abolition of dividend controls on companies' shares in 1979, again to encourage finance to find the most profitable corporate investments.

Third, abolition of controls on bank lending in 1980. Previously, bank loans were effectively rationed by central government's administrative controls over credit creation. This had been the microeconomic means of controlling inflation noted above. The abolition of controls reinstated lending decisions to financial markets.

Fourth, abolition of hire purchase (HP) controls in 1982 in order that HP (offered by companies selling consumer durables such as kitchen appliances and cars) could compete equally with bank loans in the market for credit.

Fifth, reform/privatisation of publicly controlled banks (the Trustee Savings Bank and Girobank) in order to allow them to compete more effectively with the commercial banks and, again, free capital markets from unnecessary control. Both banks subsequently merged with mainstream commercial banks.

Sixth, reform of building societies in order to allow them to compete more fully with banks, for example by offering cheque accounts and non-housing loans. Previously, building societies had been restricted to providing mortgages and deposit accounts. The commercial banks were increasingly competing with the building societies for mortgage business but the societies were not allowed to compete with the banks for provision of general banking services. This was regarded as increasingly anti-competitive. Following the liberalising reforms, all the societies provided more or less the full range of banking services. Indeed, some subsequently demutualised, their members voting for conversion to banks, receiving free shares and so being transformed from members or policy holders to shareholders. Critics of conversion bemoaned the loss of the supposed benefits and philosophy of mutuality. Advocates of conversion highlighted the benefits of shareholding (i.e. former members received free shares typically worth several thousand pounds).

Seventh, reform of the operations of the Stock Exchange and stockbrokers to increase competition in brokerage services and improve the service to the public, so encouraging more widespread shareholding.

Eighth, encouraging wider share ownership by privatisation of former state-owned enterprises, reducing stamp duty on Stock Exchange transactions, abolishing the investment income surcharge component of income taxation, providing tax incentives for the profit-sharing schemes noted above, and providing tax relief on government-approved personal savings and investment schemes (see Chapter 10).

Ninth, abolition of income tax relief on the premia of new life assurance policies in order to reduce distortions of the savings market.

Finally, reform of corporation tax in order to remove the distortions to investment caused by differential tax relief on different sorts of company finance (e.g. debt and equity financing). The intention was to make investments in physical plant and machinery more truly profitable, rather than only profitable after qualifying for tax relief (see Chapter 10).

Land and property markets

Reforms of land and property markets during the 1980s and 1990s were intended to remove unnecessary controls inhibiting economic development both nationally and in particular regions and cities. Measures included the following.

First, removal of unnecessary planning controls, so as to remove unnecessary restrictions on the development of land for commercial and other purposes. Some degree of control over the location of economic activity is necessary in order to deal with, say, negative externalities arising from industrial processes. In promoting the public interest, governments have typically prevented the location of polluting activities in cities or otherwise in close proximity with residential areas (see Chapter 2). However, various developments have arguably increased the need for flexibility in those controls. These include de-industrialisation, the shift of people and jobs from urban to rural areas and the development of the service sector. Governments are increasingly concerned with the need to restore the economic, social and demographic base of cities. Such restoration may have been increasingly inhibited by unnecessarily stringent controls over physical redevelopment.

Second, reducing the public sector's holdings of land and property by requiring or encouraging local government and other public sector bodies to sell land and buildings to the private sector. Again, the objective is to facilitate physical and economic redevelopment, particularly in depressed local economies. During the 1980s local authorities were required to prepare registers of land and to make them available for consultation by potential private developers. Nevertheless, according to an Audit Commission report, local governments were still holding on to surplus land and buildings at the end of the 1990s. The Commission estimated that about a fifth of council property was surplus to requirements, that surplus having a value in the region of £15 billion. Many councils own prime properties and enterprises, including airports and the freehold of shopping centres. Both Conservative and Labour governments have taken the view that such holdings are not the essence of local government. Sale of such assets could raise several billion pounds a year and reduce the need for wasteful maintenance expenditures on surplus properties, so releasing funds for education and welfare services. The 1997 Labour government's projections of privatisation receipts up to and beyond the year 2000 show local government contributing the major part of such revenues (see Chapter 13).

Third, stimulating regional land markets by abolishing Industrial Development Certificates and Office Development Permits, which had previously constrained development in prosperous regions, as a complement to regional policy financial incentives to encourage firms to locate new investment in depressed regions. Payment of regional policy financial assistance was also made more selective and less automatic in order to target private firms genuinely in need of financial encouragement to relocate activities to depressed regions.

Fourth, stimulating inner-city land markets through the creation of redevelopment bodies and tax incentives for physical redevelopment. Examples of the former include urban development corporations and the Urban Regeneration Agency, with remits to redevelop long-derelict inner-city sites by maximising the involvement of private companies. Examples of the latter include enterprise zones which, *inter alia*, offer relief against local property taxes. Simplified planning zones have also been designated in certain areas.

Fifth, liberalising housing markets to facilitate choice of residential location and housing sector. The UK differs from other European countries, not just in terms of the predominance of owner-occupation of housing, but also in terms of the dominance of the state (traditionally local government) in providing rental housing. Not-for-profit organisations and the private sector are relatively undeveloped as providers of rental housing. Councils have near monopolies and give prospective tenants very little effective choice, tenancies being allocated strictly according to bureaucratically assessed need. Encouragement of both owner occupation and greater diversity in the rental sector is thought to enable workers to move in search of jobs, thus removing a supply constraint in labour markets (as noted above). This has been achieved in large measure by reducing the housing role of local government in four ways. **Firstly**, by giving council tenants the *right to buy* (RTB) their rented houses and flats, purchase being encouraged by increasing council rents and by giving discounts (on the market value of the dwelling) of up to 60 per cent. The longer their tenancy the greater the discount, the average being 50 per cent. Just over 2 million dwellings had been sold under RTB by the year 2000, nearly one third of council tenants having exercised their RTB. The eventual sale of RTB properties will lubricate housing markets in cities and neighbourhoods once dominated by council housing. **Secondly**, by not allowing councils to use the capital receipts from council house sales to build more homes. **Thirdly**, by severely restricting their use of borrowing to finance repairs whilst allowing housing associations (some charitable, others not-for-profit companies) access to such private finance, secured against future rent payments. **Fourthly**, by allowing council tenants to vote for transfer of whole council estates to alternative 'registered social landlords' (RSLs), namely housing associations. Nearly half a million council homes were transferred during the late 1980s and 1990s, increasing numbers of transfers being expected over the first decade of the twenty-first century. The incentive for tenants to vote for transfer is that they benefit from improved repairs and customer-oriented service. The incentive for councils to seek transfer is that any housing debt remaining after sale to RSLs will be written off by central government. Notwithstanding the cumulative impact of these reforms, the market value of the remaining council housing was still around £200 billion in the year 2000.

Markets for goods and services

Here the intention of reforms during the 1980s and 1990s was to strengthen competition by freeing producers (including nationalised industries) of government control and subjecting them to full market discipline. Bureaucracy has to be replaced by market pressures in order to stimulate more effective management. Market prices and costs would therefore be minimised, thus keeping inflation in check and allowing unemployment to be reduced further before inflationary pressures begin to build. Measures included the following.

First, abolition of pay and price controls in 1979 in order to allow factor and product prices to adjust to market-clearing levels. Previously, governments had from time to time attempted to implement *prices and incomes policies*, typically reaching (formal or informal) agreements with trades unions to moderate their wage claims on condition that prices of basic food items and domestic energy supplies were frozen or tightly controlled (see Chapter 13). The success of such controls was questionable even under collective bargaining arrangements between powerful national unions and major employers. They were certainly inconsistent with the supply-side labour market reforms described above because they obstruct the free operation of markets.

Second, strengthening competition policy in 1980 and 1998. The 1980 Competition Act gave the Office of Fair Trading (OFT) powers to investigate individual firms and refer anti-competitive practices and mergers to the then Monopolies and Mergers Commission (MMC). The Commission was also given powers to investigate the efficiency of nationalised industries in a regular rolling programme of reviews. The 1998 Competition Act outlaws cartels and abuse of dominant market position. It gave the OFT and post-privatisation sector regulators (see Chapter 13) strong powers, including the power to impose penalties of up to 10 per cent of UK turnover. Measures to control the growth of monopoly power date from 1948, having been strengthened in a succession of legislative measures in 1956, 1964, 1965, 1968, 1973 and 1976, as well as in 1980 and 1998. Hence concern with the control of monopoly power was apparent even during periods when the efficacy of Keynesian demand management was accepted. However the earlier measures were primarily directed at the growth of monopoly power in the private sector, by controlling mergers of firms and their use of restrictive trade practices. It was not until the 1980 Act that the investigatory powers of the then MMC were extended to the former nationalised industries and to other bodies operating in markets where competition was limited by statute or by other special circumstances. This extension of monopoly legislation to the public sector marked an explicit recognition that the potential abuse of monopoly power was not restricted to the private sector. It was a tacit recognition that the public sector may not always act in the public interest (see Chapter 7). The 1998 Competition Act focused much more on conduct of dominant firms than on structure of the industry. This change of approach is captured in the renaming of the MMC as the Competition Commission.

Third, abolishing opticians' monopoly in the supply of spectacles. This subsequently led to much greater competition based, *inter alia*, on increased use of national advertising, 'free prescription sunglasses' type offers and same-day dispensing guarantees.

Fourth, abolition of solicitors' monopoly on conveyancing, i.e. dealing with the transfer of the legal title to property from seller to buyer. This subsequently led to estate agents, building societies and banks offering conveyancing services in addition to advertising properties for sale, providing mortgage finance and so on. Conveyancing became much more competitive as a result.

Fifth, liberalising bus services (both long distance and local) by ending the regulation of long-distance coach fares, abolition of road service licensing for bus transport and privatisation of the National Bus Company.

Sixth, deregulating domestic airline routes (in conjunction with EU aviation policy), ultimately allowing airlines to compete for landing rights at individual airports and to charge whatever fares they like. This subsequently led to the establishment of companies offering flight-only (i.e. no catering and so on) low-cost fares between major UK cities.

Seventh, liberalising shop opening hours, especially allowing Sunday trading. Prior to liberalisation, shop opening hours largely coincided with working hours in factories and offices, making it difficult for workers to shop at convenient times. Today, many shops and supermarkets are open until late in the evenings, all weekend and on most public holidays. Whilst some trades unions have criticised employers for putting pressure on shop staff to work unsociable hours, such flexibility in opening hours has been welcomed by shoppers generally and by two-earner households in particular.

Finally, encouraging the formation of small firms, thought to be more flexible and responsive to market conditions than large firms. In addition to the initiatives to encourage self-employment noted above, measures have included a lower rate of corporation tax for small firms, raised VAT thresholds (to relieve many small firms of its payment), the Business Expansion Scheme (providing tax relief for small unquoted companies' investments), local enterprise agencies (providing business advice for small firms) and a loan guarantee scheme.

8.6   Supply-side policies for the public sector

Monopoly power was not restricted to the private sector or to nationalised industries within the public sector (see Chapter 13). In whole areas of the economy, the public sector has been either the only supplier or so large in relation to total provision that its monopoly was near absolute. Rather than being the result of overwhelming economies of scale (and therefore efficiency), such monopolies were often the result of statutory constraints (e.g. formerly in public transport and energy) or of tax-financed provision free at the point of consumption (with the result that private producers found it virtually impossible to compete in education and health care).

Supply-side policies for the public sector can be divided between macro- and micro-policy responses. Each of these two categories took a number of forms.

Macro-policy responses

Macro-policy responses seek to improve supply-side conditions at the level of the **total** economy.

First, providing a stable macroeconomic framework based on permanently low inflation and sound public finances (the reasons for this fiscal prudence are explained above).

Second, cutting (or controlling the growth of) public expenditure such that its share of GDP would fall, so reducing any direct crowding out (see Chapters 3 and 9).

Third, cutting taxation so as to allow people to retain more of what they earned (a moral argument) and improve incentives to work (see Chapters 4 and 10).

Fourth, cutting the budget deficit, based on the moral view that the state should live within its means and on the economic theory that excessive public sector borrowing crowds out private expenditures through higher interest rates and/or inflation (see Chapters 5 and 11).

Fifth, reforming the social security system in order to reduce a perceived growing dependency culture (an assertion rather than a proven fact), to increase incentives to work, to reduce spending, and to promote equity by targeting benefits more accurately on needs (see Chapters 4, 9 and 12).

Finally, reducing (or constraining the increase in) public sector pay. Public expenditure restraint, the control of public sector borrowing and the pursuit of efficiency are all crucially dependent on trends in public sector pay, simply because of the importance of wages and salaries in total input costs. Wages and salaries account for about half of exhaustive public expenditures but more than two-thirds for the education service and three-quarters for the police service. The government seeks greater flexibility in public sector pay through local determination and performance related pay (PRP). For example, central pay bargaining in the Civil Service ended in 1996, all government departments and agencies now negotiate their own pay and grading. PRP was introduced for school teachers in 2000.

Micro-policy responses

Micro-policy responses seek to improve supply conditions for **individual** public sector activities.

First, transferring the activity to the private sector wherever possible. Provision of a public service need not necessarily require its production within the public sector itself. The sale of former state-owned enterprises such as British Telecom and British Gas demonstrates that the private sector is capable of providing many services previously provided by the public sector. The popular meaning of privatisation is the sale of the assets of the former nationalised industries and of local government (e.g. council houses). The sale of nationalised industries was intended to stimulate management reform, release their investment from public expenditure controls and raise revenue for the Exchequer (see Chapter 13). The sale of council houses was intended to increase labour market flexibility (as noted above). However the remit of the privatisation programme is much broader than simply the sale of assets. Privatisation also includes encouraging private sector provision of activities that remain the responsibility of the state (e.g. prisons). These will be considered below.

Second, questioning whether there is a continuing need for those activities which cannot be privatised. There may be activities carried out within the government that have outlived the need that gave rise to them, for example in the Civil Service.

Third, market testing through the creation of external markets. External markets have been created by the use of **competitive contracting**. Competitive tendering for provision of service **inputs** has long been the case, for example for major construction projects (e.g. motorways, hospitals and prisons) and provision of supplies and services (e.g. refuse sacks for local government refuse collection services). Private companies are invited to bid (tender) for contracts to supply such inputs. Opening public procurement practices to greater international competition is expected to reduce the costs of inputs for public sector services and so improve economy.

There has also been increasing use of private companies to supply public sector final and intermediate **outputs**. Where full privatisation of a service or activity is inappropriate, decisions to provide services remain within the public sector. Nonetheless their delivery may be entrusted to private sector companies by **contracting out**. There are two forms of contracting out: non-competitive and competitive.

- **Non-competitive contracting**: local governments for example, may contract out residential care of the elderly by approaching private residential companies directly, rather than seeking competitive bids from a number of alternative private residential homes. Such non-competitive contracting is thought to be more suitable for ensuring quality care for heavily dependent and vulnerable old people.

- **Competitive contracting**: companies and organisations are invited to submit competitive bids (tenders) for contracts in such areas as catering, cleaning and vehicle maintenance, areas where substantial private sector capacity exists. This is intended to stimulate competition in the supply of public sector services by making markets contestable between producers in the public and private sectors, the expectation being lower unit costs through increased efficiency. The emphasis is on achieving value for money rather than on the implementation of ideological dogma. Whilst private sector provision of public services is being encouraged, private companies must demonstrate that they can offer better value for money than any in-house providers. If they do, then **contracting out** occurs. If in-house providers win service contracts in competition with private companies, the result is **contracting in**. Hence the government does **not** insist on contracting out for its own sake. What it does insist on is competition (see below and Chapter 15).

Fourth, internal markets. Internal markets can be created **within** the public sector by creating a plurality of public providers. This is effectively 100 per cent contracting, whereby competitive bureaux seek to win government service contracts. Internal (or quasi) markets are most suitable where provision of services cannot be made by the private sector. Although problematic, they have been used, for example, in education and health whereby educational establishments (schools, colleges, universities) and hospitals compete for pupils/students and patients respectively. The NHS internal market was abolished by the 1997 Labour government because, for whatever reason, it did not work. Likewise, critics argue that schools do not openly compete for pupils, the 'educational market' being subdivided and school places often being allocated according to non-educational criteria such as the socioeconomic groupings of parents and so on. Put simply, experience shows that internal markets are much more complex than expected and they may not be appropriate for some public services (see 'Further Reading').

Fifth, creation of agencies. Agencies have been created where whole public services cannot yet be put out to tender and where internal markets cannot be created. They are given specific remits and are subject to performance appraisal. Agencies with which the reader may have been in contact include the Social Security Benefits Agency, the Child Support Agency, the UK Passport Agency, the Driver and Vehicle

Licensing Agency and the Employment Service. Agencies also provide weather forecasts, manage prisons, care for historic monuments and undertake local economic development activities.

Civil Service agencies are not an entirely new phenomenon, three having been created in the 1970s. However the widespread use of agencies had been implemented by the early 1990s. The formerly monolithic Civil Service was broken up into separate agencies focusing on individual services. The primary aim of the government's reform of the Civil Service is to raise standards of public service and improve value for money. Only a small part of the Civil Service is not suitable for agency status, namely the centres of government departments concentrating on policy making, strategic management, central purchasing and financial and personnel functions.

Agencies, as well as departments, must identify which of their activities can be contracted out or subjected to market testing. Whilst often associated with internal markets, they may also operate in non-competitive environments, the intention being to reduce day-to-day political intervention and allow more management freedom whilst acting in accordance with strategic objectives. These are also referred to as non-departmental public bodies or, more commonly, as quasi-autonomous non-governmental organisations (**quangos**), created by the deconstruction of former unitary provision by central and local government into a plurality of providers.

Whilst the introduction of agencies cannot be interpreted as privatisation by the back door, there have been criticisms from Civil Service trades unions, the Public Accounts Committee and others about possible job losses, poorer pay and conditions, poorer quality of service, problems of confidentiality and security of information, risks of corruption and loss of the Civil Service ethos. Of particular concern are any undesirable impacts on integrity, impartiality and parliamentary accountability (see Chapter 7). Many of these potentially adverse outcomes are held to be due to the financial and profit imperatives of commercialisation, market forces and working to contract. The validity of these claimed adverse effects, and the increases in quality and cost effectiveness claimed by central government, can only be assessed by objective research.

Finally, **user charges**. Charges could be used to make supply more responsive to demand. This will only be the case where service users have a genuine choice whether to use the service or not, for example a municipal leisure facility. They can also help to inform the voter/consumer of the 'true' cost of service provision. For example paying a proportion of dentistry costs may clarify the size of the tax-financed component (see Chapters 6 and 14).

8.7   The purchaser–provider split

The above examples have shown the increasingly clear distinction between the role of government in policy making, inspection and regulatory activities, and the way in which services are delivered or purchased. Separation of the specification and delivery of service distinguishes between the purchaser and provider of services (the purchaser–provider split). For example local government or hospital trusts could make contracts with private sector companies for the delivery of catering and cleaning services. In this example local authorities and hospitals are the purchasers, and private catering and cleaning companies are the providers. Chapter 15 provides details of the purchaser–provider split in central and local government. Hence this section restricts itself to a discussion of general principles.

Four separate stages can be distinguished for the delivery of services:

- provision of inputs
- the processing of inputs
- the resultant output
- the subsequent outcome.

The purchaser buys output from the provider. It is the purchaser's (not the provider's) responsibility to ensure that the output achieves the desired outcome and that the contract secures the output at cheapest cost. Payment provides the means for the provider to buy inputs and manage the process.

Figure 8.1 illustrates the purchaser–provider split for local government. The initial situation is Box 1, where a local authority is not the purchaser but the direct provider of service. Indeed there is no purchaser *per se*. Central government merely gives local government money to spend locally at its discretion without clearly specifying service levels or other contractual criteria. Three shifts from Box 1 are possible. A shift to Box 4 represents **contracting out** service provision to a private producer (e.g. residential care of the elderly). In this scenario local government is the purchaser but not the provider. A shift to Box 2 represents **contracting in**, where local government employees are successful in winning the service contract in competition with bids by private firms (e.g. for refuse collection, catering or cleaning). A shift to Box 3 represents **opting out**. Where schools choose to transfer control to central government (i.e. become grant-maintained schools), or where former council house tenants choose other public sector landlords, the purchaser–provider relationship remains within the public sector. However, where former council house tenants choose private sector landlords the purchaser–provider relationship is formally reconstituted within the private sector.

Figure 8.1 The purchaser–provider split

Purchaser
(e.g. a local authority
or a hospital trust)

		No	Yes
	Yes	1	2
	No	3	4

Provider
(e.g. a private catering
or cleaning company)

The diagram illustrates the change in emphasis brought about by the purchaser–provider split. Previously the emphasis was placed on controlling inputs and processes. Auditing and 'value for money' studies emphasise inputs. Management initiatives such as efficiency studies and performance review emphasise processes. Outputs and outcomes have traditionally been regarded as very difficult to measure and the impetus of service provision de-emphasised them in practice. However the purchaser–provider split emphasises outputs and outcomes. Individual production units are now responsible for their own inputs and processes since they must compete within the competitive contracting or internal markets framework, or have delegated financial management and budgeting responsibilities where public provision continues. Local and central government attention switches to securing the desired outputs and outcomes, resulting in a transformation from a producer-oriented public organisation to a consumption-oriented regulatory body.

The four main issues for evaluation include:

- the degree of individual choice
- the cost effectiveness of services
- equity
- the degree of control over total expenditure.

Evaluation is problematic and requires detailed ongoing research. However, outcomes ultimately depend on:

- market structure (whether truly competitive or not);
- accurate information about service costs and quality;
- the motivations of purchasers and providers (e.g. in terms of service development or profits);

- the potential for 'cream skimming' (e.g. taking the lowest cost cases only, to the exclusion of high-cost or needy clients);
- the enforceability of contracts in practice.

Results therefore differ service by service, between different geographical areas for the same service and over time as these key factors vary (see Chapter 15). These differential results demonstrate the inherent variability of supply-side initiatives in promoting both allocative efficiency and X-efficiency.

8.8   Private financing of public sector projects

Sale of former state assets and contracting out apply to activities previously undertaken by the state itself. Therefore the further development of these two initiatives is finite, limited by the number of activities that can be sold or contracted out. Potentially much more substantial over the longer term is the development of arrangements in respect of the private financing of public sector projects. There are two main initiatives.

The Private Finance Initiative

Mention has already been made of the introduction of private finance into public sector rental housing. Increased user-charges (i.e. rents) are other means of raising private finance. However, a specific initiative, the Private Finance Initiative (PFI) was launched by the former Conservative government in 1992 and was retained by the 1997 Labour government. Its objective is to increase the involvement of the private sector in the financing and management of projects and services that have traditionally been provided by the public sector. Hence it involves more than just private finance and, indeed, entails the use of public money. Nonetheless, the PFI has considerable potential to reduce total public expenditure, particularly capital spending. The aim is to involve the private sector in the provision of infrastructure and capital-intensive services. By the end of the 1990s it accounted for about an eighth of total publicly sponsored capital spending.

The 1997 Labour government subsumed the PFI under its Public Private Partnerships (PPPs) initiative. Perhaps more important than finance, PPPs were seen as a vehicle for improving service quality as they became increasingly concentrated in transport, health and local government. 'Partnerships between the public and private sectors are central to the Government's programme for modernising public services. By drawing on the best of both sectors, PPPs can help the public sector to deliver modern, high quality public services' (HM Treasury, *Budget*, March 2000, para. 3.91).

The PFI falls within the general supply-side principle of 'rolling back the frontiers of the state' by expanding the scope for private enterprise and its associated financial and management skills. Privatisation in the form of sales of assets was the major policy instrument during the 1980s and continued to a lesser extent during the 1990s. Competitive contracting is also enabling the private sector to provide services such as cleaning, catering and vehicle maintenance, mostly current expenditures (see Chapter 15). The PFI extends this philosophy to the provision of infrastructure. Contracting out and the PFI blur the conventional distinction between the public and private sectors (see Chapter 1).

Under the PFI the private sector is expected to bear the risks of project design, construction and subsequent management. The public sector continues to bear the risks pertaining to planning and Parliamentary processes. The private sector is also expected to contribute management expertise, provide access to world capital markets and avoid costs exceeding initial estimates. Public sector provision of infrastructural projects has often been characterised by time and cost over-runs created by over-elaborate, over-engineered projects that are frequently changed and poorly managed. The result is provision of infrastructure at excessive cost. Improved management and increased value for money would increase the provision of infrastructure financed by restricted public sector budgets. Hence the government expects the PFI to improve both the quantity and quality of the UK's infrastructure.

The PFI facilitates continued investment in infrastructure whilst simultaneously allowing the government both to control public sector borrowing and to reduce the tax implications of infrastructural investments (see Chapter 11). Hence it is argued both that the efficiency of individual projects will be increased and that there will be wider efficiency gains at the economy-wide level. Moreover, as was noted above, the public sector holds on to surplus capital assets and to assets which are unnecessarily expensive to maintain. Under the PFI, the private sector has greater incentives to dispose of such assets because their retention reduces profits.

Broadly three types of project fall within the remit of the PFI.

Financially free-standing projects, where private sector contractors recover all costs through user charges (e.g. bridge tolls). The public sector simply provides the usual planning permissions and so on. No other public funds are involved. The projects must generate sufficient social, economic or other non-user benefits. For example, the road bridge to the Isle of Skye was justified in that it would remove congestion and queues for the ferry services it replaced, and it was therefore expected to act as an important catalyst for the future development of the island. On the other hand the private operator was given monopoly power because the government required the nationalised Caledonian Macbrayne ferry company to withdraw its ferry service serving the same route and private sector ferry operators were unable to establish a competitive sea crossing. Monopoly tolls could jeopardise the development of the Isle of Skye. Similarly, second road bridge schemes over major rivers inevitably have to allow operators also to take over the operation of the first bridge (or tunnel) in order to prevent traffic switching between crossings. Hence, there is a possible trade-off between supply-side initiatives: stimulating greater competition inevitably reduces private sector interest in the PFI. For example, the privately financed cable bridge crossing of the River Thames at Dartford (called the Queen Elizabeth II Bridge) operates in parallel with two older tunnels under the River Thames. It provides a key link in the M25 orbital motorway round London and has to operate in conjunction with the two existing tunnels under the River Thames if traffic is not to divert to other crossings. The private sector consortium that built and financed the bridge consisted of a construction company, a merchant bank, a foreign bank and an insurance company. The consortium was given a concession to collect tolls for up to 20 years, but once the consortium breaks even on the bridge, ownership transfers to the government.

Joint ventures involving contributions from both public and private sectors but where private sector partners retain overall control and where the government's contribution is clearly defined and limited. Private sector partners in joint ventures should normally be secured through competition. They are expected to recover costs from user charges. The government's contribution can be in the form of concessionary loans, equity (but not a controlling share), transfer of existing assets (e.g. land for approach roads to a bridge), ancillary or associated works or any combination of these. In general, any subsidy or financial interest would be limited to the minimum amount necessary for the project to go ahead and secure the wider social benefits (e.g. from reduced congestion) that cannot be recovered through charges. In this way, public finance is said to lever private finance although, in practice, leverage works in both directions.

Services sold to the public sector by private firms, often where capital expenditure is a significant part of the total cost. Examples include residential care for the elderly, prison places, the incineration of clinical wastes on hospital sites and provision of kidney dialysis services to hospitals.

Other examples of private finance include the Lewisham extension of the Docklands Light Railway in London, the Manchester Metrolink tram system, the Heathrow Express rail link, and the Channel Tunnel rail link (the Channel Tunnel itself was constructed without any support from the taxpayer.)

The PFI requires a radical change of culture within the public sector. It has to negotiate deals with the private sector rather than operate in accordance with rules and fairly rigid procedures. Any public spending continues to count against a government department's capital allocation but the private sector's contribution is treated as additional to public provision, therefore representing net additionality. Hence it is intended that private finance plays a key role in improving the quantity and quality of the UK's capital stock.

However, public sector purchasers have to ensure achievement of value for money by comparing the costs of services provided in these ways with the cost of alternative means of provision. For example the cost of private sector provision of kidney dialysis services to hospitals should be compared with the hospitals' own costs of constructing the facilities and buying the equipment themselves. It is generally cheaper for central government to raise capital funds than for a private company (e.g. because central government cannot go bankrupt, the risk premium therefore being lower than for private companies). Hence higher private company borrowing costs must be more than offset by savings in other capital and operating costs in order for private provision to be cheaper than public provision. If not, total costs would increase and the public sector would incur unnecessarily high costs in enabling infrastructure to be provided.

Whatever the political hue, it appears that political parties have redefined the conventional dividing line between the public and private sectors (see Chapter 1). This is not peculiar to the UK, other countries in Europe and elsewhere also having PFI-type projects. The intention is not simply to shift costs from the public to private sector accounts. The PFI still requires the public sector ultimately to fund projects' assets and services unless there are user-charges (e.g. bridge tolls) which fully fund the project. The objectives for both main political parties are to achieve efficiency gains (by making use of more efficient private sector management and facilitate closer control of capital-spending budgets), transfer risk to the private sector and reduce pressure on public sector borrowing. Various PFI project studies by the National Audit Office suggest cost savings of between 10 and 20 per cent. These studies are 'snap shots' of long-term, highly disparate, projects. PFI schemes are not necessarily cheaper than public provision and not all achieve the same cost savings, again illustrating the variability of outcomes from supply-side initiatives. The Committee of Public Accounts concluded that estimates of costs depended upon highly complex calculations involving the exercise of judgement. Any savings depend upon the trade-off between relatively low early costs and relatively high future costs and, in particular, on the rate at which future costs are discounted to present values (see Chapter 5). Small changes in the discount rate have large impacts upon the assessment of cost savings. Too high a discount rate tends to overstate the net savings of PFI projects. Nevertheless, the NAO studies do illustrate the potential cost savings resulting from a contestable approach to the provision of service infrastructure.

Problems for the PFI

The general problem facing such initiatives is whether the private sector will be interested enough to make substantial capital expenditures. Private sector companies or consortia will only be interested in the cash flows that can be generated from such investments and will not take into account any public good or positive externality justifications for provision (see Chapter 2). Bridges or railway tracks have no inherent value for private commercial companies, nor for the banks from which they may have to borrow the funds to finance them. Where they are financed almost solely from debt (rather than from equity), interest payments may extend capital redemption periods beyond 20 or 25 years. Generally the longer the time span and the higher the real interest rate, the greater the financial risk of losses. Rapid inflation would reduce the real value of the borrowed sum and may lead to high nominal but low (even negative) real interest rates. In that case lenders would be subsidising borrowers and so the risk of loss would be reduced. Equity is an alternative to debt, private companies selling shares in order to finance an infrastructural project. The risk would then be transferred to shareholders, who would face the possibility of receiving low or no premium payments and/or capital loss (i.e. reduced resale value of their shares). Alternatively a tradeable infrastructure bond could be used to reduce risk (simply because it is tradeable), tax exemptions possibly being used to encourage this form of financing.

The key risk factors for (say) a bridge with tolls include:

- the gearing ratio (i.e. the balance between equity and debt finance)
- real interest rates
- the volume and mix of traffic (tolls differ for cars and light and heavy goods vehicles)
- the length of the franchise
- the real value of the toll
- the various elasticities of demand.

Price elasticity of demand measures the responsiveness of demand to a change in price at a particular point in time. The lower it is the less the risk of financial loss. Price elasticity of demand is significantly reduced in the case of second river crossings by giving the private company control of the first river crossing and its tolls. This arrangement reduces the substitutability of one crossing by another at lower cost and so reduces price elasticity. However, given the long time period over which the concession will operate, income elasticity of demand is also likely to be important. Rising real incomes will influence car ownership and the volume of retail and other goods sent by road. Hence the prosperity of the local and regional economy will ultimately determine the volume of traffic using a bridge. Similar caveats pertain to cross elasticities of demand between substitutes (e.g. rail), complements (e.g. petrol prices) and non-related goods (e.g. the cost of housing) that influence disposable incomes.

The operator is entirely dependent on the revenue stream where infrastructural assets revert to the public sector at the end of the concession period (i.e. there is no residual capital value relating to the land or assets constructed on it). Hence, in general, the longer the franchise the less the risk of financial loss. However, beyond a certain time horizon, longer franchises will entail expenditure on structural repairs as well as maintenance, so reducing net revenue and increasing risk. Banks issuing loans on such ventures will therefore prefer shorter payback periods (i.e. the time taken for the investment to generate sufficient funds to repay the outstanding debt) as a way of minimising risk. However, motoring organisations such as the Automobile Association argue that fast payback periods demonstrate that tolls are too high (i.e. are effectively monopoly prices).

As already noted, most of the PFI projects require a financial input (in cash or in kind) from the public sector. Ideally that contribution is the minimum amount necessary for the project to go ahead and no more than the marginal public policy benefit. If, however, such projects are regarded as effectively underwritten by the state, then the degree of risk transferred to the private sector is reduced, with the consequential loss of the potential benefits of private sector involvement. The PFI would then become simply a means of bypassing public expenditure control, leading to excessive (rather than insufficient) investment. In that case this supply-side initiative would have failed. Hence the public sector should identify projects that satisfy its policy objectives and seek private partners to secure their implementation in the most efficient way. Private partners need not necessarily be sought through competitive tendering but, if they are, the number of bidders is normally limited to three or four. Competitive tendering is not used where it may impair the stimulation of innovation; for example where a private company undertakes preparatory work prior to submitting a private finance proposal to the government. Again, this illustrates the complexity of an apparently simple supply-side initiative.

Planning gain

The PFI initiative has a smaller-scale precedent within the local government area called 'planning gain'. This usually refers to the situation where a private sector developer builds a capital facility and donates it to the relevant local authority; for example a road bypassing a small town or village where the developer is building a large housing estate. The increased road congestion resulting from the development requires the local authority to increase the capacity of the local road network. However, if the local authority is short of finance it will not be able to incur expenditures on the local road network and so the granting of planning permission by the local authority to the developer may have to be delayed. In order to expedite development, the developer may voluntarily offer to build a bypass in order to circumvent the local authority's budgetary constraint. In this way, private finance has long been used to expand the public sector's infrastructure at the local government level. The end result is similar to the PFI in that infrastructure is provided by the private sector. Its use increased markedly during the 1980s and 1990s, becoming formalised as *planning obligations*.

8.9 Conclusions

The casual observer may regard the many and varied reforms listed above as largely incoherent. A political scientist may rationalise the reforms as purely ideological, cuts in taxation and in public spending being an attempt to redistribute national income and wealth back towards a privileged minority. Alternatively the difficulty in actually cutting expenditure may suggest that political pragmatism explains the shift of emphasis to other reforms. However the analytical framework of Part I provides a coherent **microeconomic** explanation of this seemingly diverse set of public and private sector reforms. There is, indeed, an element of pragmatism in seeking to make existing resources go further by improving efficiency. More generally, achieving better value for money requires improved economy, efficiency and effectiveness in the provision of public and private sector outputs – the '3 Es'. Economic theory suggests that the most effective ways of promoting the '3 Es' is to stimulate competition, reward enterprise and effort, and give the customer (or service client) more economic power. Hence there is also a theoretical base in terms of the increased attention given to microeconomic reforms as a prerequisite of macroeconomic growth.

Keynesian economists argue that demand-side macroeconomic factors explain the bulk of the rise in unemployment during the first half of the

1980s. They argue that the main factors were an appreciating exchange rate (which makes UK goods less competitive), restrictive fiscal and monetary policies and slower growth of the world economy. However, both the Conservative and Labour governments came to see demand-side issues as essentially short-term concerns. Actions in response to unemployment were increasingly regarded as counterproductive to long-term economic growth. Hence economic policy focused on the supply-side, creating what were seen as the necessary and sufficient conditions for economic growth to occur spontaneously.

The examples of supply-side measures given above display considerable variation in scale and significance. However they are all intended to create the conditions necessary for the freer play of market forces, which in turn are expected to make the economy work more effectively. Individually they may appear to be insignificant but collectively they have the potential to make aggregate supply much more responsive to changing economic conditions. Whether this is the case in practice is not just a theoretical and empirical issue. It also reflects a lack of political will to continue the Keynesian-style interventions of the past few decades, there no longer being a belief in a macroeconomic 'magic wand' in the form of expansionary fiscal policy. It also reflects a moral stance that emphasises the responsibilities as well as the rights of the individual in preference to direct intervention by the state in economic and welfare issues.

Whilst the supply-side policies listed above are intended to **enable** markets to work properly, they are obviously not limited to the private sector. They are more generally known as the **enabling approach** that underpins the reform of the public sector generally. Enabling local government service provision operates not only through the purchaser–provider split but also, more generally, through the shift from government to governance. Enabling the Civil Service to function more efficiently involves the creation of executive agencies. Provision of physical infrastructure is being enabled by private finance. These examples make clear the all-pervasive nature of supply-side policies.

Refocusing on the theory, policy and practice of public sector economics, the emphasis on supply-side rather than demand-side measures illustrates how microeconomic reforms have become the foundation for sustainable macroeconomic growth. Whilst privatisation and trade union reforms have received the most public attention, supply-side reforms have been much more pervasive than this. As the formal privatisation programme approached its limits, increasing emphasis was placed on extension of competitive forces throughout the public sector as a whole and on improved management procedures for services even where competition was not feasible. The 'supply-side revolution' is an ongoing process as will be made evident in the following chapters.

Further reading

Audit Commission (online). Available from <http://www.audit-commission.gov.uk>.

Bartlett, W., Roberts, J. A. and Le Grand, J. (1998) *A Revolution in Social Policy: Quasi-market Reforms in the 1990s* (Bristol: The Policy Press).

Board of Trade (1994) *Competitiveness: Helping Business to Win*, Cm 2563 (London: HMSO).

Committee of Public Accounts (1998) *The Private Finance Initiative: The First Four Design, Build, Finance and Operate Roads Contracts*, Forty-Seventh Report Session 1997–98, House of Commons (London: The Stationery Office).

Department of Health (1997) *The New NHS: Modern, Dependable*, Cm 3807 (London: The Stationery Office).

Grout, P. (1997) 'The Economics of the Private Finance Initiative', *Oxford Review of Economic Policy*, vol. 13, no. 4, pp. 53–66.

Hasluck, C. (2000) 'Early Lessons from the Evaluation of New Deal Programmes', *Institute for Employment Research* (Sheffield: Employment Service).

Hasluck, C. (2000) 'The New Deal for the Long Term Unemployed – A Summary of Progress', *Institute for Employment Research* (Sheffield: Employment Service).

HM Treasury (1993) *The Private Finance Initiative: Breaking New Ground* (London: HMSO).

Holterman, S. *et al.* (1999) *Lone Parents and the Labour Market: Results from the 1997 Labour Force Survey and Review of Research* (London: Employment Service).

Jarvis, T. (1997) 'Welfare-to-Work: The New Deal', *House of Commons Library Research Paper 97/118* (London: House of Commons).

Joseph Rowntree Foundation (online). Available from <http://www.jrf.org.uk>.

Millar, J. (2000) 'Keeping Track of Welfare Reform: The New Deal Programmes', *Joseph Rowntree Foundation* (York: York Publishing Services).

National Audit Office (1999) *Examining the Value for Money Deals under the Private Finance Initiative* (London: NAO).

ONS (1999) *Social Trends 29*, Office for National Statistics (London: The Stationery Office).

Office of Public Service and Science (1993) *Next Steps Agencies in Government Review 1993*, Cm 2430 (London: HMSO).

Sargeant, G. and Whiteley, P. (2000) *A Good Deal Better: Reforming the New Deal* (London: Industrial Society).

Van Reenen, J. (2001) *No More Skivvy Schemes? Active Labour Market Policies and the British New Deal for the Young Unemployed in Context*, WP01/09 (London: Institute of Fiscal Studies).

Whitty, G., Power, S. and Halpin, D. (1998) *Devolution and Choice in Education: the School, the State and the Market* (Buckingham: Open University Press).

Wistow, G., Knapp, M., Hardy, B., Forder, J., Kendall, J., and Manning, R. (1996) *Social Care Markets: Progress and Prospects* (Buckingham: Open University Press).

Woods, P. A., Bagley, C. and Glatter, R. (1998) *School Choice and Competition: Markets in the Public Interest?* (London: Routledge).

9 Public Expenditure Policy and Practice

9.1 Introduction
9.2 The Public Expenditure/GDP Ratio
9.3 Cutting the Public Expenditure/GDP Ratio
9.4 Expenditure Components
9.5 Controlling Social Security Expenditure
9.6 Is Social Security Spending Out of Control?
9.7 The Changing Philosophy for the Welfare State
9.8 Conclusions

The Government's objective for public expenditure is that it should take a declining share of national income over time, while value for money is constantly improved. To meet this objective, public spending needs to grow more slowly over time than the economy as a whole. (*Financial Statement and Budget Report 1993–94*, London: HMSO, 1993, p. 74).

To give everyone the chance, through education, training and work, to realise their full potential and build an inclusive and fair society and a competitive economy (*Comprehensive Spending Review: Aims and Objectives*, London: HM Treasury, 1998, p. 3).

9.1 Introduction

Public services have a profound effect on people's standard of living and life chances or opportunities. Spending on public services is classified as exhaustive expenditure, that in the form of cash payments being classified as transfer expenditure (see Chapter 3). Cash transfers through the national social security system and public services such as education, health and housing are major components of the welfare states in all developed countries. Whilst both total transfer payments and total exhaustive expenditure are of approximately equal importance in the UK, exhaustive expenditure on public services is more than twice the size of social security payments. This emphasises the importance to living standards of payments in kind as well as those in cash.

Issues of social justice (including equity) are at least as important as efficiency criteria in the provision of services – many would argue that

163

they are more so. It is sometimes argued that efficiency improvements must not be achieved at the expense of equity. However inefficiency in the provision of public services has the result that opportunities for improved equity are lost because of the wasteful use of resources. This result may be exacerbated to the extent that both the provision and financing of public services crowds out the private sector and leads to reduced economic growth (see Chapters 4 and 5). Lower economic growth results in fewer resources being available to pursue social programmes.

Moreover, it has to be recognised that the provision and financing of public services is not simply concerned with the redistribution of income in favour of disadvantaged socioeconomic groups in society. Social justice is not only concerned with distributional issues, but also with equality of opportunity, individual responsibility for self-improvement and reward for merit and effort (see Chapter 12). In sharp contrast with the idea that the state promotes social justice, the leviathan state model of government suggests that rather than being socially enlightened, governments are rent-seeking, self-serving distributional coalitions benefiting those with the greatest effective political power (see Chapter 7). In this scenario, improvements in efficiency and in equity are not necessarily mutually exclusive. For example, where middle-class capture of public sector outputs occurs, the increased use of charges (supplemented by means-tested subsidies) can promote both efficiency and equity by relating payment for service to the costs of provision and the income of users (see Chapter 6).

Government public expenditure policies during the 1980s and 1990s became increasingly focused on supply-side initiatives (see Chapter 8). **First**, reducing crowding out by limiting the share of public spending in national income. **Second**, seeking more value for exhaustive public expenditures by introducing competition into public procurement and service provision. **Third**, seeking more value for money for transfer expenditures by requiring recipients of social security payments to pursue self-help strategies in finding paid work. **Fourth**, restructuring spending towards investments in human and physical capital.

Hence, public expenditure policy is much more than simply reducing spending as a proportion of national income. Put rather simplistically, public spending increasingly shifted away from **public consumption** and towards **public investment**. Public expenditure policy became highly **proactive in microeconomic terms** in seeking to improve the supply side of the economy. It became **passive in macroeconomic terms**, seeking stability on the demand side of the economy in order that supply-side measures could be effective. This crucial distinction helps understand the myriad of changes in public expenditure, for example on education and social security.

9.2   The public expenditure/GDP ratio

The long-term growth of public spending is shown in Table 9.1. It can be measured in absolute or relative terms.

Absolute measures: figures for cash spending reveal huge increases over the past few decades but take no account of the reduction in their purchasing power due to inflation. An assessment of changes in the purchasing power of public expenditure uses *constant prices* net of inflation. For example, the *constant 1998–9 prices* used in **Table 9.1** required cash figures for previous years to be increased (inflated) by an appropriate index of inflation over the intervening period, whilst those for later years have been reduced (deflated). This requires the inflation index used to derive real expenditures to be highly accurate. Whilst it may be fairly accurate in converting total expenditure to real terms it is much less reliable when applied to individual services or parts of services. This is because some services are highly labour intensive (e.g. education) whilst others are very capital intensive (e.g. transport). Hence, there will be differential inflation between services that will not be adequately reflected in a standardised index. For this reason, the published real expenditure series for individual services shown below in **Table 9.3** should be treated only as broad approximations rather than precise measures.

Although much less dramatic than those for cash expenditures, increases in real spending also reveal substantial increases over the past few decades. Whilst the cash figure never fell from one year to the next, the real figure has occasionally fallen: in the late 1960s, in the mid 1970s, in the mid 1980s, and in the mid 1990s. However real (constant price) expenditures do not give any appreciation of their size relative to the economy as a whole. Relative measures are more useful in this respect.

Relative measures: the size of the public sector is normally measured by the ratio of public spending to gross domestic product (GDP) at market prices, a measure of the resources available to society. This ratio is thought to be a more accurate representation of relative size than that for gross national product (GNP) because GNP includes earnings on overseas investments that are not part of domestic productive potential and can fluctuate sharply from year to year. **Table 9.1** reveals that the ratio of public expenditure to GDP rose from just over a third in the early to mid 1960s to almost a half in the mid 1970s, thereafter falling to just below two-fifths in the late 1980s and again in the late 1990s.

The public expenditure/GDP ratio is influenced by the following factors.
   First, the absolute level of exhaustive expenditures. Rising exhaustive expenditures do not only increase public expenditure. They also directly increase GDP in accounting terms. Hence, for the public

Table 9.1 The growth of public expenditure 1963–4 to 2001–2

Year	General Government Expenditure		
	Cash (£ billion)	Real terms* (£ billion)	Percentage of GDP
1963–4	11.4	140.3	36.7
1964–5	12.3	145.4	36.4
1965–6	13.7	154.4	37.8
1966–7	15.1	164.2	39.5
1967–8	17.5	184.7	43.1
1968–9	18.3	184.1	41.7
1969–70	19.2	183.2	40.6
1970–1	21.6	190.0	41.0
1971–2	24.3	195.6	41.4
1972–3	27.3	203.8	40.8
1973–4	31.5	219.4	42.4
1974–5	42.4	246.7	47.9
1975–6	53.2	246.8	48.2
1976–7	58.9	240.4	45.6
1977–8	63.8	229.1	42.4
1978–9	74.2	240.0	43.1
1979–80	89.0	246.6	43.1
1980–1	108.5	254.3	46.1
1981–2	120.6	258.0	46.7

Year	General Government Expenditure		
	Cash (£ billion)	Real terms* (£ billion)	Percentage of GDP
1982–3	131.9	263.9	46.6
1983–4	139.6	267.1	45.6
1984–5	150.0	272.5	45.5
1985–6	157.3	271.5	43.5
1986–7	161.8	270.9	41.6
1987–8	171.1	272.0	39.8
1988–9	178.2	265.2	37.2
1989–90	200.1	277.9	38.3
1990–1	216.4	287.7	38.5
1991–2	240.5	291.7	40.8
1992–3	262.5	308.1	42.8
1993–4	277.8	317.6	42.9
1994–5	289.4	326.3	42.2
1995–6	304.3	333.5	42.1
1996–7	308.9	327.9	40.3
1997–8	318.7	329.1	39.1
1998–9	328.4	328.4	38.3
1999–00**	342.4	334.0	38.0
2000–1**	369.9	352.9	39.1
2001–2**	391.5	364.5	39.5

Notes:
* Cash figures adjusted to price levels of 1998–9.
** Data for 1999–00 are estimates and those for the last two years are plans.
Source: *Public Expenditure Statistical Analyses 2000–1*, Cm 4601 (HM Treasury April 2000).

expenditure/GDP ratio to rise, exhaustive expenditures must rise faster than all other (private sector) spending. Increased public spending on goods and services caused the huge increases in the ratios during the two world wars (1914–18 and 1939–45) because of armaments production and so on. Since military output was substituted for civilian output the impact on GDP was not as pronounced as the effect on exhaustive expenditures. The latter showed little if any rising trend relative to GDP both before and between the two world wars and only a slowly rising trend during the 1960s and 1970s. Thereafter falling exhaustive expenditure/GDP ratios occurred (being less than 23 per cent in the mid 1980s) as governments attempted to cut exhaustive expenditures to offset rapidly rising transfer payments.

Second, the absolute level of transfer payments. Unlike exhaustive expenditures, transfer payments are not part of GDP as such and so have no effect on the published GDP figure. Hence, any rise in transfer payments increases the public expenditure/GDP ratio. In general, the greater the amount of income redistribution through transfer payments the larger the public expenditure/GDP ratio. Transfer payments were relatively insignificant before the First World War. They increased substantially during the interwar period (1919–38) but remained largely stable as a share of GDP. They then increased substantially relative to GDP during the 1960s and 1970s to reach 24 per cent in the mid 1980s. In particular, sharp short- to medium-term increases occurred during recessionary periods in the early 1970s, early 1980s and early 1990s. This occurred because of the demand-determined nature of many social security payments such as unemployment benefits, an example of the automatic stabilisers in the Keynesian model of aggregate demand.

Third, the absolute level of GDP. The public expenditure/GDP ratio also rises if GDP falls and vice versa, for example during the economic recessions of the early 1980s and early 1990s (see **Table 9.1**). Such short-term changes in GDP may occur as a result of changing world trading conditions, which affect export earnings. They may also occur because of changes in domestic savings ratios, for example where increased savings and/or reduced personal debt lead to the collapse of a consumer boom.

Finally, the relative growth of public expenditure and GDP. The ratio rises if public expenditure rises faster than GDP. In 1984 the Conservative Government published a discussion document, *The Next Ten Years: Public Expenditure and Taxation into the 1990s* (Cmnd 9189). Called the 1984 Public Expenditure Green Paper (because of the colour of its covers), it noted that public spending had increased by 90 per cent in real terms over the previous twenty years whilst real GDP had only risen by 50 per cent. The result was that the public expenditure/GDP ratio rose from 36.7 per cent in 1963/4 to a peak of 48.2 per cent in 1975/6 (see **Table 9.1**).

9.3   Cutting the public expenditure/GDP ratio

Unless purely ideologically driven, the primary economic reasons for cutting public expenditure are in terms of the possible adverse effects of high levels of taxation on both allocative efficiency and economic growth. The Conservative governments of the 1980s and 1990s laid great emphasis on stimulating the growth of GDP through the development of an entrepreneurial culture, which it considered to be crucially dependent on the achievement of the correct structure of economic incentives. Those governments believed that incentives are influenced by the tax and transfer payments systems. High marginal rates of taxation (i.e. tax rates) were thought to lead to strong disincentive-to-work effects, exacerbated by high levels of social security payments creating poverty and unemployment traps (see Chapter 4). Similar disincentives to economically productive investment were believed to be created by high levels of corporate subsidy and complex tax reliefs against corporation tax (see Chapter 10).

The greater these disincentive effects, the slower the growth of GDP, the faster the growth of public expenditure and the greater the public expenditure/GDP ratio. The government believed that if the UK's ratio exceeded that of its trading partners then its economy would become increasingly impoverished in a relative if not an absolute sense. Hence the relative growth of public expenditure and GDP were seen as crucially interdependent, a negative rather than positive relationship. This is a particular manifestation of the crowding-out hypothesis (see Chapter 5) and clearly qualifies the development and organic state macromodels of public expenditure growth (see Chapter 3).

This emphasis on economic and financial incentives was criticised, both as assertion rather than as proven fact and for its adverse impact on equity. Cuts in high marginal rates of tax mainly benefit affluent groups whilst cuts in social security payments have the greatest impact on low-income groups. A cynical interpretation of the restructuring of economic incentives during the 1980s was 'to give the rich more and the poor less'. However, as already noted, equity is not solely concerned with a more equal distribution of income. It is also concerned with creating opportunities and rewards for personal effort. Reforms of tax and social security systems were paralleled by other radical measures intended to increase the flexibility of markets (see Chapter 8).

Stated intentions during the 1980s had changed from reducing public expenditure in real terms to maintaining it broadly constant in real terms (at least up to 1990), then to restraining its increase below that of GDP. Whilst the reduced public spending/GDP ratio objective was achieved, it proved difficult to constrain public expenditure in real terms (see **Table 9.1**). This is perhaps not surprising since real public expenditure had almost doubled between 1963/4 and 1983/4 and many of the same forces continued to apply upward pressure on spending. As a result it increased by over a quarter between 1983/4 and 1999/00.

There were both accusations of public expenditure cuts and claims of public expenditure increases during the 1980s. These seemingly contradictory claims can be explained in terms of the particular base or measure chosen for public expenditure. Public expenditure was indeed cut in terms of its share of GDP (see **Table 9.1**). However, **total** public expenditure increased enormously in cash terms and modestly in real terms. Nonetheless, critics could still claim cuts against previously planned increases, particularly when the newly-elected Conservative government cut back on the previous Labour government's spending plans in 1979. In 1997, the newly-elected Labour government committed itself to keeping to the previous Conservative government's expenditure plans for its first two years of office, thereafter planning substantial increases in real expenditure (see **Table 9.1**).

Even though expenditures were rising in real terms, it was often claimed that they were still falling when judged against rising expenditure needs. For example the 1984 Green Paper estimated that real expenditure on health and personal social services would have to rise by 1 per cent per annum from 1983/4 to 1993/4 simply to take account of demographic change. Failure to achieve this led to allegations by the 1988 House of Commons Social Services Committee that the NHS had experienced a shortfall in funding of some £1.8 billion between 1981/2 and 1987/8. Adding the cost implications of advances in medical technology and policy initiatives to demographic change raised the required real increase to 2 per cent per annum over the ten-year period.

The revised objective of restraining the share of public expenditure in GDP recognised that the forces that drove up public spending in the past were likely to continue in the future. The practical policy option was to restrict the growth of public expenditure half a percentage point or so below that of GDP. Whilst even this option proves difficult during recession as GDP stagnates or falls, it could be achieved over the longer term.

The 1984 Green Paper argued that **finance should determine expenditure**, not **expenditure determine finance**. During the post-war period as a whole emphasis had been laid on the 'volume' of public sector outputs rather than on the *cash outlay* required to finance them. Outputs of public services such as education and health are difficult to measure. Hence public expenditure planning focused on the levels of **inputs** required to provide them (e.g. teachers, nurses, police officers). Whilst the desired volume of public sector services was inevitably influenced by what the economy was thought to be able to afford, the emphasis was on real (rather than cash) expenditures. Public expenditure was effectively **index-linked**, automatic adjustments being made to take account of inflation over the years (as many as five) between the initial plans and the actual delivery of services. This led to many different sets of financial figures (on differing price bases) for a given financial year. For example, during the 1970s **survey prices** reflected price levels at the time of the Public Expenditure Survey, a quadrennial projection of estimated public expenditures on the basis of existing policies. Survey prices would then be revalued to derive **main estimates**, which were presented to parliament one year after the survey and still a year or more before expenditures would actually be incurred. **Supplementary estimates** would then be presented to parliament during the financial year to which the main estimates related so as to fund subsequent inflation. Actual final expenditures were referred to as 'outturn' expenditures.

These differing price bases for given financial years caused considerable confusion when comparing expenditure outcomes with plans, leading to the term **funny money** and obscuring financial accountability. Of course the Keynesian view is that **money doesn't matter**, since it is real resources that are important for economic policy. However this guarantee of additional funds did little to promote financial accountability. Moreover, whilst such repricing of expenditure plans was administratively convenient, it meant that changes in the relative prices and costs of public sector outputs were not explicitly considered by the planning process. And yet basic economic theories of markets clearly demonstrate that changing relative prices lead to a reallocation of resources. In effect the public expenditure planning system pre-empted any reallocation of resources between the public and private sectors in response to changing relative prices, a manifestation of direct crowding out (see Chapter 5). This is of considerable importance if the **relative price effect** occurs for public sector services (see Chapter 3).

If the public sector has less scope for productivity improvements than the private sector and yet grows at the latter's expense due to index-linking of public expenditure, then the productive potential of the economy is reduced. This will be exacerbated to the extent that the higher levels of taxation required to finance those public expenditures lead to disincentive-to-work effects (see Chapter 4). Alternatively, higher levels of public sector borrowing may lead to higher interest rates and less private sector investment, or to further inflation (see Chapter 5). The scenario is that direct and indirect crowding out ultimately leads to reduced rates of economic growth and to living standards that are lower than they otherwise would have been. Whilst not provable, this scenario helps to explain the government's increasing concern with the need to control public expenditure and clearly demonstrates the interrelationship between the numerator and denominator of the public expenditure/GDP ratio.

In its 1984 Green Paper the then Conservative government argued that the country should decide first what could and should be afforded and then set expenditure plans for individual programmes consistent with that decision. In fact general government spending had increased during the 1960s and 1970s despite the recurrent attempts of successive governments to restrain it. **Cash limits** had already been introduced by the previous Labour government in 1976 and were tightened under Conservative governments during the 1980s and early 1990s. The subsequent Labour government introduced departmental expenditure limits, set for three years at a time. Hence the perceived need to restrain public expenditure is not driven solely by ideology. Nor is this preoccupation with public expenditure control peculiar to Britain. It is common amongst advanced industrial nations.

Cash limits covered 60 per cent of total public expenditure, directly or indirectly. They excluded demand-determined expenditures such as social security, where the volume of spending depends on the number of claimants eligible for benefit. Cash limits set an upper limit on the financial provision for inflation within both the main and supplementary estimates. The latter were effectively abandoned in the late 1970s when main estimates were presented to parliament at price levels forecast for the forthcoming year, including the cash limit. If inflation turned out to be greater than forecast and allowed for in the cash limit, then the volume of public services had to be reduced in order for spending departments to remain within their own cash limits. In effect public expenditure plans continued to be in volume terms but it was no longer guaranteed that they would receive full compensation for inflation.

In 1981 the government announced a major shift in the planning of public expenditure from volume to cash. **Volume planning** in terms of physical inputs such as teachers and hospitals had been consistent with what had then been the main role of macroeconomic policy, namely the management of aggregate demand through fiscal policy. However the shift of emphasis towards the financial or monetary aspects of macroeconomic policy necessitated close control of cash amounts.

Financial accountability was said to be improved by **planning in cash** in that ministers are able to discuss the money that will actually be spent, rather than 'funny money' figures that could be significantly different from actual outturn spending, and because expenditure figures can be more closely related to revenue projections. Hence, in principle if not in practice, **finance determines expenditure** rather than the reverse. From a managerial perspective, programme managers previously had little incentive to adapt their expenditures in response to changing relative costs. Cash planning supposedly gives them more incentive to consider alternative ways of sourcing resources and/or using resources in different ways to achieve programme objectives. In other words there is increased emphasis on the achievement of **value for money**.

Nevertheless the major problem with cash planning is that realistic assumptions must be made about inflation, otherwise expenditures may either be constrained much more than was intended or cash plans be regarded as unrealistic. For example, during the 1980s and early 1990s successive Conservative governments set targets for the control of inflation, initially wishing to reduce it to zero but later setting ceilings such as 4 per cent per annum. In the late 1990s, the Labour government likewise set an even tighter inflation target of 2.5 per cent. Monetary and fiscal policy had to be consistent with such inflation targets. There is a natural tendency for the government to use its target rather than any more realistic assessment of future inflation in its projections of public expenditure over the planning period. Too wide a discrepancy between government and market expectations of inflation would throw into question the credibility of the government's public expenditure plans. In fact both Conservative and Labour governments have explicitly recognised the powerful forces driving up public expenditure. These include increasing numbers of elderly people and other benefit recipients, increased educational spending on schools, colleges and universities, increased health spending, and expenditure on capital infrastructure. The sharp increases in planned public expenditure after 1998/9 in **Table 9.1** reflect Labour's priorities for increased expenditures on health, education and physical infrastructure whilst restraining expenditures on other services.

9.4   Expenditure components

The economic categories of exhaustive and transfer expenditures do not figure explicitly in public expenditure statistical series since, whilst useful for analytical purposes, they have little value for accounting or planning purposes. The published public expenditure figures are the summation of many accounting components. Indeed, exactly what constitutes public spending is open to question and the definition of public expenditure has changed on many occasions. Such changes are normally justified on technical grounds and, generally, have attempted to separate that part of public expenditure over which central government has little or no control from that part over which it does have (or could reasonably be expected to have) control.

However, such changes may also be politically expedient in allowing central government to claim success in controlling (reducing) public expenditure. For example, when central government was committed to cutting public expenditures during the 1980s, privatisation revenues were treated as negative public expenditure rather than as a source of public revenue. (Justification of the treatment of privatisation proceeds as negative expenditure is considered in detail in Chapter 11.) This had the effect of reducing the accounting figure for public expenditure by several billion pounds a year. During the 1990s, cyclical social security expenditures (primarily on unemployment benefits) were excluded from the then new control total (along with debt interest and privatisation proceeds) because central government could not be expected to control such transfer payments during recessions. The net effect of these accounting adjustments can be quite substantial. For example, the control total in 1993/4 was only 85 per cent of General Government Expenditure (GGE) excluding privatisation proceeds.

According to standardised figures published by the Institute of Fiscal Studies, real expenditures had risen by 1.5 per cent per annum under the former Conservative governments, while in the subsequent 1997 Labour government's first two years in office it had risen by only 0.2 per cent per annum. This broadly confirms the Treasury's own figures in **Table 9.1** above which show public spending was virtually unchanged in real terms in 1999/2000 compared with the mid 1990s.

Accounting components

The 1997 Labour government introduced a new expenditure budgeting and control regime in 1998. It clearly distinguishes between current and capital expenditure, sets departmental expenditure limits (DEL) for three years at a time, and distinguishes annually managed expenditures (AME) which cannot reasonably be subject to multi-year limits, most notably social security benefits and debt interest. Total managed expenditure (TME) is the sum of DEL and AME. TME is defined as public sector current expenditure plus net investment and depreciation (see **Table 9.2**).

Current expenditure includes spending on wages and salaries, supplies and services, rent and rates and so on. These are broadly considered to be consumable items, the benefits of which are consumed or exhausted within each financial year. **Capital expenditure** includes spending on fixed assets such as land, buildings and plant and machinery, the benefits of which are more durable, lasting several years or decades. Both components involve exhaustive and transfer expenditures. For example social security payments are categorised as current expenditures, as are the interest payments on debt used to finance capital expenditures. **Table 9.2** demonstrates the relatively small scale of capital expenditure, the capital budget being less than 10 per cent of the DEL in all years. Moreover, depreciation is greater than net investment in all years. It was noted above that investment in human and physical

Table 9.2 Public expenditure 1997–8 to 2001–2: Summary

	£ billion				
	1997–8 outturn	*1998–9 outturn*	*1990–00 outturn*	*2000–1 plans*	*2001–2 plans*
Departmental Expenditure Limits					
Current budget	149.7	155.3	165.1	177.3	184.1
Capital budget	12.6	12.1	13.8	16.4	18.5
Departmental Expenditure Limits	162.3	167.4	178.9	193.7	202.6
Annually Managed Expenditure					
Main departmental programmes	104.0	105.8	112.5	114.4	118.9
Locally financed expenditure	15.6	16.1	17.2	18.1	19.1
Other	40.8	41.7	36.7	44.7	45.6
Annually Managed Expenditure	160.4	163.6	166.3	177.2	183.6
Budget 2000 addition					5.9
Total Managed Expenditure	322.7	331.0	345.2	370.9	392.1
of which:					
current expenditure	305.0	312.5	325.6	348.2	365.6
net investment	4.6	5.0	5.5	8.2	11.4
depreciation	13.1	13.6	14.1	14.5	15.0

Source: Public Expenditure Statistical Analyses 2000–1, Cm 4601 (HM Treasury, April 2000).

capital is a supply-side initiative. Nevertheless, there seems to be a lack of investment in physical infrastructure, notwithstanding the private finance initiative (see Chapter 8) and the restrictions on public borrowing of the Maastricht Treaty (see Chapter 11). Historically, it has been capital expenditure that bore the brunt of public expenditure restraint as cash limits began to bite, capital projects easily being shelved or postponed. The new system of public expenditure budgeting and control now makes a clear distinction between capital and current expenditure (see **Table 9.2**). The government's intention is thus to avoid worthwhile capital expenditures being squeezed out.

Governmental components

Table 9.2 shows that local government self-financed expenditure accounts for less than 5 per cent of the total managed expenditure in all years. Whilst total local government expenditure typically accounts for about a quarter of public expenditure, less than a fifth of local spending is financed by local authorities themselves. About 85 per cent of their expenditure net of income from sales, fees and charges is financed by grants from central government through intergovernmental grants. The main programmes for **central government** are social security, health and defence. Other central government programmes, relatively minor in expenditure terms, include trade and industry, overseas development, transport and agriculture, fisheries and food. The main **local government** programmes are school education (accounting for about half of local spending), personal social services, housing and the police. Other local government programmes include local environmental health, refuse collection and disposal, and leisure and recreation.

Public sector pay

The importance of wages and salaries in exhaustive expenditures was noted in Chapter 8. The public sector pay factors contained within public expenditure plans since the 1970s are average allowable increases in labour costs, a broad measure of what the government considers reasonable and affordable. As for any average, some pay increases can be more but others must be less. To the extent that the aggregate of pay increases exceed the average, then labour costs have to be reduced by reductions in manpower. Hence both Conservative and Labour governments during the 1980s and 1990s claimed that pay factors are not a public sector incomes policy despite such claims by public sector trades unions and other critics.

However in early 1994 the Conservative government announced a freeze on the public sector wage bill for the following three years. With the 1997 Labour government committed to maintaining the Conservatives spending plans during its first two years in office, the pay freeze continued. This does not necessarily imply a freeze on wages since if costs can be reduced through more efficient working practices the savings can be used to finance higher wages. Hence recommendations by the independent pay review bodies are not necessarily vetoed by the public sector pay freeze. Nor is greater freedom necessarily denied for public sector managers setting pay levels in a decentralised system of financial management involving quangos and agencies (see Chapter 8). However, in practice there may be an inherent contradiction between a centrally imposed pay freeze and local managerial accountability. This is the case when there is little or no scope for productivity improvements.

Reforms include a shift from national to local public sector pay negotiations, performance-related pay and other work-incentive schemes, reducing the use of 'comparability' with the private sector when setting public sector wage levels and paying increased attention to the wage levels (which could be higher or lower) required to attract and retain staff.

The shift to agencies involves changes to Civil Service recruitment, promotion, management development, and pay and grading arrangements, part of the pursuit of cost effectiveness. The application of standardised Civil Service pay and conditions is no longer considered appropriate for such a diverse range of organisations. Agencies are responsible for reviewing their own pay and grading systems with the objective of increasing the cost effectiveness of their pay bills. Besides pay levels, staffing economies are also being sought through competitive contracting and so on (see Chapter 15).

Notwithstanding the apparent flexibility of payment systems in the public sector, the fact is that pay levels in the private sector have grown substantially faster. Between 1982 and 1997, the gap between the (lower) average earnings of public sector workers and the (higher) average earnings of private sector employees grew by 16 per cent. Relatively low pay in the public sector has resulted in shortages of nurses, doctors, teachers and so on, and the public sector is having increasingly to recruit from abroad. Nevertheless, many vacant posts remain unfilled, thus jeopardising the government's commitment to increase spending on education and the NHS. This, in part, explains underspending on these services compared with the Labour government's planned increases.

Service components

Table 9.3 demonstrates the overwhelming size of social security, accounting for over a third of total expenditure on services, and spending more than health and education (the next two largest services) combined. Notwithstanding the impact of the trade cycle, social security expenditures have generally grown at least as fast as GDP over the period as a whole. For example, the later 1980s and later 1990s were outside the recessions of the early 1980s and early 1990s and yet social security expenditures accounted for a higher proportion of GDP in the later 1990s compared with the later 1980s. Health expenditures accounted for only a very small rise in terms of their share of GDP over the period. Education expenditures grew marginally and then actually declined as a share of GDP during the later 1990s. These trends illustrate the Labour government's prioritisation during the early twenty-first century of reducing the social security budget and redirecting the financial savings to investments in human (as well as physical) capital as part of its supply side strategy.

Trends in services' real expenditures correspond with the discussion above and in Chapter 8. **First**, the decline in real expenditures on housing, defence, transport and public sector debt interest payments even though real total expenditure on services grew by 23 per cent over the period as a whole. In sharp contrast, social security expenditures rose by 40 per cent over the full period, health expenditure rose by 59 per cent, education by 35 per cent and law, order and protective services rose by 61 per cent (on a relatively small base). **Second**, the policy to reduce total public expenditure as a percentage of GDP. **Table 9.2** shows that real total managed expenditure rose by 17 per cent over the period. Nevertheless, **Table 9.3** shows that it has accounted for a consistently diminishing trend share of GDP since the early 1990s. Thus, public expenditure grew less fast than GDP over a complete trade cycle. This reflects not only general measures of public expenditure restraint but also privatisation programme, competitive contracting and so on (see Chapters 13 and 15).

Whether this falling ratio of public expenditure to GDP will be maintained remains to be seen. After holding real total managed expenditure in check between 1997/8 and 1999/00, the Labour government's Comprehensive Spending Review announced plans for sharp increases in TME over the following three years, and particularly for education and the National Health Service. Being exhaustive expenditures, control of education and health spending can, in principle, be achieved through genuine efficiency savings without reducing service levels and quality. Other diverse measures include control of the drugs bill for the National Health Service by encouraging general practitioners to reduce the amount of drugs and medicines they prescribe, and to switch to cheaper generic drugs where prescriptions are necessary. General practitioners' prescriptions account for 10 per cent of the NHS budget and improved prescribing could save up to £500 million a year, according to estimates by the Audit Commission. Such reforms are not

Table 9.3   Total managed expenditure (TME) for major services 1984–5 to 1999–00

(a) Real spending (£ billion)

	1984–5	1985–6	1986–7	1987–8	1988–9	1989–90	1990–1
Education	29.6	29.0	30.9	32.2	32.5	33.8	33.9
Health**	30.0	30.2	31.3	32.6	33.6	34.0	35.3
Transport	12.2	11.8	11.2	10.7	10.3	11.1	12.5
Housing	8.4	7.2	6.8	6.7	4.9	7.2	6.3
Law & order***	11.6	11.4	12.0	12.8	13.4	14.1	14.8
Defence	31.3	31.1	30.5	29.8	28.3	28.6	27.7
Social Security	71.9	74.5	77.6	77.0	73.9	73.1	75.9
All services	240.1	239.9	245.9	246.1	241.2	248.8	254.5
Debt Interest	31.4	32.9	31.7	31.7	30.2	29.0	26.2
TME	287.6	284.3	285.7	287.0	279.5	287.2	287.7

(b) Percentage of GDP

	1984–5	1985–6	1986–7	1987–8	1988–9	1989–90	1990–1
Education	4.9	4.6	4.8	4.7	4.6	4.7	4.7
Health**	5.0	4.8	4.8	4.8	4.7	4.7	4.9
Transport	2.0	1.9	1.7	1.6	1.4	1.5	1.7
Housing	1.4	1.2	1.1	1.0	0.7	1.0	0.9
Law & order***	1.9	1.8	1.8	1.9	1.9	1.9	2.0
Defence	5.2	5.0	4.7	4.4	4.0	3.9	3.8
Social Security	12.0	11.9	11.9	11.3	10.4	10.1	10.5
All services****	40.1	38.5	37.8	36.1	33.8	34.3	35.1
Debt Interest	5.2	5.3	4.9	4.6	4.2	4.0	3.6
TME	48.0	45.6	43.9	42.0	39.2	39.6	39.7

Notes:
*   Data for 1999–00 are estimated outturn, all other years being actual outturn.
**   Health expenditures exclude personal social services.
***   Law and order also includes protective services.
****   'All Services' is referred to in the Public Expenditure Statistical Analyses as 'Total expenditure on services'.

In addition to the services listed above 'All Services' also includes trade and industry, agriculture, culture, medial and sport, and so on (not shown).

The difference between 'All services' and TME is public sector debt interest plus other accounting adjustments (the latter not shown).

Source: Public Expenditure Statistical Analyses 2000–01, Cm 4601 (HM Treasury, April 2000).

1991–2	1992–3	1993–4	1994–5	1995–6	1996–7	1997–8	1998–9	1999–00*
35.3	36.9	37.9	39.1	39.0	38.3	38.4	38.4	40.1
37.8	40.3	40.7	42.3	43.0	43.1	43.8	44.6	47.8
13.2	14.8	13.4	13.6	12.6	10.7	9.4	8.6	8.5
7.1	7.4	6.1	6.0	5.6	4.9	3.8	3.7	3.5
15.7	16.6	16.9	17.3	17.3	17.2	17.4	17.4	18.7
27.5	26.6	25.8	25.3	23.7	22.6	21.6	22.6	22.4
84.8	93.0	98.9	100.1	101.7	102.5	100.6	99.5	101.0
266.7	284.3	289.4	293.1	290.7	290.6	285.4	286.9	295.6
22.3	22.3	23.7	26.5	28.8	29.9	31.0	29.6	25.0
303.3	318.3	324.1	334.5	333.4	335.5	333.3	331.0	336.8

1991–2	1992–3	1993–4	1994–5	1995–6	1996–7	1997–8	1998–9	1999–00*
4.9	5.1	5.1	5.1	4.9	4.7	4.6	4.5	4.6
5.3	5.6	5.5	5.5	5.4	5.3	5.2	5.2	5.4
1.8	2.1	1.8	1.8	1.6	1.3	1.1	1.0	1.0
1.0	1.0	0.8	0.8	0.7	0.6	0.5	0.4	0.4
2.2	2.3	2.3	2.2	2.2	2.1	2.1	2.0	2.1
3.8	3.7	3.5	3.3	3.0	2.8	2.6	2.6	2.6
11.9	12.9	13.4	12.9	12.8	12.6	12.0	11.6	11.5
37.3	39.5	39.1	37.9	37.3	35.7	33.9	33.5	33.6
3.1	3.1	3.2	3.4	3.7	3.7	3.7	3.5	2.8
42.4	44.3	43.8	43.3	42.8	41.2	39.6	38.6	38.3

feasible for social security expenditures as they are transfer payments. Spending cuts therefore mean a reduction in the provision of financial support to individuals.

9.5   Controlling social security expenditure

The dramatic rise in social security spending identified in **Table 9.3** makes clear that its control must feature prominently in the attempt to restrain public expenditure over both the medium and the long term. As already noted, social security expenditure is by far the biggest area of public spending, accounting for more than a third of the total expenditure on services. To the nearest whole number, social security expenditure has accounted for at least 12 per cent of GDP in 12 of the 16 years in **Table 9.3**, compared with at most 5.1 per cent for education and 5.6 per cent for health. A 'ratchet effect' seems to cause expenditure to rise with each recession but it does not return to earlier levels in subsequent recovery. Hence radical reform of the social security system seems necessary.

For given eligibility criteria and rates of benefits, spending is non-discretionary. Expenditure can only be cut or controlled by making eligibility criteria much more restrictive and/or cutting the real levels of benefit. This is, of course, both highly controversial and highly politicised. It involves a redefinition of what constitutes need for state assistance, and inevitably certain (possibly highly dependent) groups will suffer a reduction in their standard of living. **Table 9.4** makes clear that social security expenditures are not simply concerned with redistribution of incomes from rich to poor since most are not means-tested but, instead, are based upon prior national insurance contributions (i.e. are contributory benefits) or are simply paid flat-rate to all in a group (e.g. child benefit). However, between 1979/80 and 1997/8, payments of means-tested benefits rose by 318 per cent compared with a rise of only 36 per cent in payment of contributory benefits. The sharp rise in means-tested benefits was largely due to the declining real value of the state retirement pension. This (ongoing) decline occurs because pensions are linked to retail prices rather than to earnings, the latter growing considerably faster than the former. This trend will be further enhanced by the minimum income guarantee (MIG) for pensioners introduced in 1999 (see Chapter 12). It is being paid through means-tested income support, rather than by increasing the value of the basic pension.

Table 9.5 shows that pensions account for 37 per cent of total social security expenditures in 1999–00. Pensions rose by 31 per cent and disability benefits by a staggering 62 per cent. In contrast, income support, social fund and housing benefits showed little or no growth over the period. Total social security spending rose by 16 per cent over

Table 9.4   Major state benefits by category 1992/3

Contributory national insurance[1]	Non-contributory means-tested[2]	Non-contributory categorical[3]
Retirement pension	Income support	Child benefit
Incapacity benefit	Housing benefit	Disability living allowance
Jobseeker's allowance (c–b)	Jobseeker's allowance (i–b)	Attendance allowance
Statutory sick pay	Council tax benefit	
Statutory maternity pay	Social Fund	
Widow's benefits		

Notes:
1. Entitlement to national insurance benefits is conditional upon prior payment of national insurance contributions. They provide for payment when earnings are interrupted or cease. Jobseeker's allowance (c–b) is contributions-based, i.e. based upon prior national insurance contributions.
2. Receipt of means-tested (i.e. income-related) benefits is subject to an assessment of personal or household income and savings. They are intended to provide support for insufficient incomes, and hence benefits are progressively reduced (to zero) as income and/or savings rise beyond set thresholds. Jobseeker's allowance (i–b) is income-based and is paid to those who do not qualify for Jobseeker's allowance (c–b) or if it does not fully meet their needs (e.g. where the claimant has dependent children).
3. Categorical benefits are payable to particular groups of people without a test of means or prior contributions. They are a recognition of the higher living costs incurred by certain groups (e.g. families with dependent children) and are payable in addition to any national insurance or means-tested benefits.
4. Rates of benefits are published annually by the Office of National Statistics in *Social Trends* (London: Stationery Office). Leaflets giving details of benefit rates are available at Post Offices.

the period even though the 'unemployment, incapacity and other benefits' group fell markedly as the economy emerged from the early 1990s recession. This is because a combination of economic, demographic, social and policy factors affect spending, these being discussed below.

Overall, **non-contributory** benefits have grown faster than **contributory** unemployment, sickness and invalidity benefits funded by NICs (see **Table 9.4**). By the mid 1990s, each were roughly half of total social security payments excluding cyclical (i.e. unemployment-influenced) social security (which showed a much bigger, fourfold increase for means-tested income support) so as to identify longer term structural trends.

The cost of benefits had been growing by 3 per cent per annum in real terms between 1979 and 1992. Assuming no change in unemployment and no policy changes, but taking account of projected demographic

Table 9.5 Social security total managed expenditure 1994–5 to 1999–00

	£ million					
	1994–5	1995–6	1996–7	1997–8	1998–9	1999–00*
Pension benefits	29 553	30 804	32 883	34 483	36 551	38 762
Widows' benefits	1057	1051	1017	1021	1009	1015
Unemployment, incapacity and other benefits	9787	9423	8723	7804	7638	7286
Industrial injury benefits	728	753	765	768	783	795
Family benefits	8663	9263	9754	10 022	10 430	11 059
War pensions	1147	1258	1351	1288	1264	1241
Disability benefits	6888	8019	9214	9942	10 547	11 141
Income support	17 037	17 359	17 295	16 720	16 215	16 904
Social fund	177	224	201	154	154	163
Housing benefits	10 572	11 386	11 921	12 058	11 970	11 977
Administration and miscellaneous services	3184	3270	3380	3170	2925	3230
Total Social Security	88 794	92 811	96 503	97 430	99 485	103 573

Notes:
* Data for 1999–00 are estimated outturn, all other years being actual outturn.
Source: Public Expenditure Statistical Analyses 2000–01, Cm 4601 (HM Treasury, April 2000).

changes, the cost was forecast to grow faster (by 3.3 per cent annually) during the rest of the 1990s. However, if unemployment were to fall by a quarter, the average annual real growth rate of non-contributory benefits would reduce to 2.6 per cent per annum, and to 1.7 per cent if unemployment were to halve. Hence very slow or zero economic growth would lead to a rising benefits/GDP ratio, but moderate economic growth of 2.5 per cent combined with a fall in the level of unemployment to around 2.75 million would leave the total social security/GDP ratio almost fixed at around 12.4 per cent of GDP. In fact, **Table 9.3** shows a sustained reduction in that ratio after 1993/4.

Whilst the growing economic burden of social security should not be overplayed, in 1993 it appeared that non-contributory benefits could rise faster than the projected growth in GDP. Since increasing the economic growth rate may be beyond the control of government, the more practical and immediate solution was to seek to reduce the growth of social security payments. Reform of social security is an ongoing process.

The 1988 social security reforms

Introduced subsequent to the 1986 Social Security Act, the major part of the 1988 reforms concentrated on means-tested income support, the former family credit and housing benefit. They attempted to:

- simplify the benefits system;
- promote value for money;
- improve the targeting of benefits on those most in need;
- restrain expenditure by directing it towards families in poverty;
- increase work incentives and private provision.

Reforms reduced the complexity of the social security system for both claimants and administrators. Complexity is inevitable in a system that attempts to tailor benefits to individual needs. However complexity also increases the administrative costs of the system and so provides poor value for money for benefits whose basic purpose is to supplement the incomes of those in need. For example, 11 per cent of spending on supplementary benefit (the precursor of income support) was accounted for by administrative costs. Hence the number of additional single payments was reduced. Complexity also reduces the take-up rate of those eligible to claim and so frustrates system objectives in terms of helping those in need.

The 1988 reforms attempted to increase the incentives to work by reducing the poverty and unemployment traps (see Chapter 4). These traps mainly affected low-income families with children. The reforms ended the disparity between benefits for children according to whether heads of households were in or out of work. Previously more generous 'out of work' benefits created the unemployment trap. Similarly the threshold for the former family credit (which replaced family income supplement), above which benefit was progressively withdrawn as income rose, was made the same as the basic personal allowance against income tax for a married couple in receipt of income support. The use of net income (i.e. disposable income after payment of income tax and national insurance contributions) rather than gross income as the basis for assessment of family credit also reduced the extent of the poverty trap. Families in receipt of a pay rise were no longer made worse off by losing benefit and by having to pay income tax and national insurance contributions.

Benefit payments were shifted from those primarily dependent on housing benefit (e.g. pensioners and young single people) towards recipients of family credit and income support (mainly families with children whose head of household was either unemployed or in low-paid part-time work). This reform was intended to avoid the state being the first port of call when financial support was required by individuals without dependants to support.

Estimates produced by the Institute of Fiscal Studies in 1988 found that, in general, the reforms improved the levels of benefits paid to low-income families with children. Conversely childless couples were made worse off (having no children to support), as were young single people (under 25 years of age) living in rented accommodation away from the parental home (largely because of the reductions in housing benefit). On average, pensioners and young people living at home saw little or no change as a result of the reforms.

Within a given tax cost, these reforms were intended to increase the financial pressures on those who were capable of supporting themselves (i.e. childless couples and young single people of working age) by reducing benefit levels and using the savings to make better provision for low-income families with children, for lone parents and for the sick and disabled. This illustrates the point that improved equity is not simply about redistributing income; it is also about taking account of need and ability (see Chapter 12). However 'need' is a highly subjective issue and normative statements abound.

The reforms of the early 1990s

Reforms introduced in 1988 had already brought about a major restructuring of benefits, so the most appropriate policy response in the early 1990s was to target the fastest growing areas of social security expenditure. Of the projected growth of social security spending during the 1990s, a third would arise from sickness and disability benefits, a quarter from housing benefit and a fifth from income support (largely attributable to increased numbers of lone parents), most of the remaining increase coming from earnings-related pension entitlements.

The disintegration of traditional notions of 'the nuclear family' (two adults with an average 2.4 children) and the rise in unmarried motherhood have profound implications for social security expenditure. Particular attention has been paid to the cost implications of lone parents. About 90 per cent of lone parents are women, over two-thirds of whom claim income support and other benefits such as housing and council tax benefits. Receipt of income support acts as a 'passport' (i.e. gives automatic entitlement) to receipt of other benefits such as free school meals, dental care, prescriptions and spectacles. Hence the full cost of supporting lone-parent families on income support far exceeds the cash outlay on this benefit alone.

General Household Survey and Social Trends data show that married and cohabiting couples with dependent children appear to be in long-term decline as a proportion of all families. Numbers of first marriages more than halved between the late 1960s and late 1990s, whilst the number of divorces doubled. By 1997 there were just about as many divorces as first marriages, with one in every five marriages ending in divorce. The number of remarriages has remained almost constant since the mid 1970s and was only three-quarters the number of divorces in the late 1990s. The extra-marital birth rate was 38 per cent in the late 1990s, compared with only 7.2 per cent in 1964.

In 1991, for the first time, the number of unmarried mothers exceeded that of divorced mothers. Research for the Joseph Rowntree Foundation found that in 1991, whilst a quarter of unmarried women bearing children were cohabiting with a male partner, they cohabited for less than two years on average.

These changes in family relationships are clearly long term in nature and are not peculiar to the UK. However, the independent Family Policy Studies Centre argues that it is too early to talk of the death of the 'traditional family' because four-fifths of dependent children still live in families with two parents and 9 in 10 of those parents are married. Nevertheless, a fifth (2.8 million) of dependent children live in single parent households, this proportion having trebled from 7 per cent in 1972. Likewise, the number of single parents has trebled, the fastest growing group being single never-married lone mothers.

Hence, there are significant ongoing long-term changes in family demographics that could have profound implications for social security payments since the economic and cultural assumptions underpinning benefit systems are changing. As a general rule, single (i.e. never married) mothers find it difficult to support both themselves and their children. They tend to be younger than other lone parents and have younger children. A substantial proportion have no educational qualifications and a majority have no job. In 1989 only 13 per cent of single mothers received child-maintenance payments from the fathers of their children and average payments were only just over half the average for all lone parents. Hence single mothers are much more likely to depend on social security benefits than are other lone (separated or divorced) parents. A 1998 report by the Policy Studies Institute confirmed that teenage mothers do overwhelmingly become dependent upon benefits, 81 per cent claiming income support – with 57 per cent receiving no other income. Department of Social Security data reveal that this group of claimants have the highest take-up rate for income support at 95 to 100 per cent. Nonetheless, research results published by the Joseph Rowntree Foundation showed that most lone mothers want to work, part-time at least, but are usually unable to do so because of lack of affordable child care. In other words, they are not part of a benefit-dependent deviant sub-culture and so should benefit from the 1997 Labour government's New Deal for lone parents (see below).

In order to reduce the growing social security bill for 'broken' families and single mothers, the Conservative and Labour governments have both attempted to introduce the following.

First, a moral code preventing family breakdown and child bearing outside marriage. The Department of Health attempted to halve the pregnancy rate among under-16 year olds during the 1990s through contraceptive advice and education in schools and elsewhere. However the liberalisation of divorce laws in 1969 made divorce easier and also made it more likely that custody of children would go to the mother. Combined with the increasing proportions of economically-active mothers no longer solely dependent on the earnings of their husbands, 70 per cent of divorces are sought by women. Hence it will prove particularly difficult for the government to reinstate traditional notions of family and of sexual morality.

Second, reduction of the higher rates of benefit payable to single mothers. During the early 1990s, some social security ministers suggested that these higher rates of benefits (i.e. the former one-parent benefit), combined with their priority status for council housing (and hence housing benefit), created financial incentives for illegitimate births by teenage girls and young single women. In fact less than a fifth of lone parents were under the age of 24 and girls under 16 accounted for only 2 per cent of births outside marriage in 1990. Indeed the rate of teenage pregnancies was lower than 20 years previously though still the highest in the EU. Hence the factors causing the changes in family relationships and the rates of household formation are not as simple as some politicians have suggested. They are not simply financial matters. Neither are they restricted to the UK.

Third, more fathers contributing larger amounts to the cost of bringing up their children instead of allowing them to transfer the financial burden onto the state and its taxpayers. To this end, the Social Security Child Support Agency (CSA) was established as an executive agency of the Department of Social Security in 1993 (see Chapter 8). Whilst more than 80 per cent of fathers still live with their children, prior to the CSA more than two-thirds of absent fathers were making no financial contribution whatsoever to the upkeep of their children. The third who were paying maintenance paid an average of only £25 a week. In part this was because the courts usually agreed to divorce settlements giving the wife and children the family house. This was usually offset by minimal maintenance payments in the knowledge that the wife could claim social security benefits. Moreover, the real value of such court awards was eroded by inflation and there was little incentive for the ex-wife or Department of Social Security to go back to court to get maintenance payments increased. This process, together with increasing rates of separation and divorce, accounted for the trebling of the number of lone parents dependent on income support and other benefits to almost one million between 1979 and 1992.

The Department of Social Security had attempted to trace 'liable relatives' prior to 1993, recouping £138 million from known and traceable absent fathers, although this constituted only 14 per cent of the £1 billion paid in income support to their former partners. Hence the CSA's remit is to recoup larger amounts from absent fathers by providing for the assessment, collection and payment of child maintenance so that parents (rather than the state) will support their children financially whenever they can afford to do so.

Although other countries such as Australia and Norway have comparable child maintenance enforcement schemes, the work of the CSA has proved highly controversial on a number of grounds. **First,** it initially targeted increased maintenance payments from easily traceable fathers already making some provision, mainly 'responsible', middle-class, middle-aged men, rather than 'irresponsible' young teenage males who were not. It is more difficult to establish fatherhood for the latter group, to trace them and to extract payments from them. **Second,** the law is retrospective with the result that the Agency's maintenance formula took no account of past agreements that provided for 'clean breaks' between former spouses. **Third,** many former husbands had subsequently remarried and begun second families or acquired step-children, the upkeep costs of whom were largely ignored by the agency's formula (housing costs were not). **Fourth,** there was no phasing-in of the additional maintenance payments determined by the agency, so that absent fathers had no time to adjust their budgets as average weekly payments trebled to £75. Widespread protests and non-payment by many of the ex-husbands required to make such payments served to restrict the phased take-up of all cases for existing absent fathers. Reforms introduced in 2001 use a much simpler maintenance formula taking less money from fathers (to encourage them to pay), allow mothers to keep some of the recovered maintenance payments additional to benefits (to encourage them to co-operate with the CSA), and will attempt to benefit children rather than simply the Exchequer.

Whilst still highly controversial, the Agency's remit demonstrates the shift in emphasis from rights to responsibilities. The normative principle upon which the agency is based is that fathers should regard maintenance payments as an obligation arising out of their responsibilities towards their children. These personal and individual responsibilities increasingly substitute for the financial burdens and collective responsibilities previously falling on the state and its taxpayers in meeting the rights to financial support of unmarried mothers and their children.

Fourth, reduction of fraudulent claims. Being difficult to identify, estimates of social security fraud vary from £2 billion to £7 billion per annum. Failure to declare earnings from part-time work is the most common form of benefit fraud. Others include exaggerating medical conditions to obtain incapacity benefit, claiming housing benefit and income support dishonestly and failing to disclose cohabitation. Some false claims may arise simply due to the complexity of qualification criteria or because of tardiness on the part of recipients in notifying the Department of Social Security of a change in personal circumstances. However, some fraud is due to organised crime.

Fifth, redefining 'homeless' to exclude those persons living with family, relatives or friends. This puts increased pressure on single people and childless couples in particular because it removes the statutory duty of local authorities to house them and reduces the associated claims against housing benefit. The Conservative and Labour governments of the 1980s and 1990s not only believed that the state should not be the first port of call in times of need, they also began to question whether the state should meet needs caused by 'irresponsible' behaviour and personal preference.

Individual benefits

Unemployment benefits

Unemployment benefit *per se* is the Jobseeker's Allowance (JSA). It is only payable if the unemployed person has a prior record of national insurance contributions (NICs). It is therefore a **contributory** benefit (but see **Table 9.4** notes 1 and 2). Those who have no NIC record, or who have been unemployed for more than six months, receive other benefits including income support, housing benefit and council tax benefit. According to the Labour Force Survey, in the mid 1990s almost 60 per cent of the unemployed received income support, only 5 per cent received both income support and unemployment benefit, 10 per cent received only unemployment benefit, the remaining 25 per cent not being in receipt of any unemployment-related benefits. Hence terms such as 'being on the dole' are misleading in that they do not differentiate the various categories of payment the unemployed person may be receiving.

Besides the supply-side initiatives referred to in Chapter 8, measures have also attempted both to reduce the growth in benefit paid to each claimant and to restrict cash benefits to those genuinely in need of them. **First**, basic unemployment benefit has been indexed to the growth in retail prices since 1980, rather than to earnings as previously. Since earnings have grown faster than prices, the result is that unemployment benefit (JSA and its predecessor) has fallen substantially relative to earnings. **Second**, in order to qualify for benefit, the unemployed have to demonstrate to the Employment Service that they are actively seeking work and are not repeatedly turning down successive offers of jobs.

The **available for work** requirement was formalised in the replacement of unemployment benefit by the JSA in 1996. It replaced unemployment benefit and income support for jobseekers and is payable for six months, after which recipients switch to income support. Prior to JSA, unemployment benefit was payable for a year. This halving of the period of entitlement to unemployment benefit to six months means the earlier transfer of unemployed people onto means-tested income support. At that point many redundant middle-class workers with only modest savings (of £8000 or more) receive no benefit at all, generating substantial savings for the Exchequer. This reform brings further into question the distinction between NICs and taxes (see Chapter 10).

As already noted, **Table 9.5** shows that expenditure on the 'unemployment, incapacity and other benefits' group fell substantially as the economy emerged from the early 1990s recession. This fall was also enhanced to the extent that adoption of supply-side measures that reduce the average period of unemployment also reduce the instability arising from recession and recovery (see Chapter 8).

The JSA was introduced by the then Conservative government. Its general 'available for work' principle was further strengthened by the subsequent Labour government in its 'Welfare-to-Work' reform. The objective is to get people off benefits and into jobs, benefiting those individuals (extra income and status), as well as the Exchequer (higher tax revenues, lower benefit spending) and the economy (higher output and lower poverty).

Labour's 1998 Green Paper *New Ambitions for Our Country: A New Contract for Welfare* placed paid work at the heart of its welfare reform plans. The basic principle is 'work for those who can, security for those who cannot'. This principle applies to all benefit recipients of working age – not just those who receive the JSA. As already noted, most of the unemployed receive benefits other than unemployment benefit (JSA) *per se*. It has been implemented in stages through the **New Deals** for young people aged 18 to 24 unemployed for six months or more, for other long-term unemployed people aged 25 and over, for lone parents, for people with a disability or long-term illness, and for the non-working partners of unemployed claimants aged under 25 without children (see Chapter 8). The element of compulsion is seen as necessary because the long-term unemployed typically become so dissociated from the labour market that they are unable to respond to rational incentives. Although compulsion and the threat of loss of benefit has been criticised it has to be seen as a measure complementary to training, education, job search and other more positive initiatives to help the unemployed. The principle of benefit sanctions being imposed when claimants fail to meet their responsibilities as benefit recipients has been accepted by all the main political parties. Essentially, payment of benefit creates a contract between the individual recipient and the state, the former being obliged to seek work if they are so capable and the latter being obliged to enable that individual to gain employment by providing them with training opportunities, job-search and other forms of assistance. The objective is to reduce the number of people who can legitimately claim benefit whilst not actively seeking employment. Research results published by the Joseph Rowntree Foundation concludes that welfare-to-work schemes have had a significant impact in assisting people move from benefits to paid employment.

Income support, housing benefit and other benefits

Income support is available to people who are unemployed or who work less than 16 hours a week and have savings of less than £8000. **Housing benefit** supports rents and mortgage costs. The former **family credit** was replaced by the **working families tax credit** (WFTC) in 1999, both schemes topping up low earnings for those in work. Like income support, family credit was a direct cash payment to beneficiaries. However, they were mutually exclusive benefits in that the former can only be received by the low-income unemployed whereas the latter could only be received by the low-income employed. As its name suggests, the WFTC is a reduction in tax liability for low-income families whose parents are in paid employment. It is therefore not a cash benefit and so is considered further in Chapters 11 and 12. Income support is the main means-tested benefit (see **Tables 9.4** and **9.5**).

Child benefit

Child benefit is a **non-contributory** benefit paid directly to mothers for each child, irrespective of whether the family is rich or poor. Hence it is the main **categorical** benefit (see **Table 9.4**). Originating from the combination of a tax allowance for dependent children (dating back to 1909) and family allowances (dating back to 1948), child benefit was introduced in 1979. It subsumed the former one-parent benefit in 1996. Its value is no longer dependent on the head of household's tax position, child tax allowance being worth more the higher the taxable income because of the tax that would otherwise be levied upon it.

Like other non-means-tested benefits (i.e. JSA (c-b) and the state retirement pension), it has the major advantage of an almost complete (98 per cent) take-up rate. However, the take-up rate for housing benefit is also high, typically 90–95 per cent, that for income support perhaps being as low as three-quarters (accurate estimates being difficult to calculate). It appears that take-up is greatest for those in most need of support (e.g. single lone parents), many pensioners apparently not bothering to claim the relatively small individual amounts of income support to which they are entitled as a supplement to their pensions.

Child benefit constitutes about a fifth of income for families in the lowest decile of earnings. However its disadvantage is its high cost, as not only poor families receive it. Means-tested benefits are more economical with public funds in that they do not give assistance to higher income families who least need it. Whilst the Child Poverty Action Group (CPAG) argues that the 'poor targeting' argument is exaggerated, it is effectively assuming that even households on average incomes should be eligible for child benefit rather than say the poorest 10–20 per cent. Possible economies include:

- **Means-testing**. Child benefit could become a means-tested (rather than categorical) benefit. This could be achieved by incorporation of child benefit into working families tax credit and income support. In principle, it would safeguard the position of low-income families. Whilst the lower take-up rates of these other benefits would mean that some low-income families would be disadvantaged, the higher benefit rate (made possible by means testing) may itself increase take-up by families most in need of child support.
- **Taxation**. Taxing child benefit would no longer recoup the large amounts originally expected because of the independent taxation of husband and wife (see Chapter 10). Independent taxation would base the means-tested benefit on the wife's income alone and therefore, if she was either not working or in low-paid part-time work, little or no tax liability would be incurred. In that case even fairly affluent families would still be eligible for child benefit whilst a single working

mother earning more than the tax-free allowance (see Chapter 10) would pay tax on the benefit. Such inequity would increase the political unpopularity of taxing child benefit. Nonetheless the estimated tax recoupment would have been £0.85 billion in 1999/2000.

- **Reduced real value**. Child benefit is generally index-linked to retail prices rather than to earnings so that its value relative to earnings tends to fall (earnings having risen faster than prices). Moreover, the government could prioritise the working families tax credit over child benefit, diverting incremental resources from the latter to the former.

Incapacity benefit

Formerly known as *invalidity benefit*, incapacity benefit is payable after 28 weeks on other sickness benefits, is the second largest **contributory** benefit and is typically more than triple the cost of unemployment benefit with which it is combined in **Table 9.5**. This is because it is thought to be a disguised unemployment benefit for many recipients. During the later 1980s fears were expressed that lax interpretation of the guidelines by general practitioners had been overly generous towards intending claimants and had significantly contributed to the rapidly rising expenditure on invalidity benefit. This hardly appears to be a marginal effect, those claiming having risen from 600 000 in 1978/9 to 1.5 million by 1992/3. Expenditure had doubled in real terms during the previous decade. Moreover sickness and invalidity benefits were forecast to account for almost a third of the growth in the social security bill during the later 1990s. In the mid 1990s, some 70 per cent of the long-term sick and disabled were ex-manual blue-collar workers, concentrated in areas with declining industries. This explains the suspicion that invalidity benefit was being misused as a form of unemployment benefit. The ongoing growth is apparently due, in part, to growing numbers of women and white-collar claimants – perhaps an inevitable reflection of the restructured labour market.

The basic rate of invalidity benefit was about 25 per cent greater than unemployment benefit and was potentially open-ended in nature, whereas unemployment benefit was only paid for 12 months at that time. Moreover, unlike both unemployment benefit and pensions, invalidity benefit was not taxable and no deduction was made to take account of any occupational pension which a recipient may have received.

These differential rates and conditions created incentives to claim invalidity benefit rather than unemployment benefit, and also to defer entitlement to the state retirement pension (possible for up to five years). Whether reflecting over-generous invalidity benefit or insufficient levels of unemployment benefit, it was thought that this disparity could account for some of the increase in the numbers of claimants of invalidity benefit. Other significant causes seem to be an ageing population, a growing consciousness of disability and a greater expectation of financial support from the state, not just in terms of invalidity benefit but also other related benefits (disability living allowance, attendance allowance and so on). Clearly, expenditure needed to be controlled, **first**, by restricting eligibility and, **second**, by means-testing or taxation.

In 1994 invalidity benefit was replaced by **incapacity benefit**, the latter being both taxable and subject to more stringent medical tests to ensure that people registering as medically unfit for work (in order to claim benefit) were genuine cases. The 1997 Labour government subsequently introduced *personal-capability assessments* for incapacity benefit recipients to determine what, if any, work they are capable of doing. The change of name to incapacity benefit was symbolic in that the new policy focuses on claimants' capacity for work instead of viewing them as disabled and so not fit for any work at all. Taxation is an indirect form of means-testing and is probably more acceptable than direct means-testing.

Not surprisingly these proposals created considerable controversy. Apparent concern with value for money became highly politicised as denying the long-term sick and invalids the benefits to which they are (or should be) entitled. Nevertheless, the long-term sick and disabled typically experience employer discrimination against them, hence reduced motivation to find work, therefore increasingly out-dated skills and lack of suitable jobs. This explains the 1997 Labour government's introduction of the New Deal for disabled people (see Chapter 8).

Statutory sick pay

As was the case for invalidity benefit, an increasing number of people were claiming sickness benefit (payable for 28 weeks). At any one time about 330 000 people were claiming statutory sick pay (approaching half those claiming unemployment benefit). Until 1992 employers were able to claim the full cost of this contributory benefit from the Exchequer. Besides the cost to the public sector, it was argued that full reimbursement of sick pay provided employers with no incentive to improve their workers' motivation and morale or to improve their attendance records. Hence in 1992 the subsidy was reduced to 80 per cent, employers bearing the remaining 20 per cent. Any further reduction would impose additional costs on business and could adversely affect Britain's competitiveness. The government would probably feel obliged to provide additional tax allowances in order to partially offset the extra costs. More problematic would be any tendency by firms to dismiss workers who fall sick and to avoid recruiting those who are more likely to claim sick pay due to illness.

Pensions

The state retirement pension is by far the largest benefit (see **Table 9.5**), being paid to about 10 million claimants. Receipt of the state retirement pension is conditional upon having a record of prior payments of national insurance contributions (NICs). This has included most male workers in the past (having predominantly worked full time). However less than 30 per cent of women aged 60 and above in 1993 qualified for a full retirement pension through their own NICs, either because they had not paid them in full (married women were previously allowed to pay reduced NICs) or because they had spent insufficient time in paid employment. The same effect will become apparent for a growing minority of men employed in part-time, casual or short-term employment or those who have become long-term unemployed.

The basic pension was index-linked to earnings prior to 1980 but to retail prices thereafter. Hence, whilst maintaining its real purchasing power, its value relative to earnings has fallen, earnings having risen faster than prices. The basic (single person) pension was equal to 20 per cent of average earnings in 1979, falling to 15 per cent by 1992 and projected to fall to 8 per cent by the year 2030. If the basic single-person state pension had been index-linked to earnings inflation instead of to retail price inflation after 1980 it would have been 44 per cent higher in 2000, costing an extra £20 billion per year by 2002. The earnings-related element of the state earnings-related pension scheme (SERPS) provides some offset against the falling value of the basic pension in relation to earnings. However SERPS excludes the 10 million or so who do not contribute to it because of their uneven NIC records. This may be due to part-time work and unemployment or because firms are instituting new forms of contract that treat employees as nominally self-employed, having to make their own provision for payment of NICs. Hence the state pension will become increasingly irrelevant to those on middle and upper incomes. At best it will become a minor supplement to other income sources from private and occupational pensions, maturing life assurance policies, home ownership and shareholdings.

About two-thirds of male workers and half of employed women have **occupational pension schemes**, to which both they and their employers contribute. An estimated five million or so people also have **personal pensions** (via life insurance company schemes). The remaining third or so of workers are solely dependent on the **state retirement pension**. Private and occupational pensions are **funded schemes** in that those who pay into them subsequently benefit. The basic state pension is an **unfunded scheme** since it is financed by those still in work. It involves a transfer from the current generation of workers to the current generation of retired people and so has implications for NICs and the tax burden faced by current workers.

Fears about the rising cost of pensions have been exaggerated, in the UK at least. The more generous pension arrangements of other countries have created much more severe financing problems. Nevertheless, British pensioners also benefit from other free welfare provisions, including those who are automatically eligible for income support. In addition, elderly British people do not have to pay for hospital accommodation, unlike the elderly in France (where state pensions are 70 per cent of average earnings). Hence international comparisons may be somewhat misleading in that the adequacy of any benefit depends on what else is received from the state.

The net result of this complex situation of retirement finances is that many pensioners (e.g. those with occupational pensions) have been growing more affluent whilst the poorest have become increasingly dependent on means-tested social security benefits to supplement the state retirement pension. Pensioners display one of the widest distributions of income of any demographic group. Hence not all pensioners are poor, but the basic state retirement pension is becoming increasingly ineffective as a means of relieving the poverty of those who are poor. Estimates produced by the Institute of Fiscal Studies show that it is much more cost effective to benefit poor pensioners through means-tested income support than by increasing the basic state retirement pension.

This declining value relative to general standards of living calls into question the contributory principle, i.e. that national insurance benefits have been earned and are paid as a right rather than as charity (see Chapter 10). The basic retirement pension will ultimately become so small relative to average earnings that a working lifetime's NICs will not be worthwhile. This also makes it clear that the basic state pension will not impose an intolerable burden on the economy into the future, notwithstanding the demographic bulge in the over-65s in the twenty-first century. On the basis of the then existing pension ages of 65 for men and 60 for women, the Office of Population Censuses and Surveys forecast a rise from 9.1 million pensioners in 1991 to 9.6 million in 2001, followed by a 50 per cent increase to 14.4 million by 2031. The question of how to respond to this demographic change is not straightforward. Options include the following.

First, raise the retirement age. The different retirement ages for men (65) and women (60) clearly discriminated in favour of women. Government calculations suggested that equalising male and female retirement ages at 63 would be cost-neutral. Equalising them at 60 would cost an extra £3.5 billion a year at 1992 prices because men would retire earlier. Equalising both at 65 would save £3 billion annually because women would retire later. Whilst remaining committed to the basic state pension the then Conservative government decided to achieve expenditure savings with a common retirement age of 65 phased in over ten years from 2010 onwards. Hence no woman aged 44 or over in 1994 will be affected and savings will not be achieved for almost two decades. Thereafter public expenditure savings will be substantial. Other countries have adopted similar responses: Japan has raised the age of entitlement to state retirement pension from 60 to 65, Germany and Italy are gradually increasing the pension age to 65 and the USA is gradually increasing it to 67.

Second, compulsory privatisation of pensions. The cost of state pensions could be reduced by privatising pensions, effectively making occupational pension schemes (or private pensions for the self-employed) compulsory for both full-time and part-time workers. Those with interrupted work records would have their pension contributions paid by the state. However there may be little real difference between such compulsory savings and taxes or social security contributions. The obvious disadvantage is that such a switch from an unfunded to a funded scheme would increase employers' costs for part-time workers and possibly choke off the fastest growing category of employment, especially for women. There is also an equity problem in that the current generation of workers would not only have to finance their own pensions but also those of the current retired generation.

Third, restrict the state pension to the elderly poor. Those with adequate private pensions would receive no support. Again there is an equity problem in that it creates a disincentive for people to save for their retirement since, by so doing, they lose entitlement to state benefits. Nonetheless, the 1997 Labour government began to progressively restrict increases in the state pension to the elderly poor through its minimum income guarantee, proposing to ameliorate any disincentive to save through the planned introduction of a pension credit in 2003 (see Chapter 12).

Finally, encourage people to opt out of the state scheme. Through tax relief on contributions, people are already being encouraged to arrange their own private pensions (see Chapter 8). This is a good example of how a private market may only be able to exist with the aid of public subsidy (i.e. the tax relief). However, opting out reduces government receipts as well as expenditures and therefore may have only a limited net impact on public finances. Nevertheless, giving employees tax incentives to opt out of state earnings-related pension schemes and replacing them with private pension arrangements appears to be the most practical reform of pensions. Since this can only be financially worthwhile for people who are at the start of their working lives, any reduction in public spending will only occur in the long term.

Personal social services

Although not part of the social security programme, the provision of personal social services has had a profound impact on the social security budget. It is forecast that there will be 79 'dependants' (children aged up to 15 and retired elderly people) for every 100 people of working age by the year 2031 compared with only 63 in 1991. Those over 75, the group making most use of health and personal social services, was forecast to rise from 3.6 million in 1991 to 6.1 million by 2031. The claims on the social security budget are clearly set to rise, as are those on health (pensioners accounting for more than 45 per cent of spending) and community and residential care.

In particular, provision of residential care for the elderly by local government and the voluntary and private sectors has led to substantial payments of income support and housing benefit. Social security support for people in private and voluntary residential care and nursing homes increased from £10 million in 1979 (12 000 claimants) to £1.6 billion in 1991 (220 000 claimants) and was forecast to grow to £4.1 billion in 1995/6 if the system were to stay unchanged.

Being demand-led, this growth was largely outside central government's control. It was primarily a result of increased numbers of claimants since national limits on the level of individual payments meant that the system was based more on flat-rate payments than on cost-related ones. It was exacerbated as health authorities devolved responsibility for funding long-term nursing care onto the social security budget and as many reduced the number of long-stay geriatric beds, including those for mentally ill patients. Moreover the need for formal systems of institutionalised care is expected to grow, given both the forecast increased dependency ratios and the diversion of unpaid, informal (particularly female) carers into paid employment.

Reforms were introduced in 1993 partly as a result of these increasing costs. Local government's role changed from one of direct provision of residential care to that of designing, organising and purchasing care provided by independent (private and voluntary) homes, an example of non-competitive contracting out (see Chapter 8). The government introduced a shift from residential care to community care, and especially to domiciliary support in elderly people's own homes. Although controversial, this was widely considered to be both more cost effective and more appropriate to the needs of most elderly people who prefer to stay in their own homes. Some cabinet ministers were openly critical of people who expected their elderly relatives to be looked after at the state's expense, even when they had the financial means to provide care themselves (e.g. from the sale of the elderly person's home upon entry into residential or nursing care).

9.6 Is social security spending out of control?

In 1949, in the first full year of the welfare state, social security accounted for 13.5 per cent of public expenditure. That proportion rose to 18 per cent by 1971 and, as already noted in **Table 9.3**, by the mid 1990s it was 30 per cent. Not surprisingly, during the early 1990s there were claims that social security spending was out of control.

Overall, the 3.3 per cent annual increase in spending on benefits in the early 1990s was projected to lead to a social security budget of £97 billion by the year 1999/2000 compared with £74 billion in 1992/3. In fact, the 1999/2000 figure was greater at £103.6 billion (see **Table 9.5**). In early 2000, taking into account the impact on the state retirement pension of the ageing population, the government forecast continuing growth at 2.5 per cent per annum, matching the growth of GDP and growing in real terms by 1 per cent per annum. Whilst a slower rate of growth than previously, this forecast assumes no increase in unemployment and no downturn in economic activity.

During the mid 1990s, estimates by the Department of Social Security showed that some 6 million people (with some 5 million dependants) claimed income support. Hence, 11 million people depended on income support, one in six of the population, compared with just over 4 million being supported by the equivalent benefit in 1979. Family credit added almost another half million claimants with over 1 million dependants. These figures, together with payments of child benefit in respect of some 13 million children in about 7 million families, demonstrate the extensive coverage of the social security system. This situation is the result of dramatic increases in welfare spending in the 1960s and also in the 1980s and early 1990s (see **Table 9.3**).

The increasingly extensive coverage and cost of social security led to claims that the social security budget was out of control and provided the basis for the piecemeal reforms outlined above. However the London School of Economics Welfare State Programme argued that the welfare state as a whole (including education, health, personal social services and housing as well as social security) is not out of control. In line with most other industrialised countries, there was rapid growth relative to GDP after 1960 but the UK remained below the Organisation for Economic Co-operation and Development (OECD) unweighted average during the 1980s and 1990s. As already noted in respect of **Table 9.3** 'all services' spending has fallen relative to GDP. In fact, from the early to mid 1990s social security expenditure remained very stable whilst that for health grew substantially, maintaining its growth since the mid 1980s.

Some of the increase in real spending on social security during the later 1980s had been a consequence of supply-side measures (see Chapter 8). These included the scrapping of Wages Councils in cleaning, catering and hairdressing and other measures leading to lower wages which therefore increased claims of family credit and other means-tested benefits. Increased payments of housing benefit reflected the government's policies regarding deregulation of rents in the private rental sector and increasing council rents in order to move closer to market-determined rents, so encouraging sitting tenants to purchase their council houses.

Moreover, some of the extra social security budget was simply a switch between accounting heads within the public sector rather than a net increase. For example the extra spending on the social security budget due to higher council rents was matched by a reduction in the need for rent subsidy within the housing budget of the Department of the Environment. This was the result of the changing role of local government from direct provider of housing to administrator of housing benefit (for which it has had administrative responsibility since 1982/3). The share of central government housing expenditure devoted to benefits rose from 40 per cent in 1979 to over 85 per cent within the subsequent decade, the remainder being general subsidies to local authorities.

The increased central government payments will eventually be substituted for by those council tenants who are not eligible for housing benefit as local authority 'ring-fenced' housing revenue accounts become increasingly self-financing. Thus there will be a shift away from the direct provision of low-rent housing to all tenants whether low income or not ('bricks and mortar' subsidies), to rental housing let at market rents with personal subsidies specifically targeted at low-income households by means testing.

9.7 The changing philosophy for the welfare state

The early 1990s debate about the welfare state became increasingly philosophical, questioning some of its fundamental principles, not just in the UK but in the EU generally. The issue is not just one of saving money. It also involves a re-evaluation of the relationship between the state and the individual. There are three basic options for reform:

1. **The status quo – but with more generous benefits**. This option would probably exacerbate the current perceived problems of high welfare dependency and disincentives to work.
2. **Dismantle the welfare state**. The Institute of Economic Affairs (a right-wing think-tank) argues that the welfare state is causing psychological and moral harm by creating and sustaining a dependency culture. Hence it proposes the dismantling of the welfare state, beginning with phasing out unemployment and incapacity benefits, and ultimately pensions and health care.

3. **Radically reform the welfare state**. The Commission on Social
    Justice (a left-wing think-tank) proposed a new conception of social
    justice. It suggested that Beveridge's *five great evils* (of want, disease,
    ignorance, squalor and idleness) should be replaced by the *five great
    opportunities* (of lifelong learning, work, good health, safe environ-
    ment and financial independence). The role of the welfare state
    would change from that of a safety-net (*from the cradle to the grave*)
    to an enabling instrument for personal development (providing a
    hand up not simply a *hand out*).

Both the Conservative and Labour parties subscribe to the third option. If
fully implemented, it will represent a radical departure from the welfare
state of the past 50 years in creating a looser compact between the
individual and an enabling government. In effect, this is a bipartisan
rejection of the universalist state-run Beveridge model and a rewriting of
the *cradle to grave* contract.

A general principle with which most people would agree is that the
welfare state should increase society's (and the individual's) ability to
cope with socioeconomic and demographic change, that ability extending across the entire population. The idea of the welfare state as a safety-
net, shielding people if normal income falls as a result of specified
contingencies, is becoming increasingly superseded by the welfare state
as enabler and facilitator. Rights and entitlements have been central to
social progress in the past but it is now being increasingly recognised
that they involve parallel responsibilities, obligations and participation
by the individual.

For example, making receipt of some benefits conditional upon
participation in training and work-experience schemes caused considerable political controversy in Britain during the 1980s and 1990s. It was
condemned for tying benefit payments to the performance of low-skilled
work. However other EU countries such as Denmark and the Nether-
lands regard such conditionality as non-punitive, as an essential aspect
of social caring.

In other words, rather than creating dependency traps, the social
security system should create incentives to new employment and self-
sufficiency. In the UK receipt of benefit had previously been conditional
upon undertaking no work at all: the unemployed had to be precisely
that. It was argued that this created dependency upon the state as the
unemployed increasingly lost both skills and the work ethic the longer
they were unemployed. Since demand-side measures based on macroeconomic fiscal and monetary expansion were no longer regarded as
effective, the policy response had to focus on supply-side retraining and
reskilling initiatives. Hence receipt of benefit had to be made conditional
on participation in such schemes (see Chapter 8).

Social caring was increasingly viewed as providing the individual with the wherewithal for self-improvement, enabling investment by individuals in their own human capital. According to this philosophy the social security system is no longer a demand-side, macroeconomic, counter-cyclical Keynesian fiscal response based on automatic stabilisers. Instead it becomes a microeconomic, supply-side, long-term response to economic restructuring.

On a more practical, less philosophical level, the social security system was created during a period of mass, standardised, industrial production based on full-time male employment and the traditional nuclear family. However by the late 1980s manufacturing accounted for less than a quarter of GDP whilst services accounted for two thirds, the remaining sectors being energy, construction and agriculture. By the late 1990s, the service sector accounted for over 70 per cent of GDP. Industrial production was becoming increasingly organised along non-standardised post-Fordist lines (i.e. small-scale, customised, batch production based on a just-in-time delivery basis) that offered less job security to male blue-collar workers.

The social security system has to take account of social and economic restructuring. The massive rises in unemployment during the recessions of the early 1980s and early 1990s were predominantly full-time male redundancies. Female employment rose dramatically amongst both married and single women and became increasingly concentrated in the service sector (both public and private). The proportion of married women in paid employment rose from a tenth in the 1930s to a fifth in the 1950s, a third in the 1960s, half in the 1970s and two thirds in the 1980s. Women now comprise half the paid labour force, although most (particularly married women) are part-time workers. In general, employment seems to be increasingly casualised, 'flexible' and low paid, especially for part-time work.

Together with the social changes noted above towards higher divorce rates, cohabiting (not married) couples and single parent families, this social and economic restructuring has created a radically different role for the social security system in the 1980s and 1990s from that which prevailed during the four decades following the 1942 Beveridge Report. Beveridge's welfare state was an instrument of strongly interventionist state paternalism based on full employment for male full-time workers and the nuclear family, wives being financially dependent on their husbands. In contrast, during the later 1980s and 1990s the social security system has increasingly become an enabling instrument for the economic and social self-improvement of individuals. In other words the social security system (and the welfare state generally) is a reflection of political, economic and social restructuring.

Of particular relevance, a shift towards part-time employment has potentially profound implications for public spending and tax revenues. Employers can reduce their expenditure on NICs by employing part-time rather than full-time workers. Neither employer nor employee have to pay NICs on very low earnings (see Chapter 10), which is often the case where employees work less than 16 hours per week. Part-time workers who do not contribute to national insurance lose all or part of their pension (depending on their previous and subsequent contribution records), as well as Jobseeker's allowance and sickness and incapacity benefits. They also pay little or no income tax. Hence an on-going replacement of full-time by part-time employment may result in NICs and income tax revenues being constrained whilst social security benefits increase. The numbers of low-paid workers will increase if the national minimum wage is not increased in line with average earnings. It will increasingly have to be topped up by the working families tax credit, as well as by housing benefit, council tax benefit and so on. It therefore appears likely that the shift from contributory to non-contributory benefits will continue, with obvious implications for tax rates.

9.8 Conclusions

Public expenditure policy and practice have concentrated on both controlling public spending and achieving increased value for money through privatisation and through internal and external markets (see Chapter 8) and, more philosophically, by enabling personal development. These objectives were highlighted by the quotations at the beginning of this chapter, the first being from the Conservative government, the second from the subsequent Labour government. This chapter has made clear that, rather than being mutually exclusive, these objectives can be mutually reinforcing and are now encompassed within a quite sophisticated policy, the basic elements of which now receive cross-party support.

Whilst both the policy and its theoretical rationale (in terms of reducing crowding out) are clear, the practice is extremely detailed and complex. It is primarily **microeconomic** in approach, dealing with the individual items of spending and the particular characteristics of service delivery. It is also **supply-side** in nature, emphasising financial and economic incentives faced by service users and providers.

The discussion of social security in particular has made it clear that public expenditure policy and practice are based both on a social code and on moral principles relating to the parallel rights and responsibilities of individuals for their own welfare and for that of their dependent children. Ongoing social security reforms have increasingly focused on getting able-bodied benefit recipients back into jobs as a condition of their continuing receipt of benefits. Notwithstanding the national minimum wage, this work-based welfare allows labour markets to create more low-wage employment. This minimises the extent to which the welfare state acts as a barrier to economic growth, complements moral arguments about the need to foster individual responsibility and self-reliance, reduces the financial burden on the taxpayer, and yet also allows low-income families to be supported by the state. In this way equity and social justice are neatly complemented by increased economic incentives making work financially worthwhile.

The social security system has, at least in part, increasingly been shaped to promote a competitive, efficient and flexible labour market, not just by making work financially worthwhile but also by encouraging (some would say cajoling or compelling) unemployed people to compete effectively for jobs. The crucial interaction of social security benefits with labour markets and labour market policy was increasingly recognised by both the Conservative and Labour governments of the 1980s and 1990s. This recognition was crystallised in the Jobseeker's Allowance, applicants no longer being able to refuse employment because they found the wage level or other conditions unacceptable. The JSA therefore reinforces labour market mechanisms because recipients have to be available for and actively seeking work. This obviates the unemployment trap, the working families tax credit essentially doing the same for the poverty trap. By such means, supply-side initiatives could create increasingly free and competitive markets whilst avoiding the unacceptable inequities for those least able to compete due to lack of skills and aptitude.

It has to be borne in mind, however, that in the late 1990s almost half of social security benefit expenditures was accounted for by elderly people, just over a quarter by sick and disabled people, a fifth by families and only 7 per cent by the unemployed. Hence, the impact on social security spending of welfare-to-work initiatives will necessarily be limited. Of more impact on the accounting figures will be the shift of the working families tax credit from the Department of Social Security budget to the Inland Revenue budget.

The discussion of social security has illustrated the fact that social and economic policies are interdependent. This interdependence highlights the highly restrictive nature of the assumptions underlying Pareto optimality (see Chapter 2). It also demonstrates the major shortcomings of the traditional approach of undergraduate textbooks in dealing separately with public sector economics and social policy. It makes clear the fundamental errors in regarding economics as concerned solely with efficiency issues whilst social policy is concerned solely with equity issues. In fact the two issues are crucially interdependent and part of a broader framework of social justice. These are all crucially influenced by the increasing complexity of family structures and working patterns.

Further reading

Allen, I. and Bourke Dowling, S. (1998) *Teenage Mothers: Decisions and Outcomes* (London: Policy Studies Institute)

Barr, N. (1998) *The Economics of the Welfare State*, 3rd edn (Oxford: Oxford University Press).

Bennett, F. and Walker, R. (1998) *Working with Work. An Initial Assessment of Welfare to Work*, Joseph Rowntree Foundation (York: York Publishing Services).

Bradshaw, J. and Millar, J. (1991) *Lone Parent Families in the UK*, Department of Social Security Research Report No. 6 (London: HMSO).

Burghes, L. (1993) *One Parent Families: Policy Options for the 1990s* (York: Joseph Rowntree Foundation).

Commission on Social Justice (1993) *Social Justice in a Changing World* (London: Institute for Public Policy Research).

DE/DSS (1994) *Jobseeker's Allowance*, Cm 2867, Department of Employment, Department of Social Security (London: HMSO).

Department of Social Security (online). Available from <http://www.dss.gov.uk>.

DSS (1993) *Equality in State Pension Age*, Cmnd 2420, Department of Social Security (London: HMSO).

DSS (1993) *The Growth of Social Security*, Department of Social Security (London: HMSO).

DSS (1993) *Containing the Cost of Social Security: The International Context*, Department of Social Security (London: HMSO).

DSS (1994) *Income Related Benefits – Estimates of Take-up for 1990 and 1991*, Department of Social Security (London: HMSO).

DSS (1995) *Piloting Change in Social Security: Helping People into Work*, Department of Social Security (London: HMSO).

DSS (1998) *New Ambitions for Our Country: A New Contract for Welfare*, Cm 3805, 26 March, Department of Social Security (London: Stationery Office).

DSS (1998) *The Case for Welfare Reform*, Department of Social Security (London: Stationery Office).

DSS (2000) *Social Security Departmental Report: The Government's Expenditure Plans 2000/01–2001/02*, Department of Social Security (London: Stationery Office).

Erens, B. and Ghate, D. (1993) *Invalidity Benefit: A Longitudinal Survey of New Recipients*, Department of Social Security Research Report No. 20 (London: HMSO).

Gardiner, K. (1997) *Bridges from Benefit to Work: A Review*, Joseph Rowntree Foundation (York: York Publishing Services).

Glennerster, H. (1997) *Paying for Welfare: Towards 2000*, 3rd edn (Oxford: Prentice Hall).

Glennerster, H. and Hills, J. (eds) (1998) *The State of Welfare: The Economics of Social Spending*, 2nd edn (Oxford: Oxford University Press).

Grover, C. and Stewart, J. (1999) ' "Market Workfare": Social Security, Social Regulation and Competitiveness in the 1990s', *Journal of Social Policy*, vol. 28, no. 1, pp. 73–96.

Grover, C. and Stewart, J. (2000) 'Modernising Social Security? Labour and its Welfare-to-Work Strategy', *Social Policy and Administration*, vol. 34, no. 3, pp. 235–52.

Haskey, J. (1998) 'One-parent Families and their Dependent Children in Great Britain', *Population Trends*, 91 (Spring) (London: Office of National Statistics).

Hills, J. (1994) *The Future of Welfare: A Guide to the Debate*, the LSE Welfare State Programme (York: Joseph Rowntree Foundation).

HoC (1993) *The Operation of the Child Support Act*, House of Commons Paper 69 (London: HMSO).

HM Treasury (online). Available from <http://www.hm-treasury.gov.uk>.

HM Treasury (2000) *Public Expenditure Statistical Analyses 2000–01*, Cm 4601 (London: HM Treasury).

Jarvis, T. (1997) *Welfare-to-Work: The New Deal*, House of Commons Library Research Paper 97/118 (London: House of Commons).

Kemp, P. (1998) *Housing Benefit – Time for Reform*, Joseph Rowntree Foundation (York: York Publishing Services).

McKay, S. and Marsh, A. (1994) *Lone Parents and Work: The Effects of Benefits and Maintenance*, Department of Social Security Research Report No. 25 (London: HMSO).

Marsland, D. and Pirie, M. (1994) *The End of the Welfare State* (London: Institute of Economic Affairs).

Millar, J. (2000) *Keeping Track of Welfare Reform: The New Deal Programmes*, Joseph Rowntree Foundation (York: York Publishing Services).

Mullard, M. (1993) *The Politics of Public Expenditure*, 2nd edn (London: Routledge).

Noble, M. *et al.* (1998) *Lone Mothers Moving In and Out of Benefits*, Joseph Rowntree Foundation (York: York Publishing Services).

Organisation for Economic Co-operation and Development (OECD) (online). Available from <http://www.oecd.org>.

PSI (1993) *Families, Work and Benefits* (London: Policy Studies Institute).

Ritchie, J., Ward, K. and Duldig, W. (1993) *GPs and IVB: A Qualitative Study of the Role of GPs in the Award of Invalidity Benefit*, Department of Social Security Research Report No. 18 (London: HMSO).

SMF (1998) *The Future of Welfare*, Paper No. 35 (London: The Social Market Foundation).

10 Tax Policy and Practice

10.1 Introduction
10.2 Principles of Taxation
10.3 The 'Burden of Taxation'
10.4 The Balance Between Direct and Indirect Taxes
10.5 The Main Principles of UK Tax Policy During the 1980s and 1990s
10.6 Extending the VAT Base
10.7 Earmarked Taxes
10.8 Integration of Income Tax and National Insurance
10.9 Conclusions
Appendix 10.1 UK Taxes
Appendix 10.2 The Impact of Applying VAT to Newspapers
Appendix 10.3 Abolition of the Local Domestic Property Tax
Appendix 10.4 Tax Harmonisation

Government activity has to be financed. A broad tax base, with a simple structure, and low marginal rates, does the least harm to enterprise and to work effort (1994 White Paper, *Competitiveness: Helping Business to Win*, Cm 2563, London: HMSO, p. 17).

The Budget sets long-term ambitions for Britain by securing economic stability based on low inflation and sound public finances, encouraging work . . . making work pay . . . and . . . promoting enterprise through a range of tax incentives, creating a fairer society and protecting our environment (*Budget 1998: The Pocket Budget*, London: HM Treasury, p. 1).

10.1 Introduction

The analysis in this chapter frequently combines taxes and social security contributions on the grounds that both forms of payment are compulsory. Taxes are unrequited payments (to general government) in the sense that the benefits to any one individual that they finance are not normally in proportion to that person's payment. Social security payments, levied in the form of national insurance contributions (NICs), resemble taxes in that their payment is related to occupational earnings and because the amount of benefits they finance is not necessarily related to the value of NICs paid. Nonetheless, receipt of benefits may depend upon appropriate contributions having been paid (see Chapter 9). Whilst their very name indicates the different purposes for which they are levied, employers' NICs have nevertheless been colloquially referred to as a *'tax on jobs'*.

In its 1984 Green Paper, *The Next Ten Years: Public Expenditure and Taxation into the 1990s*, the then Conservative government noted that, year after year, higher taxation had been required to finance ever higher public expenditure. It was explicit in its view that increases in taxation have had a serious impact on Britain's economic performance over many years. This view is clearly consistent with the crowding-out hypothesis in general and the disincentives-to-work hypothesis in particular (see Chapters 4 and 5).

The 1984 Green Paper provided the basic rationale for the tax reforms of the 1980s and early 1990s. The overriding emphasis had been to reduce the rates of taxation on personal and corporate incomes (so as to reduce disincentive effects) and, ideally, reduce the overall burden of taxation in the economy. However if (as the 1984 Green Paper noted) there is an in-built tendency for spending to rise and an in-built resistance to public expenditure reductions, then cuts in the levels of income and corporate taxes necessitate increases in taxes on goods and services. This is, in fact, what happened during the 1980s and 1990s, together with a broadening of the tax base. That broader tax base facilitated the simpler structures and the lower marginal rates of personal and corporate taxes referred to in the first quotation above (from the then Conservative government).

The second quotation above (from the then Labour government) makes clear that government policies during the 1990s were also intended to encourage investment and raise skill levels, this being regarded as essential for long-term prosperity. Such a *long-term microeconomic supply-side emphasis* (see Chapter 8) requires stable public finances and so the avoidance of *short-term macroeconomic measures* based upon fiscal boosts and retrenchments. This long-term perspective has fundamental implications for assessment of the annual Budget, at which the government sets its tax rates and bases for the forthcoming financial year. The media typically assesses each Budget in terms of the distributional impact on the different income groups of tax changes on the cost of cigarettes and tobacco, wine and spirits, beer, income tax rates and allowances and so on. The media typically assesses whether Budgets are broadly socialist (in reducing the tax burden on low-income groups) or anti-socialist (resulting in the reverse outcome). However, a *microeconomist's assessment would focus on the extent to which a Budget introduces or reinforces supply-side reforms*, for example reducing any disincentives to work, to invest and to stimulate enterprise generally. In practice, budgets of the 1980s and 1990s attempted to achieve elements of both redistribution and supply-side improvements.

10.2   Principles of taxation

The key principles of any tax system include equity, efficiency and economy.

Equity

There are two concepts of equity.

First, horizontal equity: it is generally accepted that taxes should treat taxpayers in similar positions in the same way, for example taking equal proportions of equal incomes.

Second, vertical equity: it is generally accepted that people with higher incomes should pay higher amounts of taxation than those with low incomes. However there is less agreement about the appropriate degree of unequal treatment of people in unequal positions. There are three alternative tax structures:

- **Proportional**, taking a **constant** share of all income levels, the marginal and average tax rates being equal (i.e. the rate of tax equals the proportion of income taken by tax – see Chapter 4)
- **Progressive**, taking a **rising** share as income increases, the marginal tax rate being greater than the average tax rate
- **Regressive**, taking a **lower** share as income increases, the marginal tax rate being less than the average tax rate

The rich pay more tax in cash terms than the poor under all of these tax structures (in the last case, as long as the marginal tax rate is above zero). However vertical equity is usually taken to mean a progressive tax system. Nonetheless, it can be argued that a progressive tax system breaches constitutional liberty by applying a different set of tax rules to a minority of citizens (i.e. the rich or affluent). Moreover, a highly progressive tax may lead to excessive public expenditure if it encourages the belief that someone else (i.e. the rich) will pay for spending.

In fact equity is also concerned with reward for effort and with responsibilities as well as rights and entitlements. Both the Conservative and Labour governments of the 1980s and 1990s argued that people should be allowed to retain more of what they earn, rather than have it taxed and spent by the state. Chapter 9 demonstrated how these changing perceptions of equity underpin reform of the welfare state.

Hence equity is not as clear a principle as it appears. It is certainly not restricted to the achievement of a more equal distribution of income (see Chapter 12).

Efficiency

In terms of the efficiency criterion, taxes are only sanctioned if they improve allocative efficiency, although 'second best' theory makes this problematic (see Chapter 2). Any economic distortions they create should specifically be designed to offset market distortions such as negative externalities caused by pollution. Otherwise taxes should be financed by economic rents (see Chapter 4) so that they introduce no allocative distortions, for example where required to finance pure public goods. At a more practical level, it is generally agreed that taxation should not lead to inefficiency through the creation of, for example, significant disincentive-to-work effects (such as those created by the poverty and unemployment traps) or of disincentive-to-save effects.

Economy

The structure of taxation should be such that the costs of collecting taxes and administering the tax system are small relative to the tax yield. This applies equally to the government and to taxpayers.

These three principles may be contradictory. For example designing a tax system that is easy to administer and simple to understand may result in horizontal inequities by failing to take account of the different circumstances of taxpayers with similar incomes. For example, of two people with identical earned incomes one may have dependent children to support whilst the other may have none. Tax allowances (tax credits) in respect of children can be used but such measures increase administrative costs.

10.3   The 'burden of taxation'

An economic interpretation of '**burden of taxation**' is that taxes that deter economic activity create an '**excess burden**' or '**deadweight loss**' of taxation (see Chapter 4). In comparison with this highly specific (and value-free) economic concept, the more general meaning of the term 'burden of taxation' is emotive and value-laden. Unlike the economic concept, the general meaning of 'burden of taxation' ignores the many benefits derived from public services financed by tax revenues. It is usually used either to indicate a regressive (inequitable) structure of taxation, or a moral or constitutional presumption that the state has no automatic right to sequester citizen's incomes. There are three main measures of the 'burden of taxation':

- **The level of direct and indirect taxes paid by hypothetical households on various multiples of average earnings**. Male full-time earnings are conventionally used as the benchmark, these being higher than female earnings (more women also working part-time). Earnings data is derived from the annual New Earnings Survey. Household types include single person households, single-earner couples with two children, two-earner couples without children, and so on. Figures calculated for each household type reflect the various standard tax allowances (e.g. income tax and NICs) and benefits (e.g. child benefit) for which they are eligible and assume a standard expenditure pattern for each household type based on the results of the Family Expenditure Survey (FES). However, they do not take account of non-standard tax reliefs (e.g. on tax-exempt savings) or expenditure patterns (i.e. relatively high saving or borrowing) and take no account of the self-employed or pensioners. Hence, the household types are not meant to be typical of the majority of taxpayers.
- **The amount of taxes paid by households at different levels within the distribution of income**. Figures are based upon the data collected by the FES, a relatively small sample survey which is necessarily subject to sampling errors. These errors limit calculations to earnings between 75 per cent and 150 per cent of the average. Moreover, the FES data for successive years are not necessarily comparable, most notably because the definition of income has changed over time (to include the value of company cars and low-interest loans from employers). These limitations also apply to the first measure of the burden of taxation.
- **The ratio of aggregate taxation to GDP**. There are different bases on which figures are compiled. All data series include social security contributions (NICs) and local and central government taxes. Data series are shown at both current and constant prices. Current prices are transformed into constant prices using the *GDP deflator* to take account of inflation during the period under consideration. Different data series include and exclude tax revenues from oil and gas production, changes in world oil prices in particular affecting the tax take quite substantially from year to year.

The first measure indicates that between 1978/9 and 1996/7 the burden of taxation fell for single-person households (from 45.6 per cent to 42.7 per cent) whilst that for a single-earner couple with two children rose (from 35.2 per cent to 37.8 per cent).

The second measure shows that by the end of the same period households in the top and bottom 20 per cent (quintiles) of the income distribution paid larger shares of their incomes in taxes than did middle-income households (in the second, third and fourth quintiles).

The third measure reveals that the aggregate tax burden rose (from 34 per cent to 36 per cent) over the same period. However, this measure fluctuated quite markedly during the period as the economy moved through the trade cycle, from recession to recovery during both the 1980s and 1990s.

Whilst these trends occurred during the Conservative Party's period of government 1979 to 1997, they continued following the election of the Labour government in 1997. For example, in 1998/9 the tax/GDP ratio was 37.1 per cent and forecast to stay almost unchanged until 2002/3, thereafter falling slightly.

This continuity is not surprising given that the new Labour government committed itself to maintain during its first two years in office the Conservatives' plans for public expenditure and taxation. The figures reflect many changes in tax and benefit regimes and economic growth in the UK (and in other countries) during the 1980s and 1990s. Furthermore, there were substantial rises in real incomes, such that those household groups paying a larger proportion of taxation nevertheless enjoyed increased spending power. Average male earnings more than tripled over the period whilst retail prices only doubled. Likewise, real GDP increased by almost half. However, the distribution of income became more unequal as incomes above the average rose faster than those below (see Chapter 12).

None of these measures establishes that taxation is a 'burden' on the economy. Chapter 4 made clear the considerable difficulty in identifying (let alone measuring) the excess burden (if any) of taxation. The first two measures ignore the value of public sector services financed by those taxes (i.e. exhaustive expenditures as distinct from transfer payments). The third measure assumes that the benefits of public services are equal to their financial costs, ignoring any public good or external (i.e. social) benefits they create.

International comparisons are also unable to determine whether or not there is an excessive burden of tax in the UK. Nevertheless, they are often used to determine whether the UK is out of step with other countries, for example having excessive levels of taxation. International comparisons (on a standardised basis) are provided by the OECD, both for the tax to GDP ratio and for taxes less cash benefits as a percentage of gross earnings for the average production worker in each country. Tax to GDP comparisons are more reliable over a run of years since different countries can be at different stages of the trade cycle, thus affecting the ratios. Whereas during the 1960s and 1970s the UK was consistently above average for taxes as a percentage of GDP, during the 1980s and 1990s the UK has been below average. By 1996, the UK figure was fully 6 percentage points below the EU average which, in turn, was higher than the OECD average (see **Table 10.1**).

The UK's recent low tax status has been mainly caused by the growth of taxation elsewhere. The ratio of total taxes (including social security contributions) to GDP in the EU as a whole rose dramatically by 10 percentage points between 1970 and 1991 (to 41 per cent) whereas the UK's ratio was unchanged (at 36 per cent). Hence the UK's shift from high to low tax status was caused by the growth of taxation elsewhere – it was not the result of radical cuts in the overall levels of UK taxation.

Despite the UK's low tax status, it is still possible for there to be high disincentive-to-work effects. The various tax to GDP ratios only indicate *average* tax rates whereas disincentive-to-work effects depend on *marginal* tax rates (see Chapter 4). Average tax rates could be low and yet marginal rates of tax could be high. In other words, the *structure* of taxation may be more important than the *share* of taxation in the economy in determining the degree of crowding out. In particular, whether or not the structure is consistent with supply-side criteria in not taxing jobs, instead taxing negative externalities such as pollution.

Over the long term, the UK's total tax revenues have depended much less on social security contributions than the EU average, the latter again being high relative to the OECD average. In 1996, the proportions of total tax receipts comprised of social security contributions were 16.8 per cent, 26.4 per cent and 22.3 per cent respectively (see **Table 10.1**). So, in summary, **the UK's tax/GDP ratio is typically relatively low and taxes on jobs (i.e. social security contributions) are a relatively low proportion of total taxes**.

The UK also tends to be below average in terms of the highest rates of personal income tax (PIT) and of corporate income tax (CIT), the latter referred to in the UK as 'corporation tax' (see **Table 10.1**). The situation in respect of taxation of the average production worker is more mixed, however. After taxation (PIT) of the average production worker's earnings, a single person had a significantly greater disposable income than the EU average, and was also just above the OECD average. However, a married man with two children had significantly less than the OECD average, although slightly more than the EU average (see **Table 10.1**). So, the average production worker in the UK seems less heavily taxed than in the EU as a whole. Nonetheless, disincentive-to-work effects could still be created as means-tested benefits are withdrawn, leading to the unemployment and poverty traps (see Chapters 4, 9 and 12). Certainly the relatively narrow base for employees' NICs can be expected to lead to high marginal tax rates on earnings

Table 10.1 The burden of taxation in the UK 1996

	Total tax receipts % of GDP	Tax structures (as % of total tax receipts)						Highest tax rates		Disposable income*	
		Personal income tax (PIT)	Corporate income tax (CIT)	Social security contributions		Taxes on goods and services	Other taxes			Single person	Married with 2 children
				Employees	Employers			PIT	CIT		
UK	36.0	25.9	10.5	7.2	9.6	35.2	11.6	40.0	31.0	74.8	76.5
EU average	42.4	26.0	7.5	10.1	16.3	31.2	8.8	49.7	36.3	69.5	75.6
OECD average	37.7	26.8	8.2	7.8	14.5	32.5	10.2	47.8	35.1	74.0	85.1

Notes:

* of average production worker as percentage of gross pay.
1. EU and OECD averages are unweighted.
2. According to the UK's budget for 2000/1, the UK tax–GDP ratio was 37.1 in 1998/9 and was estimated to be 37.0 in 1999/00. Other up-to-date UK figures are available in Table 10.2, Appendix 10.1.

Source: OECD Figures, 1999 Edition.

within that band (see Appendix 10.1). **Hence, the UK's 'low tax economy' status is not necessarily indicative of stronger incentives to work than elsewhere**.

In particular, the reader may be surprised to see (in **Table 10.1** and in **Table 10.2**, Appendix 10.1) that income tax typically raises only a quarter of total tax receipts in the UK. Whilst NICs typically raise another 16 per cent or so, unlike PIT they are not levied across the full range of earnings and so are higher than they would be if raised over that full range. One way of reducing any disincentive effects caused by relatively high NICs would therefore be to abolish the upper earnings limit for employees, above which NICs are not payable (see Appendix 10.1). However, during the late 1990s and early 2000s the Labour government's policy was instead to reduce the income tax paid by families by introducing tax credits for children and for working families (see below). Abolition of the upper earnings limit for employees would be tantamount to an increase in PIT and would inevitably lead to proposals to merge PIT and NICs (see section 10.8 below).

Tables 10.1 and **10.2** also reveal that whilst taxes on goods and services typically raise over a third of tax revenues, corporation tax typically raises only a tenth. The remaining 10 per cent or so of tax revenues is raised by other taxes, including council tax, capital gains tax, inheritance tax, and stamp duties (see Appendix 10.1).

10.4   The balance between direct and indirect taxes

Direct taxes are broadly Inland Revenue taxes, including income tax, corporation tax, and NICs. Indirect taxes include VAT and duties on alcohol, tobacco, fuel and so on, (collected by Customs and Excise), vehicle excise duty (collected by the Department of Environment, Transport and Regions), stamp duties (collected by the Inland Revenue) and property taxes (collected by local governments). Direct and indirect taxes are defined in Chapter 4. The balance between them changes over time by default, that is unless the government takes action to achieve a desired balance. This changing balance results from the following:

- **Fiscal drag**. Inflation erodes the real value of indirect taxes fixed in cash terms (i.e. most excise duties). Hence real revenues raised by most excise duties tend to fall. The major exceptions are the *ad valorem* (percentage) taxes, especially VAT, whose 'tax takes' rise in line with inflation. In contrast, more people begin paying income tax for the first time and more pay higher rates of tax as inflation raises their **cash** incomes above the thresholds for the tax-free personal allowance and different tax rates respectively. They are therefore 'dragged into' the fiscal net as inflation increases the effective rate of income tax. More families on low incomes become liable for income tax as the first part of earnings free of tax falls in real terms during inflationary periods. Fiscal drag therefore leads to particularly severe poverty and unemployment traps (see Chapter 4).

- **Growth of real incomes**. Even with inflation-indexed tax thresholds, temporal growth in real incomes will lead to increased payments of income tax under a progressive structure of direct taxation.

The net result of both of these effects is threefold:

- **More workers became liable to pay income tax and more paid higher proportions of their earnings in tax**. In the 1950s a married man did not pay income tax until his pay rose up to average earnings. By the mid 1990s, a married man began paying income tax when he reached 30 per cent of average earnings.
- **Many more workers were both paying income taxes and receiving social security benefits** (referred to as *'churning'*).
- **A switch in the balance of revenues from indirect to direct taxation occurred**.

The 1984 Green Paper noted that revenues from indirect taxes rose by less than half of those from income tax and NICs between 1963/4 and 1984/5. Hence rising public expenditure was not the only cause of increased direct tax deductions from average earnings over those two decades. There was also a shift in the balance of tax revenues from indirect taxes on commodities to direct taxes on incomes. Many of the tax reforms of the 1980s and 1990s sought to reduce the increasing dependence upon revenues from direct taxes.

10.5   The main principles of UK tax policy during the 1980s and 1990s

The then Conservative government's 1984 Green Paper expressed a desire to return to the relative tax levels of the early 1960s. Although not expressed in such terms, the subsequent Labour government adopted the same broad aims during the later 1990s. Policy objectives have generally been to shift the balance of taxation towards indirect taxes and away from direct taxes. At the same time tax reform has attempted to reduce any disincentives to work and to enterprise by cutting the rates of direct taxes whilst broadening their tax bases. Where possible, both the tax rates and tax bases of indirect taxes have been increased. Broadening the tax base facilitates lower marginal tax rates and reduces the allocative distortions created by narrowly based taxes that divert demand and activities towards commodities and occupations subject to lower or zero rates of taxation. The main tax changes are now considered.

Income tax

Cutting the rates of income tax

As already noted, the government's general policy has been to stimulate incentives to work, save and invest by reducing taxes on incomes. The means of achieving this have been:

- **Abolition of the investment income surcharge**. In 1979 the highest rate of tax on earned income was 83 per cent. Adding the investment income surcharge of 15 per cent (on unearned income – basically interest on bank deposits) raised the top tax rate to 98 per cent. The new Conservative government's first budget of 1979 reduced the highest tax rate on earned income to 60 per cent and the investment income surcharge was abolished in 1984. Very few people paid the 98 per cent tax rate. It encouraged **tax avoidance** (i.e. the *legal* ordering of one's income and wealth into non-taxable forms) and **tax evasion** (i.e. the *illegal* non-declaration of taxable income earned in the so-called *black economy*).
- **A single higher rate**. In 1988 the government replaced the five higher rates of income tax of 40, 45, 50, 55 and 60 per cent with the single higher rate of 40 per cent.
- **A reduced basic rate**. The basic rate of income tax was progressively reduced from 33 per cent in 1979 to 22 per cent by 2000/1, the lowest level for 20 years.
- **A lower rate** of 20 per cent was introduced in 1992, subsequently replaced by a 10 per cent rate in 1999/2000. This halved the marginal tax rate for 1.9 million low paid workers. Besides earnings, the 10 per cent rate also applies to income from pensions and savings up to the basic rate threshold.

Cuts in the highest tax rates made the formal structure of income tax much less progressive during the 1980s. Introduction of the lower rate (and its subsequent reduction) together with reduction of the basic rate reintroduced greater progressivity into the tax structure during the 1990s, but at the bottom (rather than top) range of earned incomes.

Whilst the total number of income taxpayers remained fairly constant during the 1990s at between 25 and 26 million, the number paying the basic rate fell sharply from 24 million at the start of the decade to 16 million by the end (a fall of a third). This was mainly caused by an increase in numbers paying the lower rate, from 4 million upon its introduction in 1992/3 to 8 million by the end of the decade. Those paying the higher rate also rose, increasing by 50 per cent from 1.6 million to 2.4 million over the decade as a whole, as higher incomes rose faster than tax thresholds (see Appendix 10.1).

Broadening the base of income tax

- **The tax base was broadened by reducing scope for tax avoidance**, namely by redefining non-taxable perquisites (called 'perks') as taxable income. Perks range from company cars to luncheon vouchers. The money equivalent of company cars and other perks is now subject to income tax. The reduced rates of tax (noted above) also reduced incentives for both tax avoidance and tax evasion.
- **Allowances against income tax were reduced**. Almost all former tax allowances were withdrawn by tax year 2000/1. Prior to that year there were allowances against payment of income tax for married couples, for interest payments on loans (mortgages) for house purchase, and for single parents. Prior to abolition, their values (in terms of reduced tax payments) were progressively reduced by both Conservative and Labour governments by limiting their values to lower rates of income tax and/or not increasing their thresholds or values in line with inflation (see Appendix 10.1).

However, reliefs against income tax were introduced by both Conservative and Labour governments in order to promote specific objectives. There are two main measures:

- **Promotion of personal savings and shareholding**. The first is by means of special savings accounts allowing interest to be earned free of income tax. The second is through equity schemes allowing tax-free dividends and capital gains on shares. These supply-side measures are aimed at stimulating financial self-sufficiency and investment respectively. The only substantive difference between the Conservative and Labour governments (which introduced separate schemes) is that the latter sought to increase the incentive to save for low-income groups by making such schemes more widely available and allowing smaller amounts to be saved for shorter periods. It was argued that low-income groups did not have easy access to complex savings and investment markets, and could not afford to save the large minimum amounts for the long periods previously required. If widely taken up, such schemes would reduce demands on the social security budget, with consequent public expenditure savings. This would help offset the tax revenues lost as a result of the tax reliefs on interest, dividends and capital gains. However, it seems that take-up of these schemes is still disproportionately concentrated on middle-income and higher-income groups, much of the tax relief (about £1 billion per annum) going to those who already save and invest without such schemes.

- **Introduction of the Working Families Tax Credit (2000) and Children's Tax Credit (2001)** avoid families with dependent children being severely disadvantaged by the general broadening of the tax base (see Appendix 10.1).

Corporation tax

Cutting the rate of corporation tax

Prior to 1984 the main rate of corporation tax was 52 per cent, the then Conservative government cutting it to 35 per cent and further to 33 per cent in 1991. The subsequent Labour government cut it further. The main rate was 30 per cent, with a small company rate of 20 per cent in 2000/1.

Broadening the base of corporation tax

Prior to 1984 companies' capital expenditures reduced taxable profits by the value of investment in buildings, plant and machinery. Known as 'free (or accelerated) depreciation', 100 per cent **capital allowances** allowed the whole of the cost of *plant and machinery* to be 'written off' (for corporation tax purposes) in the year of purchase. Firms could accumulate these tax reliefs, carrying unused allowances over from years when profits were low to years when profits were high. They allowed companies to postpone tax liability indefinitely as long as they reinvested profits in new plant and machinery each year. A similar arrangement applied to *industrial buildings*, with a 75 per cent write-off. The result was that corporation tax raised little revenue despite a high rate of tax.

The intention of those tax allowances was to provide a major boost to new manufacturing investment. However, many investments were not truly profitable in an economic sense but only as a means of avoiding taxation. Moreover, the commercial (as distinct from industrial) sector received no such allowances. This was justified on the grounds that commercial buildings generally retain or increase their capital value whereas industrial buildings do not. Nonetheless banks and other financial institutions captured some of the value of the tax allowances aimed at manufacturing by buying industrial capital equipment and leasing it back to industrial companies. This arrangement also suited manufacturing firms since many had accumulated such large allowances against tax that they paid no corporation tax at all during a prolonged period of low profits. Hence the value of additional allowances associated with new investment was nil. Manufacturing firms could, however, benefit by hiring industrial capital equipment and buildings from banks at rents that were lower as a result of the tax allowances gained by those financial institutions. In other words a share of the tax benefits gained by banks was passed on to industry. Hence the effect of industrial investment allowances was that both manufacturing and financial companies paid little or no corporation tax during the early 1980s. This extraordinarily roundabout way of giving tax concessions to manufacturing companies was inefficient on two counts:

- **It resulted in a loss of tax revenue to the Exchequer** since the banks retained some of the value of tax concessions that were not intended for them.
- **The accounting profitability of manufacturing investments became unduly dependent on tax allowances.** There was evidence that pre-tax rates of return were low relative to other countries. In other words the UK's system of company taxation seriously distorted investment, resulting in too much investment with low economic productivity.

Hence the then Conservative government concluded that tax allowances subsidised projects with poor returns and therefore did not lead to the high performance investments intended by the allowances. This led to the phased abolition of capital allowances during the mid 1980s, allowing a lower tax rate on an unbiased and enhanced tax base – a classic supply-side improvement.

In 1997, and for much the same reasons, the incoming Labour government abolished another major allowance against corporation tax, namely **advance corporation tax** (ACT). ACT was a tax on distributed company dividends, levied in advance of the collection of main corporation tax – hence the name. In 1997, a company paying shareholders a dividend of £0.80 would also pay £0.20 to the government as ACT. The company could then offset that £0.20 payment against main corporation tax, such that it had no impact on the total tax bill. The potential distortion was caused by allowing pension funds and life-assurance companies (which are major shareholders, controlling about 45 per cent of quoted equity investments) to claim a refund of the £0.20 ACT. The refund was meant to be a subsidy to pension funds to encourage people to make provision for their own retirement. However, as major shareholders, pension funds were able to influence companies' decisions about what proportion of profits to pay as dividends and what proportion to retain to finance new investment in productive plant and machinery. About 90 per cent of new investment is financed by retained earnings. The government came to the view that the subsidy to pension funds led them to require companies whose shares they owned to distribute a higher proportion of profits as dividends than they would have done without this tax refund. **Once again, the tax system distorted company investment, in this case leading to under-investment – a classic supply-side constraint**. Hence, ACT was abolished despite the Labour government's wish to encourage private, company and occupational pensions (see Chapter 9). Put simply, there are less distortionary ways of encouraging pension provision, savings and shareholding (see above).

Despite the protestations of pension funds, they are not necessarily disadvantaged by this reform. Abolition of ACT refunds made more equal the tax treatment of dividend income and capital growth. If companies retain higher proportions of their earnings for investment in profitable ventures that otherwise would have been blocked by excessive dividend payments, then pension funds will benefit from higher share values and higher future earnings. Abolition of ACT therefore encourages pension funds to take a longer-term view of their shareholdings and more interest in company investment programmes.

This experience of reform under both Conservative and Labour governments is consistent with other conclusions relating to income tax and VAT (see below) that tax allowances often lead to unintended and inefficient market distortions. The Labour government's policy was to target allowances much more effectively. **First**, introducing 40 per cent capital allowances for small and medium sized enterprises (SMEs) in 1997/8, subsequently made permanent in 2000/1. This is intended to encourage SMEs to invest from their own resources in capital stock. **Second**, subject to EU approval, introducing 100 per cent first year capital allowances for energy saving investments in 2001/2. **Third**, introducing 100 per cent first year capital allowances for small enterprises investing in computers and other e-commerce information and communications technology (ICT) equipment, to help them invest in the 'knowledge economy' (available until 2003).

Inheritance tax

Cutting the rates of inheritance tax

Reforms have been intended to increase the incentive to work and invest by allowing a greater proportion of estates to be passed on to offspring or other inheritors. Prior to 1981 there were 14 different rates of tax. This was gradually reduced to a single rate of 40 per cent in 1988.

Broadening the base of inheritance tax

By 2000/1 inheritance tax was being charged on only about 23 500 estates each year, around 4 per cent of all deaths. The outgoing Conservative government had proposed abolition of inheritance tax (and capital gains tax – see below), ostensibly because it raised so little tax revenue (at least in relative terms). The incoming 1997 Labour government decided to retain the tax because abolition would probably have required an increased rate of income tax (which Labour was committed to avoid). Moreover, the growth of owner occupation and personal pensions could result in many more people becoming liable for inheritance tax, many houses costing around £200 000, especially in London and the South East in the late 1990s. In that case, foregone tax revenues would be much greater.

Capital gains tax (CGT)

Cutting the rate of CGT

In 1988 the single 30 per cent rate was replaced by the relevant top income tax rate for each payer. The basic and lower rates were subsequently reduced so that CGT was payable at 10, 20 or 40 per cent in 2000/1. The Labour government introduced further reforms in 1998/9 to strengthen the incentive for entrepreneurial investment. Equity investment by individuals is seen as a vital source of capital for SMEs. Those reforms progressively reduce the rate of CGT faced by a higher rate taxpayer to 10 per cent for such investments held for more than four years (this period reflecting investment patterns). This was complemented by the introduction of a new comprehensive all-employee share ownership plan allowing employers to give their employees up to £3000 of shares each year free of tax and national insurance contributions. It replaced an earlier scheme introduced by the previous Conservative government.

Broadening the base for CGT

As for inheritance tax, whilst the outgoing Conservative government had proposed abolition of capital gains tax, Labour chose to retain it. In fact, the loss of tax revenue would have been potentially much greater than the loss of revenue from CGT itself. This is because abolition would have created incentives for people to convert income into capital gains and so avoid payment of income tax. Hence, there would probably also have been substantial losses of income tax revenues. The most effective way of broadening the base would be to extend CGT to gains arising on disposal of a person's only or main residence (currently exempt). According to government estimates, this would have raised £2.2 billion in 1999/2000. It would probably be politically unacceptable given that over three-quarters of households own their own homes.

National Insurance Contributions (NICs)

Cutting the rates of NICs

Both Conservative and Labour governments have argued that higher social security taxes would make UK goods uncompetitive in both home and overseas markets, an aspect of crowding out (see Chapters 4 and 5). Moreover, both Conservative and Labour governments have sought to minimise any supply-side constraint created by NICs being a 'tax on jobs'.

The 1997 Labour government reduced *employers'* NICs in 1999 by replacing the previous tiered structure of contributions (the rate rising as weekly earnings rose to a maximum 10.2 per cent) with a flat rate of 12.2 per cent. Although higher, this rate only became payable above a threshold set at the same level as the standard personal income tax allowance (an example of the two systems coalescing – see section 10.8). This reform was meant to be neutral in terms of government revenue as a whole, whilst making it more attractive to hire workers at the bottom of the pay scale but more expensive at the top. It supposedly provides a stimulus to the creation of low-paid jobs for the unskilled unemployed. This was meant to complement other initiatives aimed at getting the low paid into jobs and helped offset any higher costs as a result of the introduction of the national minimum wage (see Chapter 8). However, critics argued that it encouraged employers to pay low wages specifically to avoid their payment of NICs.

The Labour government also made the 10 per cent standard *employees'* NIC rate only payable on earnings above the pay threshold, namely the lower earnings limit (LEL). Previously all earnings became subject to employees' NICs once the LEL had been passed. This served to reduce the marginal effective tax rate for low-paid workers. It will be further reduced in 2001/2, at which point the Labour government plans to align the LEL with the income tax personal allowance (previously the LEL has been less than that allowance).

Broadening the base of NICs

There would appear to be plenty of scope to broaden the base for NICs. UK social security contributions are only just over half of those in the EU (at about 6 per cent and 12 per cent of GDP respectively) and they are also a relatively small proportion of total taxation in the UK (see **Table 10.1**). The EU's ratio has equalled or exceeded a quarter since 1965 whilst the UK's ratio has been well below a fifth of total tax revenue.

The coverage of NICs could be increased by applying the 10 per cent standard rate to *employees'* earnings above the upper earnings limit

(UEL), *employers'* NICs having no such limit. Alternatively either or both the employees' or employers' rates could be increased and/or the LEL abolished for both employers' and employees' NICs. However, given the worries about NICs being a tax on (especially low paid) jobs and a commitment not to increase direct taxes generally, these possible reforms would appear to be ruled out for the time being. A radical means of extending that tax base (through integration of NICs and income tax) is considered in detail in Section 10.8 below.

Property tax

Cutting property tax rates

Both Conservative and Labour governments have controlled property tax rates, either directly (for business properties) or indirectly (for residential properties) in order both to control local government spending and to limit crowding out. In particular, the former Conservative government believed that locally variable tax rates on business properties created a supply constraint, driving business investment out of relatively highly taxed localities (see Appendix 10.1).

Broadening the base of property taxes

Compared with industrial and commercial property, **owner-occupied** housing has traditionally been relatively favourably treated for tax purposes:

- **Capital gains tax is not payable on principal residences**. However the net benefit of this exemption is limited because proceeds from sales are usually used to buy other houses at correspondingly inflated prices (see Appendix 10.3 on **tax capitalisation**).
- **No tax is payable on imputed rents**. Landlords pay tax on rents received from their properties whereas owner-occupiers (effectively their own landlords) pay no tax on the notional incomes earned by their properties. The notional income is the rent that would be payable were the owner and occupier not the same person. Such rents are known as 'imputed rents'. They were calculated and taxed prior to 1963, being calculated with reference to the net annual rental values used for local property tax purposes. However massive increases in tax liabilities consequent upon revaluation of rental values in 1963 caused such a political furore that the tax was abolished.
- **Mortgage interest payments were formerly given relief against income tax**, although the value of this allowance was progressively restricted and finally abolished (as noted above).

- **There was no domestic property tax during 1990–3** (see Appendix 10.3).

Hence, notwithstanding the abolition of mortgage interest tax relief and reintroduction of the local property tax, the tax base for indirect taxation could still be broadened by phasing out the continuing favourable tax treatment of owner-occupied housing. In addition, second homes (i.e. holiday homes) are taxed by local government *council tax* at only half the rate of first homes (i.e. main residences). Hence, the tax base could also be extended by subjecting them to the full rate of council tax.

Customs and excise duties

Increasing tax rates

Both Conservative and Labour governments increased the excise duties on cigarettes, alcohol and road fuel duty faster than inflation during the 1990s. However, a *taxpayer revolt* occurred in 2000 in respect of the relatively high UK road fuel duty. This led to blockades of oil refineries and road fuel distribution depots leading to closure of virtually all UK petrol stations as they ran out of fuel. Severe economic disruption would have occurred had the blockades lasted much more than a week. Even though most blockades ended within a week there was mounting disruption to public services (most notably the NHS began cancelling non-emergency operations because its staff could not get to work) and to food distribution to supermarkets and so on. Panic buying of petrol, diesel and food occurred. Hence, whilst demand for cigarettes, alcohol and road fuel is highly price inelastic, it does not mean that consumers will happily pay high (inclusive of tax) prices. Ultimately, a taxpayer revolt occurs – as also happened for the local government poll tax in the early 1990s (see Appendix 10.1).

Broadening the base of excise duties

The main changes introduced to broaden the base of excise duties during the 1980s and 1990s were to broaden the base of VAT (see below), introduce a tax on most general insurance premiums (the main exclusions being life insurance and pensions), and introduce an airport departure tax (air passenger duty). The relatively high rates of UK taxes on tobacco and alcohol led to widespread tax evasion by obtaining cheaper supplies from the Continent, leading to potentially critical erosion of their tax bases (see Appendix 10.4). Hence the main concern here was to protect (rather than broaden) the tax base for cigarettes and alcohol by more rigorous anti-smuggling procedures at cross-Channel ports.

Value Added Tax

Increasing the rate of VAT

Before 1979 the standard rate of VAT was 8 per cent, 12.5 per cent being levied on certain 'luxury' goods. Both rates were replaced by a single standard rate of 15 per cent by the newly-elected 1979 Conservative government. The standard rate was increased to 17.5 per cent in 1991. A reduced rate of 5 per cent was subsequently introduced on domestic fuel and power (see Section 10.6).

Broadening the VAT base

The tax base was extended on a piecemeal basis during the 1980s and 1990s, for example to cover building repairs, home extensions, take-away meals (restaurant meals have always been taxed), advertising in newspapers and magazines, and domestic fuel and power. However, there is considerable scope for extending the tax base for VAT, both now and in the future. This is discussed separately in the following section.

10.6 Extending the VAT base

About 80 per cent of food products are **zero-rated** (i.e. not subject to VAT), as are public transport, young children's clothes, books, news-papers and prescription drugs. Zero-rating is usually defended on vertical equity grounds, expenditures on the above items generally being proportionately greater relative to household budgets for low-income than for high-income families. Certain other commodities have been **exempt** from VAT since 1973, including financial services provided by banks and building societies. Contrary to expectations, exempt activities are much less favourably treated than zero-rated ones because input tax can be reclaimed by the latter but not by the former (see Appendix 10.1).

Banks have been exempt from VAT on the grounds of practice rather than of principle. Contrary to the case for other traders, the output of banks (i.e. potentially chargeable banking services) is not properly measured but rather is hidden and financed from the differential interest rates charged to borrowers and lenders. The increased computerisation of banking services and the growth of discrete services for which charges are being levied (e.g. direct debits) may ultimately lead to banking services becoming liable for standard rate VAT. However the gross revenues raised by ending exemption would be partially offset by other companies' ability to deduct itemised banking charges from their own VAT bills.

Possible future extensions of the VAT base

Consideration has been given to extending VAT to, for example, newspapers, books, newly-built homes and to foods. Government estimates of the extra tax revenue that could be gained from extension of standard rate VAT to goods and services which are currently zero-rated, reduced-rated, exempt or outside the scope of VAT are crude. In particular, they make no allowance for changes in behaviour in response to consequential changes in relative prices and in real incomes (see Chapter 4). For that reason the following individual figures cannot be added together. In 1999/2000 extension of 17.5 per cent VAT would have raised £7.75 billion on food, £2.75 billion on construction of new dwellings, £2.65 billion on rents of domestic dwellings, £1.8 billion on each of domestic and international passenger transport, £1.8 billion on domestic fuel and power, £1.7 billion on rents of commercial properties, £1.3 billion on books, newspapers and magazines, £1.1 billion on children's clothing, and £0.95 billion on water and sewerage services. Water and sewerage are the only domestic utility services not subject to VAT, the others being subject to 5 per cent VAT. Hundreds of millions of pounds could likewise be raised from each of betting, gaming and lottery, prescription drugs, private education, health services, postal services, burial and cremation, finance and insurance and so on.

Whilst most other countries apply reduced rates of VAT to many items (most commonly food, books, water, pharmaceuticals and newspapers and periodicals), billions of pounds could clearly be raised by such extensions. These amounts are many times greater than the extra revenues raised by increasing the basic rate of income tax by 1 penny. In reality, the additional *net* revenues may be much less because:

1. **Social security expenditure may rise**. Extra payments would probably have to be made to low-income groups in order to offset politically unacceptable distributional consequences. This could occur both as a discretionary act of policy and as an automatic outcome. The latter would occur since extensions to the base of VAT would lead to cost-push inflation and so increase retail prices, against which most benefits are automatically indexed (see Chapter 9).
2. **Other government expenditures may increase**. For example, levying VAT on public transport (i.e. trains, buses, coaches, taxis and planes) may cause a shift to private transport. If so, there may be significantly increased social and economic costs of congestion and other such negative externalities (see Chapter 2). More roads may have to be built to accommodate the increased use of private vehicles.
3. **Consumption of newly taxed commodities may fall**. If so, tax receipts may be less than expected. The key factor is the sensitivity

of demand to the price of each of these items, that is the price elasticity of demand (see Chapter 4). The example in Appendix 10.2 illustrates the in-practice complexity of this fairly simple concept.

Extending VAT to remove anomalies

Except where used to deal with market failure (see Chapter 2), tax anomalies can create substantial unintended market distortions. In the case of VAT, anomalies arise:

1. **Between food items**. For example ice cream and soft drinks are taxed but not caviar and smoked salmon. The reader may have difficulty appreciating the rationale for taxing the first two relatively low-cost items but not the last two 'luxuries', especially as this arrangement apparently favours affluent groups and is therefore contrary to vertical equity.
2. **Between given food products containing the same ingredients**. For example, biscuits *coated* in chocolate carry VAT at 17.5 per cent whilst those which *contain* chocolate chips are zero-rated (as are those without chocolate). In this case the difference in the presentation of the same ingredients is of critical importance for tax liability but is hardly rational.
3. **Between virtually identical brand products**. For example, ginger-bread men, whose heads are coated in chocolate, are subject to standard rate VAT whereas gingerbread women, whose heads are coated in caramel (to make them 'blondes') are zero-rated. In this case the difference between caramel and chocolate is of critical importance for tax liability but again defies rational justification.

VAT anomalies also arise for non-food products. For example clothes of the same size are subject to different tax liability depending on whether they are designated as children's clothes (in which case they are zero-rated) or as adults' clothes (in which case they are not). The increasing average height of young teenagers makes the distinction between adults' and children's clothes increasingly problematic.

The Customs and Excise department accepts the dubious nature of these apparently irrational distinctions. They arise from the attempt to zero rate (most) food products but tax supplies in the course of catering. The problem is that tax law does not define food of a kind used for human consumption. Moreover, many anomalies arise from inherited tax laws combined with incremental decision-making by successive governments regarding the extension of VAT since 1973. The zero-rated and standard-rate categories originate from the predecessor of VAT (*purchase tax*) which discriminated between 'luxury' consumer goods and 'essentials'. For example potato crisps were subject to purchase tax prior to 1973 because they were regarded as a non-essential food item (and therefore a luxury), and therefore became subject to standard rate VAT. However the more recently developed tortilla chips and pork scratchings are zero-rated. Hence rapid innovation of snack-food products since 1973 has led to an increasing number of anomalies that severely distort the market for food and drink.

The tortuous legal aspects of tax law relating to VAT were highlighted by the infamous case of Jaffa Cakes. In 1993 Customs and Excise tried to have VAT levied on Jaffa Cakes on the ground that, despite their name, they are a chocolate-coated biscuit and are therefore liable to standard rate VAT. Whilst the Court was not convinced that Jaffa Cakes are really cakes, it was sure that they are not biscuits! Hence they remain zero-rated.

Whilst these examples seem to verge on the trivial they are indicative of both the widespread incidence of tax anomalies and of the severe distortions they can create for certain products and their manufacturers. Some anomalies are being removed on a piecemeal basis. For example the ending of zero-rating for freshly squeezed orange juice in the early 1990s was justified on the grounds that both apple juice and orange juice made from concentrates were already subject to VAT. This anomaly came about because the pasteurisation of other orange juices and the addition of citric acid to apple juice (to prevent discoloration) resulted in their being prepared or 'manufactured' foods and thus subject to VAT. It had been argued previously that freshly squeezed orange juice is non-pasteurised and additive-free and therefore should not be liable for VAT.

However, piecemeal extension of the VAT tax base is unlikely to significantly reduce such anomalies and it may create new anomalies in other areas. Moreover, anomalies have been exacerbated by the more than doubling of the tax rate from 8 per cent to 17.5 per cent since 1973. In general, the narrower the tax base the higher the rate of tax necessary to raise a given tax revenue. Hence removing anomalies would allow a lower tax rate. However many items of expenditure would still be free of VAT and so a much more comprehensive reform is required. VAT would have to be levied on all expenditures, including food.

Extending VAT to food

There are two main options in respect of food. Either: **all food should be zero-rated** or **all food should be subject to standard (or reduced) rate VAT**. The first option would be inconsistent with government policy to shift the balance of taxation towards indirect taxes whereas the second option would not. The latter would also possibly be consistent with tax harmonisation at the EU level (see Appendix 10.4).

The UK differs from other EU countries in being one of the few countries not to levy VAT on most foods. However the British system is thought to be very slightly progressive, in that a higher proportion of a poor family's budget is spent on zero-rated goods compared with that of an affluent family. VAT systems in other countries are thought to be slightly regressive. Broadening the VAT base to cover all foods would, if revenue neutral, allow a reduced rate for foods, a rate as low as 5 per cent being consistent with EU directives. Whilst a multiplicity of rates would reverse previous reforms to fewer rates and cause administrative complexity, reducing the rate of VAT on politically sensitive items would be more politically feasible. Certainly 5 per cent on all foods would have a much less regressive impact than 17.5 per cent.

The impact of applying VAT to all foods would be of much more limited effect today than in the past because of rising real incomes. Family Expenditure Survey figures show that the average family spends only a sixth of its disposable income on food and soft drinks (1999), compared with nearly 40 per cent before 1945. However a VAT rate of only 5 per cent on all foods would still create significant distributional impacts since food accounts for a relatively high proportion of the spending of low-income groups. Expenditure on food and soft drinks remains the largest expenditure item for the five lowest of the ten income groups in the UK. It typically accounts for about a third of the expenditure of lowest income decile households, an eighth for middle income decile families and a tenth for higher deciles. Hence welfare groups stress the adverse distributional aspects of extending VAT to all food.

Whilst noting problems with take-up rates and the fact that benefit payments increase some time after prices rise, these distributional effects could be offset by increased welfare payments being financed by the increased VAT revenues. Indeed , as already noted, benefits are generally automatically increased in line with retail prices (see Chapter 9). However, unless the increased tax revenues are also used to finance real increases in the income thresholds below which families become eligible for welfare payments, the position of those with incomes rising above benefit thresholds will be made worse off. Critics would argue that the additional tax revenues would be used either to reduce public sector borrowing (see Chapter 11) or to finance further income tax cuts that most benefit middle-income and affluent groups. In neither case would poor groups benefit.

Although the absolute sums are smaller, the difference between the domestic fuel expenditure patterns of rich and poor is even greater than that for food and hence the impact of VAT on domestic fuel is more regressive then would be VAT on food. The poorest decile (i.e. 10 per cent) of families spent 13 per cent of their household budgets on fuel, light and power in 1993 (i.e. before the imposition of 8 per cent VAT in 1994, subsequently reduced to 5 per cent in 1997 by the incoming Labour government), compared with 3 per cent for the richest decile. Extension of VAT to domestic fuel but not to food therefore seems anomalous (see Appendix 10.1).

Efficiency issues

If it is government policy that extra tax revenues be raised from VAT, then – in efficiency terms – extending its base is preferable to increasing its rate. To the extent that a wider base allows a lower tax rate, both outcomes would reduce (rather than increase) the market distortions and anomalies identified above. It could also reduce the adverse distributional aspects noted earlier, though this would depend on the particular commodities that become newly liable for standard rate VAT and which particular socio-economic groups consume them.

In fact, both Conservative and Labour governments raised extra indirect tax revenues during the later 1990s by increasing vehicle fuel duty, tobacco duty and insurance premium tax. They seemed reluctant to extend the coverage of VAT, refusing for example to levy VAT on new houses. This exemption is thought to discourage the redevelopment of inner cities, builders modernising older properties having to pay the full rate of 17.5 per cent. Widening the tax base to all house building/ rehabilitation would allow a 5 per cent rate and remove the tax bias towards greenfield development outside cities. Thousands of homes are lying empty in Britain's cities.

Both governments had to take action to prevent *erosion of the tax base* as a result of *tax avoidance*. By the later 1990s holiday insurance was taxed at the 4 per cent insurance premium tax rate whereas holidays were (and still are) taxed at the full 17.5 per cent VAT rate. Tour operators therefore began to rebalance holiday costs by classifying more as insurance and less as the other costs of the holiday in order to reduce costs and compete with other holiday companies. The government reacted by taxing holiday insurance at 17.5 per cent as from 1998. A similar tax-avoidance strategy was pursued by electrical retailers offering their customers extended warranties. Insurance was offered against breakdown for household appliances such as washing machines and televisions, typically for three to five years. The VAT bill on appliances could be slashed by inflating the value of the insurance element sold as part of a package. Again the government had to increase insurance premium tax to 17.5 per cent.

These examples pale into insignificance when compared with the distortions created by widely varying tax rates within the EU's single market, resulting in substantial cross-border shopping solely to take advantage of differential taxes (see Appendix 10.4). Tax anomalies can lead to gross distortions of investment in retailing, much only being profitable as a result of tax differentials. Broadening the tax base for both VAT and other customs and excise duties and tax harmonisation within the EU would remove such distortions, demonstrating the supply-side benefits of a truly comprehensive tax base. The alternative is to spend much larger amounts on enforcement. However, enforcement is costly, not necessarily very successful and the need for it only arises because of the incentives created by tax differentials. The ultimate solution is to remove those tax differentials, yielding a net windfall gain in terms of reduced enforcement expenditures and more economically (rather than tax) efficient investment.

10.7 Earmarked taxes

An earmarked tax directly identifies tax payment with provision of the service it finances. The revenues of an earmarked tax are dedicated to a public sector service, either in whole or in the form of a predetermined and fixed percentage. Such earmarking (*hypothecation*) is the basis of the *fiscal exchange model* of government (see Chapter 7). Tax earmarking may be used within the *despotic benevolent model* of government as a means of widening the tax base according to willingness to pay, so minimising any disincentive-to-work effects. Earmarking may be used within the *fiscal transfer model* whereby the majority of taxpayer-citizens exploit a minority, forcing them to pay the bulk of costs for a service benefiting the majority. Earmarking may also be used by a *leviathan* government to increase tax revenues in order to maximise its own welfare instead of that of its citizens.

There are six examples of earmarking in the UK. **First, national insurance contributions**. Earmarking is, of course, one of the supposed advantages of NICs. However revenues raised from NICs are usually insufficient to fund all contributory benefits, and in practice an additional Treasury grant is made available to the National Insurance Fund. **Second, the television licence fee**, the revenues being used to finance the British Broadcasting Corporation. **Third, revenues from the National Lottery** are earmarked to the so-called *good causes*, including sports, the arts, national heritage, charities, and certain educational and health projects. **Fourth, council tax and the national non-domestic (i.e. business) property tax**, revenues from both being earmarked to local government services in general. **Fifth, the landfill tax credit scheme** (see below). **Sixth, the one-off windfall tax** on the excess profits of the privatised utilities raised £5.2 billion and was used to finance the 1997

Labour government's Welfare to Work programme (see Chapters 8 and 9). The rationale for linking particular taxes to particular services is as follows:

Functional earmarking, where one commodity is taxed in order to finance another part of the same functional system. Examples include the dedication of road fuel duty to finance the building and maintenance of roads (used in some developing countries), of revenues from the road fund licence fee to subsidise public transport (discussed in the UK – see below), of carbon taxes on fuel to finance environmental improvement programmes (proposed by environmental groups), of a supplementary graduate income tax to fund universities (discussed extensively in the UK in the 1990s), of taxes on cigarettes to pay for public health services (a rise in UK tobacco duties of 5 per cent in real terms in 2000/1 being used to provide an additional £2 billion for the NHS), of bed taxes on overnight stays in hotels to fund general tourist facilities (levied in the English Lake District and other national parks) and of increased property taxes in a particular neighbourhood to finance improved pavements or street lighting in that neighbourhood (used in the USA and called *special assessments*).

Temporal earmarking, where tax revenues are transferred to different stages of the lifecycle. It would appear that some of the contributory benefits financed by NICs are of this kind, for example the state retirement pension. However it has already been noted that state retirement pensions are not a funded scheme in that NICs are not stored in an account until the individual contributor retires but instead are paid to the current generation of pensioners.

Distributive earmarking, where one group pays earmarked taxes to finance benefits for other groups. NICs paid by current workers and employers to finance the pensions of the retired are, in fact, an example of distributive (rather than temporal) earmarking, as is their use to finance unemployment, sickness and invalidity benefits. The eligibility requirement for national insurance benefits (i.e. making them conditional on a record of prior contributions) only serves to limit, rather than negate, the distributional effect.

Any one earmarked tax can simultaneously display elements of functional, temporal and distributive hypothecation. NICs have elements of both temporal and distributive earmarking. A functionally earmarked tax can also have distributive effects, for example where the consumption patterns for both the commodity that is subject to the earmarked tax and the service it finances diverge between different socio-economic groups.

Besides proposing the transfer of the provision of services to the market sector (wherever it is possible and sensible so to do) and the increased use of charges to limit demand, the 1984 public expenditure Green Paper's possible solutions to the problem of public expenditure control included earmarking tax revenues to individual expenditure programmes (especially in the social field) in order to highlight their costs. However, by the end of the twentieth century arguments for increased use of earmarked taxes came from those wanting *higher* public expenditures. **First**, public opinion surveys consistently found willingness on the part of substantial majorities of respondents to pay higher taxes to fund increased spending on health, education and pensions. **Second**, motoring organisations argued for taxes on road fuel to be limited to the revenue necessary to finance the building and maintenance of roads (i.e. a return to the earmarking of the early twentieth century) and/or for financing improvements in public transport. **Third**, environmental organisations argued for taxes to be levied on polluting activities, the resulting revenues being used to fund environmental improvements. There are a number of considerations if increased use is to be made of earmarked taxes:

Constitutional

In 1993, Demos (an independent think-tank) argued that the separation (*disconnection*) of taxes from public services and other benefits financed by taxes has led to an opaque and excessively centralised governmental structure. It argued that people are increasingly less willing to sign 'blank cheques' to the state. As already noted, surveys have shown that a majority of people would be prepared to pay additional taxes in order to secure higher levels of funding for the National Health Service, education and pensions. However, those same surveys have found majorities against paying higher taxes for other social security expenditures (such as unemployment benefits), for housing, for help for industry, and for police and prisons. Hence the more general use of earmarking would *reconnect* taxes and services, sharing sovereignty between elected representatives and citizens by giving voters an effective choice over the real levels of specific public services, rather than decisions being made downwards from the top.

However governments often dislike earmarked taxes precisely because they reduce their freedom to allocate resources. Moreover earmarking is based on a particular conception of democracy that may not be acceptable to the government or the citizens. **First**, that conception is one where the electorate takes decisions on particular issues rather than (as now) voting for a package of issues contained within a manifesto. **Second**, that conception is one where governments act as vote-counting mechanisms rather than (as now) taking decisions in the public interest without direct consultation with voters on each and every issue. Hence full earmarking of all taxes would raise complex constitutional issues. Nevertheless, increased use of earmarking (for the NHS) was again advocated in a report published by the Fabian Society (a left-wing think-tank) in 2000. Of course, earmarking tax revenues to the NHS could be used to constrain (rather than finance) the seemingly inexorable increase in real spending on the NHS (see Chapter 9, Table 9.3).

Economic efficiency

The efficiency case for earmarking depends on the complex interaction of a set of factors, including the following.

The model of government. Judged against general-fund financing, earmarked taxes are potentially inefficient in the despotic benevolent government model (by definition) and in the fiscal exchange model (specific services in return for specific tax payments) because they create budgetary rigidities and fiscal inflexibility irrespective of changing costs and needs. However, earmarked taxes are potentially efficient in the fiscal transfer model (where the majority can over-tax the minority and direct services to themselves) and in the leviathan model (where revenue-maximising, self-serving political agents expand service provision for their own benefit) because they serve to limit such behaviour (see Chapter 7).

Joint equilibria. In the general-fund financing case, decisions regarding taxation and expenditure are conceptually distinct so that allocatively efficient equilibria can be determined separately for the commodities subject to tax and the services the resulting tax revenues finance. However, if an earmarked tax is the sole means of financing a particular service then the outcome for the service will depend on the equilibrium market situation for the taxed commodity. For example, if a tobacco tax were used to finance public health services, expenditures on public health would be determined in the market for tobacco. However there is no *a priori* reason why optimal equilibria should be jointly determined for both commodities at any one point in time nor over time under such an arrangement.

Market conditions. Even if joint equilibria were to be optimal at a particular point in time the revenue derived from an earmarked tax will change over time as market conditions vary. That change will not necessarily coincide with the incremental revenues required to finance desired or optimal changes in service provision. The main factors influencing incremental revenues are as follows.

First, income elasticity of demand. A high income elasticity of demand causes demand for a commodity to increase faster than income. The tax base provided by such a commodity would increase and the earmarked service would enjoy a rising income, possibly more than that required to finance service expansion for the purposes of allocative efficiency or equity. However, if the earmarked tax were levied on a commodity with a low income elasticity of demand then the tax base would be largely static and the earmarked service would experience increased, and perhaps unintended, fiscal constraints.

Second, price elasticity of demand. An earmarked tax levied on a commodity whose demand was highly sensitive to price would obviously raise little additional revenue if the tax rate were to be increased (see Chapter 4). Hence finance derived from the earmarked tax would tend to be static in real terms (unless it had a high income elasticity of demand), as would the resulting levels of service. Services financed from earmarked taxes on commodities whose demand is highly insensitive to price would be more able to finance expansion. However earmarked taxes on commodities with price-inelastic demands may still fail to deliver sufficient resources if there is a change in tastes away from the commodity. For example, if the National Health Service were to be financed by an earmarked tobacco tax, a health campaign highlighting the health risks of smoking would thereby create a funding crisis for the service.

Third, cross elasticity of demand. Changes in tastes for complements and substitutes of the commodity subject to the earmarked tax will necessarily impinge on the amount of revenue raised by that tax. For example road fuel and motor vehicles are complements. If road fuel duty were to be earmarked for a service and the other costs of motoring rose (e.g. an increase in the purchase price of vehicles, increased insurance costs, charges levied for driving on urban roads, taxes on work-place parking and so on), then demand for and use of motor vehicles would fall (unless demand were perfectly inelastic). Therefore demand for road fuel would also fall, as would the tax revenues derived from it. This may lead to unintended financial constraints on the service financed by the earmarked road fuel duty. Similar effects could occur for substitutes.

Equity

Differing consumption patterns for the commodity subject to an earmarked tax and the service it finances could have significant distributional consequences for different social classes. This outcome is more likely when demand for a commodity subject to an earmarked tax is highly price inelastic, so leading to a tendency to raise that tax rate much more than would be the case without earmarking. Take, for example, a tax on cigarettes earmarked to finance health services. Whilst it would finance increased provision of public health services, the distributional outcome would be regressive because, on average, low-income groups spend a higher proportion of their income on cigarettes than high-income groups. Over a third of men and women in manual occupations smoke, compared with less than a fifth of those in non-manual occupations. This vertical inequity would be exacerbated to the extent that high-income groups are relatively more successful than low-income groups in gaining access to public health services. Such 'middle-class capture' of the benefits of public services could combine with socioeconomic stratification of consumption patterns with regard to the earmarked commodity to lead to increasing vertical inequity over time.

Ethics

Earmarking may also raise ethical dilemmas. Taking the 'cigarette tax for public health services' example, some hospital surgeons refuse on clinical grounds to operate on heavy smokers because of their very poor prognosis compared with non-smokers. In that case, earmarking tobacco tax to health services would deny care to those who were financing a disproportionate share of NHS costs. This may be regarded as unethical.

Behavioural responses

With general fund financing, those advocating increased service provision do not have to identify a specific source of finance for it. In contrast, with tax earmarking the source of finance has to be clearly identified, so highlighting the costs as well as the benefits arising from service expansion. This could promote both efficiency and account-ability. However earmarked taxes may be used to promote the interests of dominant political groups, for example if they are presented as a form of 'sin tax' for self-abuse (e.g. using tobacco and alcohol) or for anti-social activities (e.g. congestion-creating, air-polluting car drivers). This is a case of self-serving distributive earmarking, an aspect of public choice theory (see Chapter 7).

Conceivably such outcomes would be made less likely if there were complementarity between the earmarked tax and the service it finances (e.g. road fuel duty and the provision and maintenance of roads, or cigarette tax and health) rather than non-related activities (e.g. cigarette tax and education). However such functional earmarking may be more apparent than real. For example it is not self-evident that consumption of cigarettes and the use of public health services are highly correlated. Since, on average, smokers die earlier than non-smokers then in fact the latter may make more use of health services than the former, especially as they grow old (Chapter 3 having noted how costly the very elderly are in public expenditure terms). Together with the fact that smokers are not exclusive users of health services, what appears to be *functional earmarking* may in fact be self-serving *distributive earmarking*.

More generally, earmarking may increase political lobbying by special-interest groups since they can gain more by lobbying for higher earmarked tax rates dedicated to their particular activities than they can gain by lobbying for increased levels of general taxation (which would be shared by all groups). However, if all taxes were earmarked the final outcome would effectively be the same as competing for shares of a fixed budget for total public expenditure. Increased lobbying would incur opportunity costs (i.e. the alternative output forgone by not using one's time productively) and so lead to allocative inefficiency.

Rather than serving as a quasi-constitutional constraint on the self-serving behaviour of governments and 'reconnecting' taxes and services so as to increase efficiency, earmarked taxes may be used by special-interest groups as instruments of fiscal discrimination to serve their own purposes. This is most likely where there is no strong positive correlation between those using the public service and those paying the earmarked tax, and where service providers exploit political antipathy to certain activities to increase earmarked taxes on them.

Hence tax earmarking is questionable both in principle and in practice. The fact that the principle has been widely accepted for NICs and the other cases noted above does not necessarily mean that the practice should be extended to all or most other public services. NICs are in effect a partially earmarked income tax, experience with which provides little guidance regarding the use of earmarked commodity taxes. Earmarking VAT would be problematic given its broad base and its single standard rate. Moreover, it has been shown that the constitutional, efficiency, equity and other cases for tax earmarking are not decisively positive. Tax earmarking may lead to public accountability being side-stepped by pre-empting democratic deliberation regarding the totality of public services. Individual services may experience increased financial instability as a result of changing market conditions for the commodity or activity subject to the earmarked tax. Changes in consumption patterns could lead to unintended revenue consequences. Similarly, the changes in work patterns towards more 'flexible' employment and 'workless' households could have substantial impacts on the revenues available for the earmarked services in the longer term (see Chapters 9 and 12). This is especially the case for NICs.

Full earmarking of all taxes would appear to be both unwarranted and politically unlikely. The Treasury is against a general expansion in the use of earmarking tax revenues, believing that it should be limited to specific cases where there is a very robust argument in favour of earmarking. The following two case studies illustrate the above analysis.

The Landfill Tax

The landfill tax was introduced in 1996, the government claiming it to be the first UK tax with an explicit environmental purpose. The aims of the landfill tax are to promote the **polluter pays principle** (see Chapter 2), reduce waste and promote recycling. The tax is payable by operators of landfill sites in respect of waste deposited therein. The tax is based on the weight of waste disposed of, rather than on its toxicity, the former clearly being less related to the resulting negative externalities than the latter. It was accepted that it would be very difficult and costly in practice to tax in accordance with toxicity, but relatively easy to tax tonnage of waste. A practical compromise was to tax *active waste* (i.e. contaminated with dangerous chemicals) more heavily than *inert waste* (such as construction rubble). The initial tax rate was £2 per tonne for inert waste and £7 per tonne for all other waste, the latter subsequently being increased to £10. The 1999 Budget announced a *tax escalator* for active waste of £1 per tonne each year until at least 2004, leading to a 50 per cent increase in the tax (at which point the policy will be reviewed). This gives waste producers a clear signal that recycling will become increasingly tax efficient.

This arrangement is designed progressively to internalise the negative externalities associated with landfill, if only crudely, so market forces control waste. This will increase incentives to find alternatives to landfill, most probably incineration of combustible wastes. Environmental groups, however, criticise incineration (as well as landfill) on environmental grounds because of toxic and polluting emissions. That criticism is all the greater when incineration is not part of an energy recovery scheme, burning waste to produce heat and power so reducing the need to burn fossil fuels in power stations (with resulting savings for the environment). Environmental groups advocate measures, **first** to reduce production of waste and **second**, to recycle that which continues to be produced. It is generally thought that the tax would have to be more than £20 per tonne (i.e. more than doubled) for recycling to become financially worthwhile. The short-term result seems to have been an increase in illegal *fly tipping* at unauthorised sites.

A **tax credit scheme** is associated with the tax whereby 20 per cent of the tax liability can be used to fund environmental projects and organisations approved by the regulatory body (ENTRUST). Hence, it is the tax credit (**not** the actual tax payment) that is earmarked to environmental projects. The revenues from the landfill tax go into general government funds and finance the generality of public services. Earmarking only of the tax credit was a compromise reflecting the Treasury's reluctance to earmarking tax revenues directly.

Landfill taxpayers qualify for a credit of 90 per cent of the payment (up to a maximum 20 per cent of his or her annual landfill tax bill). In other words, the remaining 10 per cent (or more) has to be financed by the operator. This is intended to make the operator contribute to the cost of remedying the adverse environmental outcomes (i.e. negative externalities) of landfill sites and to ensure that such expenditures do not count as public expenditures. Environmental projects can be designed simply to compensate communities in the vicinity of the landfill site for the *disamenity effect* of landfill (noise, smell, traffic and so on.). Such compensation includes the provision of public parks, football grounds, nature reserves, even the repair and restoration of nearby churches and building of historical or architectural interest. Approved projects not designed specifically for compensation include land reclamation (i.e. restoring old sites for community use, including removal of pollutants) and research into more sustainable waste management practices. The bulk of the money has been used to finance local amenity and nature conservation projects, rather than waste reduction and recycling. New relationships have thereby been forged between the landfill industry and some of its strongest opponents, namely environmental and local residents' organisations.

The landfill tax was designed to be fiscally neutral, being offset by a matching reduction in employers' NICs (see above). The tax has therefore been regarded as a part of a broader movement towards increasingly *taxing bads* (i.e. negative externalities such as pollution) and away from *taxing goods* (employers' NICs being described as a tax on jobs). In this sense, the landfill tax is a supply-side initiative as well, because it (and its associated tax credit scheme) is intended to stimulate market forces in the waste disposal industry.

However, critics argue that the tax is too crude in taxing tonnes of waste rather than polluting methane emissions and leachates directly, that it has actually increased pollution because of insufficient resources for the policing of illegal disposal, that it unjustifiably taxes only one form of waste disposal (i.e. landfill but not incineration), that it is not set within a proper waste management strategy, that the tax credit scheme is insignificant, and that the tax revenues should also be earmarked to more ambitious environmental projects (particularly waste reduction and recycling). Put simply, the tax needs to be reformed (rather than abolished) if it is to be an effective supply-side economic instrument for protection of the environment.

Road Fuel Duty

Taxes paid on the use of vehicles have clear conceptual links with road building and maintenance in that revenues and expenditures can logically be matched. For example, the Automobile Association (AA) has long argued that much more money is raised by taxes on vehicle use (£31 billion in 1997/8) than is spent on the building and maintenance of local and national roads, parking and public transport (£6 billion): a ratio of 5 to 1. The £31 billion was raised from fuel duty, VAT and the road fund licence, of which about two-thirds was levied by fuel duty. Tax accounted for 82 per cent of the cost of road fuel in 1999 compared with 44 per cent in 1980. Not surprisingly, the AA (and reportedly over 70 per cent of motorists) believe that drivers have been exploited by excessive levels of taxation, greatly in excess of spending on the roads and public transport programmes.

Both Conservative and Labour governments claimed 'green credentials' in arguing that higher road fuel duty would reduce emissions of carbon dioxide, as required by the Kyoto Protocol (see Chapter 2). Such emissions are thought to cause the 'greenhouse effect' (i.e. global warming) and the resulting adverse environmental consequences. These include rising sea levels, extreme weather patterns, increasing geographic coverage of climate-related diseases (e.g. malaria) and the resulting humanitarian and economic problems.

These claimed green credentials were disputed. **First**, the Institute of Fiscal Studies calculated that a 1.0 per cent rise in the *total* cost per mile of motoring would reduce the number of miles driven by less than 0.5 per cent. This was corroborated by a 1999 survey that found that the price per gallon of petrol would have to rise from its then £3.50 to £5 before having any appreciable effect on use of cars. The greater part of vehicle costs are fixed (purchase price, insurance, road licence, annual servicing, depreciation). Hence, notwithstanding the fact that road fuel in the UK has been the most highly taxed fuel in the EU, the fuel running costs are a relatively small part of total costs of vehicle ownership and use. Hence, demand for road fuel is *highly price inelastic*. **Second**, the AA argued that there are much more effective ways of reducing emissions, for example the recent voluntary agreement by European motor manufacturers to improve fuel efficiency for new vehicles by 25 per cent by 2008. It noted that the surplus tax revenues were not even used to fund schemes to reduce emissions of carbon dioxide.

The 1997 Labour government effectively acknowledged these criticisms when it argued that any cuts in fuel duty or earmarking of revenues for transport projects would mean less money for education and health, its two spending priorities. In effect, it was admitting that a very narrow tax base was being used disproportionately to finance major services. This situation was the result of both the shift from direct to indirect taxes and introduction of the *fuel duty accelerator* (which increased fuel duties faster than inflation), both of which had begun under the previous Conservative government. As already noted in Chapter 9, the incoming Labour government had committed itself to maintaining the spending plans of the outgoing Conservative government. It had also promised not to increase income tax and was committed to reducing public sector borrowing (see Chapter 11). In effect, road fuel duty was being treated as a 'cash cow' precisely because demand is so price inelastic (although the escalator was later scrapped in 1999).

The economic (rather than financial) justification of the fuel duty accelerator is that expenditure on road fuel tends to rise faster than real incomes, car use having a *high income elasticity of demand*. This means that demand will rise year on year even if road fuel duty (and the post tax price) rises in line with inflation. The high price *inelasticity* combines with the high income *elasticity* to require a relatively large increase in the real price of road fuel if demand is to be held constant. It has been calculated that the price of road fuel would have to rise by 4 per cent above inflation every year simply to hold consumption of road fuel constant.

Following the theoretical analysis in Chapter 2, it is not self-evident that all of the revenues from taxes on vehicle use should, in fact, be used for roads, public transport and emission reduction schemes. All the theory requires is for those taxes to internalise the negative externalities created by use of vehicles, namely congestion, pollution, accidents and noise. Chapter 2 reported calculations that road users pay only about a third of these social costs they impose on others. Estimates of social costs range from £28 billion to £61 billion per annum, fuel duty raising £23 billion in the late 1990s. Neither the road fund licence nor VAT revenues should be included in the comparison, VAT being a general tax levied on a wide range of commodities whilst the licence fee is not related to use of vehicles. The AA's figures should therefore be reduced by the amount of these two taxes. Moreover, the AA's figures are simply based upon reported accounting costs. They exclude social costs as well resource costs (i.e. the opportunity costs of land, labour and capital used in road programmes). Add to these the global costs of that part of the greenhouse effect attributable to the growing ownership and use of cars in the UK and the AA's figures begin to look increasingly questionable.

Internalisation of social costs does not require revenues to be earmarked. It would, of course, be negated if the road fuel duty revenues were to be use to finance increased expenditures on road building which, in turn, encouraged greater use of cars and other vehicles resulting in more pollution and accidents. Use of revenues to improve safety standards would be justifiable since it would reduce social costs (assuming no change in driver behaviour, such as driving faster and more dangerously on improved roads). Internalisation of social costs is specifically intended to help markets work better by increasing private costs to match social costs.

Whilst fuel duty does increase private costs it is not based directly upon any estimate of these social costs. Nor can it be described as a carbon tax since it is extremely partial in coverage. A true carbon tax would be applied across all energy-intensive sectors of the economy. Nor is it part of a comprehensive transport strategy. It is simply a 'cash cow' used to raise finance for the generality of public services.

The case for earmarking road fuel duty to finance the construction and maintenance of roads and public transport is a political argument; it cannot be justified on the basis of economic theory which simply requires internalisation of social costs in order for allocative efficiency to be achieved.

A robust argument for earmarking could therefore only be made for *partial* earmarking of fuel duty revenues. No such case can be made for earmarking VAT and the road fund licence. Making more efficient use of transport infrastructure is clearly a supply-side initiative but earmarking will not itself bring this about. Reducing the total of fuel duty, VAT and the road fund licence fee to the amount spent on roads and public transport would probably have precisely the opposite effect. Earmarking above inflation increases in these taxes, as the AA advocates, has no foundation in economic theory: it is simply a political ploy.

10.8   Integration of income tax and national insurance

There has been ongoing discussion of the integration of income tax and social security benefits and of the integration of NICs and income tax. The first issue is discussed in Chapter 12 since it has the potential radically to influence the distribution of income. Whilst NICs and income tax are clearly distinct in government accounts, it has often been argued that employees' NICs are effectively a tax on incomes and should therefore be fully integrated with personal income tax. Integration would:

- **Reduce administrative costs** (both for employers and the government) caused by running two separate systems. Potential cost savings should not be exaggerated, however, since collection arrangements are already substantially integrated (although this would make full integration easier).
- **Remove the various anomalies and problems relating to vertical equity** (discussed below).
- **Broaden the tax base** by applying employees' NICs to the full range of occupational and other incomes.

The main technical differences between income tax and NICs are as follows.

First, the base for the levy: income tax is levied on a much wider range of incomes than are NICs. Income tax is levied on occupational earnings, pensions, investment income and social security benefits. NICs are only levied on occupational earnings and on the equivalent income benefit of cars and car fuel provided by companies to their employees (NICs on this major perk having been introduced in 1991/2).

Second, the structure of the levy: employees' NICs have both an upper and a lower earnings limit (UEL and LEL) between which NICs are payable (see Appendix 10.1). Income tax makes use of personal allowances, has no ceiling on assessable income and uses different tax rates.

Third, reliefs and rebates: income tax has a range of reliefs that reflect individual circumstances, for example the working families tax credit and superannuation. No reliefs are allowed against NICs.

Fourth, the period of assessment: liability for income tax is assessed over the full tax year (6 April to 5 April) whereas NICs are levied in each pay period (usually weekly or monthly).

Fifth, the basis of deduction: income tax is deducted on a cumulative basis, taking account of earnings, allowances and reliefs that have accrued since the start of the tax year. Employees' NICs are deducted on a non-cumulative basis, each pay period being treated separately.

Combining income tax and NICs into a single payment levied on the same basis as income tax would extend allowances and reliefs to NICs, which could reduce the resulting revenue. This would depend on the balance between the loss of revenue resulting from extending allowances and the gain in revenue arising from the abolition of the UEL and the extension of NICs to pensions and the other sources of income not previously subject to them. If revenue did fall, the combined levy would have to rise in order to make the reform revenue neutral.

Strong distributional consequences would occur, low-paid workers generally paying less (because of the effect of extending the tax allowance to NICs) whilst the highest paid (earning above the UEL) would generally pay more. Whilst this may seem more equitable, people most dependent on state and occupational pensions and investment incomes (generally the elderly retired) would also pay more (NICs now effectively applying to these non-occupational incomes). Long transitional periods would be necessary to avoid pensioners 'paying twice' in the sense that they would effectively be paying NICs on the state retirement pension, which they had earned as of right on the basis of their earlier NICs.

Hence, whilst technical difficulties could be overcome, such integration may prove to be politically unpopular, especially given the

244 POLICY AND PRACTICE

increasing numbers of retired people in the near future. Moreover NICs are supposedly based on the social insurance principle, payment of various benefits being conditional upon prior contributions. In its 1985 White Paper, *Reform of Social Security*, the then Conservative government stated its belief that it was right to retain a link between contributions paid in and benefits received. The subsequent Labour government concurred with this belief. The reasons for retaining such a link are supposedly that:

- **People value the unqualified right to benefit** that their contributions confer upon them, a conclusion supported by a government survey showing that just over half of respondents regarded NICs as clearly distinct from income tax, only a third seeing both forms of payment as equivalent.
- **Contributions provide security in that they are a form of insurance**, providing both cover against temporary loss of earnings and income during retirement.
- **Contributions promote higher levels of take-up** compared with means-tested benefits because, being earned as a right, they are supposedly regarded as less stigmatising and less intrusive of privacy than means-tested benefits (see Chapter 9).
- **The qualifying test restricts benefits** to those who have made a long-standing contribution to the economy (i.e. it excludes recent immigrants).
- **Contributions make clear the cost** of national insurance benefits, although a substantial minority of employees apparently do not know how much they pay in contributions.
- **There are no disincentives to saving or to a partner earning** since the benefits are not means tested.
- **Social insurance fills in the gaps that would be left by private insurance** in that it is not based on strict actuarial principles and so pools good and bad risks, providing security for everyone, or at least those who have earnings from which to make contributions.
- **The long history, broad political support and wide international practice** of social insurance makes its abolition untenable.

However the link between contributions and benefits has been criticised as at best a comforting illusion and at worst a meaningless charade. Chapter 9 showed how increasingly tenuous this link is. More specifically, the main criticisms include the following:

First, the tenuous link between the values of contributions and benefits received. The values of contributory benefits have been steadily eroded since 1979 by the practice of uprating them in line with prices rather than with (faster growing) earnings, by subjecting more of them to taxation, by reducing or eliminating the value of earnings-related entitlements, and by reducing the period of entitlement to benefits (especially the Jobseeker's Allowance (see Chapter 9). In contrast contributions are fully earnings-related between the lower and upper earnings limits.

Second, the lack of security, because the system's 'pay as you go' nature means that the tenuous link between contributions and benefits is easily broken.

Third, the compulsory nature of the system and its associated paternalism, although 'contracting out' of the state retirement pension is now possible (see Chapter 9).

Fourth, increased administrative costs caused by the lack of integration with income tax.

Fifth, the high public expenditure costs and low values of national insurance benefits, further reduced by means testing in an increasing number of cases (see Chapter 9).

Sixth, the exclusion of many who need support, either because they have no earnings from which to make contributions or because those earnings are irregular. As already noted above, the Labour government made the 10 per cent standard *employees'* NIC rate only payable on earnings above the lower earnings limit. Previously all earnings had become subject to employees' NICs once the LEL had been passed. Whilst this reduced the marginal effective tax rate for low-paid workers, the Trades Union Congress expressed fears about low-paid workers being deprived of contributory benefits, including state pensions. This could particularly affect women part-time workers, Labour Force Survey data showing that they already accounted for over three-quarters of workers earning less than the lower limit for employees' NICs in 1996/7.

Seventh, the system is based on a male model of full-time permanent employment within the traditional family. However, approximately two-thirds of employment growth in the UK during the 1980s and 1990s was in part-time work, 90 per cent or so of part-time jobs being filled by women. Hence the system discriminates against women. In addition there are no such benefits for cohabitees, despite changing family structures (see Chapter 9).

Eighth, benefits take no account of extra needs (e.g. arising because of disability or dependent children) because the system is focused on income replacement. It is therefore a highly partial system of support.

Ninth, the regressive nature of the contributions schedule in that high-paid workers pay nothing on contributions in excess of the UEL.

Tenth, the regressive nature of the uprating mechanism. The UEL is set in relation to the LEL, both limits being uprated in line with prices rather than with earnings. Hence, whilst their real values (in relation to prices) are constant, their value as a proportion of earnings declines. This declining value relative to earnings causes more low-paid workers to make contributions whilst relieving more of the earnings of high-paid workers from contributions (i.e. those earnings in excess of the upper earnings limit). This mechanism detracts from vertical equity.

Eleventh, the incentive towards low pay created by the contributions schedule because of the employers' liability for employers' NICs once earnings reach the LEL.

Twelfth, the anomalous fall in the effective marginal tax rate at the UEL. Once earnings exceed the UEL they are no longer subject to NICs and therefore the withdrawal of combined income tax and NICs falls.

Finally, the differential 'taxation' of earned and investment incomes because NICs apply to the former but not to the latter, a problem for both horizontal and vertical equity and possibly for allocative efficiency.

There is no clear policy conclusion to be drawn from these lists of advantages and disadvantages since it is not possible to assess the balance between them. Indeed it is not even possible to agree whether some aspects are an advantage or a disadvantage. For example, the advantage of risk-pooling necessitates compulsory contributions so that compulsion and paternalism may be regarded as an advantage rather than a disadvantage. The best approach would appear to be to attempt to build on the broad political support for, and the advantages of, the contributory principle whilst recognising the changing patterns of employment by further widening the coverage of contributions and insured contingencies. Any such reform will inevitably be subject to policies favouring public expenditure restraint and limiting taxes on incomes.

These objectives could be achieved by extending the NIC system to include part-time and irregular employment and by its partial (rather than full) integration with income tax. **First**, the LEL could be aligned with the personal allowance for income tax and the UEL abolished. The 1997 Labour government only plans to implement the former (in 2001/2), not the latter. **Second**, the base for NICs could be further extended beyond occupational earnings and company cars to include all non-monetary forms of earnings. **Third**, employers' NICs could be retained as a separate payroll tax, which is what they are in practice. **Fourth**, the other technical differences between the two systems outlined above (e.g. period of assessment) could be fairly easily dealt with. **Fifth**, transitional arrangements could be made for current pensioners as suggested above. **Sixth**, and most crucially, the equivalent of NICs in the combined payment could be specifically earmarked to particular purposes. About a tenth of NICs are paid to the NHS and nine tenths are spent on social security benefits. This division, as well as the ratio between income tax and social security receipts (generally around 1.5 including employers' NICs) could either be maintained indefinitely or changed in accordance with the electorate's wishes.

The critical distinctions between the two systems are conceptual and appreciative rather than technical or financial. The fact that NICs are used for specific purposes whereas income tax contributes to general revenues, makes no substantive difference to the total tax take, to total public expenditure, or even to expenditure on individual services. Whilst the national insurance fund typically goes into deficit in a recession and into surplus during economic recovery and boom these fluctuations do not impact directly upon the exhaustive expenditures and transfer payments to which NICs are earmarked.

10.9 Conclusions

The examination of the various taxes in the UK has served to demonstrate that tax policy and practice is both multifaceted and incremental in nature. Tax policy and practice are not static. It is not simply a question of setting rates in accordance with redistributional and revenue objectives. Neither is it simply a case of setting the structure of those rates so as to minimise any disincentive-to-work effects or to take account of the elasticities of demand and supply analysed in Chapter 4.

Equity, efficiency and economy, the main principles of taxation, are all interdependent and may be contradictory. In addition they are all constrained by the need to raise sufficient revenue to finance the provision of public services. This overriding pragmatic imperative means that the other objectives of tax policy and practice may have to be compromised. Another overriding constraint is the inheritance of past practice. In particular the discussion of VAT made clear that economic efficiency has been compromised by the inheritance of past practices regarding indirect taxation.

In that taxation is a necessary concomitant of public expenditure, many of the fundamental principles underpinning the sequential restructuring of the welfare system identified in Chapter 9 also underpin reforms of the tax system. One of the most fundamental of principles is that of social justice. Both tax and expenditure policies have to be consistent with conceptions of social justice, both in terms of the extent to which individuals can be helped by the state and the extent to which individuals can be required to support it (see Chapter 12).

More specifically, the pragmatism of incremental reform has served to preclude radical reforms seeking to fully integrate the income tax and national insurance systems or the income tax and benefit systems. The exclusion of such radical reforms may be regarded as rather unfortunate given the ongoing structural changes in labour markets and their consequences for social security expenditures and income distribution which will be identified in Chapter 12. Nonetheless, many of the reforms described above and analysed in the following appendices can be seen to be aimed at removing supply-side constraints caused by tax distortions. Removal of those supply-side constraints has been seen to involve much more than simply reducing tax *rates*. Removing the economic distortions caused by tax *bases* that have less than universal coverage is of perhaps greater importance in allocative efficiency terms.

Appendix 10.1 UK taxes

Table 10.2   The main UK taxes 2000/1

	£ billion	Per cent
Income tax	96	25.6
Value added tax	60	16.2
National insurance	59	15.9
Excise duties	37	10.0
Corporation tax	34	9.2
Business rates	16	4.3
Council tax	14	3.8
Other	55	14.8
Total	371	100

Notes:
1. 'Other' includes stamp duty, inheritance tax, capital gains tax, petroleum revenue tax, vehicle excise duty, and so on.
2. Components do not exactly total 100.0 due to rounding.
3. Subsequent years' figures can be obtained from the website address at the end of this chapter.
Source: HM Treasury

Income tax

Personal income tax is levied on incomes from *wages, salaries and other earnings* including interest on savings. It is also levied on the monetary value of most *fringe benefits* (i.e. payments in kind), such as the provision by employers to employees of cheap or interest-free loans, private medical insurance, company cars for private use and the value of fuel for private use. The *pay as you earn* (PAYE) structure of income tax deducts tax payments directly from employees' pay. Hence, it is relatively simple to administer, the bulk of administration being undertaken by employers and the Inland Revenue. Introduction of *self-assessment* in 1997 has, in practice, had little impact upon the vast majority of employees, the

Inland Revenue still calculating tax liability for people submiting their tax returns on time.

In tax year 2000/1 there were three rates of income tax: (i) the **lower rate** of 10 per cent payable on the first £1500 of taxable income; (ii) the **basic rate** of 22 per cent levied on the next £26 500 of taxable income; and (iii) the **higher rate** of 40 per cent deducted from taxable income in excess of £28 000. The levels of income at which the taxpayer transfers from one tax rate to the next is referred to as the **tax threshold**. These thresholds are normally raised in line with inflation at each budget, referred to as '*indexation*'. However, incomes have risen faster than prices with the result that real value of the higher rate tax threshold has been reduced. This results in rising numbers of taxpayers paying the higher rate of income tax.

Not all income is subject to income taxation since there are various tax-free allowances – specified amounts (or maximum amounts) that are not liable for tax. Hence, the above description of rates of tax refers to **taxable income**, which is gross income minus the value of tax-free allowances. Different people pay different amounts of income tax on the same amount of income if they have different entitlements to tax allowances and reliefs. The main allowances and reliefs in 2000/1 were as follows.

Personal allowance. Each taxpayer receives a personal allowance, income on which they do not pay tax. There were three levels of personal allowance in 2000/1; (i) the basic amount of £4385 for taxpayers below the age of 65; (ii) a higher amount of £5720 for those aged 65–74; (iii) the highest amount of £5980 for those aged 75 and over.

Other allowances. Almost all other allowances were withdrawn by the tax year 2000/1 (but see below). Prior to that year there were allowances against payment of income tax for married couples, for interest payments on loans (mortgages) for house purchase, and for single parents. Married couples allowance was abolished for all couples aged under 65 on 5 April 2000 and for couples who reach 65 after that date. Married couples can still claim the married couple's allowance for 2000/1 if either partner was borne before 1935. It had been progressively reduced in value, having been frozen in cash terms during the mid 1990s and further eroded by limiting its value to the lower tax rate rather than the basic rate (those rates also being reduced). Maintaining the 1935 cut off will effectively abolish the allowance as that generation dies out. The former Conservative government regarded the allowance as an anomaly, given the switch from the joint taxation of married couples to the independent taxation of individuals in 1990/1. The subsequent Labour government regarded the allowance as poorly targeted in benefiting both affluent and poor married couples subject to income tax. The allowance also became increasingly anomalous in discriminating against the rising number of households formed by cohabiting (i.e. unmarried) couples. Both governments also saw abolition of the allowance as a means of broadening the tax base, simultaneously with cuts in tax rates.

Reforms of income tax legislation during the 1990s sought to remove the penalty on marriage, remove sex discrimination and adapt the tax system to the modern economy. Prior to the introduction of independent income taxation in 1990/1 a wife's earnings were treated as those of her husband for tax purposes. Joint taxation of husband and wife also gave wives no privacy in their tax affairs. It was based on outdated Victorian conceptions of marriage and work in treating wives as dependent on husbands' employment earnings. In particular it failed to recognise the fact that two-thirds of married women had their own employment incomes by the mid 1980s. The aggregation of two incomes could lead to higher tax liabilities being incurred by causing them to exceed tax thresholds, thus making them subject to higher tax rates. However, independent taxation prevents integration of the tax and benefits systems and so reduces the flexibility of the tax and benefit systems (but see later).

Working Families Tax Credit (WFTC). The WFTC was introduced in 1999. It guarantees a minimum weekly take-home pay for families with children where at least one parent is in employment (i.e. works at least 16 hours a week). There is an *age-related tax credit* for each child and a *Childcare Tax Credit* that reimburses up to 70 per cent of employees' childcare costs. The WFTC is paid directly through employees' pay packets. Low-paid families are eligible provided they have savings of no more than £8000. The WFTC replaced the former Family Credit paid in cash via social security offices, benefits more people and withdraws benefit at a slower rate as net income (after tax and NICs) rises (55p compared with 70p for each £1 above the £91.45 per week net income threshold). Hence, a transfer payment previously treated as public expenditure is now treated as a tax allowance. Take-up of family credit was relatively low, in part at least due to the stigma associated with claiming benefits at benefits offices. Being paid via pay packets, it is hoped that take-up of WFTC will be much higher. It is part of the Labour government's policy of redistributing wealth to low income groups and removing the poverty and unemployment traps (see Chapters 4, 9 and 12). Critics have usually argued that the most effective way of helping the low paid is to raise tax allowances so they do not pay tax, rather than cut the tax rate. However, both reforms also benefit higher paid groups since they also pay less tax. The WFTC effectively limits the additional allowance to poor working families claiming it (from the Inland Revenue) and it directly relates the value of the tax credit to the number of dependent children, the level of income and the value of savings. It illustrates how the tax system can be made more progressive without changing the rates of income tax. Also, it effectively begins to address the dichotomy created by assessing taxes on individual earnings whilst basing benefits on the needs of the whole household. It reduces the amount of churning for low-income families and is a partial return to joint taxation. Extending the WFTC to families without children would further fuse tax and welfare, avoiding giving benefits in one hand and taking them away as tax in the other hand. In principle, this is ultimately the most effective way to abolish the unemployment and poverty traps. In practice, it remains to be seen whether incentives to work will be increased. Indeed, they could be decreased since means-testing is being applied to more working families under WFTC than under the former Family Credit. Chapter 9 noted that it is *administrative barriers* (uncertainty, insecurity and delays) to claiming benefit that create the strongest disincentives to work whereas the WFTC addresses *financial disincentives*. If work incentives are increased, then the WFTC will be a successful supply-side initiative. Recent research published by the Institute of Fiscal Studies predicted that the WFTC would have a greater incentive-to-work effect than the simultaneously introduced 10p starting rate for income tax and reforms to NICs.

Children's Tax Credit (CTC). This tax credit is being introduced in tax year 2001/2. It replaces the former Married Couple's Allowance and the Additional Personal Allowance (for single parents). It therefore concentrates the tax allowance on families with children (aged under 16), whether single parent or married or cohabiting couple. Previously, married couples could claim the married couple's allowance whether or not they had any children. Only **one** CTC can be claimed even if there is more than one dependent child (the claim therefore normally being made in respect of the youngest child so as to maximise its duration). The tax credit is withdrawn at the rate of £1 of credit for every £15 of income taxed at the higher rate, based on the tax position of the partner with the larger income. An **integrated child credit** (ICC) has been proposed by the 1997 Labour government for introduction in 2003. It would combine child payments embedded within income support, the WFTC and the disabled person's tax credit with the CTC. In this way children of unemployed parents would receive support in the same way as children whose parents are in low-paid jobs. Hence, there would be no need to transfer from one system to another as parents move into and out of work. This would facilitate the *seamless transition from welfare to work* that the Labour government has been attempting to achieve for benefit recipients. In this way an ICC would complement a WFTC extended to families without children, the latter thus becoming an **employment tax credit** (its introduction again being planned by the Labour government for 2003). This would effectively constitute a **negative income tax** scheme, combining the tax and social security systems (see Chapter 12).

Corporation tax

Levied on company profits, the main rate of tax will be 30 per cent in 2001/2, with small companies paying 10 per cent (see the main body of this chapter).

Stamp duty

The oldest Inland Revenue tax, dating from 1694. It is payable on many documents used in commercial and legal practice, including those relating to the transfer of land and buildings, such as the purchase of a house or of stocks and shares. In 2000/1 stamp duty of 1 per cent was payable on purchases of land and buildings above £60 000 in value, 3 per cent for transactions over £250 000 and 4 per cent for those over £500 000. In 2000/1 only 5 per cent of residential transactions in the UK paid at rates above 1 per cent, but just over 10 per cent in London and the South East (reflecting higher property values there). In 1990/1 the then Conservative government announced plans to abolish stamp duty on shares and on all other property except land and buildings. However, the subsequent Labour government chose to retain stamp duty.

Inheritance tax

This is a tax on capital (i.e. wealth) as distinct from a tax on the income which it produces. Precursors include **estate duty**, replaced by **capital transfer tax** in 1975, itself replaced by **inheritance tax** in 1986. It is levied on the value of assets transferred by an individual, whether after death or as a gift during a person's lifetime (*inter vivos*). As for income tax, there are various reliefs and exemptions. The first £234 000 of a transfer in 2000/1 was exempt, as are transfers between spouses and gifts between individuals, the last provided that the donor survives for another seven years. Unlike income tax, however, planning one's tax affairs allows inheritance tax to be avoided completely, as long as inheritances are transferred well in advance of death. Not surprisingly, therefore, typically less than 4 per cent of estates are subject to inheritance tax.

Capital gains tax

This tax is levied on profits accruing from the disposal of assets, generally the difference between the buying and selling prices adjusted for inflation during the interim period. In 2000/1 the first £7200 of capital gains was free of tax and owner-occupied housing is exempt from it.

Petroleum revenue tax

Levied in addition to corporation tax and payments of royalties and licence fees, it is levied on profits net of operating costs and capital expenditures on a field-by-field basis for North Sea oil and gas operations. Reliefs and allowances are made for exploration and development costs in order to encourage further finds and the initial volume (barrelage) of production is tax free in order to encourage earlier production. Its theoretical rationale is the capture of **economic rent** (see Chapter 4).

Value added tax (VAT)

Levied throughout the EU, it was introduced in the UK upon accession in 1973. It replaced Purchase Tax and Selective Employment Tax. A broadly based tax, applying to most goods and services, it is collected at every stage of production and distribution: that is, upon sale from manufacturer to wholesaler, from wholesaler to retailer and from retailer to customer. Tax liability is the product of the value added and the tax rate. Value added at each stage is calculated by subtracting the input cost from the selling price at each stage. The input cost is inclusive of VAT (referred to as the **'input tax'**). The seller charges VAT on the selling price (referred to as the **'output tax'**). Hence the amount each trader pays to Customs and Excise is the net difference between the input tax and the output tax. This is therefore a tax on the **value added** at each stage of production and distribution. The annual turnover threshold above which traders are required to register for VAT is raised annually by the rate of inflation. In 2000/1 it was £52 000. Being unable to reclaim the input tax, it is the final consumer who pays the full amount of tax. Note, however, that the legal and economic incidences of taxation may differ (see Chapter 4 and Appendix 10.2).

The UK's rate of VAT has varied over time. It was introduced in 1973 at a standard rate of 10 per cent, subsequently reduced to 8 per cent and supplemented by a 12.5 per cent rate on certain 'luxury' goods. The newly-elected 1979 Conservative government replaced both rates by a single standard rate of 15 per cent in that year. The standard rate was increased to 17.5 per cent in 1991, the extra revenue being used to reduce levels of local government taxation and so switch about £4 billion of tax revenues from local to central government. This was a response to the widespread unpopularity of the 'community charge', which was later abolished (see below). A reduced 5 per cent rate of VAT applies to domestic fuel and power, installation of energy saving materials, and women's sanitary products. The UK agreed with its EU partners not to extend its zero rates beyond those in place in 1975 and 5 per cent is the minimum rate allowed when any reductions are made to the standard rate.

Vehicle excise duty (VED)

Generally referred to as road tax and collected by the Driver and Vehicle Licensing Agency, it is in effect a licence fee, a licence (tax disc) being required to drive motor vehicles on public roads. In 1999/2000 VED was graduated into two bands, a reduced rate applying to vehicles with an engine size up to 1100cc (subsequently raised to 1200cc). Cars with engine capacities above 1200cc pay the higher standard rate for a licence (the standard rate being about 50 per cent greater than the reduced rate). This is a reflection of cars' rate of emission of carbon dioxide, engine size being the best available indicator of emissions, albeit crude. Smaller engine cars tend to use less fuel. VED for new cars registered from March 2001 will be based on its carbon dioxide emission figure and the type of fuel it uses. This will enable the graduated licence fee to be more closely related to emissions. The government hopes that these tax differentials will provide an incentive for motorists to choose smaller, more fuel-efficient cars. At the very least, it complements the incentives resulting from relatively high UK fuel duty.

Excise duties

Excise duties are mostly set in *absolute* terms as pounds or pence (e.g. on each bottle of spirits or per litre of petrol). Unlike other duties, that on cigarettes also includes an *ad valorem* (i.e. percentage) element based on the selling price. Excise duties typically account for between half and three-quarters of the final selling prices of these commodities. In addition, VAT is charged on top of excise duties since they are included in the final selling price.

Justification of these **specific taxes** on alcohol, cigarettes and tobacco on the grounds that they are intended to deter consumption is misplaced because demand is relatively unresponsive to price (although the price elasticity of demand seems to be higher for wines and spirits than for beer). Hence the potential health benefits arising from reduced consumption are not achieved, such taxes being more successful in raising revenue than in deterring consumption. Perhaps a more convincing practical argument for these taxes and excises is that there is less tax-payer resistance precisely because taxpayers accept (to some extent at least) the 'demerit good' arguments related to these goods (i.e. a tax on 'bad habits').

Unlike the possible extension of VAT to all foods and the relatively high level of fuel duty, excise taxes on alcoholic drinks do not raise the same volume of protest in the UK. This is despite the fact that alcohol features prominently in the consumption patterns of most people. Family Expenditure Survey data shows that alcohol accounts for 4 per cent of total household spending, and 19 per cent of spending on food and drink. Over four-fifths of adults regularly drink alcohol. The probable reasons for this relative lack of controversy are that alcoholic drinks are not a necessity and that high levels of consumption are generally regarded as undesirable on both social and personal grounds.

Business rates and council tax

Both these taxes are a form of **property tax**. Business rates (national non-domestic rates) are levied by *central* government. Council tax is levied by *local* government and is the only tax over which central government has no direct control.

The national business rate was introduced in 1990 and the council tax was introduced in 1993. Prior to 1990 there had been a single property tax applied to both domestic and non-domestic properties. Householders paid **domestic rates** on their homes, and businesses paid **non-domestic rates** on their business premises. In each case the tax rate was determined by the local government in whose area the properties were located. Whilst the tax base (the annual rental value of property net of maintenance costs and insurances) was determined by the Inland Revenue in England and Wales and by the independent Board of Assessors in Scotland, the property tax was a local tax to all intents and purposes.

Central government took control of the local government tax on business properties on the grounds that widely varying tax rates between different local government areas distorted the location of industry. In particular, the then Conservative government believed that many left-wing local authorities had effectively driven businesses out of their areas by levying relatively high tax rates. The result was run-down inner city areas with relatively high levels of unemployment. It argued that a national standard tax rate would remove this unnecessary supply-side constraint on the location of industry. In fact, empirical research failed either to support or deny the government's argument. This was because many factors affect industrial location (e.g. availability of skilled labour and transport links). The so-called *'urban–rural shift'* of industry, employment and residential location was common across Europe, not just occuring in a few UK cities. In practice, it was not possible to separate all the other effects on industrial location from the effect of the locally-variable business property tax. However, assuming *ceteris paribus*, relatively high taxes in one area will deter new investment by existing and potentially incoming firms. **The neoclassical economic theory of industrial location** therefore supports the hypothesis that *relatively* high local business taxes deter investment. Nevertheless, it has to be noted that the actual tax bill depends on both the tax rate and the tax base. The *tax base* still varies widely between different parts of the country, notwithstanding nationalisation of the *tax rate*.

Domestic rates were replaced by the short-lived and highly unpopular *community charge* (a *local poll tax*) between 1990 and 1993. Hence for three years there was no UK domestic property tax. Absence of such a tax could have profound allocative effects (see Appendix 10.3). The local poll tax was replaced by the *council tax* in 1993 following a sustained and growing taxpayer revolt during the previous three years. Whilst nationally over 85 per cent of adults paid the local poll tax, such high levels of non-payment occurred in some local authorities (particularly the multiply-deprived inner cities) that administrative and legal processes attempting to enforce payment became grossly overburdened. Notwithstanding a means-tested benefit to help low-income people, many of those who paid (rather than withheld) the tax also thought it was a grossly unfair tax. Put simply, the poll tax was not a viable tax in political, administrative or equity terms.

The council tax has many similarities to the former domestic rates in that both are local property taxes. There are, however, two major differences between domestic rates and the council tax. **First**, the tax base for the council tax is the *capital* (i.e. market) value of the property, rather than the *rental* value for rates. **Second**, properties are allocated to eight *valuation bands* for council tax purposes, rather than there being a precise individual valuation for each property subject to rates (see Chapter 14). Hence the council tax has many of the characteristics of a crude wealth tax, in that it only relates to housing and because its valuation system is imprecise.

Critics such as the New Policy Institute argue that the council tax is highly regressive, making it little better than the poll tax it replaced. **First, properties in the lowest valuation band are proportionately more highly taxed than properties in the highest valuation band.** House-holders in the most expensive properties (band H) pay only three times as much as householders in the least expensive properties (band A), although the formers' properties are valued as worth at least eight times as much as the latters'. This regressive effect occurs because the eight valuation bands are too narrow. It disadvantages low income groups and distorts investment towards large houses. **Second, second homes (i.e. holiday homes) are taxed at only half the rate of first homes (i.e. main residences).** Again, this distorts investment in housing. **Third, owner-occupiers do not pay tax on the imputed rents of their properties** whereas landlords have to pay income tax on rents. This discriminates against the market for rented properties. **Fourth, council tax rebates exacerbate the poverty and unemployment traps.** Almost half of households living in properties in the lowest tax band receive means-tested *council tax benefit.* Whilst this makes council tax less regressive, it exacerbates the poverty and unemployment traps by increasing the effective marginal tax rate (see Chapters 4 and 9).

These issues relating to both business rates and council tax are discussed in more detail in the author's 1999 'Local Government Economics' text.

Social security taxes

Social security taxes are formally known as **national insurance contributions** (NICs). During the 1980s and 1990s about 60 per cent of NICs were paid by *employers* as a form of *payroll tax,* the rest being paid by *employees* out of their earnings. They are used to finance specific contributory benefits, such as those for unemployment and retirement (see Chapter 9). In being 'earmarked' for such benefits (see section 10.7 above) they are therefore supposedly conceptually distinct from (unrequited) income tax. Nevertheless, they are often informally referred to as 'a tax on jobs'. These terms reflect two features.

First, NICs are paid by *employers* in accordance with their payrolls. The amount they pay increases as they recruit more workers and/or pay them higher wages and salaries. NICs may therefore deter firms from employing more workers. In 2000/1 the standard rate for *employers'* NICs was 12.2 per cent on weekly earnings above £84.00, a threshold set at the same level as the standard personal income tax allowance. **Second, NICs are also payable by *employees* in accordance with their earned incomes.** In 2000/1 the standard rate for *employees'* NICs was 10 per cent on weekly earnings between £76.01 and £535, the lower earnings limit (LEL) and upper earnings limit (UEL) respectively. Whilst not levied on the full range of earnings, nevertheless they have the effect of increasing the effective rate of income tax by 10 per cent for earnings between the LEL and UEL. This may deter unskilled workers from seeking jobs because low-paid workers may be little better off in work than when unemployed and in receipt of means-tested benefits (see Chapter 4).

The standard rate of NICs was 10 per cent for employees not 'contracted out' of the state earnings related pension scheme (SERPs – see Chapter 9). A lower standard rate (8.4 per cent) was payable by employees with their own occupational pension schemes (and who were therefore 'contracted out' of SERPs).

The 1997 Labour government plans to align the *employees'* LEL with the personal allowance in 2001/2). The UEL for *employers'* NICs was abolished in 1985 and the *employers'* LEL was aligned with the personal allowance in 1999. Whilst the earnings of most employees in receipt of major taxable perks (such as company cars) already exceed the upper earnings limit for NICs, this would no longer be the case if the UEL were to be abolished.

The climate change levy and other environmental taxes

The 1997 Labour government announced plans to introduce a **climate change levy** in 2001/2 to encourage energy efficiency in business and help reduce greenhouse gas emissions. An offsetting cut in employers' NICs means that this tax on energy consumption is *revenue neutral*. The government also announced a new **aggregates levy** from 2001/2 to address the environmental costs associated with quarrying and encourage the use of recycled materials (thus reducing the need for landfill). The levy will apply to virgin sand, gravel and crushed rock subject to commercial exploitation in the UK. It will be charged at £1.60 per tonne. Again, the tax will be made *revenue neutral* by reducing employers' NICs. Both taxes are examples of the **shift from taxes on job creation to taxes on polluting activities**. This policy is more generally referred to as a *shift from the taxation of goods to bads*. Other new and existing environmental tax measures include extension of the reduced rate of VAT for the installation of energy saving materials in all homes, the planned 100 per cent first year capital allowances for energy saving investments in 2001/2, the landfill tax and a series of taxes on use of vehicles. The last include graduated vehicle excise duty (see above), the lower duty rate on road fuel gases (frozen as from 1996, cut by 29 per cent in 1999 and then frozen again in 2000), the lower rate of duty on ultra-low sulphur diesel (ULSD) introduced in 1997, and the introduction of a similar tax differential on ultra-low sulphur petrol (ULSP) in 2000. This last tax measure is a follow-on from the introduction in 1987 of a tax differential in favour of unleaded petrol, the success of which helped facilitate the phasing out of leaded petrol on 1 January 2000. Basically, the governments' message is that the less motorists pollute, the less tax they pay.

Appendix 10.2 The impact of applying VAT to newspapers

In 1993, as part of its campaign to prevent an extension of value added
tax (VAT) to newspapers, the Newspaper Society commissioned
consultants Price Waterhouse to estimate the impact of VAT on sales
of newspapers. Whilst recognising that each title faces different market
conditions (depending on whether it is a 'tabloid' or a 'quality' paper, or
a local, regional or national newspaper and so on), their broad estimates
suggested that the **price elasticity of demand** was −0.3 for provincial
morning and Sunday papers, −0.4 for evening papers and −0.5 for paid-
for weeklies. So, adding the standard 17.5 per cent rate of VAT to the
price of morning papers would reduce demand by 5.25 per cent. Tax
revenues would be reduced accordingly (see Chapter 4).

However the main problem with such estimates is that they are based
on what happens when the price of a single title is increased. In this case
price elasticity of demand is higher since many consumers switch to
lower-priced substitute titles. Raising the price of all newspapers
simultaneously can be expected to reduce switching between titles with
the result that the price elasticity of demand will be lower for
newspapers taxed as a whole than for a single title. However if VAT
were to be extended to cover all consumer expenditures (see the main
body of this chapter), then possibly quite strong income effects could also
be expected, leading to more severely reduced purchasing of newspapers. These effects would vary amongst different income groups,
depending on their **income elasticities of demand**. Hence any revenue
gains would depend on a myriad of complex factors and the above
estimates may be quite inaccurate.

Moreover, in comparison with the opposition to VAT on all foods
(which stresses distributional aspects), the newspapers case stresses a
much broader set of problems, appropriate responses to which may not
be so readily available. Despite the questionable blanket 'tax on
knowledge' argument against extension of VAT to newspapers, books
and periodicals, there is a more focused concern about the impact of VAT
on reading materials at a time when illiteracy seemed to be a growing
problem. Surveys during the mid 1990s found that a third of 14 year olds
had a reading age of 11 or below and that 40 per cent of 16 to 19 year olds
at further education colleges lacked basic literacy and numeracy skills.
Lack of such basic skills already imposes additional costs on industry
and commerce. Those costs could possibly be exacerbated by the
extension of VAT to reading materials. However the relevance of VAT
to the illiteracy problem is probably exaggerated since zero-rating of
reading materials is not the most effective way of improving literacy.

A more forceful argument, advanced by the Periodical Publishers'
Association, is that many magazine publishers would leave Britain if

VAT were to be so extended. It argued that production would move to other EU countries with lower VAT rates on magazines, with subscription mailing to Britain. This would reduce the financial gains to the Treasury and cause economic and cultural losses to the local and national communities. This example stresses the importance of *tax harmonisation* within the EU (see Appendix 10.4).

Such broad multidisciplinary arguments demonstrate that indirect taxation (including excise duties) is not simply a matter of raising revenue. Neither is it simply a matter of distributional equity or of economic efficiency. All these factors are simultaneously relevant, along with cultural, educational and other issues.

Appendix 10.3 Abolition of the local domestic property tax

The temporary abolition of the local domestic property tax in 1990 and its replacement by the community charge (dubbed the 'poll tax') resulted in owner-occupied housing being completely tax free. The distortionary effects of this tax anomaly for housing markets were potentially profound. Making use of some of the theory in Chapter 4, it can be shown that the abolition of domestic rates in 1990 had the following effects:

- **A price effect** as the price of housing fell relative to other commodities. The consequent increase in demand would depend on the price elasticity of demand for housing.
- **An income effect** due to the reduction in tax liability. However the resulting increase in demand was largely offset by the replacement of domestic rates by the poll tax.
- **A supply response** as more new houses were provided to meet the increased demand.

The then Conservative government originally intended that the substitution of one tax for another would be *revenue neutral*, in which case the **income effect** would have been zero. In practice, however, it was argued (with some supporting evidence) that local authorities had used the reform of local taxation to increase their real tax revenues. Hence, ignoring any offsetting change in the value of public services received, the average income effect was negative, so depressing the aggregate demand for housing. However social security benefits were amended to take account (at least in part) of the higher local tax payments of low-income groups. Moreover, within the average income effect, there were some redistributive income effects in favour of high-income groups (which was expected to increase their demands for housing). Clearly, calculation of the average income effect is highly complex and the dispersion about that average could vary substantially for particular socioeconomic groups. Hence, for simplicity of analysis, assume an income effect of zero so that the only influences on the demand for housing are the price effect and the supply response.

The supply of housing is inelastic in the short run. Increases in supply would take months (for conversions of properties such as warehouses into flats and subdivisions of existing houses) or years (for land purchase, securing planning permission and the subsequent new building). However, even in the long run the supply of housing may be inelastic in particular areas. This would be the case if no new housing developments were allowed in 'green belt' areas or if particular areas were already subject to over-development and congestion. In contrast demand could rise immediately upon abolition of the domestic property tax and so the **price effect** is expected to have the greatest impact.

The **price effect** can be best demonstrated by the following example. Suppose that there is a range of financial assets each costing £100 and earning a 10 per cent return (i.e. £10) in perpetuity. Income tax levied at 25 per cent reduces the post-tax yield to 7.5 per cent (i.e. £7.50). If one of the assets is now exempted from tax then demand for it will rise. Increased demand will continue until its post-tax yield is the same as that for all the other assets. Hence its capital value rises to £133.33 (£10 now being equivalent to the post-tax yield of 7.5 per cent on other assets). Hence the owner of an asset that is made exempt from tax experiences a capital gain. This is referred to as **tax capitalisation** because the value of the tax exemption becomes capitalised into the selling price of the asset.

By analogy with this example, house prices were already higher than they otherwise would have been as a result of favourable tax treatment, namely freedom from taxation of imputed rents and of capital gains and interest on mortgages qualifying for relief against income tax (see above). The abolition of domestic rates in 1990 was expected to have compounded this effect by leading to substantial capital gains for existing owner-occupiers. Some estimates calculated the average property tax rate on housing services to be in excess of 30 per cent. Combined with a price elasticity of demand for owner-occupied housing of about −0.75 per cent and a highly inelastic supply, the result expected by some researchers was an increase in house prices of around 15 per cent and contributing substantially to house price inflation. However, provided that supply was elastic, the elimination of such a relatively large specific commodity tax would reverse the large deadweight welfare losses it caused (see Chapter 4).

This conclusion is based on two assumptions. **First**, whilst supply increases, the town and country planning system minimises the social costs (i.e. negative externalities) of land development (see Chapter 2). **Second**, that existing owner-occupiers are not able to influence the outcomes of the planning system in order to restrict development and so preserve their potential capital gains, an example of distributional coalitions (see Chapter 7).

Given that the poll tax survived for such a short period, these potential impacts were shortlived. In fact house prices fell in response to other more powerful influences on demand for owner-occupied housing, especially the onset of recession. However other tax concessions on capital gains and imputed rents remain and may similarly be capitalised into house prices. Capitalisation of the relief of mortgage interest payments against income tax will have benefited the people who were owner-occupiers at the time the relief was introduced. Subsequent new (first-time) house buyers did not benefit if there was an immediate 100 per cent tax capitalisation, simply because they had to pay the resulting higher prices. In this case the favourable tax treatment stimulates owner-occupation (as a form of tax avoidance) rather than benefits new entrants to the owner-occupied housing sector. However new buyers would have benefited if tax capitalisation were less than 100 per cent. This is quite possible since building societies and banks ration mortgage funds (e.g. by restricting finance to those in 'eligible' occupations). Similarly, to have withdrawn the tax concession in one fell swoop would have caused possibly large capital losses to be incurred by existing owner-occupiers, explaining why it was phased out over a number of years (see the main body of this chapter).

Appendix 10.4 Tax harmonisation

Tax harmonisation is required if the single market of the EU (established in January 1993) is to function effectively. As already noted, differences in the rates and bases of indirect taxation can lead to distortions in the pattern of demand. In other words, those tax differentials lead people and companies to make choices and decisions different from those they would have made had tax rates been equal. For example, tax avoidance in respect of so-called **duty-free** purchases of cigarettes and tobacco, alcohol, watches, cameras, jewellery, clothes, perfumes and so on, led to huge distortions in the pattern of investment in retailing. Duty-free goods have long been available for international journeys made by sea and air – but not by train or coach. Potential profits made on such purchases arguably distort investment decisions – witness the major shopping malls at airports and on passenger ferries. Such tax anomalies are also inconsistent with tax harmonisation. Hence, 'duty-free' was abolished in 1999 for international journeys *within the EU*. It still exists for travel beyond EU boundaries.

Abolition of inter-EU duty-free has not affected the tremendous cross-Channel '**duty-paid**' tax-avoidance activity that takes advantage of the lower rates of customs and excise duties on the Continent. The giant stores in Cité Europe near Calais attract large numbers of British shoppers purchasing goods subject to much lower indirect taxes. The post-1993 boom in cross-border shopping followed abolition of limits on the amount of alcohol travellers can bring into Britain from other EU countries. If used for personal consumption this is *tax avoidance* (legal). However, much of this activity is clearly illegal *tax evasion*, quantities being brought back being much greater than those allowed for private consumption. Customs and Excise estimated that in 1998 up to 70 per cent of beer brought into the UK was sold illegally, costing pubs an estimated £900 million in lost sales and the government £300 million in lost duty. A similar, and increasingly serious, situation results for cigarettes and tobacco. The government estimated that tobacco smuggling cost the Exchequer £2.5 billion in 1999. UK tobacconists, off-licences and pubs lose business as a result (not just those in the south-east of England).

The government fears that the tax base is being eroded at an accelerating rate. Such erosion will be compounded with development of retailing over the Internet if it effectively becomes a VAT-free and duty-free zone. Whether tax avoidance or tax evasion, the fact is that such activity is the result of very large differences in tax rates either side of the English Channel. Tax rates on drink, cigarettes and tobacco are much lower on the Continent than in the UK. In October 1998, amongst the 15 member states of the EU, the retail price of a packet of 20 cigarettes was highest in the UK at just over £3 and lowest in Spain at just under £1. The price in France was just under £2.

Although substantial, the distortionary effect created by these tax differentials is reduced for most goods by transport costs, especially when they are high relative to the retail value of the commodity. For a given tax differential, these distortions are of greater magnitude on the Continent, where travel between a number of bordering countries is easier. Moreover, even if relatively minor in terms of total trade, it has been seen that these distortions can have substantial impacts on individual industries, especially where the ratio of product transport costs to value added is low.

Excise duties apart, the UK has relatively low tax rates compared with the rest of the EU. It was noted above that the UK tends to be a low tax state in respect of income tax, corporation tax and so on. In 1998, the UK's standard rate of VAT was less than that in nine member states, greater than that in four and equal to that in one. Moreover, it was also noted above that the UK is one of the few member states not to levy VAT on most foods, such that both its tax rate and tax base differs from those in other member states. Hence, tax harmonisation will not necessarily be restricted to reducing taxes on alcohol and cigarettes. It may also require higher taxes on incomes and on company profits. However, the UK government's view is that the way to create jobs is by cutting taxes on incomes and profits and so it is against harmonisation of income tax (including NICs) and corporation tax, as are several other member states. It wants to retain sovereignty in fiscal policy as well as in monetary policy, the latter explaining why the UK did not join the single currency in 1999. Differences in tax rates and tax systems would be highlighted if and when the UK does adopt the Euro.

The UK government believes that a single European market is still possible *without* tax harmonisation and that full tax harmonisation would have profound implications for the budgets of member states, leading to fiscal deficits in countries formerly with relatively high taxes. Most progress towards harmonisation has been made in respect of VAT, progress obviously being much slower in respect of excise duties, particularly on alcohol, fuel and tobacco. In respect of VAT, the European Commission recommended a standard rate of 15 per cent and a minimum rate of 5 per cent. Given the wide disparities within the EU, it believed that a single rate would be politically unacceptable to many member states. Any member state changing its VAT rates should move closer to (rather than further from) these two rates. The rates were considered close enough to avoid serious trade distortions. Nevertheless, many member states are reluctant to adopt the standard rate because it would cause substantial budget shortfalls for those whose rates are above 15 per cent.

There are two broad options for indirect tax harmonisation. First, the **destination principle**, currently adopted by the EU. Exports are effectively zero-rated for VAT purposes under the destination principle because the rate of taxation of the destination country applies after exportation. Hence there is no significant distortion to trade within a given country. Nonetheless, it has been made clear that there can still be severe distortions caused by cross-border shopping for those commodities which can be transported very cheaply relative to tax savings caused by proportionately wide tax differentials..

This distortionary effect could perhaps be overcome by adopting a second principle – **the origin principle** – for indirect taxation. Under the origin principle, the tax rate levied upon exports is that of the country of manufacture. Hence tax revenue accrues to the country of production, rather than to the country of consumption (as under the destination principle). This revenue effect occurs because, under the origin principle, VAT is neither rebated for exports nor levied upon imports. The problem with this principle is that other EU countries have a multiplicity of VAT rates, so adoption of the origin principle may create more distortions to trade than it removes.

For example, internationally mobile companies that sell their output in many countries would face incentives to relocate their production plants in the country with the lowest rate of VAT on their product since it is no longer rebated for exports (nor levied on imports). The greater the value added the greater the tax differential between countries, and the more alike the other factors of production (e.g. labour skills and costs) the greater the incentive for companies to relocate. Whilst subject to empirical testing of the (net of tax) price elasticities of supply for such industries (see Chapter 4), there could be substantial relocation of export-based factories producing cars, pharmaceuticals, electronic goods (e.g. video recorders and computers) and internationally tradeable financial services (e.g. marine insurance).

Put simply, replacing the destination principle with the origin principle for VAT may simply turn a **consumption** distortion into a **production** distortion. Hence this distortionary effect can only be overcome by full tax harmonisation, that is where the rates and bases of indirect taxation are identical in all EU member states. However, full tax harmonisation is unlikely since the EU has adopted a partial approach in only setting minimum rates for VAT and for certain excise duties. Finally, tax harmonisation is only required for internationally tradeable commodities.

The question arises: why bother with tax harmonisation if the destination principle still applies, given that this offsets potential distortions to trade? The reply is that differential *indirect* taxes require differential *direct* taxes for a given amount of tax revenues. For example, low indirect taxes require offsetting higher direct taxes. Differential direct taxes may create fiscal barriers to the free movement of labour. They may also create fiscal barriers to the pattern of trade. For example, if the supply of labour is highly elastic an increase in the rate of income tax (to offset the revenue consequences of a cut in indirect taxation) will be passed on to employers in the form of a rise in the gross wage. Hence employers face higher unit labour costs, leading to higher product prices and/or lower profits, with consequent impacts on the patterns of production and therefore trade. Hence differential indirect tax rates can still have distortionary effects on trade, despite adoption of the destination principle. It is likely, therefore, that the issue of VAT zero-rating food and other items in the UK will become of increasing concern in terms of the fiscal barriers created in frustration of the Single European Market.

Further reading

Bennett, F. (1993) *Social Insurance: Reform or Abolition*, The Commission on Social Justice (London: Institute for Public Policy Research).

Giles, C. and Johnson, P. (1994) 'Tax Reform in the UK and Changes in the Progressivity of the Tax System 1985-95', *Fiscal Studies*, vol. 15, no. 3, pp. 64–86.

Gregg, P., Johnson, P. and Reed, H. (1999) *Entering Work and the British Tax and Benefit System* (London: Institute of Fiscal Studies).

HM Customs and Excise (online). Available at <http://www.hmce.gov.uk>.

HM Treasury (online). Available at <http://www.hm-treasury.gov.uk>. Extend the website address to include </budget2001> for an update on the figures in this chapter.

HM Treasury (1984) *The Next Ten Years: Public Expenditure and Taxation into the 1990s*, Cmnd 9189 (London: HMSO).

HM Treasury (1986) *The Reform of Personal Taxation*, Cmnd 9756 (London: HMSO).

Hayek, F. A. (1979) *Law, Legislation and Liberty*, Volume 3: *The Political Order of a Free People* (London: Routledge and Kegan Paul).

Hirsch, D. (1998) *The Working Families Tax Credit: Options and Evaluation*, Joseph Rowntree Foundation (York: York Publishing Services).

House of Commons (1999) *The Operation of the Landfill Tax*, Environment, Transport and Regional Affairs Committee, Thirteenth Report Session 1998–99 HC 150–I (London: The Stationery Office).

Hughes, G. A. (1988) 'Rates Reform and the Housing Market', in Bailey, S. J. and Paddison, R. (eds), *The Reform of Local Government Finance in Britain* (London: Routledge).

Institute of Fiscal Studies (online). Available at <http://www.ifs.org.uk>.

James, S. and Nobes, J. (2000) *The Economics of Taxation*, 7th edn (Harlow: Pearson Education).

Kay, J. A. and King, M. A. (1996) *The British Tax System*, 6th edn (Oxford: Oxford University Press).

Meadows, P. (1997) *The Integration of Taxes and Benefits for Working Families with Children: Issues Raised to Date*, Joseph Rowntree Foundation (York: York Publishing Services).

Mulgan, G. and Murray, R. (1993) *Reconnecting Taxation* (London: Demos).

Organisation for Economic Co-operation and Development (OECD) (online). Available at <http://www.oecd.org.uk>.

OECD (1999) *OECD Figures: Statistics on the Member Countries*, 1999 Edition (Paris: Organisation for Economic Co-operation and Development.

Pearce, F. (1998) 'A Wasted Chance: Britain's Landfill Tax', *New Scientist*, 30 May, pp. 22–3.

Pocklington, D. N. and Pocklington, R. E. (1998) 'The United Kingdom Landfill Tax – Externalities and External Influences', *Journal of Planning Law*, pp. 529–45.

Rosenthal, L. (1999) 'House Prices and Local Taxes in the UK', *Fiscal Studies*, vol. 20, no. 1. pp. 61–76.

Teja, R. S. and Bracewell-Milnes, B. (1991) *The Case for Earmarked Taxes: Government Spending and Public Choice* (London: Institute of Economic Affairs).

Twigger, R. (1997) *The Burden of Taxation*, Research Paper 97/50, House of Commons Library, Economic Policy and Statistics Section (London: House of Commons).

Wagner, R. E. (1991) *Charging for Government: User Charges and Earmarked Taxes in Principle and Practice* (London: Routledge).

Wilkinson, M. (1994) 'Paying for Public Spending: Is There a Role for Earmarked Taxes?', *Fiscal Studies*, vol. 15, no. 4, pp. 119–35.

11 Public Sector Borrowing: Policy and Practice

11.1 Introduction
11.2 The Changing Economic Role of Budget Deficits
11.3 Defining and Measuring Public Sector Borrowing
11.4 A Structural or Cyclical Budget Deficit?
11.5 Forecasting the Budget Deficit/Surplus
11.6 Financing a Budget Deficit
11.7 Medium-term Debt Targets
11.8 Stocks and Flows of Debt
11.9 Conclusions

If a government cannot keep its own finances in order, it adds to the uncertainty that businesses face. The risk of unsustainably large deficits makes it more difficult to operate monetary policy. High levels of government borrowing increase the burden of public debt, raising interest rates and ultimately forcing higher taxes or cuts in public spending (1994 White Paper, *Competitiveness: Helping Business to Win*, Cm 2563, London: HMSO, p. 21).

Low and stable inflation helps individuals and businesses to plan for the long-term. This in turn improves the quality and quantity of long-term investment, both in physical and human capital, and helps raise productivity. The monetary policy framework is delivering low and stable inflation. The fiscal policy framework has restored the public finances to a healthy and sustainable position, while allowing fiscal policy to support monetary policy through the economic cycle. The Budget maintains the commitment to stability and prudence and ensures the Government remains on track to meet the fiscal rules [the golden rule and the sustainable investment rule] and deliver steady growth (*Budget*, March 2000, Chapter 2, London: HM Treasury).

11.1 Introduction

Public sector borrowing is not simply a means of 'balancing the books' nor simply a Keynesian or monetarist macroeconomic tool for controlling the level of economic activity in the short term. The policy and practice of public sector borrowing has increasingly become an essential under-pinning of microeconomic supply-side measures aimed at improving the productive potential of the economy in the longer term. Increasing attention has been paid not just to the total amount of borrowing but also to the purposes to which it is put. The rationale for this transition is explained in this chapter.

Chapter 5 provided a fuller appreciation of the possible economic effects of public sector borrowing. Briefly, if the government wishes to borrow more than the market is willing to lend at the current equilibrium, it can persuade lenders to supply more borrowable funds by increasing the interest rate earned by government stock. The interest rate will also rise automatically if an excess supply of government debt causes the selling price to fall against its fixed redemption value. Increased interest rates on government stock lead to a general rise in interest rates, simply because other borrowers must compete with the government for borrowable funds. Interest-sensitive expenditures are crowded out by increased interest rates. If investment is highly interest elastic, then economic growth will be reduced as investment in productive capacity falls.

If the government wishes to avoid any such crowding out of investment it can finance its borrowing requirement by receiving credit from the Bank of England. This expansion of bank deposits is referred to as **printing money**. Whilst avoiding higher interest rates, an increased money supply could lead to inflation according to the **quantity theory of money**. *Ceteris paribus*, UK goods therefore become uncompetitive relative to foreign goods so imports rise and exports fall. Hence domestic production falls, unemployment rises and economic growth is reduced. This is the same end result as that caused by the rise in interest rates.

Moreover borrowing leads to an accumulation of public sector debt, which must ultimately be repaid. If borrowing is not used for self-financing investments then future tax levels will have to be greater than they would have been in the absence of debt. Higher levels of taxation may lead to disincentive-to-work effects, another manifestation of crowding out leading to reduced economic growth.

These outcomes will not result if there is a surplus supply of borrowable funds (e.g. in a recession when private industry is unwilling to invest), if investment is insensitive to rising interest rates (e.g. in an economic boom), or if the quantity theory of money is invalid. However, the two quotations above demonstrate that both the Conservative (1994 quote) and Labour (2000 quote) governments of the 1980s and 1990s believed that such effects were likely. This belief provides the analytical framework by which to understand the policy and practice of government borrowing.

This economic rationale is not the only reason for the control of public sector borrowing. There is also a view that borrowing is morally undesirable: like a household, the state must live within its means. This is the **balanced-budget rule** of classical economics. However Keynes demonstrated the **paradox of thrift** in that if all households *save for a rainy day* that undesirable event is more likely to occur. This is because increased savings lead to increased withdrawals from the circular flow of income so that aggregate demand falls, production is reduced and unemployment ensues. Keynes argued that the government must offset recession by using a budget deficit to finance expansionary fiscal policy. This assumes **crowding in** rather than **crowding out** and that there are no supply constraints (i.e. aggregate supply is elastic). Nonetheless, the Keynesian analysis demonstrates that whilst balancing one's budget is prudent for a household it is not necessarily prudent for a government.

However, the Keynesian analysis does not justify **continual** borrowing over an indefinite period. Use of budget deficits as part of Keynesian counter-cyclical policy is only legitimate for the short to medium term. Hence the following analysis adopts the view that public sector borrowing has to be controlled because of the potential crowding-out effects. The need for control is therefore analysed in terms of efficiency criteria rather than in terms of any moral stance.

11.2   The changing economic role of budget deficits

For much of the second half of the twentieth century budget deficits were viewed in Keynesian terms as a **macroeconomic instrument** which governments could use to control the level of **aggregate demand**. Put simply, until the very late 1970s, governments believed that they could spend their way out of a recession by increasing public expenditure and/ or cutting taxation and so running budget deficits. Moreover, during recovery and boom phases of the economic cycle governments found it more politically expedient to use the increased tax revenues to raise spending further rather than to repay debt. The result was that budget deficits were a persistent phenomenon irrespective of which particular phase of the trade cycle the economy was in.

By the mid to late 1970s, it began to be accepted that such 'overspending' resulted in inflation which, in turn, had to be restrained by deflationary policies involving cuts in expenditure, resulting in large-scale unemployment. The desire to be re-elected led many governments to engineer pre-election economic booms in order to persuade voters to return them to power. Pre-election booms were followed by post-election cut-backs as attempts were made to curb double-digit inflation and reduce looming balance of payments deficits. The latter occurred as high domestic demand was met by higher imports, leading to a depreciation of the pound and a further inflationary stimulus. These periodic economic **booms and busts** were also referred to as **stop-go** policies. The resulting economic and financial instability and loss of international confidence in the stability of the pound were increasingly seen as severely damaging the efficient functioning of the economy. This instability was thought to deter both domestic and foreign investment in the UK, resulting in relatively low economic growth.

As a result, there was a fundamental change in the economic role of the budget deficit in the mid to late 1970s. It was no longer to be used as a **Keynesian macroeconomic instrument** for the management of aggregate demand. Instead, it was integrated into **monetarist anti-inflation policies**. More fundamentally, the **demand-side** view that budget deficits could help an economy in times of crisis was replaced by a **supply-side** view that budget deficits caused severe economic distortions that hindered economic growth. The **demand-side perspective** focused on the supposed ability of budget deficits to smooth the trade cycle by engineering offsetting variations in aggregate demand. The **supply-side perspective** focused on the long-run trend growth of GDP and the need to help (not hinder) the functioning of markets (see Chapter 8). Essentially a **short-term** policy perspective was replaced by a **long-term** view stretching way beyond the immediate trade cycle.

This fundamentally changed view of budget deficits was shared by both Labour and Conservative governments during the 1980s and 1990s as illustrated by the two quotations at the beginning of this chapter. However the emphasis changed from regarding control of the budget deficit primarily as an **anti-inflationary strategy** to regarding its control as a means of implementing **sound public finances**, simultaneously with low inflation, so as to deliver economic growth through increased productivity.

During the 1980s, the over-riding emphasis was on controlling the deficit in order to meet inflation targets, this being consistent with a broadly monetarist perspective. **Printing money** to finance a deficit was to be avoided because of its inflationary impact (see Chapter 5). Inflation targets were still specified during the 1990s but increasing emphasis was placed on setting fiscal policy within a medium-term plan based on abiding by the so-called **golden rule** of public finance (see below).

The prevailing view by the late 1990s was that problems controlling the budget deficit are synonymous with the structural weaknesses of the UK economy. **Rather than being used to cope with short-term economic crises and for expanding the welfare state, any budget deficit can now only be justified by the capital expenditure investments it finances.** Those capital expenditures are seen as a microeconomic supply-side instrument for increasing the long-term productivity of the economy, certainly **not** a macroeconomic demand-side means of boosting aggregate demand in the short term for counter-cyclical purposes.

Put concisely, the use of budget deficits as a politico-economic instrument focused on building the welfare state through short-term demand-side interventions has been replaced by its use as a medium-term supply-side instrument to build the long-term productive potential of the UK economy.

11.3 Defining and measuring public sector borrowing

Whilst economists refer to any need to borrow resulting from public expenditure exceeding tax and other receipts as a budget deficit, UK governments refer to budget deficits in ways which symbolise their view of this accounting item. Between 1966 and 1998 the budget deficit was referred to as the 'public sector borrowing requirement' (**PSBR**). In 1998 the PSBR was renamed the 'public sector net cash requirement' (**PSNCR**), reflecting the fact that the public sector can finance any deficit by other means in addition to borrowing. Neither of these definitions are consistent with the internationally accepted definition used by the OECD in comparing budget deficits in member states. They both encompass the whole of the public sector whereas most EU countries use the general government borrowing requirement (**GGBR**) as a measure of the budget deficit. The GGBR excludes the *own account* borrowing of public corporations and so is smaller than the PSBR/PSNCR. The GGBR is broadly consistent with the definition of government borrowing used in the convergence criteria set out in the Maastricht Treaty for economic and monetary union via the Euro (see below). Clearly, there are many possible definitions of 'the budget deficit' and one has to be careful not to confuse them.

The UK's budget deficit includes borrowing by central government, local government and public corporations. Strictly speaking, central government borrowing (own account) excludes on-lending from central government to other parts of the public sector. For example central government borrows not just for its own needs, but also to meet the bulk of the borrowing needs of local authorities and public corporations. This arrangement affords central government close control over the totality of public sector borrowing. Local authorities and public corporations may also borrow from the market or from overseas sources, for which central government must give its prior consent. Hence the budget deficit includes all sources of borrowed funds but avoids double-counting by netting out on-lending from one part of the public sector to another.

Local authorities can only borrow for specified purposes (generally **not** to finance current spending) and must obtain central government's

272 POLICY AND PRACTICE

permission to borrow. Nationalised industries and other public corporations are also generally subject to limits on their external financing. Following the substantial privatisation programme of the 1980s and 1990s (see Chapter 13), the public corporations now include the remaining nationalised industries such as the Post Office and other bodies such as the National Health Service Trusts and various development and enterprise agencies. Given the fairly tight central control over borrowing by local authorities and public corporations, the main cause of fluctuations in the budget deficit have been due to changes in central government borrowing (own account). Central government borrowing on own account is occasionally more than total public sector borrowing, this being referred to as 'over-funding' the budget deficit. The reasons for this practice are explained below.

The combined total of central and local government borrowing is referred to as **general government borrowing**. It is the difference between general government receipts and expenditures and includes on-lending from central government to local authorities and public corporations. **In accounting terms**, the budget deficit is a **balancing item** in the government's financial accounts, being whatever sum is necessary to bring equality between expenditures and receipts. It is therefore the **bottom line** in the budget forecasts presented to Parliament. **In economic terms**, the budget deficit provides a measure of the government's **fiscal stance**, i.e. the degree to which fiscal policy is expansionary, contractionary or neutral in terms of Keynesian-style management of aggregate demand.

The former PSBR

The **PSBR** measured the extent to which the public sector borrowed from other sectors in the domestic economy and from overseas to finance the gap between expenditure and receipts. During the 1980s, it was a key component of the money supply (Sterling M3), targets for the growth of which were set under the then Conservative government's anti-inflationary strategy. Hence, control of the PSBR was seen as crucial, both to meet monetary targets and to control inflation. It was, however, a rather simplistic short-term financial instrument that arguably gave a very inaccurate indication of the government's fiscal stance, caused severe economic distortions and yet had little basis in either theory or fact.

- **It was a cash measure that took no account of the impact of the trade cycle or inflation on its value or of its own impact upon aggregate demand** (see below).
- **It treated privatisation receipts as negative expenditure rather than as a form of financing.** Thus, privatisation always improved the

government's financial position, even if shares in the former nationalised industries had been under-priced relative to the value of the assets sold (see Chapter 13).

- **It created a bias against public sector investment**. This was because it did not distinguish between borrowing to finance consumption and that used to finance investment. In generally finding it easier to cut public sector capital expenditures than to cut current expenditure, control of the PSBR required public sector investment to be severely curtailed. Lack of an adequate infrastructure may act as a supply-side constraint, slowing down economic growth (see Chapter 3).
- **It assumed a direct impact on inflation**. In fact, neither economic theory nor empirical evidence confirm conclusively that high levels of government borrowing directly affect the money supply or that the money supply directly affects inflation (see Chapter 5).

Despite these deficiencies, the PSBR became the almost exclusive indicator of fiscal stance for decisions regarding the budget during the 1980s. Nevertheless, budget deficits persisted for most of the 1980s and 1990s. The budgetary deficit turned into surplus in 1988 and 1989, largely due to privatisation receipts and additional tax revenues from North Sea oil reflecting rising world oil prices. Thereafter, a budget deficit recurred as the economy went into recession in the early 1990s. The next budgetary surplus was not for another ten years, at which time the PSNCR was being used as the measure of budgetary policy.

The new PSNCR

Whilst the **PSNCR** is subject to the same technical criticism as the PSBR in terms of being a short-term cash measure, its use for economic policymaking differs quite fundamentally in that it is not the sole or even main focus of budgetary policy or indicator of fiscal stance. Whilst both the PSBR and PSNCR ultimately need to be financed, attention now focuses on the 'golden rule' and on the 'sustainable investment rule'. **The golden rule** states that current income and current expenditure should be in balance over the economic cycle. This means that, over the economic cycle, the government will **borrow** only to invest in public infrastructure and not to fund current spending (i.e. consumption). **The sustainable investment rule** is that public sector **net debt** as a proportion of GDP will be held over the economic cycle at a stable and prudent level. The sustainable investment rule is effectively a rider to the golden rule to indicate that borrowing for investment will not be used for counter-cyclical purposes. The two rules together mean that, if spending cuts are required, they have to be found from within current spending. Thus, the Labour government's intention is that any budget deficit will not fluctuate widely from year to year. Sustainability emphasises a long-term approach, specifically to avoid the economic distortions caused by the earlier short-term emphasis.

However, the budget deficit (or surplus) is a relatively small residual between two very large sums, government receipts and expenditure. Small percentage changes in receipts and/or expenditure cause large percentage changes in the budget deficit (or surplus). Hence the budget deficit or surplus displays tremendous variability:

- as a percentage of general government income
- as a percentage of GDP

This suggests that, in practice, the Labour government will find it difficult to control the budget deficit/surplus, and sharp fluctuations can be expected from year to year. Clearly, if budget deficits have the crowding-out effects suggested by Chapter 5, there would appear to be great cause for concern about this tremendous variability. The control of interest rates and/or inflation would appear to be highly problematic. Moreover the variability of public sector borrowing would appear to be inconsistent with the Labour government's stated aim to control it at a stable and prudent level. That variability is caused by a number of factors largely outside the government's control. For this reason the published figure is **not** an accurate reflection of the government's fiscal stance, either in terms of the restrictive or expansionary nature of discretionary fiscal policy or in terms of supporting monetary policy through the trade cycle. There are various definitions of the budget deficit that can be used to assess fiscal stance and the impact of borrowing on the economy.

The actual or out-turn budget deficit/surplus

This is simply the figure reported by the government at the end of the financial year to which the budget deficit/surplus relates. As already noted, it is heavily influenced by revenues from the privatisation programme being treated as negative expenditures rather than a (positive) source of income. Revenues derived from the sale of shares in state-owned enterprises therefore reduce the published expenditure total by the amount received from the sale. Therefore any budget deficit is reduced or surplus increased. Hence, given the stochastic nature of privatisation revenues, the reported deficit/surplus will also be highly variable.

Such asset sales raised over £2 billion per annum in the mid 1980s and exceeded £5 billion per annum during the late 1980s and early 1990s. In the mid to late 1990s asset sales were raising about £4 billion per annum, although by then it was mainly from sales of council houses and other local authority assets. Whilst small in terms of total public expenditure these sums were large relative to the former PSBR, reducing it by as much as 10 per cent. The then Conservative government was criticised for *massaging the figures* by its treatment of privatisation revenues as negative expenditures, on the grounds that such arbitrary adjustments were made in order to make reported figures fit its previously stated objectives for control of the PSBR.

This accounting convention meant that privatisation revenues reduced the PSBR whereas sales of government gilt-edged securities ('gilts') financed it. The implication was that higher public spending is acceptable if it is financed by selling shares in the former nationalised industries such as British Telecom and British Gas, but unacceptable if it is financed by selling gilts. This distinction seems to be rather arbitrary since the financial effects may be much the same. Both forms of finance compete within broadly the same financial market and both have similar implications for future government finances, whether in terms of debt to be repaid or of revenues forgone after sale.

The then Conservative government's view was that purchases of capital assets are usually financed by borrowing and therefore they increased the PSBR. Hence their sale has the opposite effect of reducing it. In addition, given its belief that the sale of gilts increases interest rates and/or leads to inflation, the government necessarily preferred the sale of assets to further sales of gilts, wherever possible. This policy also complemented its attempts to widen share ownership beyond financial institutions such as pension funds, building societies and insurance companies, as part of the move towards *popular capitalism*.

From an economic perspective asset sales are a means of *financing* rather than *reducing* expenditure. The pursuit of efficiency requires the organisation to finance its activities using the cheapest means possible. Asset sales would only be used if they were the method of finance with the lowest **opportunity cost**. Critics of privatisation argued that asset sales had a higher opportunity cost than borrowing. **First**, they argued that the assets had been undervalued (i.e. sold too cheaply). In support of this claim, most of the sales were heavily oversubscribed, demand for shares being much greater than their supply at the fixed selling price. Substantial rises in share values were usually recorded shortly after sale. **Second**, critics argued that the government was *selling the silver in order to pay the servants*. In other words the opportunity cost was future revenues forgone as a result of the sale. Certainly the privatised gas, telecommunications, electricity and other industries subsequently reported substantial profits now lost to the public purse.

However it is questionable whether those profits would have been earned had the industries remained under public ownership. The ensuing political controversy over large-scale redundancies and other forms of labour-shedding, closure of capacity and rising product prices (all of which led to those substantial profits) gives some credence to the counter-argument that, had those industries remained in public ownership, they would have made continuing demands on the public purse. In other words the opportunity cost of their sale was low, especially once the tax receipts levied on those profits are taken into account.

Many of the same considerations and criticisms apply to the PSNCR.

The cyclically-adjusted budget deficit/surplus

Fluctuations in economic activity lead to changes in the budget deficit/surplus even if the rates and coverage of both taxation and social security benefits are held constant. The budget deficit tends to rise during recessionary periods as tax revenues fall and as payments of unemployment benefits rise. The reverse occurs in a recovery. The cyclically-adjusted budget deficit/surplus takes account of these 'automatic (built-in) stabilisers' by adjusting each of the main revenue items separately (i.e. income tax, corporation tax, indirect taxes and national insurance contributions) and by adjusting those state benefit expenditures that are related to unemployment. Deducting the total of these adjustments from the actual budget deficit/surplus leaves a residual measure of discretionary changes in fiscal policy. Hence the true measure of the government's fiscal stance can be assessed. Clearly a cyclically-adjusted budget deficit is less than the actual budget deficit in a recession and greater in a boom.

However, derivation of the former figure is problematic since it requires an estimate of the 'normal' level of economic activity, based either on the assumed secular trend in the growth of GDP or on a 'constant employment' level of output. In assessing the 'normal' level of economic activity, the cycle is defined in terms of the discrepancy between actual output and the trend. Referred to as the **output gap**, this discrepancy is used to estimate the effect on the budget deficit/surplus. However the supposed deviation from trend could be a change in the trend itself. Hence it is not easy to define either the trend or the cyclical component and therefore assessment of the 'normal' level of activity is problematic.

For this reason it is more straightforward to estimate the budget deficit/surplus for a constant employment level of output. Whilst this method can be expected to be reasonably accurate over short periods (e.g. for short phases of the trade cycle), it becomes increasingly inaccurate the longer the period over which successive cyclically-adjusted budget deficits/surpluses are calculated (e.g. during prolonged recession – or is it a change of trend?). Moreover the cyclically-adjusted measure depends on whether a broadly monetarist or broadly Keynesian macroeconomic model is used to model the state of the economy. Hence there is no unique measure of the cyclically-adjusted budget deficit.

Nevertheless, the cyclically-adjusted budget deficit is useful in indicating fiscal stance. For example, OECD figures for the early 1980s revealed that the then Conservative government was engineering one of the strongest 'fiscal squeezes' of the post-1945 period in any OECD country. It reflected the Conservative government's medium-term financial strategy (MTFS), the objectives of which included reduction of government borrowing as a proportion of GDP as a key factor in securing lower interest rates. This reduction in borrowing had to occur despite very low rates of economic growth and increasing unemployment, rising from under one million unemployed in 1979 to three million by 1983. Whilst built-in stabilisers (i.e. increased social security and unemployment benefits and lower tax receipts) caused the deficit to increase, the government cut the discretionary element of fiscal policy so that the *actual* budget deficit fell from 3.3 per cent of GDP in 1979 to 2.5 per cent of GDP in 1982. The *cyclically-adjusted* measure shows the full extent of the restrictive nature of the government's fiscal stance at that time, falling from 6.2 per cent of GDP in 1979 to 1.0 per cent in 1982.

Keynesians argued that the MTFS was highly deflationary since it would normally be expected that the actual budget deficit would rise during a recession. However, whether such actions are deflationary or not depend on the long-run impact on private spending. If substantial crowding out occurs, then reducing budget deficits crowds in private spending in the longer term by facilitating lower future (income) tax rates and therefore reduced disincentive-to-work effects (see Chapter 4).

The *actual* budget deficit had turned into an actual budget *surplus* in 1988 and 1989, of 1.0 and 0.9 per cent of GDP. However, this being the boom phase of the trade cycle, the OECD's figures showed cyclically-adjusted deficits of 2.0 and 2.1 per cent of GDP respectively. In other words, the *actual* budget surplus should have been considerably higher than it was given the rapid economic growth, falling unemployment, falling expenditures on unemployment benefits and rising tax revenues from increased incomes and expenditures. This makes clear that, far from being a sign of sound and prudent public finances, the relatively small and short-lived actual budget surplus was in fact a cause for considerable concern. Indeed, the actual surplus returned to an actual deficit in 1990, rising to 7.7 per cent of GDP in 1993 in the depths of the early 1990s recession.

So, during the Conservative government's period in office (1979–97), actual budget surpluses occurred in only two of those 19 years and cyclically-adjusted budget deficits occurred in every year. Hence, even in terms of the actual budget deficit, the Conservative government had not been successful in its efforts to control public sector borrowing and this led to speculation that the UK had a **structural budget deficit** persisting through all phases of the trade cycle (see below).

As already noted, the OECD's definition of the budget deficit is narrower than the UK government's in not covering the whole of the public sector: it excludes borrowing by state industries. Moreover, the 1997 Labour government had adopted the golden rule and sustainable investment rule. These rules require a more disaggregated measure of the budget deficit/surplus. Hence, the Labour government began publishing both actual and cyclically-adjusted figures in its annual budget, for both the *current balance* and *net borrowing*.

- **The current balance**. In both 1998/9 and 1999/00 the actual *surplus* on the *current* budget was greater (at 0.9 and 1.9 per cent of GDP respectively) than the cyclically-adjusted surplus (0.6 and 1.8 respectively). This indicates that the Labour government was tightly controlling current expenditure as tax and other revenues rose during a period of strong economic growth. Its projections of the planned current budget and expected revenues to 2004/05 show that it expects the excess of actual over cyclically-adjusted current budget surpluses to continue.
- **Net borrowing**. This is equal to net investment minus the surplus on the current budget. In both 1998/9 and 1999/00 actual net borrowing was negative, indicating that the current surplus was greater than net investment. Hence, there was a *repayment* of public sector debt in those two years. Moreover, actual net borrowing was marginally more negative than cyclically-adjusted net borrowing, indicating a greater repayment of debt than would be expected during that phase of the trade cycle. Again, this shows just how tightly the Labour government was controlling both current and capital expenditure during its early years in office.

The Labour government had adopted a restrictive fiscal stance following its pre-election promise to keep public expenditure within the restrictive plans of the previous Conservative government for the two years following 1997. The Labour government projected further debt repayments for the following two years, diminishing and returning to net borrowing as the planned share of net investment in GDP rises. The cyclically-adjusted *current balance* moved from a budget deficit of over 2 per cent of GDP in 1996/7 to a surplus of 0.5 per cent in 1998/9 and 2 per cent in 1999/00. All of these forecasts (for both the current balance and net borrowing) are, however, subject to great uncertainty (see below).

The demand-weighted budget deficit/surplus

This measure shows the result of weighting various revenues and expenditures by their respective multipliers. The multipliers depend on withdrawals from the circular flow of income, being smaller if the marginal propensities to save, import and pay tax are high. For example, increased social security payments are likely to have higher multipliers than cuts in income tax. This is the case since social security recipients are likely to spend all their income whilst payers of income tax are likely to save some of the extra disposable income arising from the tax cut. The latter group may also spend higher proportions of their income on imports. Hence social security payments would be given greater weight than tax cuts in adjusting the reported budget deficit/surplus figure by the multiplier effects of the expenditures it finances. Similarly, increased public spending on construction activities is likely to have a higher multiplier than tax cuts since construction typically has a low import content. However, calculation of accurate multipliers is difficult because the marginal propensities to save, import and pay tax (direct and indirect) at each successive round of spending differ between socio-economic groups and are not known with any great degree of accuracy. Moreover the size of the multiplier also depends on the time period adopted, shorter periods reducing its value.

More fundamentally, the size of the multiplier is again dependent on the macroeconomic model used. In that such calculations assume **crowding in** (of private by public expenditures), they are situated within a Keynesian macroeconomic model of the economy. However, in assuming **crowding out**, a broadly monetarist macroeconomic model would yield much smaller multipliers (possibly even negative ones) if disincentive-to-work effects were caused by the higher levels of future (income) taxes that would be necessary to finance repayment of a budget deficit. The reverse would occur in the event of tax cuts financed by a budget surplus. Hence there is no unique measure of the demand-weighted budget deficit/surplus.

The inflation-adjusted or real budget deficit/surplus

This is the actual budget deficit/surplus adjusted for the erosion by inflation of the real value of the stock of public sector debt (i.e. the national debt) to which borrowing contributes. In the case of a budget deficit, the greater the rate of inflation the lower the real deficit. This adjustment appears to be more straightforward than that for the cyclically-adjusted or demand-weighted figures. However, in practice it is the actual budget deficit that affects interest rates, the money supply and, through the quantity theory, inflation. Hence there is little interest in the inflation-adjusted budget deficit/surplus, particularly given the emphasis on the cash planning of public expenditures.

11.4 A structural or cyclical budget deficit?

A cyclical budget deficit is caused by recession and removed by recovery. A structural budget deficit persists even when the economy returns to full employment. Given that the UK has not experienced full employment for several decades, until the budget surpluses of 1998/9 and 1999/00 it was at no time during that period self-evident whether the near perennial budget deficits were structural or cyclical. Hence any answer to the above question was speculative.

As was noted above, the Conservative government had only achieved an actual budget surplus in 2 of its 19 years in office. After the two years of relatively small actual budget surpluses (1988 and 1989), actual deficits rose sharply, exceeding 6 per cent of GDP in 1992, 1993 and 1994. The early 1990s was a recessionary phase of the trade cycle and so the cyclically-adjusted deficits were only two-thirds of the actual deficits. Nonetheless, the former figures still exceeded 4 per cent of GDP in those three years, leading to speculation that the UK had a structural budget deficit. That speculation continued throughout the 1990s decade, notwithstanding the budget surpluses at the turn of the century and the surpluses forecast to continue into the early years of the new millennium. As already noted, forecasts of budget deficits/surpluses are subject to considerable uncertainty, the margin of error increasing the further into time those projections are made. Moreover, despite its assumptions of relatively rapid economic growth, the Labour government projected only very small surpluses on current budget (falling below 1 per cent of GDP), these being exceeded by projected net borrowing in 2003/4 and 2004/5 (exceeding 1 per cent of GDP). Hence, one cannot be sure that the UK has escaped for long from the apparent structural budget deficit of the 1980s and 1990s.

This imbalance between public expenditures and receipts can be clarified by using the distinction (noted above) between the cyclical component and the trend in borrowing. The trend is the non-cyclical, or **structural**, component. Changes in the cyclical component can be interpreted as an **effect** of fluctuations in output, that is they are non-discretionary. Likewise changes in the structural component can be regarded as a **cause** of output fluctuations. Hence changes in the structural component can be taken as largely indicative of discretionary policy changes. The only qualification to this categorical distinction is that changes in oil prices (and therefore in the tax revenues derived from them) and interest rates (and therefore in the payments on accumulated debt) are neither cyclical nor purely discretionary.

Comparing the actual and the cyclically-adjusted deficits, the OECD estimated that roughly 70 per cent of the deterioration of the UK's budget balance in the first half of the 1990s was due to cyclical factors and 30 per cent was due to structural changes. In other words, nearly a third of the imbalance in the UK's general government financial balances was discretionary. This **structural imbalance** was in stark contrast to the severely deflationary deficits of the early 1980s (identified above). The conclusion drawn from the OECD's figures was that, whilst the larger part of the deterioration in public finances would be reversed as recession turned to recovery, it would not disappear completely. This conclusion was correct in that the actual budget deficit did not turn to surplus until 1998/9, and only then following remedial action. The apparent permanence of the structural imbalance during the early to mid 1990s justified the increased concern over the size of the budget deficit and supported calls for fairly urgent and drastic action to reduce it. Commonly espoused explanations of the causes of the structural imbalance were:

1. **Over-generous tax cuts for affluent groups,** particularly the cuts in the highest rates of income tax from 60 per cent to 40 per cent in 1988. Here the solution seemed obvious: reinstate higher tax rates. In fact, neither Conservative nor Labour governments raised the top tax rate. However, in terms of their proportions of GDP, it was noted in Chapter 10 that the UK's low tax status has been largely due to relatively low rates of social security contributions (NICs). Hence tax increases would have to be much more widely spread beyond affluent groups in order to remove the structural deficit. Again, both the Conservative and Labour governments were unwilling to substantially increase NICs for either the low paid or the high paid. Increasing the 'tax on jobs' would have been contrary to policies to reduce the unemployment trap for low-paid unskilled workers and also contrary to the (largely illusory) insurance principle underlying NICs. More generally, higher rates of income tax would have been inconsistent with both the Conservative and Labour governments' general policy towards taxation of incomes and the need to strengthen incentives to work. Instead, both governments sought to widen tax bases (for both direct and indirect taxes) and use sharp increases in the real levels of taxes on tobacco and fuel duty in particular to raise substantial amounts of tax revenue (see Chapter 10).

2. **The rise in social security expenditures** in exemplifying growth of a dependency culture. Here too the solution seemed obvious: restrain the growth of social security expenditures wherever possible by

restricting eligibility for benefits (e.g. for unemployment) and encouraging the progressive privatisation of the welfare state (e.g. through private pensions). This policy was followed by both Conservative and Labour governments during the 1990s, Labour adding its 'welfare to work' (New Deal) policy to earlier reforms by the Conservatives (see Chapters 8 and 9).

Whether the ongoing broadening of the tax bases and the ongoing piecemeal reforms of social security benefits during the 1990s have permanently removed the structural budget deficit remains to be seen. The budget surpluses at the turn of the century took economic commentators by surprise and were substantially greater that the Labour government had forecast only a year before. For example, in the March 1999 Budget the government expected a surplus on the current budget of only £2 billion in 1999/00, but by the 2000 Budget it was over £17 billion. Likewise, the expected *net borrowing* of £3 billion had, within a year, become a *net repayment* of £12 billion. This extremely rapid and huge apparent turnaround in the state of the public finances was widely regarded as truly remarkable. It arose largely because the economy's output was much greater than expected. Income tax receipts were greater than expected because of the higher than expected growth in wages and salaries. Corporation tax receipts were higher than expected because company profits were higher than forecast. Higher than expected consumer spending led to VAT receipts being greater than forecast. Social security expenditures were lower than expected.

However, there were also significant one-off boosts to the Labour government's income, most notably the £22.5 billion from the sale of licences for 'third generation' mobile phones. Moreover, the above discussion of the inherent volatility of budget deficits/surpluses makes such a sharp turnaround somewhat less remarkable. It would not be too surprising if large surpluses quickly turned into equally large deficits. This distinct possibility explains the 1997 Labour government's emphasis on stable and **prudent** public finances. The government believes that it would be inadvisable to assume that the structural budget deficit is a problem of the past and that the recent surpluses are permanent and so can be spent on extra public services or on further tax cuts. This could lead to a return to the 'boom and bust' cycle of the 1980s and 1990s if those surpluses turn out to be short-lived. Hence, they are largely being used to repay debt (see below).

The crucial question is whether the unexpectedly higher output is largely or wholly cyclical (in which case surpluses will be temporary) or largely or wholly trend (in which case Labour's projected budget surpluses will actually occur).

11.5   Forecasting the budget deficit/surplus

Forecasting the budget deficit/surplus is inherently difficult simply because it is the difference between two very large aggregates of spending and receipts. As made evident by the preceding analysis, the actual and forecast budget deficit figures will diverge if there are unforeseen changes in the number of social security claimants or in the pattern of consumer spending, earnings and other economic developments caused by recession and increased unemployment. Furthermore the precise timing of expenditures and receipts affect the budget deficit/ surplus figure for a given financial year, for example if firms delay payment of taxes such as VAT (paid quarterly) and make earlier claims for payment for government contract work during recessionary periods. Hence the budget deficit/surplus is volatile both between and within financial years, being subject to large monthly, quarterly and annual fluctuations.

During the later 1990s, an error of just 1 per cent in the forecasted level of total cash receipts would typically have resulted in a forecasting error of more than 10 per cent of the budget deficit. In the past, actual budget deficits have tended to be lower than forecast when GDP rose and higher than forecast when GDP fell.

The average absolute error (whether positive or negative) for forecasts of net borrowing one year ahead during the second half of the 1990s was over 1 per cent of GDP. This was plus or minus £9 billion at 2000 price levels. As already noted, forecasting errors tend to grow as the forecasting horizon lengthens, rising to 4 per cent of GDP four years ahead during the second half of the 1990s. This suggests either inaccurate forecasts of GDP or an imprecise model of the relationship between GDP and the budget deficit at different stages of the economic cycle. The latter may be caused by a higher propensity for people to register as unemployed during economic decline (when jobs are increasingly difficult to find) than during recovery (when jobs are readily available), with consequent impacts on demand-determined expenditures such as social security. However, the larger part of forecasting errors arises because of errors in the forecasts of GDP.

Errors in short-term forecasts of economic growth tend to be offsetting over the trade cycle and so have only a temporary effect on the public finances. For example, for a given trend in output, if the trade cycle is subject to greater fluctuation than expected, underestimates of growth will be followed by underestimates of decline, these cancelling out over the cycle as a whole. Errors in estimating the cyclical position of the economy in relation to its trend (the 'output gap') are of greater consequence because they will have a permanent affect on the public finances. A larger output gap would reduce the budget surpluses expected by the Labour government.

The key assumptions underpinning the Labour government's projected surpluses include those relating to further revenues from future privatisations (£4 billion per annum being expected, three-quarters from the sale of local authority assets), trend GDP growth (2.25 per cent per annum being expected), constant levels of UK claimant unemployment (1.16 million), interest rates, constant real world oil prices, success in preventing tobacco smuggling (which, as noted in Chapter 10, is leading to serious erosion of the tax base) and so on. Some unexpected changes may be offsetting. For example, the subsequent rise in world oil prices unexpectedly increased tax revenues and this would help offset lack of success in reducing tobacco smuggling.

Judging by the history of forecasting errors, it would be more surprising if the forecasts were fairly accurate than if they proved to be seriously wrong. Nevertheless, the Labour government believes that much of the improvement of the public finances has been structural because the cyclically-adjusted figures show current surpluses.

11.6 Financing a budget deficit

Whether the outcome of structural or cyclical factors, a budget deficit has to be financed and this may have the implications for interest rates and inflation that were identified in Chapter 5. A budget deficit is financed from three main sources:

- sales of debt to the non-bank private sector (NBPS);
- borrowing from the banking system;
- borrowing from overseas.

Borrowing uses a mixture of floating (or short-term) debt such as 90-day treasury bills and medium- to long-term debt such as gilt-edged securities ('gilts'), National Savings certificates and Premium (savings) Bonds. The budget deficit figure relates to net borrowing for the financial year as a whole and so nets out most of the borrowing in the form of 90-day treasury bills, most of which are redeemed during the course of the year. Gilts are marketable securities in that they can be traded on the financial markets after purchase from the government. Whilst primarily used as stores of value, there is also a speculative element in that their market value is inversely related to changes in interest rates (see Chapter 5). National Savings and Premium Bonds are non-marketable securities sold to the NBPS, mainly the general public (or 'personal sector'), industrial and commercial companies and other non-bank financial institutions such as pension funds and insurance companies.

In being sold to the NBPS, National Savings and Premium Bonds have no direct influence on the money supply in that they do not lead to a multiple expansion of deposits. However the sale of gilts can directly affect the money supply in that they form part of banks' reserve assets upon which credit creation (i.e. a multiple expansion of deposits) is based. Hence sales of gilts have been primarily targeted on other (non-bank) financial institutions (e.g. insurance companies and pension funds) as part of the government's open-market operations to control the money supply. The sale of gilts was the principal means of funding the budget deficit during the 1970s, individual issues usually having redemption periods of over five years and many over 15 years. However National Savings (and particularly index-linked) certificates were increasingly used during the 1980s to reduce long-term interest rates.

Chapter 5 covers the economic theory on all these points. An alternative explanation uses the following accounting identity: Budget deficit = OMO + NMD + BPF+ΔRA, where OMO is the sale of bonds (e.g. gilts) through open-market operations, NMD is the sale of non-marketable debt (e.g. National Savings), BPF is the finance available from a balance of payments deficit and ΔRA is the change in banks' reserve assets (e.g. notes and coins).

This accounting identity shows how the budget deficit influences the money supply. If the exchange rate is freely floating then BPF is zero since the government makes no attempt to control the value of the pound by using its holdings of gold and foreign exchange (i.e. buying and selling sterling to influence its price in foreign currency terms). If the government is committed to controlling the growth of the money supply then ΔRA must be controlled. Hence OMO and NMD become the residual means of financing the budget deficit. Interest rates therefore have to vary in order to ensure that the government can sell enough gilts and National Savings to finance its borrowing requirement. Hence the greater that requirement the higher the interest rate must be to equate supply and demand for government securities. Alternatively, if the government wishes to constrain the rise in interest rates due to a borrowing requirement in excess of the market's willingness to lend, it must control OMO and NMD and instead use ΔRA to finance the budget deficit. In that case it forgoes control of the money supply. This is the same result as that derived in Chapter 5.

Sales of debt to the NBPS and borrowing from both the banking system and overseas were of broadly comparable importance until the late 1960s. However the NBPS was used to raise the bulk of finance during the 1970s, 1980s and 1990s, occasionally being used to over-fund the budget deficit. Over-funding is the sale of gilt-edged stock above the amount needed to finance the difference between government spending and receipts. It was used in the 1980s to finance the purchase of commercial bills from the banking sector, which would otherwise fund this private company lending by means of an expansion of bank deposits. Use of the NBPS as the major source of borrowed funds (and to over-fund the budget deficit on occasion) reflected the government's concern to restrain monetary growth since the sale of gilts to the banking sector allows a multiple expansion of deposits (see Chapter 5). Over-funding the budget deficit allowed net repayments of debt to be made to the banking sector (as well as overseas), so creating a multiple contraction of bank deposits. Contraction occurs since NBPS purchases lead to cheques being drawn against the commercial banks' reserves. Hence, whilst the budget deficit is an indicator of the government's fiscal stance, the means of financing it are of critical importance for the conduct of monetary policy.

11.7 Medium-term debt targets

There are three alternative medium-term debt targets.

Full-cycle balanced budgets

If used solely for Keynesian-style demand management purposes, it would be expected that the budget would balance over the course of the economic cycle. The budget would be in deficit during the recession and depression phases of the trade cycle and in surplus during the recovery and boom phases. Full-cycle balanced budgets assume that surpluses offset deficits so that the debt is fully repaid from taxation. Hence the level of public sector debt relative to GDP would decline over time as GDP grew. Future generations would not have to be taxed as heavily as current generations in order to repay public debt.

However, the budget was in deficit for all but four or so of the last 30 years of the twentieth century (depending upon whether one uses the broader UK definition or narrower OECD definition). Net repayments of debt were negligible in terms of total borrowing over that period. This suggests intergenerational inequity in that the current generation is enjoying a higher standard of living (i.e. consumption) at the expense of future generations of taxpayers, who will have to pay higher taxes in order to service the public debt used to finance that extra consumption. Vertical inequity would be reduced if future generations have higher real incomes than current generations and/or if rapid inflation erodes the real value of public sector debt. Whilst both events have been the case historically, they cannot be taken for granted in the future. Moreover there is a question about the morality of the current generation living off the presumed affluence of future generations, obviously not represented in the democratic processes of the present day.

Constant debt/GDP ratios

This arrangement would prevent intergenerational income redistribution. If the ratio falls then income is redistributed from the current generation of taxpayers to the future generation. If the ratio rises the intergenerational redistribution is reversed.

The golden rule

The first two medium-term debt targets make no distinction between borrowing used to finance productive capital investment and that used to finance current spending (i.e. consumption). They clearly affect intergenerational equity in different ways but otherwise there is little to choose between them. Whilst they both effectively set ceilings on government borrowing, they provide no guidance on the uses to which borrowing should be put. In contrast, the golden rule states that the budget deficit should not exceed the net capital spending of the public sector. No ceiling is set on government borrowing since higher deficits are acceptable as long as they do no more than finance net capital spending. In this way current taxpayers do not increase their standard of living at the expense of future taxpayers. This is not the case when borrowing is used to finance current consumption, so creating an intergenerational redistribution of income.

If a budget deficit is used to finance the building of toll bridges and tunnels, public sector rental housing, student accommodation and so on, the investment can become fully self-financing, imposing no tax burden on future generations of taxpayers. There will still be some tax burden if these capital investments are less than fully self-financing but this would effectively represent an income transfer between future taxpayers and future users of the capital facility, the latter paying subsidised charges. If such capital investments are more than self-financing (i.e. earning an economic profit) then the subsidy is reversed. Even those infrastructural investments that do not raise finance from user-charges could still effectively be self-financing if they raise the productive potential of the economy and so lead to higher future tax receipts on profits, incomes and expenditures.

The former PSBR was less than net capital spending (by central and local government and the nationalised industries) throughout the 1960s and early 1970s, but exceeded it when the PSBR peaked in the mid 1970s. The golden rule was not met again until the late 1980s. However the PSBR again exceeded net capital spending from 1991/2, rising dramatically in the following two years to exceed it by 5 per cent of GDP during 1993/4. Whilst reflecting the cost of unemployment and other state benefits, it also reflected the structural imbalance noted above. This situation was paradoxical given the then Conservative government's determination to control the PSBR because of its potential crowding-out effects. The PSBR was being used to finance consumption, so the current generation really was *living beyond its means* and this was clearly in contradiction to the moralistic statement that borrowing for such purposes is undesirable.

Net capital spending fell steadily after its 1975 peak of 9 per cent of GDP, fluctuating around 2 per cent during the early 1990s. This was a result of the privatisation programme, which shifted much **capital** spending out of the public sector. The Private Finance Initiative is having much the same effect (see Chapter 8). The PSBR also fell during the 1980s (becoming net repayment in the late 1980s) but its rapid rise in the early 1990s to over 7 per cent of GDP meant that its ratio exceeded the net capital spending ratio by 5 percentage points. This indicates that the PSBR was primarily used to finance consumption after 1991/2.

The then Conservative government had planned to reduce the PSBR to zero by the turn of the century in order to rectify this unwanted outcome. However, the recurrent budget deficits continued until the Conservatives lost office in 1997 and continued in the first year of the Labour administration. This means that the 1997 Labour government and its successor will have to run current budget surpluses for a number of years in order to meet the golden rule. In fact, the golden rule has not been met over any economic cycle since the early 1970s. To meet the golden rule in the early twenty-first century will therefore be a reversal of past experience.

11.8 Stocks and flows of debt

An important distinction can be made between a budget deficit and public sector debt. A budget deficit is the annual flow of borrowing during a financial year that adds to the existing stock of public sector debt. Whilst a budget deficit has potential implications for current interest rates, the money supply and inflation, it is the stock of repayable debt that has implications for future levels of taxation. There are two measures of public sector debt:

1. **Gross public sector debt**. Gross debt is known more widely as the 'national debt'. It is simply the total debt of the entire public sector, including central and local government, the nationalised industries and so on. It increased markedly as a result of expenditures incurred during the two world wars (1914–18 and 1939–45) and by the major phase of nationalisation of coal, steel, gas and railways under the 1945–51 Labour governments. It also increased when the government borrowed foreign currencies from overseas and used them to support the exchange rate.

2. **Net public sector debt**. Net debt is gross debt of the general government sector minus its holdings of financial assets. These assets include cash, bank deposits, loans to the private sector, holdings in public corporations and private companies, and foreign exchange reserves. Clearly it is net (rather than gross) debt which has implications for future tax levels, unless debt is used solely for self-financing investments.

The Maastricht Treaty conditions for joining the European single currency (the Euro) relate to both the stock and flow of government debt. Regarding the **flow of debt**, *general government net borrowing* (the **Maastricht deficit**) should be no more than 3 per cent of GDP. The UK figure was –0.6 per cent of GDP in 1998/9 (i.e. net *lending*). The Labour government did not expect a return to net borrowing until 2002/3, rising to 1.2 per cent of GDP by the end of the forecast period in 2004/5. Regarding the **stock of debt**, levels of general government **gross** public debt (the '**Maastricht debt ratio'**) must be kept below 60 per cent of GDP. In 1998/9 the UK figure was 47 per cent and was projected to fall sharply to 40 per cent by 2001/2, thereafter remaining around 39 per cent until 2004/5. In fact, the UK's gross public debt ratio has long been below 60 per cent. It fell fairly steadily from 59 per cent in 1978 to 35 per cent in 1990. In 1978 it was substantially greater than the OECD average (40 per cent) but by 1990 it was substantially below the OECD average (58 per cent). Having fallen below the OECD average during the mid 1980s, UK gross public debt remained well below it thereafter, despite the subsequent rise to over 50 per cent in the mid 1990s. By 1998/9 the debt to GDP ratio had fallen back to 47 per cent and was projected to fall sharply to 40 per cent by 2001/2 as expected debt repayments took place. Thereafter the ratio was projected to remain around 39 per cent until 2004/5.

The 1997 Labour government set a target for a reduction in **net** public sector debt to below 40 per cent of GDP. It had exceeded 40 per cent for much of the 1980s and 1990s, having been as high as 52 per cent in 1978 and as low as 28 per cent in 1990. Net debt has declined continuously as a proportion of GDP since 1996/7 when it was 44 per cent of GDP. In 1998/9 it was 40 per cent of GDP and, like gross debt, the Labour government expects it to fall sharply to 34 per cent by 2001/2. Thereafter, the ratio is forecast to remain around 33 per cent until 2004/5. These projections reflect the Labour government's sustainable investment rule (see above) and are consistent with the planned doubling of net investment over the same period.

Clearly, the UK easily meets the Maastricht criteria for joining the single currency. Whether or not it should join is another matter beyond the scope of this text.

11.9 Conclusions

Although referred to earlier as the 'bottom line' of the government's accounts, to regard the budget deficit/surplus as simply an accounting item is highly misleading. The preceding analysis demonstrates that the budget deficit/surplus is not simply a technical financing problem, nor simply something only of esoteric interest for economic analysts. Whilst it is indeed the most salient aspect of the government's fiscal policy, the objectives for the budget deficit/surplus crystallise the interaction of economic and social policies as they are affected by changing economic, social, demographic, even constitutional, conditions. In fact the budget deficit/surplus encapsulates the implications of the broader social, moral and ethical issues that underpin the welfare state and its financing and which were considered in Chapters 9 and 10.

Within the more restrictive framework of economic policy, the analysis of this chapter and that of Chapter 5 effectively questions whether it is sensible to set precise annual targets for the control of the budget deficit/surplus. **First**, the theoretical links between the budget deficit/surplus and interest rates and inflation are not indisputable. **Second**, even if they do exist, such links are not the sole or even the main cause of increases in interest rates and inflation. Interest rate movements in other countries affect those in the UK as countries compete for mobile foreign currency holdings and downward fluctuations in the exchange rate can cause domestic cost-push inflation. **Third**, the practicalities of forecasting the budget deficit/surplus and taking any measures necessary to control it seem to be very imprecise and possibly even counterproductive. This is especially the case given the huge proportionate impacts of relatively small unforeseen changes in government expenditures and receipts on the budget deficit/surplus.

Such problems eventually led to the then PSBR being downgraded as a precise **macroeconomic** policy measure, in much the same way as targets for the growth of the money supply had previously been downgraded. Despite Keynesian and monetarist schools continuing to offer apparently straightforward macroeconomic solutions to economic problems, both Conservative and Labour governments of the 1980s and 1990s decided that the economic cure lay in a much broader and yet more detailed **microeconomic** approach. This latter approach centred on the stimulation of competitive forces throughout the public and private sectors, pursued by means of a multitude of supply-side measures (see Chapter 8). Macroeconomic solutions increasingly became subservient to microeconomic measures. Policy and practice for the budget deficit/surplus has to be consistent with the latter.

If the then Conservative government had ever believed in a monetary panacea in terms of control of the money supply through the PSBR, that belief largely evaporated in the late 1980s and early 1990s. This paralleled the steadfast refusal by the government to use Keynesian remedies for treating the economic malaise of the early 1980s. Instead the strategy became one of reducing the PSBR over a number of years. However even that proved difficult to achieve. Not only did the economy move into recession during the early 1990s, but a substantial structural imbalance between public expenditures and receipts became evident.

Both the Conservative government and its successor Labour government attempted to remove that structural imbalance in the public finances. In general, attention focused on a much broader array of supply-side measures, of which reducing the budget deficit was only one. To these measures the Labour government added the **golden rule** and **sustainable investment rule**. The economic reasons for controlling the budget deficit/surplus appear to have been largely based on the need to reduce levels of income tax and NICs as part of both the Conservative and Labour governments' broader supply-side initiatives relating to incentives to work. **The budget deficit/surplus therefore saw a change of role from being a traditional Keynesian short-term demand-side measure to a medium- to long-term supply-side measure**. Keynesians argue that any budget deficit/surplus still has demand-effects. Nevertheless, the fact is that under the supply-side approach fiscal policy has now to support monetary policy. Monetary policy uses interest rates (rather than the money supply) to control inflation as a key supply-side macroeconomic measure. This complements microeconomic measures aimed at improving incentives to work by removing the unemployment and poverty traps. This is clearly distinct from the usual perception of a budget deficit/surplus as a demand-side instrument of Keynesian discretionary fiscal policy, or as the financial instrument of monetary policy.

Put simply, profound changes in social, demographic, industrial and occupational structures created fundamental problems for the policy and practice of public sector borrowing. Responses to those problems involved a fundamental reinterpretation of the budget deficit/surplus as a longer-term supply-side, rather than a shorter-term demand-side, instrument.

Further reading

Board of Trade (1994) *Competitiveness: Helping Britain to Win*, Cm 2563 (London: HMSO).

Cm 3978 (1998) 'Stability and Investment for the Long Term', *Economic and Fiscal Strategy Report 1998* (London: HMSO).

HM Treasury (online). Available at <http://www.hm-treasury.gov.uk>.

HM Treasury (1994) 'The public sector borrowing requirement', *Economic Briefing*, no. 6 (February), pp. 9–12.

HM Treasury (1995) *Better Accounting for the Taxpayer's Money: The Government's Proposals – Resource Accounting and Budgeting*, Cm 2929 (London: HMSO).

Organisation for Economic Co-operation and Development (OECD) (online). Available at <http://www.oecd.org.uk>.

Robson, M. H. *et al.* (1998) 'Symposium on Forecasting the State of the Public Finances', *Fiscal Studies*, vol. 19, no. 1 (whole volume).

12 Income Inequalities and Economic Restructuring

12.1 Introduction
12.2 Definitions of Poverty
12.3 The Distribution of Income and Wealth
12.4 Limits of Principle and Practice
12.5 The Distributional Effects of Economic Policy
12.6 Dispelling Distributional Myths
12.7 Conclusions

In 1942 Sir William Beveridge recommended that a comprehensive social insurance scheme should be introduced to cover loss of income resulting from loss of earnings caused by unemployment, sickness and retirement. . . The social security system must be consistent with the Government's overall objectives of the economy. The tax burden on future generations should be reduced; incentives for people to take up or remain in work should be improved; and the system should encourage greater individual responsibility and choice. (Department of Social Security, *The Growth of Social Security*, London: HMSO, 1993).

The government believes that work is the best route out of poverty and that helping people to move from welfare to work can tackle the underlying causes of deprivation and break the intergenerational cycle of poverty. Expanding the effective labour supply will also allow the economy to grow more rapidly without running into skills shortages and inflationary pressures. The government is committed to building a fairer and more inclusive society in which everyone has the opportunity to benefit from higher living standards. But macro-economic stability is not enough to ensure employment opportunity for all (*Budget*, March 2000, Box 4.1 and paragraph 1.23, London: HM Treasury).

12.1 Introduction

Chapters 9 and 10 made clear the importance of public expenditure (including social security) and taxation in terms of influencing the disposable income and living standards of individuals. However the influence of those factors was not assessed in a systematic way. This

293

chapter remedies that deficiency. It shows how and to what extent income and wealth are redistributed through public finance mechanisms. It also attempts to illustrate how such redistribution interacts with economic policy and economic restructuring and how it is constrained, not just by economic factors, but also by considerations of social justice.

As illustrated in the first quotation above (made by the then Conservative government), the social security system has never been simply a mechanism for redistributing income from rich to poor. In the past it has been more concerned with contributory benefits (see Chapter 9). Nearly a third of benefits are paid to the most affluent 70 per cent of the population. Hence the social security system does more to even out income over people's lifetimes (i.e. between childhood, working age and retirement) than it does to redistribute incomes between different income levels at any one point in time. Much the same applies to other parts of the welfare state, such as health and education. Moreover, the relative and absolute growth of social security expenditures (on both contributory and non-contributory benefits) led to increasing concerns about the impact of that growth on tax levels and incentives to work (see Chapter 10). It also led to increasing reference to individual responsibility and social justice, the latter referring to *equality of opportunity* (as distinct from *equality of outcome*). This is reflected in the second quotation above (made by the then Labour government).

Neither Labour nor Conservative governments of the 1980s and 1990s sought full equality in the distribution of income and wealth. Instead, they tried to encourage people to meet their responsibilities, namely to support themselves through work wherever possible. Many government measures affecting the distribution of income for those groups of working age specifically address the supply side of the economy by improving incentives to work and otherwise getting people back into jobs. In effect, the distributions of income and (to a lesser extent) wealth become a *supply-side microeconomic instrument*, getting into work those socioeconomic groups who do not get jobs as a result of near-full employment and macroeconomic stability.

Nonetheless, the distribution of income and wealth is important in humanitarian terms because of the increasingly well-documented association between low standards of living and poor health. As the distribution of income became more unequal during the 1980s and 1990s (see below), so too did health inequalities between poor and affluent socioeconomic groups. Research published during the 1990s in the *British Medical Journal* and by the Joseph Rowntree Foundation reveals that *relative* poverty, rather than personal behaviour, is the greater risk to health. People and families living in relative poverty have higher incidences of almost every medical ailment from stroke to lung cancer.

Mothers in the poorest socioeconomic group are much more likely than those in the most affluent socioeconomic group to be malnourished and to give birth to underweight babies which, in turn, have increased incidences of illness in later life. The result is that people in the poorest socioeconomic group have a shorter life expectancy than those in the richest group.

This serves to emphasise that *economic factors* are the underlying influences determining a person's life chances and health status. Nevertheless, whilst rates of ill-health, morbidity and life expectancy are statistically linked to socioeconomic status, it does not follow that a much more equal distribution of income will automatically reduce or eliminate all such variations. Poor health status correlates not just with low income, but also with unemployment, poor housing, inadequate diet, polluted local environment and so on. Low incomes and relatively poor health status have become increasingly geographically concentrated in areas of multiple deprivation (see Chapter 3). More generally, there are marked differences in life expectancy, healthy life expectancy and survival of a range of diseases by occupational class, gender, region and ethnicity. Risk factors such as smoking, drinking and diet typically explain the smaller part of these health inequalities. Middle-income and higher-income groups may be more adept at getting better and earlier medical care than low-income groups because they are more articulate. Put simply, (relative) poverty kills but elimination of poverty and associated health inequalities is much more complex than simply redistributing income from high to low income groups.

Bearing this caveat in mind, the link between income distribution and life chances highlights the deficiencies of the allocative efficiency analysis of Chapter 2, used to derive the Pareto optimum. It has already been noted that the Paretian analysis of the 'first best' allocation of resources takes no account of the various forms of market failure, such as negative externalities. Nor does it take account of how the distribution of income resulting from any equilibrium point on the contract curve can itself generate adverse health consequences for the individuals on that contract curve. In other words, in creating a particular distribution of income and wealth, a free market system may create its own negative externalities in terms of the economic costs of providing medical services to those whose health suffers as a result of relative poverty.

The traditional treatment of distributional questions in economic textbooks is to argue that there is inevitably a trade-off between efficiency and equity. The second quotation above and the analysis of Chapter 6 challenges this supposed trade-off in practice since it may be possible to improve both efficiency and equity simultaneously through supply-side improvements in labour markets. However, the earlier analysis of the disincentive-to-work thesis (Chapter 4) and of the poverty and unemployment traps (Chapter 9) are consistent with the trade-off hypothesis. After identifying a trade-off between efficiency and equity, the convention is simply to state that the distribution of income and wealth is a subjective issue that has to be treated separately from efficiency issues. In contrast this chapter goes on to examine in much more detail the interrelationship between economic restructuring, economic policy and the distribution of income and wealth.

12.2   Definitions of poverty

If it is agreed that every person should receive sufficient income to meet the basic needs of food, clothing and shelter, then an **absolute** definition of poverty is appropriate. Alternatively, if it is agreed that every person should share in the generally rising economic prosperity of society, then a **relative** measure of poverty is appropriate (e.g. in relation to average incomes).

Unlike a number of other Western countries, the UK government has set no absolute or relative minimum income level below which people and households can be defined as being in poverty. However, both absolute and relative measures of poverty are commonly used in the UK. The former is based on income support, a state benefit paid to qualifying low-income households. The latter defines as poor anyone living in a household with income less than half the UK average.

An absolute definition of poverty

The **income support level** for particular types of household (e.g. those with and without children) is often used as a benchmark by which to define absolute poverty (see Chapter 9). People and households with incomes no greater than income support levels are defined as in poverty. There are two main problems with this definition of poverty:

1. **The greater the real level of benefit the greater the number of people defined as living in poverty**. The number of people on or below the income support level (or that of its predecessor) rose rapidly during the 1980s, in part because of real increases in the level of benefit in the mid 1980s.
2. **Indexing income support rates to the retail prices index has resulted in the relative level of poverty increasing whilst the absolute level remains constant in real terms**. This reflects the fact that retail prices have increased at a slower rate than earnings measured by male full-time earnings. Hence the relative level of

poverty has increased over time. However **male full-time earnings are becoming increasingly less representative of earnings as part-time employment grows and as a higher proportion of women enter the labour market. Using male full-time earnings as the income base may therefore exaggerate relative poverty.**

A relative measure of poverty

Households with incomes less than half the UK average are often said to be in relative poverty. However, this measure suffers from two main imponderables:

1. **The poor get poorer even if their real income remains unchanged**. If the higher income groups experience a rise in real income whilst the lowest income group experiences no change, then whilst the latter's absolute poverty remains unchanged they have become relatively poorer. In this example, the poor are no poorer in absolute terms. Nevertheless, the relative measure of poverty leads to the conclusion that the poor are poorer simply because the rest of society got richer. Likewise, the poor become less poor if the rest of society experiences a fall in income. This hardly seems credible.
2. **It is impossible to eradicate relative poverty**. Nevertheless, on the basis of ownership of consumer durables and housing standards, absolute poverty already seems to have been eradicated. Almost all of the poorest 20 per cent of households now own a television and refrigerator, about 90 per cent own a washing machine, three-quarters have a telephone and central heating, over half have a video cassette recorder, almost half have a car and a fifth have a home computer. Housing standards have also improved significantly over time and all income groups have access to clean water and adequate food supplies.

On the 'less than half average incomes' relative measure of poverty, almost a quarter of the British population was poor in the mid 1990s and a third of children were living below the poverty line. This compares with only 9 per cent of the population and 10 per cent of children in 1979. In the late 1990s, a quarter of children (totalling 3 million) were living in persistent poverty. The 3 million figure is three times greater than that for 1979. The population share below half average income had shown no trend between 1961 and 1981, fluctuating within narrow margins around 10 per cent. Thereafter it rose sharply. So, either poverty was alarmingly high by the mid 1990s (according to the relative measure), or the poor were better off than ever before (according to the absolute measure).

These contradictory conclusions lead to considerable confusion in public policy debates relating to poverty. They also lead to a degree of incredulity that so many people are truly poor. **In fact, what the relative poverty measure is actually measuring is not poverty** *per se* **but, instead, inequality of income**. Moreover, surveys of British social attitudes in the mid and late 1990s found that almost all of the general public agree that poverty is living below the subsistence level and only just over a third feel that the government should definitely be responsible for reducing income differences between rich and poor.

A comprehensive definition of poverty

Inequality of income is only a very partial indicator of poverty. As already noted, poverty is associated with higher incidences of many illnesses and is increasingly spatially concentrated within run-down inner city areas. It is also associated with lack of educational qualifications, relatively high accident and suicide rates, homelessness and so on. The official EU definition of poverty is '**the poor shall be taken to mean persons, families and groups of persons where resources (material, cultural and social) are so limited as to exclude them from the minimum acceptable way of life in the member states where they live**'. This *resource-based* definition is captured in the term 'social exclusion', this being a *dynamic* concept whereas the distribution of income and wealth is a *static* concept.

Poverty therefore has very many facets and cannot be eradicated simply by increasing the payments of state benefits to the poorest groups. Whilst the government has little influence over the long-run structure of employment (see Section 12.5 below), the measure of success of policies dealing with social exclusion is in the *new employment opportunities* they create – basically through *supply-side* initiatives.

These caveats have to be borne in mind when examining the distribution of income and wealth below. Whilst the level of state benefits is obviously important in the short term, supply-side initiatives are probably a more effective long-term solution to poverty. These initiatives include helping poor workless households find jobs and improving their educational and skill levels. International studies by the OECD show that gaining employment is the main factor in reducing the length of time spent in poverty. In this way the *transmission of poverty* from one generation to the next can hopefully be broken.

Both Conservative and Labour governments have sought to improve incentives to work. The Conservatives emphasised income tax cuts and unemployment benefits conditional upon seeking work and/or on participation in retraining programmes. The subsequent Labour government continued the same broad thrust of policy initiatives with further cuts in income tax and also in national insurance contributions, together with its New Deal programmes, the national minimum wage (NMW), and the Working Families Tax Credit (see Chapters 9 and 10). The WFTC is not merely redistributing income from rich to poor: it also emphasises the importance of work as a route out of poverty. It replaced the former Family Credit (introduced by the then Conservative government) and is part of the Labour government's objective to end child poverty in the long term by encouraging parents to work. Child poverty reflects household and labour market restructuring more than changes in the level of benefits (see Chapter 9 and Section 12.5 below).

A sustainable policy for abolition of child poverty cannot be based simply on paying higher benefits to such a large number of non-working families. Nevertheless, there will always be some workless households and so benefits remain an important poverty measure, as does creating greater educational opportunities for children in poor households. Besides the WFTC and higher child benefit, other initiatives to end (or at least substantially reduce) child poverty include the children's tax credit and the integrated child credit (planned for 2001 and 2003 respectively – see Chapter 10, Appendix 10.1). The irresolvable problem is that the greater and more closely targeted support is for the poorest families the faster it has to be withdrawn as income from earnings increases. This serves to increase the poverty trap (see Chapter 4)

The impact of the NMW (introduced in 1999) on poverty is uncertain because relatively few low-income households contain low-paid workers. Instead, there is an increasing polarisation between dual-earner and no-earner families (see Section 12.5 below). The NMW mainly benefits low-paid women who make up about 80 per cent of employees who benefit and most of whom work part-time. Reduction of gender pay discrimination is a worthy goal (women's average hourly earnings being only 80 per cent or so of men's in the late 1990s), but the NMW will benefit relatively few women in poor households. Low-paid women workers are usually living with better-paid male partners. Less than a fifth of households in the bottom two deciles of the income distribution benefit from the NMW according to some estimates. Hence, **wage regulation is largely ineffective in reducing poverty**, the benefits of minimum wages largely bypassing the poor. What the NMW can do is reduce the disparity between low and high earnings. Nevertheless, even in these terms, the NMW will only be effective in the longer term if it is increased in line with the growth of average earnings. If the NMW were to substantially reduce the disparity in earnings it could actually increase poverty by creating an adverse impact on employment, leading to more workless households. Lack of evidence of any such adverse impact may simply reflect the very low level of the NMW, set at less than half of median earnings.

12.3　The distribution of income and wealth

The distribution of income and wealth can be examined in a number of ways, for example on a regional, demographic, social, gender or racial basis. Different classifications or groupings for the analysis of income distribution are relevant in different contexts. They may also be used in combination in order to provide a more complete picture of the multifaceted nature of income distributions.

Definitions of income

Various definitions of income are used in government statistical series:

- **Original income** is that from employment (i.e. wages and salaries), occupational pensions, investment income (e.g. dividends on shares and interest paid on savings in banks and building societies) and from other households.
- **Gross income** is original income plus cash benefits from the state (e.g. the state retirement pension and income support).
- **Disposable income** is gross income minus income tax, national insurance contributions (NICs) and council tax.
- **Post-tax income** is disposable income minus that part of household spending accounted for by indirect taxes such as VAT.
- **Final income** is post-tax income plus the value of public services consumed, for example education and health.

These definitions of income are conceptually distinct. They are usually assumed to be independent of each other, except insofar as their calculation is sequential, from original to final income. However, in that high marginal rates of effective income tax (including withdrawal of welfare payments) may lead to disincentive-to-work effects, lower disposable income may lead to lower original income. The same reversal of the sequential relationship may occur between final income and original income. This theoretical interrelationship between final income and original is not easy to test empirically. However if the relationship is substantial it would serve to qualify conventional conclusions about the redistributive properties of taxation and public expenditure.

Bearing this caveat in mind, the data for each of the five definitions of income do suggest fairly substantial redistribution. Before examining the figures, note first that the accuracy of data is probably greatest for estimates of original income and least accurate for estimates of final income. This is because the Inland Revenue provides fairly accurate data on original incomes (qualified by tax evasion), whilst final income depends on other financial flows as well as on the consumption patterns of public services. In addition the UK system of income taxation is based on the individual. However the household or family is more consistent with the administrative mechanisms used to assess eligibility for receipt of social security benefits and is probably also more relevant for in-kind benefits such as education and health care.

Research funded by the Joseph Rowntree Foundation found that the poorest 10 per cent of the population got significantly poorer during the 1980s and early 1990s. This fall in post-tax income seemed to disprove the **trickle down effect**, which states that both high- and low-income groups benefit from top rate tax cuts, top rates having been substantially reduced during the 1980s (see Chapter 10). The hypothesis is that these tax cuts allow higher income groups to spend more, so creating jobs for low-income groups. However, whilst research by the Institute of Fiscal Studies also found that the **real post-tax income** of the lowest decile fell (by 18 per cent 1979 to 1992), the amount they spent actually increased (by 14 per cent). There are several possible explanations of this very marked discrepancy. **First**, many of those in the poorest 10 per cent are self-employed and may find it relatively easy not declare all their income for tax purposes. **Second**, others in the lowest decile may also not declare all their income because, in so doing, they lose means-tested benefits. **Third**, as many as half of those in the lowest decile are only in it for a short period and so may be living off past savings. Therefore, income may be a poor indicator of standard of living.

Other data also put income distribution figures into perspective. As already noted, even the poorest households (lowest quintile) have very high and increasing rates of ownership of consumer durables. Nevertheless, whilst the poorest income group increasingly has better housing and better-equipped and serviced homes and whilst many move out of the lowest decile, the spatial concentration of poverty has increased and an increasingly intractable group of households became trapped in the poorest income group. Particular types of household are most likely to be in poverty, in particular those whose head of household is unemployed, unskilled, retired, disabled or a lone parent. Data published annually in *Social Trends* show that in the late 1990s typically two-fifths of lone parent families were in the lowest 20 per cent (quintile) of **equivalised disposable incomes** (i.e. adjusted to take into account the size and composition of the household). Likewise, a quarter of pensioner households (single and couple) were in the bottom fifth of equivalised disposable incomes, a fifth of couples with children, under a fifth of single adults, and a tenth of couples with no children. Correspondingly, two-fifths of the last household group were in the top fifth of incomes but less than a twentieth of lone parent families were (over three-quarters being in the lowest 40 per cent of incomes group).

Two conclusions can be drawn. **First**, it is not necessarily the same people who are in the highest or lowest income groups during a certain period, for example as they move into and out of employment, or replace single parenthood with marriage, or grow old and die. **Second**, increasing the levels of benefit for all households in any particular group(s) would benefit those in the higher quintiles of income as well as those in the lowest quintiles, leading to poor targeting of public finance.

The distribution of income

Redistribution of income occurs when households receive a greater or lesser monetary equivalent from social security benefits and public services than they pay in taxes. Figures published in *Social Trends 1999* show that, in 1996–7, average **original** income ranged from £2310 per household in the bottom quintile group (i.e. the poorest 20 per cent) to £44 780 for the top quintile group (i.e. the richest 20 per cent), a ratio of about 20 to 1. However, the range of **final** incomes was much narrower: between £8310 and £31 790 respectively, a ratio of about 4 to 1. Hence, in combination, benefits in-cash and in-kind lead to a substantial redistribution of income in favour of the lowest income groups.

The original and final income figures for 1996–7 demonstrate that government intervention has the greatest **relative** effects on low-income households but the greatest **absolute** effects on high-income households. The final income of the bottom quintile group was 360 per cent greater than its original income, whilst that of the top quintile group was only 29 per cent less. However the latter group lost £12 990 as a result of that redistribution, much greater than the gain of £6000 for the former.

Not surprisingly, given the discussions of social security, other public expenditures and taxation (in Chapters 9 and 10), this is essentially a **redistribution from households whose heads are employed and highly-paid to households headed by someone who is retired, unemployed or otherwise economically unoccupied**. Hence much of the redistribution is **lifecycle**, including **redistribution from households without children to those with children**. It is therefore **not** simply a case of redistributing incomes among different *income groups*. It is also a case of redistributing incomes amongst different *household types* (i.e. those with no, one or multiple incomes, and whose head is working, retired or supporting many or few dependants).

At any point in time, about half of adults within the bottom quintile experience persistent low income and the other half move in and out of the bottom quintile from year to year. Change in employment status is a major cause of movement between the different quintile groups, wages and salaries generally constituting only a twentieth of income of the lowest income quintile but over half for the middle quintile. Other common causes are when a grown-up child leaves the parental home and when women separate from their partners (usually moving to a lower quintile in both cases).

Graphic and numeric measures of the distribution of income

The inequality of original incomes and the subsequent redistribution through payments of taxes and receipt of benefits is demonstrated in **Figure 12.1**. The 45 degree line depicts complete equality in the distribution of income because both axes are of the same length and both cover the range from zero to 100 per cent. Hence the first (or bottom) 10 per cent (or decile) of the population receive 10 per cent of total income, the first quintile (20 per cent) of the population receive a fifth of the income, the first quartile receive 25 per cent of total income, and so on. Curves to the right of the 45 degree line depict inequality in the distribution of income, those furthest away indicating greater inequality. Hence curve 1 shows that the first quartile of the population receive only 3 per cent of total income, whilst curve 2 shows that they receive 15 per cent.

Curves 1 and 2 are known as **Lorenz curves**. Since payment of taxes and receipt of cash benefits reduce inequality, the Lorenz curve depicted by curve 1 can be taken to represent the distribution of original income, whilst curve 2 represents disposable income. Lorenz curves depicting post-tax and final incomes would lie in between curve 2 and the 45 degree line. The shift from curve 1 to 2 is not drawn to scale (i.e. **Figure 12.1** exaggerates the extent of redistribution). Moreover, both curves are

Figure 12.1 Redistribution of original income

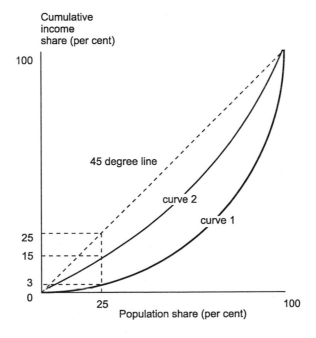

stylised in that they are not necessarily smooth curves. Their actual shape depends on the cumulative percentages of income held by successive deciles of population.

This **graphic** measure of the distribution of income can be used to derive a **numeric** measure, simply by taking the area bounded by the Lorenz curve and the 45 degree line as a ratio of the total area to the right of the 45 degree line (bounded by the axes). This numeric measure is known as the **Gini coefficient**. Clearly it will be larger for curve 1 than for curve 2. Hence, the greater the inequality the greater the value of the Gini coefficient. A value of zero indicates complete equality, one indicating total inequality.

Measures collated by the Institute of Fiscal Studies show that, although there were fluctuations from one year to the next, the value of the Gini coefficient for **disposable household income** showed a falling trend throughout the 1960s and 1970s, from about 0.26 to about 0.23 (i.e. inequality was reducing). However from 1978 it began to rise quite consistently, reaching almost 0.34 by 1991 (i.e. inequality was increasing, the degree of inequality in 1991 being greater than that in 1961). Although there had been short-term reverses of trend on previous occasions, that which occurred during the late 1970s and 1980s was particularly marked and of sustained duration.

This trend toward increasing inequality was associated with an increased dispersion around the average (mean) income. **Figure 12.2** illustrates this point. It depicts two stylised versions of the distributions of disposable household income for 1961 and 1991, which were calculated by the Institute of Fiscal Studies. The Institute also calculated distributions for 1971 and 1981 that displayed a progressive and fairly consistent shift towards the 1991 distribution over the full 30 year period.

The 1961 distribution is heavily clustered around the mean but is *skewed* slightly to the left (in comparison with a normal bell-shaped distribution). The 1991 distribution is much more heavily skewed to the left and has a less well-defined peak, an increasingly long tail and a greater number of people whose incomes are more than three times greater than the mean. Hence the dispersion about the mean increased, indicating an increased disparity between the highest and lowest incomes. The number of people with incomes less than the average rose simultaneously with an increase in the number of people with incomes more than double the mean.

Whilst this changing distribution was evident during the 1960s and early 1970s, it accelerated during the later 1970s and 1980s, consistent with the trend (noted above) for the rising Gini coefficient. The then Conservative government was heavily criticised for reversing a thirty-year trend towards greater equality in the distribution of **disposable household income**, which narrowed steadily between the late 1940s and

Figure 12.2 Distribution of income around the mean

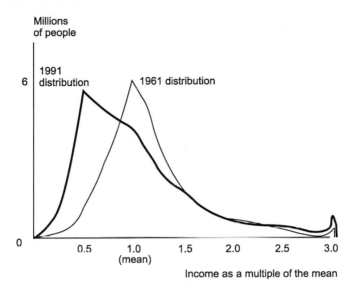

Income as a multiple of the mean

latc 1970s. In fact, between 1979 and 1991 the share of the bottom quintile group fell from 10 per cent to 7 per cent of **net equivalent disposable household income** before housing costs and to 6 per cent after housing costs. In comparison, the share of the top quintile group rose from 35 per cent to 41 per cent of disposable household income before housing costs and to 43 per cent after those costs. Hence the gap between the top and bottom groups widens after taking account of housing costs. Moreover only the top quintile group experienced an increased share of disposable income.

Net equivalent disposable income adjusts gross household incomes to take account of differing family composition, so increasing the incomes of single-person households and reducing those of households with three or more persons, in both cases relative to the income of married couples. The 'before and after housing costs' measures are intended to allow for the significant cost variations between regions, cities and other areas that are not the result of variations in housing quality.

There was a short-lived shift towards greater income equality in the early to mid 1990s. This was mainly caused by abolition of the poll tax in 1993 and reductions in tax allowances that had most impact on higher incomes (see Chapter 10), falling unemployment, slow growth in real incomes (so reducing the disparity between earnings and benefits index-linked to prices), and a declining proportion of pensioners dependent entirely on state benefits.

However, the gap between rich and poor continued to widen during the 1990s as a whole, including the first two years of the 1997 Labour government. The proportion of people living on less than half average income rose in the first two years of the Labour government as the income of the highest income decile rose more than three times faster than the lowest income decile. This is because many factors affect the distribution of income, the government not having control over all of them. The immediate causes of increasing inequality during the 1980s and 1990s were as follows.

First, increasing long-term unemployment was the greatest single cause of low incomes because wages and salaries accounted for 57 per cent of average gross household income in 1992 (and still 56 per cent in 1997). *Unemployment* rose from around one million in 1979 to three million by 1983, remained at that level until 1986 then fell to 1.5 million in 1990, rising again to over two million in 1991, falling to just over 1 million by 2000. At the same time *employment* rose from around 25 million in 1979 to 27 million.

Second, reductions in income tax rates, the highest rates having been cut the most (see Chapter 10).

Third, abolition of the investment income surcharge and extension of tax reliefs to equity investments and special savings accounts (see Chapter 10).

Fourth, the ending of restraints on the distribution of dividends on company shares.

Fifth, increased indirect taxes, which take twice as great a proportion (about 30 per cent) of the disposable household income of the bottom quintile of incomes (of non-retired households) as that of the top quintile (although their payments are much greater in absolute terms).

Sixth, the indexing of social security benefits in relation to retail prices rather than to faster growing earnings, cash benefits comprising about 70 per cent of the gross household income of the lowest quintile (see Chapter 9).

Seventh, abolition of wages councils and the ending of pay restraint on incomes, which led to a greater disparity between low-paid and high-paid workers. Real weekly earnings for men at the lowest decile point increased only half as fast as that for the highest decile. This increasing disparity is unlikely to be significantly affected by the national minimum wage, especially given its low level.

Eighth, increased real housing costs. Higher mortgage interest rates combined with higher mortgage debt (reflecting the rise in real house prices) affected owner-occupiers during the 1980s. Rents for council housing also rose in real terms as part of the move to encourage tenants to buy (see Chapter 8). Mortgage costs (but not rents) fell as interest rates fell during the later 1990s.

Ninth, restraints on local government spending. Whilst there is some evidence that affluent groups benefit most in absolute terms from post-16 education, roads, parks, libraries and waste tips, local government services are still of great relative importance to the living standards of low-income households, especially through provision of subsidised council housing and public transport, and free school meals and milk.

Finally, changing composition and size of the lowest income groups. For example the number of people living in families containing at least one full-time employee fell sharply during the 1980s as unemployment rose. The unemployed and self-employed are most likely to be on low incomes, full-time employees being under-represented amongst those with the lowest incomes. Similarly single parents have a relatively high chance of having a low income (as noted above). Together with the increasing numbers living in single parent families and the marked fall in the percentage of single parents who were in full-time or part-time work, this group became increasingly represented amongst the lowest decile and quintile income groups. Increases in other unoccupied groups, notably the long-term sick and disabled (see Chapter 9), also affected the income distribution.

Perhaps surprisingly, despite the increasing number of pensioners, this group's representation in the lowest income groups fell in both absolute and proportionate terms. The explanation is their rising relative income level, the result of both an increase in the number of those in receipt of occupational pensions and the substantial real increases in investment incomes over that period. However the relative improvement in pensioner incomes also reflects an increase in the sizes of the other socioeconomic and demographic groups containing people most at risk of being on a low income, particularly the unemployed and self-employed.

Clearly, changes in the distribution of income ultimately reflect the complex interactions of a variety of factors. These interactions cannot be explained by a purely economic theory of income distribution. In fact, the **economic theory of distribution** only seeks to explain the division of national income between rent, profits and wages, these being payments to land, capital and labour respectively. The competitive theory of factor pricing explains that distribution with reference to factor productivity. Alternative economic theories try to explain the distribution of national income with respect to imperfect competition. **However, these theories of distribution (of payments between factors of production) cannot explain the distribution of personal income amongst the population.** They can perhaps explain the increasing *dispersion* of earnings in terms of a fall in demand for unskilled workers and a rise in demand for skilled labour (competitive theory). Alternatively, this could be the result of the changing balance of monopoly/monopsony power between trade unions and employers as they engage in collective bargaining and as modified by legislation on minimum wages (imperfect competition). However, the share of household income derived from employment has been falling over time, being not much more than half in 1997. Hence, **any theory of the distribution of income has to be multidisciplinary and include economic, sociological, constitutional, cultural and other factors. It has to explain changes in the distribution of income in terms of economic, social, demographic and tax/benefit factors**.

In general, and based on the analysis contained in this chapter and in Chapter 10, it would be expected that tax/benefit and economic factors are the most important. This expectation is confirmed by research (published in the *Economic Journal* in 1993) suggesting that, of the increasing income inequalities between 1979 and 1988, half arose due to changes in the tax and social security systems, one third arose due to changes in the pattern of economic activity and the remaining sixth were due to differential earnings growth. However that research did not attempt to measure the effects of the growth of part-time working and the other factors mentioned above, which may be of growing influence in the future (see Section 12.5).

It has been made clear that it would be much too simplistic either to attribute all changes in the distribution of income to changes in taxes and benefits on the one hand, or to changes in the level of unemployment on the other. In so doing, exaggerated expectations would be raised about the possibility of achieving a more equal distribution simply by changing taxes and benefits or by increasing employment (itself not so simple to bring about). In fact changes in demography, housing costs, family structures and other factors are, in combination, also of substantial importance for the distribution of income.

Likewise, it is much too simplistic to say that people at the bottom of the income distribution have become worse off in either a relative or absolute sense. **First**, because the membership of that group changes fairly rapidly over time. This is particularly the case for families whose head of household moves from unemployed to employed status. **Second**, because the 'widening income gap' argument takes no account of the value of public services included in final income (defined above). Despite claims of 'middle class capture', *Social Trends* data show that the value of public services is almost twice as great for the lowest quintile group of households (£3880 in 1996–7) than for the highest quintile group (£2030). This is often referred to as the **social wage**. The social wage can be made more redistributive by the introduction of means-tested charges and subsidies for public services. Such measures have been introduced under both Conservative and Labour governments, including charges for long-term care of the elderly and tuition fees for university education respectively.

The distribution of wealth

Wealth is accumulated as **savings** from income, **capital gains** on investments (including housing), and through **inheritances**. *Social Trends* defines wealth to include ownership of securities and shares; dwellings net of mortgage debt; other fixed assets; notes, coins and deposits with banks and so on; life assurance and pension funds; and other financial assets net of liabilities. In 1987 residential buildings net of loans was the largest component, accounting for just over a third of the net wealth of the household sector; but by 1997 it had fallen to just under a quarter. It swapped places with life assurance and pension funds, this component rising from just under a quarter to over a third of wealth between 1987 and 1997. Securities and shares rose from 10 to 15 per cent over the period. Notes, coins and deposits remained fairly constant, accounting for 15 per cent in 1997. No other component accounted for more than 5 per cent in 1997.

All of the reduction in the share of dwellings occurred in the early 1990s recession when the average price of dwellings actually fell. This led to **'negative equity'** for many house buyers, whereby the value of outstanding mortgages exceeded the reduced value of the houses those mortgages were being used to purchase. Over the long term, however, property prices have risen in real terms. Likewise, share prices have risen in real terms over the long term but display considerable volatility in the short term. So-called stock market 'crashes' occurred in late 1987 and late 1998. The share of wealth accounted for by life assurance and pension funds increased particularly sharply between 1991 and 1995 reflecting growth in personal pensions and increases in the price of equities.

In contrast with this marked change in its *composition*, there has been little change in the *distribution* of wealth since 1976. In 1995, the most wealthy one per cent of the population owned almost a fifth (19 per cent) of total marketable wealth, that share having fallen only marginally from 21 per cent in 1976. The most wealthy 10 per cent owned 50 per cent of marketable wealth at the beginning and end of that period, whilst the least wealthy half of the population owned only 8 per cent in both years. These percentages show that what little change did occur was restricted to the richest tenth or so of the population.

Removing the value of dwellings (net of mortgage debt) results in wealth being much more concentrated among the wealthiest groups. For example, the 1995 share of the most wealthy 10 per cent rises from half to almost two-thirds when the value of dwellings is excluded from marketable wealth. Hence, on the basis of this more restricted definition, the distribution of wealth has become much more unequal. This reflects the fact that only several tens of thousands of people pay inheritance tax each year and capital gains tax is paid by less than a hundred thousand people each year. Such low levels of payment occur because of exemptions and allowances (see Chapter 10).

Wealth is clearly much more unequally distributed than income. For example, whilst the 10 per cent of the population with the highest incomes had just under a quarter of total income in 1995, the most wealthy 10 per cent owned half of the total wealth of the household sector in that year (as noted above). Of course, the highest income decile and the wealthiest decile do not necessarily contain the same people. Nevertheless, income and wealth are closely correlated simply because higher income groups are able to save and invest in housing, equities and bonds, and pensions.

In fact part of the unequal distribution of wealth arises due to age, older people usually having paid off mortgages and accumulated wealth in the form of housing, inheritances, occupational pensions and other savings. As already noted, taking account of these forms of wealth reduces the inequality of its distribution. Taking account of the equivalent value of state retirement pensions reduces that inequality even further (although its shrinking value relative to earnings was noted in Chapter 9).

Besides its unequal distribution, the other main policy issue is the concentration of wealth in illiquid forms (notably pensions and housing). The apparently increasing degree of job insecurity (see below) emphasises the need to hold a greater proportion of household wealth in liquid forms (e.g. savings accounts). Whilst low-income groups already hold most of their wealth in savings accounts, about a third of families have no financial savings at all. Both Conservative and Labour governments have attempted to encourage people of working age to save for their retirement in order to reduce demands on public finance. Favourable tax treatment has long applied to occupational pensions. More recently, tax-exempt savings and investment schemes were introduced in the 1980s and 1990s (see Chapter 10).

This policy is based on the **economic lifecycle theory of wealth accumulation**. This states that when people are young and on low incomes they borrow money (for house purchase and so on), expecting their real incomes to rise as they approach middle age. At that point in the lifecycle they repay debt and begin saving to make provision for their retirement. Return to low income in old age means that consumption is increasingly financed by dissaving. This theory therefore predicts an **'inverted-U' shaped distribution of wealth** over a person's lifetime. However, this distribution would occur due to the growth of real earnings over time resulting in younger generations becoming better off than older generations. *Cross-sectional studies* of different age groups would therefore find an inverted-U shape irrespective of any lifecycle effect. Hence, a cross-sectional inverted-U does not prove the theory. The lifecycle theory could only be tested by following a particular cohort of people as they aged over time (i.e. undertaking *time-series studies*).

In fact, there is little evidence that retired people do dissave. This may be because they are uncertain as to how long they will live (and so hold onto wealth), because it is difficult to convert wealth into income (e.g. one always needs a house to live in), or because people wish to leave money to their children (particularly in the form of owner-occupied houses).

Research by the Policy Studies Institute found that people often save money more by accident than by design, for example by being given shares by their employer or by their building society when it demutualised and became a bank. People prefer savings schemes that require little positive action on their part, especially those taking money directly from wages (e.g. 'save as you earn' schemes) or from current accounts (through a standing order). This, of course, is one of the benefits of occupational pension schemes, the 'compulsory' nature of which is often valued by those who otherwise would not save unless forced to do so. However, taxing interest on ordinary bank accounts, lack of financial knowledge regarding savings and investments, means-testing state benefits and charges for residential care of the elderly, and the very existence of the 'safety net' welfare state may all discourage savings.

This supposed **disincentive to save** bears comparison with disincentives to work supposedly caused by high rates of income tax (see Chapter 4). If such a disincentive to save does exist then only radical reform of the welfare state would lead to a substantial change in the accumulation and distribution of wealth. Nonetheless, recent changes in household, family and labour market structures may make any such radical reform largely ineffective. Rising rates of divorce, separation and single parenthood and (apparently) of insecure employment make it increasingly difficult for those affected groups to save for their retirement. For example, half of lone parents and young single people had no housing wealth at all in the late 1990s. Certainly, radical changes in the distribution of wealth are beyond the capacity of governments to achieve, especially in the short term. In the longer term, some redistribution has occurred as a result of government encouragement of owner-occupation of housing and of pensions through tax incentives and tenants' 'right-to-buy' their council houses (see Chapters 10 and 13). As already noted above, however, this redistribution has completely bypassed the least wealthy half of the population. Irrespective of political ideology, no government has sought a near equal share of incomes and/or wealth because of perceived limits of principle and practice.

12.4   Limits of principle and practice

The distribution of income and wealth is clearly susceptible to influence (if not to direct control) by central and local government by means of taxation and public expenditure. However redistribution of income is a means to an end rather than an end in itself. That end is based on social, moral and ethical values, which in turn determine the limits of both principle and practice in the redistribution of living standards.

Limits of principle

In its most extreme form, citizenship is no longer about what the state can do for the individual but rather what the individual can (and should) do for society and the economy. Public finance is as much about *ethics and morals* as it is about *equity and efficiency*. Both Conservative and Labour governments of the 1980s and 1990s saw great moral hazards in allowing the state to become too big. They also emphasised individual ethics regarding personal (rather than state) responsibility for making adequate provision for old age and other eventualities such as unemployment. Increasingly equity was seen as not simply concerned with a more equal distribution of income but also with rewarding individual effort and enterprise. *Collective rights* became qualified by *personal responsibilities*.

This perspective is not simply one party's political philosophy. Many of the same principles were also espoused by the Commission on Social Justice, set up in the mid 1990s at the instigation of the Labour Party. The very name of the Commission is indicative of its basic principles. The term **social justice** provides a much more comprehensive analytical base than 'equity'. The Commission argued that social justice is concerned with much more than redistribution from rich to poor. It argued that few people believe that a simple arithmetic equality of incomes and wealth is either feasible or desirable. Social justice relates not only to **equality** but also to **need, entitlement, merit and desert**. If ever the free market could be both defined and implemented, it cannot ensure social justice in these broad terms.

In the Commission's and subsequent Labour government's view, **equality of opportunity** lies at the heart of social justice. This highlights the changing perceptions of equity. It also highlights the potential contribution of microeconomic supply-side policies in removing restrictions on opportunity, so promoting this particular conception of equity. Inequalities are not necessarily unjust. The real policy decision is deciding which inequalities are unjust and how to eliminate them. Inequalities in income and wealth that arise from personal effort, talent and contribution to the enterprise (or lack of these) are generally regarded as just. Inequalities that arise from discrimination on the grounds of race, sex, age or disability are generally regarded as unjust. Similarly inequalities arising solely from power relationships are generally regarded as unjust.

Social justice requires that institutional and market structures be adapted to break down barriers that prevent people from being given the opportunity for self-improvement. The Commission argued that people should have opportunities to earn resources for themselves rather than having to depend on welfare handouts from a paternalistic, dependency-creating, welfare state. The former approach arguably engenders self-respect and self-sustainability. Such conceptions of social justice appear to be increasingly held by all the major political parties. Creating opportunities is increasingly seen as requiring an enabling and facilitating approach by the state, rather than it being a direct provider of services. The welfare state is itself becoming increasingly pluralistic and adaptive, facilitative of opportunity rather than guarantor of outcome.

Limits of practice

Since long-term unemployment, as already noted, is the greatest cause of inequality, it may be thought that the most effective means of reducing inequality is to create more jobs. However inequalities would still exist even if everyone had paid employment since:

- unequal incomes are inherent in a market economy because payments for factor services (including labour) are in large part determined by market forces.
- institutional, managerial, trades union and political factors are also influential.
- earnings differ in accordance with differences in work effort (hours worked, productivity and so on), even if pay rates are the same.
- the distribution of income depends on both monetary and non-monetary items.
- increasing inequality of earnings has been caused by structural changes within labour markets.

Structural changes within labour markets resulted in the 1980s and 1990s being characterised by the simultaneous occurrence of both increasing employment and increasing dependency on social security benefits (see Chapter 9). This puzzling coincidence of events is explained by the trends towards more multi-income and more no-income households, a dichotomy caused by the apparent trend towards the casualisation of labour through the use of 'flexible' jobs. This growing dichotomy imposes particularly severe limits on the extent to which incomes can be redistributed and explains that part of the structural mismatch of social security benefits and receipts not caused by demographic ageing and lone parent families (see Chapter 9).

Bearing in mind these limits of principle and practice, a more equal distribution of **disposable** income could be brought about by integrating the income tax and social security systems. Such integration is usually suggested as a means of improving the position of the poor and of achieving cost savings in administration. Cost savings could be achieved by replacing the two separate systems for taxes and benefits with an integrated system making more efficient use of information common to both, particularly for benefits that are assessed on the basis of income. For example about a tenth of households both claim housing benefit and pay income tax, and about two-fifths of retired households both receive the state retirement pension and pay income tax. More importantly the poor would receive benefits automatically, so avoiding both the stigma of separate means-testing and the resulting low take-up rates for such benefits (see Chapter 9).

There are two main options for integration: negative income tax and a basic income scheme. Before considering these in detail, note that 'the poor' are not separately or explicitly defined within either scheme and so make unnecessary the definition of this particular group within society. However the first scheme is not applicable to all groups in society, so there is still a need for the separate identification of poor groups existing outside the scheme. Only the basic income scheme is capable of dispensing with the need to define 'the poor'.

The negative income tax scheme

The negative income tax (NIT) scheme uses the existing income tax return to calculate the right to benefits and so avoids the need for separate means testing. It is depicted in **Figure 12.3**. The vertical axis records net income after payment of income tax and receipt of cash benefits. The horizontal axis records gross income before tax and benefits. Assuming equal scales on each axis, gross and net income are equal along the 45 degree line. People with gross incomes equal to or less than $Y1$ pay no tax and automatically qualify for receipt of social security payments. These payments vary between Y_{min} and zero. Y_{min} is received when gross income is zero. No payments are received when gross income is $Y1$. Hence the crossover point (C) of the pre- and post-tax/benefit schedules occurs at $Y1$ (where $Y1 = Y2$). Below the crossover point the individual receives payments so that net income is greater than gross income. In other words income tax is negative below $Y1$, hence the name of this scheme. Above the crossover point the individual receives no payments and pays tax, so net income is less than gross income.

Figure 12.3 Integration of income tax and social security: negative income tax

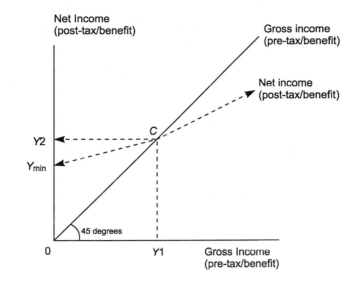

The slope of the net income schedule changes at the crossover point, indicating that the marginal rate of tax/benefit differs above and below it. The marginal tax rate for incomes below Y1 is greater than that for incomes above Y1 because, for successive equal increments of gross income, net income rises more slowly below Y1 than above it. The NIT system must be designed so as not to create strong disincentives to work. For example, if the minimum income were Y2 there would be no financial incentive to earn extra income as long as gross income remained less than Y1. This is because a net income of Y2 would be guaranteed. Hence for every pound of gross income the individual earned, one pound of benefit would be withdrawn (i.e. the marginal tax rate would be 100 per cent, resulting in the horizontal line CY2). Hence, as long as it remains below Y1, any attempt to increase gross income is pointless since it has no effect on net income. In comparison the schedule CY_{min} does provide an incentive to work for levels of income below Y1 since the marginal tax rate is less than 100 per cent. Hence net income rises, although at a slower rate than gross income. Several major problems need to be addressed.

First, differences in assessment periods: that for income tax is 12 months, whilst benefits are assessed as often as weekly (e.g. for income support). Assessing income tax liabilities over such short periods would be administratively expensive and unpopular, the majority of taxpayers not even completing an annual return. Alternatively, assessing eligibility for benefits on an annual basis would fail to identify short-term needs.

Second, differences in assessment units: that for benefits is the family or household unit whilst that for income tax is the individual. Either the relatively recent change to independent taxation would have to be reversed or benefits would have to be paid on an individual basis. The latter option would fail to accurately assess total household needs and resources.

Third, differences in the measurement of resources. For example entitlement to income-related benefits takes into account both the incomes and the capital resources of claimants (see Chapter 9). The income tax system does not need to collect information on the latter.

Fourth, the NIT scheme is only relevant to those in work and registered with the Inland Revenue for tax purposes. The unemployed would specifically have to register with a separate agency or system, much the same arrangement as now and involving similar problems with take-up of benefits.

Finally, abolition of the contributory principle would probably be unpopular, as already noted for the integration of income tax and national insurance contributions (see Chapter 10).

Besides these problems, the supposed savings in administrative costs by integrating the income tax and social security systems are exaggerated since:

1. **They serve largely separate groups of people**. Since the replacement of child tax allowances by child benefit (see Chapter 9), the Inland Revenue's most frequent contacts are with the self-employed and the higher-rate tax payers. The social security system deals mainly with the unemployed and those claiming income support. There is very little overlap between these groups.
2. **Little information is common to both systems even where they do deal with the same people**. The Inland Revenue does not need to hold information about whether or not a taxpayer has children, nor about each taxpayer's housing costs.
3. **Integration would create additional information requirements**. The administrative simplicity of the income tax system was noted in Chapter 10. The long basic-rate band and the deduction of tax on interest at source means that, in many cases, there is no need for the Inland Revenue to bring together information about the total income of individual taxpayers. With integration, both this information and benefits information would be required for everybody, not just those in receipt of net benefits.
4. **Integration would only relate to benefits whose payment is based on income**, whereas four-fifths of families with children both receive (non-means-tested) child benefit and pay income tax.

Hence the benefits of integration through a **full NIT scheme** would seem insufficient to offset the problems. A version of the NIT scheme was actively considered in the early 1970s (see 'Further Reading') but blocked in 1974 by a change of government (from Conservative to Labour). Many of the advantages of that particular scheme have been subsequently adopted. For example, child tax allowances and family allowances have been integrated into a single child benefit, unemployment and short-term sickness benefits are taxed, and the working families tax credit and children's tax credit effectively replace benefits with tax credits for low income families (see Chapters 9 and 12). The 1997 Labour government also proposed an integrated child credit and an employment tax credit (see Chapter 10, appendix 10.1). According to the government's calculations, the result of these measures is that by 2001 the tax burden on a family with two children will be negative until their income reaches nearly £16 000 a year. They will pay less in income tax and NICs than they receive in tax credits and child benefit. A family on the national minimum wage with two children will have their income topped up by 90 per cent. This reinforces the point (made above) that the NMW is unable to eradicate poverty. This applies as much to low-paid working families with children as to workless families.

Ultimately the intention is to integrate the increasingly complex system of child support (through the working families tax credit, children's tax credit, child benefit and income support) into one seamless system. The same objective underpins the pension tax credit (see below). In combination, these measures are effectively introducing a **partial NIT scheme** that, over time, is becoming less partial and more comprehensive in coverage. A fully comprehensive system would have to include other major benefits, housing benefit in particular. The problem created by a tax credit for housing costs would be the enormous cost of extending it to all families, this cost having been the justification for abolition of the tax credit for mortgage interest payments (see Chapter 10).

The basic income scheme

Under this scheme everybody would be paid an age-related sum, people of retirement age receiving more (and children receiving less) than those of working age. Hence, unlike the NIT scheme, the existing benefits described in Chapter 9 and the tax credits described in Chapter 10, the basic income scheme is based on a truly 'universal' benefit in that it would be paid to every resident or citizen (defined by a test of residence). In Chapter 9 benefits were classified as **contributory, means-tested or categorical** in order to stress the fact that eligibility for receipt of those benefits is based on set criteria, namely a record of prior contributions together with occurrence of a particular contingency, lack of an adequate income, or relevant physical or other characteristics. **Universal benefits** are paid to every person regardless of previous contributions, need and circumstances or income or wealth. Hence the basic income scheme provides a truly universal benefit.

The major advantages of the basic income scheme are:

1. **It has the potential to eliminate poverty** (in an absolute if not relative income sense) since it provides a universal benefit. However, it would not eliminate poverty in terms of the comprehensive definition based on the concept of social exclusion (see Section 12.2 above).
2. **It would eliminate the poverty and unemployment traps** (as defined in Chapter 4), since the basic income would be received as a lump sum irrespective of employment status.
3. **It is conceptually and administratively simpler and yet more redistributive in favour of the poor than the NIT scheme**. Most current benefits would be abolished, namely income support, child benefit and the state retirement pension. As already noted, non-working households (the greatest component of 'the poor') do not benefit from the NIT.
4. **It can accommodate changing working patterns** since, unlike other welfare schemes, it is payable irrespective of contributions and whatever the reason for absence (full or partial) from the labour market.
5. **It makes unnecessary a national minimum wage** and its attendant problems (see Section 12.2 above).

However there are major problems:

1. **Administrative savings would be reduced** by the need to retain separate housing and disability benefits because of their highly specific and variable nature.
2. **Many more people would begin to pay income tax** since personal tax allowances would be abolished (as well as national insurance contributions). It was noted in Chapter 10 that both the Conservative and Labour governments would ideally like proportionately fewer workers to pay income tax.
3. **Potentially enormous disincentives would be created because the rate of income tax would have to be as high as 70 to 85 per cent** (or other taxes raised instead) if the basic income benefit was to be sufficient to live on. Besides questioning its political acceptability, such a high marginal rate of income tax would probably lead to strong *disincentive-to-work effects* (see Chapter 4). Whilst elimination of the unemployment trap would improve the incentive to work for the

relatively small number of people previously subjected to it, this may be more than offset by the application of such high marginal tax rates to all workers. More generally, the unconditional nature of the benefit and the high *replacement ratio* (income out of work divided by income in work) may erode both personal responsibility and the work ethic, two characteristics both the Conservative and Labour governments wished to promote during the 1980s and 1990s. More specifically, it may act as a *disincentive to building human capital* through education and training, with consequent adverse effects on economic growth. There would also be strong *tax-evasion incentives*, leading to a growth of the so-called 'black economy'.

4. **Public expenditure would appear to soar as cash benefits replace tax reliefs**. Both Conservative and Labour governments of the 1980s and 1990s had committed themselves to controlling public expenditure and reducing its share of GDP (see Chapter 9).

A **partial basic income scheme**, paying a lower basic income, would avoid the need for such high rates of tax but would lose many of the benefits of integration in that it would have to be supplemented by other means-tested benefits. The main beneficiaries of such a partial scheme would be those with low incomes but not currently in receipt of benefits, namely 18-year-old trainees living with their parents, and women with part-time jobs whose husbands are in employment. In general, such groups do not currently receive benefits because, by definition, their needs are not sufficiently great and their resources not sufficiently low. Hence paying benefits to them would contradict policy objectives to help those other groups most in need of assistance. In addition, the abolition of child benefit would discriminate against families with children, despite the government's continuing commitment to them, whatever their income levels. Hence those living in poverty or with the greatest need of assistance would see little if any benefit, in effect negating one of the main reasons for reform. Indeed, to the extent that the system diverted public expenditure from other programmes (e.g. education, health and personal social services), those with the greatest poverty and needs could actually be made worse off in terms of the 'social wage' (namely final income).

Politically feasible alternatives

Neither the Conservative or Labour governments of the 1980s and 1990s regarded integration of tax and benefit systems as an overriding objective in its own right. Both governments had serious reservations about the basic income scheme since payment of a sufficient basic income to everybody, irrespective of their circumstances, would result in

unacceptable increases in public expenditure and the taxes required to
finance it. Hence those governments preferred to avoid 'big-bang'
solutions. Instead, they chose to pursue closer integration where this was
consistent with the primary objectives of the tax and benefit systems,
where practical and where greater efficiency seemed achievable.

Those governments also wished to retain the contributory principle for
national insurance benefits, otherwise the state retirement pension and
other contributory benefits would have to be abolished. Hence there
were only two feasible partial reforms:

- **Integration of income taxes and means-tested benefits for the
  retired**, on the grounds that their needs tend to be more stable and last
  for longer periods than those for non-retired groups. Integration
  would be feasible, either of different benefits (i.e. income support and
  state retirement pension) or of benefits and income tax. The 1997
  Labour government pursued both avenues. **First**, it introduced a
  Minimum Income Guarantee (MIG) aimed at the four million poorest
  pensioners. This is less costly in public finance terms than increasing
  the basic state pension for all pensioners regardless of income from
  other sources. The MIG is means-tested against capital and
  progressively withdrawn as savings exceed the lower capital limit
  (£6000 in 2000/1), being completely withdrawn when the upper limit
  is reached (£12 000 in 2000/1). Unlike the basic state pension which is
  index-linked to retail prices, the MIG is up-rated by earnings. In this
  way, additional money for pensioners is better targeted on those with
  low incomes. It is a response to the rising numbers of pensioners
  living in poverty as revealed in the government's annual poverty
  audit (*Opportunity for All*). The 2000 audit showed that the proportion
  of pensioners with income below 60 per cent of the median, before
  allowing for housing costs, rose from 21 per cent in 1996/7 to 23 per
  cent in 1998/9. The proportion measured after housing costs, though
  higher, was constant at 26 per cent, the poorest pensioners being able
  to claim housing benefit. The rising proportion of pensioners below 60
  per cent of median income before housing costs is the inevitable result
  of index-linking the basic state pension to retail prices rather than to
  earnings (see Chapter 9). This is simply because the latter rise faster
  than the former. **Second**, the Labour government also plans to
  introduce a pension tax credit in 2003 targeted at four million middle-
  income pensioners with modest occupational pensions or with limited
  savings. Although housing benefit will remain separate, the Labour
  government plans to end pensioner poverty through this partial
  reform. Hence, for pensioners, there is a mixture of basic income
  and NIT.

- **Integration of in-work and out-of-work benefits for the non-retired,** by removing the distinction between income support and the former family credit. This distinction caused discontinuity and delay in changing from one benefit to another as people moved between unemployment and employment and vice versa. The 1997 Labour government attempted to create a 'seamless transition' from welfare to work, but through a tax credit scheme rather than through a basic income payment. As already noted, it introduced the working families tax credit and children's tax credit and plans to introduce the integrated child credit and the employment tax credit

These smaller-scale reforms automatically increase take-up rates by avoiding the need for claimants to take the initiative and by avoiding the apparent stigma of means-testing. They are consistent with the tendency for incremental changes to be made to the tax and benefit systems (described in Chapters 9 and 10). They also avoid the political risks of adopting a completely new system whose effectiveness is in doubt. A full-blown NIT system would give tax credits to those in work whilst a full-blown basic income scheme would require enormous public expenditure. Both would therefore have substantial impacts on the public finances but neither would create job opportunities for those out of work. And yet paid employment is seen as the most effective means of dealing with poverty defined as social exclusion. Instead, the 1997 Labour government has increasingly created a **hybrid system** incorporating elements of the basic income scheme (the pensioners' minimum income guarantee), an NIT (the working families tax credit, children's tax credit and so on), whilst retaining means-tested benefits (e.g. housing benefit). The government has attempted to take the best from each scheme whilst avoiding their major drawbacks. This hybrid system demonstrates, first, that the basic income and NIT schemes are complementary rather than mutually exclusive and, second, that even in combination they are unable to deal comprehensively with the diverse range of needs facing the social security system. Put simply, complete integration of the tax and benefit systems is a chimera.

12.5 The distributional effects of economic policy

The major ideological differences of principle between the two major political parties lie in the choice of the strategic approach to ensure ability to cope with change. Whilst in opposition, the Labour Party accused the Conservative government of pursuing a low unit-labour cost economy by minimising social security taxes whilst stimulating competition within and outside the public sector. The Labour Party claimed that it would pursue the alternative high innovation, high skill and high investment economy. The Conservatives argued that this would require higher levels of taxation, increased government intervention and so lead to further crowding out (see Chapter 5).

Although the 1997 Labour government subsequently introduced the national minimum wage, critics argued that it was set at too low a rate. Moreover, it cut national insurance contributions (NICs) for low paid workers and introduced low-wage supplements through the working families tax credit (replacing the former Conservative government's version, family credit). In effect, these measures facilitated (some would argue encouraged) low pay as a means of getting unskilled workers into jobs. This seems to be contrary to the Labour government's long-term aim of transforming the UK into a high wage, high skills, high productivity economy. However, Labour hopes that people will move up the job ladder into higher skilled jobs, though it remains to be seen if this happens. In fact the growing dichotomy between multi-income and no-income families is likely to be the case irrespective of the apparent choice between the 'low unit-labour cost' strategy and the alternative 'invest and grow' strategy (i.e. high innovation, high skill and high investment).

The low unit-labour cost strategy

Lowering labour costs is likely to require the increasing casualisation of labour (i.e. sporadic and/or part-time working) so as to allow low wages to be paid and avoid imposition of employers' NICs and so on (see Chapter 10). These new flexible jobs tend to be taken by people from households seeking a second income (i.e. where the head of household is already in employment). In the late 1990s, 75 per cent of women whose male partners were in work also had jobs, compared with 40 per cent of those whose male partners were unemployed. Whilst these rates had increased from those of the early 1990s (at 60 and 24 per cent respectively), women with working partners remained about twice as likely to have jobs than those without working partners. This counters income-maintenance objectives since the need for income is greater when the head of household is unemployed. The explanation is that such unemployed households would usually be made worse off if either partner took up low-paid part-time or temporary employment. **First**, means-tested benefits were still being withdrawn in the late 1990s at rates of up to 90 per cent of incremental original income (the unemployment trap, see Chapters 4 and 9). **Second**, there were still considerable time-lags (three months or more) and uncertainties in reapplying for in-work and out-of-work benefits.

Put simply, the certainty of benefits (once in receipt of them) is better than the uncertainties created by sporadic, low-paid employment. This **low pay, no pay cycle** is another aspect of the unemployment trap. Hence the interaction of the social security system with structural changes in labour markets (i.e. flexible employment) results in the growth of jobs with low skill requirements, largely bypassing the unskilled unemployed. Paradoxically, those jobs have tended to be taken by educated women whose husbands are already in employment, who therefore receive no social security payments, and who consequently face no unemployment trap. Hence the increasing shift in the pattern of employment from full-time unskilled males towards part-time females is asymmetrical in that it disproportionately benefits educated females married to working husbands (also usually educated), so explaining the growing distinction between **work-rich** (i.e. dual-earner couples) and **work-poor** (i.e. no-earner) families. Despite ongoing reforms to a social security system attempting to deal with this problem, the proportion of workless households has been on a secular upward trend since the mid 1970s. That proportion trebled from 6 per cent of all households in the mid 1970s to 18 per cent by the end of the 1990s. This increasing **polarisation of work** is a major cause of the increasing **polarisation of incomes**. Hence the low unit-labour cost strategy is likely to increase disparities in **original household incomes**.

The 'invest and grow' strategy

This strategy is likely to accelerate the impact of technological change in manufacturing towards better-educated labour by increasing the degree of instability of employment. The more rapid pace of technological change seems to have resulted in people changing jobs more frequently than was the case for previous generations of workers. Whilst both skilled/educated and unskilled/uneducated workers face broadly the same chance of being made redundant as a consequence of such economic restructuring, those who are uneducated and unskilled have a much lower chance of re-employment than their opposite numbers. Research for the Commission on Social Justice found that, of those people with degrees who were unemployed in 1990, more than two-thirds had found a job one year later. However, of those with no qualifications, the proportion was less than one third. The proportion for those with intermediate qualifications was less than half.

Hence more rapid innovation has two effects. **First**, it results in higher wages (financed by higher productivity) for educated/skilled workers relative to those who are uneducated/unskilled. **Second**, it also increasingly excludes the latter group from the labour market. Combined with the exclusionary effect of the social security system's unemployment trap, the end result is an increasing disparity in the **original** incomes of households populated by those two groups of workers.

It is not clear whether the 'low unit-labour cost' strategy or the 'invest and grow' strategy is the best choice since both appear to result in an increasing disparity in original household incomes. The 'invest and grow' strategy would be most appropriate if labour-intensive production were to be transferred from developed to newly industrialised (particularly Asian) countries as part of an increasing international division of labour within manufacturing. Because of their low unit-labour costs the newly industrialised countries seem to have a comparative advantage in labour-intensive, low-skilled manufacturing activities such as textiles and clothing. Developed countries appear to have a comparative advantage in areas of manufacturing requiring more advanced capital stocks that require educated and skilled labour. Hence the 'invest and grow' strategy would seem to be the most appropriate. However the newly industrialised countries may also develop comparative advantages in technologically advanced manufacturing sectors, much in the same way as Japan has done. In that case the 'low unit-labour cost' strategy may be most appropriate. In practice different strategies may be appropriate in different industrial sectors (e.g. textiles and information technology).

Whatever the strategy, increasing inequality of **original household incomes** seems to be inevitable since the growth of skill-intensive manufacturing (in both the UK and other developed countries) has only partly offset the job losses in unskilled manufacturing activities. Combine this outcome with an increasing structural gap between social security revenues and expenditures arising as a result of demographic ageing and family restructuring, and the result is increasingly severe limits of practice for achieving greater equality of **gross** incomes.

Indeed the combination of structural gaps in both labour markets and social security could create a combined **structural gap in the public finances** whose total is greater than the sum of its individual parts. For example, if the dual-earner/no-earner households dichotomy increases it will have implications for increased social security expenditure. It would also serve to reduce tax revenues compared with what they would have been if employment had been more evenly distributed amongst households. This would be the case because personal allowances would combine with low pay and independent taxation to result in relatively little extra income tax revenues accruing to the Exchequer from extra part-time jobs in dual-earner households. Hence the extra taxes paid as a result of second incomes would be insufficient to pay for the extra benefits payable to no-earner households, so exacerbating the structural gap for social security.

12.6 Dispelling distributional myths

First, it is much too simplistic to attribute sole responsibility for the increasing inequality of incomes during the 1980s and 1990s to the Conservative and/or Labour governments' fiscal and monetary policies. The distribution of income and wealth is ultimately the outcome of a complex series of social, demographic, economic, institutional and political factors. For example, lone parent families have increased rapidly in both proportionate and relative terms and are at much greater risk of unemployment (in part because of lack of adequate and affordable child care), low income and lack of savings than other family groups. Growing unemployment and long-term benefit-dependency amongst unskilled, uneducated workers and their families is due to a combination of:

- more rapid technological change within domestic industries
- an increasingly competitive market for unskilled jobs (including foreign competition from developing countries)
- the unemployment trap.

Second, the achievement of a more equal distribution of income requires much more fundamental policy measures than simply tinkering with public finances. The much lower re-employment chances of unskilled, uneducated workers emphasises the point that long-term changes in the distribution of income are crucially dependent on improving the provision of education and training. Some analysts argue that there is an over-supply of better-qualified pupils and graduates, and that they are taking jobs that would otherwise have gone to the less well qualified. Even if this is the case, the argument is based on a static or short term view of the economy which ignores long term dynamic economic restructuring. Moreover, it denies the Labour government's attempts to use education and training to create employment opportunities for deprived groups as a way out of poverty.

Third, it is over-simplistic to argue that increased inequality is an inevitable concomitant of increased economic efficiency. Indeed, there is some evidence that the link between increasing equality and economic growth is positive, i.e. the greater the inequality the lower the growth. This appears to be the case for both developed and developing countries. Nevertheless, the direction of causation remains uncertain: does low growth lead to inequality or *vice versa*? Increasing inequality may reflect the loss rather than the achievement of economic potential, through unemployment, lack of investment and growth of low-paid low-productivity jobs. However it would be over-simplistic to expect faster growth simply because income was more evenly distributed. The association between these two variables is probably the joint outcome of other more general social and economic policies, for example investment in improved education and training.

Fourth, it would be inappropriate to attempt to further increase incentives to work by giving affluent groups more through further tax cuts whilst giving the able-to-work poor less through further benefit cuts. During the 1980s and 1990s social and economic changes were already so effective in encouraging affluent households to seek second incomes that the relative role of further tax cuts was probably unimportant. Whilst benefit cuts have undoubtedly increased financial pressures on the unemployed, they are not going to be effective as a means of encouraging re-employment among unemployed people who lack basic vocational skills. The comprehensive definition of poverty in Section 12.2 above demonstrates the wide range of measures needed to get those living in multiple deprivation into paid employment.

12.7 Conclusions

The combination of tax, social security and public service systems has been seen to lead to a considerable redistribution of income in favour of low-income groups. However within that aggregate redistribution there are other redistributions based on lifecycle and other factors. Redistribution, like taxation, is a multifaceted policy area.

Critics who argue that the distribution of income is too unequal have traditionally argued for more progressive tax and public expenditure systems and have been vehemently opposed to increased use of (even means-tested) charges for public sector outputs (see Chapter 6). Nevertheless there are limits to the use of taxation and public spending for these purposes.

Besides the need to avoid possible efficiency losses due to disincentive-to-work and other crowding-out effects, public spending and taxation have to be set within the much broader context of social justice. Social justice encompasses the meaning of citizenship (its responsibilities and rights) as well as efficiency and equity. The concepts of personal responsibility (i.e. for self-support) and of undue calls on the state and taxpayer, necessarily limit the degree of equalisation of income and wealth. Redistributional objectives are set within terms of need, benefit and potential for self-improvement. The formulation and achievement of those objectives are necessarily modified and limited by rapid socio-economic and demographic restructuring.

Many critics would still argue that greater use could be made of public finances in order to achieve greater equality in the short term. However there is an increasingly accepted view that the best way to promote equality in the longer term is to enable individuals to support themselves and their families through the creation of employment opportunities. Both Conservative and Labour governments of the 1980s and 1990s believed that those employment opportunities can only be created by supply-side initiatives, demand-side measures being counter-productive in the long term (see Chapter 8).

They believed that the most appropriate long-term supply-side approach is to enable individuals, families and households to cope with economic changes by increasing their flexibility. This requires investment in human capital on an ongoing basis. It is increasingly recognised that education and training should not stop after school, college or university, or at a particular age. The modern economic system increasingly requires a diverse and continuously changing range of vocational skills and abilities. However, despite the mantra of **lifelong learning**, current schemes are still largely discontinuous in being concentrated on people either before they enter the labour market or after they become unemployed.

In these terms, radical tax reforms such as the negative income tax and basic income schemes are at best short-term solutions to current problems and they may frustrate long-term measures. They have the capability of addressing many of the adverse consequences of rapid technological change, particularly in terms of constraining or reversing the increasing distributional inequality of income. However, these schemes were seen to be of high political risk, to have considerable implications for the levels of taxation and public expenditure and to magnify the very dependency culture that recent reforms have sought to eliminate. They could therefore lead to crowding out (see Chapter 5), having undesirable effects on the supply side of the economy.

The distribution of income and wealth is therefore as much a supply-side issue as it is an issue of equity. This is captured in the concept of social justice, that individual effort, talent and enterprise should be facilitated, encouraged and rewarded, inevitably leading to a degree of inequality in the distribution of income and wealth. Complete equality would be as unjust as inequality due to discrimination on the grounds of race, gender, age, disability or patronage.

Further reading

Atkinson, A. B. (1995) *Public Economics in Action: The Basic Income/Flat Tax Proposal* (Oxford: Clarendon Press).

Atkinson, A. B. (1997) 'Bringing Income Distribution in from the Cold', *Economic Journal*, vol. 107, no. 441, pp. 297–321.

Atkinson, A. B. (1999) 'The Distribution of Income in the UK and OECD Countries in the Twentieth Century', *Oxford Review of Economic Policy*, vol. 15, no. 4, pp. 56–75.

Balls, E. and Gregg, G. (1993) *Work and Welfare: Tackling the Jobs Deficit* (London: Institute for Public Policy Research).

Brittan, S. and Webb, S. (1990) *Beyond the Welfare State: An Examination of Basic Incomes in a Market Economy*, The David Hume Institute (Aberdeen: Aberdeen University Press).

Clinton, D., Yates, M. and Dharminder, K. (1994) *Integrating Taxes and Benefits?* (London: Institute for Public Policy Research).

Commission on Social Justice (1993a) *Social Justice in a Changing World* (London: Institute for Public Policy Research).

Commission on Social Justice (1993b) *The Justice Gap* (London: Institute for Public Policy Research).

Dilnot, A. and Low, H. (1994) *The Distribution of Wealth in the UK* (London: Institute of Fiscal Studies).

Dorling D (1997) *Death in Britain: How Local Mortality Rates have Changed: 1950s–1990s* (York: Joseph Rowntree Foundation).

DSS (1994) *Households Below Average Income: A Statistical Analysis 1979–1994/95* (London: The Stationery Office).

DSS (1998) *A New Contract for Welfare Cm 3805*, Department of Social Security (London: The Stationery Office).

DSS (1999) *Households Below Average Income 1994/95–1997/98* (London: The Stationery Office).

DSS (2000) *Opportunity for All*, Department of Social Security (London: The Stationery Office).

Glyn, A. and Miliband, R. (eds) (1994) *Paying for Inequality: The Economic Cost of Social Injustice* (London: Rivers Oram Press/Institute for Public Policy Research).

Goodman, A., Johnson, P. and Webb, S. (1997) *Inequality in the UK* (Oxford: Oxford University Press).

Hills, J. (1996) *New Inequalities: The Changing Distribution of Income and Wealth in the United Kingdom* (Cambridge: Cambridge University Press).

Hills, J. (1998) *Income and Wealth – The Latest Evidence*, Joseph Rowntree Foundation (York: York Publishing Services).

HM Treasury (1972) *Proposals for a Tax-Credit System*, Cmnd 5116 (London: HMSO).

Howarth, C., Kenway, P., Palmer, G. and Miorelli, R. (1999) *Monitoring Poverty and Social Exclusion 1999* (York: Joseph Rowntree Foundation).

Jenkins, S. P. (1996) 'Recent Trends in the UK Income Distribution: What Happened and Why?', *Oxford Review of Economic Policy*, vol. 12, no. 1, pp. 29–46.

Johnston, P. and Webb, S. (1993) 'Explaining the Growth in UK Income Inequality: 1979–1988', *Economic Journal*, vol. 103, pp. 429–35.

Joseph Rowntree Foundation (online). Available at <http://www.jrf.org.uk>.

LPC (2000) *The National Minimum Wage – the Story so Far* (London: Low Pay Commission).

Mitchell, R. et al. (2000) *Inequalities in Life and Death: What if Britain Were More Equal?*, Joseph Rowntree Foundation (York: York Publishing Services).

ONS (1999) *Social Trends 29*, Office for National Statistics (London: The Stationery Office).

Oppenheim, C. and Harker, L. (1996) *Poverty: The Facts* (London: Child Poverty Action Group).

Phillimore, P., Beattie, A. and Townsend, P. (1994) 'Widening Inequality of Health in Northern England 1981–91', *British Medical Journal*, vol. 308, no. 6937, pp. 1125–8.

Rowlingson, K., Whyley, C. and Warren, T. (1999) *Wealth in Britain: A Lifecycle Perspective* (London: Policy Studies Institute).

Townsend, P. and Davidson, N. (1992) *Inequalities in Health: The Black Report* (London: Penguin).

Wilkinson, R. G. (1997) 'Socio-economic Determinants of Health: Health Inequalities: Relative or Absolute Material Standards?', *British Medical Journal*, vol. 314, pp. 591–5.

Part III

Case Studies of Theory, Policy and Practice

13 Nationalisation, Privatisation and Regulation

13.1   Introduction
13.2   Privatisation Versus Nationalisation
13.3   The Efficiency Case for Nationalisation
13.4   The Efficiency Case for Privatisation
13.5   Comparing Efficiency under Nationalisation and
       Privatisation
13.6   Forms of Privatisation
13.7   Privatisation and Industry Structure
13.8   The Rationale for Regulation
13.9   Alternative Forms of Regulation
13.10 Regulatory Philosophy in the UK
13.11 The Form of Regulation in the UK: RPI minus X
13.12 Reconsideration of Rate of Return Versus Price Cap
       Regulation
13.13 Allocatively Inefficient Regulation
13.14 Conclusions

Often the Government can help most by getting out of the way. In the 1970s the state ran the phone company and the main airline. It manufactured cars and steel and ran a high street bank. Privatisation has expanded the market sector, transferring the ownership of almost 50 major businesses to the private sector where efficiency has been improved by market disciplines (1994 White Paper, *Competitiveness: Helping Business to Win*, Cm 2563, London: HMSO, p. 16).

The Government . . . plans to strengthen the regulation of the utilities, putting consumers – including business consumers – first (1998 White Paper, *Our Competitive Future: Building the Knowledge Driven Economy*, Cm 4176, London: Stationery Office, p. 56).

13.1   Introduction

Privatisation was the most high profile supply-side policy of the 1980s and 1990s. It is generally referred to as *rolling back the frontiers of the state* through the sale of state assets (see Chapter 8). Indeed the **first** quotation

333

above (from the then Conservative government) refers specifically to the sale of major public sector businesses to the private sector. However, in its more general form, privatisation also refers to any measures that are specifically designed to stimulate provision by the private sector of goods and services previously produced solely or mainly by the public sector. These various forms of privatisation will be defined below.

The sale of formerly state-owned telephone, energy, water and similar 'public utility' companies is not the end of the matter. Where sale of assets transforms a former public sector monopoly into a private monopoly, continued government intervention is required for the purposes of both allocative efficiency and X-efficiency (see Chapter 7). Changing the ownership of a monopoly does not in itself dispense with the need for government intervention when addressing market failure (see Chapter 2). Such a redefinition of property rights changes the form of, but not the rationale for, government intervention. Regulation of a newly created private sector monopoly replaces direct government ownership and control of the former public sector monopoly. In other words, the pursuit of efficiency takes another form but the objective of achieving it remains the same.

This chapter considers the opposing rationales for nationalisation and privatisation, and the need for (and form of) regulation subsequent to privatisation. It provides a general overview of these issues rather than a detailed account for individual industries. A detailed case study of water and sewerage is provided in the following chapter. Here the intention is to provide a thorough appreciation of the theoretical, methodological and institutional underpinnings of privatisation and regulation, rather than a mass of descriptive detail. The latter creates the danger of 'not being able to see the wood for the trees'.

13.2   Privatisation versus nationalisation

It is instructive to consider the earlier case of the state purchase of the industries and assets that have now been privatised (see **Table 13.1**). These industries were generally in private ownership prior to nationalisation and were returned to private ownership after five decades or so of public ownership. Nationalisation had legislative force (implemented by an Act of Parliament specific to each nationalised industry) in **compelling** private owners to sell their industries to the state, for example iron foundries and coalmines. Such compulsory purchase is quite distinct from the government's purchase of company shares on the Stock Exchange (a **voluntary** transaction with sellers of shares). The latter method has also been used on occasion, for example for British Petroleum and British Leyland (a car manufacturer). The sale of both nationalised and publicly owned limited companies falls within the broad definition of privatisation.

Comparison of the arguments in support of privatisation with those for nationalisation demonstrates a surprising degree of commonality as well as a significant degree of difference. Moreover it would be too simplistic to see nationalisation and privatisation as simply opposing actions resulting from ideological and political polar extremes.

Some public enterprises (e.g. the former Central Electricity Board and London Passenger Transport Board) were established by Conservative, Liberal and National governments before 1945. Local governments of similarly differing political persuasions had also created their own municipal electricity, gas, tram and water and sewerage undertakings. In that sense, nationalisation was a cross-party initiative, essentially a response to the failure of private markets to make such services available in sufficient quantity and quality. In general, however, neither central nor local government carried their nationalisation initiatives into the manufacturing sector before 1945.

The main period of nationalisation is associated with the election of a UK Labour government immediately after the Second World War. This led to a major programme of nationalisation, namely the purchase by the government of major industries *at the commanding heights of the economy*. Iron and steel, coalmining, electricity generation, gas and various forms of transport were nationalised in the late 1940s and early 1950s. The Labour Party regarded ownership of the means of production, distribution and exchange as the foundation of political and economic power. Exploitation of the people by the capitalist system could therefore be controlled by state ownership of the means of production, distribution and exchange. As recently as the mid 1970s Labour Party conferences were passing motions for the nationalisation of the banking system. However, during the 1990s it abandoned its commitment to nationalisation (see below).

The common rationale for nationalisation and privatisation

Social and political objectives as well as an **economic** efficiency rationale underpinned the nationalisation programme of the late 1940s and early 1950s. A similar multidisciplinary rationale underpinned the privatisation programme 40 to 50 years later. Many of the same economic and social concerns existed, particularly the need to ensure:

● **The development of industries and their services** to business and domestic customers through technological change and innovation. Such development was manifestly lacking in many of the industries prior to their nationalisation (e.g. steel) and also became increasingly apparent prior to privatisation (e.g. British Telecom). In both examples there was a lack of new investment in new technology, leading to allocative inefficiency (i.e. a supply constraint).

- **High quality and universality of service**, both geographically and by sector. For example urban and industrial development is critically dependent on the security (i.e. continuity) of supplies of electricity and gas in virtually all parts of the UK.
- **Production efficiency** in terms of minimisation of costs (i.e. X-efficiency), whether through the achievement of economies of scale and/or through competitive forces.
- **Equity** in terms of consumers' ability to pay for natural monopoly services such as electricity and water. Potential abuse of monopoly power has to be pre-empted (whether by nationalisation or regulation) particularly where demand is price inelastic.

The changing context

The relevant question is which form of intervention best promotes the achievement of these objectives? So much happened in the UK during the five decades between nationalisation and privatisation that it would be over-simplistic to assume that the political, social, industrial and economic conditions relevant for each industry were directly comparable between the time of nationalisation and the time of privatisation. A full appreciation of the privatisation debate requires a comprehensive awareness of the historical development of each nationalised industry. Limited space does not allow a detailed discussion but the main changes include the following forms of restructuring.

First, economic and industrial restructuring. The public utility industries in question experienced substantial technological change, e.g. in telecommunications. The energy sector saw the development of oil and natural gas in parallel with electricity, and a shift away from coal-fired electricity generation and domestic heating. The non-rail transport sector expanded enormously. The relative and absolute shift of industry, employment and residential location away from the centre of conurbations towards suburbs and free-standing towns put a premium on personal mobility: transport of people by car and of goods by lorry, instead of by rail. The wider economy experienced substantial growth and economic restructuring towards services as distinct from manufacturing. Mass production in manufacturing gave way to methods of industrial organisation based on small-batch production processes and just-in-time delivery systems requiring a highly flexible and highly responsive transport infrastructure.

Table 13.1   Nationalisation and privatisation in the UK

Nationalised industries privatised between 1979 and 1999

British Aerospace	British Shipbuilders
British Airports Authority	British Steel
British Airways	British Telecom
British Coal	Electricity generation and distribution*
British Gas	National Bus Company
British National Oil Corporation	National Freight Consortium
British Railways (Railtrack)	Water and sewerage (England and Wales)

Nationalised industries remaining within the public sector in 2000

British Waterways Board	London Transport
Caledonian MacBrayne (ferries)	Post Office
Civil Aviation Authority	Water and Sewerage (Scotland)

Other privatised companies/enterprises/assets

Amersham International	Jaguar
Associated British Ports Holdings	Rolls Royce (aeroengines)
British Gas Onshore Oil (Wytch Farm)	Rover Group
British Petroleum	Royal Ordnance Factories
British Rail Hotels	Sealink
Britoil	Short Brothers
Cable and Wireless	Trustee Savings Bank
Enterprise Oil	Unipart
Girobank	British Technology Group and others**
Her Majesty's Stationery Office	Local government seaports, airports etc.
International Aeradio	Local government housing

Notes:

* *England and Wales*: Area Boards, PowerGen, National Power, Nuclear Electric, National Grid Company.

Scotland: South of Scotland Electricity Board, North of Scotland Hydro-Electric Board, Scottish Nuclear (excluding the Magnox power stations, these remaining in the public sector for decommissioning)

** Fairey, Ferranti, ICL and Inmos.

Second, social and political restructuring. Although at least partly endogenous to the political party in power, society and state have also been transformed. A predominantly paternalistic, monolithic, standardised, collective form gave way to more emphasis on a pluralistic and enabling state, facilitating individual self-sufficiency, independence and personal achievement (see Chapters 9 and 12). Employment in the primary (e.g. coal) and secondary (i.e. manufacturing) sectors declined whilst that in services grew. This led to a dramatic decline in the rate of unionisation of workers and of the political influence of trade unions. This, in turn, led to the growth of increasingly 'flexible' employment patterns in the tertiary sector (i.e. public and private services).

Despite such profound change the UK has retained its mixed economy, and so the institutional and constitutional context within which privatisation has occurred has remained essentially the same. In contrast, political and socio-economic restructuring has been much more profound in some other countries, most notably in Central and Eastern Europe. Privatisation in the UK has therefore been a relatively small adjustment to the size and scope of both public and private sectors. Nevertheless, its significance both as a supply-side measure and in heralding a socio-political cultural shift is profound.

Privatisation may require continuing and increased government intervention in terms of the public sector providing the strategic services that underpin private activity. Privatisation renders market failure concepts and the macro and micro models of public expenditure growth no less relevant (see Chapters 2 and 3). For example allocative efficiency subsidies paid in respect of particular industries (i.e. where marginal social benefit is greater than marginal private benefit) can be justified (e.g. for rail services) whether they are privatised or nationalised. However the amount of subsidy may be reduced under private ownership of industries if there are significant efficiency gains in production.

The Conservative government's objectives

The Conservative governments' *economic* objectives are summarised in the first quotation at the beginning of this chapter, namely to improve efficiency through improved market discipline. Its **political** objectives of the privatisation programme were as follows.

First, to reduce public expenditure, taxation and borrowing, particularly by raising revenue and reducing the need for public subsidy to finance the frequent and substantial deficits of nationalised industries (see Chapters 9, 10 and 11). However, a number of the industries became highly profitable in the run-up to privatisation, most notably electricity and gas, and so their sale reduced future revenue streams accruing to the public sector. Moreover privatisation receipts were not maximised since shares were typically sold at a substantial discount relative to their actual market value the day after sale. Whilst valuation of state assets for stock market purposes is difficult, share prices were deliberately discounted in order to encourage their purchase. However, since privatisation typically involved an initial sale of only 51 per cent of the shares, followed by the sale of subsequent tranches in later years, the value of the government's remaining shareholding also rose. Hence subsequent privatisation receipts were higher so that the initial revenue loss was substantial but limited. Moreover, subsequent tax revenues paid by privatised companies typically exceeded the subsidies that had previously been paid to them whilst under public ownership.

Second, to facilitate 'popular capitalism' by encouraging more widespread share ownership by the public generally and by the employees of individual privatised companies in particular (so as to give them more incentive to support economic reforms and industrial efficiency and profitability). There was a substantial increase in the number of adults owning shares, from 7 per cent in 1979 to 25 per cent in 1991. Some 14 per cent of adults owned shares in privatised companies, 5 per cent holding shares in only one company. Hence privatisation does seem to have facilitated popular capitalism. However, following market trading in shares subsequent to privatisation, share ownership once again became increasingly concentrated among the affluent professional and managerial socio-economic groups and among major institutional shareholders such as pension funds and insurance companies. Demutualisation of former building societies and some life assurance companies created many more shareholders than privatisation (see Chapter 8).

Third, to reduce the political and economic power of trades unions in line with the Conservative government's attempt to destroy the collective philosophy of socialism. However privatisation's impact is not clear in this respect. There has been a decline in the membership and political influence of trades unions throughout the economy. This would probably have occurred (though perhaps more slowly) within the nationalised industries even in the absence of privatisation, for example as a result of technological change. Certainly there was substantial labour-shedding by many of the nationalised industries prior to their sale (e.g. steel). Such employment reductions have been a long-term feature of the nationalised coal industry.

Finally, to reduce political intervention in the operations of the former nationalised industries by using a systematic but controlled approach to intervention through the establishment of a regulatory body for each privatised industry. However the extent to which political intervention is reduced in practice depends on the relationship between the secretary of state and regulator for each industry and the extent to which the regulator chooses to intervene in the operations of the industry. It is arguable that the privatised British Telecom has been subject to more detailed intervention by its regulator than it had been to government intervention whilst still nationalised. The same applies to water and sewerage in England and Wales (see Chapter 14).

The Labour government's objectives

The Labour governments' *economic* objectives are summarised in the second quotation at the beginning of this chapter, namely ensuring regulatory bodies put consumers first. Its **political** objectives were effectively transformed. In opposition prior to 1997, the Labour Party was initially strongly and ideologically opposed to privatisation and stated that it would re-nationalise the major privatised companies upon its election to power. Such a reversal of policy became less practical the more the privatisation programme progressed and the more widespread the associated shareholding became. A re-nationalisation programme would be enormously expensive in public expenditure terms (re-nationalisation without compensation at full market value would probably not be politically feasible). Moreover the Labour Party reconsidered the role of the state (see Chapter 12) and, upon attaining office in 1997, it announced plans for further privatisations or forms of privatisation including the Private Finance Initiative and Public-Private Parnerships (PPPs) for hospitals, schools, prisons and the London Underground (see Chapter 8), and contracting out (see Chapter 15).

In its approach to privatisation, the Labour government distinguished between services that can be left to the market to provide and those that cannot. The latter, according to Labour's view, include education, the health service, the armed forces, the police and the Post Office (the PO already facing strong competition and performing well). Labour's policy is that these services should remain within the public sector. All other services can be privatised, leaving the government to concentrate on key strategic public services such as education and training (see Chapter 8). In other words, there should be a presumption in favour of private ownership except where competitive conditions make it unrealistic or where Labour's interpretation of 'the public interest' dictates it. However, whilst Labour would have preferred to keep rail services in the public sector had they not been privatised by the Conservative government, it does not propose to re-nationalise them.

Labour announced plans to privatise National Air Traffic Services (NATS), British Nuclear Fuels Limited (BNFL), the Tote (a state-owned betting business), the Royal Mint, London Underground (using a PPP), the Commonwealth Development Corporation, motorway service stations and so on. Being controversial and delayed by various problems, some of these privatisations may not take place until 2002. Other possible privatisations include Manchester Airport, the Meteorological Office, Forestry Commission forests, land and buildings owned by the Ministry of Defence which are no longer used for military purposes. The Labour government privatised the student loan portfolio in 1998 and raised

£22.5 billion from the sale (in early 2000) of licences to operate *third generation* mobile phones.

Central government receipts from sales of assets, running at several billion pounds per year under the former Conservative government prior to 1997, continued under the 1997 Labour government and were planned to continue at that level well beyond 2000/1. Between two-thirds and three-quarters of privatisation receipts were derived from sale of **local government** assets during the late 1990s, revenues from the sale of 2.2 million council houses and flats under the former Conservative governments' *right-to-buy* policy having dwarfed any single public utility privatisation such as British Telecom. The Labour government planned further **local government** privatisations by continuing the Conservatives' later policy of so-called *large scale voluntary transfers* (LSVTs) of council housing to housing associations and other not-for-profit *registered social landlords* (RSLs), these being regulated by the Housing Corporation.

Economic, industrial, social and political restructuring combined to change the politico-economic context of government intervention in general and nationalisation/privatisation in particular. These interactions are highly complex and require much greater and more sophisticated analysis than can be provided in this chapter. However this sketchy analysis serves to illustrate that nationalisation and privatisation occur in political, cultural, social and institutional contexts. It would be oversimplistic to suggest that privatisation is simply an economic phenomenon, resulting from the prescriptions of economic theory. Equally it would be grossly misleading to see the arguments for and against privatisation as purely political. The privatisation debate is subsumed within a complex amalgam of multidisciplinary perspectives.

13.3 The efficiency case for nationalisation

Economic arguments are concerned with the achievement of allocative and X-efficiency (see Chapter 7). These are as follows.

First, to prevent the abuse of monopoly power. For example water, gas and electricity companies could exploit their local or regional monopolies. However it could be argued that the nationalised electricity and gas industries earned monopoly profits immediately prior to privatisation when, at the then Conservative government's behest, they raised prices much more than inflation.

Moreover public sector monopolies may still abuse their monopoly position even if they do not earn abnormal profits from high prices. Excessive costs of production (including management costs) and/or inferior quality of product or service may have much the same impact on market price as monopoly profits. In such cases nationalisation simply changes the form in which monopoly power is made manifest. Abnormally high profits are politically and publicly unacceptable. Unnecessarily high costs are less salient (especially where there is no company with which to make a comparison) and soak up profits.

Some nationalised industries operated partly as social services. In general they did not pursue profit maximisation and provided uniform, universal services at flat-rate prices. For example the cost of posting a letter is the same in remote rural areas as in urban areas, despite the higher cost of providing services in the former. They were often used to maintain employment in economically depressed regions, for example by keeping uneconomic coalmines open in order to provide jobs. However, such social arguments were often used as blanket justifications for subsidy, much of which was required to finance inefficient production methods rather than provide social protection. It was increasingly accepted that social programmes or factors should be separately justified and individually costed. Such an approach would clarify management's responsibility for achieving efficiency and the government's responsibility for social programmes. Whether high profits or high costs, the consumer is exploited in each case. The taxpayer may also be exploited where losses require payment of tax-financed subsidies.

Second, to achieve economies of scale. For example the transmission of electricity through a national grid achieves considerable economies of scale by avoiding duplication of facilities by competitor companies. This provided the economic rationale for the creation of the Central Electricity Board, referred to above. However the achievement of economies of scale requires considerable investment and many of the nationalised industries experienced considerable delays in having investment plans agreed by the government, for example the railways and water and sewerage. During the 1980s the Conservative government became concerned about the implications of new capital equipment for public expenditure (see Chapter 9). Trade unions were also concerned with the implications for jobs (i.e. if investment were to involve capital substitution for labour). Furthermore, even if economies of scale were to be achieved in technical production processes, they do not guarantee lower prices for the consumer.

The resultant cost savings could be soaked up by monopoly profits, by excessive management costs or by over-production of unsaleable output. For example, an excess supply of coal and basic steel during the 1980s led to large stocks being held, which added considerably to the industries' costs. Put simply, economies of scale may be a necessary but not sufficient condition for cost reduction. Such reduction requires the driving force of competition, something which the natural and statutory monopolies lacked.

Third, some industries were nationalised in order to promote national security, a public good (see Chapter 2). In particular steel, shipbuilding and aerospace are important inputs for a country's military capacity for self-defence. Fourth, some industries were nationalised in order to avoid substantial negative externalities, for example radioactive pollution from nuclear energy (though pollution incidents did subsequently occur). Fifth, nationalisation may have been motivated by a desire to benefit particular special-interest groups such as railwaymen, steel workers and miners as well as helping 'the poor' by keeping low the prices of essential services. This is as much an 'economic' as 'social' argument. Sixth, nationalisation may also have been motivated by the rent-seeking activities of public choice theory (see Chapter 7). Of course public choice arguments could also be applied to privatisation (see below).

In general, for nationalisation to occur the industry had to be **both** on the 'commanding heights' of the economy **and** experiencing acute problems in dealing with economic and industrial restructuring. This rationale explained nationalisation of most of the industries listed in **Table 13.1**. Without the limitations of this rationale many other industries could have been nationalised, for example petrochemicals, banking and insurance.

As already noted, nationalisation did not necessarily put an end to labour shedding. Most of the industries experienced large and sustained decreases in employment (British Telecom being a notable exception). However labour shedding was probably at a much slower rate than would have occurred under private ownership (most notably for coalmining). Moreover the improvements in efficiency achieved under nationalisation seemed to do little in terms of reducing the need for government subsidy. As losses rose during the 1960s and 1970s governments became increasingly concerned with the need to control public sector borrowing and levels of taxation for the theoretical reasons outlined in Chapters 4 and 5.

Successive attempts (in White Papers of 1971, 1976 and 1978) to move towards allocatively efficient pricing and investment regimes were unsuccessful. In practice it proved very difficult (if not impossible) to base consumers' retail prices on long-run marginal cost (see Chapters 6 and 14). Some industries had to set prices in response to market forces (e.g. British Airways), some simply could not operationalise long-run marginal cost (e.g. in electricity and gas meter readings) and most found it difficult to derive this cost concept from accounting data.

Although the former Monopolies and Mergers Commission found much to praise when it reviewed the activities of individual nationalised industries during the 1980s, it was highly critical of the industries for their poor management structures, often fairly critical of their methods of financial control, use of manpower and investment appraisal and sometimes critical of their pricing policies. Interference by Ministers in the operations of the industries was not found to be an important problem, suggesting that the 'excessive political interference' argument for privatisation had been overstated (see below).

13.4 The efficiency case for privatisation

The earlier achievements of the nationalised industries were not sustained in the long term and their perceived failings eventually provided the rationale for their privatisation.

First, the lack of competition stifled innovation and ongoing development of the industries, resulting in poor quality services and lack of service. The monopoly position of many of the nationalised industries protected them from competition. For example in the mid 1970s the nationalised industries' share of output in their respective industrial sectors was 94 per cent for communications (postal and telephone), 84 per cent for coal and 77 per cent for gas, electricity and water. Few monopolies are absolute in the sense of having no substitutes. Coal competes with gas, electricity and oil within the energy sector and railways compete with road and air transport services. However their very substantial monopoly positions shielded the nationalised industries from competition within their own markets. For example, it was argued that industry and commerce was being held back by a shortage of capacity in telecommunications due to inadequate investment in new technologies (electronic exchanges and so on).

Second, the lack of a profits incentive for the nationalised industries resulted in excessive costs. Any profits earned by these companies were subject to political criticism as 'exploitation of the consumer' and so there was no incentive to maximise monopoly profits by reducing costs (as distinct from raising prices). One of the conditions for allocative efficiency throughout the economy is that all productive units operate at full X-efficiency (see Chapters 2 and 7). As already noted, the main economic rationale for *nationalisation* was to improve the efficiency of erstwhile private steel, rail, coal and other such companies by financing large-scale investment programmes. The same economic efficiency rationale underpinned *privatisation* of the former publicly owned industries.

Third, control of public expenditure, public sector borrowing and taxation was compromised by their increasingly severe financial and economic problems. Conservative governments of the 1980s and 1990s were committed to cutting public expenditure, taxation and borrowing (see Chapters 9, 10 and 11). Such cuts were being jeopardised by the need to subsidise loss-making nationalised industries, particularly coal mining and nuclear power. Nevertheless, ongoing subsidies continued to be paid in respect of train services and the nuclear industry after privatisation and a one-off subsidy was paid to the privatised coal mines in 2000 in order to save coal pits from closure.

Fourth, there was increasing emphasis on supply-side measures, efficient nationalised industries being crucial for the efficiency of the rest of the economy, much more so than their demand-side impacts on employment and so on, (see Chapter 8). However, constraints on public expenditure, taxation and borrowing meant that the nationalised industries were being starved of finance for the major investment programmes they needed to undertake to maintain efficiency. The need for large-scale investment was instrumental in the British Telecom, water and rail privatisations. Except for water and rail, the other privatised utilities absorbed the cost of those capital expenditures through efficiency savings, regulation requiring reductions in prices.

Fifth, growing scepticism of the efficacy of government intervention also served to question the rationale for nationalisation. After three or four decades of government control the nationalised industries were clearly not as efficient and effective as they could be in terms of either cost control or quality of service. This was increasingly seen as the inevitable result of short-term political interventions in the running of the industries.

In combination, these arguments provided a strong rationale for privatisation. That rationale was subsequently endorsed by the 1997 Labour government which, as already noted, introduced its own proposals for further privatisations. However, critics of privatisation argued that the nationalised industries were efficient in terms broader than simply profit maximisation and/or could easily be made as profitable as their privatised counterparts. In practice, it is very difficult to determine which is the most efficient form, nationalisation or privatisation.

13.5   Comparing efficiency under nationalisation and privatisation

In principle it is possible to assess the relative efficiency of the nationalised industries by comparing their returns on capital employed with those achieved by private sector companies. There are, however, a number of methodological difficulties in making such a comparison.

First, differences in risk. The natural or statutory monopoly positions of many of the nationalised industries served to reduce the economic risks faced by them. In many cases their markets were virtually guaranteed: for example the former Central Electricity Generating Board was virtually the only seller of electricity and the British Gas Corporation had a statutory monopoly for domestic mains gas supplies. Such predictable markets served to reduce risk. Hence a lower risk-premium was required within the return on capital employed for nationalised industries than for private sector companies.

Second, lack of monopoly profits. The economic theory of the firm assumes profit maximisation. Hence the return on capital employed would necessarily be less for nationalised industries (which were not allowed to maximise profits) than for private monopoly companies. In practice, even private sector firms may not maximise profits, for example if they are satisficers earning only a satisfactory level of profits. However the threat of takeover by more profit-oriented firms can be expected to limit such deviations from the profit maximisation objective by private sector companies.

Third, lack of comparable private sector companies. In practice there were no private monopoly companies that could legitimately have been compared with British Coal, the Central Electricity Generating Board, British Rail and so on. Comparing them (individually or jointly) with the average rate of return on capital employed achieved by private sector manufacturing is methodologically suspect since many of the nationalised industries were in the primary (i.e. extractive) and tertiary (i.e. service) sectors rather than in the secondary (i.e. manufacturing) sector. Some limited public–private comparisons were possible when there was direct competition between public and private sector enterprises. For example an early 1980s study found higher costs for the public sector cross-channel ferry company (Sealink) than for one of its rival private sector companies (European Ferries). Similar results were found for airlines and for gas and electricity appliance retailing. However it would be invalid to generalise such findings for specific activities across the whole range of nationalised industries' outputs.

Fourth, lack of standardised accounting methods. Valid comparison of returns on capital employed requires standardisation in the measurement and valuation of capital and revenues. It would be methodologically invalid simply to compare profit levels as reported in the annual reports of public and private companies. Capital employed can be measured in various ways, the main option being the choice between *current cost accounting* and *historic cost accounting*. Inflation serves to reduce the real value of the historic cost of capital equipment whilst raising nominal prices for the outputs currently produced by that plant and machinery. Hence nominal profits will be both larger and earned sooner than if capital equipment is revalued (upwards) each year according to its current *replacement cost*. In essence historic cost accounting serves to increase reported profits (or reduce reported losses), whilst current cost accounting reduces reported profits (or increases reported losses). Hence there was an incentive for nationalised industries earning high levels of profits to use current cost accounting, whilst those incurring losses could use historic cost accounting. Different accounting methodologies both between the public and private sectors and amongst the nationalised industries themselves served to qualify any straightforward comparisons of efficiency as measured by the return on capital employed.

Fifth, use of nationalised industries as macroeconomic instruments. The nationalised industries accounted for almost a fifth of fixed investment (gross domestic fixed capital formation), just over a tenth of national output and a twelfth of employment during the 1970s. Hence they were used for macroeconomic purposes. For example they were sometimes required by central government to accelerate or slow down their investment programmes as part of the management of aggregate demand. They were also sometimes required to restrict increases in their prices to below the levels required to cover rising costs, for example during periods of prices and incomes policy in the early 1970s.

Finally, social functions. Many of the nationalised industries undertook social as well as economic functions, for example in supplying services to remote or sparsely populated rural areas where market potential was too limited for private companies. Such loss-making services (financed by cross-subsidy from more profitable outputs) served to reduce returns on capital employed compared with those earned by private companies. In principle it would be possible to take account of the extra costs of such social functions in order to compare like with like. In practice, such functions were not separately costed and so accurate comparisons were not possible.

Given these methodological problems, it proved extremely difficult to make accurate comparisons of the economic efficiency of the nationalised industries relative to private companies. Many of the nationalised industries did earn profits in most years, at least before account was taken of interest payments on outstanding debt and any liability for corporation tax. However Treasury figures showed that their real rate of return on capital employed had generally been well below that of private industry, and debt charges were often so large that they turned operating profits into accounting losses. Unlike private companies, the nationalised industries could not finance their investment programmes by issuing equity. With very limited exceptions, they had to borrow funds from central government in order to finance that part of their investment programmes which was not financed from internal sources. The subsequent interest charges were unavoidable. Private companies are not so highly geared towards debt and can reduce dividends paid to shareholders during periods of low operating profits.

In more general terms, social and political objectives serve to qualify the economic definition of efficiency. The return on capital employed became only one (and perhaps not the most important) component of efficiency. The political economy context within which the nationalised industries operated meant that, in practice, much broader concepts of efficiency overrode the narrower concept of X-efficiency. Social and allocative efficiency clearly encompass a much broader range of factors than simply the return on capital employed for a particular monopoly company. For example, if prices rise due to (public) inefficiency, social gains to employees are at the expense of losses to customers.

The use of the nationalised industries as instruments for the pursuit of social and political (as well as economic) objectives created particularly profound problems when comparing them with private companies. Given such overwhelming methodological problems, comparison of the rates of return on capital employed achieved by the nationalised industries with those of private companies was at best subject to severe qualification and at worst grossly misleading.

Other partial measures are possible, most notably **productivity**. This is usually measured in terms of output per person employed. Again, however, there are difficulties in that it is generally not possible to compare the output of different companies in physical terms (e.g. cars and coal), so a financial measure has to be employed. The financial value of a company's output depends upon both volume and price. Many of the nationalised industries could have used their monopoly positions to raise prices and therefore productivity, as many were required to do during the run-up to privatisation in the 1980s, most spectacularly electricity and gas.

Nonetheless, despite such methodological problems the general picture was one of relative inefficiency. That inefficiency was not judged in terms of the **historic** situation (i.e. compared with the situation when the industries were privately-owned). Nor was it judged in terms of **comparable** private companies (since they were few and far between). Instead it was judged in terms of the **potential** improvements in efficiency when stimulated by a more competitive environment. Both theory and evidence suggest that the most important influence on economic performance is competition, not which sector (public or private) owns the enterprise. Hence, whether on the basis of theory or of empirical evidence, to conclude that the nationalised industries were inefficient because of lack of competition does **not** lead to a subsequent conclusion that privatisation is an economic panacea. Transformation of a public monopoly into a private monopoly does not change competitive conditions and so cannot be validated by the theory of perfect competition.

In fact a rapid improvement in productivity for the industries remaining nationalised during the 1980s (e.g. the Post Office) was charted by the Treasury. Previously less than that for manufacturing and for the whole economy prior to 1981, the then remaining nationalised industries' productivity rose so rapidly thereafter that it exceeded both of the other two measures by the mid 1980s (even though they were also rising). The rise in the productivity of the then remaining nationalised industries was achieved by reductions in their labour forces whilst simultaneously increasing output. Previously the nationalised industries were generally considered as having substantial levels of over-manning. This was possibly the outcome of central governments' earlier commitment to full employment and use of the industries for social as well as economic functions.

Nevertheless the efficiency case for privatisation rests simply on the assertion that privatisation makes markets more competitive or **contestable**. In fact it is not evident that privatisation does stimulate competition. The degree of competition engendered by privatisation is crucially dependent on the **form of privatisation** and the **market restructuring** with which it is associated. As already noted, the transfer of a monopoly company from the public to the private sector does nothing to stimulate competition since it has no effect on market structure. Much criticism was made of the initial privatisation measures, which left the monopoly positions of British Telecom and British Gas virtually untouched.

The rapid improvement in the nationalised industries' economic and financial performance, both before and after privatisation, led to claims that privatisation was unnecessary since such improvements could have been achieved by changes in government objectives and management practices. Improved trading performance could certainly have been achieved in this respect. However retention of public sector ownership would still have restricted competition and removed the threat of bankruptcy. It would have been inconceivable for a government to allow one of the major nationalised industries to become insolvent and cease trading. The impact on the wider economy would have been too severe. However, much the same could be said of the arrangements for regulation of the same industries subsequent to privatisation. In fact such an outcome would be most unlikely for a statutory or regulated monopoly since it could always raise its prices with relative impunity.

Despite criticism that privatisation was usually merely transforming public sector monopoly into private sector monopoly with no change in market conditions, both the potential and actual effect of privatisation is much more far-reaching. The effect of privatisation is not simply dependent on the structure of the industry at the time of sale. Competition may not be increased overnight, but over the longer term industrial restructuring and technological change may make markets much more contestable and so create a spur towards increased efficiency. Telecommunications is a case in point, British Telecom now facing strong competition from mobile phone companies and others. The initial criticism that privatisation did nothing other than change ownership of property rights failed to recognise the dynamic nature of privatisation, and instead analysed it in a very short-term, static framework. The effect of privatisation is dependent on the form of privatisation, on the (changing) form of regulation and on the development of technology and associated market structures.

13.6 Forms of privatisation

Privatisation is most commonly thought of in terms of denationalisation, that is the sale of state-owned industries. This perception arises because of the public prominence of the initial privatisation measures involving the sale of British Telecom, British Gas and other companies or enterprises (see **Table 13.1**). However the term 'privatisation' has become much more widely used over time, also being used to categorise the increasing use of user charges for public sector outputs and even the Private Finance Initiative (see Chapter 8). There are three main forms of privatisation.

Sale of state-owned assets to the private sector

This includes not just the sale of former public utilities such as British Gas and British Telecom (i.e. denationalisation) but also the sale of government shareholdings in British Petroleum, the sale of council houses by local government and the sale of surplus land and buildings by hospital trusts, former water boards, the Ministry of Defence and so on. Sale of companies can take four forms:

1. **Public flotation on the Stock Exchange**, share prices either being fixed in advance of sale (e.g. as for British Telecom and British Gas) or tenders being invited. In the latter case, potential purchasers offer to buy at prices specified by themselves (e.g. as for Britoil and Enterprise Oil).
2. **A trade sale**, where the company is sold to a single firm or consortium (e.g. as for BR Hotels and Sealink).
3. **Placing the company with a group of investors**. This approach was attempted for the electricity supply industry, but subsequently abandoned due to lack of interest.
4. **A management or employee buyout**, (e.g. as for the National Freight Consortium).

Some privatisations used a mix of approaches. For example a combination of offers and tenders was used for Cable and Wireless and Associated British Ports. British Rail was sold using trade sales for the rolling stock companies and a public sale of Railtrack. In general small companies were sold by means of trade sales where capacity for trade purchase existed and where such a sale would not lead to a significant accumulation of market power. Former public utilities were sold through the offer of shares at fixed prices.

Liberalisation

Markets can be liberalised by dissolving former statutory monopolies so as to allow freedom of entry for competitors. Examples include deregulation of road passenger transport, less strict licensing for operators of long-distance coaches and local bus services, and allowing other companies to start operations in telecommunications, electricity generation and in supply of gas to households.

Encouraging private sector provision of public services

This can be achieved in two ways:

1. **Franchising**, that is, selling the right to supply a regulated market whose product generates revenue, for example the provision of scheduled rail passenger services on the separately owned railtrack network. The contract will generally go to the **highest** bidder and/or the bidder who promises the best quality of service.
2. **Contracting out** to private companies the provision of public services that do not generate their own revenue and were previously internally produced, for example the collection and disposal of domestic refuse. The contract will generally go to the **lowest** bidder, that is, the company that requires the lowest payment to provide the service to a given quantity and quality of output (see Chapter 15).

Both franchising and contracting out retain the monopoly nature of services in that there is no competition for market share **within** the service. Instead they generate competition **for** the monopoly as an alternative means of achieving cost reductions. Both approaches confer monopoly rights for a limited period only.

These three forms of privatisation can be pursued simultaneously and independently of each other. For example the sale of state-owned assets is not a necessary precondition for liberalisation and neither of these is a prerequisite for contracting out. Some forms of privatisation involve neither the sale of public sector assets (i.e. liberalisation) nor the withdrawal of the public sector from any of its activities (i.e. leasing and contracting out).

The rationale for, and ultimate outcomes of, these three forms of privatisation (together with the effects of any associated regulation) could be analysed in terms of the rent-seeking assumptions of public choice theory (see Chapter 7). In particular it has already become clear that the four forms of sale described above have the potential to benefit particular groups of purchasers. These groups could be expected to apply political pressure in support of privatisation. Much the same could be said for liberalisation, franchising and contracting out.

It is generally agreed that **liberalisation** (i.e. reductions in barriers to market entry) increase competition simply by increasing the number of *actual or potential* suppliers. However new entrants may engage in *cream skimming*, producing highly profitable outputs whilst leaving unprofitable services to the public sector. The loss of ability of the nationalised or privatised industry to cross-subsidise from profitable to unprofitable services could lead to the closure of loss-making services, especially as the true subsidy cost would be made both explicit and visible rather than hidden in the industry's accounts. Of course this serves to question why the unprofitable (presumably social) services should be undertaken at all and, if so, whether they should be financed by the consumers of the industry's profitable services rather than by general taxpayers. The Conservative and Labour governments' commitment to a universal letter postal service with flat-rate prices for first and second class mail delivery clearly requires cross-subsidisation between different parts of the country.

The extent to which the other forms of privatisation actually increase competition, and therefore efficiency, depends on the precise conditions in each area or sector. For example the **sale of former state shareholdings** in companies such as British Petroleum did little to increase competition, simply because it already operated in a competitive market and no deficit guarantee was provided by the government. The **sale of state-owned assets** such as British Airways, British Rail hotels and public sector ferry companies was expected to increase efficiency by reintroducing (or increasing) the possibility of bankruptcy, so spurring the companies to search for more cost-effective strategies. This assumed that market structure was already competitive and that privatisation would not subsequently lead to a concentration of market power. However government intervention in the markets for land and housing (e.g. through planning and rent controls) have been so pervasive that there may have been little net effect on competition as a result of the **sale of land and council houses**.

Encouraging private provision through **contracting out** the provision of public services does not necessarily lead to increased competition and increased efficiency. In particular the past use of non-competitive, cost-plus contracting for defence items was found to lead to unnecessarily high costs. Even where contracting is made competitive, as in the case of certain local government and hospital services, there may be little competition in terms of the number of companies actually bidding for contracts (see Chapter 15).

Hence whilst generally categorised as a supply-side policy, privatisation will not necessarily make supply more responsive (elastic) and therefore will not necessarily stimulate greater competitiveness. Therefore the economic case for privatisation cannot be taken for granted since the implications for efficiency depend on the consequent and subsequent changes in market conditions, if any. It depends crucially upon:

- **The initial form of privatisation**, i.e. liberalisation, sale of state-owned assets or the encouragement of private sector provision of public services.
- **The initial industrial structure consequent upon privatisation**, i.e. whether the monopoly powers of the former nationalised industries are retained or deconstructed.
- **The initial form of regulation** in controlling any remaining monopoly power.
- **Subsequent market restructuring**, e.g. because of technological, regulatory, or market changes.

An unquestioning acceptance of privatisation as a desirable policy measure (as an end in itself) can only be ideologically-driven or justified on much broader moralistic and constitutional criteria relating to the role of government in society. In fact, by allowing the public sector to continue to produce a service if it submitted the lowest bid under the former compulsory competitive tendering regime, the then Conservative government clearly accepted the principle that **it is competition rather than ownership that provides the spur to increased efficiency**. It explicitly accepted that the public sector is not necessarily less efficient than the private sector (see Chapter 15).

13.7   Privatisation and industry structure

The sale of major public utilities such as British Telecom and British Gas was criticised for simply transferring monopoly power from the public to the private sector. In particular the then Conservative government was accused of justifying privatisation in terms of seeking to create greater competition and efficiency and yet creating private monopoly companies that could maximise their profit potential and so maximise the revenues from privatisation. For example the Treasury believed that the sale of British Telecom as a single company would raise more revenue than the sale of its individual parts. In other words it put greater privatisation revenues before greater efficiency.

The benefits of higher privatisation receipts were immediately obvious. They helped the government achieve its stated objectives of controlling public sector borrowing and/or reducing (or avoiding the need for higher levels of) taxation. The benefits of greater competition are less immediately obvious, more diffuse and of much longer time scale. Hence British Telecom and British Gas were sold as single entities in order to maximise privatisation receipts. Although telecommunications was partially liberalised, by allowing a second company (Mercury) to start operations, the immediate impact was extremely small in terms of market penetration.

However, these asset sales were amongst the first acts of privatisation, were by far the largest in value terms and were a severe test of privatisation policy. In effect the sale of these public utilities had to be made so attractive that the policy could be heralded as a success and provide a pragmatic justification for the privatisation programme to continue. The Conservative government also claimed that it did not have the financial data necessary to differentiate the various operations of British Telecom if they were to be sold separately. Privatisation as a policy had to evolve and change, adapting to a learning curve of political, social and economic experiences.

The Conservative government began to pay more attention to competition as it became more confident of the financial and political success of its privatisation programme, of the capacity of the private financial markets to absorb such large sales and of the irreversibility of the programme by any future Labour government. The emphasis on creating competitive market structures upon privatisation increased over successive privatisations. For example, unlike the earlier privatisations of British Telecom and British Gas, the Central Electricity Generating Board for England and Wales was not sold as a single entity but instead was split into three competing generator companies (National Power, PowerGen and Nuclear Electric) and one transmission company (the National Grid Company) responsible for the transmission of high voltage supplies. The 12 area boards that distributed retail electricity were privatised as 12 regional electricity companies (RECs). The RECs originally did not compete directly with each other since they were given regional monopolies in retailing electricity purchased wholesale from the generators. However comparisons of relative performance afforded some scope for *yardstick competition* (see Chapter 14).

At the time of the RECs' privatisation, the three electricity production companies generated electricity from coal, oil and nuclear power. However many of the RECs subsequently built their own gas-fired power stations so that the degree of competition increased over time.

Competition was further enhanced as the fully integrated production and distribution companies in Scotland began seeking market share in England and also when Nuclear Electric and Scottish Nuclear were privatised in 1996 as British Energy (see **Table 13.1**). Likewise, the electricity retailers are now offering to supply gas and the gas retailers are offering to supply electricity. This restructuring of the gas and electricity markets led to OFFER and OFGAS being merged into OFGEM, the Office of Gas and Electricity Markets (see below).

Privatisation of British Railways separated the suppliers of scheduled passenger and freight services (franchised train operating companies) from the rail network. Although simple in terms of principle, the structure created by privatisation (and consequently its regulation) is very complex. Railtrack was set up prior to its privatisation in 1996. It owns the stations, track and signalling systems and levies access charges on the train operating companies, these charges being controlled by the Rail Regulator. Nevertheless, it continues to receive government subsidy (capital grants of between £1 billion and £2 billion a year) to finance investment in the rail network, partly because of the sharp growth in the number of trains using the network. The 25 train operating companies were privatised sequentially between 1995 and 1997. They own franchises to operate passenger services and continue to receive operating subsidies, though these are diminishing over time. Only four franchises are held singly, 21 being held by 6 companies with one company holding 9 franchises in late 2000. Passenger carriages, freight wagons and engines were sold to 3 rolling stock leasing companies in 1996/7. There are also separate rail freight operators, freight grants continuing to be paid to encourage a shift of freight from road to rail.

The 1997 Labour government created the shadow Strategic Rail Authority (SRA) in 2000 (see notes to **Table 13.2**). It replaced the Office of Passenger Rail Franchising and British Railways Board and has a remit to develop the network as part of an integrated transport policy at a time of rising rail passenger numbers. The SRA gains extra powers to deal with concerns about poor quality of service (particularly reliability, punctuality, overcrowding and safety), operational fragmentation (e.g. lack of through-ticketing and co-ordinated services) and sharply rising fares (half of companies having increased their fares by more than inflation between 1995 and 1999 – see **Table 13.2** below). The Labour government wants the 25 train operating companies ultimately to be owned by just a few large holding companies as a means of stimulating investment in passenger services and rolling stock. Hence, the SRA intends to replace all short-term franchises with fewer long-term franchises requiring higher standards of service and profit sharing. Franchises vary between 5 and 15 years, most being for 7 years and expiring in 2004.

The complicated privatisation structures for the electricity supply industry and for rail services contrasted sharply with that for British Gas and British Telecom, where the single unified privatised company format was followed. However there has been an increasing element of liberalisation in the gas and telecommunications industries. Only Mercury was allowed market entry to compete with BT at the time of privatisation. Since then, however, the scope for market entry has been massively increased by new technologies using radio, satellite and cable as well as the wired means of transmission. Development of a single digital data transmission network (the 'information superhighway') will increase the scope for competition amongst operators, not just in telecommunications but also in broadcasting, publishing and computing. The Labour government intends BT's local loop to be opened for use by other service providers in 2001. This will allow rival operators to install their own equipment in BT exchanges and pay a fee on the same terms as for BT's own use.

Likewise, liberalisation of the gas market followed privatisation of British Gas as a single company. The only restructuring that took place initially was that the former British Gas Corporation was forced to sell its offshore and onshore oil fields, Enterprise Oil and the Wytch Farm operations respectively. British Gas subsequently lost its statutory protection as the sole authorised gas utility and was later required to separate its transmission business (now called 'Transco') from its other activities (still operating under 'British Gas'). It also lost its exclusive right to supply gas through the pipe network and lost its monopoly for supply to domestic users. It already faced competition from other companies for industrial and commercial customers.

If competition and efficiency is to be increased as far as possible for such national network industries, privatisation or subsequent liberalisation should ideally create a **separate national grid company** selling transmission services to competing production companies who use the network to supply retail distribution companies. A single transmission company can be justified in terms of economies of scale, avoiding unnecessary duplication of infrastructure. Given its natural monopoly position, such a company would have to be subject to regulatory control. However, regulation of production companies would not be necessary if there was a high degree of competition to supply the network.

As already noted, separate transmission companies owning the national grids for electricity and for gas were set up after privatisation. Power stations generally display constant (rather than increasing) returns to scale and so replication of many separately owned production facilities creates considerable potential for competition. In this sense privatisation of the electricity supply industry was not radical enough in only creating a few production companies. Much the same can be said for production of natural gas. The separation of production and transmission (referred to as *'unbundling'*) facilitated liberalisation of these three industries. However it was not thought suitable for water and sewerage since these services are generally organised on the basis of water catchment areas, there being no national pipeline transmission network (but see Chapter 14).

13.8 The rationale for regulation

Regulation refers to the direct control by the government of an industry's structure, conduct and/or performance. It usually requires a free-standing regulatory body that, formally at least, operates independently of politicians but within a policy framework and regulatory system determined by the national government. This form of state intervention is usually confined to cases of gross market failure that are not amenable to anti-trust (i.e. anti-monopoly) legislation, namely cases of natural monopoly and chronic market instability. It is the chosen form of intervention where nationalisation is eschewed.

Although it may be thought of as a post-privatisation development, direct regulatory intervention was used for the UK steel industry for 15 years prior to its renationalisation in 1967. There are also regulatory agencies of the banking and financial sectors, of the National Lottery, of public sector rental housing, of school education, of the press and broadcasting, of employment (health and safety, equal opportunities and so on), of pharmaceutical prices and of the environment (see Chapter 14). Commercial, consumer and other UK business laws are, of course, examples of indirect regulatory intervention. However the rapid growth of regulatory institutions consequent upon denationalisation of the former public utility industries is a new development simply because of its sheer scale. Other countries have considerable experience of regulation, most notably the USA, but the UK only began to accumulate significant regulatory experience during the late 1980s and 1990s. Regulation is concerned with the following.

Preventing abnormal or monopoly profits

Monopoly profits can be earned by electricity, gas and water and sewerage companies with local, regional or national monopolies. Such companies could seek to restrict their output and so drive up market price and profits. This is particularly effective if the demand for their outputs is highly insensitive to increased prices (i.e. is highly price inelastic). Such exploitation causes particularly severe inequities if expenditure on their outputs forms a much higher proportion of the budgets of low-income than of high-income households, as is generally the case for energy and water (see Chapter 10).

The usual approach in other countries has been to control the **rate of return on capital employed**. This method therefore controls the *relative* rather than *absolute* level of profits. Its main disadvantage is that companies can increase the absolute level of profits by expanding the capital base upon which rates of return are assessed. They will have an incentive to substitute capital for labour since the latter does not augment the base used to assess company profitability. Hence regulation may prevent the attainment of a cost-minimising mix of factors of production and so lead to **X-inefficiency** for the regulated company (see Chapter 7) and **allocative inefficiency** for the economy (since the marginal rates of transformation of any two factors of production will not be equalised, see Chapter 2).

Preventing market instability

Stability of supply is deemed necessary for the energy and water industries, for example, because continuous availability of these services is an essential input for the economic, social and physical infrastructure and underpins the standard of living. Hence the regulator has to protect the companies (in order to promote allocative efficiency) as well as their consumers. Like privatisation, regulation does not necessarily guarantee allocative efficiency because:

- **It may simply guarantee survival of inefficient companies** and so lead to ossification of the regulated industry, particularly in terms of a lack of technological development and innovation.
- **Regulation itself uses factors of production**, which themselves have an opportunity cost.
- **Public choice theory** suggests that regulatory officials will have a self-interest in expanding the regulatory regime beyond that which is strictly necessary for efficiency purposes (see Chapter 7).
- **The regulatory body may be 'captured' by the regulated industry**. For example regulatory officials may become too sympathetic towards the industry or be implicitly or explicitly bribed with the prospect of higher paid jobs with the regulated company as long as they deal leniently with it in the interim period.
- **Regulatory officials may not be free of government influence and pressures**, particularly where their decisions have political consequences and because they are dependent on the government for renewal of their contracts, for approval of their budgets and so on.

Hence the possibility of **regulatory failure** cannot be ignored. Regulation can only be justified in efficiency terms if it leads to a net improvement in allocative efficiency. It has to be compared with the possibility (and potential degree) of **state failure** (caused by political interference in the operations of nationalised industries) and **market failure**. If state and regulatory failure are each of greater magnitude (i.e. more distortionary) than market failure, then such forms of government intervention cannot be justified. Since the relative degree of regulatory, state and market failure is an empirical question that cannot be answered, there is a *prima facie* case for:

- **The restriction of direct regulation to the most gross forms of market failure**, namely the natural monopolies providing national transmission and network systems. Direct regulation is not necessary where a reasonable degree of competition already exists or where the indirect regulation provided by the Competition Commission is thought to be sufficient. Hence not all privatised undertakings have been subject to direct regulatory control (compare **Tables 13.1** and **13.2**).
- **The progressive encouragement and facilitation of liberalisation**. This would ensure that regulation does not result in structural ossification of the industry.

13.9   Alternative forms of regulation

There are two main forms of regulatory control, each with a number of advantages and disadvantages:

Rate of return control

The perceived advantage of rate of return regulation is that it is fair in preventing the exploitation of customers by a company with monopoly power. However monopoly profits may also be dissipated by unnecessarily high costs such that there is no benefit to consumers in the form of lower prices, nor to the economy in terms of lower costs. The main disadvantages are:

- **The lack of incentive to reduce costs**, since any increased profits would lead to the company breaching its rate of return ceiling with the result that prices would have to be reduced.
- **The bias towards capital-intensive production methods**, since this expands the 'rate base' (i.e. the value of capital employed) against which the rate of return is measured and so allows a higher absolute level of profits for a given relative rate of return.
- **The extremely detailed nature of regulation** in terms of defining the rate base and monitoring the rates of return actually achieved.

Price control

This involves setting a maximum price ('price cap'), either **individual price caps** set on each individual output, or **a tariff-basket price cap**, a ceiling being set on the average of prices for a specified range ('basket') of services.

Individual price caps provide more guarantees for consumers in controlling the prices of individual services; the tariff basket price cap cannot do this. However individual price caps are more complex to administer. They require much greater information about the costs of individual services and become out of date more quickly as service-specific costs change. They may also restrict the actions of companies in terms of their ability to rebalance costs and tariffs or respond to market developments. Put simply, individual price caps lack the basic simplicity of the tariff basket price cap. However a tariff basket price cap allows the regulated company to alter its relative prices as it wishes. It may afford the company too much freedom to manipulate prices.

Essentially, the advantages of price control are that it avoids the disadvantages of rates of return control:

- **Companies face incentives to reduce costs** because they retain any profits arising from improved internal efficiency.
- **There is no bias towards capital investment** since there is no rate base against which rates of return are judged.
- **A price cap is simple to administer**, market prices being much more salient than costs of production.

However, price control has a number of disadvantages:

- **The maximum price may become the minimum price**. In other words, the regulated company may view the maximum price as a right and fully exploit the price cap.
- **It creates considerable uncertainty regarding the actual outcome of regulation**. Uncertainty becomes greater the longer the price cap is in place. Profit levels could be much higher or much lower than those envisaged when the price cap was set, depending on changes in both costs and volume of sales.
- **Quality and universality of service may be reduced**, contrary to public policy objectives, because the price cap creates a great incentive to reduce costs (in facilitating increased profits).

In practice, however, the control of prices or of rate of return may not be radically different and so may not have clearly distinct advantages and disadvantages. Whilst the price cap regime does not consider rate base and rates of return explicitly, these concepts are implicit in the price cap actually set. The regulator must ensure continuity of supply and therefore must allow regulated companies to earn sufficient returns to encourage them to remain in the industry. In more formal terms, their profits must at least match their *transfer earnings*. That is, they must cover the *opportunity costs* of their factors of production, their earnings in their next best alternative use (see Chapter 4).

Rate of return and price control methodologies will be more similar:

- **The shorter the time period** over which any set of regulatory rules are applicable, an annual price cap for individual services being little different from rate of return control; and
- **The greater the propensity of the regulator to 'claw back' any unwarranted and unforeseen increases in profits**, since this will reduce incentives towards increased efficiency through cost reductions.

13.10 Regulatory philosophy in the UK

Regulation in other countries typically involves detailed control of company operations, for example specifying maximum prices, influencing the capital intensity of the mix of factors of production, in requiring a mass of detail about the companies' cost structures and revenues, and so on. In the UK regulatory regime there is no direct control of profits whatsoever, only indirect control of prices.

In the UK culture, specifying exactly how a company should behave is too restrictive in that it is likely to stifle increased competition, innovation and product development, the very supply-side objectives of privatisation. It may also be too prescriptive for a government that is seeking to distance itself from paternalism, dependency cultures and intervention generally. Regulatory arrangements should be cost effective, able to accommodate changes in technology and market structure, and yet maintain the basic financial health of the company.

Hence the UK system of regulation is based upon 'lightness of touch'. Regulation does not have to be totally intrusive into company operations. Instead it has been based upon a much broader approach in terms of creating incentives that will motivate companies to operate in ways that satisfy the regulators' objectives. This recognises that neither the government nor its regulators have sufficient business acumen to take decision-making away from the regulated companies. Regulation should therefore avoid attempting to 'fine tune' the industry and instead allow as much commercial freedom as is consistent with the achievement of public policy objectives.

In the words of the director general of telecommunications, 'regulation is a second-best alternative: wherever possible competition should be preferred as the means of preventing a company from earning excessive profits or otherwise exploiting its customers . . . regulation should, so far as possible, seek to mimic the pressures of a competitive market [and] be widely accepted as fair' (DGT, 1988, pp. 2–3). The latter qualification suggests that the 'random stewardship' of the competitive market may not always be acceptable and therefore implies some degree of social regulation, as distinct from economic regulation. Social regulation is usually subsumed within the arrangements for economic regulation. It typically involves protection of 'vulnerable' groups of consumers, such as those with low incomes, the elderly or disabled (see Chapter 14).

As noted in the second quotation at the start of this chapter, the 1997 Labour government sought to strengthen the regulation of the utilities so that consumers would get more of a share of profits through lower prices. The profits of the regulated utilities had been much greater than expected by their regulators when setting price caps, even though prices fell in real terms for telecommunications, gas and electricity. Regulators were criticised in the media and elsewhere for being too lenient and primarily benefiting the industries and their shareholders. Regulatory regimes were subsequently made harder on the companies, the regulators being given a primary responsibility to promote the interests of and protect consumers, becoming consumer champions as well as promoting competition (see below and Chapter 14). In effect, the Labour government intends regulation to achieve a more acceptable balance between economic efficiency and consumer protection, ensuring a reasonable distribution of gains from increased efficiency.

13.11   The form of regulation in the UK: RPI minus X

The UK's price cap regime takes the form of RPI minus X (conventionally written as RPI − X). This was the prototype first developed for British Telecom and subsequently modified for gas, and for water and sewerage (see **Table 13.2**). RPI refers to the percentage rate of inflation as measured by the retail prices index. X refers to a percentage **efficiency factor** set by the regulatory body over the period the price cap is in force.

It is clear from this very simple formula that the price cap is set in real terms and that the negative X efficiency factor requires **real** prices to fall over time. For example, if over the course of a year inflation is 5 per cent (i.e. RPI = 5) and X is fixed at 3 per cent (X = 3), then the maximum price increase in that year is 2 per cent. Whilst the **real** price falls by a constant percentage amount each year (i.e. by X), the **nominal** price change in any one year is dependent on the relative values of the RPI and X. In the above example, if inflation fell to 2 per cent then the **nominal** price would fall by 1 per cent. Regulated companies do not have to increase prices by the full amount of the resulting figure if it is positive. However they **must** reduce prices by the full amount if the resulting figure is negative.

Table 13.2   Regulatory bodies and formulae

Regulatory body	Company/industry	Regulatory formula*	
OFGEM	Electricity	RPI − X	see note 1
OFGEM	British Gas	RPI − X + Y	see note 2
OFTEL	British Telecom	RPI − X	see note 3
OFWAT	Water	RPI + K	see note 4
ORR	Rail services	RPI − X	see note 5

Notes:

* RPI refers to the retail prices index. X is the efficiency factor. RPI − X denotes RPI minus X.

1. OFGEM, the Office of Gas and Electricity Markets was created by merger of the Office of Electricity Regulation (OFFER) and the Office of Gas (OFGAS). The merger reflected market restructuring as gas and electricity companies now compete in offering both fuels to consumers. Separate values of X are set for each company in the various parts of the UK.

2. Separate values of X are set for British Gas Trading and for Transco. Y originally provided for full cost pass-through of wholesale gas purchase costs to retail customers. The allowable cost pass-through was indexed to a gas price index in 1992 and subject to a 1 per cent reduction each year to provide an efficiency incentive. Cost pass-through was also allowed for energy efficiency schemes.

3. Office of Telecommunications. The value of X increased in stages from 3 in 1984 to 7.5 in 1993 but then was subsequently cut to 4.5 for the period 1997–2001.

4. Office of Water Services. K is effectively X + Q, where Q reflects the costs of meeting the improved quality standards required by UK and EC legislation. K therefore provides cost pass-through for capital programmes (see Chapter 14).

5. Office of Rail Regulation. ORR's responsibilities overlapped with those of the Office of Passenger Rail Franchising (OPRAF). This led to confusion about their respective roles and so the 1997 Labour government established the 'shadow' Strategic Rail Authority (SRA) for the management of passenger rail franchises and the administration of subsidy for passenger services. It will also support integrated transport initiatives, including freight. The SRA is **not** an independent regulator: it is guided by Ministers. The ORR **is** independent in the same way as OFGEM and so on. Only train companies operating within a 50 mile radius of London have their fares controlled. Fare increases are restricted to RPI minus 1 per cent but control has to be relaxed if the companies demonstrate they have improved reliability and punctuality. In practice, whilst some companies' fares have fallen in real terms others have risen by 2 per cent above inflation. Many popular fares such as APEX, cheap day singles and returns are set entirely at the discretion of individual train operators and have complex and varying conditions attached to them (see Chapter 6).

RPI − X applies to a range of specified services, rather than to a single product. It is therefore a **tariff basket** type of price cap. This is an aggregate price cap applicable to the generality of regulated services, rather than there being an individual price cap for each specific regulated service provided by a particular company. The services allocated to the basket are those which are thought to be most in need of regulatory control; that is, where possible abuses of monopoly power are thought most likely. In the case of British Telecom, for example, price control was limited to essential network services relating to business and residential line rentals and directly dialled local and national (i.e. long distance) calls. The director general of telecommunications can seek a licence to bring other services into the regulated basket if their prices seem to reflect an abuse of monopoly power. Likewise progressive liberalisation leading to the development of effective competition ultimately allows individual services to be taken out of the basket as competition from Mercury and other newly evolving telecommunications companies increases (e.g. price controls on international calls were relaxed in 1999).

Such a minimalist approach has generally been adopted for the other regulatory regimes. For example, OFGEM expects rapidly developing competition in electricity and gas retailing to domestic consumers to enable removal of their respective price caps in 2001 or shortly thereafter. As already noted, electricity and gas are now offered by gas and electricity retailers respectively. However, the 1997 Labour government expressed concern that, despite liberalisation, 80 per cent of customers had remained with their original supplier two years after these markets were progressively opened to competition in the late 1990s. This may be because customers are confused by complicated bill options. Charges per kilowatt hour vary in terms of whether they are 'standard' or 'saver', or 'supersaver' or other such option and whether they offer discounts for other products (e.g. free air miles). Furthermore, standing charges and discounts for payment of bills by direct debit (rather than by cheque or by pre-payment meters) also vary from company to company. Hence, it can be difficult for consumers to compare companies' bills and work out which is the cheapest. A 1999 study by the National Audit Office found that over a third of gas consumers were unaware that new suppliers were offering lower prices than they were currently paying. Nevertheless, more than 5 million customers had changed their suppliers of gas and electricity.

The increasing threat of switching can be expected to force companies to become more competitive and offer less complicated illustrative bills. British Gas cut prices to its customers and announced abolition of its standing charges in early 2000 for both gas and electricity in response to new suppliers' lower prices. The major multinational oil companies could also become major providers of gas and electricity direct to households as they further their ambitions to become all-round energy providers.

RPI – X also applies to the weighted average of prices for services within the tariff basket. Individual tariffs within the basket are weighted by the revenues generated by their respective services. Prices for individual commodities may deviate from the RPI − X figure as long as the average tariff is consistent with the price cap. Whilst dispersion about the average can be large or small, the degree of deviation is controlled by other regulatory requirements: that companies should discriminate neither in favour of nor against particular (groups of) customers (i.e. should not practise price discrimination, see Chapter 6), and that they should gradually adjust their prices in order to keep them in line with the cost of providing services.

Tariff structures can be quite complex in practice. There may be separate peak and off-peak period tariffs, separate standing charges and running rates, regional and local price variations and so on. In comparison with actual tariff structures, the UK's RPI − X price cap is a **highly simplified** form of control in that:

- **It requires no detailed assessment of company-specific costs**, of their annual increases, of the capacity for innovation and technological change nor of the impact of rising volume of sales on unit costs.
- **It is an aggregate price cap**, rather than a multitude of individual caps for specific services provided by a particular regulated company.
- **It only controls annual real changes in tariff baskets**. The regulator has no power to determine the charges actually levied for individual services, although, of course, increases in the value of X at periodic price cap reviews serve to reduce average charges in real terms (as has been the case for British Telecom, see **Table 13.2** and British Gas).
- **It is set for periods of between three to five years rather than annually**. The rationale for this medium-term price cap period is that a time horizon of more than five years involves excessive uncertainty, whilst one of less than three years would lead to excessive regulation. The shorter period would effectively result in ongoing, uninterrupted reviews (given their time-consuming nature) and would lead to results similar to those of rate of return control, already rejected as unsuitable.
- **It does not dictate a particular tariff structure**. Nonetheless the regulators have generally expressed a preference for price structures where charges for particular services are related to costs, and they expect companies to move their prices towards (rather than away from) costs in any 'rebalancing' of tariffs. The regulators generally have the power, or can exercise suasion, to require companies to justify any such rebalancing of tariffs.
- **It does not directly control profits**. Within their given price caps, companies are free to maximise their returns on capital employed. This is achieved by cost reductions in the form of reducing

overmanning and adopting business development strategies involving rapid innovation and technological development. The very
adoption of the RPI − X price cap assumed that such cost-effectiveness
strategies would be adopted.

With regard to the last of these it was assumed that British Telecom
would take advantage of rapidly developing telecommunications
technologies (e.g. the replacement of electromechanical switch gear by
electronic telephone exchanges), which would lead to significant cost
reductions. The RPI − X formula ensured that the benefits of
technological change would be fairly reasonably shared between
companies, their shareholders and customers. Such a distribution of
benefits (even if crude and approximate) was thought to provide the best
balance of incentives and rewards. In the British Telecom case, the RPI −
X formula also recognised the fall in unit system capital costs as the
number of subscribers increased over time.

   **Periodic reviews of the price cap afford regulators the opportunity to
adjust the value of X if profits have been greater or less than expected
at the time the last price cap was set.** However the regulators have
generally taken the view that it would be both improper and unwise to
'claw back' higher than expected levels of profits during earlier price cap
periods since this would diminish incentives for companies to seek
continuing cost effectiveness and could deprive them of necessary
investment funds for the future. Nevertheless, the 1997 Labour
government imposed a £5.2 billion **windfall tax** on what it regarded as
'excess profits' earned by the utilities and imposed other obligations on
them. Note that those excess profits were not used to finance a price
reduction for consumers. Instead, the windfall tax was used to finance
the New Deal scheme to reduce youth unemployment (see Chapter 8).

Suitability of the RPI

Whilst simple, transparent and readily understood, the RPI is not
necessarily the most appropriate index of inflation because:

- **It includes irrelevant items** as it refers to retail prices, not to the costs
  of individual regulated companies. Many factors cause changes in the
  RPI but do not cause comparable changes in company costs, for
  example changes in mortgage interest rates and indirect taxes.
- **Its value already reflects economy-wide improvements in factor
  productivity** arising from technological change and innovation, such
  that regulated companies must increase their own productivity by
  more than X. However immediate improvements in productivity may
  be substantial because of initial pre-privatisation inefficiencies that can
  be easily remedied. This hypothesis is corroborated by the substantial

labour shedding for the core activities of many of the privatised industries. In the long run they may still find it relatively easy to reduce real prices if their scope for innovation is greater than average (e.g. for British Telecom), if monopsony powers can be used to reduce wholesale prices (e.g. for British Gas), or if productivity improvements are facilitated by volume growth against indivisible capital (e.g. for both British Telecom and British Gas).

The *producer price index* could be used, but it is not widely known and – in being an average – may not reflect changes in input costs for individual regulated companies any more accurately than does the RPI. Much the same can be said of the *GDP deflator at factor cost*. Construction of cost-inflation indices for individual companies would be complex and expensive and may create the wrong incentives for companies regarding both the cost-minimisation of inputs and the combinations of factors used in production. *Company-specific cost indices* would:

- **Fail to recognise that regulated companies often have considerable monopsony (i.e. sole purchaser) powers**, which they could exercise to restrain increases in the costs of their inputs (the Y factor for gas can be criticised in these terms: see **Table 13.2**, note 2);
- **Provide companies with no real incentives towards rapid innovation and technological change**, which can be expected to reduce the unit costs of their outputs;
- **Allow companies to pass increasing costs directly on to consumers** such that regulation would afford them little protection against monopoly exploitation (the K factor for water and sewerage companies can be criticised in these terms: see **Table 13.2**, note 4);
- **Lack transparency for consumers in comparison with the RPI**, the basis of which is generally understood by consumers and is a headline inflation figure.

13.12 Reconsideration of rate of return versus price cap regulation

It has been argued here that the RPI $-$ X price cap is a highly simplified form of regulatory control. It is, however, simpler in its abstract form than in its practical application. It could be argued that the apparent simplicity of the RPI $-$ X price cap is illusory. It was noted earlier that price cap regulation more closely approximates rate-of-return regulation the shorter the period for which price caps are set. It is not simply a case of the regulator setting the price cap by arbitrarily setting a value for X and then taking no further interest in the regulated industry until the next price cap is set. In practice regulation is an ongoing process. Periodic reviews of company performance tend to be highly detailed, intensive, take a considerable length of time and be an essentially ongoing exercise. The two forms of regulation become more similar the more the regulator takes account of the rates of return actually achieved by the company when setting its price cap for the subsequent period. Whatever the method chosen, regulation is a highly complex and politically contentious affair.

The regulatory system provides each regulator with considerable leeway in terms of ability to negotiate outcomes with the regulated company. They have considerable discretion in determining precisely how regulation is undertaken. Its form is less dependent on quasi-judicial process (as in the USA) and more dependent on the persuasive, competent and dominant personalities appointed as directors general. Regulatory adaptability is arguably required because of the following differences between regulated industries.

First, differences in the structures of the regulated industries that were created upon privatisation. These different industrial structures create differences in the competitiveness of the industries and therefore differences in the degree and nature of regulatory intervention. For example British Gas was a single company where there was little immediate scope for competition. In contrast with gas, the potential for competition was greater in the electricity supply industry since, as noted above, it contains a number of competing companies.

Second, differences in the degrees (and rate of development) of liberalisation. In general, the greater the degree of liberalisation the greater the degree of competition existing within any one industry, and the less the need for regulatory intervention. As already noted, a measure of liberalisation was built into the privatisation of British Telecom (in the form of Mercury), but was introduced as an afterthought in the gas and electricity supply industries. Such liberalisation measures are particularly slow to develop.

Third, their different requirements for major capital programmes. The greater the need for investment in new capacity and new technology, the more the regulator has to allow companies the opportunity to increase current and future profits in order to finance that investment, whilst at the same time paying sufficient dividends to shareholders. The degree of such flexibility can be expected to vary between companies, both between and within regulated industries. For example the requirement for capital investment varies quite substantially between the water and electricity supply industries and also between different companies within the water and sewerage industry (see Chapter 14).

Fourth, differences in the interaction with environmental regulation. The complexity of economic regulation, and the subsequent need for flexibility, is exacerbated when it has to coexist and be consistent with other forms of regulation, most notably environmental regulation. Environmental legislation dealing with such negative externalities as pollution is a particularly binding constraint for water and sewerage. The director general of water services has had to be increasingly accommodating of UK and EU legislation when setting price caps for individual companies (see Chapter 14).

In conclusion, the distinguishing features of the UK price cap regulation are as much in terms of the considerable discretion afforded to regulators as in its broad brush (tariff basket) approach. The choice between price control and rate-of-return control regulation therefore reflects not so much the balance of advantage of one method over the other as the cultural dimensions in the nature of polity. The differences between price cap and rate-of-return regulation may be more apparent than real. Of more importance in influencing the choice of regulatory method has been the desire to avoid mechanistic and legalistic systems and to promote adaptability and organic development of the regulatory process.

In particular, the separation of production and transmission and subsequent liberalisation of the electricity, gas and rail service industries means that the main regulatory problem now relates as much to the **conditions determining access to networks** (termed *'common carriage'*) as it does to **implementation of the price cap formula**. Determination and preservation of those access conditions has led to increasingly detailed regulation synonymous with increasing liberalisation. For example, should charges for interconnection be based on marginal or average costs and how are those costs determined? Hence, the belief that increasingly liberalised utility industries would reduce the need for regulation seems to have been somewhat naive.

13.13 Allocatively inefficient regulation

It was noted above that, as far as possible, regulation should mimic competitive forces that promote allocative efficiency. However regulation may create a market structure that has the perverse effect of raising rather than reducing costs of production. Mention has already been made of regulatory capture and other public choice (rent-seeking) distortions that may detract from the pursuit of efficiency. Besides these general problems of regulation, the regulatory arrangements for the electricity supply industry may serve to stifle rather than increase competition.

Under nationalisation the *merit order* system for the electricity supply industry brought successive power stations 'on stream' by using the lowest-cost supplies first (to meet 'base load' demand), only using the highest-cost supplies for short periods to meet peak demands. That cost-minimisation system was abandoned upon privatisation. However, most of the RECs in England and Wales built their own gas-fired power stations in order to reduce their dependence on supplies from the two generators, National Power and PowerGen. This *dash for gas* continued even though gas-fired power stations may produce electricity at higher cost than that which could be purchased from the generator companies. The RECs can pass on the capital costs to consumers. Hence, once built, there is a strong incentive for RECs to replace (possibly) lower-cost wholesale electricity supplies from the generators with the (possibly) higher-cost supplies from their own gas-fired power stations.

Any such inefficiency will not be restricted to the electricity supply industry since there would be knock-on consequences for the demand for other fuels. The demand for coal for burning in power stations fell sharply, with further consequences for unemployment in economically depressed coalmining regions. Before privatisation, coal-fired power stations generated three-quarters of the UK's electricity. By the end of the 1990s that proportion was only one-third. The share of electricity generated from gas rose from less than one per cent to one-third over the same period and could reach three-quarters by 2020. This would lead to early exhaustion of gas supplies for the domestic market where gas is a 'premium' fuel (i.e. creates no ash and can be easily switched on or off, unlike coal) and a competitor with electricity. Coal production would have virtually ceased. The UK would then be highly dependent upon imported supplies of both gas and oil, leaving it vulnerable to political turbulence in producing countries such as Algeria, Russia and the Middle East.

In effect the regulatory system could lead to greater allocative inefficiency and greater X-inefficiency. **First**, it could distort the marginal rates of transformation of the factors of production (i.e. alternative fossil fuels) in the electricity supply industry such that **input costs are not minimised**. **Second**, it could distort the balance of fuel consumption within the wider economy such that **energy resource costs are not minimised**. An allocatively efficient energy policy minimises the resource costs of energy supply. This requires account to be taken of the resource costs of alternative primary fuels, namely coal, oil, gas, nuclear power and hydroelectric power. Such an energy policy was attempted in the UK in the past under the regime of the nationalised fuel industries, even if it was not wholly successful. However, energy policy was effectively privatised along with the energy industries. **Third**, in generating lower real gas and electricity prices, **consumers are encouraged to use energy inefficiently**, this being contrary to the Kyoto Protocol which requires reductions in carbon dioxide emissions (see Chapter 2). The gas and electricity industries contribute well over half of the UK's carbon dioxide emissions. More research into renewable energy sources is needed if dependence on fossil fuels is to be reduced. The alternative would be to increase the proportion of electricity generated by nuclear power.

13.14 Conclusions

In economic terms, regulation (subsequent to privatisation) and nationalisation are simply different forms of government intervention to deal with the potential efficiency problems of natural monopolies. Ultimately the choice between them is based less upon any clear economic rule and more upon the political and social culture of any one country. In that it assumes rent-seeking on the part of all participants in democratic and governmental processes, the economic theory of public choice has the potential to explain the shift from nationalisation to privatisation with regulation. This analytical framework adds another dimension to the traditional economic arguments relating to privatisation. It had not been well developed by the time of writing this text, but some (admittedly very limited) attempt will be made to apply it to the privatisation of the water industry (see Chapter 14).

In the UK the balance of argument (or of power) shifted in favour of privatisation and against continuing nationalisation as the technological and market conditions within which the nationalised industries operated changed over four decades or so. The form of privatisation has also changed, with increasing emphasis on achieving a more competitive industrial structure upon privatisation and subsequently extending the degree of liberalisation. This has meant that the unitary form of privatisation for British Telecom and British Gas became less representative of subsequent asset sales and that the form of regulation has correspondingly become more complex.

Regulation is not simply concerned with preventing the potential abuse of monopoly power. It is also concerned with promoting the development of the regulated industry and its services to consumers, while ensuring adequate returns to shareholders and taking into account other factors such as environmental protection. Hence the efficiency case for regulation has to be seen in a much broader framework than simply that of the market model of monopoly. That framework has become increasingly *microeconomic* in approach and less *macroeconomic*. Use of the former nationalised industries as macroeconomic instruments has taken second place to the growing emphasis on the need to improve their microeconomic characteristics. This development is part of the *prioritisation of supply-side over demand-side policy* throughout the economy. Price control through the RPI − X formula is the microeconomic instrument being used to achieve efficiency improvements.

Economic efficiency criteria increasingly came to be prioritised over social considerations. Such a shift in relative emphasis is also evident in the reforms of social security and taxation. The inevitable links between the form of intervention, the necessity for subsidy and the implications for public expenditure, public borrowing and taxation came to the fore during the late 1970s, 1980s and 1990s. More generally the moral, cultural and political emphasis on rolling back the frontiers of the state also required the government to divest itself of the nationalised industries. But, notwithstanding rolling back those frontiers, state intervention in the economy has actually increased as it moved from the *production state* to the *regulatory state*. This highlights the argument in Chapter 1 about the nature of 'public'.

The emphasis on microeconomic factors may have constrained consideration of macroeconomic and sectoral issues, for example those relating to the balance of fuels as part of energy policy. Moreover, there is ultimately a limit to the extent of real cuts in prices, after which the development of an industry and increases in the quality of its output may suffer. Besides changing the value of X, the RPI − X formula will have to be reformed in the future. Alternatively liberalisation may be so extended that regulation is no longer necessary. This may be more likely for telecommunications than for electricity, gas or water because of more rapid technological progress in telecommunications.

These profound links between political philosophy and polity are at least as important (if not more so) than any of the economic theories relating to nationalisation and privatisation reviewed earlier in this chapter and throughout the book. What the limited multidisciplinary analysis contained within this chapter has demonstrated is that the privatisation debate is not a free-standing issue. It is highly integrative with other economic issues relating to fiscal and monetary policies as well as with social and constitutional issues relating to equity and democratic rights. The reader should not lose sight of these integrative themes when going on to consider the complex details of individual privatisation measures in any subsequent case studies. Two such integrative case studies are provided in the next two chapters. Others can be found in the following list.

Further reading

Beesley, M. E. (1997) *Privatisation Regulation and Deregulation*, 2nd edn (London: Routledge).

Beesley, M. E. (ed.) (1997) *Regulating Utilities: Broadening the Debate* (London: Institute of Economic Affairs).

Bishop, M., Kay, J. and Mayer, C. (eds) (1994) *Privatisation and Economic Performance* (Oxford: Oxford University Press).

Bishop, M., Kay, J. and Mayer, C. (eds) (1994) *The Regulatory Challenge* (Oxford: Oxford University Press).

Department of Trade and Industry (1994) *The Future of Postal Services: A Consultative Document*, Cm 2614 (London: HMSO).

Department of Transport (1992) *New Opportunities for the Railways: The Privatisation of British Rail*, Cm 2012 (London: HMSO).

DETR (1988) *A New Deal for Transport: Better for Everyone* (London: Department of the Environment, Transport and Regions).

DGT (1988) *The Regulation of British Telecom's Prices: A Consultative Document* (London: OFTEL).

DTI (1988) *A Fair Deal for Consumers: Modernising the Framework for Utility Regulation* (London: Department of Trade and Industry).

Ernst, J. (1994) *Whose Utility? The Social Impact of Public Utility Privatisation and Regulation in Britain* (Buckingham: Open University Press).

Foreman-Peck, J. and Millward, R. (1994) *Public and Private Ownership of British Industry 1820–1990* (Oxford: Clarendon Press).

Foster, C. D. (1992) *Privatisation, Public Ownership and the Regulation of Natural Monopoly* (Oxford: Blackwell).

Helm, D., Jenkinson, T. and Morris, D. (1997) 'Competition in Regulated Industries', *Oxford Review of Economic Policy*, vol. 13, no. 1 pp. 1–103 (whole issue).

Helm, D. and Jenkinson, T. (1998) *Competition in Regulated Industries* (Oxford: Oxford University Press).

Jackson, P. M. and Lavender, M. (1998) *Public Services Yearbook 1997–98* (London: Pitman Publishing) (see chapters 10 and 11 on regulation).

Jackson, P. M. and Price, C. M. (1994) *Privatisation and Regulation: A Review of the Issues* (Harlow: Longman).

Kennedy, D. (1996) *Competition in Regulated Industries*, Centre for the Study of Regulated Industries, Regulatory Brief 7 (London: CIPFA).

National Consumer Council (1989) *In the Absence of Competition: A Consumer View of Public Utilities Regulation* (London: HMSO).

Office of Gas and Electricity Markets (online). Available at <http://www.ofgas.gov.uk>.

Office of the Rail Regulator (online). Available at <http://www.rail-reg.gov.uk>.

Railtrack (online). Available at <http://www.railtrack.org>.

Ramanadham, V. V. (1991) *The Economics of Public Enterprise* (London: Routledge).

Ramanadham, V. V. (1993) *Privatisation: A Global Perspective* (London: Routledge).

Ramanadham, V. V. (ed.) (1994) *Privatisation and After: Monitoring and Regulation* (London: Routledge).

Ramanadham, V. V. (ed.) (1995) *Privatisation and Equity* (London: Routledge).

Rees, R. (1994) *The Economics of Regulation and Public Enterprise* (Hemel Hempstead: Harvester Wheatsheaf).

Vickers, J. and Yarrow, G. (1988) *Privatisation: An Economic Analysis* (Cambridge, Mass: MIT Press).

Weyman-Jones, T. and Price, C. (1993) *Regulating Public Utilities* (Hemel Hempstead: Harvester Wheatsheaf).

14 Water – A Case Study of Regulation and Charging

14.1 Introduction
14.2 General Characteristics
14.3 Economic Characteristics
14.4 Dealing with Market Failure
14.5 Regulation
14.6 Restructuring Water and Sewerage in Scotland
14.7 Charging for Water and Sewerage Services
14.8 Other Forms of Demand Management
14.9 Conclusions

The aim of the Government's energy and water policies is to ensure secure and sustainable supplies at competitive prices. . . . Efficient and reliable energy and water networks . . . underpin competitiveness. . . . The Government believes that this will best be achieved through privatisation . . . and so long as monopolies remain in some areas, a regulatory system which acts as a proxy for the competitive process (1994 White Paper, *Competitiveness: Helping Business to Win*, Cm 2563, London: HMSO, p. 121).

The driving principles behind the Government's policy are to deliver a system which provides for fair and affordable water charges, particularly for vulnerable customers, while ensuring the sustainable use of water supplies and protection of the aquatic environment. Increased customer choice is an essential ingredient (*Hansard Written Answers*, 18 November 1998, p. 670, Secretary of State for the Environment, Transport and the Regions).

14.1 Introduction

The purpose of this case study is to demonstrate how the themes treated separately in preceding chapters come together at the stage of policy implementation. It attempts a coherent synthesis of market failure concepts, other reasons for government intervention (e.g. social and distributional), charging, public sector borrowing, taxation and the level and form of government intervention through the creation of quangos (water boards), privatisation and regulation. In highlighting the interaction of these separate themes, it demonstrates the complexity of policy implementation through apparently simple supply-side measures.

Of all the public utilities, water is the most essential for health and life and many people believe, as a matter of principle, that this natural resource should be free at the point of use, access being denied to no one. Nevertheless, the other utilities such as electricity and gas are essential for a reasonable quality of life and yet they are not free at the point of use. Moreover, the above quotations emphasise the need to take a broader view of water as both an economic resource and an environmental resource, charges for which can and should be levied. Unlike air, water can be appropriated into the ownership of public and private sector organisations and firms building reservoirs, pipelines, treatment facilities and so on, by means of which to supply end users.

The first quotation is from the then Conservative government. It emphasises the need to introduce competition into the water and sewerage industry as a broad supply-side measure. The second quotation is from the then Labour government. It endorses the principles of customer choice through competition and of sustainable supplies but also highlights the principle of fairness and affordability for vulnerable groups. Such groups include low-income households and families with children. The Labour government wanted the levels of water and sewerage charges for such groups to be consistent with its policy to reduce the numbers of children and pensioners living in poverty (see Chapter 12).

Essentially, Conservative and Labour governments shared common objectives. They sought an efficient water and sewerage industry providing a quality low-cost service that is also consistent with their environmental and social policies. However, notwithstanding privatisation of the water and sewerage industry in England and Wales and structural reforms elsewhere in the UK, neither the Conservative nor Labour governments were able to introduce a substantial degree of competition into the industry during the 1990s. Moreover, prices of water and sewerage services rose substantially in the decade following privatisation. A 1996 survey by National Utility Services found water charges in the UK to be the sixth most expensive of 15 industrialised countries studied, those costs rising at double the rate of inflation.

It would be invalid, however, to conclude that supply-side policy has failed in the case of water and sewerage. That policy has to make up for years of under-investment in the infrastructure, meet increasingly tough EU requirements for the treatment of water and sewerage, respond to industrial, household and geographic restructuring (all of which affect the patterns of demand), and reflect increasingly critical environmental and sustainability issues. Water and sewerage is often referred to as a 'long term industry' with a long planning horizon. Introduction of competition would be a slow process even without having to take account of this complex mix of issues. These issues reflect the general, economic, environmental and social characteristics of the industry.

14.2   General characteristics

Water is used for domestic household purposes and for industrial and commercial processes. The industry has 22 million water customers and 21 million sewerage customers. Households account for over 90 per cent of customers and for 70 per cent of water delivered. Household demand continues to rise even though total population is stable. This is because more houses are required as average household size falls. More houses mean more gardens to water, cars to wash and so on. Smaller household size leads to more wasteful use of water through half-empty clothes washers and dishwashers. This exacerbates rising demand due to increased use of baths and showers ('power showers' actually use more water than baths on average), more frequent washing of clothes and so on. However, water delivered to business customers is falling, reflecting industrial restructuring away from heavy users. For example, water is used for industrial cooling, cleaning and other purposes. About 30 000 litres of water are used in the production of the average car and eight pints are used to produce one pint of beer. Decline in the number of steel mills, engineering works and breweries has led to falling industrial demand for water.

For the UK as a whole, about 30 per cent of mains water is metered, supplied mainly to industry, and 70 per cent is unmetered, supplied mainly to domestic and commercial customers. On average only 2 per cent of the water supplied daily to each home is used for drinking purposes. A third is used for flushing toilets, a fifth for personal washing (bath/shower), an eighth for washing machines and dishwashers, 3 per cent for outside use, the remaining third being for other uses. Consumption rises by about 10 per cent over the summer (May to August), outdoor use increasing to over 25 per cent of monthly consumption as people water their gardens and wash their cars more frequently when the weather is dry. This seasonal peak in demand is the opposite of that for electricity and gas (demand peaking in the winter).

Water costs usually represent a relatively low proportion of industrial and commercial costs and of household income, in the latter case the national average being a little over 1 per cent. However, together with the above quotations, the examples of use emphasise that provision of the appropriate quality and quantity of water is of vital importance in underpinning both improved standards of living and economic growth. This is demonstrated by the fact that total water use per head was 70 per cent more in the early 1990s than in the early 1960s. However, between 1992/3 and 1999/2000 the volume of drinking water delivered in England and Wales actually fell by 0.6 per cent. This partly reflected the fall in business use but was mainly due to the water companies taking action to prevent the substantial rates of leakage of water whilst in the mains system (see below). It is, however, a one-off saving and so demand for water will increasingly return to its long-term rising trend as the scope for further such savings diminishes.

Much depends on whether households and commercial customers become more economical in their use of water. Growth rates are likely to be affected by the growing use of metering and associated volumetric charges (see below). Increasing attention is being paid to the need for water conservation measures, for both economic and environmental reasons. Nevertheless, high rates of growth for water use are likely to be maintained in prosperous regions experiencing rapid economic development and in-migration of working population.

Unfortunately, regional growth in demand coincides with shortage of supply, especially in the south east of England and East Anglia. This increasing mismatch between supply and demand is made more problematic because there is no national grid for water and sewerage. Unlike gas and electricity, water is extremely costly to pump around the country and so, historically, the industry has developed in a way that minimises the need to pump water. Even so, some water companies spend half as much again on storing and pumping water around their networks as on abstracting it (from rivers, lakes and acquifers) and treating it. Adoption of the principle of integrated river basin management to minimise pumping costs has necessarily led to a geographically fragmented industry. This has profound implications for the level of competition (see section 14.3).

14.3   Economic characteristics

Allocatively efficient provision of water and sewerage services may fail to exist because of the lack of perfect competition in the market for each service and/or because their economic characteristics would cause a perfectly competitive market to fail to achieve allocative efficiency. The latter would be the case if water and sewerage had public good, externality or merit good characteristics (see Chapter 2).

Lack of perfect competition

The water and sewerage services are both systems-based utility industries, requiring prior installation of a capital-intensive network of reservoirs, mains pipelines, pumping and distribution facilities and so on. Hence entry costs to the industry are high and economies of scale are considerable. This leads to the formation of natural local or regional monopolies, such that the conditions for perfect competition do not exist. Monopoly theory demonstrates that output will be lower and price higher than would be the case for a perfectly competitive market because equilibrium price exceeds marginal cost. Hence allocative inefficiency results. Bearing in mind 'second best' caveats, allocative efficiency may be improved by appropriate forms of monopoly control, either nationalisation or regulation (see Chapter 13).

A public or private good?

Water does *not* have the pure public good characteristics of non-rivalness and non-excludability. Consumption of water is rival in use, as made evident by periodic droughts, the 1995 drought leading to water shortages and interruption of supplies in many parts of the UK. Moreover, exclusion is possible in that, subject to any legal constraints, water supply can be disconnected if consumers refuse to pay charges. Whilst disconnection of water supply to households with unpaid bills is no longer allowed by law in any part of the UK, the rapidly growing purchases of bottled (mineral, spring and table) water demonstrates that water is a tradeable commodity. Sales of bottled mineral water exceeded a billion litres in 1999 (a 10-fold increase since 1986) and were greater than the consumption of fruit juice. Hence water has the economic characteristics of a private good in that its use is both rival and excludable. The same is true for sewerage services.

Negative externalities

The provision of unpolluted water and the removal and treatment of sewage are both crucial for the maintenance of public health. The improper disposal of sewage (including domestic, industrial, commercial and agricultural liquid wastes) causes negative externalities in terms of water-borne diseases and other longer-term health problems (e.g. caused by chemical pollution). Little more than a century ago there were many instances of local wells contaminated by open sewers, leading to a proliferation of water-borne diseases, often with fatal consequences for those infected. British local governments took the initiative in providing integrated water and sewerage services during the nineteenth century in order to secure public health.

In general, where water and sewerage services were supplied by separate companies, a sewerage company had every incentive simply to dump untreated sewage into water courses since this practice minimises costs and maximises profits. However dumping untreated sewage into rivers from which drinking water supplies are abstracted by water companies increases water treatment costs. Hence a negative externality occurs since not all costs are reflected in market prices for sewerage services. Internalisation of the negative externality is possible by combining, into a single company or organisation, both the water and sewerage companies of a particular geographical locality. In that case the previous negative externality becomes an internal cost. This solution has been adopted at various times by means of local government provision, nationalisation and privatisation with regulation.

However, not all negative externalities have been internalised by such restructuring. Ironically, of the ten organisations most heavily fined for UK pollution offences in 1999, seven were integrated water and sewerage companies. The British practice of dumping largely untreated sewage and toxic wastes into the sea led to the UK being referred to as the 'Dirty Man of Europe'. Many beaches have been heavily polluted by sewage and sanitary products and there was growing evidence of adverse health effects on people using beaches and those involved in water-based sports. Untreated sewage contains high levels of pathogenic viruses and bacteria, causing vomiting, diarrhoea, gastro-enteritis and other illnesses. In accordance with the EU's Bathing Water Directive (see below), most companies now kill bacteria using a combination of chemical and biological treatment and irradiation with ultraviolet light. Adverse consequences for health have also been attributed to deposition of industrial wastes in major rivers and surrounding coastlines.

Besides adverse health effects for people, the tourist industry can also be adversely affected by polluted beaches. Failure of a tourist resort beach to win an EU 'Blue Flag' bathing-water quality rating can lead to a loss of tourists and their spending power. Similarly, the dumping of bovine slurry into rivers, and the seepage into them of chemicals from fertilisers and pesticides applied to crops, are further examples of a continuing negative externality that was unaffected by the integration of water and sewerage functions. At a global level, environmental and wildlife organisations (e.g. the World Wide Fund for Nature) are increasingly concerned about depletion of freshwater resources drying up wetlands and causing extinction of wetland habitat species. These negative externalities emphasise the need for regulation on health and environmental grounds, irrespective of whether water and sewerage is under local government control, nationalised, or privatised (see below).

Merit good characteristics

The individual consumer may undervalue the personal (as distinct from external) benefits of adequate supplies of potable water and proper disposal of sewage. Besides greater publicity of the potential consequences for personal health and hygiene, the government also uses planning law, water byelaws and building regulations to make compulsory the provision of adequate water and sewerage facilities for dwellings and for industrial and commercial buildings. These quality standards are now part of the EU's Drinking Water Directive (see below). For example, whilst many houses in remote rural areas have their own private water supply (from springs, wells and boreholes, rivers or lakes) they still have to comply with water quality regulations requiring freedom from contamination by bacteria (often from animal droppings on farm land), chemicals (e.g. from nitrates, pesticides and sheep dip), lead (dissolved from pipes and tanks), and other materials (e.g. iron or peat). Likewise, such houses also have to conform with sewerage byelaws, for example requiring use of septic tanks. Without such regulations, there would be potentially serious health problems for people living in these households, especially the very young, elderly or sick people. Most people seem to be generally unaware of these adverse health consequences.

14.4   Dealing with market failure

It is clear that the market conditions and economic characteristics of the water and sewerage industries require some form of government intervention to deal with market failure. There are four broad options.

- **Municipalisation.** Throughout Europe, the usual form of regulation has been to vest statutory responsibility for water and sewerage services in local (or regional) government (OECD, 1999). As already noted, this was previously the case in the UK. Local governments may combine to form inter-municipal enterprises in order to gain economies of scale. The alternative would be to vest responsibility for the service into regional government. Whilst formally there is local (or regional) democratic control of the industry, municipalisation does not foster competition and cost minimisation. Municipal enterprises typically operate in a non-competitive environment and are often heavily subsidised, charges not fully covering operating costs. Moreover, local taxpayers often resist the tax increases necessary to finance maintenance and investment programmes, thereby leading to deteriorating service quality and higher social and environmental costs.

- **Nationalisation**. Prior to their privatisation, English and Welsh water and sewerage services were taken out of local government control in 1974 and nationalised in the form of Water Boards, these being non-elected quangos. There had previously been almost 1600 separate water and sewerage undertakings. Creation of the 10 Water Boards offered considerable cost savings through economies of scale. Water and sewerage services in Scotland were likewise taken out of local government control in 1996 but remain within the public sector under three geographically separated quangos (see below). The Northern Ireland Water Service is a state enterprise, reflecting the different arrangements for local government in the province. These quangos are subject to the 'lack of democratic accountability' argument and also to the lack of competition/higher costs arguments noted for municipalisation

- **Privatisation**. Consistent with the Conservative government quotation at the beginning of this chapter, the English and Welsh Water Boards were privatised in 1989, the third major public utility to be privatised after telecommunications and gas. Privatisation of both assets and management is rare within the OECD countries (OECD, 1999). Privatisation in the UK created the 10 water and sewerage companies (WaSCs) listed in **Table 14.1**. They deliver water to three-quarters of the population of England and Wales and remove sewage from virtually all homes, the exceptions being those with septic tanks. The remaining quarter of water supply is provided by private water-only companies (WoCs), these existing prior to privatisation but having been substantially reduced in number by mergers and takeovers. **Tables 14.1** and **14.2**. only list the WoCs existing in 2000. Privatisation is subject to the usual argument against monopoly exploitation of consumers, although this may be moderated by effective regulation. Although regulation does not foster democratic accountability, the UK system does provide for consultation with consumers and other stakeholder groups. Indeed, it has been argued that the regulatory arrangements for protecting customers' interests are a substantial improvement on those existing under the previous public ownership, notwithstanding the fact that prices rose substantially in the decade following privatisation (see below).

- **Mutualisation**. Privatisation vests ownership of the company in its *shareholders* who put up equity capital by purchasing shares. In contrast, mutualisation vests ownership in the users of the company's services, users becoming *members*. Whereas a shareholder's voting power depends on the number of shares held (more shares equals more votes), each member only has one vote irrespective of the amount of capital he or she contributes. The mutualisation, or co-operative, principle underpins building societies, members putting up cash (in the form of savings accounts) which other members borrow to finance mortgages for house purchase (see Chapter 8). Mutualisation of water and sewerage was proposed by the Institute for Public Policy Research and even by some WaSCs in the later 1990s (the latter wanting to concentrate on waste management and infrastructure engineering in the UK and abroad). The apparent advantages to water and sewerage customers would be the shift to a non-profit organisation, inviting competing private sector companies to bid to manage the assets and provide the service. However, users would ultimately have to finance mutualisation because the privatised companies would sell their assets to the newly created mutual companies. The mutuals would have to finance the purchase and the subsequent ongoing investment programmes by issuing long-term bonds, those borrowings being repaid by revenue from charges. They would also, of course, have to cover the costs of the companies operating the service. Hence, charges would not immediately be lower as a result of mutualisation – they could well be higher. Moreover, in the longer term, mutualisation could inhibit the development of competition and, with it, lower prices. This would be the case, for example, if one very large company won most of the mutuals' service-operation contracts. In effect, regional monopolies would be replaced by a national monopoly. For these reasons, neither the 1997 Labour government nor the industry regulator believed that customers' best interests would be served by a switch from equity ownership with strict regulation to mutualisation and so it was prohibited.

Clearly, there is no single option for dealing with market failure that is necessarily superior to the others. As already noted in Chapter 13, the immediate advantage of privatisation was the finance so raised and the fact that it was treated as negative expenditure, so aiding achievement of public expenditure targets (see also Chapter 9). Additionally, the necessary infrastructural investments would be financed by the private sector, again leading to public expenditure savings, to lower levels of taxation and borrowing, and so to the potential supply-side improvements from reduced crowding out (see Chapters 4 and 5). The then Conservative government recognised the need for regulation to prevent monopoly exploitation of consumers.

14.5 Regulation

Water and sewerage services are subject to two separate forms of regulation.

Environmental regulation

Privatisation in England and Wales related only to the fresh water and wastewater functions of the former regional water authorities in providing public water supplies. Public water supply accounts for only about half of water abstracted from non-tidal surface water and groundwater. Power generation accounts for over a third of water abstraction, other industry an eighth and agriculture 1 per cent. Hence, environmental regulation is not restricted to the public water supply and related sewerage services.

Responsibility for pollution control, conservation, management of water resources and other functions was vested in a separate environmental body that subsequently became the Environment Agency in 1996. The Agency inherited the responsibilities of the former National Rivers Authority, HM Inspectorate of Pollution and the Waste Regulation Authorities. The equivalent body in Scotland is the Scottish Environment Protection Agency (see below). The Drinking Water Inspectorate remains a separate body. The government thought that to give these responsibilities to the privatised companies would create a conflict of interest. Their incentives to cut costs would probably lead to increased pollution (through discharge of untreated sewage and so on) and also to excessive abstraction of water resources (destroying wetland and river habitats and so on).

In essence these regulatory bodies are concerned with safeguarding and improving water quality. The Environment Agency is the licensing authority for water abstraction. It has a statutory duty to secure the proper use of water resources, including assessing the need for new developments and taking into account their environmental impact and the impact on existing users. The Agency's management of water resources is underpinned by three key concepts:

- **Sustainable development** – avoiding systematic deterioration in the water environment;
- **Precautionary principle** – erring on the side of caution in avoiding environmental damage;
- **Demand management** – controlling or influencing the consumption or waste of water.

These environmental regulators operate within the framework of UK and EU legislation. Quality standards for both water supply and sewage disposal are increasingly being dictated by the EU through its Drinking Water Directive, Bathing Waters Directive and Urban Waste Water Treatment Directive. The market failure rationale for these directives is based on the negative externality and merit good characteristics considered above.

Of course various interest groups are also concerned with environmental protection, including Friends of the Earth and the Council for the Protection of Rural England. Such pressure groups have attempted to highlight the adverse environmental impacts of the ever-expanding demand for water and the dumping of largely untreated sewage into water courses.

Economic regulation

Economic regulation in England and Wales is carried out by the Office of Water Services (OFWAT), a non-ministerial government department that supports the Director General of Water Services. The director's remit is to ensure that the companies are able to finance their operations whilst at the same time seeking to secure both efficiency and consumer protection. In effect, the director has to serve a number of stakeholders whose interests may conflict. First, the companies and their shareholders by ensuring a rate of return on capital sufficient to finance investment programmes and dividends to shareholders. Second, consumers by ensuring that companies do not exploit their local and regional monopolies by restricting output or quality and/or raising water charges. Third, the government by avoiding politically embarrassing rises in charges and company profits and/or deterioration in quality of service.

It was noted in Chapter 13 that for allocative and X-efficiency to be improved privatisation should be designed to introduce a substantial degree of competition and that, where this is not immediately possible, regulators should subsequently progressively introduce competition via liberalisation of the market. Neither outcome has occurred in the case of water and sewerage.

First, privatisation did not change the structure of the industry. The WaSCs have regional monopolies, their boundaries being identical to those of the former regional water authorities and which had been drawn in accordance with the principle of integrated river basin management. Put simply, each WaSC has its own river catchment areas. There being no national water network, there is little possibility of direct competition between WaSCs because of the lack of interconnection between local and regional distribution networks. These constraints on competition also apply to the WoCs. A number of mergers between WoCs and WaSCs reduced the potential for competition in particular areas. Competition is also limited by the high entry costs, new companies having to provide their own network of water mains and sewerage systems.

Second, introduction of competition has subsequently been minimal. There are five broad types of competition:

- **Direct competition** where firms compete to supply water and sewerage services. As already noted, the prospects for direct competition are limited because of the very high set-up costs and because the geographically fragmented nature of the industry. Nonetheless, legislation allows a limited degree of product market competition by *inset appointments*. These were originally limited to new customers on greenfield sites not connected or adjacent to the WaSC's network within whose area those sites were located. However, inset appointments were subsequently opened up for existing large customers, initially those using at least 250 megalitres (55 million gallons) of water a year, subsequently reduced to 100. Though reduced, this minimum threshold requirement effectively limits inset appointments to the largest 1500 or so customers in the non-household sector (e.g. power stations, chemical companies, brewing companies or large hospitals). Inset appointments for existing customers are based on *common carriage*. This refers to the possibility of one company using another company's distribution network in order to supply an existing customer. It has been allowed since 2000 under the 1998 Competition Act and the director general told companies to develop access codes for common carriage.
- **Yardstick competition** whereby the regulator compares the relative efficiencies of the WaSCs (for example in cutting costs and improving service levels) when determining the RPI+K formula for each company (see below and Chapter 13). Such comparisons would be inhibited by mergers between the 10 WaSCs and so several proposed mergers/takeovers were disallowed by the then Monopolies and Mergers Commission during the 1990s, notwithstanding the lost potential for further economies of scale. Nevertheless, by late 2000, five of the WaSCs were owned by foreign companies.
- **Competition for the market** via auction of franchises, as is the case for train services (see Chapter 13). This option was not followed because of the need for large investments required by EU legislation relating to water quality and sewerage treatment (see above). These investments would have made it difficult for franchisees to recover sunk costs. Current companies' licences last until 2014 so franchising is ruled out for the time being at least.
- **Contracting out services**, used in large parts of the public sector via competitive tendering (see Chapter 15). The WaSCs have incentives to

contract out when costs can be reduced and so profits maximised without the need for such a regulatory requirement.

- **Capital market competition** whereby inefficient companies are threatened with takeover because they do not maximise profits. In such cases share prices are lower than those that would arise if profits were maximised and so a predatory firm will offer to pay a premium for shares in order to buy a controlling interest and introduce profit maximisation. As already noted, this type of competition has been limited in order to maintain yardstick competition. Takeovers would also have to be blocked if they were intended to achieve profit maximisation via monopoly pricing.

Economic regulation depends heavily on yardstick competition and is based on the price-cap regulatory model set out in Chapter 13, adapted for the particular circumstances of water and sewerage. The director general sets price limits for each company, within a remit of ensuring that the water companies are provided with incentives for operational efficiency.

Besides expansion of common carriage, the Labour government (in its 2000 Green Paper) also proposed a new licensing regime to make it easier for companies to enter the market. Only one newly licensed water company (supplying non-potable water to a large industrial user) has been set up, and then only ten years after privatisation. The Green Paper also considered more radical options including separation of the service infrastructure (pipes, treatment works and so on) from supply and service, as has been the case for gas and electricity. This would allow competition for the market. It is already happening to a limited extent. Canals owned by British Waterways have long been used to supply drinking water to Bristol and to industries in the Midlands. They will also be used as from 2001 to supply water from the north-west of England and from Wales to the south-east of England.

The regulatory formula

The regulatory formula is a modified case of the RPI − X framework (see Chapter 13). RPI − X relates only to economic regulation whereas water and sewerage are also subject to environmental regulation. Hence, the regulatory formula was modified to RPI + K. The RPI is the percentage increase in the retail price index in the year to the November before the charging year. The value of the K factor is different for each company since it is intended to allow them to recover the capital invested in improving water quality and sewage treatment in line with EU standards. Those costs vary from company to company. For example the degree of industrial and agricultural pollution of water supplies varies between different parts of the country, as does the age of existing network capacity and the practice of dumping untreated sewage into rivers and the sea. Hence both the level of charges and their annual rates of increase vary between companies. The one K factor applies to water and sewage jointly for the 10 WaSCs. However the director general has sought to eliminate cross-subsidy between water and sewerage so that charges can be directly related to relevant costs for each service. The K factors are much higher for the water and sewerage companies than for the water-only companies, reflecting the high cost of wastewater treatment.

RPI + K can be thought of as RPI − X + Q. Factor X relates to economic regulation and reflects the potential for future cost reduction through improved efficiency. Factor Q relates to environmental regulation and reflects the costs of meeting the improved quality standards required by UK and EU legislation. Whilst not a requirement in law, regulators of all the public utilities are seeking improved service standards with respect to continuity and reliability of service, dealing with customer complaints, accuracy of billing systems and so on. However, quality standards for water and wastewater treatment are quite separate from these general aspects of standards of service. The director general is concerned to keep the price increases as low as possible whilst allowing the companies sufficient finance to meet their legal obligations.

The K factor is subject to periodic review by the director general every 5 to 10 years, there having been 'Periodic Reviews' in 1994 and 1999. K is effectively a cost pass through, with the result that consumers pay for extra capital costs through prices, rather than companies financing them through lower profits, or investors financing them through lower dividends. Hence the advantages claimed for the RPI − X formula in Chapter 13 are less applicable for water and sewerage. Cost reduction objectives gave way to the recognised need to catch up on the backlog of investment arising from the restraints on capital spending during the 1970s and 1980s as well as from the need to meet the EU Directives on water quality. The RPI − X formula would have made privatisation unattractive to potential shareholders by significantly increasing the possibility of low profits and even trading losses. It would also have substantially delayed conformity with EU quality standards.

The RPI + K formula effectively gave the water and sewerage companies a guaranteed rate of return on all investments, thereby encouraging them to meet environmental and water quality standards. The greater the rate of investment the greater the absolute profit, even though the rate of profit (i.e. return on capital employed) remains the same. The formula sets a price cap on the five groups of standard charges that make up the so-called 'basket' of charges. Their increases overall are weighted by the amount of revenue they yield. The basket items for the combined water and sewerage companies are:

1. Unmeasured water
2. Unmeasured sewerage
3. Measured water
4. Measured sewerage
5. Trade effluent.

Only (1) and (3) apply to water-only companies.

Basket items may increase at different rates, as may their individual components (e.g. standing and volumetric charges within measured water), as long as the overall price cap for the total basket is not breached. Moreover not all charges are subject to the RPI + K formula. For example, maximum infrastructure charges to property developers are set down in licences and there are no limits on connection charges. However, the director general requires that all prices are related to costs and that the companies show no discrimination between classes of customer in setting their charges (see Chapter 6 on price discrimination). Companies have therefore had to 'rebalance' their tariffs accordingly.

The impact on charges

The impact on charges can best be assessed by considering separately the effects of the separate price determinations at the time of privatisation and at the two subsequent periodic reviews.

The first charging period, 1989–1994/5

The original 1989 price cap was set by the secretaries of state for the environment and for Wales at the time of privatisation. **Table 14.1** shows the increases in unmeasured water and sewerage bills in **cash terms** (i.e. including the effects of inflation) between 1989/90 and 1994/5. The rates of increase of charges for *unmeasured water* varied from less than 50 per cent to almost 150 per cent and the level of water charge varied between £67 and £153 in 1994/5. The rates of increase of charges for *unmeasured sewerage* (obviously not applicable for the water-only companies) varied between 52 per cent and 122 per cent whilst the level of sewerage charge varied between £83 and £185. The **average real increase** in charges was 5 per cent a year between 1989 and 1994. In allowing prices to increase in real terms, the price cap was quite unlike the cases for British Telecom and British Gas, where 1994 prices fell by about 7.5 per cent and 5.0 per cent after inflation, respectively.

In respect of the *water and sewerage companies only*, the combined average bill of £200 was 67 per cent greater than bills in 1989 before privatisation, compared with an increase in retail prices of 25 per cent. Average water bills rose by 69 per cent and average sewerage bills by

Table 14.1   Average unmeasured household water and sewerage bills, 1994/5

| Company | Water | | Sewerage | |
| | increase | | increase | |
	1989–1994 (%)	1994/5 (£)	1989–1994 (%)	1994/5 (£)
Water and Sewerage Companies (WaSC)				
Anglian Water Services Ltd	93.8	124	52.2	140
Dwr Cymru Cyfyngedig	69.8	129	78.4	127
North West Water Ltd	65.4	85	64.0	97
Northumbrian Water Ltd	68.9	88	80.3	99
Severn Trent Water Ltd	69.7	80	67.7	99
South West Water Services Ltd	89.5	119	122.4	185
Southern Water Services Ltd	65.3	84	58.4	117
Thames Water Utilities Ltd	55.9	79	67.4	83
Wessex Water Services Ltd	67.9	102	57.1	121
Yorkshire Water Services Ltd	53.7	97	61.3	96
WaSC average (weighted)	69.0	94	66.0	106
Water-Only Companies (WoC)				
Bournemouth & W. Hampshire Water Cos	92.3	87		
Bristol Water plc	60.2	91		
Cambridge Water Company	88.9	96		
Chester Waterworks Company	49.1	107		
Cholderton & District Water Co Ltd	67.2	120		
East Surrey Water plc	101.4	151		
Essex & Suffolk Water plc	78.2	101		
Folkestone & Dover Water Services Ltd	95.9	109		
Hartlepools Water Company	75.6	79		
Mid Kent Water plc	64.1	119		
Mid Southern Water plc	90.0	108		
North East Water plc	66.3	89		
North Surrey Water plc	102.3	89		
Portsmouth Water plc	52.5	67		
South East Water Ltd	89.1	153		
South Staffordshire Water plc	55.2	73		
Sutton District Water plc	97.4	106		
Tendring Hundred Water Services Ltd	149.4	141		
Three Valleys Water Services plc	65.9	91		
Wrexham & E. Denbighshire Water Co	85.4	130		
York Waterworks plc	53.7	82		
WoC average (weighted)	N/A	98		
Industry average (weighted)	N/A	95		106

Note:
Consumers supplied by a WoC also pay a sewerage charge to the WaSC in whose area they live.
WaSC and WoC averages calculated by the National Consumer Council.
Source: Office of Water Services, *Water and Sewerage Bills 1994-5* (Birmingham: OFWAT 1994).

66 per cent. The levels and rates of increase of charges were relatively high compared with those in Scotland, where water and sewerage remained a local government responsibility. The £132 average figure for Scotland was much less than the average £200 bill in England and Wales. However, many of the necessary investment costs would have resulted whatever the form of the industry and it is difficult to compare like with like (see below).

The need for the director general to make trade-offs between protecting companies, consumers and the environment had previously led to criticisms of OFWAT from a wide range of interest groups. Consumer groups such as the National Consumers' Council and the Consumers' Association criticised OFWAT for allowing substantial price increases and inflated profits. For example in 1992/3 the privatised companies achieved a real rate of return of 13 per cent on capital value, almost three times greater than the 5 per cent rate of return that the nationalised water boards had to achieve prior to 1989. Known as the 'privatisation effect', it is this higher rate of return that makes charges higher when water and sewerage are under private ownership than they would have been under public ownership, assuming *ceteris paribus*. Increased capital spending would have been required whether water and sewerage services were privatised or not. Whilst the other privatised utility industries had been able to respond to concerns about high profits by demonstrating price reductions and efficiency improvements, the water and sewerage companies' high profits could not be so defended.

Profits rose by an average of 20 per cent a year between 1989 and 1993, dividends rose by 40 per cent and average share prices doubled (the *Financial Times* all-shares index only rising by 39 per cent) – all this for a low-risk industry with little opportunity of growth in the volume of output (unlike telecommunications and gas). High profit levels were made all the more conspicuous as salaries for company executives tripled over the same period to around £150 000 per annum (plus share options worth much more than that).

The second charging period, 1995/6–1999/00

At the time of the 1994 periodic review the director general was of the view that a return of 5–6 per cent after corporation tax would be adequate to attract sufficient investment funds. This return was allowed for in the post-1995 price limits (OFWAT, 1994). Nevertheless the legal powers of the director general relate to prices, not to profits. Profits remain high if the companies achieve cost reductions through improved productivity and by adopting new technology. However OFWAT specifically stated that it does not want to move towards annual rate of return legislation, effectively cost-plus arrangements. The director

Table 14.2   Charge limits for water and sewerage, 1995–2000

Company	Per cent above inflation	
	1995/6	*1996/7 to 1999/00*
Water and Sewerage Companies		
Anglian Water Services Ltd	1.5	1.5
Dwr Cymru Cyfyngedig	0.5	0.5
North West Water Ltd	2.5	2.5
Northumbrian Water Ltd	2.5	2.5
Severn Trent Water Ltd	0.5	0.5
South West Water Services Ltd	1.5	1.0
Southern Water Services Ltd	4.0	4.0
Thames Water Utilities Ltd	0.5	0.5
Wessex Water Services Ltd	1.5	1.5
Yorkshire Water Services Ltd	2.5	2.5
WaSC average (weighted)	1.5	1.5
Water-Only Companies		
Bournemouth & W. Hampshire Water	−0.5	−0.5
Bristol Water plc	1.0	1.0
Cambridge Water Company	−2.0	−2.0
Chester Waterworks Company	−1.0	−1.0
Cholderton & District Water Co Ltd	0	0
East Surrey Water plc	−1.0	−1.0
Essex & Suffolk Water plc	2.0	2.0
Folkestone & Dover Water Services Ltd	−0.5	−0.5
Hartlepools Water Company	1.5	1.5
Mid Kent Water plc	1.0	1.0
Mid Southern Water plc	−1.0	−1.0
North East Water plc	0	0
North Surrey Water plc	2.0	2.0
Portsmouth Water plc	−1.5	−1.5
South East Water Ltd	−1.0	−1.0
South Staffordshire Water plc	−0.5	−0.5
Sutton District Water plc	−1.5	−1.5
Tendring Hundred Water Services Ltd	−0.5	−0.5
Three Valleys Water Services plc	2.5	2.5
Wrexham & E. Denbighshire Water Co	−2.0	−2.0
York Waterworks plc	0	0
WoC Average (weighted)	0.6	0.6
Industry average (weighted)	1.4	1.4

Note:
Determinations for South West Water and Portsmouth Water were referred to the MMC but the MMC tightened rather than eased the price controls.
Source: Office of Water Services, *Future for Water and Sewerage Services, The Outcome of the Periodic Review* (Birmingham: OFWAT 1994).

general espoused a continuing belief that 'price cap regulation can respond better to the needs of customers and provide more incentives for companies than rate of return regulation' (OFWAT, 1993a, p. 2). This is consistent with the analysis of regulation in Chapter 13.

Despite the need for substantial ongoing investment, the 1994 price cap was much less generous for the companies, having been reduced from 5 per cent faster than the rate of inflation from 1989–95 to 1.4 per cent faster from 1995 to 2000 (see **Table 14.2**). The substantial reduction from 5 per cent to 1.4 per cent reflected the director general's view that maintenance of the original price cap would generate profits for the companies that could not be justified in terms of the risks they faced by the mid 1990s.

As already noted, the original 1989 price cap was set by the secretaries of state for the environment and for Wales. It reflected their assessments of the risks faced by the companies at the time of privatisation. The director general felt that those initial levels of risk had subsided by the time of the 1994 periodic review and therefore he reduced the price cap in order to reduce the profits that would otherwise have been achieved.

Table 14.2 shows considerable variation between companies in their maximum allowed price increases above inflation. This variation is explained by the implications of EU legislation on improving water quality, particularly that covering the treatment of sewage. For example companies with long coastlines and many tourist beaches (e.g. South West Water) have to spend large amounts in order to prevent pollution caused by the dumping of raw sewage into the sea. This largely explains the particularly high percentage increase for sewerage charges for South West Water in **Table 14.1**. Another example is that provided by the 14 water-only companies, whose price limits for 1995–2000 restricted them to increases below the rate of inflation (**Table 14.2**). This is largely because the bulk of investment is required for the treatment of sewage.

The third charging period, 2000/1–2004/5

The 1999 periodic review brought the first price reductions since privatisation. Across the industry as a whole, the average price reduction in 2000/1 was 12.3 per cent, with an expected reduction of 2.1 per cent over the full period up to 2005 (see **Table 14.3**). No company was allowed a price increase in 2000/1. Prices remain broadly flat for the following two years but then begin to rise slowly. Unlike **Table 14.2**, these price limits do not include inflation and therefore the reductions will be even greater in real terms. They cover the tariff basket which includes metered and unmetered charges for water and sewerage and charges for trade effluent.

Table 14.3   Price limits for 2000–1 to 2004–5

	2000–1	2001–2	Annual Price Limits 2002–3	2003–4	2004–5	Average
Water and Sewerage Companies						
Anglian	−10.0	1.0	2.2	2.5	2.5	−0.5
Dwr Cymru	−10.5	−0.5	0.0	1.2	1.0	−1.9
North West	−9.3	−1.0	0.0	4.0	4.5	−0.5
Northumbrian	−19.4	−2.0	0.0	0.0	0.0	−4.6
Severn Trent	−14.1	−1.0	−1.0	0.0	1.0	−3.2
South West	−12.2	0.0	2.0	2.0	2.0	−1.4
Southern	−13.0	0.0	0.0	1.6	0.8	−2.3
Thames	−11.7	0.0	0.0	−0.8	0.0	−2.6
Wessex	−12.0	0.0	0.0	3.8	4.7	−0.9
Yorkshire	−14.5	0.0	0.0	0.0	1.0	−2.9
WaSC average (weighted)	−12.3	−0.4	0.2	1.3	1.7	−2.0
Water-Only Companies						
Bournemouth & W. Hants	−3.0	−1.7	−1.7	0.0	1.7	−1.0
Bristol	−10.0	1.0	1.0	0.0	−1.9	−2.1
Cambridge	−14.3	0.0	−1.2	−0.4	−0.9	−3.5
Cholderton	−8.0	−5.0	0.0	0.0	0.0	−2.7
Dee Valley	−10.6	−2.6	−3.0	−3.0	0.0	−3.9
Essex and Suffolk	−13.8	0.0	0.0	0.0	0.0	−2.9
Folkestone & Dover	0.0	1.0	3.0	3.0	3.2	2.0
Mid Kent	−19.7	0.0	0.0	0.0	1.6	−4.0
North Surrey	−15.0	0.0	0.0	2.0	2.2	−2.4
Portsmouth	−3.0	−1.2	−1.3	−0.5	−1.0	−1.4
South East	−16.1	−1.0	−1.5	0.0	0.0	−3.9
South Staffordshire	−2.7	−1.0	−1.0	−1.0	−1.0	−1.3
Sutton & E. Surrey	−17.0	−5.0	−2.4	0.0	0.0	−5.1
Tendring Hundred	−6.9	1.0	2.0	2.0	2.0	0.0
Three Valleys	−15.2	0.0	0.0	0.0	0.0	−3.2
York	−9.0	−1.0	0.0	0.0	0.0	−2.1
WoC average (weighted)	−12.4	−0.6	−0.5	0.0	0.0	−2.8
Industry average (weighted)	−12.3	−0.4	0.1	1.1	1.5	−2.1

Notes:
1. Price limits do not include inflation.
2. Mid Kent and Sutton and East Surrey appealed to the Competition Commission. The Commission ruled that the price cuts required in this table are too onerous and so reduced them. Likewise, Anglian Water, Welsh Water and Tendring Hundred appealed to the new director general appointed in 2000.

Source: Office of Water Services 1999 Periodic Review, *Future Water and Sewerage Charges 2000–5: Final Determinations* (Birmingham: OFWAT 1999).

The regulator took account of the Labour government's views as set down in *A Fair Deal for Consumers* (1998) and effectively passed on to customers the efficiency savings achieved by the companies. Consumers are now benefiting not just from lower prices but also from a higher quality service and an improved environment. In fact, the 1999 review superceded the remainder of the 1994 periodic review which had already set price limits for the period covered by the 1999 review. The expectation in 1994 was that price limits could be set for 10 years for this 'long term' industry characterised by long term investments and low rates of technological change. However, the companies were able to cut costs much faster and much more substantially than had been expected by both the government and the regulator. Hence, the 1994 review's price limits beyond 2000 were re-determined and the regulatory period reduced to five years. Whereas the 1994 review had set industry-wide charge limits at 0.4 per cent above inflation between 2000/1 and 2004/5, the 1999 review requires a reduction in nominal (cash) prices of 2.1 per cent irrespective of the change in the retail price index.

The director general's calculations of the likely charges resulting from the 1999 periodic review are set out in **Table 14.4**. The average household bill of £248 in 1999/00 is expected to fall to £218 in 2004/5, a 12 per cent reduction in real terms. Actual bills will depend on the companies' charging schemes, as approved by the director general. They will also depend on whether a household is on a metered or unmeasured supply and, if the former, the extent to which a household tries to save water and therefore money. The director expects metered (measured) bills to fall faster than unmeasured bills and be 20 per cent less than unmeasured bills in 2004/5.

Variations in the figures for individual companies in the above tables reflect the different K factors which, in turn, reflect the different phasing of investment programmes over the three charging periods. For example, the figures for North West in **Tables 14.3** and **14.4** towards the end of the period reflect the environmental obligations placed on the company and the consequently large investment expenditures. The K factors also reflect scope for further efficiency savings by individual companies, some companies having already secured a greater proportion of potential efficiency gains than others.

The experience of the water and sewerage industry is similar to that of the other privatised industries, all of whose X factors were initially set at too low a level. They were successively tightened in subsequent price reviews as evidence of greater efficiency (resulting from the incentives of price regulation) became apparent. The price limits for water and sewerage determined at the time of privatisation in 1989 were based on expected cost savings of £6 in the average household bill between 1990

Table 14.4   Average expected household bills (£)

	1999/00		2004/5		Total
	Water	Sewerage	Water	Sewerage	change
Water and Sewerage Companies					
Anglian	120	157	105	142	−30
Dwr Cymru	134	168	114	150	−38
North West	104	143	117	121	−9
Northumbrian	101	143	86	111	−47
Severn Trent	113	118	102	91	−38
South West	119	237	115	205	−36
Southern	112	166	83	156	−39
Thames	104	102	94	86	−26
Wessex	126	146	113	138	−21
Yorkshire	115	126	99	111	−31
WaSC average (weighted)	112	135	103	116	−28
Water-Only Companies					
Bournemouth & W. Hants	101		98		−3
Bristol	113		100		−13
Cambridge	97		83		−14
Cholderton	139		121		−18
Dee Valley	120		96		24
Essex and Suffolk	128		108		−20
Folkestone & Dover	117		126		9
Mid Kent	147		117		−30
North Surrey	125		107		−18
Portsmouth	81		74		−7
South East	138		108		−30
South Staffordshire	88		82		−6
Sutton and E Surrey	133		96		37
Tendring Hundred	148		132		−16
Three Valleys	125		103		−22
York	96		84		−12
WoC average (weighted)	119		100		−19
Industry average (weighted)	113	135	102	116	−30

Notes:
1. May 1999 prices.
2. The actual impact on bills will also be governed by companies' charging
   schemes as approved by the regulator.
Source: Office of Water Services 1999 Periodic Review, *Future Water and Sewerage Charges 2000–5: Final Determinations* (Birmingham: OFWAT 1999).

and 1995. The subsequent periodic reviews in 1994 and 1999 expected even greater efficiency savings. Allowing for its interruption, expected savings almost doubled in the 1994 review. The 1999 review's assumptions of even more substantial efficiency savings led to a corresponding expected reduction in average bills of £60 between 1999/00 and 2004/5. That £60 comprised £35 made possible by higher than expected past efficiency savings and £25 from further efficiency savings up to 2004/5. However the actual expected reduction in the average bill was only half the £60 figure, the costs of improvements in drinking water and environmental quality reducing the actual reduction to £30.

Financing the investment programme

The combination of the high capital expenditures for water supply with the increasingly substantial investment in wastewater treatment facilities in line with EU and national environmental regulations make this already highly capital-intensive industry increasingly so. Under the 1999 periodic review's price limits, operating costs will account for approximately 40 per cent of revenue, capital charges for 30 per cent, the remaining 30 per cent being the return on capital.

The bulk of new investment has been financed on a 'pay-as-you-go' basis, from revenue raised from charges rather than from borrowing. This resulted in current consumers paying several billions of pounds each year for investments that will benefit future consumers over the next 40 years or so. Consumer groups argued that it would be fairer to finance the investment programme through borrowing so as to spread the cost over the lifetime of the capital assets in order that the current generation of consumers do not subsidise future consumers. In fact, it could also be argued that current consumers were being asked to make up for the lack of investment in water and sewerage during the 1970s and 1980s, the cost of which would otherwise have fallen on taxpayers.

Indeed it is arguable that water and sewerage were privatised specifically to pass the costs of necessary investments on to the private sector and so avoid the significant implications for public expenditure, taxation and public borrowing. The Conservative government was trying to constrain or reduce all three at the time of privatisation (see Chapters 9, 10 and 11). Similarly, it could be argued that the 'pay as you go' financing of capital investments relieves shareholders of the costs and risks associated with relatively high levels of debt charges, payment of which takes precedence over dividends on equity.

If valid, these criticisms mean that privatisation and regulation exploited rather than protected consumers by appropriating finance:

- from current to future consumers,
- from current consumers to holders of equity, and
- from current consumers to taxpayers.

This exploitation has been facilitated by:

- the continuing monopoly nature of the industry
- the price inelasticity of demand for water and sewerage services
- the K factor cost-pass through.

In the early to mid 1990s, nationally over a quarter of water was lost in mains leakage between leaving reservoirs and reaching final users. In some areas the rate of leakage was almost 40 per cent. Bizarrely, the K factor meant that companies earned much greater profits if they spent lots of money building new reservoirs, pumping stations, and so on, than if they spent much more modest sums repairing leaking pipes (see below). Put simply, consumers were being asked to finance unnecessarily high costs so that shareholders benefited from higher profits.

These distributional issues could be analysed in terms of the rent-seeking public choice framework (see Chapters 7 and 13). Any such exploitation of consumers has particularly adverse effects on low-income groups and large families, two groups that the 1997 Labour government has sought to protect (see Chapter 12) and which may be adversely affected by introduction of metering (see below). Hence, the social implications of regulation cannot be ignored.

OFWAT has had some sympathy with these arguments. The 1994 and 1999 periodic reviews required the companies to progressively increase the proportion of profits used to finance the remaining investment programme necessary to meet EU legislation. As already noted, the 1999 review brought the first price reductions since privatisation. The K factor became negative for all 10 of the WaSCs and for all but two of the WoCs (see **Table 14.3**). In the 1994 periodic review all WaSCs had been allocated positive K factors (see **Table 14.2**). In effect, expected efficiency savings were more than double the allowance for cost-pass through under the 1999 periodic review with the result that household bills fall and, likewise, so do the companies' operating profits.

This led to claims by the companies of a harsh regulatory regime and to proposals for mutualisation of several water companies (see above). Water UK, which represents the industry, warned of resulting substantial job losses, reduced maintenance expenditures, reduced profits and dividends and heavy borrowing to finance investment programmes. The companies have not been reluctant in the past to reduce their workforces in order to improve efficiency, reduce costs and increase profits. Their workforce was cut by over a quarter during the 1990s. Moreover, the director general argued that shareholders have no automatic right to increased dividends – they have to be earned through greater efficiency (rather than through monopoly pricing). Ultimately, however, companies disputing price determinations can ask the director general to refer the matter to the Competition Commission (the successor to the Monopolies and Mergers Commission). See the notes to **Tables 14.2** and **14.3**.

Whether the regulatory regime is too harsh remains to be seen. Certainly, in the past review periods, the companies have consistently outperformed the director general's expectations about how efficient they could become. The director general has tried to strike a reasonable balance between passing efficiency savings back to customers through lower bills; continuing to seek improvements in water quality and the environment; improving levels of service (e.g. increased reliability of supply and reduced sewer flooding); and allowing companies also to profit from their greater efficiency. The progressively greater expected cost savings at each periodic review demonstrate the benefits of yardstick competition, even if direct competition could achieve even greater efficiency gains were such competition feasible.

Paying for environmental regulation

Environmental regulation has implications for water and sewerage charges: in general, the more the environment is protected the greater the cost and the greater therefore the charges necessary to fund it. In the 15 years between 1990 and 2005 a £50 billion investment programme will have been implemented to refurbish and improve water supply and the treatment and disposal of sewage, all financed by consumers. OFWAT calculated that this investment programme (averaging over £3 billion a year) would cause water and sewerage charges to rise 50 per cent faster than the rate of inflation during the 1990s. Hence there is interdependence between both economic and environmental forms of regulation. This interdependence differentiates the regulatory regime for water and sewerage from the regulatory regimes for the other public utilities: gas, electricity and telecommunications

Whilst the director general acknowledged his statutory obligation to ensure that companies are able to finance the standards set by the UK government and the EU, he preferred to treat companies as service providers rather than as environmental contractors because the latter function would require high K factors. In effect, water consumers would be paying the costs of environmental protection, something which the water companies and many environmental bodies have claimed they would be willing to do but which the director general has been unwilling to accept. Moreover, OFWAT has consistently advocated that all quality initiatives should be fully costed and compared with the resulting benefits, something that calls for a full cost–benefit analysis. In questioning whether the benefits justify the costs, the director general created an element of tension between OFWAT and the environmental regulator. This tension was enhanced when the director general advocated renegotiation of the EU directives, or delays in their implementation, so as to allow time for more cost-effective planning and for new technological developments to reduce costs. He was concerned that current consumers would also be paying for unnecessarily expensive environmental protection programmes and for some costs that should be financed out of general taxation.

The regulatory framework results in the consumer being made to pay for the costs of cleaner water. This is allocatively efficient for that part of pollution resulting from the dumping of untreated sewage into rivers from which the same company abstracts water (i.e. the externality is internalised). However, it is not allocatively efficient to require consumers of water and sewerage services to pay for the costs imposed by other forms of pollution (e.g. from agricultural chemicals or road drainage). Most of the extra investment costs relate to the costs of meeting the EU's Urban Waste Water Treatment Directive of 1991.

14.6 Restructuring water and sewerage in Scotland

As already noted, the then Conservative government restructured water and sewerage in Scotland into three quangos in 1996. These three water authorities remain within the public sector and serve different parts of Scotland: east, west and north. The limited political representation of the Conservative Party in Scotland made privatisation of Scottish water and sewerage too politically controversial. A vigorous anti-privatisation campaign in Scotland led to opinion polls and a referendum (the latter financed by the former Strathclyde Regional Council) which showed overwhelming opposition (in excess of 80 per cent of respondents) to privatisation of water and sewerage in Scotland. A similar response followed publication of the 1992 White Paper on reorganisation of water and sewerage.

Instead, the industry was reorganised. Prior to 1996 the then nine Scottish regional councils were already of such large geographical area that they had probably already fully exploited economies of scale. However, reform of Scottish local government in 1996 tripled the number of local authorities such that some structural reform was required if economies of scale were not to be lost. Hence, the three public water authorities were created. Whilst they could easily be privatised, any remaining economies of scale are limited by their already large size. Moreover, privatisation would create even less competition in Scotland than what little has been created in England and Wales.

When in opposition prior to 1997, Labour had promised that the water and sewerage industry in Scotland would remain democratically controlled, but without specifying how. Following establishment of the Scottish Parliament, this became an issue for the Scottish Executive. Mutualisation was an option (see above) but reform was less radical in simply appointing local politicians to the boards of the three authorities and establishing a consultative committee for each water authority.

Whatever the governance structure, Scottish water and sewerage services face many of the same regulatory issues as the privatised companies in England and Wales. Economic regulation of the industry was vested in the Water Industry Commissioner for Scotland in 1999. The Commissioner is responsible for promoting the interests of customers and advising the Scottish Executive on the level of charges. Environmental regulation was vested in the Scottish Environment Protection Agency (SEPA) in 1996.

Both Conservative and Labour governments stated their intention to attract private sector investment in order to finance the massive investment programme required to meet EU quality standards. Both governments used the private finance initiative to introduce private sector finance and management into the provision of infrastructure (see Chapter 8). The private companies recover costs through treatment charges or other arrangements. Whilst competition could be encouraged by competitive franchising, it would not transfer the necessary capital expenditures to the private sector and may lead to high transaction costs. Nevertheless, awarding franchise contracts through competitive tendering could bring efficiency gains through cost reduction (see Chapter 15). Although the division of property rights may lead to opportunisitic behaviour as franchisees seek to exploit ambiguities in contracts for the operation of these highly specific assets (see Chapter 2), this may not be a significant problem for water and sewerage since quality of output is readily assessable.

Opponents of privatisation made much of the fact that average water and sewerage charges were substantially lower in Scotland than in England and Wales during the1990s (see above). However, rather than reflecting greater efficiency under public ownership, those relatively low charges resulted from substantially lower levels of capital expenditure per head. This resulted in a lower quality of service. For example, in 1992 a third of Scottish households were drinking water contaminated with lead and over half of water mains pipes were more than 50 years old and in need of replacement, especially unlined cast-iron mains pipes. Moreover it was claimed that the environmental regulatory regime for sewage disposal was not as strict in Scotland, since a third of the members of the then river purification boards were nominated by the councils they were supposed to regulate. Hence sewerage treatment investments had not been forced upon Scottish local authorities to the same extent as the then NRA had imposed them on the private companies in England and Wales. This confusion of roles provided the rationale for the separation of monitoring and control of discharges (subsequently by SEPA) from the sewerage authorities.

Whilst the English and Welsh privatised companies cut costs by substantial reductions in employment (of over a fifth during the 1990s), employment in the Scottish industry was virtually unchanged and much greater per thousand resident population than in England and Wales. Charges in Scotland began to catch up with those in England and Wales after the 1996 reorganisation as infrastructural investments were made in accordance with EU standards. Scottish charges continued to rise under the new regulatory regime in 2000, at a time when charges were being cut in England and Wales (see above).

Hence, it would be over-simplistic to argue that public ownership is superior to privatisation based only on charge levels at a particular point in time. Account also has to be taken of differing water and sewerage service standards, differing balances between demand and available water resources, differing demographic, household and industrial structures, different population densities and so on. As already noted in Chapter 13, it is very difficult to compare like with like when judging the relative efficiencies of public and private sector ownership of enterprises.

14.7 Charging for water and sewerage services

The charges listed in **Tables 14.1** and **14.4** are not derived from the costs imposed by use of the service. Students often appear incredulous of the notion that payment should be directly related to use, the frequent claim being that water is a free natural resource ('manna from heaven') to which people have a moral right of use, much like access to breathable air. Unlike air, however, water has to be collected (in reservoirs), purified (in treatment works) and then distributed (through the water mains and pipes networks) to the houses, shops, offices and industrial and commercial premises where people live and work. Hence water is **not** free simply because it falls out of the sky. In fact it has many of the system-based characteristics of gas and electricity, charges for which are universally accepted in principle. The first quotation at the beginning of this chapter highlights such comparability. In addition, once used, wastewater has to be disposed of in a sanitary manner, untreated sewage being hazardous to public health.

Water and sewerage have traditionally been supply-oriented (rather than demand-oriented) and dominated by an engineering approach to service provision: what is demanded must be supplied. As reservoirs and natural water sources have become progressively depleted by increasing demand, water providers have looked for supplementary sources of supply, building more reservoirs, increasing the levels of abstraction from rivers and drilling more wells. The emphasis on increasing supply rather than on constraining demand has resulted in the structure of charges being viewed as simply a way of recovering the inescapable costs of supply. Crude flat-rate charges unrelated to volume of use have therefore been preferred to sophisticated tariff structures related to volume and cost of use.

If charging for water consumption reduces demand, there will be knock-on effects for the sewerage service since sewage is almost the reverse flow of the supply of water, being about 99 per cent water. This may affect the ability of both services to cover costs, each having high proportions of fixed (network) costs within total costs. Hence joint supply relationships must be recognised.

The joint provision of water and sewerage services creates difficulties in separating joint overheads such as administration and interest payments. These are in addition to the standard accounting problems of current versus historic cost accounting which are more salient for such capital-intensive services. It is also important to distinguish costs directly attributable to use and those independent of use. Bearing these caveats in mind, it appears that almost a quarter of sewerage costs are related to highway drainage, almost a quarter to properties and other (impermeable) surface drainage and just over half to foul drainage (OFWAT, 1991).

Private companies in England and Wales are prohibited by the 1989 Water Act from charging highway authorities for drainage costs. This inconsistency is important since run-off from roads is increasingly polluted and disposal costs are rising as a result. It is perhaps more acceptable for the general taxpayer to bear such costs but questionable whether the water user (rather than road user) should pay.

Alternative charging methodologies can be judged in terms of seven objectives:

1. **Financial**: to raise sufficient revenue to cover operating costs, finance investment programmes and provide a reasonable rate of return to shareholders or to government.
2. **Economic**: allocating water and sewerage services between customers and over time so as to maximise economic welfare. This requires tariff structures to create sensible incentives for both customers and companies.
3. **Equity**: defined in the second quotation at the beginning of this chapter as 'fair and affordable'. This suggests that customers in similar circumstances pay similar bills and that differences in bills properly reflect relevant differences in circumstances.

4. **Simplicity and comprehensibility**: so customers can appreciate what determines their bill and how they can influence it.
5. **Public health**: avoiding charging systems that endanger health and the environment (e.g. by making potable water too expensive).
6. **Environmental protection**: aided by charges that create incentives to conserve water and reduce sewage pollution.
7. **Economic development**: ensuring that the water and sewerage infrastructure can accommodate economic growth.

The alternative charging methodologies are as follows:

Rateable Values

Rateable values are the values attributed to individual properties in determining the tax base on which the local government tax is levied. Most domestic customers in England and Wales pay a charge that is related to the rateable value of their property plus a fixed standing charge (see below). The calculation of the charge is as follows:

$$\text{Bill (£)} = \text{standing charge (£)}$$
$$+ \frac{(\text{rateable value (£)} \times \text{variable rateable value charge (p)})}{100}$$

Both elements of the bill are flat-rate charges in that they are not related to volume of use. The standing charge and the variable rateable value charge are common to all customers of a particular company. Hence variations in bills between customers of a particular company reflect variations in the rateable values of the properties in which they live. Water and sewerage charges are greater the greater the rateable value of the property. Hence this is a **tax methodology** since it relates charges to property values rather than to the actual costs of meeting demand by individual consumers.

Payments are easily recovered from occupiers of properties and are reasonably simple and comprehensible, hence satisfying finance and development objectives. Customers know exactly what they will pay and suppliers know exactly what they will receive and therefore can be reasonably sure of covering costs. Public health objectives are satisfied to the extent that additional use of water is free once the fixed payment has been made. This charging method also promoted equity during the nineteenth century when rateable values were an accurate indicator of income and therefore of ability to pay. However they are no longer an accurate proxy for income or wealth. It is also not self-evident that rateable values reflect the benefit of provision of these services. Hence this tax methodology creates many anomalies for equity.

The other major disadvantages are that such a charging scheme fails to meet economic and environmental objectives. It does not relate payment to use of service, costs of provision or quality of service, nor does it provide any incentive to avoid wasteful use of water. Once the flat-rate charge is paid water and sewerage become free goods (at zero marginal cost to the consumer) and so there is no incentive to conserve water and reduce pollution from sewage.

The advantage of rateable values prior to 1974 was that such a billing system was cheap to administer in that the same system was used for financing other local government services. Indeed, despite the 1974 separation of responsibility in England and Wales, local government continued to collect charges on behalf of the water authorities on the same basis. This arrangement ended with the replacement of the rates by the community charge (see Chapter 10) but the private companies in England and Wales can still make use of the (ageing) system of rateable values at much cheaper cost than devising their own system. The 1989 Water Act had prohibited the use of rateable values in England and Wales after the year 2000 but prohibition was dropped because companies were unable to develop a viable alternative. Dwellings built since 1 April 1990 do not have rateable values. Hence, in having no specific rateable values, properties built since 1990 have had to be metered in order that companies can charge for provision of water and sewerage services. This accounts, in part, for the growing use of meters (see below).

It would be possible to make use of the banded rateable values now used for the purposes of local government's council tax. This is the option favoured by the water companies and is already the case in Scotland. **Table 14.5** provides data for one of the three Scottish public water authorities. The valuation bands are the same as those for the council tax (see the note to the table). The bills for each band are set as proportions of band D properties, whose households pay the average council tax set by each authority. Bills for houses in band A are two-thirds of those in band D whilst houses in band H pay twice as much as those in band D. However, the discounts available for the council tax also apply to water charges. For example there is a 25 per cent discount for single adult households.

Use of banded rateable values is subject to many of the same criticisms as use of rateable values. The director general of OFWAT has stated that he would only approve property banding (based on rateable value or any other property characteristic) if differences between bands reflect the likely differences in water use and hence in costs. This is unlikely to be the case for valuation bands in general and for the Scottish bands in particular, households in the highest band paying three times as much as those in the lowest band. Some of the privatised companies have suggested banding with a ratio of as much as 9:1, this having the

Table 14.5   Water and sewerage charges, West of Scotland Water, 2000/1 (£)

Valuation bands	A	B	C	D	E	F	G	H
Water charge	79.60	92.87	106.13	119.40	145.93	172.47	199.00	238.80
Sewerage charge	69.20	80.73	92.27	103.80	126.87	149.93	173.00	207.60
Total charge	148.80	173.60	198.40	223.20	272.80	322.40	372.00	446.40

Note:
The valuation bands are the same as those for the local government council tax:

Band A up to £27 000	Band E £58 000 – £80 000
Band B £27 000 – £35 000	Band F £80 000 – £106 000
Band C £35 000 – £45 000	Band G £106 000 – £212 000
Band D £45 000 – £58 000	Band H over £212 000

Source: West of Scotland Water (Glasgow).

advantage of bringing about a substantial reduction in the bills of (generally poor) households in the lowest council tax band. However, it is a question of principle whether private profit-seeking companies should have powers to tax their customers, this objection already applying to use of rateable values.

A fixed standing charge (licence fee) per property

Use of only a licence fee would be equivalent to a single property valuation band, clearly unrelated to use. As already noted, most domestic consumers in England and Wales still pay a charge based on rateable value plus a standing charge. Whilst the proportions vary between different companies, the standing charge typically accounts for about a quarter of the total bill. Rateable values typically account for the other three-quarters. Both are flat-rate charges. The major advantages of a standing charge are the revenue certainty for the supplier and the administrative simplicity, subject to defining adequately a 'chargeable unit' (e.g. within bedsit or subdivided properties). However it is unrelated to costs, benefits, use, volumetric supply, quality of service, need to encourage economies or ability to pay. The level of charge is essentially arbitrary (depending on the water and sewerage companies' accounting definitions of fixed and variable costs) and therefore varies widely (OFWAT, 1991). It also ignores distance-related costs and therefore tends to favour low-density housing far from the treatment facilities and existing network. This favourable treatment may become capitalised into house prices (see Appendix 10.3) and encourage urban sprawl. Some companies have abolished standing charges in order to encourage customers to opt for meters, all of the bill thereby being related to volume of water used.

Charges based on the number of residents

This flat-rate charging methodology has been used in parts of Britain. The previous Scottish system of community water charges charged on the basis of the number of **adults** resident in each household, coincident with liability to pay the community charge, effectively a poll tax (see Chapter 10). It utilised the poll tax register, so economising on data collection, but experienced many of the non-collection problems of the poll tax. It was comprehensible and satisfied public health objectives in that it did not deter additional consumption. Otherwise it met none of the other charging objectives listed above. It was not related to income or to use. It effectively assumed that each adult uses the same volume of water and ignored use of water by children and teenagers under the age of 18, these not being classified as adults.

Charges based on other housing characteristics

Charges could relate to the physical characteristics of the property such as floor area of house and/or garden, whether detached, semi-detached or terraced, diameter of the service pipe, number of rooms (in total or just bedrooms), the number of water-using appliances (possibly including outside taps, hosepipes and sprinklers), and so on. There appear to be few advantages for these options. Most are expensive to administer (existing powers of entry may need extending for inspection), they are not demonstrably more accurate than rateable values in terms of service use, and they become complex when used in combination with each other and with rateable values. They provide no incentives to economy or to environmental protection and, again, the director general is unlikely to favour property banding. Case law would be required to define a bedroom.

Metering and charging in accordance with volume used

Metering is already extensively used for non-domestic users but traditionally has not been used for households. The UK is therefore unusual in that two-thirds of OECD member states meter over 90 per cent of single family households (OECD, 1999). Only 3 per cent of households in England and Wales were metered (i.e. charged on a measured basis) in 1992/3. However, that proportion rose sharply to 11 per cent in 1997/8 and, further, to about 18 per cent by 2000/1. As already noted, metering is required for new domestic properties built since 1990 (because no rateable value exists). However, companies were also introducing increasingly attractive meter option schemes for other properties (the Water Industry Act 1999 requiring free installation of meters).

The director general of OFWAT is in favour of metering as the fairest way of apportioning charges in relation to water use and costs and because it gives customers the choice of reducing their bills by economising on their use of water. Likewise, the Environment Agency also favours metering to promote sustainability via demand management (see above). However, metering will not of itself promote the achievement of economic efficiency because of four qualifications.

First, the associated capital costs make it uneconomic in regions with surplus capacity or low water development costs. In other words, metering may be more expensive than building new reservoirs and so on.

Second, households switching from unmeasured to measured charges may not be any more economical in their use of water and sewerage services. Optional metering is more attractive:

- the higher the rateable value and therefore the bill derived from it, and
- the fewer the number of people in the household, which therefore uses less water.

Hence, affluent small households occupying expensive properties (with high rateable values and, therefore, charges) are increasingly opting to have meters installed simply as a means of reducing their bills, without reducing their consumption. As already noted in respect of **Table 14.4**, the director general expects metered (measured) bills to fall faster than unmeasured bills and be 20 per cent less than unmeasured bills in 2004/5. This will increase the rate at which affluent households switch to optional metering. In fact, the rise in household demand for water is driven mainly by new households which are generally metered.

Third, water and sewerage costs are an extremely low proportion of average household income (just over 1 per cent), such that measured charges may have little or no impact.

Fourth, the tariff structure may not relate charges to the incremental cost of supply. The tariff structure is of crucial importance in relating charges to marginal costs (see Chapter 6). Any charge directly related to the volume of water consumed will cause the marginal cost of consumption to rise, marginal cost being zero for the previous four charging methodologies. Assuming *ceteris paribus*, this will have a redistributive effect on demand irrespective of whether the average cost per household rises, falls or remains constant. Average cost would rise in the short run if the introduction of volumetric charging causes aggregate demand to fall against fixed capital costs.

The metered volumetric rates could rise, remain constant or fall as the rate of consumption increases. The first may be most efficient where increased use leads to a shortage of capacity, necessitating new investment. The last variant may be justified where greater use spreads high fixed costs over a larger output and there is no capacity constraint in the foreseeable future and no adverse environmental effects arising from over-abstraction or pollution. The intermediate case may be most efficient where costs are constant over all realistic rates of use.

Figures 14.1 and **14.2** illustrate two tariff schedules in respect of a metered rate (R), which falls as the volume of water consumed (V), increases.

A continuous tariff schedule

This is shown in **Figure 14.1**. As the level of consumption rises from $V2$ to $V3$ the rate paid by the consumer (or household) falls from $R2$ to $R3$. The economic rationale for such a structure is based on the economies of scale associated with the indivisible distribution network costs of utility industries (see Chapter 6). In being convex to the origin, the schedule assumes that economies of scale are ultimately exhausted and so the metered rate falls more slowly (moving from R_{max} to R_{min} as the volume of water consumed increases (from V_1 to V_4). R_{min} is the minimum rate that must be paid, irrespective of volumetric consumption above V_4. R_{max} is the maximum rate that must be paid for all levels of consumption below V_1.

Figure 14.1   A continuous water rate schedule

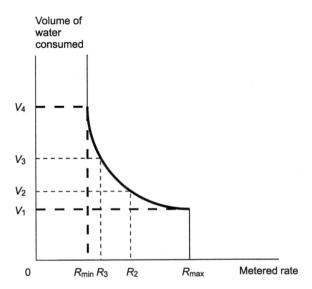

A stepped tariff schedule

This is shown in **Figure 14.2** where three separate charges are associated with three separate bands of consumption. All levels of consumption falling within band 1 (i.e. between zero and V_1) pay a metered rate of R_{max} All levels of consumption falling within band 3 (i.e. above V_4) pay a metered rate of R_{min}). This is the same as for the schedule in **Figure 14.1**. However, unlike the multiplicity of rates between V_1 and V_4 in the continuous water rate schedule in **Figure 14.1**, the schedule in **Figure 14.2** has only a single rate (R_s) payable on all levels consumption falling within band 2 (i.e. between V_1 and V_4).

Stepped tariff schedules are simpler for billing procedures. There is a multiplicity of rates between R_{min} and R_{max} in **Figure 14.1** but only one in **Figure 14.2**. Such a multiplicity of rates causes increased complexity in billing procedures.

Stepped tariff schedules are common for large industrial and commercial customers, most comprising only two blocks but a few as many as five blocks. They are commonly referred to as 'discounted falling block tariffs', discounts generally being around 30 per cent but varying widely. They are less able to reflect economies of scale but have the advantage (to the water companies) of encouraging use, price elasticity of demand being high for the non-household sector.

Stepped tariff schedules are increasingly common for metered household customers, but are typically 'rising block tariffs', the opposite of

Figure 14.2 A stepped water rate schedule

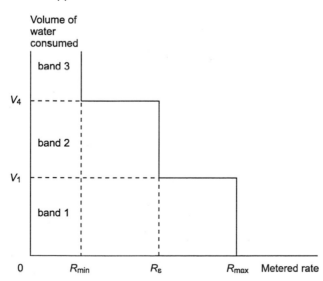

those for the non-household sector. Rising block tariffs may be justified because, as already noted, households account for about 70 per cent of water used. They may also be justified on merit goods and negative externalities grounds (see above). Protection of the environment from over-abstraction and from critical pollution thresholds may require rising water rate schedules, at least beyond some level of consumption. Moreover, protection of low-income families and other vulnerable groups, together with the argument that people have right of access to an amount of water sufficient for normal living, may require the schedule to be flat up to an agreed minimum level of use, thereafter rising rapidly with increasing consumption. From the water companies' perspective, the major advantage is the greater level of profits of a rising block tariff when applied to the price inelastic demand of the household sector.

However, all volume charges create uncertainty in respect of their revenue yield, volume consumed varying with weather patterns and with the state of local and regional economies. Billing would be made simpler for the household sector by the fact that no separate licence fee would be required for hosepipes, sprinklers or swimming pools if all domestic properties in a company's area were metered. Flat-rate charges for such uses provide inappropriate incentives and, besides, bans on use of hosepipes during periods of water shortage deny use at the very time they are most required.

Efficiency problems may still arise in that the time-averaging of metered rates causes cross-subsidy between peak and off-peak use, whether daily, weekly or seasonally (see Chapter 6). This may be dealt with in the future as metering technology improves (e.g. electronic metering by time of use or dual-flow meters that register relatively faster as the rate of flow increases). Meanwhile, some companies have introduced seasonal tariffs for large and medium business users and others require households with lawn sprinklers and swimming pools to install meters, as a means of discouraging peak use.

Arguments that metering would be too expensive to introduce relative to the resource savings it would engender only relate to accounting costs for water companies and users. Reductions in water use yield cost savings for the treatment of sewage, the costs of which are rising dramatically as a result of the EU directives referred to above. Moreover accounting cost analyses ignore wider environmental costs and concentrate on short-term perspectives. Where demand is approaching a capacity constraint, meter installation costs may be cheaper than the capital expenditures required to build new reservoirs, the associated land and distribution network costs and the subsequent sewerage costs. Hence the timing of the installation of meters is crucial in determining their cost effectiveness.

The time horizon will be much shorter for areas experiencing rapid demographic and economic development (e.g. the south-east of England and East Anglia) than it is for those experiencing decline (e.g. Northumbria), simply because existing capacity constraints will be more immediate for the former than for the latter. Anglian has introduced meters for about half of its homes because it faces water shortages resulting from a growing population and rainfall only two-thirds of the UK average. Northumbrian, however, meters less than 5 per cent of houses in its region because it has substantial spare capacity, resulting primarily from falling industrial demand. There is an increasing shortage of suitable sites for reservoirs in the South East and a national water grid would probably be impractical in terms of cost. Transfer from one river system to another (i.e. from the Severn to the Thames) seems to be the cheapest of these options (NRA, 1994).

Metering and volumetric charges will ultimately be the most effective measure unless demand is perfectly price inelastic. Empirical evidence is difficult to derive and interpret but it appears that water used inside the home for washing and other purposes is relatively price inelastic, much more so than that used outside the home (e.g. for car washing and lawn watering), but which only accounts for about 3 per cent of household water consumption. However the water conservation incentives will be much more pervasive in terms of encouraging the development of more water-efficient domestic appliances. Metering also provides essential management information, for example regarding the extent of water loss due to mains leaks in the distribution network. Hence the purported price inelasticity of demand may be overstated in the longer term and does not provide a complete assessment of the potential for water conservation through metering.

Limited metering trials indicate that total domestic use falls by 10–15 per cent upon introduction of metering (Bird and Jackson, 1966; Warford, 1966; Jenking, 1969; Rees, 1973a, 1973b; Herrington, 1973; Phillips and Kershaw, 1976; Thackray et al., 1978; WSA, 1993; WRC, 1994). This does not, however, mean that a universal switch to metering will reduce water use by a tenth or so. As already noted, some households are opting for meters because bills can be reduced without any change in use. Widespread use of metering may reduce demand by no more than, say, 5 per cent. Nevertheless, the proportionate reductions in peak use may be much greater, easing what is a critical supply constraint in some areas. It is this component of demand that effectively determines the required capacity of the system.

Assuming *ceteris paribus*, it could be expected that consumers would wish to reduce (rather than increase) their bills. Such reductions may depend on the precise structure and levels of tariffs and on the socioeconomic mix of customers, all of which vary by area. However it appears that any metered rate above zero has an immediate impact on demand, irrespective of whether it is rising, declining or constant with increasing consumption. The probable explanation is that consumers (rightly or wrongly) think that metering allows them to determine the total value of their water bills, whereas previously (with flat-rate charges) they could not (except at the expense of moving house).

This manifestation of consumer psychology (see Chapter 1) suggests that a complex tariff structure based on long-run marginal cost is not strictly necessary, which is just as well since the tariff structure may become so complicated as to be either unworkable or not publicly acceptable. Indeed the household metering trials in England suggested an unfavourable customer reaction to complex rising block, seasonal and peak-load tariffs. Ultimately, however, the question is not whether to introduce metering, but when to do so.

Metering promotes a particular definition of equity in relating payment to use. However, The Water Industry (Charges) (Vulnerable Groups) Regulations 1999 require water companies to include special provisions in their charging schemes for 'vulnerable groups' (referred to in the second quotation at the beginning of this chapter). They include those persons in receipt of council tax benefit, housing benefit, income support, disabled person's tax credit, working families tax credit, or income-based jobseeker's allowance (see Chapter 9) and:

- is either entitled to receive child benefits for three or more dependent children, or
- is a person suffering from and receiving treatment for desquamation, weeping skin disease, incontinence, abdominal stoma and renal failure requiring dialysis at home, and
- in both cases, water is not used for watering a garden, other than by hand, by means of any apparatus or automatically replenishing a pond, or a swimming pool, with a capacity greater than 10 000 litres.

In this way, fairness and affordability are secured in that vulnerable groups are protected when faced with potentially high metered charges beyond their control, but they are not allowed to abuse that protection. Vulnerability is caused by the combination of low income and many children or by low income and specific medical treatments requiring copious amounts of water. However, fairness and affordability come at a price. Vulnerable groups are protected at the expense of other customers (whose bills must be higher to finance the resulting cross-subsidies) rather than the general taxpayer. This is already the case, however, with flat-rate charges and vulnerable groups can continue to be protected because metering is optional. Moreover, the administrative burden of identifying vulnerable groups falls on the companies who will have to ask eligible claimants for proof of social security status, family size and health status. Whilst it is possible to make offsetting additional payments directly through welfare benefits, these are more difficult to assess accurately for volumetric charges than for standard flat-rate charges. Moreover, low income on its own does not cause vulnerability. The need for such complicated mechanisms to promote fairness and affordability could be largely avoided by rising block tariffs (see above).

Infrastructure charges

Various types of infrastructure charges could be used to recover capital costs for renewal/upgrading and new construction. Infrastructure charges are allowed by law and have the potential to improve both efficiency and equity. They would reduce the level of standing charges and so allow a closer link between volumetric use and bills. This would make it easier for consumers significantly to reduce bills by regulating the use of metered water. At the moment a high proportion of costs are fixed. As a very broad figure, only about a quarter of the average unmetered household bill for water and sewerage would have related to the metered element and only a small proportion of this could feasibly be reduced. Greater use of a separate infrastructure charge would allow the metered rate to account for a higher proportion of recurrent bills and so have more influence on demand. However there may be a tendency to overuse infrastructure charges to finance service expansion, resulting in double payment by some users.

A trade effluent charge

Whilst water metering provides a useful indicator of sewage disposal for the domestic sector, a separate trade effluent charge is used throughout Britain for the non-domestic sector. The Mogden formula (OFWAT, 1991) takes account of both volume and (at least partially) strength of effluent. However the charge does not encourage location in the least-cost area (i.e. where there is existing spare capacity), nor does it specifically take account of environmental costs. Even if such a premium were added to the charge it would not eliminate effluent completely since it will often be cheaper for the firm not to treat fully its own effluent. Similar outcomes are likely to arise from any polluter-pays tax on agricultural fertilisers, pesticides and herbicides that pollute water supplies. Hence the polluter-pays principle is not a cure-all for pollution and the water consumer will inevitably have to bear some of the cost of ensuring potable water. The trade effluent charge should relate only to the costs incurred in excess of treatment of the average strength of domestic sewage.

A combined charge

The above analysis has shown that no single charge is ideal in terms of simplicity and comprehensibility, providing the right incentives to both suppliers and users of services, being fair and equitable, reflecting benefits or costs and so on. Various combinations of metered rates, standing charges, infrastructure and other charges are used in different countries, the emphasis varying between countries and between water and sewerage authorities in any one country (OECD, 1999). Such variations in tariff baskets may partly reflect costs, but more often they seem to be the rather arbitrary outcomes of historical and statutory constraints. A number of alternative combined charges are in use.

First, a combined water and sewerage charge, the sewerage surcharge simply being 'piggy-backed' onto the water charge, irrespective of whether the latter is flat-rate, metered rate and so on, as in the UK. Given that sewage treatment is generally more costly than provision of potable water, it will tend to more than double the original water bill and so magnify any reduction of water consumption caused by metering. Hence, if estimates of price and income elasticities of demand are being undertaken, cross elasticities of demand must also be used so as to recognise the complementary nature of the two services. If not, then inaccurate and potentially grossly misleading estimates of the sensitivity of demand to price will be made (see Chapter 6).

Second, a standing charge plus payment related to property values – as used in England and Wales.

Third, a charge based on property bands with a single person discount – as used in Scotland.

Fourth, a two-part tariff – composed of some form of a standing charge and volumetric charge. This would be consistent with the traditional economic option if the standing charge covered fixed system capital costs with the running rate set at marginal cost to regulate consumption (see Chapter 6). However the actual two-part tariff structure may not be consistent with these economic prescriptions, especially if the standing charge is too high and the running rate too low.

The water standing charge in England and Wales has generally been relatively much higher than those of the electricity and gas industries. This tariff structure defeats the purpose of metering, increases the costs of billing and causes inequity in that low-volume users bear an unduly high share of costs, a single-person household paying the same standing charge as a multi-person household.

Most OECD countries use a two-part tariff, the volumetric charge comprising at least 75 per cent of the total water bill (OECD, 1999). There has been a gradual shift towards a two-part tariff where the per unit volume charge rises as consumption increases. Economic and environmental factors have provided the rationale for the increasing use of this tariff structure in Australia, Canada, Japan, Switzerland and the USA. In Belgium, Greece, Italy, Portugal and many developing countries it is also justified on the grounds that it is thought equitable that affluent households using large amounts of water should pay more per unit of water than poor, low-volume users. The lower initial rate is also assumed to ensure that households have enough water for personal hygiene, so satisfying public health objectives, especially for low-income families. However problems remain for low-income families with a large number of children.

Fifth, a multi-part tariff. OFWAT believes that accounting costs should match economic costs as far as possible, and be reflected in the charges for water and sewerage. It is sceptical of the argument that fixed costs should be recovered through capital contributions or a standing charge and variable costs through a volumetric charge because of the imprecision of definition of these costs in practice. It suggested that an appropriate structure would be as follows:

- **Connection charge** – to recover the capital cost of connection to the system (i.e. the cost of the service pipe from the system to the property boundary, the boundary stop valve and the meter, where appropriate).
- **Standing charge** – to recover billing and meter reading (i.e. customer-related operating costs).
- **Use-related charges** – to recover all other operating costs of water and sewerage (including surface drainage).
- **Infrastructure charges** – to recover the average capital cost of enhancing the capacity of the entire water and sewerage system so as to accommodate new connections to it (i.e. the cost of provision of remote infrastructure to accommodate premises that have never been connected to the water and sewerage system).
- **Requisition charges** – to recover the cost of enhancement of the local water and sewerage network (e.g. in providing new or enhanced mains, tanks, service reservoirs, treatment facilities and pumping stations). Requisition charges must be accommodated by the K factor and income from this charge will rise substantially as more stringent quality standards require additional treatment facilities for local water and sewerage networks.

Given its restricted coverage, the standing charge would be broadly similar across companies, whereas the other charges would differ in line with differences in cost structures. Such variability in charges between regions and localities can, of course, be justified in terms of allocative efficiency and the benefit principle (i.e. matching the incidence of costs and benefits). Water and sewerage charges can therefore be expected to be inherently more geographically variable than are electricity and gas prices.

This recommended tariff structure is radically different from those for electricity and gas, neither of which have a component comparable to an infrastructure charge. However OFWAT has not imposed such a tariff structure on the water and sewerage companies. Whilst it will probably attempt to persuade companies to adopt such a tariff structure, its formal powers of control are based on price-cap regulation.

Implementation of a new tariff structure

Different charging structures can have profound effects on the balance between various groups of users. The residential share of charges is highest when the charge formula includes a large **flat-rate** component; the commercial share is largest when the charge is based on **property values**; the industrial share is largest if the charge is based on **sewage strength** or volume (Johnson, 1969). Within the industrial sector, the chemical industry bears a particularly heavy burden if the charge is based on the biochemical oxygen demand of sewage. Within the residential sector, a tariff basket with a relatively high standing charge will bear most heavily on low-income and low-consumption households. Infrastructure charges also affect the share of costs.

To the extent that many industrial and commercial premises are already metered, the main impact of metering would be on household consumption. There would also be a redistribution of bills between households. Although equity has been considered in general terms for each of the above charging methods, the distributional effects of a changing tariff structure can only be judged in terms of the system being replaced. Those effects will be crucially dependent on the particular characteristics of the new charging structure.

For example, in England and Wales a move to a system of charges based on household size or metering would tend to benefit single-person households (mainly pensioners). However the greater the level of the standing charge relative to the volumetric rate for metered charges, the less the benefit to such households. High-income households tend to be made better off by any system that is not based on a tax methodology (i.e. standing charge, household size and water metering). Low-income families would tend to be worse off under a system solely based on standing charges and better off with charges based on metering or household size, unless they are large households with many children.

In general the differences between alternative charging methods are much more heavily influenced by household size than they are by household income, and it is here that water metering raises the most concern. Whilst social security payments such as income support can take account of the factors influencing household size and ability to pay (i.e. number of children and adults and household income), the extent to which adverse distributional impacts can be offset by changes in welfare payments is reduced the greater the variation in charges across the country (Rajah and Smith, 1993).

A phased introduction of metered prices is therefore necessary to avoid radical shifts in liability overnight. Phasing will also be necessary because any reduction in use (for both the water and sewerage services) will lead to higher costs per unit of output due to the relatively high short-term fixed costs relating to network capacity. The standing charge component may have to be relatively large to start with, the running rate gradually accounting for an increasing proportion over time until the correct balance is achieved.

Not all users could be metered at once, so discrimination (i.e. the rebalancing of charges unrelated to costs) between metered and unmetered users as well as between domestic and non-domestic users should be avoided as far as possible. This could be achieved by reference to rateable values, retaining the existing balance between sectors and even within the domestic sector until metering was complete. The rateable value banding for the council tax could be used as a guide for the phased introduction of metering. The single-person discounts for the council tax could also be used to adjust interim bills pending full introduction of metering.

A high proportion of revenue from metered charges will make revenues more sensitive to annual fluctuations in consumption, causing financing problems for suppliers. Hence a 'charges stabilisation fund' will be required to prevent erratic changes in charges from year to year. Customer relations would be improved if volumetric rates were increased at the start of periods of lower consumption. In southern areas of Britain this is likely to be the winter whereas in Scotland it is likely to be the summer (since summer lawn watering is rarely necessary but winter bursts and leaks are more likely in the colder north). Similarly, volumetric charges should be increased on a regular basis (in line with costs) in order to avoid infrequent but large rises in bills.

14.8   Other forms of demand management

Widespread use of metering is still years away and, even when introduced, the impact on demand will be limited. Metering would probably have had little impact on demand during the successive droughts in 1976, 1984, 1989–92 and 1995–7. Hence, other forms of demand management have also to be considered. This is where environmental regulation can have the greatest impact. As already noted above, the Environment Agency's management of water resources is based upon the three concepts of sustainable development, the precautionary principle and demand management. The 1995 Environment Act places companies under a duty to promote the efficient use of water. Some surprisingly simple options are available, others being more radical and potentially more costly.

Following the 1995 drought, the 1997 Labour government told the water companies that leakages had to be substantially reduced before any new reservoirs could be built. The companies blamed water shortages on the weather (i.e. lack of rainfall). Whilst this was clearly a factor, those shortages were severely exacerbated by substantial rates of leakage (i.e. by poor management of water resources). Companies were therefore set mandatory targets to reduce leakage, these subsequently being based on the economic level of leakage (ELL) determined for each company. A company would determine its ELL as the point at which further spending on leakage control would cost more than the value of water saved. By comparison, OFWAT defines the ELL as 'the point at which further leakage control activity would cost more than alternative means to bridge the gap between supply and demand'. The cost of leakage control activity will rise increasingly fast as the level of leakage is progressively reduced (assuming the largest and easiest to stop leaks are repaired first). The cost of alternative means of bridging the gap between supply and demand will also rise increasingly sharply because it has to include the environmental and social costs of further river abstractions, more reservoirs and so on. Hence, the economically optimum level of leakage will generally be less than the optimum level based solely on company operating costs. Over the longer term, ELLs could be expected to show a downward trend due to both technical improvements in finding and dealing with leaks and growth in demand.

In the short term, the major part of reduced leakage seems to have resulted from simply reducing water pressure in the mains (so less leaks out), rather than from spending large sums actually repairing the leaks, digging up roads and so on, being particularly disruptive. Water saved as a result of these measures in the later 1990s was enough to supply an extra 13 million people, accounting for the marginal fall in the amount of water delivered after 1992/3 noted above. Nevertheless, in some areas, it led to shortages of mains pressure for fighting fires and for refilling pressurised central heating systems and it also takes longer to run a bath or fill a sink. This represents a reduction in the quality of service.

In addition to leakage control, many low-cost water saving technologies are available. Some water companies now offer 'hippos' or similar devices (effectively plastic bottles full of water) that are placed in toilet cisterns in order to reduce the amount of water flushed down the toilet. Low-flush toilets are required under 1999 regulations for installations from 2001. More generally, public education may be more effective than metering in convincing people that they should conserve water and be less wasteful in its use. For example, they could be encouraged only to operate washing machines and dishwashers on full loads, not to use hosepipes to wash cars or water gardens, to grow plants that thrive in dry conditions, to install water butts for rainwater collection, not to leave the water running whilst washing or cleaning teeth, to buy low-water-use appliances, to fix dripping taps, leaks and continuously running overflows, to fit spray nozzles and spring-loaded levers on taps and so on.

People may not realise just how much water they are using. For example, a garden hose left running for one hour uses seven times as much water as the average consumer uses in a day. A dishwasher uses 10 times as much water on its normal cycle as washing the same pots in the sink. A power shower typically uses more water than a bath. Use of seep hoses, low flow shower heads and/or supply restrictor valves, and dishwashers that reduce water consumption by as much as 20 per cent are all currently available.

Besides being set leakage targets, the water companies could also be made responsible for public education regarding water conservation. Their profit motive encourages them to sell more water not less. However, climate change is expected to impose considerable costs on the water industry because of reduced and more variable precipitation and because of reduced water quality (due to leaching of agrochemicals, urban pollution and algal blooms). Although climate change effects and its associated costs are inherently uncertain, government projections are for a 30 per cent shortfall in supplies by 2030, shortfalls being confined to England and Wales. It will be much cheaper to conserve water by the above means than to build more reservoirs, invest in bulk transfer schemes and desalination plants and so on. Hence, the 1997 Labour government has required water companies to submit 25-year water resource plans that take climate change into account.

A radical demand management option is to adopt the principle of 'appropriate quality water for appropriate use', in this case not flushing the toilet with drinking water. Instead, 'grey water' from washing machines (but not from dishwashing – it contains grease and food particles) and rainwater from roofs could be recycled for flushing toilets, washing cars or watering gardens. Such recycling would only require low-cost, domestic-scale technology. Waterless WCs and urinals are also available.

Clearly, water conservation involves much more than simply introducing metering along with tariff structures designed to encourage efficiency in the use of water. Effective conservation requires a judicious mix of market mechanisms **and** regulation (see Chapter 2). Nevertheless, pricing mechanisms do provide a financial incentive for people and firms to be more 'environmentally friendly' in their use of water. People and firms are more likely to 'go green' if it saves, rather than costs, money. Those cost savings can only be realised at the individual user level if metering is in place.

14.9 Conclusions

This case study has demonstrated how apparently disparate themes treated elsewhere in this book interact in the implementation of policy. It has brought together a number of themes relating to market failure, the need for government intervention, public choice theory, the level at which government intervention can take place, the creation of quangos (water boards), privatisation, regulation, transaction costs, charging, public sector borrowing, taxation and equity. It has demonstrated the complexity of policy implementation in terms of how to operationalise an apparently simple supply-side policy.

This case study has made clear the government's continuing concern with service costs, charges, availability and quality, even after privatisation. It provides an excellent example of just how little difference privatisation makes to the need for public intervention in the case of the utility industries. Privatisation has most definitely **not** led to a 'hands-off' approach by central government. In fact there is **increasing** intervention in areas such as tariff structures and service quality and availability with **more** (rather than less) attention being paid to efficiency and equity through the regulatory framework. This is probably because privatisation did not create a highly competitive market structure but rather a series of local and regional monopolies.

Demand-side factors are increasingly recognised as complementing engineering supply-oriented solutions to water shortages. Nevertheless, in general, the tariff structure for domestic water and sewerage still does not relate bills to use. It has to be acknowledged that the problem of recurring water shortages in parts of the south and east of England is as much a problem of demand as it is of supply. Proposals for a national piped water grid, for the transfer of water by river and canal systems, for increased river abstractions, for bringing water by ship, for towing icebergs from the Arctic and for seawater desalination plants are all part of the supply-oriented engineering approach upon which the industry has been built. The price regulation regime administered by OFWAT is consistent with the supply-oriented, engineering tradition of water and sewerage in that real increases in charges sufficient to finance capital costs of increased volume and quality of supply are in effect guaranteed. However it is also attempting to persuade (rather than compel) the water and sewerage companies to supplement the emphasis on supply with measures designed to influence demand, basically by relating water and sewerage bills to long-run marginal cost.

Even with such measures, periodic water shortages will continue in some parts of the country, if only because charging structures do not differentiate between off-peak and peak demands. Water shortages will remain a political as well as an economic issue. The British government's response to water shortage on a previous occasion was to appoint a minister for drought (in 1976), which was as likely to solve the problem as 'praying for rain' (another supply-oriented measure)! Suggestions by the minister that two people should share a bath (a demand-side response) caused a moral maelstrom. Fortunately it started to rain immediately!

References and further reading

Bird, P. A. and Jackson, C. I. (1966) 'Economic Methods of Charging for Water', *British Waterworks Association Journal*, vol. 48, pp. 614–28.

Consumers' Association (1996) *Policy Report: Water Consumption and Charges* (London: Consumers' Association).

CRI (1994) *The UK Water Industry: Charges for Water Services 1993/4* (London: The Centre for the Study of Regulated Industries).

Department of the Environment (1990) *This Common Inheritance: Britain's Environmental Strategy*, Cm 1200 (London: HMSO).

Department of the Environment (1994) *This Common Inheritance: The Third Year Report*, Cm 2549 (London: HMSO).

Department of the Environment, Transport and Regions (online). Available at <http://www.detr.gov.uk>.

DETR (1998) *Water Charging in England and Wales: Government Decisions Following Consultation* (London: Department of the Environment, Transport and the Regions).

DETR (2000) *Climate Change: Assessing the Impacts – Identifying Responses. The First Three Years of the UK Climate Impacts Programme* (London: Department of the Environment, Transport and the Regions).

DETR (2000) *Potential UK Adaptation Strategies for Climate Change: Technical Report* (London: Department of the Environment, Transport and the Regions).

Environment Agency (online). Available at <http://www.environment-agency.gov.uk>.

Environment Agency (Wales) (online). Available at <http://www.environment-agency.wales.gov.uk>.

Ernst, J. (1994) *Whose Utility? The Social Impact of Public Utility Privatisation and Regulation in Britain* (Buckingham: Open University Press).

Helm, D. and Jenkinson, T. (1998) *Competition in Regulated Industries* (Oxford: Oxford University Press).

Herrington, P. R. (1973) *Water Consumption in the Trent River Authority Area: An Economic Analysis* (Leicester: University of Leicester).

Herrington, P. R. and Price, C. (1987) *What Price Private Water? A Study of the Economic Regulation of Privatised Utilities in the UK with Particular Reference to the Water Industry* (London: Public Finance Foundation).

Hewett, C. (1999) *Testing the Waters: The Potential for Competition in the Water Industry* (London: Institute for Public Policy Research).

Jenking, R. C. (1969) *Metering at Malvern* (London: Institute of Municipal Treasurers and Accountants, December).

Johnson, J. A. (1969) 'The Distribution of the Burden of Sewer User Charges Under Various Charge Formulas', *National Tax Journal*, vol. 22, pp. 472–85.

Merret, S. (1997) *Introduction to the Economics of Water Resources: An International Perspective* (London: UCL Press).

NRA (1994) *Water: Nature's Precious Resource. An Environmentally Sustainable Water Resources Development Strategy for England and Wales*, National Rivers Authority (London: HMSO).

OECD (1999) *Household Water Pricing in OECD Countries* (Paris: Organisation for Economic Co-operation and Development).

Office of Water Services (online). Available at <http://www.open.gov.uk/ofwat/>.

OFWAT (1991) *Paying for Water: A Time for Decisions* (Birmingham: Office of Water Services).

OFWAT (1993a) *Setting Price Limits for Water and Sewerage Services: The Framework and Approach to the 1994 Periodic Review* (Birmingham: Office of Water Services).

OFWAT (1993b) *Paying for Quality: The Political Perspective* (Birmingham: Office of Water Services).

OFWAT (1994) *Future Charges for Water and Sewerage: The Outcome of the Periodic Review* (Birmingham: Office of Water Services).

Ogden, S. and Anderson, F. (1995) 'Representing Customers' Interests: The Case of the Privatised Water Industry in England and Wales', *Public Administration* vol. 73, pp. 535-59.

Peiser, R. (1988) 'Calculating Equity-Neutral Water and Sewer Impact Fees', *Journal of the American Planning Association*, vol. 54, no. 1, pp. 38–48.

Phillips, J. H. and Kershaw, C. G. (1976) 'Domestic Metering: An Engineering and Economic Appraisal', *Journal of the Institution of Water Engineers and Scientists*, vol. 30, pp. 203–16.

Rajah, N. and Smith, S. (1993) 'Distributional Aspects of Household Water Charges', *Fiscal Studies*, vol. 14, no. 3, pp. 86–108.

Rees, J. A. (1973a) *Review of Evidence of the Effects of Prices on the Demand for Water Services* (London: Department of the Environment, June).

Rees, J. A. (1973b) 'The Demand for Water in South East England', *Geographical Journal*, vol. 139, part 1 (February), pp. 20–42.

Save the Children (1996) *Water Tight: The Impact of Water Metering on Low-income Families* (London: Save the Children).

Sawkins, J. W. and Dickie, V. A. (1999) *Regulatory Reform in the Scottish Water Industry: Recent Progress and Future Prospects*, Discussion Papers in Economics no. 99/12 (Edinburgh: Heriot-Watt University).

Sawkins, J. W. and Mackay, D. F. (1996) *Charging for Water in Scotland: Options for Change*, Fraser of Allander Institute Quarterly Economic Commentary vol. 21, no. 2, pp. 32–9.

Scottish Environmental Protection Agency (online). Available at <http://www.sepa.gov.uk>.

Scottish Office (1991) *Consultation Paper: Charging for Water and Sewerage Services* (Edinburgh: Scottish Office).

Scottish Office (1992) *Water and Sewerage in Scotland: Investing for Our Future. A Consultation Paper* (London: HMSO).

Thackray, J. (1990) 'Water Charging: Options for the 21st Century', *Public Finance and Accountancy*, (28 September) pp. 20–3.

Thackray, J. E., Cocker, V. and Archibald, G. (1978) 'The Malvern and Mansfield Studies of Domestic Water Usage', *Proceedings of the Institution of Civil Engineers*, vol. 64, part 1 (February), pp. 483–502.

Warford, J. J. (1966) 'Water Requirements: The Investment Decision in the Water Supply Industry', *The Manchester School of Economic and Social Studies*, vol. 34, no. 1, pp. 87–112.

WRC (1994) *The Effects of Metered Charging on Customer Demand for Water from 1 April 1989 to 31 March 1993* (London: Water Resources Council).

WSA (1993) *Water Metering Trials: Final Report*, National Metering Trials Working Group (London: Water Services Association).

15 Market Testing and Contracting Out

15.1 Introduction
15.2 Market Testing in Central Government
15.3 Market Testing in Local Government
15.4 Is Contracting Out Privatisation?
15.5 The Degree of Competition
15.6 The Extent and Nature of Cost Savings
15.7 Justifying the Choice of Services Subject to Market Testing
15.8 Interactions Between Competition and Service Objectives
15.9 Conclusions

Public services should be delivered efficiently. Government itself need not be a large scale provider. Market testing the delivery of services, and contracting out where appropriate, brings commercial disciplines to bear and stimulates private sector activity (1994 White Paper, *Competitiveness: Helping Business to Win*, Cm 2563, London: HMSO, p. 17).

We believe that the best public sector managers and the best in public services can match anything achieved in the private sector (1991 White Paper, *Competing for Quality: Buying Better Services*, Cm 1730, London: HMSO, p. ii).

We will use market testing and contracting out when in individual cases these can be shown to offer better value for money: that is, better quality services at optimal cost. Our approach to this is pragmatic not dogmatic (*Better Quality Services: A Handbook* 1998, London: Stationery Office, p. 8).

What matters is what works ... services should not be delivered directly if other more efficient and effective means are available. Competition will therefore continue to be an essential management tool for securing improvement, and an important means of demonstrating in a transparent way that best value is being obtained (1998 Green Paper, *Modernising Local Government: Improving Local Services through Best Value*, London, DETR, paras. 1.6 and 4.16).

15.1   Introduction

Contracting out the supply of public services to the private sector is one of the forms of privatisation discussed in Chapter 13, namely **liberalisation**. It is a supply-side measure, the intention of which is to improve efficiency by subjecting the provision of public services to competitive supply (see Chapter 8). **Contracting out** only refers to the situation where an external contractor wins the service contract (see **Figure 8.1**). For that to happen external organisations (e.g. private sector companies) must bid for and win the contracts put out to tender. If in-house production units (e.g. in a local authority) win the contract, the service is **contracted in** (see **Figure 8.1**). Hence market testing is **not** synonymous with contracting out.

Market testing (i.e. competitive contracting) has long been used by British governments of differing political persuasions for the purchase of supplies and services from external contractors. The 1967 Labour government, for example, contracted out the cleaning of *central government* offices. However the scope of contracting out was significantly extended by the Conservative government during the 1980s and 1990s by making competitive contracting compulsory for a specified range of *local government* services and activities. The 1997 Labour government abolished compulsion, which it regarded as too inflexible in securing best value for money spent. Nevertheless, it retained the emphasis on competition and shared with the previous Conservative government a belief in the benefits to be derived from market testing the supply of public services. This is indicated by the quotations above, the 1991 and 1994 quotations being the former Conservative government's, the two 1998 quotations being those of the 1997 Labour government. Hence market testing and contracting out is a bipartisan non-ideological policy of both Conservative and Labour governments. It underpins the **purchaser–provider** split (see Chapter 8).

15.2   Market testing in central government

Both Conservative and Labour governments have recently used market testing in **central** government.

The Conservatives' Competing for Quality (CfQ) Initiative

Prior to the Conservative government's CfQ initiative, market testing and contracting out had been confined almost exclusively to ancillary manual ('blue-collar') support services such as cleaning and catering, mostly within the Ministry of Defence. The 1992 CfQ initiative extended competition to a much wider range of professional and 'white-collar' support services. These included facilities management (e.g. prisons), office services, estate management, information technology support services (the largest group of services contracted out), and scientific/technical/research and development. During the 1990s the private sector won most of the Civil Service work put out to tender. A government-appointed scrutiny team found CfQ achieved gross savings in its first three years of about 18 per cent, reduced to between 13 and 15 per cent net of the costs of running the competitive process. The main source of savings was new working practices, irrespective of whether the work was contracted in or contracted out. It believed that even greater gross and net savings were possible as CfQ became more systematic in stimulating competition and in identifying services with the greatest potential for economies of scale and changes in management practices. These conclusions were supported by other independent studies of market testing in central government (CIPFA 1996).

Labour's Better Quality Service Reviews

The 1997 Labour government extended market testing beyond support services. In early 2000 it announced that every central government service would be subject to *'a better quality service review'* over the following five years. *Inter alia*, those reviews are to consider market testing and introduction of strategic contracting out to the private sector (i.e. where private companies are invited to bid but no in-house bid is sought). These reviews are paralleled by Labour's contracting private companies to provide support services to the NHS (including pharmacy and information technology – as well as ancillary services), administer teachers' pensions, manage state prisons, undertake prisoner-escort services, administer benefit payments, provide non-emergency ambulance services for patient transport and take over the running of 'failing institutions'. Such institutions include local education authorities judged (by OFSTED, the Office for Standards in Education) to be providing inadequate school support services (e.g. payroll, personnel, governor support, special education needs, and information technology services). Private companies, not-for-profit organisations and other consortia have been invited by the Labour government to bid to provide central education services in 'failing councils'. Likewise, 'education companies' are being invited to take over the management of 'failing schools'. Labour regards such measures as key to its attempts to raise educational standards in schools as part of its supply-side strategy of investing in human capital. Similar central government interventions are in hand for other council services, ranging from housing management to social care.

15.3 Market testing in local government

Market-testing initiatives during the 1980s and 1990s became progressively more extensive within **local** government.

The Conservatives' Compulsory Competitive Tendering (CCT) Regime

CCT was a central plank of the Conservative government's philosophy for almost 20 years. The rationale was a diverse mixture of motives including promoting competition in order to increase efficiency, reducing (or constraining the rise in) public expenditure, reducing the power of public sector trades unions, downward pressure on pay and conditions, rolling back the frontiers of the state by encouraging private enterprise, and facilitating an enabling role for local government.

Very few local governments (less than 10 per cent) had voluntarily introduced competitive tendering (i.e. market testing) for ancillary services prior to the introduction of CCT. Besides political and trades union opposition to competitive tendering, the explanation of this situation lies in the structural reforms of the mid 1970s, which specifically created local governments large enough to make efficient direct provision of services. Hence, compared with the relatively small local governments in other European countries, those in the UK did not need to contract out service provision to the private sector in order to secure economies of scale.

However large size is a necessary but not sufficient condition for securing economies of scale. There also has to be an incentive to achieve cost reductions. Since local governments are effectively tax-financed monopoly providers of services, and are specifically not seeking to make or maximise profits, there is no strong economic incentive for them to reduce costs. Indeed high levels of trade union organisation provide strong political incentives not to seek efficiency gains by reducing costs because it would lead to a loss of jobs, of union members and probably of votes. This is a particular example of distributional coalitions (see Chapter 7). Hence the maximisation of economies of scale may only be achievable if strong incentives are provided by competition for service contracts. Much the same scenario exists for private monopolies so that, in theory, it is competition rather than ownership that is important if cost reductions are to be secured through economies of scale.

CCT was introduced in 1980 for local government construction-related activities (i.e. new building and renewal, building repairs and maintenance, and highways construction and maintenance), in-house production units being known as direct labour organisations (DLOs). CCT was extended in 1988 to include the cleaning of buildings, refuse collection, street cleaning, school and welfare catering, other catering (e.g. town halls), vehicle maintenance, ground maintenance, and management of sports and leisure services. In-house production units for these services are known as direct service organisations (DSOs).

By the mid 1990s competition had been introduced to most 'blue collar' (i.e. manual) services and, thereafter, was progressively applied to 'white collar' (i.e. professional and administrative) services. These included housing management, construction-related professional services (architecture, engineering and property management services), computing, legal services, financial services, personnel, and corporate and administrative services.

Labour's best value regime

As already noted, the 1997 Labour government abolished compulsion, which it regarded as too inflexible. It accepted criticisms that CCT had been too heavily focused on achieving cost savings (much like the CfQ initiative in central government), with the result that service quality had often been neglected. Moreover efficiency gains had been uneven and uncertain and compulsion had bred local government antagonism. It argued that the process of competition had become an end in itself rather than a means of achieving best value for money spent. Hence, the Labour government replaced CCT with its Best Value regime. The 1998 quotations above demonstrate, however, that the Labour government still wished to use competition as a primary means of delivering best value in the provision of local government services.

Therefore abolition of CCT does not mean that the private sector is being excluded. Indeed, liberalisation seems to be being strengthened. By the late 1990s even traditional Labour local authorities, though having opposed the compulsory element of CCT, began voluntarily to invite the private sector to carry out town hall functions such as collecting council tax payments, paying staff salaries and pensions, administering housing benefit and so on. Contracting out had become de-politicised and was increasingly referred to as *out-sourcing*, this term including both strategic and competitive contracting out.

CCT had initiated a programme of analysing and questioning the levels of local authority costs relating to staffing, equipment, central overheads and so on. It prompted a trend towards *activity-based costing* upon which the Best Value regime has been built. Attention has shifted from the *process* of tendering towards the *outcomes* achieved by routine comparisons of service costs.

Besides the services listed above, market testing and out-sourcing can be used for almost all of the tremendous range of technical services undertaken within local government. Other examples include library support services, management of theatres and art facilities, management of parking and traffic warden services, home-to-school transport, minor highway works, various police support services, maintenance of fire service vehicles and so on. Pilot out-sourcing projects can help identify potential problems which must be resolved before more extensive market testing.

As a very approximate figure, by the late 1990s contracts totalling over £12 billion had been awarded for local government services. Assuming average cost savings of 20 per cent (based on the evidence referred to above and in **Table 15.1**), the annual saving in public expenditure is £2.4 billion. This saving could be used to increase expenditure on education by about 6 per cent or on health by about 5 per cent, both services being Labour's priorities for increased spending (see **Table 9.3**).

Both the CCT and Best Value regimes reflect the development of **enabling** local government. This involves a shift away from a vertically integrated, monolithic, corporate institutional form of direct service provision by local governments to one of an enabling function within a horizontally co-ordinated network of multi-agency service provision. The overall shift is towards *functional decentralisation*: from *government* to *governance* (Bailey, 1999). Governance implies a clear distinction between local authority provision of a policy framework and the provision of services within that framework. Put simply, local authorities 'steer rather than row'. Hence market testing and contracting out are not simply economic instruments applied in isolation. They are part of a much more fundamental and ongoing reform of local government and of the public sector in general.

15.4 Is contracting out privatisation?

Contracting out is **not** privatisation in terms of **asset sales**. Whilst contracting out results in private sector companies providing services, their specification and delivery remains the statutory responsibility of local government. Whether contracted in or contracted out, the contract is for a finite period. Contracting does not require the public sector to sell its assets nor even to relinquish control over how they are managed. This remains the case even if DSOs are subsequently sold to the private sector, or if management buyouts occur. Contracting out is therefore a very partial form of privatisation compared with the sale of public sector utilities in energy and transport (see Chapter 13).

As already noted, a more accurate description of contracting out is that it is a form of **liberalisation**. It enables potential private sector involvement but does not necessarily secure it (except in the special case of strategic contracting out noted above). Under market testing there

Table 15.1   Cost savings from competitive contracting: international evidence

Country	Activity	Reported savings
Australia	Water supply	Estimated potential cost savings of 15 per cent.
Canada	Refuse collection	Public collection up to 50 per cent more costly.
Denmark	Fire services	Public provision almost three times more expensive than private contractors.
Germany (West)	Office cleaning	Public sector provision 42–66 per cent more expensive.
Japan	Refuse collection	Municipal collection 124 per cent more costly.
Sweden	Road and park maintenance, water supply, sewerage	Cost reductions of 10–19 per cent in several municipalities.
	Waste collection	Average cost reductions of 25 per cent.
	Leisure activities	Cost reductions of 13–15 per cent.
	Child care	Cost reductions of 9–15 percent in nurseries.
Switzerland	Refuse collection	Costs of private contracts 20 per cent cheaper.
UK	Domestic services in local government and the NHS	Savings of 20–26 per cent, costs being reduced by more than a third in some cases.
	Refuse collection	Cost reductions of about 20 per cent.
	Central government (e.g. IT and printing)	Average savings of 25 per cent.
USA	Refuse collection	Savings of 29–37 per cent.
	Street cleaning	Savings of up to 43 per cent.
	Office cleaning	Savings of up to 73 per cent.
	Federal government	Cost savings of up to 35 per cent with an average saving of around 20 per cent.
	Mass transit	Potential savings of 20–50 per cent.

Source: *OECD Economic Outlook*, no. 54 (December 1993) and Parker (1990). Domberger and Jensen (1997), Parker (1990) and Walsh (1995) provide synopses of most of the research.

is no presumption in favour of private sector provision, only a presumption in favour of competition, as made evident by the quotes at the beginning of this chapter. Since the intention of market testing is primarily to promote competition and efficiency, local authority in-house units are not precluded from bidding for contracts. Indeed, in facilitating comparisons between public and private sector providers, DSOs are an effective means of regulation in respect of contract prices and service quality.

The outcome of market testing ultimately depends on the active interest of private companies and the competitiveness of their bids for contracts compared with in-house bids. If no bids are received or only the DSO bids then the contract remains in-house, i.e. contracted in. This result is most likely where potential profits are low. Private sector contractors will have a greater incentive to bid for service contracts when internal service provision is highly inefficient, for example where capital assets are underemployed and labour costs excessive. Hence the extent of private sector involvement can be expected to be (and indeed is) highly variable, both between different services and between different local authorities (Pinch and Patterson, 2000).

Whether contracted in or out, the activity will still be subsidised by central and local government. Local authorities usually retain ownership of assets and facilities (e.g. for catering, refuse collection and leisure and recreation) so that they are not privatised, even though their operation may be. At best it is highly misleading to use the terms 'privatisation' and 'contracting out' in a generic sense. At worst it displays a fundamental misunderstanding of the role and results of market testing the activities of local authorities.

Privatisation may result in the longer term, however. Since DSOs operate as 'arms-length' agencies they become less useful to local governments as instruments for achieving social and political goals. Increasingly there will be less incentive for local governments to retain ownership of DSOs. Many DSOs will become more commercially competent and their management more ambitious. In that case both DSOs and their respective local authorities may increasingly see the balance of advantage shifting towards management and/or employee buy-outs. This would allow DSOs to compete for contracts not just in other authorities, but also in the private sector. It is forbidden for DSOs to compete for private sector contracts because they are protected from commercial risks by taxpayers' money. Hence, if they wish to expand their business, managers will have to opt for a management buy-out of the DSO. Local authorities may regard growth of the former DSO as a desirable contribution to local economic development and therefore may actively support a buy-out. That would constitute full privatisation, but only a handful of buy-outs had occurred by the end of the 1990s.

15.5 The degree of competition

The degree of competition depends on potential profits to be earned from contracts. Annual surveys by the Local Government Management Board (LGMB) of the former CCT regime in England and Wales found that the degree of competition (measured by the number of bids per contract) varied dramatically between services. The proportion of contracts won without any competition was highest for catering (almost two thirds) and lowest for refuse collection and ground maintenance (a tenth for each). Not surprisingly DSOs were more successful in winning contracts where competition was limited, initially securing over 90 per cent of catering contracts for education and welfare and 84 per cent of sports and leisure management contracts.

DSO success rates tended to fall as the average number of contractors tendering for each contract rose. Factors influencing private sector bids include the relative size of market entry and exit costs (e.g. the requirement for specialist equipment), the degree of trades unionisation of activities, the capacity of the private sector to undertake individual activities, an individual local government's attitude to contracting (positive or negative) and any anti-competitive behaviour by councils.

Rather than reflecting lack of interest by the private sector, low recorded levels of competition and private sector involvement could reflect attempts by local authorities both to restrict bids and to bias their subsequent acceptance of tenders in favour of DSOs. However successive surveys of CCT produced little evidence of anti-competitive behaviour and very few allegations were made and statutory action was taken in even fewer cases. Moreover, government guidelines became progressively more specific regarding anti-competitive behaviour.

Instead, limited competition could itself reflect a high *ex ante* probability of DSOs winning the contract, such that the number of outside bidders was reduced. If so, the market for these contracts was still highly **contestable** even though the number of *bids* was very low. Hence, to claim that CCT was a waste of time and money because few bids were received for service contracts fails to understand the nature of competition. **Contestability theory** argues that the very threat of competition is more effective at stimulating improved efficiency than the actual number of bids received for service contracts.

15.6 The extent and nature of cost savings

Competition for service contracts is in terms of given levels and qualities of service. Hence competitive contracting can only reduce organisational slack, namely X-inefficiency (see Chapter 7). It does not reduce allocative inefficiency because service levels are fixed and there is no explicit mechanism for comparing incremental costs and benefits for differing levels of service output. Consequently any allocative inefficiency arising out of defective public decision-making (i.e. government failure) remains (see Chapters 2 and 7).

There is evidence for a wide range of public sector services in the UK and other countries that market testing leads to significant savings in *direct costs*. In the UK, **gross cost savings** seem to be 20 per cent or more with respect to refuse collection and other local government services. Such savings occur irrespective of whether contracts were won by private contractors or by in-house DSOs (Audit Commission, 1984, 1987, 1988; Carnaghan and Bracewell, 1993; Chaundy and Uttley, 1993; Cubbin et al., 1987; Domberger et al., 1986, 1988; Ganley and Grahl, 1988; Kerley and Wynn, 1991; Parker and Hartley, 1990; Uttley and Harper, 1993; Vining and Boardman, 1992; Voytek, 1991; Walker, 1993; Walsh, 1991). The extent of savings seems to be broadly comparable with cost reductions in other public services in the UK, including health (Uttley, 1993; Whitbread and Hooper, 1992) and central government departments (Cabinet Office, 1996; CIPFA, 1996), and in other countries (see **Table 15.1**).

However, some research suggests **net cost savings** of only 6–7 per cent if account is taken of the cost of tendering, other client-side administrative costs and contract monitoring costs, particularly the need to recruit extra specialist staff (see CPS, 1989; Szymanski and Wilkins, 1993; Walsh, 1991; Walsh and Davis, 1993). However, section 15.7 below questions whether the difference between gross and net cost savings is as substantial as claimed.

Boyne (1998) criticises much of the research on methodological grounds arguing that most studies are restricted to analysis of only a single service or to only a few (not necessarily representative) local authorities, fail to test whether their results are statistically significant, and fail to control for other influences on service costs including any reductions in quality of service. Moreover, it is invalid to generalise from studies of particular services in particular regions or countries. This is because market forces can be expected to vary dramatically service-by-service (e.g. refuse collection versus housing management), area-by-area (urban versus rural, north versus south) and over time. Economic theory predicts that market testing and contracting leads to greater reductions in costs, **first**, the greater the availability of competitive supply in the market, **second**, the fewer and less specific the assets required to provide the service, **third**, the easier it is to specify quality in contracts (Domberger and Jensen 1997). These features vary between services, for example cleaning services versus sports facilities management.

Research that considers only the **production function** (i.e. *economy* and *efficiency*) is seriously deficient. Its results simply cannot be accepted at face value since it has ignored **quality of outcome** (i.e. *cost effectiveness*). Explicitly or implicitly, it makes the heroic assumption that quality is constant. Existing research has only been able to make anecdotal statements about quality. Some research gives highly specific examples of deterioration of quality, usually derived from complaints by customers or trades unions. Other research refers to the subjective impressions of managers in concluding either that there is no evidence of deterioration of quality or that there has been an improvement. Whilst feasible, such assessments are neither wholly impartial nor comprehensive.

Since quality of service was not systematically and objectively assessed prior to the introduction of contracting, it is not possible to come to firm conclusions that contracting (and its associated incentive to reduce costs) has led to reduced quality of service. Without a formal system of quality assessment it is not possible categorically to state whether quality of service has changed, and if so, in which direction. If services are provided at maximum efficiency, it can be expected that there is a real trade-off between cost and quality, lower costs requiring lower quality of service. However, if there is substantial inefficiency in service provision, it may be possible to reduce costs whilst simultaneously maintaining or improving quality of service. A formal model of cost effectiveness with two service quality case studies is developed elsewhere (Bailey, 1999).

It is clear, therefore, that evidence of cost savings has to be treated with caution. Nevertheless, the overwhelming consensus of the research is that competitive contracting has reduced the costs of providing services. The reported gross and net cost reductions may as easily underestimate as overestimate actual cost savings. British local authorities are large relative to those in other countries and so may have already been more able to achieve substantial economies of scale (e.g. in rationalising refuse collection and disposal depots and sites), so reducing potential cost savings. Nevertheless, potential cost savings may be understated, in that competition, in terms of significant numbers of competing suppliers often takes time to arise. Ongoing surveys by the Local Government Management Board revealed that the private sector share of contracts increased at subsequent contracting rounds of cleaning, vehicle maintenance, refuse collection and ground maintenance.

On the other hand, private contractors may collude to form a cartel by means of which to raise contract prices at subsequent tendering rounds. Moreover, post-tender renegotiation of contracts raises costs if tenders were under-priced, deliberately or accidentally, when competing for contracts. This effectively occurs automatically for *deficit-guarantee contracts* whereby a local authority guarantees to cover higher than expected costs.

Not all the identified cost savings were the direct result of competition. Instead they may have reflected more general financial restraints and service restructuring independently of competitive contracting. Cost savings to the public sector as a whole are further reduced by the costs associated with any lower wages or increased unemployment arising from competition. These include increased payments of social security, lost revenues for taxation and the cost of retraining schemes. Such revenue losses will, of course, be partially or wholly offset by any extra tax payments made by private contractors out of profits derived from contracting. Furthermore, cost savings may not be preserved at subsequent rounds of contracting, for example if nominally competitive bidders act collusively through market-sharing arrangements.

Whilst not denying the general validity of these arguments, it would be easy to exaggerate their cost implications. Certainly research has identified specific cost savings arising from *improvements in technical efficiency, changes in the capital–labour mix, better asset management* and *reductions in overheads,* as well as from *cuts in wage costs.* Research by the Institute of Local Government Studies (CoE, 1993) found efficiency savings arising from the reorganisation of rounds for refuse collection and street cleaning, limited mechanisation in the cleaning of premises, greater mechanisation and centralisation of depots for ground maintenance, decentralisation of administration in catering, and fuller use of vehicle fleets facilitated by more efficient scheduling of vehicle maintenance. It also suggested that the greatest potential future savings by DSOs will come when questioning the levels of overhead costs attributed to central services, and their reduction by a shift towards *time-charging systems* in particular (i.e. charging according to the use made of central service officers and so on) and to *service-level agreements* in general.

Overstaffing seems to be the most important cost factor. Reductions in manual jobs of between 10 per cent and 25 per cent seem to have been fairly commonplace (CoE, 1993). Cuts in employment have also been identified in ongoing surveys by the *Municipal Journal* and *Local Government Chronicle.* However the scale of job losses is very small relative to total employment in local government and has largely been achieved without substantial compulsory redundancies (the exception being the cleaning of premises). Natural wastage, early retirement and redeployment have generally been used to secure the necessary reductions in the number of workers.

The general lack of systematic evidence of decline in the quality or quantity of services, together with the evidence of increased productivity, provides corroboration of substantial overstaffing prior to introduction and extension of market testing in the 1980s and 1990s. An example is the *'task and finish' scheme.* Commonly used in the past for refuse collection, this scheme allows refuse disposal operatives to finish work once their collection round has been completed, regardless of time taken. It has been criticised for making insufficient use of vehicles and other equipment, so raising costs. The scheme also fails to take account of ongoing changes that speed up collection times, for example increasing mechanisation and changes in the geographic distribution of premises and in working methods. Costs are unnecessarily high in such cases and may be reduced simply by rearranging the sequence of tasks, without necessarily having any adverse effects on quality of service.

Other significant cost savings have been achieved by changes in **pay and conditions**. Evaluation of pay and conditions is complex, involving not just standard working week wages and salaries but also overtime, shift and bonus payments, performance-related pay schemes, fringe benefits, holiday entitlements, pensions and other conditions of service for the employees concerned. Savings appear to have been achieved by greater discrimination in the use of **bonuses** (which, in the past, accounted for a quarter of labour costs in refuse collection), and **overtime**. Cuts in **basic pay rates** have been less common. More discriminatory use of supplementary payments on top of basic pay is not necessarily unwarranted. For example the value of **occupational pensions** is very limited for manual work forces characterised by high rates of employee turnover, employers' pension contributions being poor value for money.

More generally, pay and conditions seem to have been more generous in local government than in comparable private sector occupations for 'blue-collar' manual workers (such as those in cleaning, catering and refuse collection), but less generous for 'white-collar' professional and administrative workers (such as those in finance, legal and computing services). Possible reasons for such a differential include stronger 'blue-collar' trade union bargaining power in the public sector, a disposition on the part of local government to protect the living standards of manual workers or, alternatively, the 'exploitation' of such workers by the private sector. In such cases it would not be surprising if competitive contracting brought cost savings by means of less generous pay and conditions. In some cases where contracting out has occurred, ex-local authority employees have been re-employed by private contractors on a less secure part-time (rather than full-time) basis.

The EU's Acquired Rights Directive is intended to protect the employment, pay and conditions of workers. Its UK equivalent is the Transfer of Undertakings (Protection of Employment) Regulations 1981 (known as TUPE). TUPE applies to both public and private sector contracts but only when there is a legal transfer of business to a new employer. It therefore relates to contracting out but not to contracting in. Changes in pay and conditions secured by in-house DSOs are not restricted by TUPE. Moreover, private companies' profits can still be obtained through improved productivity, as distinct from cuts in the pay and conditions of workers. Since it was noted above that the bulk of savings seem to have been achieved through higher productivity, the constraints imposed by TUPE (in terms of its preservation of pay and conditions) are strictly limited and not always adhered to (Adnett and Hardy, 1998).

Definitive conclusions on pay and conditions are clearly not possible without detailed, complex research, and generalisations are of dubious validity. Whether better pay and conditions for local government employees are desirable or not depends on one's view as to whether local authorities should be *model employers* in exceeding market rates of pay or other (statutory minimum) working conditions. Put more bluntly, should local authorities use their general revenues to benefit particular groups of employees, including low-paid unskilled male, part-time female, disabled and ethnic minority workers? Similarly should local government be a direct employer, protecting jobs at the expense of overstaffing? If the answer to both questions is negative, then the increasing disparities in rates of pay and employment for skilled/educated managers and unskilled/uneducated operatives identified in Chapter 12 becomes increasingly evident for local government contracted services. Rates of unionisation are much lower for employees in contracted-out services and wages increasingly reflect local labour market conditions. In contrast, individual performance-related pay seems to be becoming the norm for managers who are paid the going private sector rates. Indeed managers are increasingly recruited from the private sector on fixed-term contracts.

All these factors may explain why cost savings have been made, even when contracts have been won by internal contractors. Even though a majority of contracts continued to be won by DSOs, competitive tendering led to increased internal efficiency and long term financial savings. The very process of contracting seems to have stimulated increased competition in *input* markets (e.g. for labour) quite separate from any limited competition for *output* markets. The research results tend to support the hypothesis that it is **competition rather than ownership** that brings greater efficiency through increased productivity.

Besides improving the efficiency of public services, competitive contracting also promotes the achievement of broader supply-side objectives in labour markets (see Chapter 8), including:

- **A shift towards the market determination of public sector wages and salaries**;
- **A shift away from national pay bargaining**, towards local pay negotiations;
- **The increased flexibility of labour markets**, through the growth of contract-specific employment (i.e. workers are made redundant if the contract is lost).

Although competitive contracting has been criticised for its claimed negative impacts on local government employees (Pinch and Patterson, 1995 and 2000), research suggests that the very act of contracting seems to improve staff morale and teamwork, particularly at the management level (CoE, 1993). The positive (rather than punitive) aspects of new work disciplines and changed attitudes in the DSOs appear to explain the reductions in absenteeism and time off work due to illness, and the greater commitment to quality of service.

15.7   Justifying the choice of services subject to market testing

There are both pragmatic and theoretical justifications:

The administrative rationale

The usual justification for the choice of services subject to competitive contracting is that they are peripheral technical and ancillary (mainly non-client) services such as vehicle maintenance. Public accountability issues are crucial for major client-based services such as education and personal social services but the direct provision of services such as construction, cleaning and catering is not necessarily a prerequisite of the democratic system. However this explanation of the services subject to competitive contracting begins to look doubtful given its subsequent extension to client-based management services (i.e. municipal sports and leisure and housing) and to internal professional services (e.g. architecture) under the successive central and local government market testing regimes.

The theoretical rationale

The theoretical justification of the services subject to competitive contracting is supposedly provided by **transaction costs** (see Chapter 2). In everyday language, transaction costs include risk factors relating to the viability and trustworthiness of the contractor, the chances and potential costs of service disruption, the feasibility and cost of the information requirements necessary for contract monitoring, the feasibility and effectiveness of penalties for non-compliance, and the availability of alternative sources of supply. These are effectively the broader value for money considerations noted above.

Quantity, quality, price, delivery times and other dimensions of supply must be capable of being precisely specified, especially where contracts are to be regularly renewed. Where these items are difficult to specify and monitor, and where potential loss arising from failure of the contractor is high, direct provision of services should be retained in order to minimise transaction costs. Only those services for which contracts are easily specified and enforced (i.e. which have low transaction costs) should be subject to contracting. However low transaction costs do not automatically mean that a service should become subject to a contracting regime. This would only be appropriate if it promoted service objectives, whether in terms of cost reductions or in securing wider benefits. Hence transaction costs theory does not provide a mechanistic cost-based formula from which to derive definitive rules and decisions. There is a large element of subjective assessment and discretion in reaching decisions.

Vehicle maintenance is an example of a service with low transaction costs, in that it is a series of easily specified tasks that can be clearly written in contractual terms. Hence performance of service can be easily monitored and therefore imperfect knowledge (i.e. **bounded rationality**) is not a serious problem. Alternative vehicle maintenance firms are readily available in the event of the supplier's failure to perform in accordance with contract, so that the scope for exploitation of the client by the contractor (i.e. **opportunism**) is limited. Nor are clients tied to a particular contractor because of the highly specific nature of plant and equipment to the contract in question (i.e. **asset specificity** is not an overriding problem). Hence market failure due to high transaction costs is not a problem for vehicle maintenance. Given a high level of competition between the large number of alternative suppliers, the service can be efficiently provided by the private sector. It is not necessary to provide the service in-house. The same conclusions would seem to apply to construction and most of the other blue-collar services formerly subject to CCT.

Transaction costs would seem to be greater for white-collar services such as management of sports and leisure facilities, and particularly significant for education and personal social services because of the difficulties in the identification, measurement and evaluation of the quality of their output. This explains why competitive contracting is not used in the case of residential care of the elderly, service provision having been strategically contracted out to private establishments since 1993. Although it does not eliminate them completely, non-competitive strategic contracting constrains any incentives to reduce quality of service because of the need for contractors to minimise costs in order to win competitively tendered contracts.

Nevertheless, the conditions for transaction costs may exist even if provision of the service is retained in-house. The public choice arguments of Chapter 7 suggest that it is an act of faith to assume that public servants are completely devoid of self-serving behaviour. In such cases, recruitment of specialist staff for monitoring performance against service objectives is necessary whether the service is contracted in or out. This largely eliminates the difference between net and gross cost savings reported above.

15.8   Interactions between competition and service objectives

The cost-saving rationale for competitive contracting is based on the 'policy-constant' assumption, namely that the client specifies the level and standard of service to be provided and then invites competitive bids from potential contractors in order to secure the lowest cost. However, competition may also change policy for the service, so that the policy-constant assumption is invalid. This is quite separate from claims that competitive contracting leads to lower standards of service as contractors cut costs.

Services such as refuse collection and vehicle maintenance involve relatively straightforward objectives that can be precisely specified in contracts. However, policy for sport and recreation tends to be formulated in terms of externalities associated with health, crime prevention, local economic development, quality of life of the disabled, the elderly, ethnic minorities and the unemployed. Lack of management information regarding the achievement of social objectives through sports provision may tip the balance of information in favour of activities that generate a financial return, thus affecting the nature of sports provision.

This would be most likely where management contracts contain an *income sharing* or *profit sharing* arrangement. For example there could be a reorientation of leisure and recreation services away from traditional sports with low capacity for income generation and towards chargeable leisure activities such as squash, sunbeds and sauna. In addition the use of sports centres for profitable non-sporting activities such as dog shows, antiques fairs and craft exhibitions is increasingly being seen as a means of cross-subsidising unprofitable sports activities. Such events generate finance from sponsorship by commercial companies and from profit-based admission charges. Whilst cross-subsidy may increase participation for some activities, this approach also encourages dilution of service objectives with possibly less priority for heavily subsidised target groups and a contraction of provision for minority sports that require space and equipment.

Unless social objectives are explicitly mentioned in contract specifications by the local authority, then the pressure is there for DSOs (who may have a different, more managerialist view of management or who may be bound by tight financial specifications and spending restraints) or commercial contractors to increase income from charges by encouraging those already attending to attend more often, or by targeting those with greater financial resources. Contracting management contracts thus has the potential to influence both the type of sports facilities provided and the groups who use them (Bailey and Reid, 1994).

High transaction costs make it difficult to combine the spirit with the letter of the contract and thus allow contractors considerable discretion as to the precise characteristics of the service. Any attempt to impose default systems comes up against the problem that contract specifications may have been written in terms of inputs rather than outputs thus limiting the power of local authorities to monitor contracts in relation to social objectives. This may shift the balance of activities away from traditional sports (with little revenue-raising potential) towards leisure activities (with greater scope for revenue generation).

For example traditional (highly unprofitable) swimming pools have often been replaced by leisure pools with flumes and wave machines, for which higher charges can be levied. Also, the increased provision of chargeable aerobics classes and fitness suites may be at the expense of traditional sports such as cricket, football and rugby, where charges per participant tend to be lower. However transaction costs analysis probably gives too much power and discretion to the contractor and too little to the local authority, voluntary clubs and other users. In particular the nature and extent of any shift from sports to leisure is crucially dependent on the balance of power between groups that are active in the formulation and implementation of policy. Moreover the adoption of a more sophisticated approach to charging can facilitate a reduction in recreational disadvantage by moving away from across-the-board subsidies (which may institutionalise recreational disadvantage) towards selective increases in charges for those who can afford to pay and who traditionally have not. This would allow income to be generated to improve the quality of facilities and equality of access to be improved by the more effective targeting of subsidy on children, the disabled, the unemployed and low-income groups.

15.9 Conclusions

Market testing through competitive contracting is concerned with more than cost savings. Benefits seem also to accrue from setting clear specifications, from improved management, from innovation, from the removal of restrictive practices, from setting performance targets and so on. Many of these benefits are intangible and therefore are difficult to measure. Hence the emphasis of research has been on the identification and measurement of cost savings. Whilst the extent of cost savings is open to dispute, there is clear evidence that they are larger where competition has been greatest.

Cost savings arising as a result of competitive contracting mean that enhanced public services can be financed from existing resources. In that respect, competitive contracting is a development of earlier attempts to achieve value for money, for example *programme planning budgeting systems, zero-based budgeting* and *efficiency audits*. Competitive contracting promotes government objectives (noted in the quotes at the beginning of this chapter) relating to increased efficiency, market testing the delivery of services, and contracting out where appropriate so as to stimulate private sector activity. It is also consistent with the objectives for restraining public expenditure set out in the quotes at the beginning of Chapter 9.

Market testing through competitive contracting is only one supply-side policy tool amongst many. It fits within a framework of other substantial changes, including a general shift towards an enabling framework for the public sector as a whole. Although popularly referred to as privatisation, contracting out does not constitute privatisation in terms of the sale of assets. Instead it is a form of liberalisation that creates competition for markets. Whether a service is contracted in or out, competition rather than ownership is the more important factor in promoting efficiency. It is this very contestability of markets that leads to cost reductions. The threat of competition led many in-house providers to seek efficiency gains irrespective of the actual number of bids for service contracts.

Moreover, over time, local governments learnt how to improve the specification and monitoring of contracts, including quality and service development issues. These issues emphasise the need for mutual trust and co-operation between client and contractor. Such partnerships are in sharp contrast with the anonymous and impersonal nature of buyer–seller relationships assumed by the model of perfect competition.

References and further reading

Adnett, N. and Hardy, S. (1998) 'The Impact of TUPE on Compulsory Competitive Tendering: Evidence from Employers', *Local Government Studies*, vol. 24, no. 3, pp. 36–50.

Ascher, K. (1987) *The Politics of Privatisation: Contracting Out Public Services* (London: Macmillan).

Audit Commission (1984) *Further Improvements in Refuse Collection: A Review by the Audit Commission* (London: HMSO).

Audit Commission (1987) *Competitiveness and Contracting Out of Local Authorities' Services* (London: HMSO).

Audit Commission (1988) *Competitive Management of Parks and Green Spaces* (London: HMSO).

Bailey, S. J. (1999) *Local Government Economics: Principles and Practice* (Basingstoke: Macmillan).

Bailey, S. J. and Reid, G. (1994) 'Contracting Municipal Sports Management: Policy-Making Interactions', *Local Government Policy Making*, vol. 21, no. 2, pp. 55–66.

Boyne, G. A, (1998) 'Competitive Tendering in Local Government: A Review of Theory and Evidence', *Public Administration*, vol. 76, pp. 695-712.

Boyne, G. A. (ed.) (1999) *Managing Local Services: From CCT to Best Value* (London: Frank Cass).

Cabinet Office (1996) *Competing for Quality Policy Review: An Efficiency Unit Scrutiny* (London: HMSO).

Carnaghan, F. and Bracewell, B. (1993) *Testing the Market: Competitive Tendering for Government Services in Britain and Abroad* (London: Institute of Economic Affairs).

Chaundy, D. and Uttley, M. (1993) 'The Economics of Compulsory Competitive Tendering: Issues, Evidence and the Case of Municipal Refuse Collection', *Public Policy and Administration*, vol. 8, no. 2, pp. 25-41.

CIPFA (1996) *Achieving Value for Money Through Competition: 27 Case Studies of CCT/Market Testing Experience in Great Britain* (London: Chartered Institute of Public Finance and Accountancy).

CoE (1993) *The Role of Competitive Tendering in the Efficient Provision of Local Services* (Strasbourg: Council of Europe).

CPS (1989) *The Price of Winning* (Sheffield: Centre for Public Services).

Cubbin, J., Domberger, S. and Meadowcroft, S. (1987) 'Competitive Tendering and Refuse Collection: Identifying the Sources of Efficiency Gains', *Fiscal Studies*, vol. 8, no. 3, pp. 49-58.

DoE (1991) *Competing for Quality. Competition in the Provision of Local Services: A Consultation Paper* (London: Department of the Environment).

DoE (1993) *Local Government Act 1992, Section 9: Competition in the Provision of Local Authority Services*, Circular 10/93 (London: Department of the Environment).

DoE (1994) *CCT and Local Government in England: Annual Report for 1993* (London: Department of the Environment).

Domberger, S. and Jensen, P. (1997) 'Contracting Out by the Public Sector: Theory, Evidence, Prospects', *Oxford Review of Economic Policy*, vol. 13, no. 4, pp. 67-78.

Domberger, S., Meadowcroft, S. and Thompson, D. (1986) 'Competitive Tendering and Efficiency: The Case of Refuse Collection', *Fiscal Studies*, vol. 7, no. 4, pp. 69-87.

Domberger, S., Meadowcroft, S. and Thompson, D. (1988) 'Competition and Efficiency in Refuse Collection: A Reply', *Fiscal Studies*, vol. 9, no. 1, pp. 86-90.

Ganley, J. and Grahl, J. (1988) 'Competition and Efficiency in Refuse Collection: A Critical Comment', *Fiscal Studies*, vol. 9, no. 1, pp. 80-5.

Harden, I. (1992) *The Contracting State* (Buckingham: Open University Press).

Kerley, R. and Wynn, D. (1991) 'Competitive Tendering: The Transition to Contracting in Scottish Local Authorities', *Local Government Studies* (September/October), pp. 35-41

Office of Public Service and Sciences (1991) *Competing for Quality: Buying Better Public Services*, Cm 1730 (London: HMSO).

Office of Public Service and Sciences (1992) *The Citizen's Charter: First Report 1992*, Cm 2101 (London: HMSO).

Parker, D. (1990) 'The 1988 Local Government Act and Compulsory Competitive Tendering', *Urban Studies*, vol. 27, no. 5, pp. 653-68.

Parker, D. and Hartley, K. (1990) 'Competitive Tendering: Issues and Evidence', *Public Money and Management*, vol. 10, no. 3, pp. 9–16.

Pinch, P. L. and Patterson, A. (1995) '"Hollowing Out" the Local State: Compulsory Competitive Tendering and the Restructuring of British Public Sector Services', *Environment and Planning A*, vol. 27, pp. 1437–61.

Pinch, P. L. and Patterson, A. (2000) 'Public Sector Restructuring and Regional Development: The Impact of Compulsory Competitive Tendering in the UK', *Regional Studies*, vol. 34, no. 3, pp. 265–75.

Propper, C. (1992) *Quasi-markets, Contracts and Quality* (Bristol: University of Bristol).

Szymanski, S. and Wilkins, S. (1993) 'Cheap Rubbish? Competitive Tendering and Contracting Out in Refuse Collection 1981–88', *Fiscal Studies*, vol. 14, no. 3, pp. 109–30.

Uttley, M. R. H. (1993) 'Contracting Out and Market Testing in the UK Defence Sector: Theory, Issues and Evidence', *Public Money and Management*, vol. 13, no. 1, pp. 55–61.

Uttley, M. and Harper, N. (1993) 'The Political Economy of Competitive Tendering' in T. Clarke and C. Pitelis (eds) *The Political Economy of Privatisation* (London: Routledge).

Vining, A. and Boardman, A. (1992) 'Ownership versus Competition: Efficiency in Public Enterprise', *Public Choice*, vol. 73, pp. 205–93.

Voytek, P. (1991) 'Privatising Government Service Delivery: Theory, Evidence and Implications', *Government and Policy*, vol. 9, pp. 155–71.

Walker, B. (1993) *Competing for Building Maintenance: Direct Labour Organisations and Compulsory Competitive Tendering* (London: HMSO).

Walsh, K. (1991) *Competitive Tendering for Local Authority Services: Initial Experiences* (London: HMSO).

Walsh, K. (1995) *Public Services and Market Mechanisms: Competition, Contracting and the New Public Management* (Basingstoke: Macmillan).

Walsh, K. and Davis H. (1993) *Competition and Service: The Impact of the Local Government Act 1988* (London: HMSO).

Whitbread, C. and Hooper, N. (1992) 'Contracting Out Ancillary Services in the NHS', in A. Harrison (ed.) *Contracts versus Hierarchies* (London: Policy Journals).

Index

Acquinas, St T.   14
ad valorem taxes   68, 70, 254
advance corporation tax   219-20
aggregate demand, deficiency of   133
aggregate supply, inelasticity of   133
aggregates levy   258
allocative efficiency   7, 8, 25, 31, 66, 84, 97, 101, 106, 119, 128, 154, 334, 358, 370, 377, 384, 415
   see also first best *and* Pareto optimum
annually managed expenditure   173
Aristotle   14
Arrow problem   117
asset specificity   41, 43, 439
Audit Commission   144, 177
Automobile Association   240

backward-bending supply curve of labour   71-2
balanced-budget rule   269
bank lending controls   142
basic income scheme   317-21
Baumol's productivity differential model   54-6, 85
benefits, contributory *v.* non-contributory   181
Best Value   424, 428-9
Beveridge, W. H.   200, 201, 293
black economy   319
bounded rationality   6, 15, 41, 43, 439
British Lung Foundation   33
budget deficit/surplus, definitions of   274-80
built-in stabilisers   276-7
bureaucratic empire building   118
Business Expansion Scheme   147
business rates   255-7

capital allowances   218-19
capital gains tax   221, 253
capital transfer tax   252
carbon trading   37
cardinal welfare   98
cash limits   56, 171
cash planning   171
categoric concessions   102

charges   12, 95-111, 151, 343, 401-17
child benefit   191, 317
Child Poverty Action Group   191
Child Support Agency   187-8
child tax allowance   317
childcare tax credit   250
children's tax credit   218, 251-2, 299
churning   215
Civil Service agencies   *see* quangos
climate change levy   258
Commission on Social Justice   200, 312, 323
common carriage   369, 385
community charge   *see* poll tax
compensation test   26
Competition Acts   146
Competition Commission   146, 359, 398
competitive contracting/tendering   *see* contracting out/in
Comprehensive Spending Review   177
compulsory competitive tendering (CCT)   *see* contracting out/in
Confederation of British Industry   34
consumer, nature of   5
consumers' surplus   69, 97
contestability theory   432
contestable markets   349
contract curve   24, 71
contracting out/in   43, 149, 150, 152, 351-2, 385, 424-44
   competitive *v.* non-competitive   149
contributory benefits   *see* national insurance contributions
corporation tax   218, 252
council tax   255-7
cream skimming   352
cross-border shopping   263
crowding in   131, 269, 279
crowding out   85-94, 130-1, 168, 170, 207, 269, 279, 326
current cost accounting   346
Customs and Excise duties   224-5, 254

dash for gas   370
deadweight loss   70, 209
deadweight subsidy   141
debt targets   286–8
demand-determined expenditures
    see built-in stabilisers
demand-side policies   131–2
democratic defect   10
Demos   233
despotic benevolent government
    model   113–14, 231
development model   48
diminishing marginal utility   22
discounted cash flow   88
disincentives
    to invest   63, 86
    to save   311
    to work   58, 71, 82, 121, 137, 168,
        170, 207, 209, 212, 251, 277, 294,
        296, 318, 326
displacement effect   49, 141
distribution of income   293–329
    economic theory of   307
distributional coalitions   45, 120, 164
dividend controls   142
domestic rates   255, 260–2
duty free/paid   262

earmarked taxes   231–8, 257
Economic and Social Research Council
    (ESRC)   5
economic rent   63–5, 209
    Paretian v. Ricardian   63
economy, efficiency and
    effectiveness   433–4
effective marginal tax rate   76, 215
efficiency
    in production/consumption/
        total   24–5
    see also allocative efficiency and
        X-efficiency
emissions trading   37
employment tax credit   252
enabling approach   161, 313, 427,
    429
energy policy   370
enterprise zones   144
equality of opportunity v.
    outcome   294, 312
equilibrium
    partial v. general   21
    partial   82

equity
    horizontal v. vertical   208
    trade-off with efficiency   7, 58, 295–6
estate duty   252
EU directives   379–80, 383–4, 436
excess burden   see deadweight loss
excise duties   see Customs and Excise
    duties
exhaustive expenditures   47, 163
    and median voter model   59
external benefits   see externalities,
    positive
external costs   see externalities,
    negative
external markets   149
externalities   28, 32, 46, 114, 377
    negative   32–8, 65, 261, 343, 378–80,
        410
    positive   38–41, 43, 70
    trading scheme in   35–7

Fabian Society   234
family allowance   191, 317
family credit   190, 250, 299
family income supplement   184
Family Policy Studies Centre   185
first best allocation of resources   27,
    105, 112, 295
    see also allocative efficiency and
        Pareto optimum
fiscal drag   49, 214
fiscal exchange model   113, 231
fiscal illusion   49
fiscal stance   272
fiscal stress   56–7
fiscal transfer model   113, 231
foreign exchange controls   142
franchising   351
free riders   31, 109
full-cost charging   99
funny money   170–1

Galbraith, J. K.   15
general government borrowing
    requirement (GGBR)   271
general government expenditure
    (GGE)   47
gilts   84, 86, 284–5
Gini coefficient   304
golden rule   267, 270, 273, 278, 287–8,
    291
governance structures   42, 429

government
  failure 359, 433
  intervention, rationale for 8, 15
greenhouse effect 240

Health Education Council 29
health inequalities 294–5
hire purchase (HP) controls 142
historic cost accounting 346
housing benefit 184
human capital 48, 267, 319
hypothecation see earmarked taxes

imputed rents 223
incapacity benefit 192–3
incentives
  to invest see disincentives to invest
  to save see disincentives to save
  to work see disincentives to work
income
  definitions of 300–1
  effect 72–3, 105, 260
  polarisation of 323
  support 184–5
  tax 216–8, 248–52
indifference curves 23
industrial development
  certificates 144
Industrial Society 141
inequality aversion 7, 59
inheritance tax 220–1, 252
inhospitality thesis 121, 128
inset appointments 385
inspection effect 49
Institute for Employment
  Research 141
Institute of Economic Affairs 95, 199
Institute of Fiscal Studies 141, 184,
  195, 301, 304
instrumental role/view 5, 10, 123
integrated child credit 251, 299
internal markets 150
internalisation 35, 379
invalidity benefit 192
investment income surcharge 143
invisible hand 10, 25, 27, 42

Jaffa Cakes 228
jobseeker's allowance 57, 137, 188–9,
  190, 203, 245, 412
Joseph Rowntree Foundation 78, 141,
  184, 294, 301

Keynes, J. M. 14, 123
Keynesian liquidity trap 90
Kyoto Protocol 37, 240, 370

Laffer curve 81
laissez-faire 26, 134
landfill tax 238–9
large-scale voluntary transfers 341
leasing 352
Leontief, W. 15
leviathan model 50, 106, 114–19, 128,
  164, 231
liberalisation 351–3, 368, 429
lifelong learning 327
Locke, J. 14
London School of Economics Welfare
  State Programme 198
Lorenz curve 303

Maastricht Treaty/criteria 289
marginal cost, long-run v.
  short-run 98
marginal cost pricing 97–101
marginal rate of substitution 23, 73
marginal rate of transformation 22,
  73
market
  failure 9, 26, 42, 45–6, 295, 359, 374
  nature of 6 8
  testing 149, 424–44
married couple's allowance 217, 249
means-testing 102
median voter model 50–4, 58–60
medium-term financial strategy
  (MTFS) 277
merit goods 28, 30, 43, 111, 114, 377,
  380, 410
merit order system 369
middle-class capture 103, 120, 164,
  236, 308
Mill, J. S. 10, 13
minimum income guarantee 180, 320
mixed goods 30, 32, 53
models of government 113
models of public expenditure
  growth 48–60
Monetary Policy Committee 92,
  135–6
money illusion 6
Monopolies and Mergers
  Commission 146, 343, 385, 398
monopolistic rent 64

mortgage interest relief   217, 249
multiple deprivation   56–7, 59, 256, 295
multiple expansion of deposits   89, 91
multiplier effects   *see* crowding in
municipalisation   380
mutualisation   381–2

National Audit Office   157–8, 364
National Institute of Economic and Social Research   141
national insurance contributions (NICs)   63, 206, 222–3, 257–8, 294
   integration with income tax   242–7
national insurance surcharge   139
national minimum wage   137, 299, 318
national savings certificates   284–5
nationalisation   334–44, 381
natural monopoly   27
negative income tax scheme   252, 314–18
neoclassical economic theory   6, 8, 256
   v. Keynesian theory   129–30
net additionality   141
New Deal   137, 141, 186, 190, 193, 282, 299
Nolan committee   123
non-domestic rates   255
non-excludability   31
non-rivalness   31
normal profits   19, 65
normative economics   3, 122

O'Connor legitimation thesis   85
office development permits   144
Office of Fair Trading   146
open-market operations   285
opportunism   41, 439
opportunity cost   21, 275, 358, 361
optimising   6
opting out   152
organic state model   48
organisational slack   119
   see X-inefficiency
Ormerod, P.   15
output gap   276, 283
over-funding   272, 285

paradox of thrift   269
Paretian welfare criterion   98

Pareto optimum   25–7, 31, 44, 96, 112–13, 295
   see also allocative efficiency *and* first best
partial overhead charging   99
payback period investment method   88
payments in kind   163
pensions   138, 194–7
performance-related pay   148
Periodical Publishers' Association   259
permanent income   46
petroleum revenue tax   253
planning gain/obligations   260
Policy Studies Institute   311
political constraints model   49
poll tax   66, 74–7
polluter pays principle   36, 109–10, 238
pollution   *see* externalities, negative
popular capitalism   275, 339
positive economics   3, 122
poverty
   definitions of   296–8
   and economic change   322–4
   transmission of   298
   trap   76, 168, 183, 203, 209, 212, 296, 299
premium bonds   284–5
price
   cap   *see* regulation
   discrimination   107–9
   effect   260–1
   makers/takers   27, 56
prices and incomes policy   146, 176
printing money   89–90, 268, 270
Private Finance Initiative   154–9, 288, 340
private goods   30–1, 52–3, 378
privatisation   11, 334–41, 344–57, 381, 431
   receipts   272, 274
producers' surplus   70, 97
production possibility frontier   21
profit-related pay   139
property tax   223–4
prudent public finances   93, 270, 282
public, nature of   8–13
Public Accounts Committee   123, 151, 157
public choice theory   40, 114, 116, 121

public debt 288–9
public expenditure
    cash *v.* real 47
    central *v.* local 175
    current *v.* capital 173
    exhaustive *v.* transfer 47, 165–7
    GDP ratio 165–72
public goods 28, 30–1, 42–3, 53, 209,
    343, 378
    pure *v.* impure 31–2
public interest 13–14
public–private partnerships 154, 340
public sector borrowing requirement
    (PSBR) 271–3, 287–8
public sector net cash requirement
    (PSNCR) 273–4
public sector pay 175–6
purchase tax 227
purchaser–provider split 152–4

quangos 122, 150–1, 375, 381, 420
quantity theory of money 90, 268
quasi-markets *see* internal markets
quasi-rents 64–5

rational economic man 4
rational ignorance 6
real balance effect 90
registered social landlords 145, 341
regulation 11, 359–70
    economic *v.* environmental 383–6,
        398–9
regulatory capture/failure 358, 369
regulatory formula *see* RPI-X
relative price effect 54–6, 170
rent-seeking 4, 122, 164, 369
replacement cost 346
replacement ratio 319
reserve price of labour 130
residential care of the elderly 197
right to buy 145, 311, 341
road fuel duty 240–2
roles of government 10, 18
rolling back the frontiers of the
    state 96, 123, 128–9, 134, 333
Rousseau J.-J. 13
RPI – X 362–9

Samuelson, P. A. 30
satisficing 6
Say's law 129, 131, 133, 139

second best 27–8, 105, 112, 209, 378
selfish gene model 4
sickness and disability benefits 184,
    193
simplified planning zones 144
sin taxes 236
single parents' allowance 217, 249
skills gap 140
Smith, A. 10
social justice 163–4, 294, 312, 327
social security
    cyclical 173
    expenditures 180–202
    reforms 183–4
    taxes *see* national insurance
        contributions
social wage 308, 319
social welfare function 13
specific taxes 254
stamp duty 252
stop-go policies 270
structural budget deficit 278
structural gaps 324
subsidies 40, 101–5
substitution effect 72–3, 141
supplementary benefit 183
supply constraints 133–4
supply-side policies 129, 132–61
sustainable investment rule 94, 267,
    273, 278, 291

tariff basket *see* RPI – X
tax
    avoidance/evasion 81, 216–17,
        230, 263, 319
    capitalisation 223, 261
    credits 238, 250–2, 321
    escalators 238, 241
    harmonisation 260, 262–5
    incidence 66–9
    on jobs 139, 207, 257, 281
taxable perks 217
taxation
    burden of 209–14
    principles of 208–9
    welfare effects of 69–71
taxes
    direct *v.* indirect 62, 214
    progressive *v.* regressive *v.*
        proportional 66, 208
    visible 49
taxing bads *v.* taxing goods 239, 258

taxpayer revolts   224
total managed expenditure   173,
    177–9
training schemes   140
    see also New Deal
transaction costs   41, 43, 438–9,
    440–1
transfer earnings   64–5, 361
transfer payments/expenditures   47,
    57, 163
    and median voter model   59
trickle down effect   301
TUPE   436–7
two-part tariffs   99, 109, 414–15

unanimity rule   26
unbundling   357
unemployment
    benefits   188–90
    natural rate of   135
    non-accelerating inflation rate
        of   135
    trap   76, 130, 137, 168, 183–4, 203,
        209, 212, 296, 323–4
unit tax   66, 68
universal benefits   321–2
Urban Regeneration Agency   144
urban–rural shift   256

value added tax (VAT)   225–31,
    253–4, 259–60
value for money   172
variable cost charging   99
Veblen, T.   15
vehicle excise duty   254
volume planning   171
voter, calculatively rational   5
voting systems   9–10

wages councils   137, 198, 306
Wagner's law   46
water   374–423
    metering 406–13
wealth
    distribution and composition
        of   309–11
    lifecycle theory of   310
welfare, measures of   98
welfare-to-work   141, 189, 282, 321
windfall tax   231, 366
work-based welfare   80
working families tax credit   137, 190,
    218, 250–1, 299, 412

X-inefficiency   106, 119, 121, 154, 334,
    336, 344, 348, 358, 370, 384, 432

yardstick competition   354, 385